THE PEN   KU-735-665

NEW SERIES

Compiled by F. R. Banks

G17

LONDON

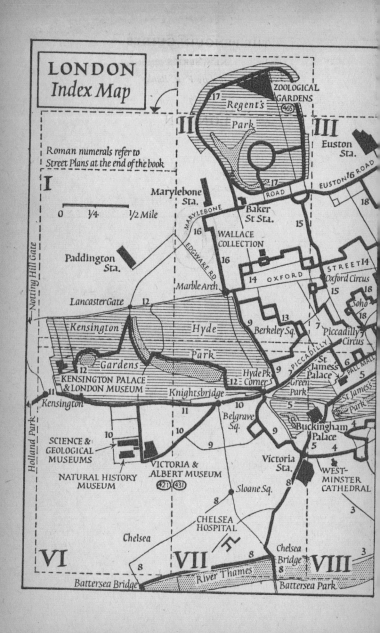

LONDON
Index Map

Roman numerals refer to Street Plans at the end of the book

I

0   ¼   ½ Mile

II

ZOOLOGICAL GARDENS
465

Regent's Park

17

2-17

Marylebone Sta.

ROAD

Baker St Sta.

III

Euston Sta.

EUSTON ROAD 16

18

MARYLEBONE

Paddington Sta.

EDGWARE RD

16

WALLACE COLLECTION

16

15

Marble Arch

14

OXFORD

STREET 14

Oxford Circus

15

18

Soho

18

Notting Hill Gate

Lancaster Gate 12

Kensington

12

Gardens

KENSINGTON PALACE & LONDON MUSEUM

Hyde

13

Berkeley Sq.

9

Piccadilly Circus

7

Park

9

Hyde Pk. Corner

12

PICCADILLY

St James's Palace

5

PALL MALL

4

St James's Park

Knightsbridge

11

10

Belgrave Sq.

5

Green Park

5

Buckingham Palace

4

11

10

9

9

Victoria Sta.

4

5

WEST-MINSTER CATHEDRAL

Holland Park

Kensington 11

SCIENCE & GEOLOGICAL MUSEUMS

10

NATURAL HISTORY MUSEUM

VICTORIA & ALBERT MUSEUM
421 431

Sloane Sq.

8

8

3

VI

Chelsea

8

CHELSEA HOSPITAL

VII

8

Chelsea Bridge

8

VIII

3

River Thames

Battersea Bridge

Battersea Park

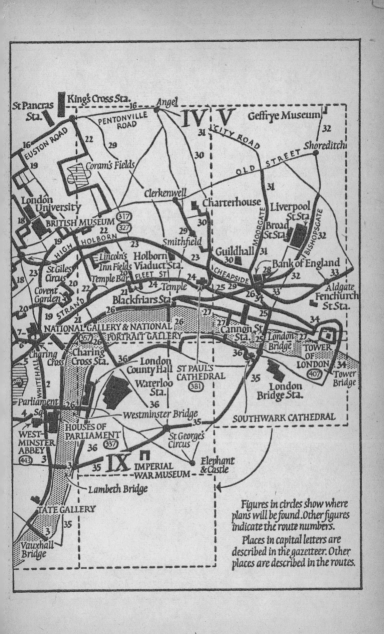

THE PENGUIN GUIDES

LONDON

F. R. BANKS

PENGUIN BOOKS

Penguin Books Ltd, Harmondsworth, Middlesex
U.S.A.: Penguin Books Inc., 3300 Clipper Mill Road, Baltimore 11, Md
AUSTRALIA: Penguin Books Pty Ltd, 762 Whitehorse Road,
Mitcham, Victoria

—

Published by Penguin Books 1958
Second edition 1960
Third edition 1963

—

Copyright © F. R. Banks, 1958, 1960, 1963

—

Made and printed in Great Britain
by Hunt, Barnard & Co., Ltd, Aylesbury
Set in Monotype Times

CONTENTS

PLACES OF INTEREST

MAPS AND PLANS

FOREWORD

THE PENGUIN GUIDE TO LONDON, now in its third edition, has established itself as the most favoured guide to the capital.

The guide is divided into three parts. The first opens with a brief introduction to the capital, telling something of its places of interest and suggesting how the visitor may employ his time to the best advantage, followed by sections offering advice regarding such practical matters as railway and motor-bus services, hotels and restaurants, postal services and useful addresses, entertainments, sport, and shopping. At the end of this part are suggestions for further reading and study.

The next part consists of a series of short routes which may be followed on foot (or partly by bus) covering the whole of central London in detail and taking in the many fine public and other buildings, parks and squares, interesting churches and small museums, and other places well worth seeing. The routes are arranged to start and finish at noted traffic points, and each may very conveniently be followed from end to end. They also mostly intersect at a number of points, so that, by comparing the index map at the front of the book, parts of several routes may easily be combined to make a longer or shorter round excursion.

The third part of the book is a gazetteer of the most important places of interest, such as Westminster Abbey, St Paul's Cathedral, and other important churches, the Tower of London and the Houses of Parliament, the great national museums and art galleries, Chelsea Hospital, and the Zoological Gardens. This is followed by a short section outlining briefly the places best worth visiting in the suburbs of London. The very full index of places and persons is preceded by a glossary of the architectural terms used in the book, which have, moreover, been kept as simple as is consistent with accuracy and clarity.

The guide is well supplied with maps and plans. The street plan of central London on nine pages at the back of the book covers the whole of the area described in the text. In addition, there are maps showing the best road routes into and around London, the railway systems, and the motor-bus routes and theatres and cinemas in the central area. Plans of the National Gallery, the British Museum and the Victoria & Albert Museum, Westminster Abbey and St Paul's Cathedral, the Houses of Parliament, the Tower, and the Zoological Gardens will be found adjoining the descriptions of these places in the guide. The Index Map at the front of the book shows clearly the arrangement of the routes and the page numbers of the various maps and plans. All the maps are based on the Ordnance Survey map with the sanction of the Controller of H.M. Stationery Office, but are amended and added to in order to bring them in line with the requirements of the guide.

London, as the capital of England and the heart of the Commonwealth, is almost certainly the most fascinating and interesting city in the world. As the centre of administration, the court, the law, learning, fashion, and pleasure, it occupies a unique position in the nation's life. An attempt has been made to deal with as wide a range of topics as is possible in the guide, consideration being given to the great public occasions and the military and civic pageantry indissolubly connected with the capital, and to the seasonal and occasional events and customs that lend colour and atmosphere to the everyday scene, as well as to the wealth of historical and literary associations. Notice has also been taken of the great amount of building, both public and private, that is going on in London, though of course not every new building can be mentioned, or indeed is worthy of mention.

For the first edition of the guide the Author explored the whole of the area considered on foot and visited every building where the stranger may expect to gain admittance at any time. In preparing a new edition, he revisited every part of the area where changes have occurred. It must be stressed, however, that changes take place rapidly in the metropolis, almost week by week in fact, and the hope that the guide will be entirely free from errors and omissions is beyond the realms of possibility. All indeed that an Author can hope for is that by constant and careful research and diligent 'field work' he may reduce the errors to a minimum. His grateful thanks are due to many anonymous helpers: to the directors of museums and galleries and their staffs, librarians and church officials, clerks of the City guilds, secretaries of companies, institutions, and societies, and private individuals, all of whom answered carefully and courteously the many questions put to them. The Author and Publishers thank the many correspondents who have made helpful comments and will be most grateful for any further suggestions for the correction and improvement of the guide, as well as for any material that will assist in keeping it up to date.

AN INTRODUCTION TO LONDON

LONDON, the capital of England and the principal city of the British Commonwealth of Nations, is situated on the river Thames, about 40 miles in a straight line, or 50 miles by water, from its mouth at the Nore. Divided into two portions by the river, it is built mainly on a tract of undulating dark brown or grey clay ('London Clay'), which extends along the river valley from about Windsor to the coasts of Kent and Essex. The clay is broken here and there by beds of sand or gravel, formed into low hills at certain places around the perimeter of London, such as Highgate, Hampstead, and Harrow on the north side, and Wimbledon, Sydenham, and Blackheath on the south. The more important part of the capital, with most of the chief buildings, lies on the north bank of the river and is bounded by Essex (on the north-east) and Middlesex; the southern portion, which includes Southwark, Lambeth, and Battersea, is conterminous with Kent (to the south-east) and Surrey.

The term 'London' has no single specific meaning: it may be applied indiscriminately to the City of London proper, which has an area of only 677 acres and a resident population of 4,771, but is usually referred to as 'the City'; to the administrative COUNTY OF LONDON, comprising both the City and the Metropolitan Boroughs (area, 117 square miles; population, 3,195,114), but by no means encompassing the whole of the inhabited area; or to the much larger and vaguely delimited GREATER LONDON, corresponding roughly to the Metropolitan Police District (area, 722 square miles; 8,171, 902 inhabitants), which extends for about 12 to 16 miles in every direction from Charing Cross, the official centre of London, and takes in the whole of Middlesex and parts of Kent, Surrey, Hertfordshire, and Essex. Transport facilities combined with the vast and rapid expansion of the built-up area have made these parts of the 'Home Counties' in effect an extension of the capital.

The County of London, though the smallest in area of the administrative regions into which England is divided (excluding only the Soke of Peterborough), is much the highest in the scale of population. The 'youngest' county in England, it was formed in 1888 out of parts of Middlesex, Surrey, and Kent, and placed under the jurisdiction of the LONDON COUNTY COUNCIL ('L.C.C.'; compare p. 310), who superseded the Metropolitan Board of Works, an authority elected by some forty-two 'vestries' or district boards. In 1899 the functions of these vestries were transferred to twenty-eight Metropolitan Boroughs, each with its own mayor and council, and in 1900 one of these was created the City of Westminster. The following are the boroughs, with their area and population:

BATTERSEA, 2,163 acres, population 105,758; BERMONDSEY, 1,503 acres, 51,815; BETHNAL GREEN, 760 acres, 47,018; CAMBERWELL, 4,480 acres, 174,697; CHELSEA, 660 acres, 47,085; DEPTFORD, 1,564 acres, 68,267; FINSBURY, 587 acres, 32,989; FULHAM, 1,706 acres, 111,912; GREENWICH, 3,858 acres, 85,585; HACKNEY, 3,287 acres, 164,556; HAMMERSMITH, 2,287 acres, 110,147; HAMPSTEAD, 2,265 acres, 98,902; HOLBORN, 406 acres, 21,596; ISLINGTON, 3,092 acres, 228,833; KENSINGTON, 2,290 acres, 170,891; LAMBETH, 4,083 acres, 223,162; LEWISHAM, 7,015 acres, 221,590; PADDINGTON, 1,357 acres, 115,322; POPLAR, 2,331 acres, 66,417; ST MARYLEBONE, 1,473 acres, 68,834; ST PANCRAS, 2,694 acres, 125,278; SHOREDITCH, 658 acres, 40,465; SOUTHWARK, 1,132 acres, 86,175; STEPNEY, 1,766 acres, 91,940; STOKE NEWINGTON, 864 acres, 52,280; WANDSWORTH, 9,107 acres, 347,209; WESTMINSTER, 2,503 acres, 85,223; WOOLWICH, 8,282 acres, 146,397.

All the figures for population given above are preliminary figures from the 1961 census.

In 1962 the Ministry of Housing and Local Government accepted recommendations for a new Council for Greater London, superseding the London County Council and administering a much larger area taking in parts of the 'Home Counties'. The thirty-two new boroughs proposed would have populations of between 170,000 and 340,000, but the City of London would remain unchanged.

Under an act of 1948 London is divided into forty-three parliamentary constituencies, the Cities of London and Westminster sharing a member, and the boroughs returning from one to four members each, except that Finsbury and Shoreditch are combined for this purpose and the boundaries of the other constituencies do not always correspond exactly with the borough boundaries.

The CITY OF LONDON, the oldest administrative unit in the

larger London, still occupying a site approximating to that of Norman London, is free of the jurisdiction of the official County of London. A corporate county in its own right, it is governed by the Corporation of the City of London, consisting of the 'Mayor and Commonalty and Citizens'. The corporation acts through the Court of Common Council, presided over by the Lord Mayor (see p. 258) and comprising twenty-five other Aldermen, who are elected annually by the ratepayers and hold office for life (or until they resign), and the Common Councilmen, likewise elected annually (their number, previously 206, was reduced to 159 by 1959). In addition, there are two Sheriffs (compare p. 273), whose forerunners served as the 'portreeves' or chief magistrates of London and Middlesex. The City is divided into twenty-six wards, each under its alderman, who is also a Justice of the Peace; the names of some of the wards (Vintry, Cordwainer, Candlewick, Portsoken) still have a strong medieval flavour.

A distinctive feature of the City, and one closely associated with its government, are the Guilds, or LIVERY COMPANIES, so named from the dress or livery adopted by the members of the guilds as early as the 14th century. There are now eighty-two such companies in the City, each with its own Master or Prime Warden, its Clerk and other officials, and about 10,000 liverymen are entitled to vote at the municipal elections. Twelve of the companies are designated 'great': of these the Mercers' Company is the foremost, while the others, in order of civic precedence, are the Grocers, the Drapers, the Fishmongers, the Goldsmiths, the Merchant Taylors and the Skinners (these two alternating in seniority), the Haberdashers, the Salters, the Ironmongers, the Vintners, and the Clothworkers. The Shipwrights have the most liveries (about 500), the Ironmongers the fewest (35). The larger companies pride themselves on their handsome halls, many of which have been carefully restored or rebuilt since the war; some of the companies are very wealthy and maintain schools and alms-houses, as well as devoting considerable sums to other charity and education, and, in several cases, to assisting the trades with which they are connected.

The City of London was described by the Roman historian Tacitus in the first century A.D. as a 'busy emporium for trade and traders', and this description could have been applied to it at almost any time since. The Saxon burgesses, predecessors of the Common Council, declared their independence after the Battle of Hastings, and William the Conqueror was forced to come to terms with them, proffering a charter which is still preserved. The City remains the most important commercial square mile in the world, the financial and business centre of the metropolis, with the chief offices of the principal banks, insurance companies, stockbrokers, and mercantile houses. The working population is estimated at nearly 500,000, and considerably more than a million people enter the City in a single business day.

The City can still show some remains of its ancient wall, built originally during the 2nd century A.D., in addition to the Temple of Mithras discovered in 1954 and a few other remains of the Roman occupation. The wall was about 2 miles long between the points where it abutted on the Thames (at the Tower and near Blackfriars Bridge); it enclosed a settlement of about 330 acres which spread over two low hills – Cornhill, where the city centre was on the site of Leadenhall Market, and Ludgate Hill, where St Paul's Cathedral now stands – and between these a small river, the Walbrook, flowed down to join the Thames. The Romans gave the place its name of *Londinium*, probably derived from a personal or tribal name, and most unlikely from the Celtic 'Llyn-din' (the 'fort in the lake'), as once popularly supposed.

The commercial centre of the City is the open space familiarly known as 'the Bank', from which many busy and congested streets radiate and round which are grouped several imposing buildings: the Bank of England, the most important bank in the world; the Mansion House, the official residence of the Lord Mayor; and the Royal Exchange, at present housing the interesting Roman and medieval collections of the Guildhall Museum. The Bank lies almost due north of London Bridge, which crosses the Thames to Southwark and is the successor of the only bridge over the river at London until the 18th century. It is still the farthest downstream, apart from the elaborate Tower Bridge, a masterpiece of engineering spoiled by its fancifully decorative appearance. Historic buildings within the City boundaries range from the noble church of St Helen's, of Norman origin, to Guildhall (north-west of the Bank), the home of the City Council and partly of the 15th century, and the magnificent bulk of the 17th-century St Paul's Cathedral, the masterpiece of Sir Christopher Wren, its famous dome one of the sights and landmarks of London. Of the incomparable series of churches rebuilt after the Great Fire (1666) by Wren, many suffered severely from air attack during the Second World War, though some fine examples survived and others have been well restored. On the edge of the City (though actually in the borough of Stepney) is the great Tower of London, the oldest part of which is early Norman work.

The City is bounded on the west, at Temple Bar, by the City of Westminster; on the north-west, at Holborn Bars, by the borough of Holborn; on the north by Finsbury and Shoreditch; and on the east by Stepney, part of the 'East End' of London, neighbouring the docks. Temple Bar stands at the point where Fleet Street, the centre of newspaper activity, ascending from the direction of Ludgate Hill, meets the Strand, running eastward from Charing Cross. The Temple, between Fleet Street and the river, is a name covering two Inns of Court or corporate legal societies; it is especially notable for its church, with a Romanesque 'round' nave and a Gothic chancel, well restored after war damage. On either side of the Strand are the Royal Courts of Justice, a Victorian Gothic edifice better known as the Law Courts, and Somerset House, a palace rebuilt in the 18th century and now converted to public offices.

The CITY OF WESTMINSTER includes the greater part of the region known as the 'West End', the residential and fashionable quarter of London, with the best shops, the chief theatres, etc., the most exclusive hotels and clubs, and the principal royal palaces and government offices. It extends from Temple Bar to Chelsea and Kensington, and from Oxford Street on the north to the Thames, though the part east of Charing Cross Road has more in common with the City than with the West End. In everyday usage the name of Westminster is confined to a much smaller region, the neighbourhood of Westminster Abbey, one of the finest Gothic churches in England, practically a cathedral in all but name, and the Houses of Parliament, the seat of British government. Both confront Parliament Square, from which Millbank leads south to the Tate Gallery, the principal gallery of modern painting and sculpture as well as of British painting in general, while Victoria Street runs south-west towards Westminster Cathedral, the sumptuous modern Byzantine-style church of the principal Roman Catholic archbishop in Britain.

Parliament Square is connected with Charing Cross by the broad Whitehall, lined by the chief government offices and traversing the site of the royal palace of the same name. Of this, however, little remains apart from the 17th-century banqueting house, a splendid work of Inigo Jones. Charing Cross, the centre of London for the tourist, opens into Trafalgar Square, with the lofty Nelson's Column. To the north of this is the National Gallery, an unrivalled collection of paintings of practically every school and period, adjoined by the National Portrait Gallery, an interesting assembly of British historical portraits, and facing these is the well-known 18th-century church of St Martin-in-the-Fields.

To the west of Whitehall is the delightful St James's Park, bounded on the north by The Mall, a spacious avenue which leads south-west from Charing Cross past St James's Palace, a Tudor royal residence, to Buckingham Palace, the principal mansion of the sovereign. To the north of this, cut through by Pall Mall and limited on the east by the Haymarket and on the west by the Green Park, is ST JAMES'S, the home of the aristocracy and men of fashion since the 17th century, and famous for its clubs. Piccadilly, which traverses it on the north, is the most fashionable street in London, with many of the most exclusive shops. Its principal building is Burlington House, the headquarters of the Royal Academy of Arts and other learned societies. Farther north, bounded approximately by Park Lane, Oxford Street, and Regent Street, is MAYFAIR, which took its name from an ancient fair held every year in May. This district, declared Sydney Smith, the 18th-century wit, 'enclosed more intelligence and ability, to say nothing of wealth and beauty, than the world had ever collected into such a space before'. It still contains many characteristic residences, though the area is being increasingly given over to large blocks of flats and offices.

Hyde Park and Kensington Gardens, to the west, together form the largest open space in Central London. Kensington Palace, on

18

the west side of the gardens, was the birthplace of Queen Victoria and now includes the very interesting collections of the London Museum relating to the capital at every period. To the south of Hyde Park is the aristocratic district of BELGRAVIA, laid out in the early part of the 19th century and still largely unspoiled, and farther west is KENSINGTON, one of the few royal boroughs and a greatly favoured residential quarter. South Kensington is well known for its important museums – the Victoria & Albert Museum, an unrivalled collection of applied art of all kinds, and the adjacent Natural History, Geological, and Science Museums, all well worth visiting – and for the Imperial College of Science and Technology, now being extended to cover the site formerly occupied by the Commonwealth Institute (transferred to Holland Park). CHELSEA, a fashionable residential district in the 17th–18th centuries and now favoured by artists, lies between Kensington and the river. It has many attractive old streets and houses, and a pleasant riverside promenade, stretching west from Chelsea Bridge and passing the grounds of the Royal Hospital, founded for veteran soldiers by Charles II, in a fine building by Sir Christopher Wren.

To the north of Hyde Park is PADDINGTON, a residential borough mostly laid out to a uniform plan during the first half of the 19th century, but including BAYSWATER, north of Kensington Gardens, with many hotels and boarding houses. To the east of Edgware Road and north of Oxford Street is MARYLEBONE (officially St Marylebone, and pronounced 'Marry-le-bun'), another mainly residential borough, with numerous secluded streets and squares of the 18th century. Its most interesting building is Hertford House, in Manchester Square, containing the Wallace Collection, the finest privately-formed art collection in London, now the property of the nation. The borough is adjoined on the north by Regent's Park, another large and attractive open space, with the popular Zoological Gardens on its north side.

On the south side of Oxford Street and east of Regent Street is the congested district of narrow bustling streets known as SOHO, the principal foreign quarter of London, where almost every nationality is to be found and many languages are spoken, French and Italian predominating. Well known for its restaurants, it extends south as far as Leicester Square, the centre of a theatrical neighbourhood, and the settlement has recently spread north across Oxford Street to the vicinity of Charlotte Street. Farther east is HOLBORN (pronounced 'Ho-burn'), a small borough deriving its name from the valley on its east side through which the Fleet River flowed. The district north of New Oxford Street, known as BLOOMSBURY, consists of quiet squares and interconnecting streets, laid out in the 18th and early 19th centuries. Once favoured by successful merchants and professional men, it is now best known for its many private hotels and as the home of two important institutions: the British Museum, the national museum of archaeology and ethnography, unsurpassed for the wealth and interest of its collections, and the growing University of London, whose new buildings, begun in 1933, are not yet finally complete. To the north of Holborn is ST PANCRAS, best known for its large railway termini, though it has a fine church of the Regency period.

To the north-east of Holborn, and traversed by Farringdon Road, which ascends from the valley of the vanished Fleet River, are the districts of SMITHFIELD and CLERKENWELL, with the church of St Bartholomew the Great, the oldest ecclesiastical building in London after the chapel in the Tower. The Charterhouse, farther north, a hostel for poor gentlemen since the 17th century, has been charmingly restored after war damage. To the north of Clerkenwell is the district of ISLINGTON, and to the east are FINSBURY and SHOREDITCH, to the south-east of which again is SPITALFIELDS. All these are mainly manufacturing districts of little interest, though Clerkenwell is well known for its watchmakers, opticians, and jewellers, Shoreditch for its cabinet-makers, and Spitalfields for its silk-weavers.

London south of the Thames is a busy commercial and industrial quarter, largely unattractive and badly damaged during the war. SOUTHWARK (pronounced 'Suth-ark'), extending along the bank of the river from London Bridge to west of Blackfriars Bridge, occupies the site of a Roman settlement, and its cathedral is the most notable Gothic building in London, except for Westminster Abbey. In the Middle Ages Southwark became a flourishing borough (in common parlance it is still 'the Borough')

20

and in Elizabethan and Jacobean times it was famous for its riverside theatres, associated with Shakespeare. LAMBETH, farther upstream opposite Westminster, contains Lambeth Palace, the London residence of the archbishop of Canterbury, partly medieval, and the Imperial War Museum, with exhibits of all kinds illustrating the two World Wars. Facing the river north of Westminster Bridge are the County Hall, the seat of the London County Council, and the Royal Festival Hall, a splendid modern concert hall, now overlooked by the vast Shell Centre, the most obvious of the many new examples of commercial architecture in London.

The fashionable LONDON 'SEASON' extends from about the beginning of May until towards the end of July, when the court is normally in residence, the Royal Academy and other annual exhibitions are open, theatres are flourishing, the chief shows and sporting events take place, dinners and receptions are given, and other social functions are held. By the end of July the great migration of Londoners to the sea and country has begun, but the capital is invaded by tourists, especially from America and the Commonwealth, for whom August and September are the favourite months. The sights and places of interest are even more crowded then than at other times. Much the best time to explore London is the spring, when the trees in the parks and squares are just coming into leaf and the atmosphere is still fresh and cool. October, after most of the crowds have departed, is another pleasant time in London.

EXPLORING LONDON. The capital is so large and intricate, and its interests so extensive, that the visitor cannot hope to obtain even a superficial impression of it in much less than a week, and a more detailed exploration will take at least a full month (the enthusiast will say a year, if not a lifetime!). Those with limited time at their disposal may well despair of gaining an adequate acquaintance with the many sights and treasures that London holds. Most of the more important features of interest, however, are confined to Central London, the area to which the major part of this guide is devoted.

The stranger freshly arrived in London cannot do better than remember W. E. Gladstone's much-quoted advice to a group of

American travellers: 'The way to see London is from the top of a bus – the top of a bus, gentlemen.' A few shillings spent on bus fares will enable the visitor to see at least the main streets, in rather better fashion than by car or taxi, and to form a mental picture of the lay-out of the capital, with the positions of the most important public buildings. He will find that two main thoroughfares run from west to east to converge at the Bank, the centre of the City, and a journey by bus along one of these, returning by the other, will be found quite a satisfactory introduction to London. The more northerly thoroughfare, beginning at Marble Arch, at the north-east corner of Hyde Park, follows Oxford Street, Holborn, Newgate Street, and Cheapside in a continuous line, passing a little south of the British Museum and just north of St Paul's Cathedral. The second through route starts at Hyde Park Corner, south-east of the park, and traverses Piccadilly eastward to beyond Piccadilly Circus, then turns southward via the Haymarket to Charing Cross, the hub of the West End, there taking up its eastward direction via the Strand, Fleet Street, and Cannon Street, and passing immediately south of St Paul's. These two long thoroughfares are joined by numerous roads running north and south, of which the most important are Park Lane, Bond Street, and Regent Street in the West End; Charing Cross Road and Kingsway (with Aldwych) in the central area; and Chancery Lane at the City's edge. A grasp of the relationship of all these streets, combined with the knowledge that the Thames flows due east and west (except for a sharp northward bend between Vauxhall Bridge and Waterloo Bridge), and the traveller is equipped to begin the exploration of London in more detail. He could then make Charing Cross and the Bank his chief centres, striking out in every direction from these, a plan followed more or less in the descriptions of the routes in this guide.

The traveller who is merely passing through London and can devote only a single day to the capital can hardly hope to receive an adequate impression. The following walk, however, takes in as many of the most interesting streets and buildings as is possible.

Charing Cross to Whitehall, Houses of Parliament, Westminster Abbey, St James's Park and Palace, Buckingham Palace, Green Park, Piccadilly (luncheon), Piccadilly Circus, Leicester Square, the National Gallery, and

Charing Cross, then to the Strand, the Temple, Fleet Street, Ludgate Hill, St Paul's Cathedral, Cheapside, Bank of England, London Bridge, Lower Thames Street, and the Tower.

Visitors with two days at their disposal can try the following walks:

FIRST DAY. Charing Cross to Whitehall, Houses of Parliament, Westminster Abbey, Queen Anne's Gate, Westminster Cathedral, Buckingham Palace, St James's Park and Palace, Piccadilly, Hyde Park Corner, Hyde Park, Marble Arch, Wallace Collection, Oxford Street, Regent Street, Piccadilly Circus, Haymarket, the National Gallery, and Charing Cross.

SECOND DAY. Charing Cross to the Strand, the Temple, Fleet Street, Ludgate Hill, St Paul's Cathedral, Cannon Street, London Bridge, Southwark Cathedral, Lower Thames Street, the Tower, Fenchurch Street, Lombard Street, the Bank of England, Cheapside, Guildhall, St Bartholomew's Church, Holborn, Lincoln's Inn, Kingsway, British Museum, Soho, Leicester Square, and Charing Cross.

The visitor who spends a week in London can devote considerably more time to the individual sights. Perhaps the best plan, if the weather be suitable, is to see the outdoor places of interest in the mornings, when the air is crisper and the streets rather less crowded, and visit the museums, galleries, and other indoor 'sights' after luncheon, particularly if the afternoons be warm. The evenings could then be spent in the parks, or at the theatre or other entertainment. Alternatively, the days could possibly be arranged as follows.

FIRST DAY. Charing Cross to Whitehall, Houses of Parliament (see below), Westminster Bridge, London County Hall, Albert Embankment, Lambeth Palace, Lambeth Bridge, Tate Gallery, Millbank, Westminster Abbey, Queen Anne's Gate, St James's Park, and Charing Cross. — SECOND DAY. Charing Cross to The Mall, St James's Palace, Buckingham Palace, Westminster Cathedral, Victoria, Belgravia, Hyde Park Corner, Piccadilly, St James's Square, and Charing Cross. — THIRD DAY. Hyde Park Corner to Knightsbridge, Brompton Oratory, Victoria & Albert Museum, Natural History Museum or Science Museum, Kensington Gardens, Kensington Palace (London Museum), the Serpentine, and Hyde Park Corner. — FOURTH DAY. Hyde Park Corner to Mayfair, Oxford Street, Wallace Collection, St Marylebone Church, Regent's Park, and the Zoological Gardens, returning via Regent Street to Piccadilly Circus. — FIFTH DAY. Charing Cross to the National Gallery, Leicester Square, Soho, British Museum, London University, Russell Square, Southampton Row, Lincoln's Inn, Kingsway, Aldwych, Victoria Embankment, and Charing Cross. — SIXTH DAY. Charing Cross to Covent Garden, the Strand, the Temple, Fleet Street, Ludgate Hill, Old Bailey, St Bartholomew's Church, St Paul's Cathedral, Cheapside, Guildhall, and the Bank of England. —

SEVENTH DAY. The Bank to London Bridge, Southwark Cathedral, Guy's Hospital, London Bridge, Lower Thames Street, the Tower, All Hallows Church, Fenchurch Street, Lombard Street, Royal Exchange (Guildhall Museum), and the Bank.

Visitors with more than a week at their disposal may prefer to follow the detailed routes given in this guide. Those wishing to draw up their own itineraries should note the following points.

Museums, galleries, and public institutions are invariably closed on Sunday mornings. The Central Criminal Court, the Houses of Parliament, and London County Hall are normally shown on Saturdays only; Lancaster House is open on Saturdays and Sundays only, and the Foundling Hospital Offices on Monday and Friday only. The Jewish Museum is closed on Saturdays, the Dickens House, Dr Johnson's House, the Guildhall Museum, and Leighton House on Sundays, the Public Record Office Museum on Saturdays and Sundays, the Soane Museum on Sundays and Mondays, the Queen's Gallery and the Geffrye Museum on Mondays, and Carlyle's House on Tuesdays. The Tower is closed on Sundays in winter.

Permits are necessary for the Royal Mint (6 weeks' notice required), the General Post Office (3 weeks' notice), the Royal Mews (open Wednesday afternoons; 2 weeks' notice), and the Mansion House and Henry VIII's Wine Cellar, both open on Saturday afternoons only. Advance arrangements must be made in writing in the case of the Charterhouse (Saturdays only), the College of Arms, Gray's Inn, Lambeth Palace (Saturday afternoons only), Royal College of Music (Donaldson Museum), St John's Gate, Trinity House, University College, and Westminster School. Where places are normally open to parties only it is often possible for an individual visitor to make arrangements to be attached to a party.

The CITY CHURCHES are now mostly open on Monday–Friday, but closed on Saturdays. In 1954 the number of parishes in the City was reduced from 108 to 24, and fifteen churches were nominated as GUILD CHURCHES. These have been assigned to specific purposes (St Lawrence Jewry, for instance, is the official church of the Corporation of London), and they may not be open on Sundays for visitors or service. The halls of the CITY LIVERY COMPANIES can often be seen by previous arrangement with the Clerks, and some of them are thrown open to the public on a few days in the year. For these occasions particulars and tickets are obtainable in advance from the City of London Information Centre, St Paul's Churchyard (see p. 61). The most interesting halls are the Apothecaries', the Fishmongers', the Goldsmiths', the Skinners', the Stationers', and the Vintners'.

The following are the principal sights of Central London, listed in such a manner as to assist the visitor to pursue his individual interests. The page numbers are those of the pages on which the times and conditions of admission are given.

STREETS AND SQUARES, etc., of interest or attraction in themselves: Bedford Square; Belgrave Square; Chelsea Embankment (and Cheyne Walk); Cornhill; Covent Garden; Dean's Yard (Westminster); Downing Street; Ely Place (Holborn); Fleet Street; Lincoln's Inn Fields; Lombard Street; Manchester Square; Pall Mall; Parliament Square; Piccadilly; Queen Anne's Gate; St James's Square and Street; the Strand; Trafalgar Square; Victoria Embankment; Whitehall.

ROYAL PALACES, PUBLIC BUILDINGS, etc.; Bank of England; Banqueting House (Whitehall Palace); Buckingham Palace; Central Criminal Court (p. 222); Chelsea Royal Hospital (p. 331); General Post Office (p. 222); Guildhall (p. 271); Henry VIII's Wine Cellar (p. 243); Horse Guards; Houses of Parliament and Westminster Hall (p. 335); Jewel Tower (Westminster Palace; p.106); Kensington Palace (p. 349); Lancaster House (p. 120); Law Courts; London County Hall (p. 309); Mansion House (p. 256); Marlborough House (p. 120); Middlesex Guildhall; the Monument (p. 239); Royal Festival Hall; Royal Mint (p. 298); St James's Palace; Somerset House; Tower of London (p. 405); Waterloo Bridge.

OTHER IMPORTANT BUILDINGS: Australia House (p. 208); Burlington House (Royal Academy); Canada House (p. 97); Charterhouse (p. 271); College of Arms (p. 251); Crosby Hall (p. 139); Gray's Inn (p. 222); India House (p. 215); Lambeth Palace (p. 301); Lincoln's Inn (p. 197); New Zealand House; Roman Bath (p. 208); Royal Exchange; Royal Institution; Royal Society of Arts (p. 207); St John's Gate (p. 262); South Africa House (p. 97); Staple Inn; the Stock Exchange; the Temple (p. 230); Trinity House (p. 294); University College (p. 184); University of London; Westminster School (p. 111).

CATHEDRALS AND CHURCHES: All Hallows Barking by the Tower (p. 294); All Souls, Langham Place (p. 169); Brompton Oratory; Chelsea Old Church; Queen's Chapel of the Savoy (p. 207); St Bartholomew the Great (p. 262); St Bride's, Fleet Street (p. 230); St Clement Danes, Strand; St Columba's Church of Scotland; St Etheldreda's, Ely Place; St George's, Bloomsbury; St Giles' Cripplegate (closed at present); St Giles-in-the-Fields; St Helen's, Bishopsgate (p. 282); St James's, Piccadilly; St Lawrence Jewry (p. 271); St Magnus the Martyr (p. 253); St Margaret's, Westminster (p.105); St Martin-in-the-Fields; St Mary Abchurch (p.239); St Marylebone; St Mary-le-Bow (under restoration); St Mary-le-Strand; St Mary Woolnoth (p. 294); St Olave's, Hart Street (p. 287); St Pancras; St Paul's Cathedral (p. 378); St Sepulchre's, Holborn (p. 222); St Stephen, Walbrook (p. 256); Southwark Cathedral (p. 394); Temple Church (p. 230); Westminster Abbey (p. 440); Westminster Cathedral (p. 460).

MUSEUMS AND ART GALLERIES: British Museum (p. 315); Carlyle's House (p. 139); Commonwealth Institute (p. 152); Courtauld Institute Galleries (p. 192); Dickens House (p. 215); Dr Johnson's House (p. 230); Foundling Hospital Offices (p. 215); Geffrye Museum (p. 283); Geological Museum (p. 389); Guildhall Museum (Royal Exchange; p. 256); Imperial War Museum (p. 346); Jewish Museum (p. 192); Leighton House (p. 152);

London Museum (p. 349); National Gallery (p. 354); National Portrait Gallery (p. 367); Natural History Museum (p. 373); Percival David Foundation of Chinese Art (p. 192); Public Record Office Museum (p. 197); Queen's Gallery (Buckingham Palace (p. 115); Royal College of Music (Donaldson Museum; p. 148); Science Museum (p. 389); Sir John Soane's Museum (p. 197); Tate Gallery (p. 398); Victoria & Albert Museum (p. 418); Wallace Collection (p. 435); Wellcome Historical Medical Museum (p. 174); Wellington Museum (Apsley House; p. 130); Wesley's House (p. 279); and several smaller or specialist museums.

PARKS AND GARDENS (see also p. 89): Archbishop's Park; Chelsea Physic Garden (p. 139); Green Park; Holland Park; Hyde Park; Kensington Gardens; Regent's Park; St James's Park; Victoria Embankment Gardens; Victoria Tower Gardens; Zoological Gardens (p. 464); etc.

PLACES OF INTEREST TO CHILDREN: Buckingham Palace and the Horse Guards (Changing of the Guard); Festival Gardens (p. 75); Geffrye Museum (see above); H.M.S. *Discovery* (p. 243); Imperial War Museum (see above); London Museum (dolls, toys, dioramas, etc.); Madame Tussauds and the London Planetarium (p. 173); Natural History Museum; Pollock's Toy Museum (p. 192); Royal Mews (p. 115); Science Museum (children's gallery); Tower of London; Zoological Gardens.

APPROACHES TO LONDON

BY RAIL. Fast through trains (including many famous 'named' trains) run to London from every important city in Great Britain. The standard 2nd-class single fare is 3*d* per mile; the 1st class fare is approximately 50 per cent more, and return tickets (available three months) are issued for both classes at twice the single fare. Seats may be reserved in advance on many trains on application to the stationmaster at the starting-point of the journey (fee 2/-), and refreshment or buffet cars are attached to most of the long-distance trains. The current charges for meals are: breakfast 5/- and 8/6, lunch 12/6, tea 3/6, dinner 13/6 (coffee 10*d*). Light meals for the journey packed in bags or cartons may be obtained from refreshment rooms, and telegrams ordering refreshments, reserving rooms at railway hotels, etc., may be sent (free of charge) from any station. Sleeping accommodation is provided on the principal night trains, but berths should be booked well in advance. 'Pullman' cars, offering a higher standard of accommodation and refreshment service for a small supplement, are included in some of the chief trains.

Timetables of 'Summer' and 'Winter' passenger services are issued by each of the regions of *British Railways* (price 1/-; the 'summer' tables extend from mid-June to mid-September). A timetable covering all the regions is also published (5/-), and is likewise obtainable from railway stations and offices, bookshops and bookstalls. The *ABC Railway Guide* (7/6; monthly), on sale at bookstalls and booksellers, gives all the journeys to and from London, as well as the fares.

Luggage will be carried free on the railways up to a maximum of 150 lb. for 1st class passengers and 100 lb. for 2nd class. For excess luggage a charge is made varying according to the distance travelled. Passengers' luggage will also be collected, conveyed, and delivered by the railways in advance for a charge of 5/6; the charge for luggage collected and conveyed *or* conveyed and delivered is 2/9.

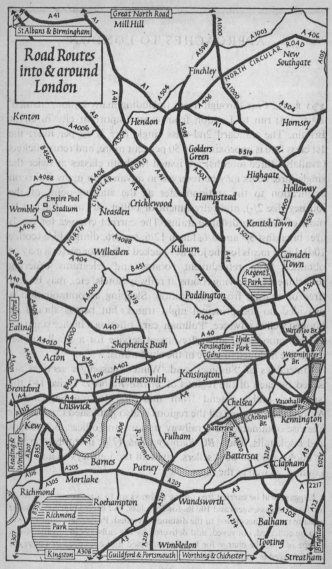

Road Routes into & around London

St Albans & Birmingham · A41 · Great North Road Mill Hill · A1

Kenton · Hendon · Finchley · Hornsey · New Southgate · North Circular Road

Wembley · Empire Pool Stadium · Neasden · Cricklewood · Golders Green · Hampstead · Highgate · Holloway

Willesden · Kilburn · Kentish Town · Camden Town

Oxford · Ealing · Shepherds Bush · Paddington · Regent's Park

Acton · Hammersmith · Kensington · Hyde Park · Waterloo Br.

Brentford · Chiswick · Kew · R. Thames · Fulham · Chelsea · Battersea · Westminster Br.

Reading & Winchester · Barnes · Putney · Wandsworth · Clapham · Vauxhall Br. · Kennington

Richmond · Roehampton · Richmond Park · Mortlake

Kingston · A308 · Guildford & Portsmouth · Wimbledon · Worthing & Chichester · Balham · Tooting · Streatham · Brighton

28

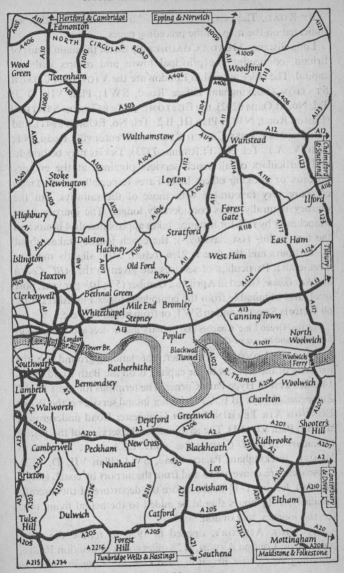

BY ROAD. The best road routes into and round London are indicated on the map on the preceding pages.

Long-distance MOTOR COACHES ply on all the main roads of Britain, connecting the principal towns and resorts with the capital. The chief termini in London are the VICTORIA COACH STATION (Buckingham Palace Road, SW1; Plan VII, D 3; Tel. No. SLOane 0202), the EUSTON SQUARE COACH STATION (Euston Road, NW1; Plan III, B 2; Tel. No. EUSton 8941), and the KING'S CROSS COACH STATION (Pentonville Road, N1; Plan IV, A 1; Tel. No. TERminus 7373). Tickets may be bought and particulars of all coach services obtained at the enquiry bureaux or booking offices here. Fares (especially return fares) compare very favourably with those of the railways, but the journey naturally takes considerably longer. The journey from Manchester by rail, for instance, takes approximately 4 hours and the fare is 46/- (1st class 69/-); the coach journey takes about 8½–10 hours and the fare is 21/6 (return 34/9; slightly more at week-ends). Particulars of services are given in the *ABC Coach and Bus Guide*, issued in April and October (5/-; 10/- per year, post free), and obtainable from the compilers, Index Publishers, Ltd, 69 Victoria Street, London SW1, or from bookstalls, etc.

For the 'Green Line' Coaches and Country Bus services in the neighbourhood of London, see p. 42.

BY AIR. LONDON AIRPORT, the landing-ground for the majority of the services to the capital, is on the Bath Road (A 4), 14 miles west of Hyde Park Corner. The terminus for most *British European Airways* (B.E.A.) and other inland services is the WEST LONDON AIR TERMINAL (near Gloucester Road underground station; Plan VI, D 1). The terminus for the services of the *British Overseas Airways Corporation* (B.O.A.C.) is at AIRWAYS HOUSE, Buckingham Palace Road, SW1 (Plan VII, D, E 3). Passengers are conveyed to and from the airport by coach (single fare 5/-), leaving 1–1½ hours before the departure of the aircraft. Similarly, 1–1½ hours should be added to the actual flying time for the journey to London.

GATWICK AIRPORT, opened in 1958 to relieve the great pressure on London Airport, is 28 miles south of London Bridge, adjoining A 23, the Brighton road (see the *Penguin Guide to*

Surrey). The airport is used by some B.E.A. services and also by *British United Airways*, whose terminus is at Victoria Station (see p. 115). Gatwick Airport station, adjoining the flying-ground, is served by frequent electric trains from Victoria.

Particulars of services, which are liable to change, are obtainable from the offices of the airway companies and the chief tourist agents. They are also given in the *ABC World Airways Guide*, published monthly (15/-) by Messrs Thomas Skinner & Co., Ltd, Liverpool House, 15 Eldon Street, London EC2, and obtainable from the publishers, at bookstalls, etc. Return tickets are obtainable on most air lines and show a considerable saving in fare. The free allowance of luggage is 20 kg. (or 44 lb.); the charge for excess luggage varies according to distance.

Regular services are operated to London at present from the following places in the British Isles: Birmingham, Chester, Manchester, Liverpool, Leeds and Bradford, Newcastle upon Tyne, Edinburgh, Glasgow (connexions from Aberdeen, Inverness, etc.), the Isle of Man, Swansea, Exeter, Belfast, Dublin, Cork, Jersey, and Guernsey.

TRANSPORT IN LONDON

RAILWAYS. The following are the chief railway termini in London. Almost all are connected by the underground railway system (see below) and by motor-bus, and an 'Inter-Station' bus service links up the most important stations before and after the times that the normal bus services operate. There are refreshment rooms at most of the termini, and hotels at Charing Cross, Euston, Liverpool Street, King's Cross, Paddington, and Victoria.

BAKER STREET (Plan II, C 2) is the terminus of the Metropolitan line (London Transport) to Amersham, Chesham, Watford, and Uxbridge, and is also on the Bakerloo and Circle lines of the underground.

BLACKFRIARS (IV, E 3) is on the Southern Region line that starts from Holborn Viaduct (but a terminus for some trains) and has a station also on the Circle and District lines.

BROAD STREET (V, D 2), adjoining Liverpool Street station (see below), is the terminus of the London Midland Region's 'North London' line to Richmond via Willesden Junction.

CANNON STREET (V, F 1) is a terminus of the Southern Region in the City (closed on Sundays) and is connected to a station on the Circle and District lines.

CHARING CROSS (III, F 3) is a terminus of the Southern Region in the West End. It is connected to the Strand station of the Northern line; Charing Cross underground station, which is also on the Bakerloo, Circle, and District lines, lies to the south on the Victoria Embankment and is reached via Villiers Street on the east side of the main station.

EUSTON (III, A 2) is one of the two principal termini of the London Midland Region, and is connected to a station of the same name on the Northern line.

FENCHURCH STREET (V, F 3) is a terminus of the Eastern Region for the Docks and places on Thames-side. It is situated about 300 yds north of Tower Hill Station on the Circle and District lines and ½-mile south-west of Aldgate Station on the Metropolitan line.

HOLBORN VIADUCT (IV, D 3) is a City terminus of the Southern Region. Its nearest underground stations are St Paul's on the Central line, just over ½-mile east, and Farringdon on the Circle and Metropolitan lines, about ½-mile north.

KING'S CROSS (III, A 3) is the principal terminus of the Eastern Region for long-distance trains to the north. It is close to St Pancras Station (see below) and is connected to the Northern, Piccadilly, Circle, and Metropolitan lines.

LIVERPOOL STREET (V, D 2) is the principal terminus of the Eastern Region for East Anglia and is connected to the Central, Circle, and Metropolitan lines.

LONDON BRIDGE (IX, E 2) is a terminus of the Southern Region south of the river and has a station on the Northern line.

MARYLEBONE (II, C 1) is a terminus of the Western Region, mostly for the shorter distance services, but used also by the London Midland and Eastern Regions. It is ½-mile west of Baker Street Station and is connected to the Bakerloo line.

PADDINGTON (I, D 2) is the chief terminus of the Western Region, and is connected to the Bakerloo, Circle, District, and Metropolitan lines.

ST PANCRAS (III, A 3) is the other principal terminus of the London Midland Region. It is close to King's Cross Station, with which it shares an underground station (see above).

VICTORIA (VII, D 3) is the principal West End terminus of the Southern Region, used by boat-trains from Dover, Folkestone, and Newhaven, and is connected to the Circle and District lines.

WATERLOO (IX, B 1) is the chief terminus of the Southern Region for trains from the West of England. It is connected to the Bakerloo and Northern lines, and is the terminus of the Waterloo & City line to the Bank, also operated by the Southern Region.

The UNDERGROUND RAILWAYS of *London Transport* provide the quickest and easiest method of getting from one part of the metropolis to another. The seven named lines are connected with each other at many points, and with their numerous branches extend into almost every quarter of London (except south of the Thames, better served by the Southern Region of British Railways) and in some cases into the country beyond. The system is electrified throughout, fares are reasonable, and trains are fast and comfortable. Frequent services operate on all the lines, starting at about 5.30 a.m. (7.30 on Sundays) and continuing until about midnight. The trains, however, like other public transport, are overcrowded on weekdays between about 8 and 9.30 in the morning and about 4.30 and 6.30 in the evening (12 and 1.30 on Saturdays). The various lines are connected at their points of intersection by subways and/or escalators, and are reached from the booking-offices (usually at or just below street level) by escalator or lift, though an ordinary staircase is always provided also. A map of the routes (free), an Underground Guide (1/-; giving the frequencies of the services, times of first and last trains, etc.), and other information may be obtained from the London Transport enquiry offices at Piccadilly Circus Station (Plan III, F 2), St James's Park Station (VIII, C 2; Tel. No. ABBey 1234), and Eccleston Bridge (near Victoria Coach Station; VII, D 3) and from the City of London Information Centre (see p. 61). Maps and information are obtainable from the Public Relations Officer at the head office of the London Transport Board (55 Broadway, London S W 1), adjoining St James's Park station, and timetables from the Publicity Officer, Griffith House, 280 Marylebone Road, N W 1.

The following are the various through routes on the London underground system. Termini, junctions, and connecting stations are shown in capital letters, but only the more important suburban stations have been included. The accompanying plan shows the system clearly.

BAKERLOO LINE. WATFORD JUNCTION, Watford (High Street), Harrow & Wealdstone, Wembley Central, Willesden Junction, Queen's Park, Maida Vale, PADDINGTON, EDGWARE ROAD, Marylebone, BAKER STREET (junction for St John's Wood, Finchley Road, Wembley Park, and STANMORE), Regent's Park, OXFORD CIRCUS, PICCADILLY CIRCUS, Trafalgar Square, CHARING CROSS, WATERLOO, Lambeth North, and ELEPHANT & CASTLE.

CENTRAL LINE. EALING BROADWAY, NORTH ACTON (junction for Northolt and WEST RUISLIP), White City, Shepherd's Bush (see below), Holland Park, NOTTING HILL GATE, Queensway, Lancaster Gate, Marble Arch, Bond Street, OXFORD CIRCUS, TOTTENHAM COURT ROAD, HOLBORN (Kingsway), Chancery Lane (closed on Sundays), St Paul's, BANK (escalator connexion to the Monument), LIVERPOOL STREET, Bethnal Green, MILE END, Stratford, LEYTONSTONE (junction for HAINAULT via Wanstead), WOODFORD (junction for Hainault via Chigwell), Loughton, and EPPING (for trains to ONGAR). The Shepherd's Bush station is not connected with the station of the same name on the Metropolitan Line.

CIRCLE LINE (trains run continuously in both directions). PADDINGTON, Bayswater, NOTTING HILL GATE, High Street Kensington, GLOUCESTER ROAD, SOUTH KENSINGTON, Sloane Square, Victoria (see p. 38), St James's Park, Westminster, CHARING CROSS, Temple (closed on Sundays), Blackfriars, Mansion House, Cannon Street (closed on Sundays), MONUMENT (escalator connexion to the Bank), TOWER HILL, Aldgate, LIVERPOOL STREET, MOORGATE, Aldersgate (closed on Sundays), Farringdon, KING'S CROSS & ST PANCRAS, Euston Square,

Great Portland Street, BAKER STREET, EDGWARE ROAD, and PADDINGTON.

DISTRICT LINE (trains are sometimes changed at the Mansion House). EALING BROADWAY, EALING COMMON, ACTON TOWN (junction for Osterley and HOUNSLOW WEST), TURNHAM GREEN (junction for Kew Gardens and RICHMOND), HAMMERSMITH, Barons Court, West Kensington, EARLS COURT – junction for KENSINGTON (OLYMPIA), for Paddington and EDGWARE ROAD (see below) and for WIMBLEDON via West Brompton, Fulham Broadway, and Putney Bridge – GLOUCESTER ROAD and thence as the Circle Line (see above) to TOWER HILL, then ALDGATE EAST, WHITECHAPEL, MILE END, Bow Road, BARKING, and UPMINSTER. This line coincides with the Piccadilly Line from Ealing Common and from Hounslow West to South Kensington, with the Circle Line from High Street Kensington to Edgware Road, and with the Metropolitan Line from Aldgate East to Barking. The service between Earls Court and Kensington (Olympia) operates only when Olympia is open. Wimbledon Station is also on the main line to the South-West from Waterloo.

METROPOLITAN LINE. HAMMERSMITH, Shepherd's Bush (see Central Line), PADDINGTON, EDGWARE ROAD, BAKER STREET (junction for Finchley Road, Wembley Park, and HARROW-ON-THE-HILL, from which lines run to UXBRIDGE via Rayners Lane and Ruislip, and to Watford, etc., see below), thence as the Circle Line (see above) to LIVERPOOL STREET (junction for ALDGATE), then ALDGATE EAST and WHITECHAPEL (junction for SHOREDITCH – during rush hours only – and for NEW CROSS and NEW CROSS GATE) and as the District Line to BARKING.

NORTHERN LINE. (a) *Charing Cross Section*: EDGWARE, Hendon Central, Golders Green, Hampstead, CAMDEN TOWN (junction for Highgate, Finchley Central, and HIGH BARNET or MILL HILL EAST), EUSTON (see below), Warren Street, Goodge Street, TOTTENHAM COURT ROAD, LEICESTER SQUARE, Strand, CHARING CROSS, WATERLOO, KENNINGTON (see below), Oval, Clapham Common, Tooting Broadway, and MORDEN. (b) *Bank Section:* as above from Edgware, etc., to EUSTON, then KING'S CROSS & ST PANCRAS, Angel, OLD STREET, MOORGATE (both junctions for Highbury & Islington and FINSBURY PARK), BANK (escalator connexion to the Monument), London Bridge, Borough, ELEPHANT & CASTLE, and KENNINGTON, and as above to Morden. Through trains run from Edgware, High Barnet, and Mill Hill East to Morden on both sections.

PICCADILLY LINE. UXBRIDGE, Ruislip, RAYNERS LANE, EALING COMMON, ACTON TOWN (junction for Osterley and HOUNSLOW WEST), HAMMERSMITH, EARLS COURT, GLOUCESTER ROAD, SOUTH KENSINGTON, Knightsbridge, Hyde Park Corner, Green Park, PICCADILLY CIRCUS, LEICESTER SQUARE, Covent Garden (closed on Sundays), HOLBORN (Kingsway; junction for ALDWYCH, during rush hours only), Russell Square, KING'S CROSS & ST PANCRAS, Arsenal, FINSBURY PARK, Wood Green, Southgate, and COCKFOSTERS. This line coincides

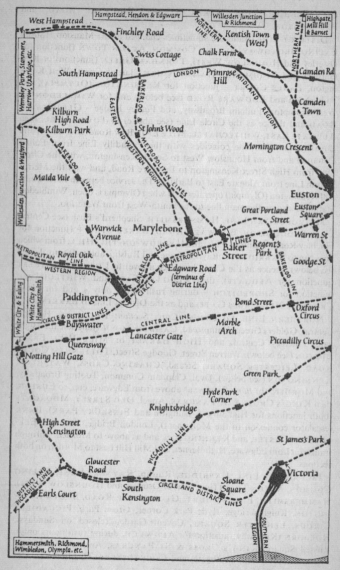

West Hampstead · Finchley Road

Hampstead, Hendon & Edgware

Willesden Junction & Richmond

Highgate, Mill Hill & Barnet

Kentish Town (West)

Wembley Park, Stanmore, Harrow, Uxbridge, etc.

Swiss Cottage

Chalk Farm

South Hampstead

LONDON

Primrose Hill

Camden Rd

Kilburn High Road

Kilburn Park

St John's Wood

Mornington Crescent

Camden Town

Maida Vale

Willesden Junction & Watford

BAKERLOO LINE

EASTERN AND WESTERN REGIONS

METROPOLITAN LINES

Warwick Avenue

Marylebone

Great Portland Street

Euston

Euston Square

Regent's Park

Warren St

Baker Street

Goodge St

Metropolitan Line

Royal Oak

Western Region

White City & Ealing

White City & Hammersmith

Edgware Road (terminus of District Line)

BAKERLOO LINE

CIRCLE & DISTRICT LINES

Paddington

Bayswater

CENTRAL LINE

Lancaster Gate

Marble Arch

Bond Street

Oxford Circus

Piccadilly Circus

Queensway

Notting Hill Gate

Green Park

Hyde Park Corner

Knightsbridge

PICCADILLY LINE

High Street Kensington

St James's Park

Gloucester Road

DISTRICT AND PICCADILLY LINES

Earls Court

South Kensington

CIRCLE AND DISTRICT LINES

Sloane Square

Victoria

SOUTHERN REGION

Hammersmith, Richmond, Wimbledon, Olympia, etc.

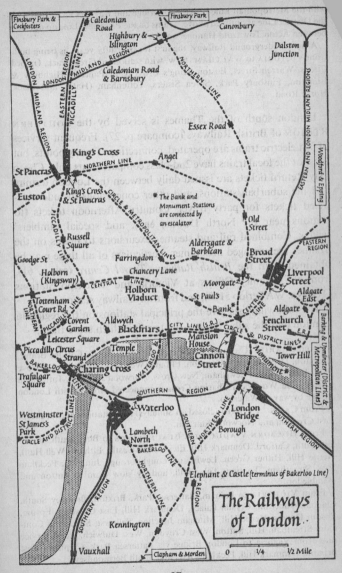

The Railways of London

...olitan Line between Uxbridge and Rayners Lane, and with
... as outlined above. Trains on the Piccadilly Line do not stop
...on Town and Hammersmith.

... Underground Railway, the first for over fifty years, is being built
... VICTORIA to WALTHAMSTOW, with stations at Green Park, Oxford
Circus, Warren Street, Euston, King's Cross & St Pancras, Highbury &
Islington, Finsbury Park, Seven Sisters, Tottenham (Hale), and Black
Horse Road.

London south of the Thames is served by the SOUTHERN
REGION of British Railways (compare p. 27). Frequent services
of fast electric trains are operated, connecting at many points, but
most of the local trains have 2nd-class compartments only. Cheap
Day Return tickets are issued daily between the London termini
and the suburban stations, and other concessions include combined tickets for party travel, Country Afternoon tickets (to
stations near the North Downs, etc.), and special ramblers'
tickets. Combined rail and steamer excursions to places on the
Thames are arranged in summer. Particulars of all these may be
obtained from the *British Railways Travel Centre* (see p. 61),
from the Enquiry Offices at Victoria and Waterloo Stations
(Tel. No. WATerloo 5100), and from any railway station.

The following lists give the principal stations on the region in
London and the suburbs, and the termini which serve them.

From CHARING CROSS to Blackheath, Bromley North, Catford Bridge,
Charlton, Deptford, East Croydon, Eltham (Well Hall), Greenwich, Grove
Park, Hither Green, Lewisham, New Cross, Norwood Junction, Tattenham
Corner, and Woolwich. Charing Cross is connected directly with London
Bridge by way of Waterloo.

From CANNON STREET (closed on Sundays) to all stations above, except
East Croydon and Norwood Junction.

From HOLBORN VIADUCT and BLACKFRIARS to Blackheath, Brom-
ley South, Catford, Denmark Hill, Elephant & Castle, Eltham (Well Hall),
Herne Hill, Hither Green, Lewisham, Loughborough Junction, Peckham
Rye, Streatham, Tooting, Tulse Hill, and by slow train to Sutton and
Wimbledon.

From VICTORIA to Balham, Battersea Park, Brixton, Bromley South,
Clapham Junction, Crystal Palace, Denmark Hill, East Croydon, Epsom,
Epsom Downs, Herne Hill, Mitcham Junction, Selhurst, Streatham Com-
mon, Streatham Hill, Sutton, West Croydon, West Dulwich, etc. A service
runs from Victoria to London Bridge via Battersea Park, Clapham, East
Brixton, Denmark Hill, Peckham Rye, and South Bermondsey.

From LONDON BRIDGE to all stations served by Victoria and to Charing Cross (see above), East and North Dulwich, New Cross Gate, Peckham Rye, Penge West, Streatham, Sydenham, and Tulse Hill.

From WATERLOO to all stations served by Charing Cross and to Barnes, Brentford Central, Clapham Junction, Epsom, Esher, Hampton Court, Kew Bridge, Kingston, Mortlake, Putney, Richmond, Sunbury, Surbiton, Twickenham, Vauxhall, Wandsworth Town, Wimbledon, etc.

The most important connecting points are CLAPHAM JUNCTION (the busiest junction in the world), where lines from Victoria and Waterloo converge, and EAST CROYDON, where lines from Victoria and London Bridge meet.

The WATERLOO & CITY RAILWAY, operated by the Southern Region, connects Waterloo with the Bank station on the underground system. There is a frequent service of electric trains (from about 7 a.m. to 10 p.m.) and the journey takes 5 minutes. Through bookings can be made to Tower Hill, Liverpool Street, and Moorgate, but no dogs or heavy luggage may be taken. The railway is closed on Sundays.

Steam trains are run by the WESTERN REGION from Marylebone Station to Wembley Hill, Sudbury Hill, South Ruislip, etc., and from Paddington Station to Acton, Ealing Broadway, West Ealing, Greenford, South and West Ruislip, etc.

The LONDON MIDLAND REGION has a useful electric line (the 'North London' line) from Broad Street to Richmond (where it connects with the Southern Region) via Dalston Junction, Highbury & Islington, Camden Road, Hampstead Heath, Finchley Road, Willesden Junction, Acton Central, and Kew Gardens. Another railway (no Sunday trains), diverging from this at Camden Road, runs via South Hampstead (closed also on Saturday afternoons), Kilburn High Road, Queen's Park, and Willesden Junction, beyond which it coincides with the Bakerloo Line to Watford Junction. Some trains start at Euston and join this line at South Hampstead. The region also runs steam trains from Euston to Willesden Junction, Wembley Central, Harrow & Wealdstone, Watford Junction, etc., and from St Pancras to Kentish Town, West Hampstead, and Hendon (for St Albans, etc.), and to Walthamstow, Leyton, East Ham, and Barking.

Steam and a few electric trains are operated by the EASTERN REGION from Fenchurch Street to Barking, Tilbury, Upminster, etc.; from King's Cross or Moorgate to Finsbury Park, Harringay Park, Wood Green (junction for Hatfield and Hertford), etc.; from Liverpool Street to Stratford, Ilford, Romford, Walthamstow, Chingford, Tottenham, Waltham Cross, Palace Gates (Wood Green), White Hart Lane, and Enfield Town; and from Marylebone to Wembley Hill, etc. (see above).

MOTOR-BUSES. The 'Central Area' motor-bus routes of *London Transport* make a criss-cross pattern extending over the whole of central London and into the suburbs, where they connect with the 'Country Buses' reaching far out into the surrounding

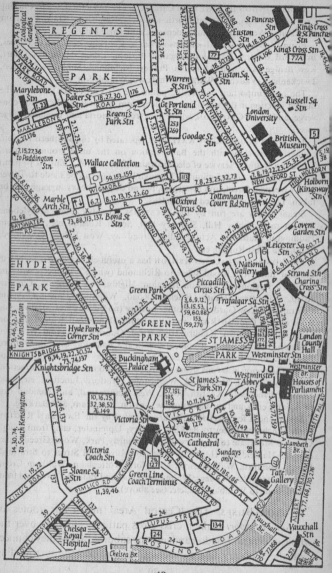

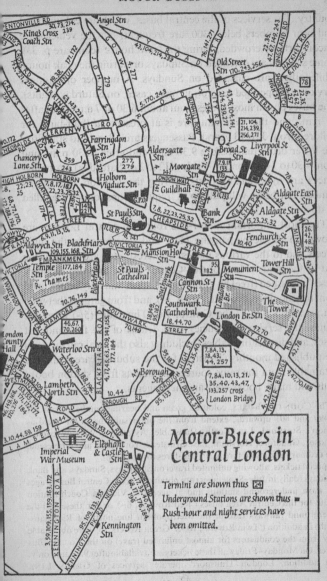

Motor-Buses in Central London

Termini are shown thus 24
Underground Stations are shown thus ■
Rush-hour and night services have
been omitted.

country. The services of the central buses, which are coloured red and bear numbers below 300, are frequent, but the vehicles are uncomfortably crowded during the 'rush hours' (compare p. 33). Some services are extended on Sundays or during the peak hours, while others are curtailed on Sundays. A number of all-night services are operated (except, in most cases, on Saturday nights). The buses ply on most routes from about 6.30 or 7 a.m. until after 11 p.m., and the minimum fare is at present 3d (half-fares for children from 3 to 13 years). Passengers are allowed to stand (on the lower deck) only before 9.30 a.m. and after 10.30 p.m., and from 4.30 to 7 on Monday–Friday (12 to 2 on Saturday). Stopping-places are indicated by posts bearing the London Transport's symbol, but buses will pull up at 'request stops' only if signalled to do so.

The most important motor-bus routes in central London are shown on the accompanying plan, and the routes in the main streets and to the various places of interest, etc., are given in the text of the guide. Maps of the 'Central Buses' and the 'Country Buses' are issued (free) by London Transport and may be obtained from the enquiry offices, etc. (see p. 34), and from garages (between 8 a.m. and 7 p.m.). The Central Bus Timetable (5/-) gives the routes, the service frequencies, and details of the first and last buses, and district timetables (including also the local rail services) are published monthly (1/- each) for the suburban areas and are obtainable from the same sources, as well as from station book-stalls and many booksellers and newsagents.

The COUNTRY BUSES, coloured green and bearing numbers from 301 to 499 and 801 upwards, extend from the outer suburbs as far afield as Bishop's Stortford, Letchworth, Dunstable, Aylesbury, West Wycombe, Windsor, Guildford, Horsham, East Grinstead, Tonbridge, and Gravesend. The ordinary minimum fare is 3d (half-fares for children).

Special tickets, allowing unlimited travel on Saturdays, Sundays, and Bank Holidays (daily in July–September) are obtainable from Central Bus garages and most underground stations and at agents of Victoria Coach Station (p. 30) for the Central Area buses ('Red Rovers'; 6/-) or for these and the underground railways (except the Metropolitan line north of Rickmansworth) in addition ('Twin Rovers'; 10/-). 'Green Rovers' (6/-) are obtainable daily from the conductors for almost unlimited travel on the Country Bus routes. On Monday–Friday all these tickets are available after 9.30 a.m. only.

In addition, London Transport operates services of GREEN LINE

42

COACHES, mostly running right across the capital from one side to the other, and reaching many places well out in the country. These coaches (numbered from 701 upwards) are much faster than the ordinary buses, but they will stop in London only at the points so indicated (fewer than the bus stops) and the minimum fare is 1/8 (usually 1/2 in the outlying districts). A timetable of all services (1/–) and a map of the routes (free) are obtainable from the London Transport enquiry offices and other sources mentioned above. The principal stopping-points in central London are Victoria (Eccleston Bridge), Hyde Park Corner, Marble Arch, Baker Street Station, Oxford Circus, Trafalgar Square, and Aldgate (where some services start), and among the termini are Tilbury, Brentwood, Bishop's Stortford, Hertford, Hitchin, Luton, Dunstable, Aylesbury, Chesham, High Wycombe, Windsor, Ascot, Woking, Guildford, Dorking, Reigate, Crawley, East Grinstead, Tunbridge Wells, Wrotham, and Gravesend.

MOTOR-COACHES also ply in summer from London on day and half-day excursions to places of interest over a wide area. Particulars are obtainable from travel agents and information bureaux (see p. 61) and from local booking-offices. Conducted coach tours are operated by *London Transport* in summer on weekdays through the City or West End (2¾ hours; fare 12/6) and to the River and East End (3¼ hours; 10/-), and daily to London Airport (4½ hours; 10/-); and on certain days to places of interest in the vicinity of London (17/6, including admission charges). The coaches start from the Victoria Coach Station, Buckingham Palace Road. A circular bus tour (2 hours; 4/-), operated daily by London Transport, starts every hour from 11 until 5 (except at 1 p.m.) from Buckingham Palace Road (near Eccleston Bridge) and affords a rapid survey of the central area covered by this guide. Other conducted tours are arranged by *Thomas Cook & Son* and *Frames' Tours* (see p. 61), *London Coastal Coaches* (Victoria Coach Station), *Evan Evans' Tours* (71 Russell Square, WC1), and *Universal Sightseeing Tours* (17 Woburn Place, WC1).

MOTOR-LAUNCHES are operated on the Thames daily in summer and provide a pleasant method of exploring the river and its neighbourhood. Services are run by *Messrs R. G. Odell, Ltd*, and *County Cruises, Ltd*, from CHARING CROSS PIER (Plan VIII, A 3) at about ¾-hour intervals from about 10.45 a.m. to the Tower of London (2/6; round trip, no landing, 3/6), to Greenwich (3/6, return 5/-), to the Festival Gardens (3/-; from noon), and to Putney, Hammersmith, Kew (4/6, return 6/-), Richmond (5/-, 7/6), Kingston (6/-, 9/-), and Hampton Court (6/6, 10/-). Evening cruises (2 hours; 6/-) and other short trips are arranged by these companies and by *Messrs Thames Launches, Ltd*, who also operate services about every 20 minutes from 10.20 a.m. from WESTMINSTER PIER (Plan VII, D 3) to Tower

Bridge and Greenwich, and at approximately ½-hour intervals to the Festival Gardens, Putney, Hammersmith, Kew, Richmond, Kingston, and Hampton Court (fares as above). Further information regarding these and other services may be obtained from the *Thames Passenger Services Federation*, York Villa, Church Street, Twickenham, Middlesex.

Cruises through the PORT OF LONDON, visiting certain of the Docks, are organized by the *Port of London Authority* on Wednesdays, Thursdays, and Saturdays from mid-July to mid-September (also Saturdays only from late May to mid-July), starting from the Tower Pier (Plan IX, D 3) at 2.30 p.m. and arriving back at about 6.15. Advance bookings (fare 9/-; children under 16, 4/6) should be made with the Chief Information Officer (Dock Cruise Section), Port of London Authority (P.O. Box No. 242), Trinity Square, London EC3. Tickets are available also at Tower Pier at 1.30 on the day of the cruise if accommodation is available.

Trips by boat are operated on the REGENT'S CANAL on certain afternoons and evenings from Easter to September, starting from the junction of Edgware Road and Blomfield Road, Paddington (Plan I, B 2), and plying through Regent's Park to Camden Town, returning thence to 'Little Venice' (fare 4/-). Particulars are obtainable from John James, Canaletto Gallery, facing No. 20 Blomfield Road, W9 (Tel. No. CUNningham 3428).

Other trips are operated by *British Transport Waterways* daily between Easter and September from 'Little Venice', near Blomfield Road (Plan I, C 2), every hour from 10 to 6 (Sundays from 2) to the Zoological Gardens (fare 6/-, including admission; children 4/-), returning at hourly intervals from 10.30 to 6.30 (Sundays from 2.30; fare from the Zoo to 'Little Venice', 1/6; children 1/-).

An excellent service of steamers is run daily in summer by *Messrs Salter Brothers, Ltd* (head-office, Folly Bridge, Oxford), from Kingston to Hampton Court, Windsor, and Oxford (see the *Penguin Guide to Surrey*). Cruises are operated also by *Messrs Eagle Steamers* (Tower Hill, London EC3) daily (except Friday) in summer from Tower Pier to Southend, Margate, and along the French coast.

TAXICABS ply on the main streets of the capital or can be hired from taxi-ranks or by telephone. Fares are indicated by meters, and if the meter-flag is up or the indicator 'For Hire' is lit the driver may be hailed, but he is under no obligation to accept a passenger unless the taxi is stationary. The present charge for hire for one person is 1/9 for three-fifths of a mile, plus 3d for each additional one-fifth of a mile. A charge of 6d extra (for the whole hiring) is made for each additional person, but two children under ten years each count as one person. Each article of luggage carried outside is charged 3*d* (bicycles and other heavy or awkward articles 9*d*). Any time spent waiting is also registered on the meter, and the driver expects a tip of about 20 per cent of the fare (1/- or 1/6 for a short journey), proportionately more if he helps with the luggage. If the journey begins or ends between midnight and 6 a.m., an extra charge of 1/- on the fare is payable. For journeys over 6 miles the fares are normally arranged by agreement.

Taxis may also be hired by telephoning the following numbers of radio taxi firms: TERminus 6444, MOUntview 3232 and WATerloo 7722. The telephone numbers of local taxi-ranks are given in the London telephone directory under the heading 'Taxi-cab'.

MINICABS do not ply for hire on the streets, but may be booked at any hour of the day or night for any period by telephoning WELbeck 4440 or HUNter 1250. The standard fare is 1/8 per mile for any distance, with a minimum charge of 4/- (payable from the time of picking up the customer).

PRIVATE MOTOR-CARS, with qualified chauffeurs, may be hired in London by the hour, day, or week, and for special occasions. Most hiring companies will meet trains, boats, or aircraft by prior arrangement. The usual charge per hour is about 15/-, for a visit to a theatre it works out at about 45/- to £3, for a day roughly £7 to £10. Self-driven cars may also be hired by the week (from £5; £10 with unlimited mileage) and for shorter or longer periods. Intending hirers should make sure that fully comprehensive insurance is included.

The following are among the many companies from which cars may be hired with or without chauffeur: *Autohall*, 302 King Street, Hammersmith, W6; *Blue Star Garages*, Queensway, W2; *John Brain*, 44 Buckingham Palace Road, SW1; *Victor Britain*, 12a Berkeley Street, W1; *Chapman's*, 12 Codrington Mews, Ladbroke Grove, W11; *Daimler Hire*, 7 Herbrand Street, WC1; *Godfrey Davis*, Davis House, Wilton Road, SW1; *J. Davy*, Arlington Street, Piccadilly, SW1; *Roy Galway*, Ansdell Street, Kensington Square, W8; *Hertz Rent-a-Car*, 243 Knightsbridge, SW7; *Kennings*, 411 Edgware Road, W2; *Martins*, 57 Park Road, NW1; *Moons Motors*, 104 Buckingham Palace Road, SW1; *Motor Rentals*, 385 Euston Road, NW1; *C. G. Norman*, 50 Vauxhall Bridge Road, SW1; *Rootes*, Abbey House, Abbey Road, NW8; *Smith and Hunter*, 376 Kensington High Street, W14; *Sussex Motors*, 22 Brook Mews North, Lancaster Gate, W2; *Victory Car Hire*, Primrose Gardens, Hampstead, NW2.

CAR PARKING. The regulation of the motor traffic has become a serious problem in the increasingly congested streets of London, and it is being tackled in three ways: by the introduction of an experimental system of one-way traffic, by the provision of parking meters, and by the building of 'multi-storey' or underground car parks.

PARKING METERS (sixpence-in-the-slot machines) were first introduced in 1960 and there are now well over 10,000 of them in almost every part of the City and Westminster, as well as many others in such neighbouring boroughs as Holborn, Marylebone, Paddington, and Finsbury. The usual charges are 6d for 1 hour and 1/- for 2 hours (the maximum period), from 8.30 a.m. to 6.30 p.m. on Monday–Friday and 8.30 to 1.30 p.m. on Saturdays. No charge is made on Saturday afternoons (on Saturday mornings also in some areas) and on Sundays and Bank Holidays.

CAR PARKS. The following large public car parks have been opened recently in central London: HYDE PARK (Plan II, E 2), with room for 1,070 cars (see p. 164) and a subway to Marble Arch station; SHOE LANE, off Fleet Street (IV, D, E 2; 280 cars); UPPER THAMES STREET, near London Bridge (V, F 1, 2; 600 cars); ALDERSGATE STREET (IV, C, D 3; 700 cars); 'ROUTE 11' (V, D 1; 250 cars; underground); FINSBURY SQUARE (V, C 2; 350 cars; underground). Others are under construction or discussion. The charges vary from 1/- to 2/- per hour (with a minimum period of 2 or 3 hours in some parks) up to 7/- to 10/- for 12 hours and 12/- for 24 hours. Weekly terms can also be arranged in some cases.

HOTELS AND RESTAURANTS

HOTELS of almost every grade will be found in most parts of London, but especially in the west and south-west quarters. The loss of many hotels during the war and the subsequent restrictions on building, however, mean that there is still a great shortage of accommodation and visitors are advised that it is essential to secure rooms as early as possible in advance. In the lists below, the sumptuous and fashionable (and proportionately expensive) hotels de luxe, all in the West End, are given first; other hotels are arranged alphabetically under their postal districts. The lists make no claim to be complete and the omission of a name certainly implies no condemnation. It is inevitable, owing to lack of space, that mostly the larger and better-known hotels are included, but there are many smaller hotels, offering adequate accommodation for rather lower charges, particularly in Kensington, Bayswater, and Bloomsbury, while even more reasonable accommodation is obtainable in such pleasant outer suburbs as Hampstead, Hendon, Dulwich, and Wimbledon.

The charges quoted below are in accordance with tariffs authorized by the hotels themselves, supplemented by information obtained by the Author or kindly provided by travellers. They are, of course, liable to fluctuation, for example owing to changes in the cost of living, but they may confidently be taken as an indication of the relative expense of the hotels. It is advisable always to verify charges before booking rooms. The 'room-and-breakfast' charge is for a single room and normally includes a bath and an 'English' breakfast; a reduction can sometimes be obtained if a light ('Continental') breakfast is taken. Almost all the larger hotels have bedrooms with private bathrooms attached, for which a relatively higher charge is made. The 'en pension' charges quoted for board and lodging are for a stay of one week, unless indicated otherwise; most hotels, however, will arrange a charge for a shorter period, though not usually of less than three days. The

47

pension charges include both luncheon and dinner (though not invariably tea), but this arrangement is generally inconvenient for holiday visitors, who will probably wish to take some at least of their meals elsewhere.

Lists of hotels are provided for the benefit of their members by the *Automobile Association* (head office, Fanum House, New Coventry Street, W 1) and the *Royal Automobile Club* (83 Pall Mall, S W 1). Handbooks of hotels are published annually by the *British Travel Association* (6/-; see p. 61) and the *British Hotels and Restaurants Association* (3/6), and are obtainable from bookstalls, etc. The Travel Association will also recommend hotels, though they cannot arrange reservations. In cases of difficulty these may be made through the *London Hotels Information Service* (for overseas visitors only), 88 Brook Street, W 1 (Tel. No. MAYfair 5414); *Hotel Accommodation Service* (Hotac), 93 Baker Street, W 1 (WELbeck 2555); or *Hotel Booking Service*, 5 Coventry Street, W 1 (GERrard 5052).

The abbreviations used below are: B. = Breakfast; gns. = guineas; pens. = pension (see above); R. = Room; T.H. = Trust House; unlic. = unlicensed. Hotels in which all (or nearly all) the bedrooms have private baths are indicated by an asterisk.

HOTELS DE LUXE (terms are obtainable on application only): BERKELEY (100 R.; all suites*), Berkeley Street, W 1 (corner of Piccadilly); CARLTON TOWER (318 R.*), Cadogan Place, S W 1 (see p. 146); CLARIDGE'S (250 R.; all suites*), Brook Street, W 1 (near Grosvenor Square); CONNAUGHT (100 R.*), Carlos Place, W 1 (off Grosvenor Square); DORCHESTER (280 R.*), Park Lane, W 1 (facing Hyde park); GROSVENOR HOUSE (550 R.*), Park Lane, W 1; HYDE PARK (250 R.*), Knightsbridge, S W 1 (overlooking Hyde Park); LONDON HILTON (495 R.*), Park Lane, W 1 (opened in 1963; see p. 147); MAY FAIR (450 R.*), Berkeley Street, W 1; PICCADILLY (250 R.*), Piccadilly and Regent Street, W 1; RITZ (132 R.*), Piccadilly, W 1 (overlooking the Green Park); SAVOY (500 R.; all suites*), Strand, W C 2 (facing the Thames); WESTBURY (285 R.*), Conduit Street, W 1 (corner of New Bond Street).

Hotels in the district W C 1 (Bloomsbury and neighbourhood): AMBASSADORS (85 R.), Upper Woburn Place, R. & B. 50/- to 60/-; AVONDALE (60 R.), Tavistock Place, R. & B. 25/-; BEDFORD CORNER (82 R.), Bayley Street, R. & B. 35/- to 45/-; BONNINGTON (240 R.), Southampton Row, R. & B. 45/- to 60/-; CORA (150 R.), Upper Woburn Place, R. & B. 36/6 to 42/6; COUNTY (175 R.), Upper Woburn Place, R. & B. 36/-; GRAND (90 R.), Southampton Row, R. & B. 30/- to 42/6; IMPERIAL (600 R.), Russell Square, R. & B. 38/6 to 49/6; IVANHOE (245 R.; unlic.), Bloomsbury Street, R. & B. 33/-; KENILWORTH (140 R.; unlic.), Great Russell Street, R. & B. 31/-; KINGSLEY (180 R.), Bloomsbury Way, R. & B. 42/6 to 57/6; MONTAGUE (100 R.), Montague Street, R. & B. 40/-; MOUNT PLEASANT (422 R.), 53 Calthorpe Street, R. & B. 21/- to 30/·; NATIONAL (308 R.), Bedford Way, R. & B. 27/6; PRESIDENT (449 R.*), Russell Square, R. & B.

60/-; ROYAL (770 R.), Woburn Place, R. & B. 27/6; RUSSELL (350 R.), Russell Square, R. & B. 55/- to 60/-; ST MARGARET'S (95 R.; unlic.), 26 Bedford Place, R. & B. 27/6 to 30/-, pens. 14–15 gns.; TAVISTOCK (301 R.*), Tavistock Square, R. & B. 55/-; WAVERLEY (100 R.; unlic.), Southampton Row, R. & B. 31/-; WHITE HALL, Bloomsbury Square (70 R.) and Montague Street (60 R.), R. & B. 35/- to 40/-.

WC2 (Charing Cross, Strand, and neighbourhood): CHARING CROSS (220 R.), Charing Cross Station, R. & B. 59/- to 93/-; CRAVEN (58 R.), Craven Street, R. & B. 30/-; GARRICK (40 R.), 3 Charing Cross Road, R. & B. 30/-; HOWARD (200 R.), Norfolk Street, R. & B. 47/6 to 67/6; NORFOLK (60 R.), 32 Surrey Street, R. & B. 28/6 to 37/6, pens. 16–20 gns.; PASTORIA (50 R.), St Martin's Street, R. & B. 50/- to 72/6; SHAFTESBURY (250 R.), Monmouth Street, R. & B. 40/- to 55/-; STRAND PALACE (850 R.), Strand, R. & B. 42/- to 57/6; WALDORF (300 R.), Aldwych, R. & B. 50/- to 80/-.

W1 (Piccadilly, Park Lane, Mayfair, and Oxford Street): ATHENAEUM COURT (140 R.*), 116 Piccadilly, R. & B. from 64/-; BERNERS (237 R.), 10 Berners Street, R. & B. 50/- to 65/-; BROWN'S (T.H.; 136 R.), Dover Street, R. & B. 49/6 to 68/6; BRYANSTON COURT (66 R.), 56 Great Cumberland Place, R. & B. 45/- to 50/-; CLIFTON-FORD (150 R.), Welbeck Street, R. & B. 45/- to 72/6; CUMBERLAND (900 R.*), Marble Arch, Oxford Street, R. & B. 57/6 to 65/-; DURRANT'S (67 R.), George Street, R. & B. 42/- to 50/-; FLEMING'S (110 R.), Half Moon Street, R. & B. 45/- to 62/6; GEORGIAN (25 R.), 87 Gloucester Place, R. & B. 45/- to 50/-; GREEN PARK (200 R.), Half Moon Street, R. & B. 45/- to 62/6; GROSVENOR COURT (100 R.*), Davies Street, R. & B. 62/6 to 72/6; MANDEVILLE (165 R.), Mandeville Place, R. & B. 45/- to 72/6; MASCOT (65 R.), York Street, R. & B. 30/-; MOSTYN (115 R.), Portman Street, R. & B. 40/- to 60/-; MOUNT ROYAL (750 R.*), Marble Arch, Oxford Street, R. & B. 62/6 to 72/6; PARK LANE (400 R.*), Piccadilly, R. & B. from 76/-; REGENT PALACE (1140 R.), Piccadilly Circus, R. & B. 42/-; ROSE COURT (35 R.; unlic.), 35 Great Cumberland Place, R. & B. 40/-; ST GEORGE'S (T.H.), Langham Place (opening in 1963); STRATFORD COURT (150 R.*), 350 Oxford Street, R. & B. 55/- to 62/6; THE LONDONER (122 R.*), Welbeck Street, R. & B. 62/6 to 72/6; WASHINGTON (190 R.), Curzon Street, R. & B. 56/- to 77/6.

W2 (Bayswater and north of Hyde Park): AMBASSADOR (77 R.*), 12 Lancaster Gate, R. & B. 40/-; ASHTON'S (34 R.), 144 Praed Street, R. & B. 32/6; BAYSWATER (40 R.), Bayswater Road, R. & B. 33/-, pens. 10 gns.; CARLISLE HOUSE (44 R.), 27 Devonshire Terrace, R. & B. 35/- to 45/-; CAVENDISH (40 R.), 77 Lancaster Gate, R. & B. 37/6 to 52/6; COBURG (150 R.), 129 Bayswater Road, R. & B. 42/6; DEAN COURT (25 R.; unlic.), 57 Inverness Terrace, R. & B. 22/6 to 37/6; DOMINIONS (80 R.), 86 Lancaster Gate, R. & B. 37/6 to 52/6; EMBASSY (60 R.; unlic.), 150 Bayswater Road, R. & B. from 35/-; GREAT WESTERN ROYAL (210 R.), Paddington Station, R. & B. 52/- to 90/-; HERTFORD (T.H.; 77 R.*), 104 Bayswater Road, R. & B. 69/6 to 78/6; INVERNESS COURT (75 R.; unlic.), 1 Inverness

Terrace, R. & B. 32/6, pens. 12½–14½ gns.; KING'S COURT (82 R.), Leinster Gardens, R. & B. 32/6 to 40/-; LEINSTER COURT (60 R.; unlic.), 19 Leinster Gardens, R. & B. 30/-, pens. 11–14 gns.; LEINSTER HOUSE (30 R.; unlic.), 45 Leinster Gardens, R. & B. 25/-, pens. 8½–10 gns.; LEINSTER TOWERS (200 R.*), Leinster Gardens, R. & B. 42/6 to 50/-; PARK COURT (100 R.*), 75 Lancaster Gate, R. & B. 45/- to 55/-; PARKWAY (100 R.), Inverness Terrace, R. & B. 37/6 to 50/-; PEMBRIDGE GARDENS (100 R.), 1 Pembridge Gardens, R. & B. 30/- to 45/-, pens. 13–16 gns.; QUEENSWAY (150 R.), Princes Square, R. & B. 35/-, pens. 13½–16 gns.; STEPHEN COURT (300 R.*), Talbot Square, R. & B. 47/6; WHITENESS (40 R.), 45 Queen's Gardens, R. & B. 27/6 to 37/6, pens. 9½–11 gns.; WHITE'S (70 R.*), 57 Lancaster Gate, R. & B. from 71/6; WINDSOR (150 R.), 56 Lancaster Gate, R. & B. 37/6 to 52/6.

W8 (Kensington): DE VERE (80 R.), De Vere Gardens, R. & B. 52/6 to 77/6; KENSINGTON CLOSE (505 R.*), Wright's Lane, off Kensington High Street, R. & B. from 50/6; KENSINGTON PALACE (320 R.*), De Vere Gardens, R. & B. 83/6 to 92/6; LEXHAM (58 R.; unlic.), 32 Lexham Gardens, R. & B. 32/6 to 35/-, pens. 12–14 gns.; MILESTONE (90 R.), Kensington Court, R. & B. 42/- to 45/-; PRINCE OF WALES (350 R.), De Vere Gardens, R. & B. 35/- to 70/-; PRINCES COURT (38 R.), 15 Prince of Wales Terrace, R. & B. 32/6 to 37/6; SUNCOURT (70 R.; unlic.), 59 Lexham Gardens, R. & B. 30/-, pens. 10 gns.

W9 (North Paddington): CLARENDON COURT (100 R.), Maida Vale, R. & B. 35/- to 63/-, pens. 14–24 gns.; COLONNADE (40 R.; unlic.), 2 Warrington Crescent, R. & B. 30/- to 45/-; WORSLEY HOUSE (100 R.; unlic.), 9 Clifton Gardens, R. & B. 21/- to 24/6, pens. from 6½ gns.

SW1 (Westminster, St James's, Victoria, and Belgravia): BELGRAVIA (30 R.), 84 Belgrave Road, R. & B. 35/- to 42/-; CADOGAN (100 R.), 75 Sloane Street, R. & B. 45/-; CHESHAM (90 R.*), 20 Chesham Place, R. & B. from 63/6; EBURY COURT (37 R.), 26 Ebury Street, R. & B. 35/- to 45/-; ECCLESTON (150 R.), Gillingham Street, R. & B. 50/- to 65/-; GORING (100 R.*), Grosvenor Gardens, R. & B. 51/- to 55/-; GROSVENOR (235 R.), Victoria Station, R. & B. 46/6 to 67/6; MEURICE (35 R.*), 16 Bury Street, R. & B. from 78/6; OLD ST JAMES'S HOUSE (40 R.*), 7 Park Place, R. & B. from 60/-; ROYAL COURT (110 R.), Sloane Square, R. & B. 45/- to 60/-; RUBENS (150 R.*), Buckingham Palace Road, R. & B. 50/- to 72/6; ST ERMIN'S (250 R.), Caxton Street, R. & B. 50/- to 72/6; ST JAMES'S COURT (250 R., all suites*), Buckingham Gate, R. & B. 45/6 to 66/6; STAFFORD (40 R.*), 16 St James's Place, R. & B. 94/6 to 115/6; WILBRAHAM (40 R.), Wilbraham Place, R. & B. 40/- to 42/6. — SW3 (Chelsea): BASIL STREET (123 R.), Basil Street, R. & B. 45/- to 55/-.

SW5 (Earls Court): BARKSTON GARDENS (T.H.; 58 R.), 36 Barkston Gardens, R. & B. 37/6 to 42/6; KING CHARLES (30 R.), 249 Cromwell Road, R. & B. 27/6 to 30/-; MAJESTIC (65 R.; unlic.), 158 Cromwell Road, R. & B. 35/-.

SW7 (South Kensington): ABAN COURT (90 R.), 19 Harrington Gardens, R. & B. 30/- to 35/-, pens. 11½–18 gns.; ADRIA (42 R.), 88 Queen's Gate, R. & B. 38/- to 56/-, pens. 12–16 gns.; ALEXANDRA (60 R.; unlic.), 5 Harrington Gardens, R. & B. 25/- to 30/-, pens. 9–12 gns.; ALWIN COURT (55 R.; unlic.), 61 Gloucester Road, R. & B. 30/-, pens. 10 gns.; ATLANTIC (47 R.), 143 Cromwell Road, R. & B. 27/6 to 35/-, pens. 13–16 gns.; BAILEY'S (180 R.), Gloucester Road, R. & B. 50/- to 70/-; BUCKINGHAM (80 R.), 94 Cromwell Road, R. & B. 37/6 to 39/6, pens. 15–18 gns.; CROFTON (63 R.), 13 Queen's Gate, R. & B. 35/- to 45/-; FROBISHER COURT (110 R.), 119 Cromwell Road, R. & B. 27/6 to 37/6, pens. 14–17 gns.; GLENDOWER (100 R.), Glendower Place, R. & B. 32/6 to 47/6, pens. 12 gns.; GORE (48 R.), 189 Queen's Gate, R. & B. from 50/-; HARRINGTON HALL (65 R.), 11 Harrington Gardens, R. & B. from 44/-; IMPERIAL (39 R.), 121 Queen's Gate, R. & B. 35/-, pens. £10; LEICESTER COURT (65 R.; unlic.), 41 Queen's Gate Gardens, R. & B. 30/-; MILTON COURT (100 R.; unlic.), 68 Cromwell Road, R. & B. 32/6, pens. 12 gns.; MONTANA (55 R.), 67 Gloucester Road, R. & B. 42/- to 65/-; NORFOLK (100 R.), 2 Harrington Road R. & B. 37/6 to 47/6; NORMANDIE (80 R.), 163 Knightsbridge, R. & B. from 46/6; ONSLOW COURT (160 R.; unlic.), Queen's Gate, R. & B. 30/- to 45/-, pens. 11 gns.; REMBRANDT (175 R.), Thurloe Place, R. & B. 40/- to 60/-; SNOW's (40 R.), 139 Cromwell Road, R. & B. 37/6 to 45/-; STANHOPE COURT (100 R.; unlic.), Stanhope Gardens, R. & B. 32/6, pens. 12 gns.; TUDOR COURT (100 R.; unlic.), 58 Cromwell Road, R. & B. 32/6, pens. 11 gns.; VANDERBILT (100 R.), 76 Cromwell Road, R. & B. from 37/6.

NW1 (Euston and Marylebone): DORSET SQUARE (50 R.), 10 Dorset Square, R. & B. 38/6 to 48/6; EUSTON (140 R.), Euston Station, R. & B. 56/6 to 85/6; SOMERSET HOUSE (30 R.*), 6 Dorset Square, R. & B. 30/- to 50/-. — N1 (King's Cross): GREAT NORTHERN (70 R.), King's Cross Station R. & B. 52/6 to 82/6.

EC (City): GREAT EASTERN (190 R.), Liverpool Street Station, EC2, R. & B. 55/- to 92/6; THREE NUNS (40 R.), 9 Aldgate High Street, EC3, R. & B. from 35/-.

BOARDING-HOUSES, some describing themselves as private hotels, are to be found in all the residential parts of London, as well as in the suburbs. They vary considerably in their charges and in the quality of the accommodation offered, and a recommendation from someone known to the visitor is advisable. The letting rooms are generally limited in number and in many cases are booked early in the season, if not all the year round. There are satisfactory boarding-houses in Bayswater, to the north of Hyde Park, and in Kensington, especially in the neighbourhood of Earls Court, where accommodation should be obtainable at an inclusive charge of about 8–10 gns. per week. Numerous cheaper and rather plainer boarding-houses exist in Bloomsbury, with proportionately lesser charges (from about 6 gns.). The visitor should come to an arrangement at the outset regarding the provision of luncheon and tea.

RESIDENTIAL HOTELS or blocks of flats, with suites of furnished apartments, and in some cases with restaurants and room attendance ('service flats'), have sprung up in many quarters of London in recent years. The most palatial (and most expensive) are in Kensington and Bayswater, where the charge for a suite varies from about 12 gns. per week upwards. In less exclusive quarters charges are proportionately less. Meals may usually either be taken in the restaurant or be ordered from it. Some of the larger blocks of flats are equipped with private bathrooms, bars and lounges, games rooms and swimming pools, and garages. FURNISHED APARTMENTS are obtainable also in private houses, but here a personal recommendation is desirable, or a house-agent of known standing should be approached. The most expensive apartments (from about 15 gns. upwards) are in St James's and Mayfair (the neighbourhood of Piccadilly and Oxford Street), where meals can often be supplied if arranged. Cheaper rooms are numerous in Bloomsbury and elsewhere (from about 3 gns. per week), but breakfast is generally the only meal that can be provided.

Furnished Houses, obtainable in parts of the suburbs, are usually fairly expensive, and are best sought through a reliable house-agent. Plate, cutlery, and linen are generally provided, but are charged as 'extras'. *En Famille Agency, Ltd*, 1 New Burlington Street, W 1 (REGent 8866), will make suitable arrangements for foreigners who wish to stay as paying guests with a private family in London. Members of the *Youth Hostels Association* (London office, 29 John Adam Street, Strand, W C 2) will find hostels in Holland Park, Kensington (see p. 156), and at Highgate (84 Highgate West Hill, N 6) and Earls Court (38 Bolton Gardens, S W 5).

RESTAURANTS, cafés, and tea-rooms of every size, grade, and range of price abound in London, the more favoured regions being the Piccadilly area, Soho, and Kensington. All the principal hotels have restaurants and grill-rooms to which non-residents are admitted, and many hotels will provide theatre suppers. Alcoholic liquor may be obtained only during the licensing hours (see p. 58), except by residents in their hotels. Some restaurants which have no licence will send out for drinks (small tip expected). Smoking is permitted almost everywhere, and evening dress is required only at a few of the more exclusive restaurants. At these and other first-class restaurants tables can usually be booked in advance.

The most expensive restaurants will be found in the neighbourhood of Piccadilly and Regent Street. Here the cuisine is mainly French or Italian, and meals are generally served à la carte; elsewhere table d'hôte meals can usually be obtained or arranged. Foreign restaurants, especially in Soho, are often unpretentious, but are greatly favoured for their cooking and unusual dishes, and charges are mostly reasonable. The grill-rooms attached to hotels and restaurants, particularly in the West End, are popular for lunch. Restaurants in the City, including some well-known and old-fashioned taverns, are usually open only on weekdays for lunch; though Pimm's and several other restaurants keep open until 7 p.m. (except Saturdays). The fare in the City is generally plainer, though well-cooked, and the special 'plat du jour' offered can be recommended. Good plain luncheons may also be obtained at reasonable charges at quite modest public houses.

Inexpensive meals may be obtained at the chains of restaurants established by *Messrs J. Lyons & Co.*, *The Aerated Bread Co.* ('ABC'), the *Express Dairy Co.*, *Kardomah*, *Messrs Forte's & Co.*, *Messrs Slater*, and other companies. The Corner Houses of Messrs Lyons at Marble Arch, Oxford Street (corner of Tottenham Court Road), Coventry Street (near Piccadilly Circus), and the Strand (Charing Cross) are especially popular. Restaurants will also be found in all the large stores.

The restaurants recommended below are arranged alphabetically under districts. Only a selection can be given, and here again the omission of a name implies no condemnation. The following abbreviations are used: L. = Luncheon; S. = open on Sundays; unlic. = unlicensed; and specialities are mentioned in brackets. For restaurants offering dancing and/or cabaret, see p. 75; for tea-rooms, see p. 57.

PICCADILLY, REGENT STREET, and their neighbourhood. First-class and fashionable restaurants: À L'ÉCU DE FRANCE, 111 Jermyn Street (French); BOULEVARD DE PARIS, Stratton Street (French; music); CAFÉ ROYAL, 68 Regent Street (S.); CAPRICE, Arlington Street; CÉLÉBRITÉ, 18 New Bond Street (from 10 p.m.); COLONY, Berkeley Square; GUINEA GRILL, 30 Bruton Place (no L. on Saturdays); HUNTING LODGE, Lower Regent Street; L'APÉRITIF, 102 Jermyn Street (French); LE CHÂTEAU-BRIAND, Stratton Street (French); LE COQ D'OR, Stratton Street (French);

L'HIRONDELLE, 99 Regent Street (no L.; French; music); MAISON BASQUE, 11 Dover Street (French and Spanish); MANETTA'S, Clarges Street (S.); MARTINEZ, 25 Swallow Street (S.; Spanish); MIRABELLE, 56 Curzon Street; MONSEIGNEUR, 16 Jermyn Street; OVERTON'S, 67a Piccadilly and 5 St James's Street (oysters, fish, etc.); PIGALLE, 190 Piccadilly; PRUNIER, 72 St James's Street (French; fish); QUAGLINO'S, 16 Bury Street (S.); SIR HARRY'S BAR, 17 Hertford Street; SOCIETY, 40 Jermyn Street (no L.).

Less expensive restaurants: AUSTRIAN, 39 Albemarle Street (Austrian; music); BEACHCOMBER, Berkeley Street (S.; no L.; Chinese and Polynesian); BENTLEY'S, 11 Swallow Street (fish and shellfish only); BRAGANZA (Wheeler's), 56 Frith Street (fish); CATHAY, 4 Glasshouse Street (S.; Chinese); CUNNINGHAM'S, 47 and 51 Curzon Street (S.; fish); DANISH (Three Vikings), 84 Brewer Street (S.; Danish); EMPRESS, 16 Berkeley Street (S.); FIFTY FIVE, 55 Jermyn Street (music); FRANK'S, 65 Jermyn Street (Italian); LO SPIEDO, 6 Jermyn Street (Italian); PREMIER, 48 Dover Street; ST JAMES'S (Wheeler's), 12a Duke of York Street (shellfish); SCOTT'S, 18 Coventry Street (S.); SHEPHERD'S TAVERN, 50 Hertford Street (closed Saturdays); STEAK AND CHOP HOUSE, 40 Haymarket (S.); STONE'S CHOP HOUSE, Panton Street (S.); TROCADERO, Shaftesbury Avenue (S.); VEERASWAMY'S, 99 Regent Street (S.; Indian); VENDÔME (Wheeler's), 20 Dover Street (shellfish; closed Saturdays); VINE GRILL, 2 Piccadilly Place; WHITE BEAR INN, Piccadilly Circus (S.; music).

SOHO AND NEIGHBOURHOOD: ALBERT, 53 Beak Street (Continental); AU JARDIN DES GOURMETS, 5 Greek Street (French; first-class); BARCELONA, 17 Beak Street (Spanish); BOULOGNE, 27 Gerrard Street (French); CAFÉ BLEU, 40 Old Compton Street (S.; Continental); CASA PEPE, 52 Dean Street (Spanish and South American); CHEZ AUGUSTE, 38 Old Compton Street (S.; music); CHOY'S, 45 Frith Street (S.; Chinese); CORONET, 9 Soho Street (L. only; closed Saturdays); DE HEMS, 11 Macclesfield Street (English); GARNER'S, 27 Wardour Street; GAY HUSSAR, 2 Greek Street (Hungarian); GENNARO'S, 44 Dean Street (S.; Italian; old-established); HONG KONG, 60 Shaftesbury Avenue (S.; Chinese); HOSTARIA ROMANA, 70 Dean Street (S.; Italian); HUNGARIAN CSARDA, 77 Dean Street (Hungarian); ISOLA BELLA, 15 Frith Street (French and Italian; first-class); ISOW'S, 6 Brewer Street (S.: Continental); KETTNER'S, 29 Romilly Street (S.; old-established); KOH-I-NOR, 29 Rupert Street (S.; Indian); LA BELLE ÉTOILE, 17 Frith Street (S.; Continental); LA COLOMBINA D'ORO, 61 Dean Street (S.; Italian); LA RESERVE, 37 Gerrard Street (French); LE MOULIN D'OR, 27 Romilly Street (S.; French); LEONI'S QUO VADIS, 26 Dean Street (S.; Italian); L'EPICURE, 28 Frith Street; L'ESCARGOT BIENVENUE, 48 Greek Street (French); LE VERSAILLES, 50 Frith Street (French); LEY-ON, 91 Wardour Street (S.; Chinese); MAXIM'S, 30 Wardour Street (S.; Chinese and English); PETIT SAVOYARD, 36 Greek Street (French); PINOCCHIO, 29 Frith Street (S.; Italian); ROMANO SANTI, 50 Greek Street (Continental: old-established); SHAFI INDIA, 18 Gerrard Street (S.; Indian); SOHO (Wheeler's), 19 Old Compton Street (shellfish); TOLAINI'S, 17 Wardour Street (French and Italian); VENEZIA, 20 Great Chapel Street (S.; Italian).

CHARING CROSS, LEICESTER SQUARE, THE STRAND, and neighbourhood: ALDWYCH BRASSERIE, 1 Aldwych; ASHOKA, 22 Cranbourn Street (S.; Indian); ASIATIQUE, 16 Irving Street (S.; Oriental); BEOTY'S, 79 St Martin's Lane (French and Greek); BOULESTIN, 25 Southampton Street (French; first-class); BRUSA'S, 50 St Martin's Lane (Continental); CARR'S, 264 Strand (near the Law Courts; closed Saturdays); CHEZ SOLANGE, 35 Cranbourn Street (French); DEVEREUX, 20 Devereux Court (opposite the Law Courts); GOW'S, 37 St Martin's Lane (noted for grills); HENRI'S GRILL, 41 Maiden Lane; IVY, 1 West Street, Cambridge Circus; LOBSTER AND STEAK, 19 Leicester Square (S.); NAG'S HEAD, Floral Street, Covent Garden (theatrical clientele); PARAMOUNT GRILL, 14 Irving Street (S.); RULE'S, 35 Maiden Lane (old-established; theatrical clientele); SHEEKEY'S, 29 St Martin's Court (fish only); SHERLOCK HOLMES, 10 Northumberland Street; SIMPSON'S, 100 Strand (old English fare); VEGA (unlic.), 56 Whitcomb Street, Leicester Square (vegetarian); YOUNG'S, 13 West Street (S.; Oriental).

WESTMINSTER AND VICTORIA: BUCKINGHAM, 62 Petty France (closed Saturdays); CHEZ GASTON, 36 Buckingham Palace Road (S.; Belgian); CHURCH HOUSE, Great Smith Street (L. only; closed Saturdays); CROW'S NEST, 17 Petty France (closed Saturdays); GAZELLE GRILL, 127 Victoria Street; LA BICYCLETTE, 61 Elizabeth Street (no L.; French); LA POULE AU POT, 231 Ebury Street (S. evening; French); OVERTON'S, opposite Victoria Station (fish, oysters, etc.); ST STEPHEN'S, 10 Bridge Street, facing the Houses of Parliament (S.; old-established); SPEEDBIRD, Airways Terminal, Buckingham Palace Road (S.); WILTON'S, 34 King Street (fish).

KNIGHTSBRIDGE, BELGRAVIA, and neighbourhood: ANTELOPE, 22 Eaton Terrace (English and French); BRIDGE, 25 Basil Street; CARAFE (Wheeler's), 15 Lowndes Street (S.; closed Mondays; Continental fish); CHARCO'S, 1 Bray Place, near Sloane Square (S.; noted for grills); COQ AU VIN, 8 Harriet Street, Sloane Street (S.; French); FISHERMAN'S WHARF, 215 Brompton Road (fish); JASPER'S EATING HOUSE, 4 Bourne Street, Sloane Square (no L.); KNIGHTSBRIDGE GRILLE, 171 Knightsbridge (old-established); LA SPERANZA, 179 Brompton Road (Italian); LA SURPRISE, 13 Knightsbridge Green (S. evening; French); LE CORDON ROUGE, 11 Sloane Street (Continental); LE MATELOT, 49 Elizabeth Street (S.; French); MARCEL, 14 Sloane Street (S.; French); MASSEY'S CHOP HOUSE, 38 Beauchamp Place (noted for grills); QUEEN'S, 4 Sloane Square (S.; Continental); SHANGRI-LA, 233 Brompton Road (S. evening; Chinese).

CHELSEA: AU PERE DE NICO, 10 Lincoln Street, off King's Road (S.; French and Italian); CHEZ LUBA, 116 Draycott Avenue (Russian and Central European); GOOD EARTH, 318 King's Road (S.; Chinese); LA

Bohème, 65 King's Road (French and Greek); L'Aiglon, 44 Old Church Street (no L.; Continental and English); Le Carrosse, 19 Elystan Street, off Fulham Road (no L.; Continental); Le Provençal, 259 Fulham Road (French); Magic Carpet, 124 King's Road (S.; French); Ox on the Roof, 353 King's Road (S.; no L.; Japanese, etc.); Shorthorn, Chelsea Cloisters, Sloane Avenue (S.); Unity, 91 King's Road (S.; English and Continental); Vivian's Pavillon, 5 Draycott Avenue (S.).

South Kensington: Balalaika, 10 Kenway Road, off Cromwell Road (S.; Russian); Brompton Grill, 243 Brompton Road (S.; Continental); Chez Cléo, 11 Harrington Gardens (French; music); Chez Vatel, 1 Old Brompton Road, opposite South Kensington Station (S.; French and Italian); Dino's, 117 Gloucester Road (S.; Continental); Jamshid, 6 Glendower Place (S.; Indian); Marynka, 232 Brompton Road (S.); Rice Bowl, 27 Pelham Street (S.; Chinese); Stable, 123 Cromwell Road (S. evening; Continental); Star of India, 154 Old Brompton Road (S.; Indian).

Kensington: Beoty's, 14 Wright's Lane, off High Street (Greek); Chez Ciccio, 38 Church Street (S.; Continental); Chez Kristof, 12 St Alban's Grove (S.; Polish and Russian); Fu Tong, 29 High Street (S.; Chinese); Hand and Flower (Silver Grill), 1 Hammersmith Road (S.; noted for grills); La Toque Blanche, 21 Abingdon Road, off High Street (French); The Buttery, 10 Church Street (S.; English and Continental); Victor's, 20 Church Street (closed Saturdays); Wolfe's, 11 Abingdon Road (French).

Oxford Street, Marylebone, and neighbourhood: Akropolis, 34 Charlotte Street (Greek, etc.); Antoine (Wheeler's), 40 Charlotte Street (S.; closed Saturdays; fish, oysters); Balon's, 73 Baker Street (Continental); Bertorelli's, 19 Charlotte Street (Continental); Chiltern, Baker Street Station; Cock and Lion, 62 Wigmore Street, and Copper Grill, 56 Wigmore Street (S.; these two noted for grills); Cordon Bleu, 31 Marylebone Lane (L. only; French); Danish (Wivex), 87 Wigmore Street (S.; Danish); El Tio Pepe, 13 Shepherd's Place, near Grosvenor Square (French); Genevieve, 13 Thayer Street, Marylebone High Street (French); Great Wall, 33 Oxford Street (S. evening; Chinese); La Belle Meunière, 5 Charlotte Street (French); La Petite Monaco, 31 Marylebone High Street (French; music); Le P'tit Montmartre, 15 Marylebone Lane (S.; French); L'Étoile, 30 Charlotte Street (exclusive); Lotus House, 61 Edgware Road (S.; Chinese); Marquis, 121 Mount Street, Grosvenor Square (French and Italian); Schmidt's, 41 Charlotte Street (S.; German and Austrian); Shearn's (unlic.), 231 Tottenham Court Road (vegetarian); Shirreff's, 15 Great Castle Street; Symond's, 34 Brook Street; Verrey's, 233 Regent Street (old-established); White House, Albany Street, near Regent's Park; White Tower, 1 Percy Street (Greek; first-class).

Holborn, Bloomsbury, and neighbourhood: Connaught Rooms, 61 Great Queen Street (L. only; closed Saturdays); Cunningham's, 32

Great Queen Street (S.; fish); SHAH, 124 Drummond Street, near Euston Station (S.; Indian).

CITY (WEST OF ST PAUL'S): COCK TAVERN, 22 Fleet Street (see p. 235); COUNTRY LIFE (unlic.), 21 Ludgate Hill (vegetarian); DIVIANI'S, 122 Newgate Street; DU CHIEN NOIR, 83 Shoe Lane (French); FALSTAFF, 70 Fleet Street; FEATHERS, 36 Tudor Street, near the Temple; OLD CHESHIRE CHEESE, Wine Office Court, 145 Fleet Street (see p. 236); PRINTER'S DEVIL, 98 Fetter Lane.

CITY (EAST OF ST PAUL'S): BARON OF BEEF, Gutter Lane, Gresham Street; BIRCH'S, 3 Angel Court, Throgmorton Street (old-established); GEORGE & VULTURE, 3 Castle Court, Lombard Street (a well-known chop-house); LOMBARD, 2 Lombard Court, Gracechurch Street; LUCULLUS, Plantation House, Mincing Lane; OLD DR BUTLER'S HEAD (Pimm's), Mason's Avenue, Coleman Street; OMAR KHAYYAM, 50 Cannon Street (Oriental); PALMERSTON, 49 Bishopsgate and 34 Old Broad Street (noted grill-rooms); PIMM'S, the Old Red House, 94 Bishopsgate; POOR MILLIONAIRE, 158 Bishopsgate; SIMPSON'S, 38½ Cornhill (first class); SWEETING'S, 39 Queen Victoria Street (excellent fish); THROGMORTON, Throgmorton Street; WILLIAMSON'S TAVERN, 1 Groveland Court, Cheapside (old established).

SOUTHWARK AND SOUTH OF THE THAMES: BRIDGE HOUSE, beside London Bridge; GEORGE, 77 Borough High Street (see p. 302); ROYAL FESTIVAL HALL (p. 311; no L.).

Reasonably priced meals may be obtained at the following chains of restaurants: *Angus Steak Houses* (31 Leicester Square, 42 Dean Street, etc.), *London Steak Houses* (116 Baker Street, 130 Kensington High Street, etc.), *Peter Evans' Eating Houses* (1 Kingly Street, near Regent Street, 225 Brompton Road, etc.), and *Quality Inns* (unlic.; 1 Coventry Street, 22 Leicester Square, 310 Regent Street, etc.).

TEA-ROOMS. Tea can be obtained at most of the hotels, many of the restaurants (practically all the lower-priced restaurants), in the principal stores, and at numerous 'cafés'. It is served out-of-doors in summer on the Victoria Embankment (p. 246), in Hyde Park, Kensington Gardens, Regent's Park, and the Zoological Gardens. Light refreshments and 'snacks' may be purchased here, in St James's Park and several other public parks, and at varying prices in the many milk, coffee, and sandwich bars. Tea-rooms are almost invariably closed on Saturday afternoons and Sundays in the City.

The following establishments specialize in afternoon tea: BARBELLION, 70 New Bond Street; BENDICK'S, 46 New Bond Street and 55 Wigmore Street; CEYLON TEA CENTRE, 22 Lower Regent Street (see p. 121); DE

BRY, 2 Marble Arch (noted for chocolate); FORTNUM & MASON, 181 Piccadilly; FULLER, 206 Regent Street, 358 Strand, and many others; SEARCY, TANSLEY, 19 Sloane Street; STEWART, 191 Victoria Street, etc.

LICENSING HOURS. Alcoholic liquor may not be sold in the County of London before 11 a.m. or after 11 p.m.; there must be a break of 2½ hours from 3 p.m.; and there is a limit of 9 hours per day. The usual 'permitted' hours are from 11 a.m. to 3, and from 5.30 to 11. Sunday hours are from 12 noon to 2 and from 7 to 10.30.

GRATUITIES in restaurants may be reckoned at about 10–12 per cent of the bill, rather more at the higher-class establishments. Some of these automatically add a surcharge or 'service charge' to the bill, while some of the lower-priced tea shops do not encourage tipping, but maintain a 'staff-box' near the cash desk. In hotels tips should amount to about 10–15 per cent of the total charge, which may still be distributed personally in some hotels, though it is a growing practice to add a stipulated service charge to the visitor's bill.

POST OFFICES, INFORMATION BUREAUX, AND USEFUL ADDRESSES

POST OFFICES. London is divided into eight postal districts, distinguished by their initials: EC (East Central), WC (West Central), W, NW, N, E, SE, and SW. These districts are further divided into delivery office areas, each distinguished by a number, the head-office of the district being in the area numbered '1'. Letters, etc., addressed to London should bear both the postal district initials and the area number (*e.g.* NW1, EC4, W12) and also the name of the locality, if possible, to avoid any confusion through the duplication of street names.

The LONDON CHIEF OFFICE (the 'General Post Office') is in King Edward Street, EC1 (Plan IV, D 3), and its telephone number is MONarch 9876. It is open from 8 a.m. to 8 p.m. for all kinds of postal and telegraph business. The new TRAFALGAR SQUARE branch office, 22-28 William IV Street, WC2 (near St Martin's; III, F2), is also open from 8 a.m. to 8 p.m., and both offices are open all night (including Sundays and holidays) for telegraph and telephone business and the sale of stamps. Other post offices are normally open every weekday from 8.30 a.m. to 6 or 6.30 p.m., but smaller offices (sometimes in shops) may be open only from 9 to 5.30 or 6 and close at 1 p.m. on the local early closing day (see p. 85). On Sundays and Public Holidays (p. 87) all the important offices in each district are open from 9 a.m. to 1 p.m. for most classes of business. The hours during which any office is open can be ascertained by telephoning MONarch 9876.

The principal delivery of letters, etc., is made between about 7 and 9 a.m., but there is usually a second delivery later in the morning, and further business deliveries are made in the central areas. The provincial night-mails can be caught by posting in any letter-box before 6 p.m., though later postings (up to 8 p.m.) may be made at certain offices. There is no Sunday delivery of letters or parcels, and the only collection on that day is made at about 4 or

4.30 p.m. Telegrams in the London postal area are delivered up to 8 p.m. (5 p.m. on Sundays and most public holidays), urgent telegrams up to 11 p.m.

Full particulars of all post office services are given in the *Post Office Guide*, published annually (2/6; supplements free); and *London Post Offices and Streets* (2/-) gives complete lists of post offices (with their addresses and telephone numbers) and of streets (with their postal districts). These publications may be obtained from H.M. Stationery Office (York House, Kingsway, WC2, and 423 Oxford Street, W1) and from the chief post offices.

POSTE RESTANTE. Correspondence marked 'poste restante' or 'to be called for' may be addressed to the London Chief Office or to any branch office, of which there are generally several in each district. Proof of identity is required before letters are given up to the addressee. Letters are kept for a fortnight (for one month, if from abroad), but the poste restante system must not be used for more than three consecutive months. Letters bearing no district initials will be delivered to the London Chief Office, while those without an area numeral go to the district head-office.

PARCELS handed in at any post office will be delivered to any address in Great Britain and Northern Ireland for a charge varying from 2/- for 2 lb. to 6/6 for 22 lb., the maximum weight. Parcels above this limit will be collected from any address and delivered by *British Railways* (compare p. 27) and in the London area by *British Road Services*, whose head-office is at 238 City Road, EC1 (CLErkenwell 7677). The charge for the delivery of a parcel within the London area varies according to weight and size (2/4 for 15 lb. and ½ cubic ft.).

TELEPHONE facilities will be found at many post offices, shops, and railway stations (including the chief underground stations), and there are numerous kiosks in the streets. The minimum charge for a call in the London area is 4*d* (3*d* in the new kiosks). Calls are made by dialling the first three letters of the exchange, followed by the number: hence the head-office of the Metropolitan Police at New Scotland Yard is dialled WHI 1212. Trunk and toll calls may also be made from most call offices, reduced rates being charged for these between 6 p.m. and 6 a.m. (all day on Sundays).

Further information on the telephone services may be obtained from the *London Post Office Telephone Directory* or by telephoning GERrard 8060 (Central Area) or CITy 8060 (City Area). After 5 p.m. (1 p.m. on Saturdays) enquiries may be made by telephoning MONarch 9876.

Information about events of interest to take place in London on the succeeding day may be obtained by dialling ASK 9211, the correct time by dialling TIM, and a weather report by dialling WEA 2211.

INFORMATION BUREAUX. The BRITISH TRAVEL ASSOCIATION maintains an information centre for tourists at 64 St James's Street (Plan VIII, A 1; MAYfair 9191). The association issues a journal of 'Coming Events in Britain' (monthly; 2/-), a diary of theatres and concerts, exhibitions, ceremonies, etc. ('This Month in London'; 1/-), and other publications for tourists, and will provide much useful information. Overseas visitors are particularly welcome. The CITY OF LONDON INFORMATION CENTRE is on the south side of St Paul's Churchyard, at the corner of Godliman Street (Plan IV, E 3; MONarch 3030). Here publications and information relevant to the City may be readily obtained, including a monthly diary of events (free).

Official guide-maps have been set up here and there in the main streets of central London. Enquiries regarding public transport in London should be made to the *London Transport Board* (see p. 34), for railways elsewhere in Britain they should be made to the Enquiry Offices at the principal termini or to the *British Railways Travel Centre*, Rex House, Lower Regent Street (Plan III, F 2; TRAfalgar 4343). Information about the weather can be obtained from the *Meteorological Office* bureau in the Kingsway (TEMple Bar 4311).

TRAVEL AGENTS. The following are the London offices of the principal travel agents, who for a fee will arrange transport, hotel accommodation, and other matters for the convenience of visitors.

American Express, 6 Haymarket, SW1; 89 Mount Street, W1; and Savoy Hotel, Strand, WC2. — *Thomas Cook & Son*, Berkeley Street, W1; 103 Cheapside, EC2; 108 Fleet Street, EC4; 98 Gracechurch Street, EC3; 123 High Holborn, WC1; 104 Kensington High Street, W8; 145 Oxford Street, W1; 125 Pall Mall, SW1; 154 and 378 Strand, WC2; etc. — *Dean & Dawson*, 81 Piccadilly, W1; 23 Baker Street, W1; 163 Fenchurch Street, EC3; etc. — *Frames' Tours*, 25 Tavistock Place, WC1; 1 Regent Street, SW1; 80 Southampton Row, WC1. — *Sir Henry Lunn*, Marble Arch House, Edgware Road, W2. — *Polytechnic Touring Association*, 309 Regent Street, W1. — *Workers Travel Association*, Eccleston Court, Gillingham Street, SW1, and 49 Cannon Street, EC4.

AUTHORIZED GUIDES to the sights of London may be obtained through the Travel Association (see above), and from the *London Appreciation Society* (see p. 63), the *Guild of Guide Lecturers* (bureau at the Washington Hotel, Curzon Street, W1), *Universal Aunts*, 36 Walpole Street, King's Road, SW3, and *Take-a-Guide*, 11 Old Bond Street, W1.

USEFUL ADDRESSES. The following lists give some addresses which may be useful to the visitor to London. Addresses, both business and private, may be found in the *London Telephone Directory* (see above) and in *Kelly's Post Office London Directory*, published yearly from 2 Arundel Street, Strand, WC2, and available at public libraries, etc.

The addresses and other particulars of people of rank and eminence are given in *Who's Who*, published annually and similarly available. The addresses of American residents in London are contained, together with other information of relevance to visitors from the United States, in the *Anglo-American Year Book*, published by the American Chamber of Commerce at 75 Brook Street, W1.

BANKS are open in London on weekdays from 10 a.m. to 3 p.m. (Saturdays, usually 9.30 to 12), except on Public Holidays (see p. 87). The following are the head offices in London of the principal English banks, most of which have numerous branches throughout the city and suburbs. The chief Scottish, Irish, and American banks also have London offices or are represented in London by English banks.

BARCLAYS BANK, 54 Lombard Street, EC3, and 168 Fenchurch Street, EC3 (foreign); COUTTS & CO., 440 Strand, WC2; DISTRICT BANK, 75 Cornhill, EC3; GLYN, MILLS & CO., 67 Lombard Street, EC3, and 1 Fleet Street, EC4 (Child's Branch), and 22 Whitehall, SW1 (Holt's Branch); LLOYDS BANK, 71 Lombard Street, EC3, and 6 Eastcheap, EC3 (overseas); MARTINS BANK, 68 Lombard Street, EC3; MIDLAND BANK, Poultry, EC2, and 60 Gracechurch Street, EC3 (overseas); NATIONAL BANK, 13 Old Broad Street, EC2; NATIONAL PROVINCIAL BANK, 15 Bishopsgate, EC2, and 1 Princes Street, EC2 (overseas); WESTMINSTER BANK, 41 Lothbury, EC2, and 53 Threadneedle Street, EC2 (overseas); WILLIAMS DEACON'S, 20 Birchin Lane, Cornhill, EC3.

CLUBS. The social and political clubs, many of which have flourished for well over 100 years, are a stable feature of London life. Below are the addresses of the best known (in the SW1 postal area unless another area is given). Largely frequented for their social advantages, all have comfortable premises with excellent licensed restaurants. Entrance fees and subscriptions vary greatly and most of the clubs are exclusive, but members may generally entertain their friends (including ladies, in the majority of cases). Clubs connected with sporting activities are included in the section on 'Sport in and around London'.

ALPINE, 74 South Audley Street, W1 (mountaineering); ARMY & NAVY, 36 Pall Mall; ARTS, 40 Dover Street, W1 (art and science);

ATHENAEUM, 107 Pall Mall (the premier literary club); AUTHORS', 2 Whitehall Court; BATH, 43 Brook Street, W1; BOODLE'S, 28 St James's Street; BROOKS'S, 60 St James's Street (Liberal); CALEDONIAN, 9 Halkin Street (Scottish); CARLTON, 69 St James's Street (the leading Conservative club); CAVALRY, 127 Piccadilly, W1; CITY OF LONDON, 19 Old Broad Street, EC2; CONSTITUTIONAL, 28 Northumberland Avenue, WC2 (Conservative); COWDRAY, 20 Cavendish Square, W1 (professional women); DEVONSHIRE, 50 St James's Street; EAST INDIA & SPORTS, 16 St James's Square; GARRICK, 15 Garrick Street, WC2 (dramatic and legal); GRESHAM, 15 Abchurch Lane, EC4 (merchants, etc.); GUARDS', 16 Charles Street, W1; JUNIOR CARLTON, 30 Pall Mall; LANSDOWNE, 9 Fitzmaurice Place, W1; NATIONAL LIBERAL, Whitehall Place; NAVAL & MILITARY, 94 Piccadilly, W1; ORIENTAL, Stratford House, Stratford Place, W1; OXFORD & CAMBRIDGE, 71 Pall Mall; PORTLAND, 18b Charles Street, W1; PUBLIC SCHOOLS, 100 Piccadilly, W1; REFORM, 104 Pall Mall (the leading Liberal club); ROYAL AERO, 9 Fitzmaurice Place, W1; ROYAL AIR FORCE, 128 Piccadilly, W1; ROYAL AUTOMOBILE, 89 Pall Mall; ROYAL THAMES YACHT CLUB, Knightsbridge (from June, 1963); ST JAMES'S, 106 Piccadilly, W1 (diplomatic); ST STEPHEN'S, 34 Queen Anne's Gate (Conservative); SAVAGE, 1 Carlton House Terrace (literature and art); SAVILE, 69 Brook Street, W1; TRAVELLERS', 106 Pall Mall; TURF, 85 Piccadilly, W1; UNION, 86 St James's Street; UNITED SERVICE, 116 Pall Mall; UNITED UNIVERSITY, 1 Suffolk Street, Pall Mall East; WHITE'S, 37 St James's Street.

The AMERICAN CLUB, 95 Piccadilly, W1, and the AMERICAN WOMEN'S CLUB, 1a Queen's Gate, SW7, cater for Americans in London. The OVERSEAS VISITORS CLUB (with bedrooms, a restaurant, a travel department, etc.), in Earls Court Road, W8, caters especially for Commonwealth visitors.

SOCIETIES. The following are among the societies that may be of particular interest to the Londoner. Visitors are usually made welcome at meetings, etc., on introduction by the secretary or a member.

The LONDON SOCIETY (secretary 3 Dean's Yard, Westminster, SW1) was founded in 1912 'to stimulate wider concern for the beauty of the capital city, for the preservation of its charms and careful consideration of its developments'; it arranges meetings, lectures, and visits, and publishes a journal (subscription 1 gn.). The LONDON APPRECIATION SOCIETY (8 Scarsdale Villas, Kensington, W8), founded in 1932, also arranges visits to places of interest of all kinds in and around the capital and issues a journal (subscription 3 gns.; after 1 August, 35/-). The LONDON & MIDDLESEX ARCHAEOLOGICAL SOCIETY (49 Mayford Road, SW12), established in 1855, likewise arranges visits, lectures, etc., publishes transactions, and maintains a useful library at the Bishopsgate Institute (subscription 2 gns.;

under 30, 1 gn.; students 7/6). The LONDON TOPOGRAPHICAL SOCIETY (9 Rivercourt Road, W6), founded in 1898, publishes facsimiles of maps and records of the history and topography of London (subscription 1 gn.). The WESTMINSTER SOCIETY (The Blewcoat School, Caxton Street, SW1) was formed in 1959 to preserve and improve the amenities of Westminster by stimulating interest in its history, protecting its buildings, preserving its river and open spaces, and encouraging good planning and architecture (subscription 1 gn.; under 18, 10/6). The ST MARYLEBONE SOCIETY (Central Library, Marylebone Road, NW1) interests itself especially in the history, topography, and social development of the borough, compiles records, and arranges lectures, visits, etc. (subscription 5/-). The KENSINGTON SOCIETY (18 Kensington Square, W8), founded in 1953 to preserve and improve the amenities of the royal borough and to stimulate interest in its history, records, and buildings, arranges lectures, visits, and exhibitions, and issues occasional news sheets and an annual report (subscription 1 gn.). The CHELSEA SOCIETY (46 Tedworth Square, SW3), founded in 1927, likewise aims to protect and foster the amenities of the borough, and carries out valuable surveys of historic buildings and places of interest, the results of which are published in its annual report (entrance fee 10/-; subscription 10/-). The CITY OF LONDON SOCIETY (34 Nicholas Lane, EC4) was founded in 1952 with the primary object of 'demonstrating that the business activities of the City are vital to the flow of trade throughout the world'; it organizes lectures, films, etc. (subscription 1 gn.).

Among the literary societies in London are the DICKENS FELLOWSHIP (46 Doughty Street, WC1), founded in 1902 (subscription 21/-); the CHARLES LAMB SOCIETY (37 Tavistock Square, WC1), established in 1935 (subscription 10/-; provincial members 7/6); and the JOHNSON SOCIETY (92 St Paul's Road, Islington, N1), founded in 1928 (subscription 10/6). All of these arrange meetings, lectures, visits, etc., and publish journals (free to members).

The NATIONAL TRUST (42 Queen Anne's Gate, SW1) owns an increasing number of fine houses, attractive open spaces, etc., in London and its neighbourhood and deserves the support of every lover of the English scene. It issues a list of its properties (3/6; free to members) and the annual subscription (minimum 10/-; new members 20/-) entitles members to free access to National Trust properties where a charge is normally made. Subscribers to the NATIONAL ART-COLLECTIONS FUND (Hertford House, Manchester Square, W1; established 1903) enjoy particular advantages, including admission without formality to the Reading Room and Students' Rooms of the British Museum, the Library and Students' Rooms of the Victoria & Albert Museum, and the Library of Westminster Abbey (subscription 21/-). Both these bodies arrange visits, etc., for their members, on some occasions to places not otherwise accessible.

Other societies worth the attention of strangers in London are the ENGLISH-SPEAKING UNION, 37 Charles Street, W1 (see p. 162); the ROYAL OVER-SEAS LEAGUE, Over-Seas House, Park Place, SW1 (p. 129);

the ROYAL COMMONWEALTH SOCIETY, Northumberland Avenue, WC2 (p. 245); and the VICTORIA LEAGUE, 38 Chesham Place, Belgrave Square, SW1.

INSTITUTES. The following institutes in or near central London offering social and recreational facilities, etc., may be worth mentioning: BISHOPSGATE INSTITUTE, 230 Bishopsgate, EC2; CITY LITERARY INSTITUTE, Stukeley Street, Drury Lane, WC2; CRIPPLEGATE INSTITUTE, Golden Lane, EC1; MARY WARD CENTRE, Tavistock Place, WC1; MORLEY COLLEGE, 61 Westminster Bridge Road, SE1; POLYTECHNIC, 309 Regent Street, W1; ST BRIDE FOUNDATION INSTITUTE, Bride Lane, Fleet Street, EC4; ST MARYLEBONE LITERARY INSTITUTE, 248 Marylebone Road, NW1; TOYNBEE HALL, 28 Commercial Road, Whitechapel, E1; WORKING MEN'S COLLEGE, Crowndale Road, NW1 (for men only). Particulars of these and other institutes (some of which also offer courses of study) may be obtained from the Education Officer, London County Hall, SE1, except in the City (EC districts), where application should be made direct.

LIBRARIES. Public libraries, where books of reference, magazines, and newspapers may be consulted without charge, are maintained by all the London boroughs and several of the institutes. In some cases books may be borrowed by arrangement through one's own library. The libraries in central London include: BISHOPSGATE INSTITUTE, see above (good London collection); CRIPPLEGATE INSTITUTE, see above; GUILDHALL LIBRARY, Guildhall, EC2 (reference only, fine London collection); HOLBORN, Theobald's Road, WC1; ST BRIDE INSTITUTE, see above; ST MARYLEBONE, Marylebone Road, NW1; and WESTMINSTER, St Martin's Street, Leicester Square, WC2.

The best of the subscription libraries is the LONDON LIBRARY, 14 St James's Square, SW1 (compare p. 123), the annual subscription to which is 10 gns. Members living within 20 miles of the General Post Office are allowed to borrow ten volumes at a time (other members, fifteen volumes). The PATENT OFFICE contains a valuable library of technical books and journals accessible without formality (see p. 221). The NATIONAL BUILDINGS RECORD (10 Great College Street, SW1) have amassed a collection of drawings, photographs, etc., freely accessible to visitors. Collections available to students and research workers (usually on written application to the director) include those at the British Museum (see p. 315), the Catholic Central Library (47 Francis Street, SW1), the Commonwealth Institute (p. 155), Dr Williams's Library (p. 196), the Geological Museum (p. 393), the Imperial War Museum (p. 346), Lambeth Palace (p. 306), London County Hall (p. 309), the National Maritime Museum (p. 486), the Natural History Museum (p. 373), the Science Museum (p. 389), Sion College (p. 248), the Victoria & Albert Museum (p. 418), Wesley's Chapel (p. 281), and Westminster Abbey (p. 439).

The NATIONAL BOOK LEAGUE (see p. 135) has a library, information bureau, and licensed restaurant, publishes book lists, and arranges interesting exhibitions. The entrance fee is 1 gn., the subscription 2 gns. (country members, 1 gn.); overseas visitors may become temporary members for 7/-. The services of the ASSOCIATION OF SPECIAL LIBRARIES and Information Bureaux (ASLIB; 4 Palace Gate, W 8) include an information bureau with a special section for industrial enquiries, a lending library, a panel of translators, and the publication of book lists and a 'Journal of Documentation', all mostly for members only.

ENTERTAINMENTS

THEATRES. Evening performances generally begin at 7.30 or 8, and end between 10 and 10.30. Matinées, beginning usually at 2.30 p.m., are given at the majority of theatres on two afternoons of the week, on Saturday and either Tuesday, Wednesday, or Thursday, but many theatres now have an early evening performance on Saturdays, starting between 5 and 6 p.m., in which case the later evening performance may be put back to 8.15 or 8.30. Particulars of times, etc., are given in the daily newspapers and in the *London Theatre Guide*, published weekly at 25 Shaftesbury Avenue, W1 (free; 10/- for 52 issues, posted to any address), and obtainable also from theatre booking-agents, etc. (see below).

The charges for seats at most London theatres are: Orchestra Stalls, 17/6 to 25/-; Pit Stalls, 8/6 to 15/6; Dress Circle, 10/6 to 25/-; Upper Circle, 5/- to 10/6; Gallery, 3/- to 5/-. Boxes, holding from 4 to 6 persons, can usually be obtained from about 2 gns. upwards. Seats (except for the gallery) should be reserved in advance, either direct or by telephone from the theatre box-office (open from 10 a.m.), or from one of the numerous booking-agents. These charge a commission of 1/- or 2/- for each ticket, but often have at their disposal better seats than can be obtained at the box-offices. For the gallery it is necessary to queue beforehand, though camp-stools (6*d*) may usually be reserved in lieu on the morning of the performance, in which case the theatregoer must return ¾–1 hour before the performance begins. For very popular plays, etc., the booking of seats (or stools) at the earliest possible moment is essential.

The following are the theatres in or within easy reach of central London (see plan on p. 69).

ADELPHI, Strand, WC2; ALDWYCH, Aldwych, WC2; AMBASSADORS, West Street, off Cambridge Circus, WC2; APOLLO, Shaftesbury Avenue, W1; CAMBRIDGE, Earlham Street, near Cambridge Circus, WC2; COMEDY, Panton Street, Haymarket, SW1; CRITERION, Piccadilly Circus,

W1; DRURY LANE (Theatre Royal), Catherine Street, Aldwych, WC2; DUCHESS, Catherine Street, WC2; DUKE OF YORK'S, St Martin's Lane, WC2; FORTUNE, Russell Street, Covent Garden, WC2; GARRICK, Charing Cross Road, WC2; GLOBE, Shaftesbury Avenue, W1; HAY-MARKET, Haymarket, SW1; HER MAJESTY'S, Haymarket, SW1; LYRIC, Shaftesbury Avenue, W1; MERMAID, Upper Thames Street, EC4 (IV, E3; with restaurant; see below); NEW, St Martin's Lane, WC2; OLD VIC (IX, B 2), Waterloo Road, SE1 (see below); OPEN AIR THEATRE (II, A 2), Regent's Park, NW1 (see below); PALACE, Cambridge Circus, Shaftesbury Avenue, W1; PHOENIX, Charing Cross Road, WC2; PICCADILLY, Sherwood Street, Piccadilly Circus, W1; PRINCE CHARLES, Leicester Place, WC2 (opened in 1962); QUEEN'S, Shaftesbury Avenue, W1; ROYAL COURT (VII, D 2), Sloane Square, SW1; ST MARTIN'S, West Street, off Cambridge Circus, WC2; SAVILLE, Shaftesbury Avenue, WC2; SAVOY, Savoy Court, Strand, WC2; SCALA (III, C 2), Charlotte Street, near Tottenham Court Road, W1; SHAFTESBURY, Shaftesbury Avenue, WC2; STRAND, Aldwych, WC2; VAUDEVILLE, Strand, WC2; WESTMINSTER (VIII, C 1), Palace Street, Buckingham Palace Road, SW1; WHITEHALL, Whitehall, near Charing Cross, SW1; WYNDHAM'S, Charing Cross Road, WC2.

The Drury Lane (especially), Adelphi, Palace, and Shaftesbury theatres are well known for musical shows, and the Whitehall specializes in farce. The Royal Court is noted for contemporary plays; the Aldwych has been taken over by the Royal Shakespeare Company. The Old Vic is famous for its performances of Shakespeare, at prices ranging from 3/- for the gallery to 21/- for the best seats in the stalls and circle. Shakespeare is also given in summer (about June–September) at the Open Air Theatre (prices 3/6 to 15/-; under cover if wet). The Mermaid (prices 7/6 to 17/6) is the only theatre in the City (see p. 253).

THEATRE TICKET AGENTS: *Abbey Box Office*, 27 Victoria Street, SW1. — *H. J. Adams*, 139 New Bond Street, W1. — *Ashton & Mitchell's*, 100 St Martin's Lane, WC2. — *Alfred Hays*, 74 Cornhill, EC3. — *Lacon & Ollier*, 60 South Audley Street, Grosvenor Square, W1. — *G. S. Lashmar*, 77 Davies Street, W1. — *Leader & Co*, 14 Royal Arcade, Old Bond Street, W1. — *Ludgate Box Offices*, 2 Broad Street Buildings, EC2. — *Keith Prowse & Co*, 90 and 159 New Bond Street, W1; 45 Aldwych, WC2; 5 Charing Cross, SW1; 50 Fenchurch Street, EC3; and at several of the larger hotels; etc. — *Rake's Ticket Agency*, 12 Great Newport Street, WC2. — *Cecil Roy*, 74 Old Brompton Road, SW7. — *Webster & Girling*, 211 Baker Street, NW1, etc. — *Webster & Waddington*, 74 Mortimer Street, Oxford Circus, W1. — and many others, particularly in the principal hotels, stores, and music-shops.

VARIETY THEATRES, offering separate acts or continuous revue, usually give two performances each evening, at about 6.15 and 8.45, while some have a weekly matinée as well. Prices are generally slightly lower than for corresponding seats in the theatres given above. The following are the principal in central London (see plan below).

PALLADIUM, Argyll Street, Oxford Circus, W1; PRINCE OF WALES, Coventry Street, Piccadilly Circus, W1; VICTORIA PALACE (VIII, C1), Victoria Street, near Victoria Station, SW1; WINDMILL, Great Windmill Street, Piccadilly Circus, W1 (continuous revue from 2.15 to 10.50; last performance at 9.15 p.m.).

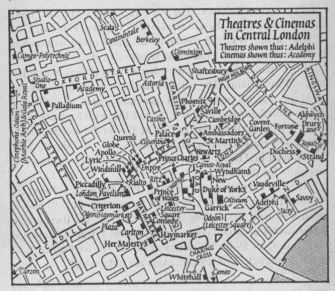

Theatres & Cinemas in Central London
Theatres shown thus: Adelphi
Cinemas shown thus: Academy

THEATRE CLUBS exist mainly for the purpose of staging new or unusual plays. Patrons must be members, but the subscription is usually small (about 5/-). Among the best known in London are: NEW ARTS, Great Newport Street, Charing Cross Road, WC2; HOVENDEN, Garrick Yard, St Martin's Lane, WC2; IRVING, Irving Street, Leicester Square, WC2 (non-stop revue); POLISH, Princes Gate, Kensington Road, SW7.

POETRY READINGS (frequently with music) are presented by the *Apollo Society* in the Royal Festival Hall, at the Arts Council (p. 123), and elsewhere. Plays (chiefly by amateur companies), concerts, ballet, etc., are given occasionally at the RUDOLF STEINER THEATRE, 33 Park Road, Regent's Park, NW1.

SUBURBAN THEATRES: HIPPODROME, Golders Green, NW11 (near underground station; see below); LYRIC, Hammersmith, W6 (near

Hammersmith Broadway; plays); MERCURY, Notting Hill Gate, W11 (near underground station); METROPOLITAN, 267 Edgware Road, W2 (I, C3; variety); STREATHAM HILL, Streatham Hill, SW2 (near Streatham Hill Station; see below); THEATRE ROYAL, Angel Lane, Stratford, E15 (plays); TOWER, Canonbury Place, N1 (repertory). Most of these are hardly less comfortable than the West End theatres, and prices of admission are considerably lower. The Golders Green Hippodrome and the Streatham Hill Theatre offer regular performances of successful London plays, etc., with the West End casts.

OPERA AND BALLET. The ROYAL OPERA HOUSE, more familiarly known as the Covent Garden Theatre (Plan III, E3), in Bow Street, WC2, is the home of grand opera in London. Performances, with international artists, alternate with ballet by the Royal Ballet (formerly the Sadler's Wells Ballet), which has acquired world fame. The season extends from about November to May; evening performances generally begin at 7.30 and matinées on Saturdays at 2 or 2.15; and the price for seats varies from 5/- to 8/- for the gallery to 27/6 or 32/- for the orchestra stalls (boxes 4–6 gns.). Booking arrangements, etc., are the same as for the West End theatres, but very early application is advisable, especially for the ballet.

The SADLER'S WELLS THEATRE (Plan IV, A2), in Rosebery Avenue, Islington, EC1, specializes in opera in English and in ballet. Performances usually begin at 7.30 p.m., but there are no performances on Mondays and no matinées. Prices of admission vary from 4/- or 5/- for the gallery to 20/- or 25/- for the best seats in the dress circle, and season tickets are obtainable.

Short seasons of opera and ballet are also given at the Palace, Scala, and other theatres, and at the Royal Festival Hall (see below). Excursions are arranged by travel agents, etc., to the summer season of opera at Glyndebourne, near Lewes (see the *Penguin Guide to Sussex*).

CINEMAS. Performances in central London usually begin between 10.30 and 12.30 (Sundays at 4.30) and run continuously until about 11 p.m., and the prices of admission vary from about 5/- to 15/-. In general, seats cannot be reserved in advance. After a season in the West End, most British and American films have a round of three weeks in the suburbs: the first week in North-West London, the second in the North-East, and the third South of the Thames. The performances here run at about the same times as the

West End, but prices are considerably lower. The following are the principal cinemas in central London (see plan, p. 69).

ACADEMY, 165 Oxford Street, W1; ASTORIA, 157 Charing Cross Road, WC2; BERKELEY, 30 Tottenham Court Road, W1; CAMEO, 152 Victoria Street, SW1; CAMEO-POLYTECHNIC, Upper Regent Street, W1; CAMEO-ROYAL, Charing Cross Road, WC2; CARLTON, Haymarket, SW1; CASINO, Old Compton Street, Soho, W1; CINEPHONE, Oxford Street, W1 (opposite Selfridge's); CLASSIC, 98 Baker Street, W1; COLISEUM, St Martin's Lane, Charing Cross, WC2; COLUMBIA, Shaftesbury Avenue, W1; CONTINENTALE, 36 Tottenham Court Road, W1; CURZON, Curzon Street, Mayfair, W1; DOMINION, Tottenham Court Road, W1 (near St Giles Circus); EMPIRE, Leicester Square, WC2; GALA ROYAL, Edgware Road, Marble Arch, W2; INTERNATIONAL, Westbourne Grove, W2; JACEY, Strand, WC2; LEICESTER SQUARE, Leicester Square, WC2; LONDON PAVILION, Piccadilly Circus, W1; METROPOLE, 160 Victoria Street, SW1, and NEW VICTORIA, Vauxhall Bridge Road, SW1 (both near Victoria Station); ODEON, Haymarket, SW1; ODEON, Leicester Square, WC2; ODEON, Marble Arch, W1; PARIS-PULLMAN (VI, E2), Drayton Gardens, South Kensington, SW10; PLAZA, Lower Regent Street, SW1; RIALTO, 3 Coventry Street, W1; RITZ, Leicester Square, WC2; ROYALTY, Kingsway, WC2; STUDIO ONE, 225 Oxford Street, W1 (near Oxford Circus); WARNER, Leicester Square, WC2. Foreign films are shown mainly at the Academy, the Berkeley, the Cameo-Polytechnic, the Cameo-Royal, the Continentale, the Curzon, the International, the Paris-Pullman, and Studio One.

NEWS THEATRES, which have programmes lasting 1 hour (admission 1/- to 3/-) with short topical, travel, and humorous films, exist at Baker Street, Victoria, and Waterloo Stations, and also include the following: EROS, 7 Shaftesbury Avenue; JACEY, Leicester Square; MONSEIGNEUR, Leicester Square, 215 Piccadilly, 523 Oxford Street, and the Strand (Charing Cross); and STUDIO TWO, 225 Oxford Street.

The NATIONAL FILM THEATRE, on the South Bank, Waterloo, SE1 (Plan IX, A 1), is open daily (prices 3/- to 7/6) to members, who may reserve seats in advance (11.30 to 7.30, except Sundays). The subscription is 30/- (associates 7/6; entrance fee 2/6) and the facilities for full members include a licensed club and a library of books and film stills. Cinema clubs, of which there are many, include the COMPTON, Old Compton Street, Soho, W1.

CONCERTS AND OTHER MUSIC. Orchestral concerts are given chiefly at the ROYAL FESTIVAL HALL (Plan IX, A 1), South Bank, Waterloo, SE1, one of the finest concert halls in Europe, both artistically and acoustically, and the ROYAL ALBERT HALL (VI, B 2), Kensington Gore, SW7. Concerts take place at one or other of these halls, if not both, almost every evening throughout the year, usually at 8 p.m. (Sundays at 7.30), and on Sunday afternoons at the Albert Hall at 3 p.m. Prices of admission at the Festival Hall normally vary from 5/- to 21/-, at the Albert Hall from 3/6 to 15/-, and tickets are obtainable at the respective box-offices and at the theatre ticket offices (see above). The Promenade Concerts given nightly (except Sundays) at the Albert Hall for eight weeks in the summer (July–September) are very popular (admission 3/6 to 10/6). Concerts are also given from time to time at the ST PANCRAS TOWN HALL, Euston Road (III, A 3); the CHELSEA TOWN HALL, King's Road, SW 3 (VII, F 1), and various other municipal halls; and the VICTORIA & ALBERT MUSEUM (on Sunday evenings in the courtyard or the Raphael Gallery). Open-air concerts are given occasionally in summer in HOLLAND PARK, Kensington, at CRYSTAL PALACE (p. 490), and on Saturday evenings by the lake at KENWOOD, Hampstead Heath (good acoustics). The Ernest Read Concerts for children, given on Saturday mornings once a month at the Festival Hall, are a valuable feature. Details of all concerts, recitals, etc., are published in the Saturday editions of *The Times* and the *Daily Telegraph*.

Recitals of chamber music and songs are given regularly at the ROYAL FESTIVAL HALL, both in the main concert hall (especially on Sunday afternoons at 3 p.m.) and in the Recital Room; at the WIGMORE HALL (II, D 3), Wigmore Street, W 1; on Sunday evenings in summer at KENWOOD HOUSE, Hampstead Heath; and occasionally at the ARTS COUNCIL, St James's Square (see below). The prices of admission usually vary from 4/- to 10/- (5/- to 15/- in the concert hall of the Festival Hall).

Lunch-time Recitals are given weekly at the BISHOPSGATE INSTITUTE (V, D 3), 230 Bishopsgate, EC2 (Tuesdays, 1.5 to 1.50 p.m.; admission 2/-), monthly at ST BRIDE'S CHURCH (IV, E 2), near Fleet Street (first Thursday at 1.15), and occasionally in GUILDHALL (V, D, E 1), near Gresham Street (Thursdays at 12.30; free). Organ (and sometimes other) recitals are given regularly at lunch-time at the following churches, mostly in the City:

ALL HALLOWS BY THE TOWER (Thursdays at 12.15 and 1.15); ALL SOULS', Langham Place (Fridays at 12.45); ST BOTOLPH'S, Bishopsgate

(Thursdays, 1.10); St Clement's, Clement's Lane (Tuesdays, 1); St Lawrence Jewry (Wednesdays, 1); St Margaret Lothbury, behind the Bank (Tuesdays, 1); St Margaret's, Westminster (Fridays, 1.10); St Martin-in-the-Fields, Trafalgar Square (Tuesdays, 1.5); St Martin's Ludgate (Thursdays, 1.15); St Mary Abchurch (Wednesdays, 12.30); St Mary Woolnoth, Lombard Street (Fridays, 1.5); St Michael's, Cornhill (Mondays, 1); St Olave's, Hart Street (Fridays, 1.5); St Peter's, Cornhill (Tuesdays, 12.30); St Stephen's, Walbrook (Fridays, 12.30); occasionally at other churches, and less frequently in the evening. Further particulars of those in the City may be obtained from the City of London Information Centre (p. 61).

Churches noted for music at their services include St James's, Piccadilly; St Paul's Cathedral; St Paul's, Knightsbridge; St Peter's, Eaton Square; Southwark Cathedral; the Temple Church; Westminster Abbey; Westminster Roman Catholic Cathedral, and Brompton Oratory; and the Church of the Jesuit Fathers, Farm Street, Mayfair.

Concerts by Brass Bands, etc., are given in summer in the Victoria Embankment Gardens, near Charing Cross (twice daily, at 12.30 and 7.30), on the steps of St Paul's Cathedral (Thursdays at 12); in Lincoln's Inn Fields; in St James's Park (p. 115), Hyde Park and Kensington Gardens (p. 157), Regent's Park (p. 180), and other parks. Concert Parties perform on Clapham Common and in various parks in the suburbs on summer evenings. Particulars of all the activities that take place in the parks etc., under the control of the London County Council are contained in a booklet (6d) published by the Parks Department and obtainable from the County Hall.

Art Exhibitions. Apart from the permanent exhibitions of paintings, etc., at the National Gallery and elsewhere (compare p. 25), loan exhibitions are held at certain galleries and by various societies. The most important of these is the 'Summer Exhibition' of the Royal Academy of Arts (see p. 133), held at Burlington House, Piccadilly, W1 (Plan III, F 1), from the first Monday in May until mid-August. It is open daily from 9.30 a.m. to 7 p.m. (Sundays 2 to 6) and admission is 3/-. The 'Winter Exhibition' of the academy, invariably well worth seeing, is held usually from November (sometimes from January) to March, and is open from 10 to 7 (Sundays 2 to 6); admission 3/6. Other important loan exhibitions are arranged frequently at the Tate Gallery (times, see p. 398; admission generally 2/- to 3/6), the White-chapel Art Gallery, Whitechapel High Street, E1 (beyond V, E 3; Tuesday–Friday 11 to 6, Sundays 2 to 6; free), and the Arts Council, 4 St James's Square, SW1 (III, F 2; weekdays 10 to 6, Tuesdays and Thursdays to 8; usually 1/6).

Other temporary exhibitions are arranged at the BRITISH MUSEUM (Prints and Drawings; see p. 315); the COMMONWEALTH INSTITUTE (p. 155); the GUILDHALL ART GALLERY (p. 274); the IMPERIAL WAR MUSEUM (p. 346); LEIGHTON HOUSE, Kensington (p. 156); the QUEEN'S GALLERY, Buckingham Palace (p. 119); the VICTORIA & ALBERT MUSEUM (p. 418); and the SOUTH LONDON ART GALLERY, Peckham Road, Camberwell, SE 5 (p. 488).

In addition, annual exhibitions are held (usually for about a month each) by the following societies: the *Royal Institute of Oil Painters* and the *Royal Institute of Painters in Water-Colours*, both at 195 Piccadilly, W 1; the *Royal Society of British Artists*, the *Royal Society of Portrait Painters*, and the *New English Art Club* (these three form the Federation of British Artists), at 6½ Suffolk Street, Pall Mall East, SW 1; the *Royal Society of Miniature Painters and Sculptors*, and the *Royal Society of Painters in Water Colours*, both at 26 Conduit Street, New Bond Street, W 1. Lunch-time recitals are also given occasionally in the Suffolk Street galleries.

Smaller art exhibitions, not to be overlooked, are held almost continuously at the many galleries and picture-dealers' shops mainly in the neighbourhood of Piccadilly and Bond Street (admission usually free). Particulars of the current exhibitions at most of the galleries, public and private, are given in the daily newspapers and in a pamphlet, *Art Gallery Guide*, published monthly by the Art Exhibitions Bureau, 6½ Suffolk Street, SW 1 (free; 5/- per year, posted to any address).

Other art exhibitions are arranged in the Victoria Embankment Gardens (usually April–May) and in summer at Kenwood House, Hampstead Heath. Exhibitions of Sculpture in the open air have been held every three years either in Battersea Park (last in 1960) or Holland Park.

OTHER EXHIBITIONS AND SHOWS. Exhibitions of widely differing kinds are held frequently at OLYMPIA, Hammersmith Road, Kensington, W 14 (adjoining Olympia station), and the EARLS COURT EXHIBITION BUILDINGS, Lillie Road, SW 5 (reached from Earls Court station by a covered passage). For the annual exhibitions, etc., held here and elsewhere, see p. 90; for the flower shows at the Royal Horticultural Society's Halls, see p. 114.

Circuses (especially during the Christmas season) are given at Olympia, and ice pantomimes, etc., at WEMBLEY STADIUM, Middlesex (Wembley Park and Wembley Hill stations). Open-air shows are held at the WHITE CITY, Wood Lane, Shepherd's Bush, W 12 (White City station).

Permanent exhibitions include that at the DESIGN CENTRE (p. 130), where the display is changed from time to time, and MADAME TUSSAUD'S

WAXWORKS (p. 175); and other exhibitions are held frequently by the NATIONAL BOOK LEAGUE (p. 135), and at the BUILDING CENTRE (p. 188), the CEYLON TEA CENTRE (p. 121), and the CRAFTS CENTRE (p. 135).

The FESTIVAL GARDENS, in Battersea Park, facing the river, were designed by John Piper and Osbert Lancaster and opened in 1951. The attractions include an ornamental lake, a concert pavilion, restaurants, bars, and tea-rooms, and an amusement section. Concerts and other entertainments are arranged during the summer; the gardens are illuminated at night, and firework displays are given on special occasions.

The gardens are open daily (free) throughout the year. The amusement section (admission 6d) is open usually from about Easter to September, daily from 1 or 2 p.m. (Bank Holidays from 10.30). The garden attractions open an hour before these times, and the amusements, etc., close at about 10.30 to 11 p.m. The gardens may be reached on foot over Chelsea Bridge (Plan VII, F 3) or the Albert Bridge (see Route 8); by Motor-Buses Nos. 44, 137, and 170 to Battersea Park and Nos. 19, 39, 45, and 49 to Battersea Bridge; by rail (Southern Region) to Battersea Park Station ($\frac{1}{2}$ m. SE.); or by motor-launch from Charing Cross or Westminster Pier (see p. 43).

Concerts, dancing, and other entertainments in the open-air are provided for in many suburban parks managed by the L.C.C. (see p. 73).

DANCING AND CABARET are offered by the following hotels, restaurants, and night clubs, mostly in the neighbourhood of Piccadilly and Regent Street. The night clubs (designated 'N.') are open to members only; the subscriptions (usually payable forty-eight hours in advance) vary considerably, and enquiry should preferably be made beforehand. Most of the restaurants and night clubs keep open until the small hours, but no drinks may be served after 2 a.m. (12 on Saturdays). Evening dress is not usually insisted on.

ASTOR (N.), Fitzmaurice Place, Berkeley Square; CABARET CLUB (N.), 16 Beak Street, Soho; CASANOVA CLUB (N.), 52 Grosvenor Street; CHURCHILL'S CLUB (N.), 160 New Bond Street; COLONY, Berkeley Square; EDMUNDO ROS' CLUB (N.), 177 Regent Street; EMBASSY CLUB (N.), 6 Old Bond Street; EVE CLUB (N.), 189 Regent Street; GARGOYLE CLUB (N.), 69 Dean Street; JACK OF CLUBS, 10 Brewer Street; LATIN QUARTER, 13 Wardour Street; L'HIRONDELLE, 99 Regent Street; PIGALLE, 190 Piccadilly; QUAGLINO'S, 16 Bury Street; SAVOY HOTEL, Strand; SOCIETY, 40 Jermyn Street; STORK ROOM, 99 Regent Street; TALK OF THE TOWN (Hippodrome Theatre-Restaurant), Cranbourn

Street, Charing Cross Road; 21 CLUB (N.), 8 Chesterfield Gardens; and several others.

Dancing (but not cabaret) may be enjoyed at the BERKELEY HOTEL, Berkeley Street; CUMBERLAND HOTEL, Marble Arch; DORCHESTER HOTEL, Park Lane; GROSVENOR HOUSE HOTEL, Park Lane; LES AMBASSADEURS (N.), 5 Hamilton Place; MAY FAIR HOTEL, Berkeley Street; PICCADILLY HOTEL, Piccadilly and Regent Street; RIVER CLUB (N.), 129 Grosvenor Road; THE STAGE DOOR, St Alban's Street; and elsewhere; and at the following ballrooms: ASTORIA, 165 Charing Cross Road; HAMMERSMITH PALAIS, Brook Green Road; LOCARNO, 158 Streatham Hill; LYCEUM, Wellington Street, Strand; MAJESTIC, Seven Sisters Road, Finsbury Park; NEW STATE, High Road, Kilburn; etc.

SPORT IN AND AROUND LONDON

THE LONDONER has an unrivalled opportunity of seeing a great many of the principal national sporting events. Particulars of these and of the facilities for individual sports and games are given below; and details of dates and times of the chief events may be obtained from the daily and Sunday newspapers.

ATHLETICS. The championships of the *Amateur Athletic Association* (A.A.A.), open to amateurs of all nations, are held at the WHITE CITY, Shepherd's Bush (White City station), usually in July, and the Oxford and Cambridge university contests also take place here (generally in May). The Women's A.A.A. championships also usually take place here, in July, and other meetings are arranged, including the British Games at Whitsun and in August. The London amateur athletic championships are held at HURLINGHAM PARK, Fulham (Putney Bridge and Parsons Green stations), in September. The annual road walk of the *Surrey Walking Club* from London (Westminster Bridge) to Brighton takes place in September, the *Stock Exchange* London to Brighton walk every May, and a relay race over the same course in April. The annual marathon race organized by the *Polytechnic Harriers* is run from Windsor Castle to their stadium at Chiswick in June. The indoor championships of the A.A.A. and Women's A.A.A. take place at Wembley (see below) in March. Particulars of all athletic events are contained in a diary (1/6) published by the A.A.A. at 54 Torrington Place, WC1.

BADMINTON. The All England Championships are held at the EMPIRE POOL, WEMBLEY (Wembley Hill and Wembley Park stations), in March, and other tournaments take place at Alexandra Palace and elsewhere.

BILLIARDS. The Amateur Championships and some heats of the Professional Championships take place at the hall of *Messrs Burroughes & Watts*, 19 Soho Square, W1. Particulars regarding other professional matches may be obtained from the *Billiards Association*, 11 Arundel Street, WC2.

BOWLS may be played in Hyde Park (see Route 12) and in Battersea Park and many other suburban parks. The L.C.C. Championship finals take place at PARLIAMENT HILL (Hampstead Heath and Gospel Oak stations) in September; the National Championships at Watney's Sports Club, Mortlake (Surrey) in August.

BOXING. Professional bouts, under the control of the *British Boxing Board of Control* (1 Hills Place, W 1), are arranged at the ROYAL ALBERT HALL, the arena at EARLS COURT (compare p. 74), the Empire Pool, Wembley (see above), and SEYMOUR HALL, Seymour Place, Marylebone. The championships of the *Amateur Boxing Association* take place in April at the EMPIRE POOL, Wembley (see above), the junior championships at the Royal Albert Hall in March.

CRICKET may be watched regularly during the season at LORD'S, the headquarters of the *Marylebone Cricket Club* (M.C.C.) and the ground of the *Middlesex Cricket Club*, at St John's Wood (see p. 181), and at the OVAL, Kennington, the home of the *Surrey Cricket Club* (p. 490). Kent play occasionally at Blackheath, and Essex at Leyton, Ilford, and Romford. Other important games, such as Gentlemen *v.* Players, Oxford *v.* Cambridge, and Eton *v.* Harrow (all in July), are played at Lord's, and international matches ('test matches') take place here and at the Oval. Club matches may also be watched on Saturdays and Sundays on grounds all around London, especially in the public parks, and cricket weeks are organized by the more important clubs.

CYCLING may be enjoyed in delightful country on almost every side of London (see the Penguin Guides to the neighbouring counties). The main disadvantages are the appalling congestion on the main roads at week-ends during the summer and the long distances that have to be covered from central London to reach open country. The interests of pleasure cyclists are looked after by the *Cyclists' Touring Club*, 3 Craven Hill, W 2 (subscription 26/-; juniors 5/6 to 16/-). The organizing body for racing is the *National Cyclists' Union* (35 Doughty Street, W C 1) and national championships (in April) and other events take place at the HERNE HILL race track, Burbage Road (North Dulwich and

Herne Hill stations), and at CRYSTAL PALACE (see Motor Racing, below), where a festival is held in August.

FENCING. The championships of the *Amateur Fencing Association* are held in April at their headquarters at 1a Tenterden Street, Hanover Square, W1 (Oxford Circus and Bond Street stations), and other contests take place at the Seymour Hall (see Boxing, above).

FISHING may be enjoyed in the Thames and its tributaries, the Lea, the Mole, the Wey, etc., but some waters are preserved. Particulars regarding permits, licences, etc., are best obtained from the *Thames Conservancy* (2 Norfolk Street, Strand, WC2) or the *London Anglers' Association* (50 Elfindale Road, SE24).

FOOTBALL (Association) may be watched at the grounds of the following professional league clubs: ARSENAL, Avenell Road, Highbury, N5 (Arsenal station); BRENTFORD, Griffin Park, Brentford (Brentford Central station); CHARLTON ATHLETIC, The Valley, Floyd Road, SE7 (Charlton station); CHELSEA, Stamford Bridge, Fulham Road, SW6 (Fulham Broadway station); CRYSTAL PALACE, Selhurst Park, Croydon (Norwood Junction and Selhurst stations); FULHAM, Craven Cottage, Stevenage Road, SW6 (Putney Bridge station); LEYTON ORIENT, Brisbane Road, Leyton High Road, E10 (Leyton station); MILLWALL, The Den, Cold Blow Lane, New Cross, SE14 (New Cross Gate station); QUEEN'S PARK RANGERS, White City Stadium, Wood Lane, W12 (White City station); TOTTENHAM HOTSPUR, White Hart Lane, Tottenham, N22 (White Hart Lane station); WEST HAM UNITED, Boleyn Ground, Green Street, E13 (Upton Park station). International matches are played at the EMPIRE STADIUM, WEMBLEY (Wembley Park and Wembley Hill stations), and the final tie of the F.A. Cup takes place here on the first Saturday in May. Amateur matches of a high standard may be seen on the grounds (mostly suburban) of clubs in the Isthmian, Athenian, Corinthian, and other leagues; the F.A. Amateur Cup final takes place at Wembley in April.

GOLF may be played on numerous courses of a high standard in the country around London. Among the best known, where national championships are held, are Moor Park (Herts), Beaconsfield (Bucks), Sunningdale (Berks), and Camberley Heath, Royal Mid-Surrey (Richmond), Walton Heath, and Wentworth (near Egham), all in Surrey. An introduction by a member is necessary at these and most other private courses, but there are public courses on MITCHAM COMMON (Mitcham Junction station), in RICHMOND PARK (near Roehampton), and at CHINGFORD and HAINAULT FOREST, in Essex, where the charge per round is about 2/6 to 3/6. Putting greens are maintained in many of the public parks.

GREYHOUND RACING. There are tracks at Catford, Clapton, Hackney Wick, Harringay, Hendon, New Cross, Park Royal, Stamford Bridge, Walthamstow, Wandsworth, Wembley, West Ham, the White City, and other places. The Greyhound 'Derby' is run at the White City in June, and the 'St Leger' at Wembley in September.

HOCKEY of a good standard may be watched at many grounds in and near London, and international matches are played at WEMBLEY STADIUM (see Football, above) and HURLINGHAM PARK (see Athletics).

HORSE RACING. The racecourses nearest London are ALEX-ANDRA PARK, N 22 (Wood Green station); EPSOM (Epsom Downs and Tattenham Corner stations); HURST PARK (Hampton Court station); KEMPTON PARK (Kempton Park and Sunbury stations); and SANDOWN PARK (Esher station). The chief events are the *Derby Stakes*, for three-year-old colts and fillies, run at Epsom on the last Wednesday in May or the first in June, and the *Oaks Stakes* (for three-year-old fillies) on the following Friday (see the *Penguin Guide to Surrey*). The fashionable Ascot Week, patronized by royalty, is held two weeks later at ASCOT HEATH (Berks), when the chief day is Thursday (Gold Cup Day).

LAWN TENNIS may be played on numerous public courts (hard and grass) in and around London (Lincoln's Inn Fields, Battersea Park, etc.), and open competitions are held at many places in summer. The All-England Championships, with the most coveted prizes of the world on grass courts, take place at WIMBLEDON, Surrey (Wimbledon and Wimbledon Park stations), at the end of June and the beginning of July, and the

Junior Championships of Great Britain in September. The London Grass Court Championships are held at QUEEN'S CLUB, West Kensington (Barons Court station), in June, the National Covered Court Championships usually in February, and the Junior Covered Court Championships in January.

MOTOR RACING takes place in summer at CRYSTAL PALACE (Crystal Palace and Penge West stations) on Whit Monday and in September, and at BRANDS HATCH (on the London–Sevenoaks road, A 20). A popular Veteran Car Rally, sponsored by the R.A.C., is held in November over a course from London (Hyde Park Corner) to Brighton. MOTOR-CYCLE RACING takes place at Crystal Palace (on Easter Monday and August Bank Holiday); speedway racing on tracks at Harringay, New Cross, Walthamstow, Wembley, West Ham, and Wimbledon. The world speedway riders championship is held at Wembley in September.

POLO is played at the fashionable ROEHAMPTON CLUB, Roehampton Lane, near Richmond Park, Surrey (Barnes station).

RACKETS. The chief competitions take place at QUEEN'S CLUB, West Kensington (see Lawn Tennis, above), the University contest in March and the Amateur Singles and the Public Schools Championships in April.

ROWING. The principal event of the year is the *Oxford and Cambridge Boat-Race*, rowed in late March or early April (usually just before Easter) on the Thames from Putney to Mortlake (nearly 4¼ miles). The nearest stations are Putney Bridge (for the start), Hammersmith, Barnes Bridge, and Mortlake. The race attracts a great concourse of spectators, who line the river bank or pay for a position in Duke's Meadows, Chiswick, or on an anchored barge or pier (about 2/- to 3/6). The *Head of the River Race*, open to Thames rowing eights and attracting over 200 crews, is rowed either on the same day or one week earlier over the same course, but generally in the opposite direction. The *Schools' Head of the River Race* is rowed from Hammersmith to Putney in March. The *Wingfield Sculls*, the chief event for solo oarsmen, is rowed between Putney and Mortlake, usually in May. *Doggett's Coat and Badge*, presented in 1715 by Thomas Doggett, an actor, is rowed for by Thames watermen each July over a course from London Bridge to Chelsea (4½ miles). Regattas are held on the

SERPENTINE, Hyde Park (in August), and on the Thames at Putney and Hammersmith, as well as at Richmond, Twickenham, Kingston, and elsewhere near London. *Henley Regatta*, the most famous of the Thames regattas, takes place during the first week in July. A Canoe Race is held annually at Easter from Devizes (Wilts) to Westminster Bridge (County Hall steps).

Boats may be hired on the Serpentine (see Route 12), on the lakes in Regent's Park (Route 16), Battersea Park, etc., as well as on the Thames from Putney upstream. For charges for sailing and rowing boats and punts, and the rule of the river, see the *Penguin Guide to Surrey*. Sailing may also be enjoyed on the Welsh Harp reservoir, between Hendon and Neasden.

RUGBY FOOTBALL may be watched at numerous grounds in the neighbourhood of London. Among the best-known clubs (all amateur) are the HARLEQUINS, who play at Twickenham (see below), RICHMOND and LONDON SCOTTISH (both at the Richmond Athletic Ground), ROSSLYN PARK (Priory Lane, Upper Richmond Road, SW15), LONDON WELSH (Old Deer Park, Richmond), BLACKHEATH (Rectory Field, SE3), SARACENS (Southgate, N14), WASPS (Sudbury, near Wembley), and LONDON IRISH (Sunbury on Thames). Other good clubs are formed from the London hospitals and public-school old boys. International matches and the Oxford *v.* Cambridge university match are played at TWICKENHAM (Twickenham station) and the final of the Rugby League Cup, a North Country professional tournament, takes place at WEMBLEY STADIUM, usually in May.

SHOOTING. The principal competitions are held at BISLEY CAMP (see the *Penguin Guide to Surrey*), the Small Bore Rifle Championships in June, the National Rifle Championships in July.

SKATING. There are rinks at the QUEEN'S ICE SKATING CLUB, Queensway, W2 (Bayswater and Queensway stations), and at Streatham (adjoining Streatham station), Wembley (Empire Pool), and Richmond (near Richmond Bridge). Skating may also be possible for short periods in winter on the Serpentine (Hyde Park), the lake in Regent's Park, Hampstead and Highgate Ponds, and elsewhere. ROLLER SKATING rinks are to be found at the Festival Gardens (Battersea), Alexandra Palace, Victoria Park, etc.

SQUASH RACKETS. The principal competitions are held at the LANSDOWNE CLUB, 9 Fitzmaurice Place, Berkeley Square, W1 (Green Park station), or the ROYAL AUTOMOBILE CLUB (p. 124), the Amateur Championship in January, the Professional Championship usually in February or March, and the Open Championship usually in November. International matches are generally played at either of these clubs. Squash rackets may also be played at Queen's Club (see Lawn Tennis, above), at the Junior Carlton Club (p. 123), at Lord's Cricket Ground, at the Blue Pool Restaurant (see below), and on courts attached to several of the West End clubs and some of the large modern blocks of flats.

SWIMMING. Among the municipal swimming pools are the CITY OF WESTMINSTER BATHS, Buckingham Palace Road (near Victoria Station), Marshall Street (near Regent Street), and Great Smith Street (off Victoria Street); CHELSEA BATHS, Manor Street, SW3; HOLBORN OASIS SWIMMING POOL, Endell Street, WC2; MARYLEBONE BATHS, Seymour Place, W1; PORCHESTER BATHS, Queensway, Paddington, W2; and MANOR PLACE BATHS, Walworth Road, SE17. Privately-owned baths include that attached to the BLUE POOL REST-AURANT, Dolphin Square, Grosvenor Road, Pimlico, SW1 (closed Sundays). Open-air bathing may be enjoyed at the Holborn Oasis Swimming Pool (April–October, daily, 9.30 to 7.30), in the Serpentine (see Route 12), and at PARLIAMENT HILL (Hampstead), HIGHGATE POND (men only), KENWOOD POND (ladies only), BROCKWELL PARK (Herne Hill), Tooting Common, Finchley, Highbury Fields, Victoria Park, etc. The County of London Swimming Championships take place at Parliament Hill in July, and other events are held from time to time.

TABLE TENNIS. The English Open Championships are held in March or April at the EMPIRE POOL, WEMBLEY (Wembley Hill and Wembley Park stations), and other national events take place here, at the Manor Place Baths (see above), and at the Royal Albert Hall.

WRESTLING may be seen from time to time at the Royal Albert Hall, Seymour Hall, the Metropolitan Theatre, the West Ham Baths, and elsewhere.

GENERAL INFORMATION

MAPS AND PLANS. The street plan of central London at the end of this guide will be found adequate for general use by the tourist and holiday-maker. By far the best map of London as a whole is that contained in the *Reference Atlas of Greater London*, published by Messrs John Bartholomew & Son, Ltd (11th edition, 1961; 50/-). The whole of the County of London is drawn on a scale of 4 inches to 1 mile, and the central area (extending from the Houses of Parliament to the Tower) on a scale of 10 inches to 1 mile, while the environs, reaching as far north as St Albans, south to Reigate, east to Tilbury, and west to Windsor, are included on a scale of 2 inches to the mile. In addition there are general and administrative maps, and an index of over 50,000 names. This atlas is exceptionally clear and detailed, but it is much too heavy to carry about, and better suited to this purpose is Messrs Bartholomew's *Plan of Central London* (6/-), on a scale of 3¼ inches to 1 mile, with an index. Other useful productions are Messrs Geographia's plans of *London*, on scales of 5¼ inches to 1 mile (3/6) and 6 inches to 1 mile (2/6), *London and Suburbs* (3 inches to 1 mile; 7/6), and *Greater London* (1 inch to 1 mile; 3/6), Messrs Stanford's *Map of Central London* (5 inches to 1 mile; 5/-), and Messrs G. W. Bacon's *City of London* (12 inches to 1 mile; 4/6), *Central London* (4 inches to 1 mile; 5/-), and *London and Suburbs* (2.3 inches to 1 mile; 5/-).

The best maps for the country round London are the Ordnance Survey 'Seventh Series' edition on a scale of 1 inch to 1 mile (for walkers) and Messrs Bartholomew's 'Half-Inch' series (½-inch to 1 mile; for motorists and cyclists). For the numbers of the sheets required see the Penguin Guides to the neighbouring counties. Maps showing recommended road routes round and across London, on a scale of 1 inch to 1 mile, are published by the R.A.C. (4/6 paper, 10/6 mounted) and the A.A. (with the environs of London on the back; 7/6, paper only).

These maps and atlases are stocked by most booksellers and many stationers. They may also be obtained from Messrs Edward Stanford, Ltd, 12 Long Acre, WC2 (near Covent Garden), who are the selling agents for the Ordnance Survey. The principal agents in London of Messrs Bartholomew are Messrs Frederick Warne & Co. Ltd, Bedford Court, Bedford Street, WC2 (near the Strand).

SHOPPING. The most fashionable shops (and hence the most expensive) are in Bond Street, Piccadilly, and the neighbouring part of Regent Street. The most popular shopping centre is Oxford Street, but other good shops will be found in Knightsbridge and Sloane Street, in Kensington High Street, and in the Strand. Shops in the City (for example, in Cheapside) are hardly inferior and generally less expensive. Burlington Arcade (Piccadilly), Shepherd Market, and the north side of St Paul's Churchyard are favoured by being free of road traffic. Certain streets have become associated with particular classes of shops; for instance, Bond Street with jewellers and exclusive dress shops, Shaftesbury Avenue with less exclusive dress shops, Savile Row with high-class tailors, Oxford Street with drapers, Tottenham Court Road with furniture dealers, and Charing Cross Road with second-hand booksellers. Most of the City and West End shops close at 5.30 p.m. (Saturdays at 1), but some of the large stores keep open on either Thursday or Friday until about 7 p.m. In the suburbs, shops generally close on Wednesday or Thursday afternoons, and keep open all day on Saturdays.

The following are among the best known DEPARTMENT STORES, where a great range of articles may be bought:

Army & Navy Stores, 105 Victoria Street, SW1; *Barker's*, 26–70 and 63–97 Kensington High Street, W8; *Bourne & Hollingsworth*, 116–28 Oxford Street, W1; *Civil Service Supply Association*, 425 Strand, WC2, and 123–5 Queen Victoria Street, EC4; *Derry & Toms*, 103–5 Kensington High Street, W8 (see p. 155); *Fortnum & Mason*, 181–4 Piccadilly, W1 (high-class); *Gamage's*, 118–28 Holborn, EC1; *Harrod's*, 87–135 Brompton Road, Knightsbridge, SW1; *Heal & Son*, 196 Tottenham Court Road, W1; *Peter Jones*, Sloane Square, SW1; *Selfridge's*, 398–429 Oxford Street, W1; *Whiteley's*, Queensway, Bayswater, W2.

Among the large drapers' stores and ladies' outfitters, where also many other ladies' requirements may usually be obtained, are: *Debenham & Freebody*, 27–37 Wigmore Street, W1; *Dickins & Jones*, 224–44 Regent Street, W1; *D. H. Evans*, 308–22 Oxford Street, W1; *Galeries Lafayette*, 188–96 Regent Street, W1; *Frederick Gorringe*, 49–75 Buckingham Palace

Road, SW1; *John Lewis*, 242–306 Oxford Street, W1; *Liberty's*, 210–20 Regent Street, W1; *Marshall & Snelgrove*, 334–48 Oxford Street, W1; *Robinson & Cleaver*, 156–68 Regent Street, W1; *Peter Robinson*, 214–34 Oxford Street, W1, and 65–72 Strand, WC2; *Swan & Edgar*, 49–63 Regent Street, W1. — *Daniel Neal's*, 3–7 Portman Square, W1, and 120–6 Kensington High Street, W8, specializes in children's clothes.

MEN'S OUTFITTERS include: *Aertex*, 177 Piccadilly, W1, 409 and 455 Oxford Street, W1, 114 Bishopsgate, EC2, and 150 Fenchurch Street, EC3; *Aquascutum*, 100 Regent Street, W1; *Austin Reed*, 103 Regent Street, W1, 1 Kingsway, WC2, 77 Cheapside, EC2, etc.; *Beale & Inman*, 131 New Bond Street, W1; *T. R. Blurton & Co*, 176 Strand, WC2, and 90 Grace-church Street, EC2; *Gieves*, 27 Old Bond Street, W1; *Hawkes & Co*, 1 Savile Row, W1; *Isaac Walton's*, 1–9 Ludgate Hill, EC4; *Jaeger Co*, 204 Regent Street, W1, and 26 Sloane Street, SW1; *Lillywhite's*, Piccadilly Circus, SW1, and 198 Sloane Street, SW1; *Morgan & Ball*, 53 Piccadilly, W1, 98 and 181 Strand, WC2, 10 Cheapside, EC2, etc.; *Moss Brothers*, 20 King Street, Covent Garden, WC2; *Savoy Taylors' Guild*, 93 Strand, WC2; *Scotch House*, Knightsbridge, SW1; *Simpson's*, 202 Piccadilly, W1; *Thresher and Glenny*, 152 Strand, WC2, and 85 Gracechurch Street, EC2; and many others, more or less expensive.

Men's clothes may be hired for almost any occasion from *Alkit*, of Cambridge Circus, *Moss Brothers* of Covent Garden, and *Young's* of Wardour Street. The charge for a morning suit (including waistcoat and top hat), shirt and collar, tie, shoes, and gloves varies from about £3 16/- to £4 4/6. Moss Brothers require a deposit of £5 (cheques accepted). Women's clothes may also be hired from Moss Brothers and Young's: evening dress, £2 12/6 to £12 12/- (with shoes, gloves, and bag, £3 2/6 to £15 12/-).

MARKETS are an integral part of the London scene and should certainly not be overlooked or avoided by the visitor. The greater part of the wholesale business is conducted early in the day, from about 5 to 8 a.m., when they are best seen, but a retail trade is carried on at least through the rest of the morning. The following are the principal markets: COVENT GARDEN (Plan III, E 3), vegetables, fruit, and flowers (retail from about 6 a.m.); SMITH-FIELD (IV, D 3), meat, poultry, and provisions (little business on Saturdays); LEADENHALL (V, E 2), meat, game, and provisions; BILLINGSGATE (V, F 2), the chief market for fish; SPITAL-FIELDS (V, C, D 3), vegetables, fruit, and flowers; and the BOR-OUGH MARKET, Southwark (IX, E 1), for general produce.

STREET MARKETS, offering almost every sort of portable goods for sale, are to be found on weekdays in BERWICK STREET, Soho (closed Thursday afternoons); LEATHER LANE, Holborn (closed Thursday after-noons and Saturdays); PORTOBELLO ROAD, Notting Hill (Fridays and

Saturdays only); BERMONDSEY SQUARE ('Caledonian'), Tower Bridge Road (Fridays only); FARRINGDON ROAD, Clerkenwell; LAMBETH WALK, Lambeth; and THE CUT, Waterloo Road. The following are best seen on Sunday mornings, when they are patronized by a cosmopolitan throng: MIDDLESEX STREET ('Petticoat Lane'), Whitechapel; CLUB ROW, off Bethnal Green Road, Shoreditch; CHAPEL STREET, Islington; and EAST LANE, Bermondsey.

BANK HOLIDAYS. Banks, shops, and business houses in London are closed on Good Friday and Christmas Day, and on Bank Holidays: Easter Monday, Whit Monday, the first Monday in August, and Boxing Day. Museums and galleries, and theatres and other entertainments are invariably closed on the first two days, but remain open on Bank Holidays, when, however, they are generally overcrowded. The public transport is also unduly congested on these days.

POLICE. The headquarters of the METROPOLITAN POLICE, who cover the whole of Greater London except the City, are at New Scotland Yard, SW1 (Plan VIII, B 3; Tel. No. WHItehall 1212). The head-office of the CITY POLICE is at 26 Old Jewry, EC2 (V, E 1; MONarch 1113). City policemen are to be distinguished by their crested helmets and red-and-white armbands; the Metropolitan police wear blue-and-white arm-bands. Strangers who require directing or information are well advised to 'ask a policeman', whose courtesy has won a world-wide reputation.

LOST PROPERTY should be sought at the Police Lost Property Office, 109 Lambeth Road, SE1 (Plan IX, D 1), open on Mondays–Fridays, 10 to 4, Saturdays 10 to 1. Enquiries cannot be answered by telephone, and a charge of 15 per cent of the value of the article is usually levied. Articles left in the trains or buses of *London Transport* should be enquired for at 200 Baker Street, Marylebone, NW1 (Mondays–Fridays 10 to 6, Saturdays 10 to 1). A charge of 1/- is made for articles up to £1 in value, and up to 2/6 in the pound above this. For articles left on the trains or at the stations of *British Railways*, enquiry should be made of the stationmaster or at the Lost Property office at the relevant terminus.

BATHS. Private hot and cold baths may be obtained at the municipal swimming baths (see p. 83). Turkish Baths include the SAVOY TURKISH BATHS, 92 Jermyn Street, SW1 (men only; open always), and 12 Duke of York Street, SW1 (ladies only), both near Piccadilly; DORCHESTER HOTEL, Park Lane, W1 (ladies only); IMPERIAL HOTEL, Russell Square, WC1 (men), and 20 Queen's Square, WC1 (ladies; near Southampton Row); PORCHESTER BATHS, Porchester Road, Queensway, W2; and METRO TURKISH BATHS, 16 Harrow Road, W2.

CHURCH SERVICES. Churches of almost every denomination can be found in London, and only a few of those most likely to appeal to visitors can be mentioned below. Several churches in the City hold mid-day services during the week, but on the other hand most of these are closed on Sundays. The times of the Sunday services, preachers, etc., at many churches are given on the preceding Saturday in *The Times*. For church music and recitals, see p. 72.

CHURCH OF ENGLAND. *St Paul's Cathedral*, see p. 378; *Westminster Abbey*, see p. 440; *Southwark Cathedral*, see p. 394; *Chapel Royal*, St James's Palace, see p. 126 (or alternatively, the *Queen's Chapel*, p. 125); *Queen's Chapel of the Savoy*, see p. 210; *St Clement Danes*, Strand, 8.30, 11, and 3.30; *Gray's Inn Chapel*, 11.15; *Lincoln's Inn Chapel*, 11.30; *Temple Church*, 8.30 and 11.15; *Tower of London* (St Peter ad Vincula), see p. 406; *Royal Hospital*, Chelsea, see p. 331.

All Hallows-by-the-Tower, 8.30, 11, and 5.30; *All Saints'*, Margaret Street, 7, 8, 9, 11 (high mass), and 6; *All Souls'*, Langham Place, 8, 11, and 6.30; *Chelsea Old Church*, 8, 12, and 6; *Grosvenor Chapel*, 8.15 and 11.15; *St Bartholomew the Great*, 9, 11, and 6.30; *St Bride's*, Fleet Street, 11 and 6.30; *St George's*, Bloomsbury Way, 8, 11.15, and 7.30; *St George's*, Hanover Square, 8, 11, and 6; *St Giles-in-the-Fields*, New Oxford Street, 8, 11, and 6.30; *St James's*, Piccadilly, 8.15, 9.15, 11, and 6; *St John's Wood Chapel*, 8, 9.30, 11, and 6.30; *St Margaret*, Lothbury, 11; *St Margaret*, Westminster, 8.15, 11, and 6; *St Martin-in-the-Fields*, 8, 9.45, 11.20, and 6.30; *St Mary Abbots*, Kensington, 7, 8, 9.30, 11.30, and 6.30; *St Marylebone*, Marylebone Road, 8, 11, and 6.30; *St Michael's*, Cornhill, 11 and 12.45; *St Olave's*, Hart Street, 9, 11, and 6; *St Pancras*, Euston Road, 8, 11, and 6.30; *St Paul's*, Covent Garden, 11 and 6; *St Paul's* Knightsbridge, 8, 9, 10.45, 11.45, and 6; *St Peter's*, Eaton Square, 8.15, 10.15, 11, and 6.30; *St Peter's*, Vere Street, 9.45, 11.15, and 8.30; *St Sepulchre's*, Holborn Viaduct, 9.15. For Guild Churches, see p. 24.

CHURCH OF SCOTLAND. *St Columba's*, Pont Street, 11, 3, and 6.30; *Crown Court Church*, Russell Street, Covent Garden, 11.15 and 6.30. — WELSH CHURCH. *St David's*, St Mary's Terrace, Paddington, 10.30 and 6; *St Benet's*, Queen Victoria Street, 11 and 6.30.

ROMAN CATHOLIC. *Westminster Cathedral*, see p. 460; *Brompton Oratory*, see p. 148; *Church of the Jesuit Fathers*, Farm Street, Mayfair, 10.50 (high mass), 12, 3.30, and 6.30.

NONCONFORMIST (all at 11 and 6.30). BAPTIST: *Bloomsbury Central*,

Shaftesbury Avenue (New Oxford Street). CONGREGATIONAL: *Westminster Chapel*, Buckingham Gate; *City Temple*, Holborn Viaduct. METHODIST: *Central Hall*, Westminster; *Kingsway Hall*, Kingsway; *Wesley's Chapel*, City Road. PRESBYTERIAN: *Regent Square*, off Gray's Inn Road; *St John's*, Allen Street, Kensington. UNITARIAN: *Essex Church*, Palace Gardens Terrace, Notting Hill. QUAKERS: *Friends House*, Euston Road (not at 6.30). — WELSH PRESBYTERIAN: Charing Cross Road, 10.45 and 6.

CHRISTIAN SCIENCE: *Third Church of Christ Scientist*, Curzon Street, Mayfair, and others, 11.30 and 7. — JEWISH: *West London Synagogue*, Upper Berkeley Street, daily at 6.30 (also Saturday at 11); *Central Synagogue*, Great Portland Street, daily at 8 a.m. (also Friday at dusk, Saturday at 9.30).

PARKS AND GARDENS. London is particularly well served with parks and open spaces accessible to the public. The best known are the Royal Parks, under the control of the Crown: ST JAMES'S PARK and the adjoining GREEN PARK (Route 5), HYDE PARK and the contiguous KENSINGTON GARDENS (Route 12), and REGENT'S PARK (Route 16), which has PRIMROSE HILL on the north. Farther out are GREENWICH PARK in the south-east suburbs (see p. 486) and RICHMOND PARK (see the *Penguin Guide to Surrey*).

Other parks and commons and numerous gardens are under the jurisdiction of the London County Council. A few of the more interesting and attractive are listed below (with their nearest stations). Open-air entertainments are given in summer in several of the parks (see p. 73) and a varied programme of sport is arranged. Facilities are provided in many parks for boating, bathing, tennis, bowls, etc., and light refreshments may generally be obtained.

BATTERSEA PARK, with the Festival Gardens (see p. 75); BROCKWELL PARK (Herne Hill station); CLAPHAM COMMON (Clapham Common and Clapham South stations); CLISSOLD PARK, Stoke Newington (Manor House station); DULWICH PARK (North Dulwich station); FINSBURY PARK (Finsbury Park and Manor House stations); HAMPSTEAD HEATH, with the adjoining Kenwood, Parliament Hill, and Golders Hill Park (Hampstead, Golders Green, Gospel Oak, and Hampstead Heath stations); HOLLAND PARK (p. 155; Kensington High Street and Holland Park stations); HURLINGHAM PARK, Fulham (Putney Bridge and Parsons Green stations); KENNINGTON PARK (Oval station); RAVENSCOURT PARK, Hammersmith (Ravenscourt Park station); SOUTHWARK PARK, Rotherhithe (Surrey Docks station); STREATHAM COMMON, with the

Rookery (Streatham station); TOOTING COMMON (Balham and Tooting Bec stations); VICTORIA PARK (Bethnal Green station); WATERLOW PARK, Highgate Hill (Archway station).

The private GARDENS of a number of houses in and around London are open to the public on certain days in summer, usually from 2 to 7 (admission 1/-). The proceeds, administered by the Queen's Institute of District Nursing, are proportioned to the Retired District Nurses' Benefit Fund and the joint gardens committee of the National Trust and the Royal Horticultural Society. Particulars are given in a booklet (2/6; postage 6d) issued yearly and obtainable from the *National Gardens Scheme* (57 Lower Belgrave Street, S W 1).

ANNUAL EVENTS. Below are listed the more important events that take place in or near London at the same (or nearly the same) period each year. For sporting events, see under 'Sport in and around London'. Information regarding dates, times, etc., may be obtained from the Travel Association (p. 61); for the ASK telephone service, see p. 60.

JANUARY: *Royal Albert Hall*, English Folk Dance & Song Society Festival; *Olympia*, Camping and Outdoor Life Exhibition; *Earls Court*, International Boat Show; *Olympia*, National Schoolboys' Own Exhibition; *Chapel Royal* (6th), Royal Epiphany Offering (see p. 126); *Drury Lane Theatre* (6th), Cutting of the Baddeley Cake; *St Martin-in-the-Fields* (26th), Australia Day Service (11 a.m.); *Trafalgar Square* (30th), Decoration of Charles I's statue, and Ceremony outside *Whitehall Palace*.

FEBRUARY: *Olympia*, Cruft's Dog Show; *St Pancras Town Hall*, St Pancras Arts Festival; *St Etheldreda's Church* (3rd; St Blaise's Day), Blessing the Throat Ceremony; *St Margaret Lothbury* (6th), New Zealand Day Service; *St Botolph's Aldgate* (20th), Girls of the Sir John Cass School attend service. — SHROVE TUESDAY: *Westminster School*, 'Tossing the pancake'. — ASH WEDNESDAY: *St Paul's Cathedral* (crypt), Stationers' Company attend service.

MARCH: *Olympia*, Ideal Home Exhibition; *Central Hall*, National Stamp Exhibition; *St Clement Danes*, Oranges and Lemons Service (see p. 214); *St Bride's*, Bridewell Royal Hospital Service. — EASTER: Tuesday in Holy Week, *St Paul's*, Bach's 'Passion Music'; Maundy Thursday, *Westminster Abbey*, Distribution of the Royal Maundy (see p. 442); Good Friday, *St Bartholomew the Great*, Poor Widows' Dole (see p. 268); Easter Sunday, *St Bartholomew's*, Bach's 'St Matthew Passion'; *Battersea Park*, Easter Parade; *Hyde Park*, Parade of Old Vehicles, etc.; Easter Monday, *Westminster Abbey*, Procession, with Carol service; *Regent's Park*, Van Horse Parade; *Hampstead Heath* and *Blackheath*, Bank Holiday Fairs; Wednesday after Easter Week, *St Lawrence Jewry* 'Spital Sermon' (see p. 272).

APRIL: *Southwark*, Shakespeare Festival (see p. 312); *St Andrew Undershaft*, John Stow Commemoration Service (see p. 289); *Parliament Square*

(19th, Primrose Day), Decoration of Disraeli's statue; *Southwark Cathedral* (23rd, St George's Day), Shakespeare's Birthday Service; *St Martin-in-the-Fields* (25th), Anzac Day Service.

MAY: *Burlington House*, Royal Academy Summer Exhibition (until mid-August); *Grosvenor House*, Royal Caledonian Ball; *Chelsea Town Hall*, Spring Antiques Fair; *Royal Hospital Grounds*, Chelsea Flower Show; *Paddington*, Festival of Little Venice; *St Olave's, Hart Street*, Pepys Commemoration Service (see p. 292); *Tower of London* (21st), Commemoration of the death of Henry VI; *Chelsea Hospital* (29th), Founder's Day; COMMONWEALTH DAY (24th), Laying of Wreaths at the *Cenotaph*; AMERICAN MEMORIAL DAY (30th), Wreaths laid at the *Cenotaph*, Lincoln's Statue in *Parliament Square*, and the grave of the Unknown Warrior in *Westminster Abbey*, and service at *St Margaret's*, Westminster. — WHITSUN: Saturday and Monday, *Hyde Park*, International Sheep Dog Trials; Monday, *Regent's Park*, Cart-Horse Parade; *Hampstead Heath* and *Blackheath*, Bank Holiday Fairs. — TRINITY MONDAY, *St Olave's, Hart Street*, Trinity House Service. — CORPUS CHRISTI: *Maiden Lane Roman Catholic Church*, Decoration by Covent Garden flower sellers.

JUNE: *Horse Guards Parade*, 'Trooping the Colour' (see p. 102); *Earls Court*, Royal Tournament; *Grosvenor House*, Antique Dealers' Fair; *Richmond* (Surrey), Royal Horse Show; MIDSUMMER (24th), *Guildhall*, Election of Sheriffs.

JULY: City of London Festival; *Hyde Park*, Meet of the London Coaching Club; *White City*, Royal International Horse Show; *Kempton Park*, Arab Horse Society's Show; Swan Upping on the *River Thames* (see p. 254); *Queen's Chapel of the Savoy* (about 20th), Beating the Bounds of the Liberty of the Savoy.

AUGUST: *Earls Court*, National Radio and Television Exhibition; *Clapham Common* (Bank Holiday and previous Saturday), County of London Horse Show; *Hampstead Heath* and *Blackheath*, Bank Holiday Fairs.

SEPTEMBER: *Kensington Town Hall*, Kensington Antiques Fair; *Olympia*, British Food Fair; *Chelsea Town Hall*, Chelsea Autumn Antiques Fair; *Farnborough* (Hants), Air Display (every two years; next in 1964); BATTLE OF BRITAIN DAY (15th), Fly-past of aircraft over London (11 a.m. to noon), and service at *Westminster Abbey* on the following Sunday (3 p.m.); *Guildhall* (28th), Admission of Sheriffs Elect; MICHAELMAS (29th), *St Lawrence Jewry*, Retiring Lord Mayor attends service before the election of the new Lord Mayor in *Guildhall*.

OCTOBER: *Wembley Stadium*, Horse of the Year Show; *Earls Court*, International Motor Show; *Olympia*, Royal Dairy Show; *Royal Albert Hall*, National Brass Band Festival; *Law Courts* open (about 1st), service at *Westminster Abbey*, followed by a procession through the main hall of the courts; *St Martin-in-the-Fields* (or other church; first Sunday), Costermongers' Harvest Festival; *St Sepulchre's*, Holborn (about 1st), Scholars of Christ's Hospital attend service, and later visit the Mansion House; *Westminster Abbey* (13th), St Edward's Day Pilgrimage; *St Katherine Creechurch*

(16th), 'Lion Sermon' (see p. 289); *Trafalgar Square* (21st), Decoration of Nelson's Monument; *St Paul's* (24th), National Service for Seafarers.

NOVEMBER: *Burlington House*, Royal Academy Winter Exhibition (to February or March); *Earls Court*, International Cycle & Motor-Cycle Show; *Royal Albert Hall* (about 5th), British Legion Festival of Remembrance; *Houses of Parliament* (about 6th), State Opening by the Sovereign; *Guildhall* (Friday before second Saturday), Admission of Lord Mayor Elect; Second Saturday, Lord Mayor's Show (see p. 258); *Whitehall* (second Sunday), Armistice Day Service at the Cenotaph (11 a.m.); *Westminster Cathedral* (16th), Relic of St Edmund exhibited; *St Sepulchre's*, Holborn (22nd), St Cecilia's Day Service and Festival; *St Paul's* (Tuesday after Advent Sunday), Handel's 'Messiah'.

DECEMBER: *Earls Court*, Royal Smithfield Livestock Show; *Olympia*, International Poultry Show, National Cat Club Show, Richmond Championship Dog Show; *Chelsea Hospital*, Ceremony of the Christmas Cheeses; *St Peter's Cornhill* (before Christmas), Nativity Play; *Westminster Abbey* (26th–28th), Procession and Carol service; NEW YEAR'S EVE: *Savoy Hotel*, Limelight Ball; Gathering of exiled Scots outside *St Paul's* (midnight).

BOOKS ON LONDON. The following is a selection from the forbidding number of books that have been published dealing with every aspect of the capital. The dates are those of the latest editions. Useful bibliographies are the Members' Library Catalogue of the L.C.C. (1939; obtainable from the County Hall) and the bibliography of the City of London by Raymond Smith, published by the National Book League (1951).

The *Survey of London* published by the London County Council and still in progress (29 vols.; 1900–61) is the standard work, though most volumes stop short at the 19th century. Parallel to this (rather than superseded by it) is the *Survey of London* in 10 large vols. (1902–12) by Sir Walter Besant, an impressive historical (mainly social) and topographical study. Other large-scale works are *London, Past and Present*, by Henry B. Wheatley (3 vols.; 1891), a historical dictionary arranged street by street, and the *New Survey of London Life and Labour*, edited by Sir H. Llewellyn Smith (9 vols.; 1930–5), a valuable social and industrial study.

GENERAL DESCRIPTION: William Gaunt: *London* (1961). — Paul Cohen-Portheim: *The Spirit of London* (1950). — H. J. Massingham: *The London Scene* (1933). — V. S. Pritchett: *London Perceived* (1962). — Colin MacInnes: *London, City of any Dream* (1962). — James Bone: *The London Perambulator* (1925) and *London Echoing* (1948), both illustrated by Muirhead Bone. — H. V. Morton: *London* (1940) and *In Search of London* (1951). — Chiang Yee: *The Silent Traveller in London* (1938), illustrated by himself. — Ivor Brown: *Winter in London* (1951). — Francis Marshall: *The London Week-End Book* (1951). — Sir Evelyn Wrench: *Transatlantic London* (1949). — Edward Carter: *The Future of London* (Pelican Books, 1962). —

D. M. Low (ed.): *London is London* (1949; an anthology). — H. and P. Massingham (eds.): *The London Anthology* (1950). — Ivor Brown: *A Book of London* (1961).

George H. Cunningham: *London* (1931; a topographical survey). — Steen Eiler Rasmussen: *London, the Unique City* (1948; Pelican Books, 1960; valuable survey by a Danish architect). — Nikolaus Pevsner: *The Cities of London and Westminster* (1962) and *London, except the Cities of London and Westminster* (1952), in the Penguin Buildings of England series. — Thomas Burke: *The Streets of London* (1949). — Gerald Cobb and Geoffrey Webb: *The Old Churches of London* (1948). — Elizabeth and Wayland Young: *Old London Churches* (1956). — Ralph Dutton: *London Homes* (1952). — Raymond Mander and Joe Mitchenson: *The Theatres of London* (1961). — Sir Ernest Pooley: *The Guilds of the City of London* (1945). — Louis T. Stanley: *The Old Inns of London* (1957). — Edwin Course: *London's Railways* (1962). — N. J. Barton: *The Lost Rivers of London* (1962). — R. S. R. Fitter: *London's Natural History* (1945).

Books mainly of interest for their photographs: Helmut Gernsheim: *Beautiful London* (1953). — Martin Hürliman: *London* (1956). — Tony Armstrong-Jones: *London* (1958). — J. Allan Cash: *The Pageant of London in Colour* (1958). — Edwin Smith: *The Living City* (1957). — O. J. Morris: *Grandfather's London* (1956).

BOOKS ON VARIOUS DISTRICTS AND PLACES: G. S. Dugdale: *Whitehall through the Centuries* (1950). — C. L. Kingsford: *The Early History of Piccadilly, Leicester Square, Soho, and their Neighbourhood* (1925). — B. H. Johnson: *Berkeley Square to Bond Street* (1952). — Simon Dewes: *Piccadilly Pageant* (1949), *Temple Bar Tapestry* (1948), etc. — Neville Braybrooke: *London Green* (the Royal Parks; 1959). — William Gaunt: *Chelsea* (1954) and *Kensington* (1958). — J. Bruce Williamson: *The History of the Temple* (1924). — Sir William Ball: *Lincoln's Inn* (1947). — Harold Rosenthal: *Two Centuries of Opera at Covent Garden* (1958). — Henry A. Harben: *A Dictionary of London* (i.e. the City; 1918). — Eilert Ekwall: *Street-Names of the City of London* (1954). — C. H. Holden and W. G. Holford: *The City of London, a record of Destruction and Survival* (1951). — Paul Ferris: *The City* (its economic background; 1960; Pelican Books, 1962). — Eric de Maré: *London's Riverside* (1958). — L. M. Bates: *The Londoner's River* (1949). — John Herbert: *The Port of London* (1947). — Grace Golden: *Old Bankside* (1951). — Harry Williams: *South London* (1949). — C. R. Dodwell: *Lambeth Palace* (1958). — Guy Eden: *The Parliament Book* (1949). — Eric Taylor: *The House of Commons at Work* (Pelican Books, 1961). — W. R. Matthews and W. M. Atkins (eds.): *A History of St Paul's Cathedral* (1957). — G. H. Cook: *Old St Paul's Cathedral* (1955). — Jane Lang: *Rebuilding St Paul's after the Great Fire of London* (1957). — G. L. Prestige: *St Paul's in its Glory, 1831–1911* (1955). — Lawrence E. Tanner: *The History and Treasures of Westminster Abbey* (1953). — W. R. Lethaby: *Westminster Abbey and the King's Craftsmen* (1906) and *Westminster Abbey Re-examined* (1925). — Philip Street: *The London Zoo* (1956).

HISTORY AND ANTIQUITIES: Of the *Victoria County History of London* Vol. I only has been published (1909), dealing with Romano-British London, Anglo-Saxon remains, ecclesiastical history, and religious houses. In the *Victoria County History of Surrey*, Vol. IV (1912) includes districts south of the Thames now in London. The *Royal Commission on Historical Monuments* has published five volumes on London: Vol. I, Westminster Abbey (1924); Vol. II, West London (1925); Vol. III, Roman London (1928; now dated); Vol. IV, The City (1929); and Vol. V, East London (1930).

R. J. Mitchell and M. D. R. Leys: *A History of London Life* (1958). — Derek Mayne: *The Growth of London* (1952; good short history). — W. H. Godfrey: *History of Architecture in and around London* (1962). — Gordon Home: *Roman London* (1948). — William T. Hill: *Buried London* (1955). — John E. N. Hearsey: *Bridge, Church and Palace in Old London* (1961). — John Stow: *The Survey of London* (1598), a classic on Elizabethan London (excellent edition in 2 vols. by C. L. Kingsford; one vol. in Everyman's Library). — Norman G. Brett-James: *The Growth of Stuart London* (1935). — Valerie Pearl: *London and the Outbreak of the Puritan Revolution* (1962). — Walter George Bell: *The Great Plague of London, 1665* (1951) and *The Great Fire of London, 1666* (1951). — T. F. Reddaway: *The Rebuilding of London after the Great Fire* (1951). — M. D. George: *London Life in the Eighteenth Century* (1925). — John Summerson: *Georgian London* (1945; Pelican Books, 1962; a delightful architectural survey). — Peter Quennell (ed.): *Mayhew's London* (1949; selections from 'London Labour and the London Poor', by Henry Mayhew, 1851). — T. Rowlandson and A. C. Pugin: *The Microcosm of London* (King Penguins; 1943).

LITERARY ASSOCIATIONS: Samuel Pepys: *Diary*, covering the years 1660–9 (3-vol. edition in Everyman's Library). — John Evelyn: *Diary* (1706). — Daniel Defoe: *Journal of the Plague Year* (1722). — James Boswell: *The Life of Samuel Johnson* (1791). — Charles Lamb: *The Essays of Elia* (1823) and *The Last Essays of Elia* (1833). — Harrison Ainsworth: *The Tower of London* (1840) and *Old St Paul's* (1841). — E. Beresford Chancellor: *The London of Charles Dickens* (1924) and *The London of Thackeray* (1923). — William Addison: *In the Steps of Charles Dickens* (1955). — Charles Dickens: *Pickwick Papers* (1837), *Oliver Twist* (1839), *Nicholas Nickleby* (1839), *The Old Curiosity Shop* (1841), *Barnaby Rudge* (1841), *Dombey and Son* (1848), *David Copperfield* (1850), *Little Dorrit* (1857), and *Great Expectations* (1861). — W. M. Thackeray: *Vanity Fair* (1848), *Pendennis* (1850), *Henry Esmond* (1852), and *The Newcomes* (1853).

Periodical publications containing valuable material on the history and topography of London include the *Transactions of the London & Middlesex Archaeological Society* (see p. 63), one Part of which is usually issued each year (three Parts make a Volume); the *London Topographical Record*, issued as and when funds allow by the London Topographical Society (21 vols.; 1901–59); and the *Guildhall Miscellany*, published by the Corporation of London (10 issues; 1952–9). Papers of value on the history and antiquities of London appear also in *Archaeologia*, issued generally every two years by the Society of Antiquaries; the *Archaeological Journal* of the Royal Archaeological Institute; the *Transactions of the Royal Historical Society*; and journals of other societies. These are usually available to members only, but can often be consulted at libraries (see p. 65).

ABBREVIATIONS. The following abbreviations are used in the guide:

b. = born	m. = mile
d. = died	N.T. = National Trust
ft = feet	r. = right
in. = inches	yds = yards
l. = left	

Places shown in black type in the routes are described in the gazetteer of Places of Interest.

ROUTES IN LONDON

1 Charing Cross and Trafalgar Square

Plans III, F 2, 3 and VIII, A 2, 3

STATIONS: TRAFALGAR SQUARE (Plan III, F 3), on the Bakerloo line; STRAND (III, F 3), on the Northern line. — MOTOR-BUSES from every part of London (compare plan, p. 40, and Routes 2, 6, 19, 21). Eastbound buses stop in Duncannon Street, south of St Martin-in-the-Fields; westbound buses in Cockspur Street, south-west of Trafalgar Square, or in the Strand; northbound buses in front of the National Gallery; and southbound buses at the upper end of Whitehall.

ADMISSION to the NATIONAL GALLERY, see p. 354; to CANADA HOUSE, Monday–Friday 9.15 to 5.30, Saturday (Reading Room only) 9.15 to 12.30; to SOUTH AFRICA HOUSE, Monday–Friday 9.30 to 12.30 and 2 to 4 (Reading Room 9.30 to 5).

CHARING CROSS (Plan VIII, A 3), the triangular open space at the head of Whitehall and on the south side of Trafalgar Square, is generally regarded as the hub of London. 'Why, sir,' said Dr Johnson, 'Fleet Street has a very animated appearance, but I think the full tide of human existence is at Charing Cross'. At this point in 1291 Edward I set up the last of the thirteen crosses that marked the stages in the funeral procession of his queen, Eleanor of Castile, from Harby in Nottinghamshire to Westminster Abbey. The cross was taken down in 1647 and its site is now occupied by a fine equestrian STATUE OF CHARLES I, by Hubert Le Sueur, cast in 1633. Before this could be erected the Civil War broke out and it was disposed of as scrap to a brazier who sold 'relics' alleged to have been made from it to Royalist supporters. At the Restoration, however, the statue was produced intact, and it was erected in 1675, on the spot where several of the regicides had been beheaded in 1660 and facing down Whitehall to the scene of Charles I's execution. On 30 January, the anniversary of the king's death, the statue is hung with wreaths by his admirers. The sculptured stone pedestal, by Joshua Marshall, is said to follow a design by Sir Christopher Wren. A bronze plaque set into the pavement in 1955 behind the statue marks the official centre of London, from which mileages are measured.

TRAFALGAR SQUARE (III, F 2, 3), named in commemoration of Nelson's great naval victory of 1805, was laid out in 1829–41 by Sir Charles Barry, partly on the site of the Royal Mews, claimed by Sir Robert Peel as the 'finest site in Europe'. The pigeons that inhabit the square are an integral part of the scene, and the square is a popular terminal point for political demonstrations. On the south side rises the NELSON MONUMENT, or Nelson's Column, designed by William Railton (1843), a fluted Corinthian column 167 ft 6½ in. high, surmounted by a colossal statue of Admiral Lord Nelson, 17 ft 4½ in. high, by E. H. Baily. On the pedestal at the base are four bronze reliefs, cast from captured French cannon, showing scenes from the battles of St Vincent, the Nile, Copenhagen, and Trafalgar; the four bronze couchant lions that guard the base are by Sir Edwin Landseer (1868). The monument is decorated every year on the anniversary of the Battle of Trafalgar (21 October).

From the column there is a noble vista down Whitehall to the clock-tower of the Houses of Parliament. To the right (south-west) is a glimpse of Admiralty Arch, the approach to the Mall and St James's Park (Route 5), and farther right is the beginning of Cockspur Street (Route 6), leading to Pall Mall and the Haymarket. To the left (east) opens the entrance to the Strand (Route 21), with Northumberland Avenue leading to the Victoria Embankment (Route 26) to the right of it. At the lower corners of the square are statues of Generals Sir Charles James Napier (d. 1853) and Sir Henry Havelock (d. 1857), and near the latter is a curious round stone police box with a lamp often erroneously said to come from Nelson's flagship, the *Victory*. Behind the Nelson monument are two ornamental fountains (1948) designed by Sir Edwin Lutyens, with bronze groups by Sir Charles Wheeler and William McMillan. Below the parapet on the north are bronze busts of Admirals Lord Jellicoe (d. 1935) and Lord Beatty (d. 1936), and the Imperial Standards of Length of the Board of Trade (inch, foot, two feet, yard, chain, and 100 ft). Above the north-east corner of the square is an equestrian statue of George IV (d. 1830), by Chantrey.

A fir-tree, the gift of the people of Norway in memory of the hospitality shown their royal family during the War, is set up in Trafalgar Square and illuminated every Christmastide.

Vehicles must proceed round the square in a clockwise direction. Entrances to Trafalgar Square underground station, at the south-east corner (near the Havelock statue), at the beginning of the Strand, and near the foot of Cockspur Street (west of Charing Cross), are connected by a subway by which pedestrians may avoid the invariably congested roadways.

On the west side of the square is CANADA HOUSE, the headquarters of the High Commissioner for Canada, built in 1824–7 by Sir Robert Smirke as the Union Club, but reconstructed by Septimus Warwick in 1925. On the ground floor are a library, reading room, and information bureau. The adjoining building on the north, also by Smirke (1827), is occupied by the ROYAL COLLEGE OF PHYSICIANS, who are to move to Regent's Park (p. 183). Over the entrance in Pall Mall East is a statue by Henry Weekes of Thomas Linacre, the humanist, founder of the college in 1518. Above the north side of the square rises the National Gallery, in front of which are a bronze statue of James II, with a Latin inscription claiming him as 'King of England, Scotland, France and Ireland', and an ineffectual bronze copy of the marble statue of George Washington by J. A. Houdon at Richmond (Virginia), presented in 1921. SOUTH AFRICA HOUSE, on the east side of the square, was designed by Sir Herbert Baker in 1931–3 as the headquarters in London of the Union of South Africa. Outside are a winged springbok in gilt-bronze by Sir Charles Wheeler, a statue of Bartholomeu Diaz, the explorer who discovered South Africa (by C. L. Steynberg), and sculptures illustrating the flora and fauna and the history of the Union. In the main hall is a tapestry map designed by Macdonald Gill and woven at Merton in Surrey, and the building contains a reference library, a reading room, and an exhibition hall.

At the foot of Charing Cross Road (Route 19), facing the east side of the National Gallery, is the church of ST MARTIN-IN-THE-FIELDS (III, F 3), a classical building of 1721–6, the masterpiece of James Gibbs, a follower of Sir Christopher Wren. A church has stood on this site at least since 1222, though in fact the previous building was erected in 1544 for Henry VIII. St Martin's is the parish church of the Lords Commissioners of the Admiralty (whose white ensign is flown on state occasions) and also of the Sovereign, most of Buckingham Palace being included in the parish. George I was the first churchwarden of the new church, the only instance of a reigning monarch holding such an office. Notable features of the exterior are the Corinthian portico and the graceful spire, 185 ft high, its weather-vane topped by a crown. The finely decorated interior has piers with Corinthian capitals, and an elliptical ceiling in the nave, the work of Italian craftsmen. At the west end of the south aisle is a bust of the architect, by Rysbrack; the font, dated 1689, in the north aisle, is from the previous church. The pulpit, introduced in 1858, has older stairs attributed to Grinling Gibbons, the famous woodcarver. On the north of the chancel is the Royal Box and on the south that of the Lords of the Admiralty. Above the chancel arch are the arms of George I, which appear also in the pediment above the portico.

The crypt, entered from the south-west corner of the church, is kept open all night as a shelter for the poor and homeless. Restored in 1937, it has massive square piers and a plain vault, and contains old memorials, a chest of 1597, the old whipping-post from Charing Cross (1752) and Gibbs' model of the church. A doorway on the south, fashioned as a memorial arch to the 'Old Contemptibles' of 1914–18, admits to a chapel furnished in 1954 as a memorial to H.R.L. ('Dick') Sheppard, vicar of St Martin's in 1914–27 and well known for his welfare work, a tradition ably carried on by subsequent vicars. The sanctuary lamp here was given in memory of George Heriot (d. 1624), founder of the famous school in Edinburgh, who was buried in the churchyard.

Nell Gwyn or Gwynne (d. 1687), the mistress of Charles II, was among the numerous others buried in the churchyard, but this was cleared in 1829 to make way for Duncannon Street. The catacombs, themselves cleared in 1938, were used during the war as an air-raid shelter. The church registers record the baptisms of Francis Bacon (1561), John Hampden (1594), and Charles II (1630), and the marriages of Benjamin West, the American painter (1765), and Thomas Moore, the poet (1811).

2 From Charing Cross to Parliament Square (Whitehall)

Plan VIII, A 3–VIII, B 3

STATIONS: For Charing Cross, see Route 1; WESTMINSTER (Plan VIII, B 3), on the Circle and District lines, for Parliament Square. — MOTOR-BUSES Nos. 3, 11, 12, 24, 29, 39, 53, 59, 77, 88, 127, 134, 153, 159, and 276 all ply down Whitehall.

WHITEHALL (VIII, A, B 3), the broad thoroughfare which runs south from Charing Cross to Parliament Square, Westminster Abbey, and the Houses of Parliament, is one of the famous streets of the world, named after a royal palace of which only the banqueting house has survived. Containing many of the principal government offices, it is generally regarded as the administrative centre of the British Commonwealth. On the right as the road descends is the WHITEHALL THEATRE, by E. A. Stone (1930), and on the left, farther on, opens GREAT SCOTLAND YARD, a street on the site of that part of Whitehall Palace occupied by visiting kings of Scotland and their ambassadors. Later it became famous as the headquarters of the Metropolitan Police, but these were transferred to new offices on the Embankment in 1891. The CROWN ESTATE OFFICE, on the south of Great Scotland Yard, is a fine building by John Murray (1910).

On the other side of Whitehall is the ADMIRALTY (VIII, A 2, 3), the offices of the governing body of the Royal Navy. The rambling edifice consists of two adjoining buildings, the older, with a classical portico in a small courtyard, erected by Thomas Ripley in 1723–6. This was the Admiralty of Nelson's day, and here the great admiral lay in state after his death at Trafalgar (1805). It is secluded from Whitehall by a charming stone screen designed by Robert Adam in 1760. Behind, a massive pile dominated by its cupolas, is the newer building, put up in 1895–1907 facing the Mall and the Horse Guards Parade. The wireless aerials on the roof keep the Admiralty in touch with ships in all parts of the world.

On the south of the old building, facing Whitehall, are ADMIRALTY HOUSE, the official residence of the First Lord of the Admiralty (by S. P. Cockerell, 1786) and the former Paymaster-General's Office (1733). Next comes the HORSE GUARDS (VIII, A 3), with its picturesque clock-tower, built by William Kent and John Vardy in 1742–52 on the site of a guardhouse for the palace of Whitehall. Two mounted troopers of the Household Cavalry (compare p. 152), in their resplendent uniforms, are posted here daily from 10 a.m. to 4 p.m., but are relieved every hour. At 11 a.m. (10 a.m. on Sundays) the ceremony of Changing the Guard is performed, a popular and colourful spectacle lasting about ½-hour, and at 4 p.m. daily a dismounted inspection takes place.

The low arch beneath the clock-tower, closed to motor-cars (except those of royalty and a few privileged persons), admits to the HORSE GUARDS PARADE, a broad open space facing the east side of St James's Park. On the north rises the Admiralty, and on the south are seen the backs of Nos. 10–12 Downing Street (see p. 104), with the Renaissance-style Foreign Office beyond to the right and the Treasury and the Scottish Office to the left. Two dismounted sentries of the Household Cavalry patrol the archway. On the parade ground near the Horse Guards are equestrian statues of Viscount Wolseley (d. 1913), by Sir W. Goscombe John, and Earl Roberts (d. 1914), a smaller copy of one at Calcutta. On the south side is a statue by John Tweed of Earl Kitchener (d. 1916), and on the west, at the edge of the park, is the GUARDS' MEMORIAL for 1914–18, by G. Ledward and H. C. Bradshaw. The Horse Guards Parade is the scene of the impressive ceremony of 'Trooping the Colour', performed by the Brigade of Guards and the Household Cavalry before the Queen on her official birthday (usually early in June).

On the east side of Whitehall, opposite the Horse Guards, is the imposing pile of the WAR OFFICE (VIII, A 3), built by William Young in 1906. The corner turrets disguise the fact that none of the angles is a right angle. In front is an equestrian statue by Adrian Jones of the Duke of Cambridge (d. 1904), Commander-in-Chief of the British Armies for nearly forty years (1856–95), and on the south is a statue of the eighth Duke of Devonshire (d. 1908), the statesman. Beyond this is the splendid BANQUETING HOUSE, practically the only surviving part of the royal palace of Whitehall and a splendid example of Palladian architecture, the masterpiece of Inigo Jones. Completed in 1622, this was the first building to be erected in England in the style evolved by Andrea Palladio, the Italian architect, and the first building in London constructed mainly in Portland stone. Over the entrance in the staircase annexe added by Wyatt in 1798 is a bust of Charles I, marking the approximate site of the window through which he stepped on to the scaffold in 1649.

The principal room is the spacious and well-proportioned BANQUETING HALL, 115 ft long, remarkable especially for its nine allegorical ceiling paintings designed for Charles I by Rubens, who received £3,000 and a knighthood for the work. The paintings were done on canvas at Antwerp with the assistance of Jordaens and other pupils, and were completed in 1635; they were well restored in 1952. The subject of the large central oval is the Apotheosis of James I, while other paintings symbolize the Birth of Charles I and his Coronation in Scotland.

A mansion on this site was purchased in the 13th century as the London residence of the Archbishops of York. Frequently altered and improved, it was known as York House until the downfall of Cardinal Wolsey in 1529, when it was seized by Henry VIII, who enlarged it and changed its name to WHITEHALL PALACE. The Tudor palace, which covered a large area now bisected by Whitehall and extending east to the river, became for a century and a half the chief residence of the court in London. Henry VIII was married here to Anne Boleyn in 1533 and here he died in 1547. Elizabeth I was taken from the palace to be a prisoner in the Tower, but returned in triumph on her accession as queen. In a new banqueting house, built in 1581, the first performance of Shakespeare's *Othello* is believed to have been given in 1604. The house was rebuilt in 1605 and here in 1612 Elizabeth, daughter of James I, was betrothed to Frederick V, Count Palatine of the Rhine, the great-grandfather of George I and ancestor of the present royal line. After this building had been destroyed by fire in 1619, plans for a new palace were drawn up for James I by Inigo Jones, but in fact only the banqueting house was completed. From a window in an annexe on the north of this (since demolished) Charles I stepped to his execution in 1649. Oliver Cromwell took up his residence as Lord Protector in the palace, with John Milton as his secretary; here he refused the crown of England and here he died in 1658. After the Restoration the court returned to the palace, which became a centre of revelry and intrigue, as related by Pepys and others, until Charles II died here in 1685. The weathercock was placed at the north end of the roof by James II to show, it is said, whether the wind was favourable to the voyage of William of Orange. In 1688 he 'stole away from Whitehall by the Privy Stairs' and in the following year the crown was offered here by the Lords and Commons to William and Mary. The new king transferred his residence to Kensington Palace and in 1698 the old palace was burned to the ground, apart from the Banqueting House. In 1724 this was converted by George I into a Chapel Royal, but it was never consecrated and in 1890 it was granted by Queen Victoria to the Royal United Service Institution, whose museum was housed here from 1895 to 1962.

The Banqueting House has been taken over by the government for official receptions and other forms of hospitality, and there is no public admission.

GWYDYR HOUSE, adjoining the Banqueting House, was built by John Marquand in 1772, and behind rises a huge block of government offices (see p. 244), which completely overshadows the statue of Sir Walter Raleigh (d. 1618), by William McMillan (1959), facing Whitehall. Dover House, now the SCOTTISH OFFICE (VIII, B 3), opposite the Banqueting House, was built by James Paine in 1755 and has a portico over the pavement added by

Henry Holland (1787). In front is an equestrian statue of Earl Haig (d. 1928), by A. F. Hardiman, and farther on is the TREASURY (see below), built by Kent in 1737, but extended by Sir John Soane in 1827 and given a new façade by Sir Charles Barry in 1847. It contains the offices of the First Lord of the Treasury (a position usually combined with that of Prime Minister) and of the Chancellor of the Exchequer. At the north end is the office of the Privy Council the private council of the sovereign, comprising princes of the blood, high officers of State, and certain Members of Parliament appointed by the Crown. At the south end, with its entrance in Downing Street, is the office of the Judicial Committee of the Privy Council. This is the highest Court of Appeal for disputes in the Colonies and in those Dominions that have no supreme court of appeal of their own.

DOWNING STREET (VIII, B 3), famous out of all proportion to its unimposing appearance, is named after its builder, Sir George Downing (d. 1684), who graduated at Harvard in 1642 and became secretary to the Treasury. No. 10, with an unpretentious exterior, is the official residence of the Prime Minister and its Cabinet Room (on the ground floor) has been the scene of many momentous meetings. The house was offered by George II in 1732 to Sir Robert Walpole, the first prime minister in the modern sense, who insisted that it be annexed to his office instead. Walpole lived here in 1735–42, but the front part of the house was rebuilt, probably by Kenton Couse, in 1766–74. The dining rooms of No. 10 and No. 11, next door (the official residence of the Chancellor of the Exchequer), were redesigned in characteristic style in 1825 by Soane.

The Treasury and Nos. 10–11 Downing Street are being rebuilt behind their façades to the designs of Raymond Erith, but most of the historic features will be incorporated. No. 12, adjoining, the office of the Chief Government Whip, is being completely rebuilt. During the demolition of the old buildings, begun in 1960, remains of the Tudor palace of Whitehall (see above), were brought to light, including part of the great hall converted by Henry VIII into a tennis court, as well as much Roman and Tudor pottery, and the remains of the wooden structure of a Saxon hall, the first work of this kind to be discovered in London.

That part of Whitehall on the east beyond Downing Street is known as Parliament Street. RICHMOND TERRACE, on this side, is a late-Georgian survival of about 1827. In the centre of the road is the CENOTAPH (VIII, B 3), simply inscribed 'To the Glorious Dead', commemorating all servicemen of the British Empire who gave their lives in the two World Wars. Designed by Sir Edwin

Lutyens, it was first erected temporarily in plaster as a saluting point for the Allied 'Victory March' of 19 July 1919, but in deference to public feeling it was rebuilt in Portland stone for the anniversary of Armistice Day on 11 November 1920. The inscription referring to the Second World War was added in 1946. A service, attended by the Sovereign, leading statesmen, and representatives of the armed forces, is held at the Cenotaph on Remembrance Sunday (second Sunday in November), when the two-minute silence in memory of the fallen is observed at 11 a.m.

On the west side of Whitehall are two large blocks of government offices, divided by King Charles Street, at the farther end of which is a statue of Lord Clive (d. 1774), by Tweed, erected in 1916. The northern block of buildings, designed by Sir Gilbert Scott (1873), contains the COMMONWEALTH RELATIONS OFFICE (northeast), the FOREIGN OFFICE (north-west), and the HOME OFFICE (south-east). Here also is the INDIA OFFICE LIBRARY, founded in 1801 by the Honourable East India Company, and the oldest, largest, and finest Orientalist library in the world. It contains about 250,000 printed books and 15,000 manuscripts (accessible to students). In the second block of buildings, by J. M. Brydon and Sir Henry Tanner (1920), are the MINISTRY OF HOUSING and Local Government, the MINISTRY OF DEFENCE, some departments of the Treasury, and the office of the Lord Privy Seal. Derby Gate, opening off Parliament Street, leads to New Scotland Yard (Route 26), while Whitehall ends on the south at PARLIAMENT SQUARE (Route 3).

3 From Parliament Square to Lambeth Bridge and Vauxhall Bridge

Plan VIII, B 3–VIII, E 2

STATIONS: WESTMINSTER (Plan VIII, B 3), on the Circle and District lines; VAUXHALL (VIII, F 3), on the Southern Region, ⅓ m. E. of Vauxhall Bridge. — MOTOR-BUSES Nos. 3, 11, 12, 24, 29, 39, 53, 59, 76, 77, 88, 127, 134, 153, 159, and 276 to Parliament Square; Nos. 3, 10, 46, 59, 77, 149, and 159 cross Lambeth Bridge; Nos. 2, 36, 57, 88, 181, 185, and 186 cross Vauxhall Bridge. No. 88 runs from Parliament Square to Vauxhall Bridge via Great Smith Street and the Tate Gallery.

ADMISSION to ST MARGARET'S CHURCH, weekdays 9 to 4; to the HOUSES OF PARLIAMENT and WESTMINSTER HALL, see p. 335; to the

JEWEL TOWER, weekdays 10.30 to 6.30 (October–February to 4; free); to the TATE GALLERY, see p. 398.

PARLIAMENT SQUARE (VIII, B 3), the attractive open space at the foot of Whitehall, was laid out by Sir Charles Barry as a kind of garden approach to his new Houses of Parliament. From the north side there is a splendid view of St Margaret's Church with Westminster Abbey towering behind, and of the massive pile of the Houses of Parliament with Westminster Hall in front. In the angle between this and the lofty clock-tower is New Palace Yard, with an entrance to Westminster Hall and the members' approach to the House of Commons. Bridge Street, skirting the clock-tower on the left, leads to Westminster underground station and Westminster Bridge (Route 26), while Great George Street runs from the north-west corner of the square to St James's Park (Route 5).

Around the grassy centre of the square, laid out afresh in 1951, are statues of Field-Marshal Smuts (d. 1950), by Sir Jacob Epstein, unveiled in 1956, and of former prime ministers: Lord Palmerston (d. 1865), the Earl of Derby (d. 1869), Benjamin Disraeli, Lord Beaconsfield (d. 1881), and Sir Robert Peel (d. 1850). Lord Beaconsfield's statue is decorated with primroses, alleged to be his favourite flower, on Primrose Day (19 April). On the west side of the square, from which there is a glimpse of the County Hall beyond the river, are statues of George Canning (d. 1827), the prime minister, and Abraham Lincoln (d. 1865), the latter a fine replica of the one by Saint-Gaudens at Chicago, presented by the American people in 1920.

Behind the Lincoln statue is the elaborate Renaissance-style façade of the MIDDLESEX GUILDHALL (VIII, B 3), the county hall and sessions hall for Middlesex (excluding the County of London), built by J. S. Gibson and opened in 1913. The relief over the door is of Henry III granting a charter to Westminster Abbey, that on the left shows the signing of Magna Carta by King John, and that on the right Lady Jane Grey accepting the crown from John Dudley, Duke of Northumberland. Illuminated panels in the entrance hall, signed by King George of the Hellenes, Queen Wilhelmina of the Netherlands, and King Haakon of Norway, commemorate the use of the court rooms by the maritime courts of foreign allies during the Second World War. On the north of the guildhall is the ROYAL INSTITUTION OF CHARTERED SURVEYORS, founded in 1868, who also occupy the fine 18th-century building adjoining in Great George Street.

To the south of Parliament Square, in the shadow of the great abbey, is ST MARGARET'S CHURCH (VIII, C 3), the mother-church of the city of Westminster, and the parish church of the House of Commons since 1614. Members attend service on certain occasions, when the Speaker occupies the pew in front of the lectern. The church, the most fashionable in London for weddings, was founded in the 11th or 12th century, but was rebuilt in the Perpendicular style in 1504–23 by Robert Stowell, master-mason of Westminster Abbey. The Solemn League and Covenant, whereby the Scottish covenanters promised military aid to the English parliament in return for the establishment of Presbyterianism in England, was signed here in 1643. The church was refaced in Portland stone in 1735 and well restored by Sir Gilbert Scott in 1878. The west porch was added to commemorate the ministry of Canon Farrar (1876–95), afterwards Dean of Canterbury. Samuel Pepys was married in the church in 1655, John Milton in 1656, and Sir Winston Churchill in 1908. It has been the custom since the 16th century to ring the bells when the sovereign drives past in state.

The magnificent Flemish glass in the east window is thought to have been made at the order of Ferdinand and Isabella of Spain to celebrate the betrothal in 1501 of their daughter, Catherine of Aragon, to Prince Arthur, elder brother of Henry VIII. It was intended for Westminster Abbey, but before it arrived Henry had become king and had married his brother's widow. The glass, dispatched to Waltham Abbey, was bought for St Margaret's in 1758.

The centre panel of the altarpiece is a copy of Titian's 'Supper at Emmaus', carved in limewood (1753). On the north side of the east door is a brass to Sir Walter Raleigh, who was beheaded in 1618 in front of the Palace of Westminster and is claimed to be interred in the chancel, though it is possible that he may be buried at Beddington (compare the *Penguin Guide to Surrey*). A tablet of 1820 on the right of the door commemorates William Caxton (d. 1491), the father of printing, who was buried in the church or churchyard. The window over the door to him, destroyed by bombing, has been replaced by one to Captain E. A. Fitzroy, Speaker of the House of Commons in 1928–

43. The second window in the south aisle is in memory of Phillips Brooks (d. 1893), bishop of Massachusetts, who often preached here. The alabaster tomb of Lady Dudley (d. 1600), near by, is one of several good 16th–17th-century monuments in the church. Farther west is a memorial of 1955 to James Rumsey (d. 1792), an American pioneer of steam navigation, who is buried in the churchyard; it incorporates an epitaph written by Robert Herrick for his niece Elizabeth (d. 1630). At the west end are windows given by Americans in memory of Raleigh (with an inscription by J. R. Lowell) and Milton (inscription by Whittier). In the north wall is a window to Admiral Blake (d. 1657), whose body was buried in the churchyard after being exhumed from Westminster Abbey.

The road leaving Parliament Square to the south-east passes between St Margaret's Church, on the right, and Westminster Hall, in front of which stands a fine bronze statue of Oliver Cromwell, by Sir Hamo Thornycroft (1899). To the south of the hall opens OLD PALACE YARD, with a striking equestrian statue of Richard I, by Marochetti (1860). The yard was the scene of the execution of Guy Fawkes and others among the Gunpowder Plot conspirators. To the left are various entrances to the Houses of Parliament (compare p. 335), while to the right are the Henry VII Chapel of Westminster Abbey and the entrance to the Poets' Corner (p. 446). With its back to the Chapter House is the NATIONAL MEMORIAL TO GEORGE V (1865–1936), by Sir W. Reid Dick and Sir Giles Gilbert Scott (1947). Nos. 6–7 Old Palace Yard, built in 1754, were until 1864 the Clerk of the Parliaments' House.

Opposite the huge Victoria Tower of the Houses of Parliament is the entrance to the moated JEWEL TOWER (VIII, C 3), the last surviving domestic part of the royal Palace of Westminster (compare p. 338). Built in 1366, probably under Henry Yevele, who completed the nave of Westminster Abbey, it stood at the extreme south-west corner of the palace (hence its L-shaped plan).

The tower was designed as the treasury for the private jewels, plate, and other valuables of Edward III and as the office of the 'clerk and surveyor of the king's works within the Palace of Westminster', who had charge of them. Here he received accessions to the king's treasure and made disbursement when called on to do so. After 1547, however, the royal treasures were dispersed by Edward VI and in 1621 the tower became a repository for the records of the House of Lords. Alterations to suit its new purpose were made in this year and in 1719–26, but in 1864 the records were transferred to the Houses of Parliament and from 1869 until 1938 the tower was occupied by the Weights and Measures Department of the Board of Trade. Though the roof was destroyed in an air raid in 1941, the building was carefully restored by the Ministry of Works in 1948–56. The ground floor rooms have vaults with carved bosses; the upper chambers contain relics and illustrations of the Palaces of Westminster and Whitehall. In a case on the first floor is a Saxon sword of the 9th century, discovered during excavations near the Houses of Parliament in 1948, and on the second floor are cases of standard weights and measures.

ABINGDON STREET, leading south from Old Palace Yard, is continued by MILLBANK to Lambeth Bridge. On the right are the offices of the CHURCH COMMISSIONERS, incorporated in 1836 (as the Ecclesiastical Commissioners) to manage the estates of the Church of England, and of the CROWN AGENTS FOR OVERSEA GOVERNMENTS and Administrations, who act as commercial and financial agents in Britain for a large number of governments and public authorities. On the left are the VICTORIA TOWER GARDENS (VIII, C, D 3), from which there are views across the river of St Thomas's Hospital (now being rebuilt) and Lambeth Palace and church, as well as of Somerset House and other buildings lining the embankment beyond Westminster Bridge. In the gardens are a bronze statue by A. G. Walker of Mrs Emmeline Pankhurst (d. 1928), leader of the women's suffrage movement, and a fine bronze replica (1915) of the group by Rodin erected at Calais in 1895 and representing the heroic BURGHERS OF CALAIS, who surrendered themselves to Edward III in 1347 rather than witness the destruction of their town.

LAMBETH BRIDGE (VIII, D 3), crossing the Thames to Lambeth (Route 35), was rebuilt in 1929–32 by Sir Reginald Blomfield and G. Topham Forrest, on the site of an ancient horse-ferry.

This is recalled by the name of HORSEFERRY ROAD, which runs west and north from the bridge towards Victoria Street (see Route 4), passing the WESTMINSTER HOSPITAL (VIII, D 3), founded in 1719 in Broad Sanctuary. The first London hospital to be supported by voluntary contributions, it was transferred to new buildings here in 1937; the medical school, also here, was founded in 1834. Dean Bradley Street, on the right, leads to Smith Square, in the centre of which is ST JOHN THE EVANGELIST'S CHURCH, with four unusual baroque towers, built by Thomas Archer in 1721–8 but gutted by bombing and still to be restored. On the south side of the square is TRANS-PORT HOUSE, the headquarters of the Labour Party, founded in 1900. On the north side and in the adjoining Lord North Street are delightful early-

Georgian terraces, and in Marsham Street, to the west, is the NINTH CHURCH OF CHRIST SCIENTIST, in a deep red brick, by Sir Herbert Baker (1929). Marsham Street is extended north to Broad Sanctuary (Route 4) by Great Smith Street, passing the NATIONAL LIBRARY FOR THE BLIND, established in 1882 and now containing over 330,000 volumes, and the offices of the BRITISH ASSOCIATION for the advancement of science (1831), at No. 3 Sanctuary Buildings.

Facing Lambeth Bridge is IMPERIAL CHEMICAL HOUSE, built by Sir Frank Baines in 1927–9 as the headquarters of Imperial Chemical Industries, the largest manufacturing company in Britain, formed in 1926. THAMES HOUSE, a similar pile of offices on the opposite corner, is the headquarters of the Ministry of Power, and other government departments. Beyond rises MILL-BANK TOWER, the tallest building in London (34 storeys and 387 ft high), designed by Ronald Ward and Partners, and completed in 1963 for Messrs Vickers. Millbank follows the bend of the river past the Tate Gallery, on the north side of which is QUEEN ALEXANDRA'S MILITARY HOSPITAL, opened in 1905, and on the south the ROYAL ARMY MEDICAL COLLEGE and Millbank Barracks (1907). It ends at VAUXHALL BRIDGE (VIII, E, F 3), built in 1906 to the designs of Sir Maurice Fitz-maurice and W. E. Riley, and crossing the river to Vauxhall Station (Route 35).

GROSVENOR ROAD, of little interest, goes on beside the Thames to Chelsea Bridge (Route 8), skirting the district of Pimlico and passing CHURCHILL GARDENS, a large housing estate in a modern style, designed by Messrs Powell and Moya and begun in 1946, with blocks of flats varying from four to eleven storeys in height, heated by hot water carried directly under the river from the Battersea power-station opposite. VAUXHALL BRIDGE ROAD, a long dismal thoroughfare, runs north-west from the bridge to Victoria Station (Route 4).

4 From Parliament Square to Victoria

Plan VIII, B 3–VIII, C, D 1

STATIONS: WESTMINSTER (Plan VIII, B 3), ST JAMES'S PARK (VIII, C 2), and VICTORIA (VIII, C 1), all on the Circle and District lines. — MOTOR-BUSES Nos. 11, 24, 29, 39, 76, 127, and 134 all ply along Victoria Street: for other buses to Parliament Square, see Route 3; to Victoria, see Route 8. Nos. 10, 46, and 149 run from Lambeth Bridge to Victoria via Horseferry Road.

ADMISSION to WESTMINSTER ABBEY, see p. 440; to WESTMINSTER SCHOOL, occasionally on previous written application to the bursar; to the BLEWCOAT SCHOOL, Monday–Friday 9.30 to 5.30 (free); to the INDUSTRIAL HEALTH AND SAFETY CENTRE, Monday–Friday 10 to 5, Saturday 10 to 12 (free; closed on Bank Holidays); to WESTMINSTER CATHEDRAL, see p. 460.

For PARLIAMENT SQUARE, see Route 3. The wide but short street running south-west from the square, and passing between the Middlesex Guildhall and Westminster Abbey, is known as BROAD SANCTUARY, a name recalling that it occupies part of the site of the sanctuary or precincts of the abbey, a place of refuge from any monarch who abused his power. Elizabeth Woodville, the queen of Edward IV, sought refuge in the sanctuary on several occasions (compare Shakespeare's *Richard III*) and her son, Edward V, was born here (perhaps in the abbots' lodging) in 1470, but the privilege was abolished by James I. In the open space opposite the west door of the abbey rises a column, 60 ft high, by Sir Gilbert Scott (1859), commemorating scholars of Westminster School who fell in the Crimean War and the Indian Mutiny. On the right, between the Middlesex Guildhall and the Central Hall, a new building to the designs of William Whitfield is to be erected as a Government conference centre, etc. (1963).

The Victorian Gothic archway on the south of the Sanctuary admits to DEAN'S YARD (VIII, C 2), enclosing the site of the abbey gardens. On the east side are entrances to the Abbey Cloisters (p. 457) and to WESTMINSTER SCHOOL, one of the foremost public schools, founded by Elizabeth I about 1560, but in effect a successor to the monastic school mentioned in the 14th century. It comprises 40 foundationers or Queen's Scholars and about 400 'town boys', about 100 of whom are day-boys. The school occupies much-restored monastic buildings on the east side of Dean's Yard and 17th–19th-century buildings round Little Dean's Yard.

The 14th-century College Hall, adjoining the Dean's Court (p. 459) and still a dining-hall, contains a minstrels' gallery and oak tables said to be made from timber salvaged from the Spanish Armada. The Great School Room, or 'School', rebuilt and heightened in 1960, was formerly the monks' dormitory. On Shrove Tuesday the ancient ceremony of 'Tossing the Pancake' takes place here, one boy from each form competing and the boy securing the largest piece being rewarded with a guinea by the Dean of Westminster. Ashburnham House, on the north of Little Dean's Yard, is a 17th-century building with a delightful interior attributed to Inigo Jones. The Dormitory of the Queen's Scholars, designed by Wren but completed by Lord Burlington (1734), was gutted during the war and has been reconstructed internally (1950). At Christmas the Queen's Scholars used to perform a Latin comedy here, as they had done since the time of the founder, with a topical epilogue, also in Latin.

Among the numerous famous pupils of the school may be mentioned Richard Hakluyt, the Elizabethan geographer; the poets Ben Jonson, George Herbert, Abraham Cowley, John Dryden, Matthew Prior, and William Cowper; Sir Christopher Wren, the builder of St Paul's; John Locke, the philosopher; the notorious Judge Jeffreys; the Earl of Mansfield, Lord Chief Justice; Charles Wesley, the Methodist hymn-writer; Warren Hastings, governor-general of India; Edward Gibbon, the historian; Jeremy Bentham, the political economist; and the statesman Lord John Russell. Robert Southey, the poet, was expelled from the school for protesting against flogging. William Camden, the antiquary, was headmaster in 1593–9; Richard Busby, headmaster for fifty-seven years (1638–95), bequeathed his valuable library to the school. The boys attend a daily service in the abbey, and are entitled to seats at all great ceremonies, including coronations, when they enjoy the privilege of crying 'Vivat' immediately after the crowning of the sovereign.

On the south side of Dean's Yard is CHURCH HOUSE (VIII, C2), rebuilt by Sir Herbert Baker in 1937–40, the headquarters of the National Assembly of the Church of England, as well as of the House of Laity and the Canterbury Houses of Convocation. It was used for a time as the meeting-place of both the Lords and Commons after the Houses of Parliament were bombed in 1941, and in 1945 it became the headquarters of the Preparatory Commission of the United Nations, the first sessions of the Security Council being held here. Visitors may see the fine circular Assembly Hall (restored in 1951 after war damage) and the Hoare Memorial Hall when these are not in use. On the front of the building are the arms of the provinces and sees of England.

VICTORIA STREET, opened in 1851 and running south-west from Broad Sanctuary towards Westminster Cathedral and Victoria Station, is now being considerably rebuilt. On the left, at the outset, is a large new office building by Ronald Fielding, to be completed in 1963 for the Legal and General Assurance Company. Abbey House, opposite, occupies the site of the Westminster Palace Hotel, where the Act of Union by which the Dominion of Canada was constituted was framed in 1867. Near the west gate of the abbey precincts, which stood hereabouts, was the Almonry, from which monastic alms were distributed, and to this building William Caxton moved his printing press in 1483 from the neighbourhood of the abbey (see p. 446). Sir Arthur Sullivan, the composer, died in 1900 at No. 58 Victoria Street.

At the corner of TOTHILL STREET, to the west of Broad Sanctuary, is the large CENTRAL HALL (VIII, C 2), the headquarters of the Methodist Church, built by E. A. Rickards and H. V. Lanchester in 1912. The dome, with a diameter of 90 ft, is the largest in London after St Paul's and the Reading Room of the British Museum. The assembly hall, which has a fine organ and seats for an audience of 2,700, is used for concerts, recitals, and meetings; in 1946 it became the first meeting-place of the General Assembly of the United Nations.

In DARTMOUTH STREET, on the right of Tothill Street, No. 11 is the offices of the FABIAN SOCIETY, a Socialist organization founded on the initiative of Edward R. Pease in 1884. Bernard Shaw and Sidney Webb were early members. The street leads to QUEEN ANNE'S GATE (VIII, B 2), a quiet close built in 1704 by William Paterson, the original founder of the Bank of England, and the most charming survival in London of the domestic architecture of the period. Outside No. 13 is a contemporary statue of Queen Anne, intended for the portico of St Mary le Strand. Lord Palmerston, the prime minister, was born in 1784 at No. 20, and Lord Haldane (1856–1928), the statesman and philosopher, lived at No. 28. The new home of the ST STEPHEN'S CLUB, a Conservative club founded in 1870, is at No. 34.

Nos. 40–42, facing Queen Anne's Gate on the west, are the headquarters of the NATIONAL TRUST (compare p. 64), founded in 1895. The street turns south to BROADWAY, the continuation west of Tothill Street, with St James's Park station, above which rise the LONDON TRANSPORT BOARD OFFICES (VIII, C 2), built by Messrs Adams, Holden, and Pearson (1929) and decorated with controversial sculptures by Sir Jacob Epstein and (higher up) by Eric Gill and others.

Broadway is extended westward by PETTY FRANCE, where John Milton occupied a 'pretty garden-house' in 1651–60 and began *Paradise Lost*. Later tenants were Jeremy Bentham, James Mill, and William Hazlitt, but in 1877 the house was pulled down to make way for the hideous 11-storey QUEEN ANNE'S MAN-SIONS (1884), long the highest residential building in London (180 ft), but now used as offices. CLIVE HOUSE farther on, designed by H. V. Ashley and Winton Newman, contains the Passport Office. Petty France ends at BUCKINGHAM GATE, which leads right to Buckingham Palace and the west end of St James's Park (Route 5) and left to Victoria Street. In Caxton Street, on the left again, is the BLEWCOAT SCHOOL (VIII, C 2), a delightful little brick building erected in 1709 for a school founded in 1688. It was bought in 1954 by the National Trust and the single lofty panelled room is now used by them as an office.

Caxton Street goes on past CAXTON HALL, which includes a noted registry office for marriages, to the southern branch of Broadway. This is prolonged beyond Victoria Street by STRUTTON GROUND (with a street-market), which emerges into Greycoat Place near the north end of Horseferry Road and the GREYCOAT HOSPITAL (VIII, C, D 2), founded in 1698 as a school for boys and girls, but subsequently enlarged and re-constituted in 1873 as a day-school for girls, who now number 500. The buildings, much damaged by bombing, were restored and again enlarged by Laurence King in 1955. On the right in Horse-ferry Road, farther south, is the INDUSTRIAL HEALTH AND SAFETY CENTRE (VIII, D 2), opened in 1927 and containing a permanent exhibition of methods and appliances designed to promote the health and safety of the industrial worker. Lectures and demonstrations are given by previous arrangement.

Behind the museum, in Greycoat Street, is the large new hall (1926) of the ROYAL HORTICULTURAL SOCIETY, founded in 1804, whose head-quarters, with another hall, are in Vincent Square, farther south-west. The halls are used for exhibitions, etc., for the fortnightly shows held by the society, and for numerous other flower-shows, of which the most notable are those of daffodils in April, rhododendrons in May, irises in June, roses in July and September, carnations in July, gladioli in August, dahlias in September, and chrysanthemums in September and November. The society's Great Autumn Show is held in odd-numbered years in its own halls, in even-numbered years at Olympia. The centre of Vincent Square is the playing-field of Westminster School.

Horseferry Road goes on to Lambeth Bridge (Route 3), while Artillery Row, north-west of the Greycoat Hospital, leads back to

Victoria Street. This passes the ends of Ashley Place, in which Westminster Cathedral is seen, and Vauxhall Bridge Road; on the right soars the new Portland House (p. 119). The street passes the VICTORIA PALACE THEATRE (1911) and runs north of VICTORIA STATION (VIII, C, D 1), rebuilt in 1909 and altered after 1923, the principal West End terminus of the Southern Region of British Railways. A passenger terminal for British United Airways was built on 'stilts' over the western platforms in 1962. Victoria Street ends at Buckingham Palace Road opposite GROSVENOR GARDENS (Route 9).

5 From Charing Cross to Hyde Park Corner or Victoria via St James's Park

Plan VIII, A 3–VII, C 3

STATIONS: TRAFALGAR SQUARE (Plan III, F 3), on the Bakerloo line; STRAND (III, F 3), on the Northern line; ST JAMES'S PARK (VIII, C 2) and VICTORIA (VIII, C 1), on the Circle and District lines; GREEN PARK (VIII, A 1) and HYDE PARK CORNER (VII, B 2), on the Piccadilly line. — MOTOR-BUSES to Charing Cross, compare Route 1; to Victoria, see Route 8; to Piccadilly and Hyde Park Corner, see Route 7.

ADMISSION to the QUEEN'S GALLERY, Tuesday–Saturday (and Bank Holiday Mondays) 11 to 6, Sundays 2 to 5 (2/6); to the ROYAL MEWS, Wednesdays 2 to 4, on application (enclosing a stamped addressed envelope) to the Superintendent (1/-; two weeks' notice advisable). — BANDS play in ST JAMES'S PARK on weekdays, June to early September, 12.30 to 2 and 5.30 to 7.

For CHARING CROSS, see Route 1. St James's Park and the Mall, leading to Buckingham Palace, are reached by passing under the ADMIRALTY ARCH (VIII, A 2) to the south-west, a triumphal arch designed by Sir Aston Webb and erected in 1910 as part of the national memorial to Queen Victoria. It serves to connect two wings of the Admiralty and the rooms above house the valuable naval library. From the arch there is a noble vista to the Queen Victoria Memorial and Buckingham Palace down THE MALL (VIII, B 1–A 2), a wide boulevard planted with double rows of plane-trees and forming an admirable processional avenue for State pageants. It takes its name from the game of 'paille-maille' (see p. 120), played here during the reign of Charles II. On the left beyond the arch is a bronze statue of Captain James Cook (d.

115

1779), the explorer, by Brock; the grimly functional building beyond, known as the Citadel, was erected by the Admiralty in 1940 as a repository.

Overlooking the Mall on the right are the once-aristocratic mansions of Carlton House Terrace, intercepted by the Duke of York's Steps, which ascend to Waterloo Place at the foot of Regent Street (see Route 6). Opposite are a road leading to the Horse Guards Parade (Route 2) and an entrance to ST JAMES'S PARK (VIII, B 1, 2), the most attractive park in London, with an area of 93 acres. It is bounded on the north by the Mall and on the south by Birdcage Walk, and stretches from the Horse Guards Parade on the east to Buckingham Palace on the west.

Once a marshy meadow belonging to the hospital of St James the Less (p. 125), it was drained by Henry VIII and converted into a deer park adjoining his new palace, which under the first two Stewarts became a favourite resort of the Court. Charles I walked across the park from St James's Palace to his execution in Whitehall (1649). After the Restoration it was laid out as pleasure grounds for Charles II by the French landscape gardener, Le Nôtre, and it remained a fashionable rendezvous for over a century. The park was remodelled in 1829 for George IV by the architect John Nash, who created the lake and made other improvements.

Facing the park and the Mall on the north are the memorial to George VI (see p. 122) and the gardens of Marlborough House and St James's Palace. From the gate opposite the road between these two mansions a path descends to the elegant bridge over the lake (rebuilt in 1957 to a design by Eric Bedford). The views from the bridge are amongst the most enchanting in London: in one direction to Buckingham Palace, in the other to the buildings in Whitehall. The lake, which extends almost the whole length of the park, is a haunt of numerous varieties of waterfowl, for whom the island at the east end is preserved as a breeding-place. The pelicans always to be found hereabouts are great favourites with Londoners. The path running southward from the bridge leads to Birdcage Walk and Queen Anne's Gate (see p. 118).

In the broad semicircular open space in front of Buckingham Palace, at the south-west end of the Mall, is the conspicuous QUEEN VICTORIA MEMORIAL, sculptured by Sir Thomas Brock, with Sir Aston Webb as architect, and completed in 1911.

From a platform embellished with marble water-basins rises a pedestal surmounted by a gilt-bronze figure of Victory, at whose feet sit Courage and Constancy. At the base, facing the Mall, is the seated figure of Queen Victoria (1819–1901), 13 ft high, carved from a solid block of white marble, and on the other sides of the pedestal are marble groups representing Truth (on the south), Motherhood (west), and Justice (north). Around the memorial are further groups in bronze symbolizing Science and Art (north), Peace and Progress (east), Naval and Military Power (south), and Industry and Agriculture (west), while the garden round the open space is enclosed by a balustrade with piers supporting sculpture including the heraldic shields of countries in the British Commonwealth.

BUCKINGHAM PALACE (VIII, B 1), the principal residence of the sovereign, overlooks the west end of St James's Park and is backed by a private garden of 40 acres. The dignified classical façade, 360 ft long, reconstructed in 1913 by Sir Aston Webb, is enclosed by a large forecourt patrolled by sentries of the Brigade of Guards in full dress uniform (see below). When the Queen is in residence, the Royal Standard is flown at the mast-head and the colourful ceremony of Changing the Guard is performed normally every day in the forecourt at 11.30 a.m.

The palace takes its name from Buckingham House, built in 1703 for John Sheffield, Duke of Buckingham, and purchased in 1762 for George III. Here in 1767 the famous interview between the king and Dr Johnson took place. The house was settled in 1775 on Queen Charlotte, from whom it passed to her son, George IV, and he in 1824 commissioned John Nash, the court architect, to remodel it. Though its name was changed to Buckingham Palace the new mansion (completed in 1830) was little used until the accession of Queen Victoria in 1837, after which it became the permanent London residence of the court. Edward VII was born in the palace in 1841 and died here in 1910, and here Charles, Prince of Wales, was born in 1948 and Prince Andrew in 1960. An east wing added in 1846 by Edward Blore gave the palace the form of a quadrangle, and it was the unimposing front of this that was rebuilt, in Portland stone, by Webb.

The interior of the palace, never open to the public, contains many splendid apartments, some decorated under the direction of Queen Mary. The state apartments include the Throne Room, 65 ft long, with a marble frieze depicting the Wars of the Roses; the State Ballroom, 120 ft long, now used for investitures; and the Picture Gallery, 150 ft long. The apartments of the royal family are in the north wing; the new Queen's Gallery, containing a selection of the valuable paintings, etc., in the royal collection, is entered on the south, from Buckingham Palace Road (see p. 119).

To the north of the palace is the GREEN PARK (VII, B 3–VIII, B 1), a triangular expanse of tree-studded grassland, 53 acres in extent, stretching up to Piccadilly. Originally added to the royal parks by Charles II, it succeeded St James's Park as the fashionable resort of society. The Queen's Walk, on its east side, probably named after Caroline, queen of George II, is overlooked by the Ritz Hotel and former palatial mansions of the aristocracy. A passage near the south end of it leads to Lancaster House and St James's Palace (Route 6). CONSTITUTION HILL, between the Green Park and the Buckingham Palace gardens, ascends to the Wellington Arch at Hyde Park Corner (Route 7). Three attempts on the life of Queen Victoria were made in this road, in 1840, 1842, and 1849, and here in 1850 Sir Robert Peel was fatally injured by being thrown from his horse.

BIRDCAGE WALK, recalling an aviary established here by Charles II, skirts the south side of St James's Park as it leads towards Westminster. Near its west end are the WELLINGTON BARRACKS (VIII, C 1), built in 1833 in a Regency style and the headquarters of the Brigade of Guards, who comprise the Grenadier, Coldstream, Scots, Irish, and Welsh Guards. All these regiments wear scarlet tunics with dark blue facings, but they may be distinguished by their cap-bands, the Grenadier Guards (originally the 1st Regiment of Foot Guards, formed in 1656) having a scarlet cap-band, while the Coldstream Guards (raised in 1659 by General Monck at Coldstream on the Tweed) wear white, the Irish Guards (formed in 1902) green, the Welsh Guards (founded 1915) black, and the Scots Guards (the oldest of the regiments, formed in 1642) a red, white, and blue chequered cap-band. All the foot regiments likewise don the high bearskin 'cap' when in full dress uniform, but the Grenadiers may be distinguished by the white plume on the left of the bearskin, the Coldstreams by the scarlet plume on the right, the Irish Guards by a pale blue plume on the right, and the Welsh Guards by a white and green plume on the left, while the bearskins of the Scots Guards carry no plume at all. These regiments of Foot Guards, together with the Household Cavalry, make up the Household Brigade (compare p. 152).

The GUARDS' CHAPEL, formerly the Royal Military Chapel, opened in 1838, at the east end of the barracks, was almost completely destroyed, with appalling loss of life, when it was hit by a flying-bomb during a Sunday morning service in June 1944. Rebuilding was begun in 1962, to the designs of George, Trew, and Dunn, incorporating the surviving apse. A fine war-memorial cloister, designed by H. S. Goodhart-Rendel and built in 1956, will lead from Birdcage Walk to the narthex of the chapel. It contains cases with seven books of remembrance, one for each of the regiments of the Household Brigade. Behind the chapel towers the huge Queen Anne's Mansions, and beyond opens an entrance to Queen Anne's Gate (Route 4). From Storey's Gate, opposite the south-east corner of St James's Park, Great George Street goes on to Parliament Square (Route 3). Just inside the gate is the INSTITUTION OF MECHANICAL ENGINEERS, founded at Birmingham in 1847 and moved to London in 1877, and outside is the INSTITUTION OF CIVIL ENGINEERS, established in 1818.

Buckingham Gate, skirting the south side of the palace, is prolonged by BUCKINGHAM PALACE ROAD towards Victoria Station. On the right is the entrance to the QUEEN'S GALLERY, formerly the private chapel of Buckingham Palace, but restored after bomb damage and opened in 1962 to show a selection (changed from time to time) of the finest paintings, drawings, furniture, and other works of art drawn from all parts of the royal collections.

In Palace Street, leading left towards Victoria Street (Route 4), is the WESTMINSTER THEATRE (1931). Part of the area north of Victoria Street is being laid out on a new plan, with large office and residential blocks. The most prominent of the buildings here (1962) is PORTLAND HOUSE (29 storeys and 335 ft high), designed by Howard Fairbairn and Partners, and overshadowing Buckingham Palace in the view from the Green Park side. Among the survivals are Stafford Cottage, dating from 1811, in Palace Street, and 18th-century houses in Catherine Place and Buckingham Place, on the left.

No. 25 Buckingham Palace Road is the headquarters of the BOY SCOUTS, started in 1907 by Lieut.-Gen. Sir Robert (later Lord) Baden-Powell and now numbering nearly 700,000 in Britain and well over 7 million in more than 100 countries of the world. No. 17 is the headquarters of the GIRL GUIDES, a similar organization established in 1910 by Lord Baden-Powell and his sister, Agnes Baden-Powell; it now has nearly 600,000 members in Britain and more than 5½ million throughout the world. Almost opposite these is the entrance to the ROYAL MEWS (VII, C 3), where the queen's horses are stabled and her coaches kept. These include the splendid state carriage (used for coronations) designed in 1762 for George III by Sir William Chambers and painted by G. B. Cipriani, a Florentine artist who had settled in England; the Irish state coach bought in 1852 by Queen Victoria and used for the state opening of Parliament; and the so-called glass state coach bought in 1910 by George V and now used for royal weddings, etc.

Lower Grosvenor Place, on the right beyond the mews, leads to the north end of Grosvenor Gardens (Route 9). In Victoria Square, a late-Regency backwater on the right farther on, No. 8 was the home in 1840–4 of the poet, Thomas Campbell. Buckingham Palace Road goes on past the west end of Victoria Street and the main entrance to VICTORIA STATION (Route 4); for the continuation towards Chelsea, see Route 8.

6 From Charing Cross to Hyde Park Corner via Pall Mall

Plan VIII, A 3–VII, B 3

STATIONS: TRAFALGAR SQUARE (Plan III, F 3), on the Bakerloo line; STRAND (III, F 3), on the Northern line; GREEN PARK (VIII, A 1) and HYDE PARK CORNER (VII, B 2), on the Piccadilly line. — MOTOR-BUSES Nos. 3, 6, 9, 12, 13, 15, 53, 59, 60, 88, 153, and 159 in Regent Street (northbound only) and Haymarket (southbound only); in Piccadilly, see Route 7.

ADMISSION to MARLBOROUGH HOUSE, Easter Sunday to last Sunday in October, Monday–Friday, at 12.30, 3, and 4.30 (conducted tours, including the Queen's Chapel), Saturdays, Sundays, and Bank Holidays, 2 to 6 (1/-), except when conferences are being held; to LANCASTER HOUSE, Easter to mid-December, Saturdays, Sundays, and Bank Holidays, 2 to 6 (1/-), except when used for government functions.

For CHARING CROSS, see Route 1. COCKSPUR STREET, lined with offices of noted steamship companies, runs west to join Pall Mall East, the extension of the north side of Trafalgar Square from the National Gallery. In the angle of the roads is a fine bronze equestrian statue of George III, by M. C. Wyatt (1836), and in Suffolk Street, north of this, are the galleries of the ROYAL SOCIETY OF BRITISH ARTISTS, founded in 1823, in a building by John Nash. Richard Cobden, the apostle of free trade, died in 1865 at No. 23 in this street. Beyond the George III statue the Haymarket (Route 7) opens on the right.

PALL MALL (VIII, A 1, 2), which leads westward from this point, derives its name from 'paille-maille' (pronounced 'pell-mell'), an old French game resembling croquet, introduced into

England during the reign of Charles I. The distinguished thoroughfare traverses the once-fashionable district of St James's, still the centre of London club life. On the south, at the corner of Waterloo Place, is the UNITED SERVICE CLUB, the oldest club for officers in London, founded in 1815 by veterans of the Napoleonic wars and occupying a building by John Nash (1827), altered by Decimus Burton in 1858.

WATERLOO PLACE, given over to large banks and insurance offices, intersects Pall Mall and is extended on the north by the lower section of Regent Street, ascending to Piccadilly Circus. On the north side of the place is the GUARDS' CRIMEAN MEMORIAL, by John Bell (1859); the figures of guardsmen at the foot were cast from Russian cannon and the guns at the back of the monument were captured from the Russians at Sebastopol in 1855. In front are statues of Sidney Herbert (Lord Herbert of Lea; d. 1861), secretary for war during the Crimean campaign, and of Florence Nightingale (d. 1910), the 'lady with the lamp'.

In LOWER REGENT STREET (III, F 2), at the corner of Charles II Street, are the head-offices (by Leslie C. Norton and others, 1960), of the UNITED KINGDOM ATOMIC ENERGY AUTHORITY, established in 1954. Varied and interesting exhibitions are held frequently at the CEYLON TEA CENTRE (No. 22), at the corner of Jermyn Street.

In the centre of the southern part of Waterloo Place is the NATIONAL MEMORIAL TO EDWARD VII (1841–1910), a fine equestrian statue by Sir Bertram Mackennal. To the left (east) are statues of Captain R. F. Scott (d. 1912), the Antarctic explorer, sculptured by his widow, Lady Scott; of Colin Campbell, Lord Clyde (d. 1863), commander-in-chief during the Indian Mutiny; and of Lord Lawrence (d. 1879), ruler of the Punjab and Viceroy of India. The statues on the west side are of Sir John Burgoyne (d. 1871), the Crimean general, and Sir John Franklin (d. 1847), the Arctic explorer. At the south end of Waterloo Place are the DUKE OF YORK'S STEPS, descending to the Mall and St James's Park (Route 5), over which there is a view to the towers of Westminster. At the top of the steps rises the DUKE OF YORK'S COLUMN, 124 ft high, designed by Benjamin Wyatt (1833) and surmounted by a bronze statue 14 ft high, by Westmacott, of Frederick, Duke of York (d. 1827), the second son of George III and Commander-in-Chief of the British Army. Though the duke was assiduous in carrying out reforms in the army, he is now chiefly remembered from a nursery rhyme; his impecuniosity was a by-word, and wits declared after the erection of the monument that he was placed so high to keep him away from his creditors. Most of the cost of the memorial, in fact, was met by stopping one day's pay from every soldier in the army.

The column stands on the site of Carlton House, the residence of George IV after 1783, when Prince of Wales, but pulled down in 1826. Its name survives in CARLTON HOUSE TERRACE, built by John Nash in 1827–32, former mansions of the aristocracy now mainly occupied by government departments, extending on either side of the southern part of Waterloo Place. No. 11, on the left, was the home of W. E. Gladstone, the prime minister, in 1856–75, and No. 1, to the right (at present housing the SAVAGE CLUB, founded in 1857), was the town house from 1894 until his death in 1925 of the Marquess Curzon, a statue of whom, by Mackennal, stands at the corner of Carlton Gardens, which leads to the right back to Pall Mall.

Another branch of CARLTON GARDENS prolongs Carlton House Terrace. No. 4 here, rebuilt in 1933, was the home of Lord Palmerston in 1846–54 and Lord Balfour in 1905–29, and the headquarters of General de Gaulle, the leader of the Free French movement, from 18 June, 1940. Louis Napoleon (later Napoleon III) occupied No. 1, opposite on the west, in 1839–40, and Lord Kitchener lived at No. 2 in 1914–15. At the south end of the open space adjoining these buildings, and facing over the Mall, is the NATIONAL MEMORIAL TO GEORGE VI (1895–1952), an excellent bronze statue by William McMillan, showing the king in the robes he customarily wore for the ceremonies of the Knights of the Garter. It stands in an architectural setting by Louis de Soissons and was unveiled in 1955.

At the south-west corner of Waterloo Place and Pall Mall is the ATHENAEUM CLUB, the leading literary club of London, founded in 1824, with a famous library in which Thackeray wrote many of his works. The building, by Decimus Burton (1830), has a frieze below the cornice reproducing that of the Parthenon at Athens. Adjoining it in Pall Mall are the TRAVELLERS' CLUB, founded in 1819 for gentlemen who had made the 'Grand Tour' (and occupying a building of 1832), and the REFORM CLUB, the premier Liberal club, established in 1832 (in a building of 1840). Both buildings were modelled by Sir Charles Barry on Italian palazzi.

The short street opposite leads to ST JAMES'S SQUARE (VIII, A 2), laid out after 1660 by Henry Jermyn, first Earl of St Albans, as a fashionable residential quarter. Most of the houses have been reconstructed at one time or another, and are now occupied for various other purposes. In the centre of the gardens is a good bronze equestrian statue of William III, by John Bacon the younger (1808). NORFOLK HOUSE (No. 31), at the south-east corner, the town house of the Dukes of Norfolk from 1723 until

1938, was rebuilt in 1939, and from it the allied commanders under General Eisenhower launched the invasions of North Africa (1942) and North-West Europe (1944). The first house on this site, lent in 1737–41 to Frederick, Prince of Wales, after he had been turned out of St James's Palace by his father, was the birthplace of George III in 1738. Norfolk House is now the headquarters of the IRON AND STEEL BOARD, established in 1953. No. 32, rebuilt in 1792 by S. P. Cockerell, was the residence of the Bishops of London from 1771 until 1919. No. 4, in the northeast corner, is a fine Georgian house designed in 1725, probably by Edward Shepherd, and now occupied by the ARTS COUNCIL of Great Britain, established in 1946 to encourage the appreciation of the fine arts, an object assisted by the interesting loan exhibitions frequently held here.

No. 8, on the north side of the Square, is the head office of the MINISTRY OF LABOUR, set up in 1916. CHATHAM HOUSE (No. 10), built in 1736 by Henry Flitcroft, was the residence of three prime ministers: the Earl of Chatham (1759–61), the Earl of Derby (1837–54), and W. E. Gladstone (1890). In 1923 it was presented by two Canadian citizens to the ROYAL INSTITUTE OF INTERNATIONAL AFFAIRS, founded in 1920 for the study of foreign affairs. On either side of the steps to the house are pillars carrying the original torch extinguishers. No. 14, in the northwest corner, houses the LONDON LIBRARY, the best-known subscription library in England (compare p. 65), founded in 1841 and now containing over 600,000 volumes. No. 15, with a fine classical façade by 'Athenian' Stuart (1763), was originally the home of the Duchess of Richmond ('La Belle Stuart'), who sat as model for the 'Britannia' on our copper coins. Nos. 16–17 are occupied by the EAST INDIA AND SPORTS CLUB (1849); at No. 17 Queen Caroline resided while the bill to dissolve her marriage to George IV was brought before the House of Lords, while Lord Castlereagh, the Foreign Secretary involved in the case, lived next door at No. 18 (since rebuilt). The design of No. 20, built in 1775 by Robert Adam, has been reproduced at No. 21.

The road from the south-west corner of the square returns to Pall Mall between the JUNIOR CARLTON CLUB, founded in 1864, and the ARMY AND NAVY CLUB (1837), familiarly known as 'The Rag'. Opposite is the long façade of the ROYAL AUTO-MOBILE CLUB, founded in 1897; the building (by Mewes and Davis, 1911) occupies the site of the old War Office, which had incorporated SCHOMBERG HOUSE, built about 1698. The west wing of this, however, survives as No. 80, and here Thomas Gainsborough, the artist, lived from 1774 until his death in 1788. No. 79 stands on the site of a house that belonged to Nell Gwyn from 1671 until her death in 1687. Here, according to the diarist Evelyn, the former orange-seller used to talk over the garden wall to Charles II as he strolled in the park. No. 71, built by the brothers Smirke (1837), houses the OXFORD AND CAMBRIDGE CLUB, founded in 1830, while No. 48, on the right, is the headquarters of the BRITISH LEGION, the organization of ex-servicemen formed in 1921 under Field-Marshal Earl Haig.

On the south side of Pall Mall is the inconspicuous entrance to MARLBOROUGH HOUSE (VIII, A 2; pronounced 'Mawl-'), built by Sir Christopher Wren in 1709–11, but subsequently heightened and enlarged, to its detriment. It was the home of Queen Mary (the consort of George V) from 1936 until her death here in 1953, and in 1962 it was renovated as a Commonwealth conference and research centre. This has a reference library of books on Commonwealth subjects, and a public information office on the ground floor.

The house was built for the first Duke of Marlborough, the victor of Blenheim, and his Duchess, the redoubtable Sarah, who after the death of the duke in 1722 until her own death in 1744 lived here in such magnificent style as to overshadow the court of George II ('Neighbour George') at St James's. Later occupants were Leopold I of Belgium (until his accession in 1831) and Queen Adelaide (d. 1849), and in 1850 the house was made the official residence of the Prince of Wales. George V was born here in 1865, and after his accession in 1910 the house became the home of Queen Alexandra, the widow of Edward VII.

On the north of the garden is a brick screen wall designed by Wren, now dwarfed by the buildings in Pall Mall; on the west is the Queen's Chapel (see below). The entrance to the house is from a porte-cochère or carriage porch, part of the extensions made by Sir James Pennethorne for Edward, Prince of Wales, between 1850 and 1863, when he took up residence. Beyond the vestibule and a passage is the Saloon, rising two storeys to the original height of the house. Above the cornice are paintings of the Battle of Blenheim, part of a series by Louis Laguerre portraying the Duke of Marlborough's campaigns. The elaborate ceiling paintings, representing the Arts and Sciences, are the work of Orazio Gentileschi (1616) and were originally in the Queen's House at Greenwich. The chimney-piece of coloured marbles was probably inserted by Sir William Chambers when he heightened the building about 1770. Beyond the saloon is the former State Drawing Room, remodelled by Pennethorne and now the main conference room. The handsome marble chimney-pieces at either end date from the mid 18th century. To the right is the Prime Ministers' conference room, to the left the former State Dining Room, containing portraits from the royal collection, including the Family of Frederick, Prince of Wales, by Knapton (1751). The room beyond, formerly the Household Dining Room, retains its original arrangements. On the staircases to the first floor (no access) are large murals by Laguerre of the Battles of Ramillies (on the west) and Malplaquet.

The NATIONAL MEMORIAL TO QUEEN ALEXANDRA (1844–1925), designed by Sir Alfred Gilbert (1932), is in Marlborough Road, facing St James's Palace, and here also is the QUEEN'S CHAPEL, designed by Inigo Jones and intended as the private chapel of the Infanta Maria of Spain, a Roman Catholic, whom Prince Charles (later Charles I) was expected to marry. It was completed for Henrietta Maria, whom in fact he did marry (1625), and refurnished for Catherine of Braganza on her marriage to Charles II in 1661. George III was married here in 1761 to Charlotte Sophia of Mecklenburg-Strelitz. The chapel is notable for its royal pews, its Carolean panelling and its elaborate coffered ceiling. Visitors are admitted to the services held on Sundays at 8.30 and 11.15 a.m. from Easter Day to the end of July, and the chapel is included in the weekday tours of Marlborough House (see p. 120).

ST JAMES'S PALACE (VIII, A, B 1), farther west, is a rambling and picturesque brick mansion of Tudor origin built round several courtyards. It was long the official London residence of the sovereign and the scene of all important court functions, and foreign ambassadors are still accredited 'to the Court of St James's'.

The palace takes its name from a leper hospital dedicated to St James the Less and mentioned early in the 12th century. This was dissolved in 1532 and in its place Henry VIII built a royal palace, traditionally to the designs of Holbein, in which Mary I died in 1558. After the fall of Wolsey in 1529, however, Henry transferred his affections to Whitehall Palace, and although Charles II (1630), James II (1633), Mary II (1662), and Queen Anne (1665) were all born at St James's, it became the official residence of the sovereign only after Whitehall was burned down in 1698. George IV was born here in 1762, but in 1809 the south-east wing was destroyed by fire and on her accession in 1837 Queen Victoria moved the court to Buckingham Palace. The royal Levees (for gentlemen) continued to be held here (until 1939, when they were discontinued), but after 1861 the Drawing Rooms or Courts (for ladies) were transferred to Buckingham Palace.

The chief relic of the Tudor palace is the picturesque four-storeyed GATEHOUSE, or Clock Tower, facing up St James's Street and retaining its original doors with linenfold panelling. It admits to the private Colour Court, which has a late-17th-century colonnade. Sentries of the Brigade of Guards (compare p. 118) patrol in front of the gatehouse and of the gate of Marlborough House. The entrance to the State Apartments (no admission) is on the east, in the open FRIARY COURT, where the guard is changed at 10.30 a.m. when the sovereign is not in residence at Buckingham Palace (see p. 117). From the balcony overlooking the court the official proclamation of a new sovereign is made by the Heralds (compare p. 249). To the west of the gatehouse is the entrance to the AMBASSADORS COURT (visitors admitted), on the east side of which is the CHAPEL ROYAL, built about 1532 for Henry VIII, but much altered from time to time and last renovated in 1955.

Visitors are admitted to the services held on Sundays at 8.30 and 11.15 a.m. (from the second Sunday in October until Palm Sunday, and on Christmas Day) and to the choral service (at 11.30) on the Feast of the Epiphany (6 January), when royal gifts of gold, frankincense, and myrrh are offered. The gem of the chapel is the magnificent coffered ceiling painted in 1540 and attributed to Holbein. Charles I attended service in this chapel on the morning of his execution (1649) and many royal marriages have been celebrated here, including those of William III and Mary II (1677), Queen Anne (1683), George IV (1795), Queen Victoria (1840), and George V (1893). The choristers wear a Tudor costume of scarlet and gold; among former choristers or organists may be mentioned the composers Thomas Tallis, William Byrd, Orlando Gibbons, Henry Purcell, and Sir Arthur Sullivan.

On the north side of the Ambassadors Court is YORK HOUSE, an extension of the palace occupied by Lord Kitchener in 1915–16 and the Duke of Windsor (when Prince of Wales) in 1919–30, and now the residence of the Duke of Gloucester, uncle of the Queen. The court opens on the west to STABLE YARD, facing which on this side is the Lord Chamberlain's Office. At the south-west angle of the palace is CLARENCE HOUSE, one of the less successful designs of Nash, carried out in 1829 for William IV, then Duke of Clarence. The interior, much altered since, was restored in 1949 for Princess Elizabeth, who occupied the house until her accession in 1952. Princess Anne was born here in 1950, and Clarence House is now the home of Queen Elizabeth, the Queen Mother.

St James's Palace is the headquarters of the Honorable Corps of GENTLE-MEN AT ARMS, founded in 1509 by Henry VIII and now consisting of about thirty army officers with distinguished service records, under a captain (always a peer) whose appointment is political. The gentlemen, who form a personal bodyguard for the sovereign at royal levees, wear a resplendent uniform composed of scarlet tail-coats with gold epaulettes and white gauntlets, dark blue pantaloons and Wellington boots, and white plumed helmets. The palace is also the home of the Queen's Bodyguard of the YEOMAN OF THE GUARD, the oldest of the household corps, formed by Henry VII in 1485 (traditionally on the battlefield of Bosworth). The yeomen, who are not to be confused with the Yeoman Warders at the Tower, wear a picturesque royal red uniform of Tudor origin with purple and gold ornaments. Their familiar nickname of 'Beefeaters', popularly claimed to be derived from their fine physique or from the rations formerly served to them, is more probably a corruption of 'buffetiers du roy'. Together with the Gentlemen at Arms, they form the sovereign's dismounted body-guard at state ceremonies.

On the south side of Stable Yard rises LANCASTER HOUSE (VIII, B 1), begun in 1825 by Benjamin Wyatt for the 'grand old' Duke of York (p. 112), who died in 1827 before he could either pay for it or occupy it. Originally named York House, it was purchased by one of the duke's creditors, the Marquess of Stafford (after-wards Duke of Sutherland), and completed by Sir Robert Smirke in 1840, Sir Charles Barry being responsible for much of the lavish decoration.

Under the second Duke of Sutherland, the house (renamed Stafford House) became a gathering point for liberal causes, as well as a fashionable social and artistic centre. Queen Victoria often visited her friend, the Duchess, saying 'I have come from my house to your palace'. The third Duke, a friend of Giuseppe Garibaldi, was visited by the Italian patriot here in 1864. In 1912 the house was bought by the first Viscount Leverhulme, who changed its name and presented it to the nation, and it became the home of the London Museum until 1941. Remains of a Roman boat of the late 3rd century, found 30 ft below the site of the County Hall, and other large objects belonging to the museum are still stored in the basement, and can be seen on application to the director of the museum. After restoration from war damage the house is now used for international conferences and for banquets and other forms of government hospitality.

The entrance from Stable Yard is through a two-storeyed portico, leading to a low Vestibule. The corridor to the left of this ends at the Garibaldi Room, which has a grey marble fireplace with a fine Italian mirror above.

To the left is the East Dining Room, with notable console-tables, and to the right is the State Dining Room, which has decorated pelmets, carved fireplaces, and an unusual 18th-century clock supposed to have belonged to Napoleon. On the other side of this room are the Red Room and the Gold Room, the latter an ante-room to the Duke of Sutherland's Library (entered by a concealed doorway). The corridor on this side of the house gives access to the magnificent Staircase Hall, in the centre, rising to the full height of the building, with a huge lantern the richly decorated ceiling of which is supported by massive black caryatids. The coffered coving below this rests at the ends on fluted Corinthian columns supported by balconies. The walls of imitation marble have good copies by Lorenzi of paintings by Veronese.

The Grand Staircase, with a rococo-style balustrade, ascends to the main state-rooms. The corridor on the west leads to an ante-room on the right of which is the West Drawing Room, formerly the Duchess's boudoir, with a ceiling painting representing the solar system, and on the left the State Drawing Room, which has a beautiful coffered ceiling and elaborate fireplaces. Beyond another ante-room is the Great Gallery, over 120 ft long, notable for its decoration, which includes a painting on the ceiling of the lantern by Guercino, previously in a church at Rome. The mantelpiece of the ornate marble fireplace supports a fine 18th-century French clock. On the north side of the building are the Veronese Room, which has a small ceiling painting by that master, and the Music Room, with another finely decorated ceiling. It was probably in this room that Chopin played before Queen Victoria in 1848, and here the Nine-Power Conference held its plenary meetings in 1954.

A passage from the west side of Stable Yard leads to the GREEN PARK (Route 5), across which paths go on to Buckingham Palace and to Hyde Park Corner (Route 7). Cleveland Row, on the north side of York House, returns to Pall Mall. On the north side of the tiny Cleveland Square rises the delightful BRIDGE-WATER HOUSE, built by Sir Charles Barry in 1849 in a rich Italian Renaissance style for the Earl of Ellesmere.

ST JAMES'S STREET (VIII, A 1), ascending north from St James's Palace, contains several well-known clubs and some interesting houses. No. 3 (wine merchants) and No. 6 (hatters) are fine examples of late-18th-century shop fronts. A passage beside No. 3 opens to the charming little court of Pickering Place. Byron House, farther up, replaces the house (No. 8) where Lord Byron 'awoke one morning to find himself famous' in 1811. No. 86, on the other side of the street, is the UNION CLUB, founded in 1805; No. 74, a building by George Basevi and Sydney Smirke (about 1843), stands on the site of the house in which Edward Gibbon, the historian, died in 1794. Nos. 69–70, built by Thomas Hopper about 1826, are now the CARLTON CLUB, the foremost Conservative club, founded by the Duke of Wellington in 1832, and moved here after its original home in Pall Mall had been bombed in 1941.

The narrow ST JAMES'S PLACE, opening on the west here, has a variety of pleasant old houses. SPENCER HOUSE, on the left facing the Green Park, is a large mansion in a classical style built in 1765 by John Vardy after designs by General Gray, and restored in 1957 after war damage.

In KING STREET, on the other side of St James's Street, is CHRISTIE'S, the famous auction-rooms, founded in 1766 and specializing in works of art (at No. 8). Louis Napoleon, later emperor of France, lived at No. 1c, also on the north side, in 1846–8.

No. 60 St James's Street, at the corner of Park Place, is BROOKS'S CLUB, founded by Charles James Fox and the Duke of Portland in 1764, and occupying a building by Henry Holland (1778). This was the leading club of the Whigs in the 18th century. At the farther end of Park Place are the headquarters and club of the ROYAL OVER-SEAS LEAGUE, founded in 1910 by Sir Evelyn Wrench to 'promote friendship and understanding amongst British subjects and Commonwealth citizens all over the world' and to encourage individual service to the Commonwealth; it now has about 50,000 members.

Opposite Park Place, at No. 28, is BOODLE'S CLUB, founded in 1762, in a building by John Crunden (1765). A United States Trade Centre was opened in 1961 at No. 58 St James's Street, on the left. Farther up, on the right (No. 37), is WHITE'S CLUB, the oldest club in London, evolved in 1693 from a coffee-house of the same name. This was the chief Tory club, the rival of Brooks's, and like both Brooks's and Boodle's was famous in the 18th century as the resort of men of fashion and wealthy gamblers. No. 50, on the other side of the street, is the DEVONSHIRE CLUB, established in 1875 in succession to 'Crockford's', a notorious 'gambling-hell', in a building by Benjamin Wyatt (1827). St James's Street ends on the north at PICCADILLY, which runs east to Piccadilly Circus and west to Hyde Park Corner (see Route 7).

7 From Charing Cross to Hyde Park Corner via Piccadilly

Plan III, F 3–VII, B 3

STATIONS: TRAFALGAR SQUARE (Plan III, F 3), on the Bakerloo line; STRAND (III, F 3), on the Northern line; PICCADILLY CIRCUS (III, F 2), on the Bakerloo and Piccadilly lines; GREEN PARK (VIII, A 1) and HYDE PARK CORNER (VII, B 2), on the Piccadilly line. — MOTOR-BUSES Nos. 9, 14, 19, 22, 25, 32, and 38 all ply along Piccadilly, but Nos. 25 and 32 go up Bond Street. For other buses in Regent Street (lower part) or Haymarket, see Route 6; to Piccadilly Circus, see Routes 15, 18; to Hyde Park Corner, see Routes 9, 10.

ADMISSION to the DESIGN CENTRE (Haymarket), weekdays 9.30 to 5.30 (Wednesdays and Thursdays to 9; free); to BURLINGTON HOUSE, see p. 133; to the CRAFTS CENTRE (Hay Hill), weekdays 10 to 5 (Saturdays to 12.30; free); to the WELLINGTON MUSEUM, weekdays 10 to 6, Sundays 2.30 to 6 (1/-; closed Good Friday and Christmas Day).

From CHARING CROSS to the foot of the HAYMARKET (III, F 2), see Route 6. This street, the site of a market removed in 1830, ascends to the junction of Coventry Street and Piccadilly near Piccadilly Circus. On the left, at the corner of Pall Mall, a large new building to the design of Sir Robert Matthew was begun in 1957 for the New Zealand Government. When complete (in 1963), it will have a library, information and exhibition rooms, etc., for visitors, and other offices in a tower 225 ft high. The Royal Opera Arcade, a survival from a theatre on this site designed by John Nash and G. S. Repton (1818), is being retained, but later the building is to be extended to incorporate HER MAJESTY'S THEATRE, where Sir Herbert Beerbohm Tree was manager from its opening in 1897 until his death in 1917. On the east side of the road is the HAYMARKET THEATRE (officially the Theatre Royal, Haymarket), built in 1820 by John Nash on the site of a theatre founded in 1720. It retains its distinctive portico, but the interior was rebuilt in 1905. Panton Street, on the right beyond this, contains the COMEDY THEATRE, built in 1881 and restored in 1955. At Haymarket House, farther up, the Council of Industrial Design opened in 1956 a DESIGN CENTRE for the display of the most recent designs in British furnishings and other products. The picturesque bow windows of the tobacconists' shop at No. 34 Haymarket, near the upper end, are a relic of late-18th-century London.

Immediately to the left at the top of the Haymarket is PIC-CADILLY CIRCUS (III, F 2), one of the busiest traffic points in London, invariably crowded with a jostling throng of vehicles and people. The centre of London for the pleasure-seeker, it is at its most characteristic in the evening, when the electric signs all round are lit up. Laid out in the late 19th century, the circus stands at the junction of five important streets: Piccadilly on the west; Regent Street (Route 15) running north-west to Oxford Street and Regent's Park, and south to Waterloo Place (Pall Mall; Route 6); Shaftesbury Avenue (Route 18) on the north-east, leading to Soho and Holborn; and Coventry Street (Route 20) on the east, giving access to Leicester Square.

In the centre of the circus is the SHAFTESBURY MEMORIAL, a bronze fountain in the form of a pyramid, designed by Sir Alfred Gilbert and topped by the figure in cast aluminium of a winged archer and his bow, intended to represent the Angel of Christian Charity, but popularly known as 'Eros' (the Greek god of Love). It was erected in 1893 to the seventh Earl of Shaftesbury (d. 1885), the philanthropist. The characteristic Victorian block of buildings on the south of the circus includes the CRITERION THEATRE (1874). Beneath the roadway, with entrances from every side, is PICCADILLY CIRCUS STATION, perhaps the largest underground station in the world, designed by Charles Holden and opened in 1928.

The Piccadilly 'tube', the busiest in London, was first opened in 1906 from Hammersmith to Finsbury Park as the Great Northern, Piccadilly, and Brompton Railway. A completely new plan for Piccadilly Circus, drawn up by Sir William Holford, is still under discussion.

PICCADILLY (III, F 2–VII, B 3), which runs west for about a mile to Hyde Park Corner, is one of the fashionable shopping streets of London. It is said to derive its name from 'Piccadilly Hall', the popular name given to a house (since demolished) in what is now Great Windmill Street, built for himself in the 17th century by a retired tailor and maker of 'piccadils' – high collars or ruffs with laced or perforated edges – popular at the time. On the north side of the street is the large PICCADILLY HOTEL, by R. Norman Shaw (1908), with another frontage on Regent Street. On the south of Piccadilly are the modern wrought-iron entrance gates of ST JAMES'S CHURCH (III, F 1), which was designed by Sir Christopher Wren and built in 1676–84. Gutted by incendiary bombs in 1940, it was beautifully restored in 1954 by Sir Albert Richardson, who is also to add a new spire to the tower. The church was the most fashionable in London in the 18th century, and three of its rectors (Tenison, Wake, and Secker) became archbishops of Canterbury. It has galleries in the aisles, and a decorated barrel vault covering the combined nave and chancel, supported by piers with Corinthian capitals. The white marble font (at which Lord Chesterfield, the Earl of Chatham, and William Blake, 'artist, poet, visionary', were baptized), the carved limewood altarpiece and the organ case, salvaged from the bombing, are all by Grinling Gibbons. The organ, built by Renatus Harris in 1685 for Whitehall Palace and given to the church by Mary II, has been restored after war damage. The fine stained glass in the east windows is the work of Christopher Webb. Among celebrities buried in the vaults are Charles Cotton (d. 1687), the angler, friend of Isaak Walton, and the Marquess of Queensberry (d. 1810), better known as 'Old Q'. The churchyard has been laid out in memory of the fortitude of Londoners during the Second World War, at the charge of Viscount Southwood (d. 1946), who is himself commemorated by a fountain by A. F. Hardiman.

Farther on is the ROYAL INSTITUTE OF PAINTERS IN WATER COLOURS, founded in 1831 and housed in a building of 1883. The Royal Institute of Oil Painters and other societies also hold exhibitions in the galleries here. SACKVILLE STREET, on the right, is the first of several streets with pleasing Georgian houses in a modest style. Beyond it, set back behind a courtyard, is THE ALBANY (or merely 'Albany'), built in 1770 by Sir William Chambers, but converted in 1802 into 'residential chambers for bachelor gentlemen'. It consists of suites of chambers flanking a covered passage running north to Burlington Gardens, but is not open to the public. Famous residents have included George Canning, Lord Byron, Bulwer Lytton, Lord Macaulay, and W. E. Gladstone.

BURLINGTON HOUSE (III, F 1), the rather ponderous Renaissance-style façade of which overshadows Piccadilly on the north, is the headquarters of the Royal Academy of Arts, the

Royal Society, and other learned societies, whose private rooms are open only by invitation. An imposing archway admits to a quadrangle in the centre of which is a statue of Sir Joshua Reynolds (d. 1792), by Alfred Drury. On the north side is Old Burlington House, rebuilt in 1715 by the third Earl of Burlington, architect and patron of the arts, who was assisted by Colen Campbell.

In 1854 the building was sold for £140,000 to the government, who in 1866-9 added the upper storey and the entrance loggia, and built the wings on the east and west of the courtyard. The south wing, with the Piccadilly frontage, was added in 1874 by R. R. Banks and E. M. Barry.

Old Burlington House is now the home of the ROYAL ACADEMY OF ARTS, founded in Pall Mall in 1768, with Sir Joshua Reynolds as its first president, moved in 1780 to Somerset House in the Strand, then in 1837 to the National Gallery, and finally in 1869 to its present quarters. It comprises 40 Academicians (R.A.) and 30 Associates (A.R.A.), and vacancies are filled by the vote of all the members. In addition there are a number of Senior Academicians (over 75 years of age), while distinguished foreign artists may be elected Honorary Academicians. The summer Exhibition of the Royal Academy, held regularly since 1769, is open from May to mid-August (admission, see p. 73) and consists of paintings, sculptures, engravings, and architectural designs by living artists completed within the previous ten years and not exhibited before in London. The private view of the exhibition, the Academy Soirée, and the Academy Dinner are all fashionable and exclusive functions. In winter (usually from November to March) special loan exhibitions of outstanding interest are held at which many works of art not otherwise accessible may be seen.

From the vestibule in Old Burlington House a staircase ascends to the exhibition galleries, added in 1869 by Sydney Smirke, then goes on up to the private rooms of the Royal Academy, which contain diploma works presented on their election by Academicians; portraits of members, including self-portraits by Reynolds and Gainsborough, and of royal patrons; sketch-books of Romney and others; and a collection of historical relics (Reynolds' easel and painting-table, etc.). Also housed in Burlington House are the ROYAL ACADEMY SCHOOLS, founded in 1768 and providing free tuition to students of approved ability. Famous pupils have included Constable, Lawrence, Turner, and Millais.

In the east wing of Burlington House are the headquarters of the ROYAL SOCIETY, one of the most important scientific bodies in the world, founded in 1660. It now numbers 560 Fellows (F.R.S.), with the addition of sixty foreign members. Among the original Fellows were Sir Christopher Wren (in whose rooms the first meeting was held) and John Evelyn, the diarist; and famous presidents have included Wren (elected 1680), Samuel Pepys (1684), Sir Isaac Newton (1703), Sir Hans Sloane (1727), Sir Joseph Banks

(1778; for 42 years), and Sir Humphry Davy (1820) and several other eminent 19th-century scientists. The rooms (admission by a Fellow's introduction only) contain a fine collection of portraits of men of science, and such interesting relics as Newton's telescope and the original model of Davy's safety lamp. Also in this wing are housed the GEOLOGICAL SOCIETY, founded in 1807, and the CHEMICAL SOCIETY (1841).

The west wing of the buildings accommodates the SOCIETY OF ANTIQUARIES of London, the oldest society of its kind, founded in 1707 and incorporated in 1751. Its private rooms contain an important collection of early paintings (Tudor monarchs, etc.) and portraits of distinguished Fellows. Also in this wing are the ROYAL ASTRONOMICAL SOCIETY, incorporated in 1820, and the LINNEAN SOCIETY (for natural history) established in 1788 and named in honour of the great Swedish botanist.

To the west of Burlington House is the BURLINGTON ARCADE, a covered promenade with exclusive shops, running north to Burlington Gardens, which may be approached also from Regent Street (see Route 15). This privately-owned arcade, the first shopping arcade of its kind in England, was built in 1819 by Samuel Ware and still retains its Regency atmosphere. Beadles (ex-soldiers of the 10th Hussars) are on duty to enforce the rules. The arcade, 585 ft long, contains seventy-two shops whose original rents were £18 a year (£34 for a double shop), but whose total annual rental value is now estimated at £50,000. Over the Piccadilly entrance (recast by Beresford Pite in 1930) are the arms of the Chesham family, who sold the arcade in 1926 for £333,000. The north end, which suffered considerably in an air raid in 1940, was well restored by W. G. Sinning in 1954.

Parallel to the arcade is BOND STREET (II, E 3–III, F 1), which leads north to Oxford Street (Route 14) and is divided into Old Bond Street (the southern part, as far as Burlington Gardens) and New Bond Street. This 'High Street of Mayfair' is renowned for its highly fashionable costumiers and jewellers, and also contains many picture-dealers' galleries at which exhibitions are frequently held. At the corner of Bruton Street, which diverges left to Berkeley Square (Route 13), is the TIME AND LIFE BUILDING, designed by Michael Rosenauer and completed in 1952, with a balustrade including carving by Henry Moore. On the opposite corner, of Conduit Street, which leads to Regent Street (Route 15), is the WESTBURY HOTEL, by the same architect, opened in 1955. At No. 34, higher up, is SOTHEBY'S, the well-known auction rooms specializing in rare books and manuscripts, and farther on New Bond Street crosses Brook Street, which runs left to Grosvenor Square (see Route 13) and right to Hanover Square (Route 15).

St James's Street, on the left of Piccadilly, descends to St James's Palace and Pall Mall (see Route 6). In Albemarle Street, opposite this, No. 7, a pleasant early-18th-century house with a modest exterior, is the headquarters of the National Book League, who hold interesting exhibitions here. Farther up is a classical building housing the Royal Institution of Great Britain (III, F 1), founded in 1799 for the 'promotion, diffusion and extension of science and useful knowledge'. Among the most popular of its lectures are those for children given during the Christmas holidays. The work of two of its most famous members, Sir Humphry Davy, appointed professor of chemistry in 1802, and Michael Faraday, his assistant after 1813 and professor in 1833, is commemorated in the Davy-Faraday Research Laboratory, next door, presented to the Royal Institution in 1896. In Grafton Street, to the left at the end of Albemarle Street, Sir Henry Irving (d. 1905), the actor, lived at No. 15A, on the corner, and Lord Brougham (d. 1868), who defended Queen Caroline at her trial, resided for thirty years at No. 4, one of a row of mansions built about 1750, probably by Sir Robert Taylor. The return to Piccadilly may be made by Dover Street, in which No. 40, rebuilt in 1957 after serious war damage, is the Arts Club, founded in 1863, while No. 37, with a fine stone façade of about 1772 by Sir Robert Taylor, incorporates part of Ely House, the town house of the bishops of Ely until 1909.

At No. 16 Hay Hill, opening on the west of Dover Street, is the Crafts Centre, devoted to the promotion of fine craftsmanship in Britain, and providing an exhibition of craftsmen's work of all kinds (changed about every six weeks).

The palatial Ritz Hotel (VIII, A 1) on the south side of Piccadilly, designed by Mewes and Davis (1906) with an arcade over the pavement, was the first steel-framed building to be put up in London, though the exterior stonework obscures this fact. In Arlington Street, on the east of it, Sir Robert Walpole, the prime minister, lived at No. 5 from 1742 until his death in 1745, while Wimborne House (No. 22) on the other side of the street, replaces another house of his in which his son, Horace Walpole, the author, was born in 1717.

BERKELEY STREET, on the opposite side of Piccadilly, leads north to Berkeley Square (Route 13), skirting DEVONSHIRE HOUSE, a huge block of flats and shops (1926), on the site of the London mansion of the Duke of Devonshire. Beyond this point Piccadilly has the GREEN PARK (Route 5) on its south side. The TURF CLUB, established in 1868, occupies No. 85, at the corner of CLARGES STREET, in which Lady Hamilton, the friend of Nelson, lived at No. 11, Edmund Kean, the actor, at No. 12, and Charles James Fox, the politician, at No. 46. The wrought-iron gates into the Green Park beyond this, attributed to Inigo Jones, were moved here from the old Devonshire House in 1921. No. 94, a mid-18th-century mansion badly damaged by bombing, was the home of Lord Palmerston from 1855 until his death in 1865 and is now occupied by the NAVAL AND MILITARY CLUB, sometimes called the 'In-and-Out Club', founded in 1862. White Horse Street, beyond this, gives access to Shepherd Market and Curzon Street (Route 13). No. 106, a fine late-18th-century building with decoration by the brothers Adam, is now the home of the ST JAMES'S CLUB (1858), founded for members of the diplomatic service; and No. 127 is the CAVALRY CLUB, established in 1890 for officers of the mounted services. Park Lane (Route 9), leading to Marble Arch, opens on the right farther on.

Piccadilly ends on the west at Wellington Place, better known as HYDE PARK CORNER (VII, B 2, 3), the busiest traffic centre in London, with over 100 vehicles passing every minute during the day. From it Knightsbridge (Route 10), connected to Piccadilly by an underground motorway, built in 1959–62, leads west towards Kensington, and Grosvenor Place runs south to Victoria Station (see Route 9). On the east side, facing Apsley House (see below), is a bronze equestrian statue of the Duke of Wellington (d. 1852), by Boehm, on a pedestal at the corners of which are a Grenadier Guard, a Highlander, a Welsh Fusilier, and an Inniskilling Dragoon. To the south-east rises the WELLINGTON ARCH, a triumphal arch designed by Decimus Burton (1828), surmounted by a large bronze quadriga or four-horse chariot with a figure of Peace, by Adrian Jones (1912). The arch stands at the top of Constitution Hill (Route 5), which descends to Buckingham Palace, and the central passage through the gate is reserved for royalty. On the north side of the roadway, beyond Apsley House, is the principal entrance to HYDE PARK (Route 12), which has a fine screen by Decimus Burton (1828), with a triple archway; the reliefs over the centre arch (by John Henning) are copied from the Parthenon frieze (p. 320).

On the island in the roadway opposite the Wellington Arch is the ROYAL ARTILLERY WAR MEMORIAL for both World Wars, by C. S. Jagger (1928), and south of this is the MACHINE GUN CORPS MEMORIAL for 1914–18, by F. Derwent Wood (1925), with a fine if inappropriate figure of David ('Saul has slain his thousands, but David his tens of thousands'). ST GEORGE'S HOSPITAL (VII, B 2), on the west side of the road, was founded in 1733 and occupies a rather austere building of 1829 by William Wilkins. The medical school was established at least as early as 1756.

APSLEY HOUSE (VII, B 3), the last house in Piccadilly ('No. 1, London'), next to the Hyde Park entrance, was long the residence of the great Duke of Wellington (1769–1852). Presented to the nation in 1947 by the seventh duke, it was opened in 1952 as the WELLINGTON MUSEUM. The house contains numerous relics of the 'Iron Duke' and valuable paintings, silver plate, and porcelain collected by him.

The house, built in 1771–8 by the brothers Adam for Henry Bathurst, Baron Apsley and Earl Bathurst, was bought in 1805 by the Marquess Wellesley, eldest brother of the Duke of Wellington, and sold by him in 1817 to the duke, who in fact had lived here since the previous year. In 1829 the house was altered by Benjamin Wyatt, who added the Corinthian portico and the west wing, including the Waterloo Gallery, and re-faced the whole of the brick exterior with Bath stone. The Duke of Wellington made Apsley House his permanent London home, quitting the army for politics and becoming Prime Minister in 1828–30. For his opposition to the Reform Bill brought in by Lord Grey he suffered a period of unpopularity; after the windows of his house had been broken by rioters in 1831, iron shutters had to be put up, but these were removed in 1856. After his appointment as Lord Warden of the Cinque Ports (1829) he lived much at Walmer Castle (Kent) and he died there in 1852 at the age of eighty-three.

To the left of the Entrance Hall is the Muniment Room, which contains a notable collection of orders and decorations conferred on the Duke, as well as his swords, batons, snuff-boxes, and many other personal relics. Remarkable are the silver-gilt Wellington Shield and two large candelabra presented by the merchants and bankers of the City of London; the Order of the Garter, awarded in 1813; and the Badge of the Order which originally belonged to the great Duke of Marlborough and was presented to the 'Iron Duke' by George IV. The Inner Hall, on the right of the Entrance Hall, contains a bust of the Duke by Nollekens (1813) and his uniform as a colonel of the Grenadier Guards. From the Vestibule beyond, which has a heroic marble statue of Napoleon by Canova, the staircase ascends to the first floor, where the rooms contain beautiful plate and services of Sèvres, Meissen, Vienna, and other porcelain given to the Duke by British and foreign royalty, and numerous fine paintings by Flemish, Dutch, and Spanish masters. The Waterloo Gallery, 90 ft long, is named from the Waterloo Banquets held here annually from 1830 until the Duke's death, and attended by his senior officers who took part in the great victory over the French. On the original banqueting table is set out the elaborate Portuguese Service, presented to the Duke in 1816 by the Prince Regent of Portugal. The two candelabra of Siberian porphyry at the ends of the table were given by the Emperor Nicholas I of Russia. In this room also are some of the finest paintings, including works by Rubens, Murillo, Ribera, Guercino, and Sassoferrato, many of which were captured after the Battle of Vitoria (1813) from Joseph Bonaparte (by whom they had been looted from the Spanish royal collections) and afterwards bestowed on the Duke by Ferdinand VII.

Here also is an equestrian portrait of the Duke by Goya (1812) and in the Striped Drawing Room are a fine portrait of him by Lawrence (1814) and others of his companions in arms. The Yellow Drawing Room holds a beautiful Correggio ('Agony in the Garden') and three superb examples of Velazquez, while the Dining Room contains the Waterloo Vase (presented in 1825), portraits of contemporary monarchs, including George IV (in Highland costume) by Sir David Wilkie, and busts of the Duke by Chantrey (1823) and Sir J. Steell (1846).

8 From Victoria to Battersea Bridge (Chelsea)

Plan VII, C 3 – beyond VI, F 3

STATIONS: VICTORIA (Plan VIII, C 1), on the Southern Region and the Circle and District lines; SLOANE SQUARE (VII, D 2), on the Circle and District lines. — MOTOR-BUSES Nos. 10, 16, 25, 29, 32, 38, 52, 76, 127, 134, and 149 to Victoria Station (others in Victoria Street, see Route 4; in Grosvenor Place, see Route 9); Nos. 11, 39, and 46 in Buckingham Palace Road and Pimlico Road; No. 137 (from Knightsbridge) in Chelsea Bridge Road; Nos. 19, 39, 45, and 49 across Battersea Bridge (the two last from South Kensington); and Nos. 11, 19, and 22 in King's Road.

ADMISSION to CHELSEA HOSPITAL, see p. 331; to CHELSEA PHYSIC GARDEN, occasionally on written application to the Clerk to the Committee, London Parochial Charities, 3 Temple Gardens, EC4: to CARLYLE'S HOUSE, weekdays, except Tuesday, 10 to 1 and 2 to 6 or dusk, Sundays from 2 (1/-); to CROSBY HALL, Monday–Friday 10 to 12 and 2 to 5, Saturdays and Sundays 2 to 5 (free).

For VICTORIA STATION see Route 4. BUCKINGHAM PALACE ROAD, leaving Grosvenor Gardens (Route 9) on the right, runs southward alongside the station, passing (at No. 90) the ROYAL SOCIETY OF HEALTH (formerly the Royal Sanitary Institute, founded in 1876), with a well-designed museum by Sir Hugh Casson (1957). Temporary exhibitions are held from time to time, and a permanent collection is being steadily built up. On the left is ECCLESTON BRIDGE (VII, D 3), a principal changing-point for Green Line services, and farther on, at the corner of Elizabeth Street, is the large VICTORIA COACH STATION (VII, D 3), opened in 1932. Buckingham Palace Road ends beyond AIRWAYS HOUSE (1939; extended 1960), the passenger terminal of the British Overseas Airways Corporation, established in 1939.

PIMLICO ROAD, branching to the right here, is prolonged beyond Chelsea Bridge Road by ROYAL HOSPITAL ROAD, which passes the main entrance to Chelsea Hospital and reaches Chelsea Embankment farther on. In EBURY STREET, a long thoroughfare on the right leading back to Grosvenor Gardens, Mozart composed his first symphony in 1764 (at the age of eight) at No. 180, and George Moore, the novelist ('the sage of Ebury Street'), died in 1933 at No. 121. In Chelsea Bridge Road are the CHELSEA BARRACKS, rebuilt in 1962 in a modern style (by Tripe and Wakeham) and quartering regiments of the Brigade of Guards (compare p. 118). The road is extended on the north by Lower Sloane Street, leading to Sloane Square (p. 144).

EBURY BRIDGE ROAD, bearing left past characteristic blocks of flats, goes on south of Chelsea Barracks to CHELSEA BRIDGE ROAD, which leads left to the LISTER INSTITUTE of Preventive Medicine, founded in 1891 and now a branch of London University (on the left), and to CHELSEA BRIDGE (VII, F 3), a suspension bridge 700 ft long, rebuilt in 1934–7 by G. Topham Forrest and E. P. Wheeler, crossing the Thames to Battersea Park.

Grosvenor Road (see p. 110) leads east along the river from this point to Vauxhall Bridge.

CHELSEA EMBANKMENT (VII, F 1–3), a fine esplanade laid out by Sir Joseph Bazalgette in 1874, extends for just over a mile from Chelsea Bridge to Battersea Bridge. From it Battersea Park and the Festival Gardens are seen on the opposite bank of the Thames. On the right the embankment skirts the CHELSEA HOSPITAL GARDENS, from which there is a noble prospect of the delightful brick buildings of the Royal Hospital (compare p. 331). The gardens are the setting of the attractive Chelsea Flower Show in May.

TITE STREET, to the west of the gardens, was once greatly favoured by artists. The White House was built by E. W. Godwin in 1878 for James McNeill Whistler, but occupied by him for a few months only; he afterwards lived at No. 13 (in 1881–5) and No. 46 (in 1888). J. S. Sargent, the American painter, occupied No. 31 for twenty-four years until his death here in 1925, and Oscar Wilde lived at No. 34 after his marriage (1884) until his trial in 1895.

Farther along the Embankment is the charming old-world CHELSEA PHYSIC GARDEN (VII, F 1; entered from Swan Walk, on the east), leased by the Society of Apothecaries in 1673. In the centre is a statue by Rysbrack (1737) of Sir Hans Sloane, who purchased the manor of Chelsea in 1712 and presented the garden to the society in 1723 for an annual rent of £5. Towards the end of the 19th century the garden became neglected and in 1899 responsibility for its upkeep was undertaken by the Trustees of the London Parochial Charities. Cotton seed was first sent from the garden to America in 1732, and seeds and specimens of plants are exchanged today with research workers all over the world.

To the west of the point where it is joined by Royal Hospital Road (see above), Chelsea Embankment is separated by a line of public gardens from CHEYNE WALK (VII, F 1; pronounced 'chainy'), a delightful row of early Georgian dwellings (1718), though with some Victorian insertions. Many of the houses retain their excellent wrought-iron gates and railings. No. 4 was the home of the painter Daniel Maclise in 1861–70, and George Eliot (Mary Ann Evans) died here in 1880 after a residence of less than three weeks. No. 16 (the Queen's House), the best of the row, was occupied in 1862–82 by D. G. Rossetti, who maintained his menagerie in the garden and who is commemorated by a fountain in the public garden in front.

Farther on is the ALBERT BRIDGE (beyond VII, F 1), a combined cantilever and suspension bridge by R. W. Ordish, opened in 1873 and crossing the river to the west end of Battersea Park. Immediately west of the approach is a figure of Atalanta by F. Derwent Wood (1871–1926), set up as a memorial to the sculptor. In OAKLEY STREET, which leads north from the bridge to King's Road, No. 56 was the residence of Captain R. F. Scott, the Antarctic explorer. Nos. 46–9 Cheyne Walk, west of the bridge, are a charming group of early-18th-century houses, and in the gardens just beyond is a good bronze statue by Boehm of the author Thomas Carlyle (1882). It stands opposite the entrance to CHEYNE ROW, a quiet street running north from the river, with a terrace of modest brick houses built in 1708. In one of these (No. 24; formerly No. 5), now called CARLYLE'S HOUSE (VI, F 3), Thomas Carlyle (1795–1881) and his wife Jane Welsh (1801–66) lived from 1834 until the end of their lives. *The French Revolution* (1834–7), *Heroes and Hero-Worship* (1840), *Past and Present* (1843), and *Frederick the Great* (1853–65) were all written here. The small but dignified house, purchased through the efforts of a group of admirers in 1895 and presented to the National Trust in 1936, remains very much as it was in the time of the Carlyles, with the furniture, etc., used by them. Cases contain books and letters of the 'Sage of Chelsea', as well as many personal relics, and on the walls hang portraits of the Carlyles and photographs and drawings of places with which they are associated. On the topmost floor is the Attic Study, with the large skylight and double walls added by Carlyle in 1853 in a vain attempt to find light and quiet. Visitors may also see the Kitchen in the basement, where Carlyle and Tennyson used to smoke until a late hour, and the little Garden, where Mrs Carlyle's favourite dog, 'Nero', is buried.

Cheyne Row ends at UPPER CHEYNE ROW, where Leigh Hunt, the essayist, lived in 1833–40 at No. 22, one of a number of houses of about 1716. Tobias Smollett, the novelist, lived in 1750–62 at No. 16, LAWRENCE STREET (at the west end of Upper Cheyne Row), and in this street the famous Chelsea porcelain works flourished from about 1745 until 1784, when they were removed to Derby. In CARLYLE MANSIONS, a block of flats facing the embankment to the west of Cheyne Row, Henry James, the American novelist, died in 1916 at No. 21.

CHELSEA OLD CHURCH (beyond VI, F 3), on the Embankment, founded at least as early as the 12th century but rebuilt at various times, was devastated by a land mine in 1941, when the tower, nave, and aisles were destroyed and the chancel and north chapel gravely damaged. The south chapel, rebuilt in 1528 by Sir Thomas More, fortunately survived the explosion, as did the single arch with its two beautiful Renaissance capitals (attributed to Holbein) opening to the chancel. In the More Chapel are monuments to Sir Robert Stanley (d. 1632) and Lady Jane Guildford, Duchess of Northumberland (d. 1556), and a tablet to Henry James (see above). The chancel, well restored in 1954 by Walter H. Godfrey, has in its south wall a 16th-century monument to Sir Thomas More, who settled in Chelsea about 1524 and counted Erasmus and Holbein among his famous visitors. His first wife was buried here in 1532 and More intended this to be the resting place of himself and his second wife, but after his execution in 1535 his head was fixed on London Bridge and his body buried in St Peter's in the Tower.

In the north or Lawrence Chapel, Henry VIII is thought to have been secretly married to Jane Seymour on 20 May 1536, several days before their official marriage. This chapel, likewise restored, contains a monument to Sara Colvile (d. 1631), with an unusual effigy (a demi-figure rising in a shroud), and a tablet to William de Morgan, perhaps best known as a novelist, who had a pottery in Cheyne Row in 1872–82 and died in Chelsea in 1917. The nave and tower were rebuilt in their former (17th-century) style by W. H. Godfrey and the whole church reconsecrated in 1958. The 17th-century font and pulpit have been replaced. On the north wall is a monument to Lady Jane Cheyne (d. 1669), attributed to Bernini, and on the south is the altar-tomb with effigies of Lord Dacre of the South and his wife (1595). Here also are chained books given to the church by Sir Hans Sloane (d. 1753), whose collections formed the nucleus of the British Museum and whose tomb is in the south-east corner of the churchyard.

Farther west is CROSBY HALL, an international hall of residence of the British Federation of University Women, built in 1927 by Walter H. Godfrey incorporating (on the east side) the great hall of Crosby Place, a sumptuous mansion erected in Bishopsgate in 1466–75 by Sir John Crosby, a London alderman and wool merchant, and later supposed to have been occupied by the Duke of Gloucester, afterwards Richard III. The hall escaped destruction when the house was burned down in the 17th century, and in 1910 it was brought from Bishopsgate and re-erected on its present site. Now used as a dining hall, it retains its fine oak roof and a lofty oriel window with the crest of Sir John Crosby in the vaulting. Behind the Jacobean high table is one of the three copies of Holbein's painting of Sir Thomas More and his family made for his three daughters.

The embankment ends at BATTERSEA BRIDGE (beyond VI, F 3), an ugly iron structure of 1887–90 by Bazalgette replacing the picturesque wooden bridge of 1772, a favourite subject of Whistler, Turner, and other artists. BEAUFORT STREET, crossing the site of Beaufort House, the manor house of Sir Thomas More and later of Sir Hans Sloane (pulled down in 1740), runs north from the bridge to King's Road, the main thoroughfare of Chelsea.

There are some interesting and pleasant old houses in that part of CHEYNE WALK extending west of the bridge. Nos. 91–2, on the corner of Beaufort Street, are notable houses of about 1771. Mrs Gaskell, the novelist, was born in 1810 at No. 93, another 18th-century house, and J. McN. Whistler lived in 1866–78 at No. 96, now the headquarters of the ROYAL HISTORICAL SOCIETY, founded in 1868. LINDSEY HOUSE (N.T.; no admission) was built in 1674 by the third Earl of Lindsey and retains its original façade, but it was altered internally in 1752, when it became the London headquarters of the Moravian brotherhood, and was subdivided into several houses in 1774. Notable residents have included Sir Marc Brunel and his son Isambard, the civil engineers (in 1811–26). No. 101 was the first London home of Whistler (1863–6), P. Wilson Steer died in 1942 at No. 109, and J. M. W. Turner lived anonymously at No. 119 (restored after war damage) from 1846 until his death in 1851. The road goes on to the huge LOTS ROAD POWER-STATION, built in 1904 to provide electricity for the underground railways, while Cremorne Road turns away from the river for King's Road and Fulham.

The return towards Victoria may be made by KING'S ROAD (VI, F 2–VII, D 2), which runs north-east to Sloane Square. PAULTON'S SQUARE, on the right east of Beaufort Street, and CARLYLE SQUARE, on the left farther on, are characteristic squares of 1830–40. In Manresa Road, also on the left, is the CHELSEA COLLEGE OF SCIENCE AND TECHNOLOGY, founded in 1891 (as the Chelsea Polytechnic) and now 'recognized' by London University. Ellen Terry, the actress, lived in 1904–20 at No. 215 King's Road, a house of 1720, and ARGYLL HOUSE, just beyond, at the corner of Oakley Street, was built in 1723 by Giacomo Leoni, the Venetian architect. Sydney Street, opposite CHELSEA TOWN HALL (by J. M. Brydon, 1887; enlarged 1908), leads to ST LUKE'S CHURCH (VI, E 3), the parish church of Chelsea, built in 1820–4 by James Savage and the earliest stone-vaulted church of the Gothic Revival. Charles Dickens was married here in 1836 to Catherine Hogarth, and the father of the novelists Charles and Henry Kingsley was rector in 1836–60, Charles serving as his curate for a time. Sydney Street ends at Fulham Road, the continuation of Brompton Road (Route 10).

ROYAL AVENUE, on the right of King's Road farther east, affords a glimpse of Chelsea Hospital as it leads to ST LEONARD'S TERRACE on the north side of Burton's Court, where Nos. 14–32 are among the best 18th-century houses in Chelsea. The main road passes the DUKE OF YORK'S HEADQUARTERS, built in 1801 by John Sanders for the Duke of York's School (moved to Dover in 1909) and now the headquarters of the County of London Territorial Army. SLOANE SQUARE (VII, D 2) is chiefly notable for Messrs Peter Jones's, one of the most striking modern department stores in London, designed by William Crabtree (in association with Slater and Moberley and Sir Charles Reilly) and built in 1936–9. In the shady centre of the square is a fountain with sculpture by Gilbert Ledward (1953), and on the east side is the ROYAL COURT THEATRE, rebuilt in 1888 and restored after war damage. In the foyer is a bust (by Michael Werner, 1955) of Bernard Shaw, whose earlier plays were produced here by Harley Granville-Barker (1904–7). From the square Cliveden Place leads north-east towards Eaton Square (Route 9) and Sloane Street runs north to Pont Street and Knightsbridge (see p. 148).

9 From Victoria to Hyde Park Corner and Marble Arch

Plan VII, C 3–II, E 2

STATIONS: VICTORIA (Plan VIII, C 1), see Route 8; HYDE PARK CORNER (VII, B 2), on the Piccadilly line; MARBLE ARCH (II, E 2), on the Central line. — MOTOR-BUSES Nos. 2, 16, 25, 32, 36, 38, and 52 in Grosvenor Place; Nos. 2, 16, 30, 36, 73, 74, and 137 in East Carriage Road (Hyde Park; northbound only) and Park Lane (southbound only). For other buses to Victoria, see Route 8; to Hyde Park Corner, see Routes 7, 10; to Marble Arch, see Routes 12, 14, 16.

For VICTORIA, see Route 4. GROSVENOR GARDENS (VII, C 3), traversed by the road hence to Hyde Park Corner, consists of two connected triangles. At its south end is a fine bronze equestrian statue of Marshal Foch (d. 1929), by Georges Malissard, a replica of one at Cassel in northern France, and on the west side (at No. 42) are the head-offices of the ROYAL NATIONAL LIFE-BOAT INSTITUTION, founded in 1824. At No. 32 (now the Commonwealth War Graves Commission) Lord Birkenhead, the statesman, died in 1930; at the north end of the gardens is the RIFLE BRIGADE WAR MEMORIAL, by John Tweed (1925).

The most direct road to Hyde Park Corner follows GROS-VENOR PLACE, with the gardens of Buckingham Palace on the right, but a more interesting route is through the district of BELGRAVIA, which vies with Mayfair as the most fashionable residential quarter in London. With its spacious squares and aristocratic mansions, it was laid out in 1825 and onwards by Thomas Cubitt, who employed George Basevi, the pupil of Sir John Soane, as his principal architect.

In Grosvenor Place are Hobart House, the headquarters of the NATIONAL COAL BOARD, constituted in 1946, and, farther up (No. 17), the IRISH EMBASSY.

HOBART PLACE leads from the north end of Grosvenor Gardens to the long EATON SQUARE (VII, D 2–C 3), its pleasant gardens traversed by the eastward extension of King's Road (compare p. 144), with distinguished terraces on both sides. Facing the north-east end is ST PETER'S, EATON SQUARE, rebuilt in a classical style by Sir Arthur Blomfield (1875) and the setting for many fashionable weddings. From the church UPPER BELGRAVE STREET runs north-west to Belgrave Square.

Nos. 10–11, in a Regency terrace (right), house the ROYAL INSTITUTION OF NAVAL ARCHITECTS, founded in 1860, and the INSTITUTION OF STRUCTURAL ENGINEERS, established in 1908. Wilton Street, Chester Street, and Chapel Street, on the same side, all have good early-19th-century terraces in a modest style. Algernon Charles Swinburne, the poet, was born in 1837 in a house in Chester Street. In EATON PLACE, on the left, Lord Kelvin, the scientist, lived at No. 15 and Lord Avebury (Sir John Lubbock) was born in 1834 at No. 29. Field-Marshal Sir Henry Wilson was shot on the doorstep of his house (No. 36) by Sinn Feiners in 1922. Chopin gave his first London recital in 1848 at No. 99, and George Peabody, the American philanthropist, died in 1869 at No. 80 Eaton Square, near by. In CHESTER SQUARE, on the other side of Eaton Square, Mary Wollstone-craft Shelley, second wife of the poet, died in 1851 at No. 24.

BELGRAVE SQUARE (VII, C 2), perhaps the most notable of London's many squares, has on each side an exceptionally fine range of building in a classical style designed by Basevi (1825), while three of the corners are occupied by large handsome mansions. SEAFORD HOUSE, on the east corner, designed by Philip Hardwick, was the residence of Lord John Russell, the statesman, in 1841–70; No. 24, on the south, built by Henry E. Kendall for Thomas Kemp, the creator of Kemp Town at Brighton, is now the SPANISH EMBASSY.

Nos. 21–3, in the south-west range, with a new building adjoining, are now the GERMAN EMBASSY. No. 19, farther on, is the headquarters of the NATURE CONSERVANCY, incorporated in 1949. No. 18 is the AUSTRIAN EMBASSY, and Nos. 14–16 house the important SOCIETY OF CHEMICAL INDUSTRY. No. 14 was formerly the residence of the Duke of Norfolk, while Nos. 15–16 were occupied by the Duke of Bedford. No. 3, on the north-west side, was the residence of the Duke of Kent (d. 1942), uncle of the Queen, and the philanthropic Earl of Shaftesbury died in 1885 at No. 5. Henry Hallam, the historian, died in 1859 at No. 24 WILTON CRESCENT, which is north-west of Belgrave Square, and in a later and more restrained style. Hence Wilton Place (Route 10) goes on to Knightsbridge. No. 32 Belgrave Square (on the east side) is the ROYAL COLLEGE OF VETERINARY SURGEONS, founded in 1844, and No. 47 houses the INSTITUTE OF PHYSICS AND THE PHYSICAL SOCIETY, two bodies who amalgamated in 1960.

South Kensington may be reached from Belgrave Square by following CHESHAM PLACE to the south-west (from the south corner) and bearing to the right into PONT STREET, which crosses CADOGAN PLACE, enclosing the largest square in London, and SLOANE STREET (VII, B 1–D 2), the long straight thoroughfare connecting Knightsbridge Station (Route 10) with Sloane Square (Route 8). William Wilberforce, the abolitionist, died at No. 44 Cadogan Place in 1833. A new hotel, the CARLTON TOWER, designed by Michael Rosenauer, was opened in the square by an American company in 1961.

The district west of Sloane Street, formerly known as Hans Town (both names were given in honour of Sir Hans Sloane), was laid out about 1780 by Henry Holland, but much of it was rebuilt in the late 19th century in a hideously ornate style satirized by Mr Osbert Lancaster as 'Pont Street Dutch'. In HANS PLACE, north of Pont Street, there survive some 18th-century houses in one of which (No. 41) the poet Shelley lived for a time. Arnold Bennett (d. 1931), the novelist, spent the latter part of his life at No. 75 CADOGAN SQUARE, farther south.

ST COLUMBA'S CHURCH of Scotland (VII, C 1), facing Pont Street at its west end, was destroyed by bombing in 1941, but rebuilt in 1950–5 by Sir Edward Maufe in an austere but satisfying style. Over the west door is a figure of the saint, and the circular window in the east gable (by Moira Forsyth) shows the cross of St Andrew. The south chapel was dedicated as a memorial to the fallen of the London Scottish Regiment in 1956. Pont Street is extended by Beauchamp Place to BROMPTON ROAD (Route 10).

From the north corner of Belgrave Square, GROSVENOR CRESCENT (VII, B 2) leads to the north end of Grosvenor Place,

passing (at Nos. 8–10), the head-offices of the ST JOHN AM-
BULANCE ASSOCIATION, founded in 1877, and (at Nos. 14–15)
those of the BRITISH RED CROSS SOCIETY, established in
1908. The route bears right (east) at HYDE PARK CORNER
(Route 7) to the beginning of Piccadilly, then turns left into
HAMILTON PLACE, where No. 4 houses the ROYAL AERO-
NAUTICAL SOCIETY, founded as long ago as 1866. This road
runs into PARK LANE (II, E 2–VII, B 3), which skirts Hyde
Park (Route 12) on the east and was long synonymous with
wealth and fashion. The opulent mansions that once bordered its
east side, however, have mostly given way to large hotels and
blocks of flats. One survivor (so far) is LONDONDERRY HOUSE,
built in 1827 by Benjamin and Philip Wyatt. It stands at the corner
of HERTFORD STREET, in which Bulwer Lytton wrote the *Last
Days of Pompeii* and *Rienzi* (1835) at No. 36. Sir George Cayley,
a pioneer of aviation, lived in 1840–8 at No. 20, and General John
Burgoyne (d. 1792) and R. B. Sheridan (in 1795–1802) lived at
No. 10. The LONDON HILTON HOTEL (24 storeys and over
300 ft high), to an unusual design by Lewis Solomon, Kaye and
Partners, was completed in 1963 north of Hertford Street. Farther
north in Park Lane is the entrance to CURZON STREET (Route
13).

To the left, within the STANHOPE GATE of Hyde Park, is
the CAVALRY WAR MEMORIAL, with a figure of St George, by
Adrian Jones (1924). The luxurious DORCHESTER HOTEL, on
the right, was built in 1931 to the design of W. Curtis Green.
Aldford Street, on the same side, leads to the Grosvenor Chapel
in South Audley Street (Route 13). Beyond in Park Lane are the
huge GROSVENOR HOUSE (1929), a hotel with a façade by
Lutyens, on the site of a mansion of the Duke of Westminster,
and the GROSVENOR GATE of Hyde Park. At No. 93 Park Lane
(then No. 1 Grosvenor Gate), the property of his wife, Benjamin
Disraeli lived during the whole of his married life (1839–72). It is
the first of a row of interesting houses with bow fronts, built in
the mid 18th century but much altered internally since, and there
are others at Nos. 129–32, farther north. Park Lane ends at
MARBLE ARCH, at the west end of Oxford Street (see Route 14).

10 From Hyde Park Corner to South Kensington

Plan VII, B 2–VI, D 3

STATIONS: HYDE PARK CORNER (Plan VII, B 2) and KNIGHTSBRIDGE (VII, B 1), on the Piccadilly line; SOUTH KENSINGTON (VI, D 3), on the Circle, District, and Piccadilly lines. — MOTOR-BUSES Nos. 9, 14, 19, 22, 30, 52, 73, 74, and 137 in Knightsbridge (for others to Hyde Park Corner, see Routes 7, 9); Nos. 14, 30, and 74 in Brompton Road; No. 74 in Cromwell Road (others to South Kensington, see p. 138).

ADMISSION to VICTORIA & ALBERT MUSEUM, see p. 418; to NATURAL HISTORY MUSEUM, see p. 373; to GEOLOGICAL MUSEUM, see p. 389; to SCIENCE MUSEUM, see p. 389; to ROYAL COLLEGE OF MUSIC (Donaldson Museum), Monday–Friday during term, on application to the registrar (free). — SERVICES at BROMPTON ORATORY, weekdays, 6.30, 7, 8, 8.30, and 10; Monday–Friday, 12.30; Fridays only, 6 p.m.; Sundays, 6.15, 7, 8, 9, 10, 10.45, 12 (High Mass), and 4.30.

For HYDE PARK CORNER, see Route 7. KNIGHTSBRIDGE (VII, B 1, 2), continuing the line of Piccadilly westward, has Hyde Park on its north side at first. Over an entrance to St George's Hospital, on the left, is a fine bronze bust by Sir Alfred Gilbert of John Hunter, surgeon to the hospital in 1768–93. AGRICULTURE HOUSE, on the same side farther on, is a handsome building erected in 1956 (by R. Ward and Partners) for the National Farmers' Union. To the left in WILTON PLACE, which has a fine 18th-century terrace on its west side, is the church of ST PAUL'S, KNIGHTSBRIDGE, a Gothic building by Thomas Cundy (1843) noted for its music. On the north wall outside is a memorial to fifty-two women of the Women's Transport Service (F.A.N.Y.) who died in the Second World War. No. 58 Knightsbridge, with No. 1 Albert Gate adjoining, is the FRENCH EMBASSY (VII, B 2); a tablet in the wall commemorates the fiftieth anniversary of the *Entente Cordiale* (1954). Beyond the north end of Sloane Street (p. 144) and KNIGHTSBRIDGE STATION (VII, B 1), Brompton Road branches left from the continuation of Knightsbridge (Route 11). Under the huge BOWATER HOUSE (by Guy Morgan and Partners, 1959) is an entrance to Hyde Park through which Epstein's vigorous bronze group, 'Pan' (1961), can be seen.

BROMPTON ROAD (VI, D 3–VII, B 1), a busy thoroughfare, runs south-west towards the South Kensington museums.

Beauchamp Place, on the left, leads to Pont Street (compare Route 9), YEOMAN'S ROW, farther on, has some good, if small, late-18th-century houses, while BROMPTON SQUARE, on the other side, has terraces of the earlier part of the 19th century. A little beyond is an avenue leading to HOLY TRINITY CHURCH, the parish church of Brompton, built in the Gothic style by T. L. Donaldson in 1829, but given a new chancel before 1899 by Sir Arthur Blomfield.

BROMPTON ORATORY (VI, C 3), or the London Oratory of St Philip Neri, is a Roman Catholic church served by a congregation of secular priests of the Institute of the Oratory, founded by St Philip Neri at Rome in the late 16th century. The institute, introduced into England in 1847 by Cardinal Newman, was first established in London in 1849 and moved to Brompton in 1854. The church, designed by Herbert Gribble and completed in 1884, is a spacious structure in the Italian baroque style, well proportioned, but perhaps rather too ornate in its decoration for English tastes. The dome, rising 200 ft above the floor to the top of the cross, was added in 1896 by George Sherrin. To the west of the oratory is a statue (by Bodley and Brindley) of Cardinal Newman (d. 1890).

The entrance to the church is through a lofty portico supported by double columns with the bases of unfinished towers on either side. The interior is notable for the width of the nave (51 ft) and the large side chapels taking the place of aisles. The arches opening into these, supported on each side by double piers of Devonshire marble, carry the arms of Popes and sculptured figures representing the principal virtues. Above the cornice are mosaics of saints connected with St Philip and windows containing the arms of notable benefactors. Between the pilasters (also of Devonshire marble) on either side of the nave are huge Carrara marble statues of the Apostles, by Mazzotti (late 17th century), which previously stood in Siena Cathedral. These, combined with the other decoration (by C. T. G. Formilli), give the nave a somewhat heavy Italianate appearance. The decoration of the chapels also follows Italian models and is notable for its use of coloured marbles. Under the altar in the chapel of St Philip, in the west transept, is preserved a relic of the saint, exposed on Tuesdays. The Sanctuary has carved walnut stalls and a marquetry floor, and altar rails of Sicilian marble. The Lady Chapel in the east transept has a magnificent Italian altarpiece of 1693 from the former Dominican church at Brescia, while the chapel of St Wilfrid, which opens on the north of the transept, contains an altarpiece of about 1710 from the cathedral of Maastricht (Holland). The organ, above a Calvary of 1952, was redesigned in 1954 by Ralph Downes. The last chapel on this side, with walls of Irish marble, contains as a war memorial a sculptured Pietà by Louis Berra.

Brompton Road bears to the left opposite the Oratory, for Fulham and Chelsea, while CROMWELL ROAD goes on past the south fronts of the **Victoria and Albert Museum** (opposite which is THURLOE SQUARE, built in 1843 by George Basevi) and the **Natural History Museum.**

PELHAM PLACE and PELHAM CRESCENT, farther south, were also laid out by Basevi (1820–30). In CROMWELL PLACE, opposite the Natural History Museum, Sir J. E. Millais, the painter, lived at No. 7 in 1862–78. In Cromwell Road, farther west, is the new building of the INSTITUT FRANÇAIS DU ROYAUME-UNI, an outpost of French culture in London. No. 49 is the ROYAL METEOROLOGICAL SOCIETY, founded in 1850. BADEN-POWELL HOUSE, on the corner of Queen's Gate, west of the Natural History Museum, was designed by Ralph Tubbs and opened in 1961 as a centre for Scouting and a hostel for visiting scouts, and also as a memorial to Lord Baden-Powell (1857–1941). Outside is a statue of B.-P., by Don Potter, and inside can be seen his numerous trophies and mementoes. Cromwell Road, a broad thoroughfare with substantial residences, goes on beyond Gloucester Road to the WEST LONDON AIR TERMINAL (VI, D 1), the principal passenger centre for British European Airways, built above the District line railway tracks in 1957 and now being enlarged (1963).

EXHIBITION ROAD, starting near South Kensington Station (VI, D 3) and skirting the Victoria and Albert Museum on the west, ascends to Kensington Road (Route 11). It gives access to a number of important public and academic buildings, occupying a site purchased out of the proceeds of the Great Exhibition of 1851. On the left are the **Geological Museum** and the **Science Museum,** on the right is the ROYAL COLLEGE OF SCIENCE (see below) founded in 1845, in a Victorian Renaissance building (1872). Beyond these IMPERIAL INSTITUTE ROAD leads to the left to Queen's Gate. On its south side are the main buildings of the IMPERIAL COLLEGE OF SCIENCE AND TECHNOLOGY (VI, C 2, 3), erected by Sir Aston Webb in 1900–6.

In reality a group of associated colleges, housed in separate buildings, the Imperial College was established in 1907 'for the most advanced training and research in science, especially in its application to industry' and affiliated to the University of London in 1908. It comprises the Royal College of Science, the City and Guilds College, and the Royal School of Mines, and has 3,000 students. The buildings in Imperial Institute Road include also the Department of Chemistry and the Science Museum Library (see p. 393). On the north of the road is the IMPERIAL COLLEGE UNION, in a building of 1903, and other buildings are now being erected here (1963) for the expanding college. The lofty Renaissance-style tower (280 ft high, with a fine peal of bells), designed by T. E. Collcutt, is all that remains of the original buildings of the Commonwealth Institute, opened here in 1893 (as the Imperial Institute). The institute was moved in 1962 to a new site in Holland Park (p. 154).

On the right in Exhibition Road, almost opposite Imperial Institute Road, is the HYDE PARK CHAPEL, the first Mormon chapel to be built in London, designed by Sir Thomas Bennett and opened in 1961, with a fine organ. In the large square of PRINCES GARDENS, the first of several new halls of residence being designed by Richard Sheppard, Robson and Partners for the Imperial College of Science and Technology was completed in 1959. No. 51 Princes Gate, on the same side of Exhibition Road, was converted in 1958 into the GERMAN INSTITUTE, with a library, reading room, etc., open to visitors.

On the left of Exhibition Road is the CITY AND GUILDS COLLEGE (founded 1885), now a branch of the Imperial College of Science (see above), built by Alfred Waterhouse in 1884 and extended in 1913, but now being rebuilt (1963). PRINCE CONSORT ROAD, parallel to Imperial Institute Road, contains a further group of academic buildings of which the most interesting (on the south) is the ROYAL COLLEGE OF MUSIC (VI, C2), founded in 1883 and occupying an elaborate building by Sir Arthur Blomfield opened in 1894.

The college has a good concert hall, and contains a valuable library and (in the Donaldson Museum) an exceptionally fine collection of over 300 old musical instruments, including Handel's spinet, Haydn's clavichord, and a guitar said to have belonged to Rizzio, the music master of Mary, Queen of Scots. Also on the south side of the road is the ROYAL SCHOOL OF MINES (established 1851) in a building by Sir Aston Webb (1909–13) embellished with statuary while new buildings farther west, completed in 1960, house the Departments of Chemical Engineering, Applied Chemistry, Aeronautics, and Physics of the Imperial College of Science. On the north are the IMPERIAL COLLEGE HOSTEL (1912–26) and the Departments of Botany and Biochemistry. HOLY TRINITY CHURCH (VI, C 2), farther west, is a lofty Gothic building by G. F. Bodley begun in 1901; the west window, a war memorial, includes the arms of the Commonwealth countries and colonies.

11   From Hyde Park Corner to Kensington

Plan VII, B 2–beyond VI, B 1

STATIONS: HYDE PARK CORNER (Plan VII, B 2) and KNIGHTSBRIDGE (VII, B 1), on the Piccadilly line; HIGH STREET, KENSINGTON (beyond VI, B 1), on the Circle and District lines. — MOTOR-BUSES Nos. 9, 46, 52, and 73 in Knightsbridge and Kensington Road; Nos. 9, 27, 28, 31, 49, and 73 in Kensington High Street; and Nos. 27, 28, 31, 46, and 52 in Kensington Church Street. No. 31 runs south to Earls Court and Chelsea, No. 49 to South Kensington and Chelsea.

ADMISSION to ROYAL SCHOOL OF NEEDLEWORK, Monday–Friday 9.30 to 5.30 (free); to ROYAL GEOGRAPHICAL SOCIETY MUSEUM, Monday–Friday 9.30 to 5.30, Saturday 9.30 to 1 (free); to COMMONWEALTH INSTITUTE, weekdays 10 to 5.30, Sundays 2.30 to 6 (free; cinema shows, Monday–Friday 12.30 and 2.45, Saturdays 2.45, Sundays 3); to LEIGHTON HOUSE, weekdays 11 to 5 (to 6 for special exhibitions; free).

From HYDE PARK CORNER to Knightsbridge Station, see Route 10. Knightsbridge, keeping to the right here, passes KNIGHTSBRIDGE BARRACKS (1879), the headquarters of the Household Cavalry.

This comprises two regiments, the Life Guards, formed originally by the followers of Charles II during his exile, and the Royal Horse Guards ('The Blues'), which began as a Cromwellian troop of horse. These regiments share the honour of providing a personal bodyguard for the sovereign on state occasions. The Life Guards wear scarlet tunics with blue collars and cuffs and white plumed helmets, while the Royal Horse Guards wear blue tunics with scarlet collars and cuffs and red plumed helmets. In full dress, white buckskin pantaloons and long knee-boots are worn, as well as the steel cuirasses revived for the coronation of George IV.

KENSINGTON ROAD (VI, B 1–3), the continuation of Knightsbridge, begins at Rutland Gardens and has Hyde Park on its right. No. 14 PRINCES GATE, the first house in a long and stately terrace of the mid 19th century, facing the park, was presented to the United States by J. Pierpont Morgan as the official residence of the U.S. Ambassador (note the Red Indian heads over the windows), but is now the head-office of the INDEPENDENT TELEVISION AUTHORITY, established in 1955. Field-Marshal Earl Haig died in 1928 at No. 21 Princes Gate; No. 25 is the ROYAL SCHOOL OF NEEDLEWORK, containing a notable collection of needlework, both old and new.

EXHIBITION ROAD, starting opposite the Alexandra Gate

of Hyde Park, leads to the South Kensington Museums (see Route 10). The next part of the main road is known as Kensington Gore; on the corner is the ROYAL GEOGRAPHICAL SOCIETY (VI, B 3), founded in 1830 and housed since 1913 in a building by R. Norman Shaw (1874). Outside are statues of David Livingstone (d. 1873) and Sir Ernest Shackleton (d. 1922), and in the forecourt is a bust of Sir Clements Markham (d. 1916), the historian of Peru. The small but interesting museum contains a model of Mount Everest, Sir John Hunt's Everest diary, and relics of Livingstone, Stanley, Shackleton, Captain Scott, Franklin, and other famous explorers. The map room has a collection of over 500,000 maps and atlases which may be consulted without obligation by visitors. ALBERT HALL MANSIONS beyond, also by Shaw (1879), were the first block of flats built in London.

The ROYAL ALBERT HALL (VI, B 2), built in 1867–71 to the designs of Captain Francis Fowke, is in the form of an immense oval amphitheatre, 273 ft across and 155 ft high, covered by a glass dome. The terracotta frieze illustrates the Triumphs of Art and Science. Capable of seating about 8,000 people, the hall is much used for concerts, balls, boxing, public meetings, and other events. The vast interior, which has three tiers of boxes with a balcony and gallery above, is open to visitors when not in use. The organ, by 'Father' Willis, with nearly 10,000 pipes, is one of the largest in Britain.

Facing the hall, in Kensington Gardens, is the ALBERT MEMORIAL, designed by Sir Gilbert Scott and erected in 1863–76 (at a cost of £120,000) as the national monument to Prince Albert of Saxe-Coburg-Gotha (1819–61), the consort of Queen Victoria. Under an ornate and lofty Gothic canopy, 175 ft high, is a seated gilt-bronze figure of the prince (15 ft high) by J. H. Foley, holding the catalogue of the Great Exhibition of 1851. Around the pedestal are fine marble reliefs of artists and men of letters of every period, 178 in all, by H. H. Armstead and J. B. Philip. At the angles of the pedestal are groups representing Agriculture, Manufactures, Commerce, and Engineering, and at the outer corners of the steps are further groups symbolizing the continents of Europe, Asia, Africa, and America.

The Albert Hall stands on the site of Gore House, famous as the residence in 1836–49 of Lady Blessington, whose salon attracted many eminent men of letters, art, and science. Behind the hall, facing the Royal College of Music (Route 10), is the MEMORIAL TO THE 1851 EXHIBITION, with a poor statue of the Prince Consort by Joseph Durham (1863). On the west of the hall are the ROYAL COLLEGE OF ORGANISTS, founded in 1864 and housed in an exotically decorated building by H. H. Cole (1875), and the ROYAL COLLEGE OF ART, founded in 1837 for training in the fine arts and industrial design, and occupying a rather severe building by H. T. Cadbury-Brown, Sir Hugh Casson, and R. Y. Goodden (1960–2), with an exhibition hall.

At the junction of Kensington Road and the broad QUEEN'S GATE is an equestrian statue by Boehm of Lord Napier of Magdala (d. 1890), soldier and historian of the Peninsular War. Sir Jacob Epstein, the sculptor, died in 1959 at his home at No. 18 HYDE PARK GATE, farther on, and Sir Leslie Stephen, scholar and mountaineer, died in 1904 at No. 22 (then No. 11). Farther west are PALACE GATE, where Sir John Millais died in 1896 at No. 2, a house designed for him by Philip Hardwick (1878), and DE VERE GARDENS, where No. 29 was the last home (1887–9) of Robert Browning (d. at Venice) and Henry James lived in 1886–1902 at No. 34. The Broad Walk of Kensington Gardens (Route 12) opens on the right beyond Palace Gate, and farther on there is a view through the trees of Kensington Palace.

Kensington Road is extended by KENSINGTON HIGH STREET (VI, B 1), the bustling shopping centre of the royal borough of Kensington. On the right is the gate of KENSINGTON PALACE GARDENS, an attractive private road shaded by plane-trees and lined with opulent mansions. No. 1 Palace Green, at the south end, was built by Philip Webb in 1863 for the Earl of Carlisle, and No. 2 was designed for himself in 1861 by W. M. Thackeray, who died here in 1863.

Thackeray wrote *Vanity Fair*, *Pendennis*, and *Esmond* at No. 16 YOUNG STREET, on the other side of the High Street, where he lived in 1846–53. Young Street opens into KENSINGTON SQUARE, built late in the 17th century and a fashionable quarter when the court was at the near-by Kensington Palace. On all sides except the east there survives a variety of old houses, though some are much altered: notable are Nos. 11–12 (originally one house), where Talleyrand, the French statesman, lived in 1792–4. Sir Hubert Parry (d. 1918), the composer, lived at No. 17 and John Stuart Mill, the philosopher, at No. 18 (in 1837–51), on the south side, and No. 33 (N.T.; no admission), built in 1695 on the west side, was the home of Mrs Patrick Campbell (d. 1940), the actress, friend of Bernard Shaw.

At the corner of Church Street is the parish church of ST MARY ABBOTS (VI, B 1), so called from its connexion with the abbey of Abingdon (Berks), which owned the manor of Kensington in 1260. There was a church on this site before 1100; the present church in the Decorated style, one of the best designs of Sir Gilbert Scott, was built in 1869–72. The lofty spire, 278 ft high, was completed in 1879 and the cloistral approach in 1893, and the church, well restored in 1956 after war damage, retains a pulpit of 1697 and some old monuments. James Mill (d. 1836), the Utilitarian philosopher, father of J. S. Mill, is buried near the west end.

CHURCH STREET, which leads north to Notting Hill (Route 12), is well known for its antique shops. Several terraces of 18th-century houses will be found in the streets to the left, particularly in HOLLAND STREET, where Walter Crane (d. 1915), the artist, lived at No. 12. Church Walk, with a quiet garden, leads back to Kensington High Street.

On the south side of High Street are several large stores, of which Messrs DERRY AND TOMS has a pleasant roof-garden with a tea-room and a terrace commanding a wide view over south-west London. Opposite is KENSINGTON TOWN HALL (1878) and to the west is High Street, Kensington, station.

A new group of municipal buildings to designs of E. Vincent Harris, and including a town hall and concert hall, is being erected between Hornton Street and Campden Hill Road, to the north-west. The first building to be completed, the KENSINGTON CENTRAL LIBRARY, was opened in 1960. Sir Henry Newbolt, the poet, died in 1938 at No. 29 CAMPDEN HILL ROAD, which ascends to the QUEEN ELIZABETH COLLEGE for women studying domestic science, nutrition, etc. built in 1915 by Adams, Holden, and Pearson and now part of London University. Campden Hill, a road farther up, leads west to Holland Walk (see below), passing HOLLY LODGE, where Lord Macaulay lived from 1856 until his death in 1859.

On the left farther west is Earls Court Road (see below) and on the right is HOLLAND PARK, a sylvan retreat on the slope of a hill, skirted on the east by Holland Walk. At the south end of the park is the COMMONWEALTH INSTITUTE, founded in 1887 (as the Imperial Institute) to commemorate Queen Victoria's Golden Jubilee, and moved from Imperial Institute Road in 1962 to a striking new building by Sir Robert Matthew and Johnson-Marshall, the roof of which is shaped, very unusually, in the form of five interconnected hyperbolic parabolas and covered in copper.

The primary objects of the institute are to assist the economic development of the natural resources of the British Commonwealth and to provide an exhibition showing its scenery, life, and industries. The exhibition galleries contain interesting models, dioramas, etc., illustrating the natural features and resources of the Commonwealth, and examples of its products and handicrafts. The building also includes a library and reading room, a restaurant, a spacious art gallery for temporary exhibitions, and a cinema where relevant films are shown daily.

In the middle of the park is the east wing, practically all that survives, of HOLLAND HOUSE, a historic and once beautiful Jacobean mansion unhappily damaged by bombing in 1941 and then left derelict.

Begun in 1605 for Sir Walter Cope, Chamberlain of the Exchequer, and doubtfully attributed to John Thorpe, the house passed by marriage to Sir Henry Rich, created Earl of Holland (a district of Lincolnshire) in 1624, but executed in 1649. The second earl became in 1673 the fifth Earl of Warwick. The widow of the third earl was married in 1716 to Joseph Addison, the essayist, who has described the then rural setting in his letters and who died here in 1719. The house was sold in 1768 to Henry Fox, afterwards Baron Holland, the father of Charles James Fox; and under the third Baron Holland (1773–1840), the politician's nephew, it became famous as the 'favourite resort of wits and beauties, of painters and poets, of scholars, philosophers, and statesmen'. The estate was sold to the L.C.C. in 1952.

The remaining wing of the house, partly restored, dates from about 1640. It has been incorporated in a Youth Hostel, new buildings for which, designed by Sir Hugh Casson and Neville Condor, were completed in 1959. On the west are the attractive gardens, with the Orangery beyond (used occasionally for exhibitions of sculpture).

Earls Court Road (compare above) leads to the large exhibition buildings (p. 74) and the huge EMPRESS STATE BUILDING, 28 storeys and over 300 ft high, completed in 1962 to the designs of Stone, Toms and Partners, and now occupied by the Admiralty.

Kensington High Street goes on to EDWARDES SQUARE (to the left) and EARLS TERRACE (on the main road), delightful terraces of the early 19th century. Leigh Hunt, the essayist, lived at No. 32 Edwardes Square in 1840–51. In MELBURY ROAD, on the right, Holman Hunt, the artist, died in 1910 at No. 18, while No. 6 (Little Holland House) was built by G. F. Watts in 1876, after the demolition of Old Little Holland House (where he had spent his brief married life with Ellen Terry, 1864–5), and he lived here until 1903. LEIGHTON HOUSE, in Holland Park Road, near by, was built in 1866 (with the assistance of George Aitchison) by Lord Leighton, the artist, who lived here until his death in 1896. The house, with its contents, was given to the Kensington Borough Council in 1926. The remarkable Arab Hall is decorated with 14th–16th-century Persian tiles and a mosaic frieze by Walter Crane, and has beautiful damascene stained glass windows. Parts of the walls elsewhere are faced with tiles by William de Morgan. Visitors may see the studios, containing paintings and drawings by Lord Leighton and other Kensington artists, and the delightfully secluded garden should not be overlooked. Loan exhibitions, lectures, etc., are held frequently in the house.

12 Hyde Park and Kensington Gardens

Plan I, F 1–VII, B 3

STATIONS: HYDE PARK CORNER (Plan VII, B 2) and KNIGHTSBRIDGE (VII, B 1), on the Piccadilly line, and HIGH STREET, KENSINGTON (beyond VI, B 1), on the Circle and District lines, for the south side; MARBLE ARCH (II, E 2), LANCASTER GATE (I, E 3) and QUEENSWAY (I, F 1), on the Central line, and BAYSWATER (I, E 1), on the Circle and District lines, for the north side. — MOTOR-BUSES in Knightsbridge and Kensington Road, see Routes 10, 11; in Park Lane and East Carriage Road, see Route 9; Nos. 12 and 88 in Bayswater Road.

HYDE PARK and KENSINGTON GARDENS are open daily, but the gates of the Gardens are closed at dusk. — MOTOR-CARS and Cycles are allowed on all the roads in Hyde Park, except that on the north side of the Serpentine; the speed limit is 30 m.p.h.

ADMISSION to KENSINGTON PALACE and the LONDON MUSEUM, see p. 349.

REFRESHMENT PAVILIONS in Hyde Park and Kensington Gardens (see below), open in summer for light luncheons and teas. — BANDS play at the bandstands on Sundays from late May to early September, in Hyde Park from 3 to 4.30 and 6.30 to 8, in Kensington Gardens from 3 to 4.30 only.

BOATING on the Serpentine, daily, 2/- to 5/- per hour. — FISHING from the shore only. — BATHING in the Serpentine, daily, all the year round: May–September, mixed bathing, from 6 a.m. to 7.30 p.m. (9d; Saturdays, Sundays, and Bank Holidays, 1/-; 6 to 10 a.m., free); children, Monday–Friday 4.30 to 6.30, Saturdays and Bank Holidays 1 to 6.30, Sundays 2 to 5.30 (3d); October–April, men only, 6.30 to 8.30 a.m. (free). — BOWLING and putting greens in Hyde Park (near Alexandra Gate). — HORSE JUMPING enclosure in Rotten Row.

HYDE PARK, with an area of 360 acres, is bounded on the north by Bayswater Road, stretching from Marble Arch to Notting Hill Gate, on the east by the long-fashionable Park Lane, and on the south by Knightsbridge and Kensington Road, leading from Hyde Park Corner to the Alexandra Gate. On the west it is conterminous with KENSINGTON GARDENS (275 acres), once the private domain of Kensington Palace, but now equally accessible to the public, so that the two form one continuous open space of well over 600 acres, the largest in London. Both parks have many fine trees and are the haunt of a surprising variety of birds, natural sanctuaries for which are provided by some of the shrubberies. The complete perambulation of the parks involves a rural walk of about 4 miles.

Curving diagonally across both parks is the SERPENTINE, an artificial lake of about 40 acres formed by damming the West Bourne, a stream that has now practically disappeared. The lake is the home of numerous waterfowl and is frequented every morning of the year by hardy bathers; the part within Kensington Gardens is known as the Long Water. The motor-road from the Victoria Gate (on the north, near Lancaster Gate) to the Alexandra Gate, crossing the Serpentine and following the boundary between the two parks, forms a pleasant and convenient method of reaching Kensington and the South Kensington museums from Paddington and north-west London. On the south side of Kensington Gardens is the Albert Memorial (Route 11) and on the west is Kensington Palace, long a royal residence but now partly occupied by the London Museum.

The manor of Hyde was the possession of Westminster Abbey from the Norman Conquest until the Dissolution (1536), when it was taken by Henry VIII and converted into a royal deer-park. In 1635 Charles I threw this open to the public and it quickly became a fashionable rendezvous; the Ring, a drive and racecourse laid out, was much frequented by the carriages of society. Later the park became the resort of duellists, while the roads across it were infested with robbers, but under the earlier Georges it was taken in hand again, and in 1730 Caroline of Anspach, the queen of George II, had a series of ponds converted into the Serpentine. It was in this lake that Harriet Westbrook, first wife of the poet Shelley, committed suicide in 1816. The park was the scene in 1851 of the Great Exhibition, the inspiration of the Prince Consort, which occupied a site of about 20 acres between Rotten Row and Knightsbridge. The famous exhibition building of glass and iron, designed by Sir Joseph Paxton, was afterwards moved to Sydenham and re-erected as the Crystal Palace (see p. 490).

Kensington Gardens owe their present appearance mainly to Queen Caroline, under whose direction they were laid out and the noble avenues of trees planted by Henry Wise and Charles Bridgman.

From HYDE PARK CORNER (Route 9), the south-east entrance to the park, three roads set out: that on the left (south) leads to the Alexandra Gate and the Albert Memorial, that in the centre to the Serpentine (see below), and that on the right (East Carriage Road) to MARBLE ARCH (see Route 14), skirting the east side of the park, with exits to Park Lane at the Stanhope and Grosvenor Gates (Route 9). A new road, connecting Knightsbridge with the East Carriage Road, was built in 1959–62 to relieve the congestion around Hyde Park Corner. On the left of this, facing the entrance to the park, is the ACHILLES STATUE, a colossal bronze figure by Westmacott, cast from captured French cannon and erected in 1822 to the Duke of Wellington and his companions in arms 'by their countrywomen'. The statue, however, is not an Achilles, but an adaptation of one of the antique horse-tamers on the Monte Cavallo at Rome.

Between the two leftward roads is ROTTEN ROW (VI, B 3– VII, B 2; perhaps originally 'Route du Roi'), a famous sandy track nearly a mile long, reserved for horse-riders. The paths on either side were long the fashionable rendezvous after church on Sunday mornings. A path opposite the ALBERT GATE (which affords access to Knightsbridge) passes the Dell, a charming glade below the east end of the Serpentine, and ascends to the SERPENTINE ROAD (once called the Ladies' Mile). This skirts the north side of the lake, passing the boathouse (near the Royal Humane Society's 'receiving house'), and leads to the road connecting the Victoria and Alexandra Gates. To the north is the RING TEA HOUSE, and some distance west is a memorial to W. H. Hudson (d. 1922), the naturalist author, comprising a 'bird sanctuary' and a much-criticized sculptured panel by Sir Jacob Epstein (1925) representing 'Rima', the Spirit of Nature in Hudson's *Green Mansions*.

The road crosses the Serpentine by the fine RENNIE'S BRIDGE (VI, A 3), built in 1826 by the brothers Sir John and George Rennie. The enchanting view eastward includes the distant towers of Westminster Abbey and the Houses of Parliament. On the south shore of the lake is the Bathing Station, while the road going on to the Alexandra Gate passes near the REFRESHMENT PAVILION. The FLOWER WALK beyond this, running west to the Broad Walk, is one of the most attractive parts of Kensington Gardens. The path on the west shore of the LONG WATER, the extension of the Serpentine, passes the PETER PAN STATUE, a delightful and popular representation by Sir George Frampton of the hero of Sir J. M. Barrie's play. At the north end of the lake are a paved garden with fountains and a pavilion, and a statue of Edward Jenner (d. 1823), the discoverer of vaccination; and beyond to the north-east is QUEEN ANNE'S ALCOVE, attributed to Sir Christopher Wren.

The path leading south-west from the fountains, leaving on the right an obelisk to J. H. Speke (d. 1864), the African explorer, ascends to a striking bronze equestrian figure by G. F. Watts (1903) representing PHYSICAL ENERGY. (A replica of this forms part of the memorial to Cecil Rhodes on the slope of Table Mountain, near Cape Town.) From the sculpture an avenue runs west to the ROUND POND, a favourite resort of model yachtsmen, and beyond this is the BROAD WALK (I, F 1–VI, B 1), running north and south in front of **Kensington Palace**, which, however, is half-hidden by trees. The elms that were once the pride of the walk were felled when they became dangerous and have been replaced by limes. In front of the palace is a poor statue of Queen Victoria by her daughter, Princess Louise (1893), and in the gardens on the south of the house is a statue of William III, presented in 1907 to Edward VII by the Emperor William II of Germany. This is seen from the path that leads out to Kensington Palace Gardens (Route 11). The path to the north of the Victoria statue passes an attractive SUNK GARDEN, enclosed by walks of pleached limes, while farther north, beside the drive leading from the Orme Square Gate to the **London Museum** entrance is the ORANGERY, designed in 1705 by Wren (or possibly Vanbrugh) for Queen Anne and a notable example of the brickwork of the period.

The avenue running north from Kensington Palace leads to BAYSWATER ROAD (I, F 1–II, E 2), which skirts Kensington Gardens and Hyde Park on this side. It runs west to NOTTING HILL GATE, a busy traffic centre at the north end of Kensington Church Street (Route 11), and east to Marble Arch, and is, in fact, the westward continuation of Oxford Street. LANCASTER GATE (I, E 2), in this direction, consists of imposing blocks of houses built in 1857–65 by Sancton Wood and others. Lancaster Terrace, a little farther on, leads to WESTBOURNE TERRACE (named after the stream which formerly flowed hence to Hyde Park) and SUSSEX GARDENS, wide boulevards (by S. P. Cockerell) that are interesting as examples of early-19th-century town planning (the best of the houses are at the north-east end of Sussex Gardens, near Edgware Road; see Route 16). Facing the junction of the roads is ST JAMES'S CHURCH (I, E 2, 3), the parish church of Paddington, rebuilt in a spacious Gothic style in 1883 by G. E. Street, who retained the tower of 1843. The fine west window, by Goddard and Gibbs (1952), is a war memorial introducing persons connected with Paddington. Lord Baden-Powell (pronounced 'Poel'), the founder of the Boy Scouts, was born in 1857 at No. 11 Stanhope Terrace (formerly No. 6 Stanhope Street), near Sussex Square, farther east.

No. 1 HYDE PARK GARDENS, parallel to Bayswater Road, is the head-quarters of the ROYAL SOCIETY OF LITERATURE, founded in 1823. Nearer to Marble Arch is the little CHAPEL OF THE ASCENSION (II, E 1), built by H. P. Horne in an Italian style (1893) but completely gutted during the war. Adjoining on the east is the restored mortuary chapel of the cemetery of St George's, Hanover Square, which lies behind and can be seen (with the chapel) on application to the caretaker in the adjacent cottage. The cemetery, opened in 1764, is now partly used as a recreation ground and contains the range of the Royal Toxophilite Society, founded in 1781. Near the middle of the west wall is the grave of Laurence Sterne (d. 1768), the author. His body is said to have been exhumed and sold to the professor of anatomy at Cambridge, who, however, recognized it and had it returned. No. 10 Hyde Park Place, to the east, is claimed to be the smallest house in London. Stanhope Place, farther on, leads to CON-NAUGHT SQUARE, with unspoiled terraces built about 1828.

13 From Hyde Park Corner to Marble Arch via Mayfair

Plan VII, B 3–II, E 2

STATIONS: HYDE PARK CORNER (Plan VII, B 2) and GREEN PARK (VIII, A 1), on the Piccadilly line; MARBLE ARCH (II, E 2) and BOND STREET (II, E 3), on the Central line. — MOTOR-BUSES in Park Lane, see Route 9; in Oxford Street, see Route 14.

ADMISSION to No. 44, GROSVENOR SQUARE, occasionally, on previous application.

This roundabout route from HYDE PARK CORNER follows Hamilton Place and Park Lane (see Route 9) at first, then turns right into CURZON STREET (VII, A 3) to thread its way through MAYFAIR, long the most fashionable part of London, and still of much interest for its associations with the distinguished people who have resided here. Curzon Street is one of several streets that retain some old houses among the modern blocks of offices. At

No. 19, on the right, Lord Beaconsfield died in 1881, while Lord Reading, the Liberal statesman, died in 1935 at No. 32. CREWE HOUSE, on the left, is a very pleasant though restored Georgian mansion, built in 1735 by Edward Shepherd and later the town house of the Marquess of Crewe.

Hertford Street opposite leads to SHEPHERD MARKET (VII, A 3), a little quarter of quaint and narrow streets, laid out by Edward Shepherd (1735) on part of the fairground where the popular May Fair that gave its name to the district had been held since 1688. The fair was revived here, after a lapse of nearly 200 years, in 1956. In Curzon Street, farther east, are the imposing THIRD CHURCH OF CHRIST SCIENTIST (by Lanchester and Rickards, 1912) and the huge office of the MINISTRY OF EDUCATION, established in 1944.

Queen Street, on the left of Curzon Street, leads to CHARLES STREET, which has several interesting houses. No. 16, a fine house of the mid 18th century facing Queen Street, is the GUARDS' CLUB, founded in 1813. Sydney Smith, the author and wit, lived in 1837–9 at No. 32, to the left; the Earl of Rosebery, prime minister, was born in 1847 at No. 20, and William IV lived here for a time when Duke of Clarence. Portland House (No. 19) is the home of the PORTLAND CLUB, established in 1816, while Dartmouth House (No. 37), to the right, is the headquarters of the ENGLISH-SPEAKING UNION, founded in 1918 to draw together the English-speaking peoples in the interest of world peace and offering assistance to American and other overseas visitors. The facilities include a club, library, and information bureau; and lectures, visits, etc., are arranged.

In this direction, Charles Street leads to BERKELEY SQUARE (II, F 3; pronounced 'Barkly'), laid out in 1739–47 and named from Berkeley House (later Devonshire House), part of whose grounds it covered. The fine plane-trees in the gardens were planted about 1790. The square was long one of the most aristocratic in London, but its character has been despoiled by the building of immense blocks of offices. LANSDOWNE HOUSE, on the south side, stands on the site of the town house of the Earl of Shelburne (later Marquess of Lansdowne), the prime minister who recognized the independence of the United States (1783), while BERKELEY SQUARE HOUSE, on the east side, covers the site of the house (No. 17 Bruton Street) where Queen Elizabeth II was born in 1926. Of old houses the best (on the west side) are No. 44, designed by William Kent (1744), and Nos. 45–6, with good 18th-century stone fronts; Lord Clive, founder of the British Empire in India, committed suicide at No. 45 in 1774.

BRUTON STREET leads to Bond Street (p. 134), while Berkeley Street runs from the south-east angle of the square to Piccadilly (Route 7). In Fitzmaurice Place, south-west of the square, No. 9 is the LANSDOWNE CLUB (founded in 1935), whose premises are now shared with the ROYAL AERO CLUB, established in 1901. Hill Street, on the west side of the square, gives access to Farm Street on the north side of which is the rather florid Roman Catholic CHURCH OF THE JESUIT FATHERS (1849), noted for its music. This street is extended to Park Lane by South Street, which crosses SOUTH AUDLEY STREET. No. 71, on the corner, with a portico, is an unusual house of 1744 attributed to Isaac Ware. No. 74, just below, is the ALPINE CLUB, founded in 1857, and No. 14, on the other side, was the home of Sir Richard Westmacott (d. 1856), the sculptor. To the right in the street is the pleasant little GROSVENOR CHAPEL (II, F 3), built in 1730 and adopted as their church by the United States Armed Forces in 1939–45.

From the north-west corner of Berkeley Square, Mount Street and Carlos Place (on the right) lead to the large GROSVENOR SQUARE (II, E, F 3), laid out during the reign of George II and named after Sir Richard Grosvenor (d. 1732). It has been associated with the United States since John Adams, first minister to Britain (1785–8) and later President, came to live at No. 9 (now derelict), in the north-east corner. On the west side is the exciting new building (1960) of the UNITED STATES EMBASSY, designed by Eero Saarinen (an American architect of Finnish extraction) and surmounted by an American eagle with a wing span of 35 ft. On the north side of the gardens is a fine statue by Sir W. Reid Dick (1948) in memory of Franklin D. Roosevelt, President in 1933–45. No. 12 on this side, occupied in 1868–73 by Bulwer Lytton, the novelist, and No. 44, on the south side, are two of the few good survivals of the 18th-century houses that once lined the square, which has been almost completely rebuilt in the last 30 years.

In BROOK STREET, which leads from the north-east angle of the square to Bond Street, are the SAVILE CLUB (No. 69), founded in 1868, and the old-established CLARIDGE'S HOTEL, one of London's most famous hotels-de-luxe. No. 25 (much altered) was the home of Handel for nearly forty years until his death in 1759, and *Messiah* and many other masterpieces were written here. In DAVIES STREET, which Brook Street crosses, No. 65 is the head-office of the BRITISH COUNCIL, established in 1934 to promote a wider knowledge abroad of British life, thought, and culture.

From the north-west corner of Grosvenor Square, NORTH AUDLEY STREET leads to Oxford Street (Route 14), passing ST MARK'S CHURCH (II, E 2), rebuilt in 1878 by Blomfield in a Victorian Renaissance style, though retaining the porch and narthex of a church of 1828. Sir Hudson Lowe (d. 1844), governor of Elba during the banishment of Napoleon, is buried here. Sydney Smith died in 1845 at No. 59 GREEN STREET, which starts opposite the church and reaches Park Lane a little south of MARBLE ARCH (Route 14).

14 From Marble Arch to St Giles Circus (Oxford Street)

Plan II, E 2–III, D 2

STATIONS: MARBLE ARCH (Plan II, E 2), BOND STREET (II, E 3), OXFORD CIRCUS (III, E 1), and TOTTENHAM COURT ROAD (III, D 2), all on the Central line. Oxford Circus is also on the Bakerloo line, and Tottenham Court Road on the Northern line. — MOTOR-BUSES Nos. 7, 8, 23, and 73 in Oxford Street from Marble Arch to St Giles Circus; Nos. 6, 12, 13, 15, 60, 88, 113, and 137 from Marble Arch to Oxford Circus only; Nos. 25 and 32 from Bond Street to St Giles Circus; Nos. 59, 153, and 159 in Wigmore Street. For other buses to Marble Arch, see Routes 9, 12, 16; to Portman Square (Baker Street), see Route 16; to Oxford Circus, see Route 15; to St Giles Circus, see Routes 18, 23.

ADMISSION to HOME HOUSE (Courtauld Institute of Art), Saturday only, 10 to 1, during term; Monday–Friday only, 10 to 5, in vacation (free; closed in August and for ten days at Easter and Christmas); to the WALLACE COLLECTION, see p. 435.

OXFORD STREET (II, E 2–III D 2), the busiest shopping street in London, is also one of the principal thoroughfares connecting the West End with the City. It runs from Marble Arch, at its west extremity, to St Giles Circus, at the junction of Charing Cross Road and Tottenham Court Road, from which it is continued by New Oxford Street and High Holborn towards St Paul's Cathedral and the Bank of England (Route 23). The MARBLE ARCH (II, E 2) was designed in 1828 by John Nash, who is believed to have been inspired by the Arch of Constantine at Rome. Intended as the main gateway to Buckingham Palace, it is popularly supposed to have been too narrow to admit the state coach and in 1851 it was moved to its present site as the north-east entrance to Hyde Park (Route 12). The reliefs on the south side are by E. H. Baily, on the north by Westmacott, and the arch has excellent wrought-iron gates.

In 1908 the park railings were set back to allow room for the traffic to pass on this side, and in 1960 the Marble Arch was further divorced from the park by a new road linking up with the East Carriage Road (p. 159) to relieve the appalling traffic congestion around the arch and in Park Lane (Route 9), which runs south to Hyde Park Corner and Piccadilly. An underground car park (entrances from Park Lane and North Carriage Drive), with room for 1,070 vehicles in an area of about 7 acres, was opened in 1962. The open space inside the park is well known as ORATORS' CORNER, where those with a message or a grievance may exercise their right of free speech unimpeded by the law, if not by hecklers.

Bayswater Road (Route 12) leads west from Marble Arch to North Kensington, and Edgware Road north-west to Paddington and the west end of Marylebone Road (compare Route 16). A tablet on the south at the beginning of Bayswater Road recalls that this is the site of TYBURN, for nearly 600 years the famous place for public executions, to which the condemned were brought through the gaping crowds from Newgate Prison or the Tower. The first recorded execution took place in 1196, the last in 1783, and among those who suffered here (usually 'hanged, drawn, and quartered') were Perkin Warbeck, the pretender (1499); Elizabeth Barton, the 'holy maid of Kent' (1534); leaders of the Pilgrimage of Grace (1537); Edmund Campion (1581) and other Jesuit martyrs; Oliver Plunket, archbishop of Armagh (1681); and the notorious highwaymen, Claude Duval (1670) and Jack Sheppard (1724). In 1661 the bodies of Cromwell, Ireton, and Bradshaw, exhumed from Westminster Abbey, were gibbeted and beheaded here before being buried at the foot of the gallows. A permanent gallows, the 'Tyburn Tree', stood from 1571 to 1759 at the place indicated by a stone in the roadway at the foot of Edgware Road.

Oxford Street is named after Robert Harley, first Earl of Oxford (d. 1724), the statesman whose collections formed part of the nucleus of the British Museum, and who held the manor of St Marylebone to the north. Though famous for its large stores and in particular for its drapery shops, it is of little interest otherwise, and a pleasanter route, taking very little longer, may be threaded through the streets to the north. Portman Street, on the left before SELFRIDGE'S, the largest store in London, founded in 1909 by H. Gordon Selfridge (d. 1947), an American businessman, leads to PORTMAN SQUARE (II, D, E 2), a fashionable quarter laid out after 1761 and still retaining many of its fine 18th-century houses. No. 20, on the north side, is HOME HOUSE, one of the most pleasing designs of Robert Adam, built in 1773–7 for Elizabeth, Countess of Home, daughter of a West Indian merchant.

The rooms are notable for their exquisite stucco decoration, with small paintings by Antonio Zucchi and Angelica Kauffmann, and their carved marble fireplaces and inlaid doors. The unusual circular staircase well rises the full height of the building and is covered by a spherical dome with a skylight. The house was carefully restored after 1927 for Samuel Courtauld (d. 1948), the textile manufacturer and a noted art-collector, who on the death in 1931 of his wife, Elizabeth, a well-known patron of music, presented it to the University of London for use as the COURTAULD INSTITUTE OF ART, established in 1932 for the teaching of art history in all its aspects. The paintings, etc., also given have been transferred to galleries in Woburn Square (p. 195). No. 20 is also the headquarters of the BRITISH ARCHAEOLOGICAL ASSOCIATION, established in 1843.

Other good houses will be found in the streets and squares to the west and north-west of Portman Square (Montagu Square, etc.; compare Route 16), and especially in GLOUCESTER PLACE, built about 1810 and preserving some of its old lamp-brackets, BAKER STREET is an important thoroughfare leading north to Marylebone Road and Regent's Park (see Route 16). ORCHARD STREET, running south from the square, is extended beyond Oxford Street by North Audley Street, which leads to Grosvenor Square (Route 13), while WIGMORE STREET, a long uninteresting thoroughfare, runs east to Cavendish Square (compare below), passing the WIGMORE HALL, opened in 1901 and used for concerts, etc.

Fitzhardinge Street leads east from the north side of the square to the smaller MANCHESTER SQUARE (II, D 2, 3), built in 1776–88 and little spoiled. On the north side rises HERTFORD HOUSE, the home of the magnificent **Wallace Collection**.

Manchester Street, on the west of the house, passes ROBERT ADAM STREET, with good, if humble, 18th-century houses, and crosses George Street and BLANDFORD STREET, at No. 48 in which (now a shop) Michael Faraday was apprenticed in 1804–12 to a bookbinder. In GEORGE STREET are Durrant's Hotel, a well-restored 18th-century mansion, and the Roman Catholic church of ST JAMES'S, SPANISH PLACE, a lofty cathedral-like building in the Early English style, by Joseph Goldie (1890). It takes its name from its predecessor in Spanish Place (leading back to Manchester Square), in which Captain Marryat (d. 1848), the writer of boys' stories, lived at No. 3.

Hinde Street, going on east from Manchester Square, is prolonged by Bentinck Street to Welbeck Street. On the right, at the

corner of Mandeville Place, is the TRINITY COLLEGE OF
MUSIC, founded in 1872, and now a teaching school of London
University. WELBECK STREET has many 18th-century houses;
in one of these (No. 29, to the left) Thomas Woolner, the sculptor
and poet, lived in 1860–92, while Anthony Trollope, the novelist,
died in 1882 at No. 34. QUEEN ANNE STREET, in which No. 56
is the ROYAL ASIATIC SOCIETY (founded in 1823), leads to the
right, crossing Wimpole Street and Harley Street, well known for
the consulting rooms of many leading physicians and surgeons.

Henry Hallam, the historian, lived in 1819–40 at No. 67 WIMPOLE
STREET, but the house (No. 50) which Elizabeth Barrett left secretly in 1846
to marry Robert Browning has unfortunately been rebuilt. J. M. W. Turner
lived in 1803–12 at No. 64 HARLEY STREET, which runs south to Cavendish
Square, passing QUEEN'S COLLEGE, founded in 1848 by F. D. Maurice
and the oldest college in England for women. The many well-known pupils
have included Gertrude Bell, Octavia Hill, and Katherine Mansfield. The
college now occupies also No. 47, once the home of Florence Nightingale.
No. 2, at the corner of Cavendish Square, though partly rebuilt, has a fine
doorframe carried up to enclose the window above.

CAVENDISH SQUARE (II, D 3) was laid out after 1719 by
John Prince for Edward Harley, son of the first Earl of Oxford,
and some of its original houses still survive. Nos. 11–14, the two
noble pairs of houses with classical façades on the north side, were
built later, about 1770. They are now the CONVENT OF THE
HOLY CHILD, and the arch connecting them carries a large
bronze Madonna by Sir Jacob Epstein which the sculptor called
his 'passport to eternity'. Lord Nelson lived in 1787 at No. 5, on
the east side of the square, while No. 20, a house partly of 1729 at
the south-west corner, long the home of the Earl of Oxford and
Asquith (d. 1928), the Liberal statesman, is now the COWDRAY
CLUB for nurses and professional women (founded 1922). Alongside and above the staircase are fine murals painted about 1730
and well restored in 1955. On the south side of the gardens in the
square, notable for their fine trees, is a statue of Lord George
Bentinck (d. 1848), the politician.

From this side Henrietta Place runs west, passing the ROYAL COLLEGE
OF NURSING (1926, extended 1934) and the ROYAL SOCIETY OF MEDI-
CINE (founded in 1805), in a building of 1912 by Sir John Belcher. Close
by is ST PETER'S, VERE STREET (II, D, E 3), a delightful little church by
James Gibbs (1721–4), the architect of St Martin-in-the-Fields, and des-

cribed by Sir John Summerson as a 'miniature forecast' of that church. Vere Street leads back to Oxford Street opposite Bond Street (Route 7). Bond Street underground station, however, is 200 yds farther west, nearly opposite the entrance to STRATFORD PLACE, a cul-de-sac built originally in 1774 by Richard Edwin in the style of Robert Adam. Stratford House, at its north end, still unspoiled, was formerly Derby House, a town house of the Earls of Derby, and is now the ORIENTAL CLUB, founded in 1824, mainly for those engaged in the East Indian trade.

In Chandos Street, running north from the square, is the quaint building of the MEDICAL SOCIETY OF LONDON, founded in 1773. CHANDOS HOUSE, facing down the street, is a fine stone-fronted mansion of Robert Adam (1771). There are other good 18th-century houses in Queen Anne Street, which leads to the left (see above), while in Mansfield Street to the north-west, a new building for the ROYAL COLLEGE OF MIDWIVES (founded in 1881) was erected in 1956–7. The third Earl Stanhope (1753–1816), 'reformer and inventor', lived at No. 20, nearly opposite.

Holles Street leads south from Cavendish Square to reach Oxford Street opposite the entrance to Hanover Square and a little west of Oxford Circus (III, D, E 1; Route 15). MARGARET STREET, starting from the south-east corner of the square, crosses Regent Street and GREAT PORTLAND STREET, a long thoroughfare with the shops of many motor-dealers, running north to Euston Road (see Route 16). The rest of the route, through a poorer quarter, is of less interest, though it is always quicker to traverse the side streets rather than face the crowds in Oxford Street. GREAT TITCHFIELD STREET, the next street crossed, is (with the neighbouring streets) the centre for wholesale furriers and costumiers. Farther on in Margaret Street is ALL SAINTS' CHURCH (III, D 1), a rather florid Gothic church in dark red brick by William Butterfield, consecrated in 1859. It has a lofty spire, 227 ft high, and an immense reredos by William Dyce.

Wells Street, at the end of Margaret Street, leads left to the parallel Mortimer Street, to the right in which is the large MIDDLESEX HOSPITAL (III, D 1), founded in 1745 and rebuilt in 1929. Rudyard Kipling died here in 1936. On the north-east (in Howland Street) are the new buildings (by Sidney Cusdin) of the medical school (founded in 1835), the first part of which was opened in 1959. A slender tower, 580 ft high, for television and radio telephony, is being built (1963) for the Post Office above the Museum telephone exchange north of Howland Street. The tallest building in Britain, it will have a revolving restaurant near the top.

On the south the Middlesex Hospital faces down BERNERS STREET, which has several 18th-century houses (Nos. 20 and 56 with stone doorways by Sir William Chambers). Mortimer Street is extended by Goodge Street to Tottenham Court Road, crossing CHARLOTTE STREET, the axis of a neighbourhood popular with artists in the 19th century and now containing many foreign restaurants. John Constable, the landscape-painter, died in 1837 at No. 76, one of the surviving 18th-century houses. The SCALA THEATRE, close by, was rebuilt in 1904. From the south end of the street, Rathbone Place goes on to Oxford Street some distance west of ST GILES CIRCUS (III, D 2), while Percy Street, built in 1764–70 and retaining some of its original doorways, leads left to TOTTENHAM COURT ROAD (Route 18).

15 From Piccadilly Circus to Regent's Park (Regent Street)

Plan III, F 2–II, B 3

STATIONS: PICCADILLY CIRCUS (Plan III, F 2), OXFORD CIRCUS (III, E 1), and REGENT'S PARK (II, C 3), all on the Bakerloo line. Piccadilly Circus is also on the Piccadilly line, and Oxford Circus on the Central line, while GREAT PORTLAND STREET (III, B, C 1), on the Circle and Metropolitan lines, is 200 yds E. of Regent's Park station. — MOTOR-BUSES Nos. 3, 6, 12, 13, 15, 53, 59, 60, 88, 153, 159, and 276 in Regent Street; Nos. 3, 53, 137, and 276 in Portland Place (northbound only) and Great Portland Street (southbound only). For other buses to Piccadilly Circus, see Routes 7, 18; to Oxford Circus, see Route 14; in Marylebone Road and Euston Road, see Route 16.

ADMISSION to ALL SOULS' CHURCH, weekdays 8 to 6 (Saturdays to 1); to the MUSEUM OF HYGIENE (Portland Place), weekdays 10 to 5.

REGENT STREET (III, F 2–D 1), one of the most favoured shopping streets of London, was laid out in 1813–23 by John Nash as part of a scheme to connect the Prince Regent's residence, Carlton House (p. 122), with his newly acquired property of Regent's Park. Now the main south-to-north thoroughfare of the West End, it begins at Waterloo Place (Lower Regent Street; Route 6), takes a sharp bend to the left at Piccadilly Circus and crosses Oxford Street at Oxford Circus. It ends on the north in

Langham Place, which bears left in turn to the foot of Portland Place, a broad street already constructed by the brothers Adam but brought into his scheme by Nash, who finished off its northern end with a noble crescent opening towards Regent's Park.

The buildings in Regent Street have all been redesigned in the present century and it is now of no specific interest, apart from its shops. The curved portion opening on the north-west from Piccadilly Circus (Route 7) and known as the Quadrant maintains the fine sweep intended by Nash, though the façades were recast in 1923, not to their improvement, by Sir Reginald Blomfield and others, who incorporated the north front of Shaw's Piccadilly Hotel. The old-fashioned CAFÉ ROYAL, on the right, is also the headquarters of the National Sporting Club.

Beyond the curve VIGO STREET leads to the left to the north entrance to the Albany (Route 7) and to Burlington Gardens, on the south side of which is a large building by Sir James Pennethorne put up in 1869 for the University of London, but now occupied by the CIVIL SERVICE COMMISSION, constituted in 1855. In the east wing are the headquarters of the BRITISH ACADEMY, founded in 1901 for the advancement of historical, philosophical, and philological studies. The former Queensborough House, at the corner of Savile Row, built in 1721 by Giacomo Leoni but altered later in the century, is now the West End branch of the ROYAL BANK OF SCOTLAND.

SAVILE ROW (III, E, F 1), which runs parallel to Regent Street, is well known for its fashionable tailors and has some interesting houses. No. 12 was the residence of George Grote, the historian of Greece, from 1848 until his death in 1871. R. B. Sheridan, the playwright, lived at No. 14, but died in 1816 in the front bedroom of No. 17, a house later occupied by George Basevi (d. 1845), the architect of Belgravia. No. 25 is the office of the FORESTRY COMMISSION, appointed under an act of 1919. CLIFFORD STREET, on the left, was built about 1720, and Nos. 6–7 and 18 in particular are excellent survivals of this time. Savile Row passes the large building of the MINISTRY OF HEALTH (1950) and emerges into CONDUIT STREET, which leads right to Regent Street and left to Bond Street. No. 9, to the right, a fine house by James Wyatt, has one of earliest stucco fronts in London (1779); to the left, opposite the Westbury Hotel (p. 134), are the galleries of the ROYAL SOCIETY OF PAINTERS IN WATER COLOURS (founded in 1804), famous members of which have included J. S. Cotman, David Cox, and Peter de Wint.

St George Street, starting close by, leads north to Hanover Square, passing the church of ST GEORGE'S, HANOVER SQUARE (III, E 1), built in 1713–24 by John James, a follower of Wren, with a large Corinthian portico and a baroque tower. The altar painting of the Last Supper is by Sir James Thornhill, and the east windows of the chancel and aisles contain good Flemish glass of 1520 from Malines (Belgium), inserted in 1843 and representing a Tree of Jesse.

The church has been noted for its fashionable weddings since the late 18th century. The registers record the marriages of Sir William Hamilton and Emma Hart (Nelson's 'Dearest Emma') in 1791, Benjamin Disraeli and Mrs Wyndham Lewis in 1839; J. W. Cross, a New York banker, and 'George Eliot' (Mary Ann Evans) in 1880; Theodore Roosevelt and Edith Carow in 1886; and H. H. Asquith and Margaret Tennant in 1894. P. B. Shelley and Harriet Westbrook were remarried here in 1814 in confirmation of the Scottish marriage in 1811.

HANOVER SQUARE (III, E 1) was laid out in 1717, but has been largely rebuilt: No. 24, of variegated brick, is an example of the original houses. Mary Somerville, the scientific writer, lived in 1818–27 at No. 12, another old house. At the south end of the gardens is a bronze statue by Chantrey of William Pitt the Younger (d. 1806).

Brook Street (see Route 13) leads west to Grosvenor Square, and Harewood Place north to Oxford Street opposite the entrance to Cavendish Square (Route 14).

Hanover Street runs east to Regent Street, which it reaches nearly opposite Great Marlborough Street. The timber-framed block of Messrs Liberty's store here (1924) represents the Tudor revival at its most exuberant. In Argyll Street, to the left, is the PALLADIUM MUSIC HALL, opened in 1910.

Regent Street crosses Oxford Street at OXFORD CIRCUS (III, D, E 1), then goes over Margaret Street (compare Route 14). On the left just beyond is the POLYTECHNIC INSTITUTE, founded in 1882 by Quintin Hogg (see below) and rebuilt in 1911. The object of the institute, the first of its kind, is to provide technical and scientific instruction for both day and evening students, and at the same time to assist the moral and physical development of youth, and it has about 15,000 members. In LANGHAM PLACE, which curves to the left to connect Regent Street with Portland Place, is ALL SOULS' CHURCH (III, D 1), built in 1822–4 by John Nash, who designed the circular classical portico and needle-like spire surrounded by its ring of free-standing columns to close the vista up Regent Street, which it did most effectively until it became overshadowed in 1958 by a huge office building. A bust of the architect (d. 1835), by Cecil Thomas, was unveiled under the portico in 1956. The church, a simple but successful basilica with no structural chancel, was badly damaged by bombing in 1940 but charmingly restored in 1951.

PORTLAND PLACE (II, C, D 3), one of the widest streets in London, was built about 1774 by Robert and James Adam, who intended it as a kind of close to be surrounded by the houses of the wealthy. Their intentions, however, were never completely carried out and many of the houses have since been rebuilt. The street is now favoured by several embassies and various institutes and societies. At the foot rises BROADCASTING HOUSE, the headquarters of the British Broadcasting Corporation (BBC), incorporated in 1927 as successor to the British Broadcasting Company (compare p. 211). The huge and rather formless building, designed by George Val Myer and F. J. Watson-Hart (1931), has over the main entrance a sculptured group of Prospero and Ariel, one of the last works of Eric Gill. The immense and ugly building opposite (the former Langham Hotel), facing up Portland Place, is also utilized by the BBC. Near the south end of the street is a statue by Sir George Frampton in memory of Quintin Hogg (d. 1903). No. 26, on the right, houses the ROYAL SOCIETY OF TROPICAL MEDICINE AND HYGIENE (founded in 1907), while No. 28 adjoining is the ROYAL INSTITUTE OF PUBLIC HEALTH AND HYGIENE, formed in 1937, with a small museum. No. 29, on the left, one of the best survivals, is now the SWEDISH EMBASSY. An equestrian statue by Tweed of Sir George White (d. 1912), the defender of Ladysmith, stands opposite No. 47 (now the Polish Embassy), the residence in 1902–6 of Lord Roberts.

On the right at the corner of Weymouth Street is the ROYAL INSTITUTE OF BRITISH ARCHITECTS (founded in 1834), in a fine building by Grey Wornum (1934). The reliefs on the façade (by Bainbridge Copnall) and the pillars each side of the entrance (with sculpture by James Woodford) have met with some criticism, but the interior, with its fine staircase and ornamented glass, is most satisfying. At No. 76 Portland Place are the headquarters (1959) of the CITY AND GUILDS OF LONDON INSTITUTE, founded in 1878.

Near the head of Portland Place is a monument to Lord Lister (d. 1912), the pioneer of antiseptic surgery, who lived in 1877–1909 at No. 12 PARK CRESCENT (II, C 3), an admirable semicircle of building distinguished by Ionic colonnades, designed in 1821 by Nash to provide a formal approach to Regent's Park. No. 20 is the office of the MEDICAL RESEARCH COUNCIL, established in 1913. The arms of the crescent abut on MARYLEBONE ROAD, which runs to the south of Regent's Park (see Route 16).

16 From Marble Arch to Euston and King's Cross via Marylebone Road

Plan II, E 2–III, A 3

STATIONS: MARBLE ARCH (Plan II, E 2), on the Central line; EDGWARE ROAD (II, C 1), BAKER STREET (II, C 2), GREAT PORTLAND STREET (III, B, C 1), EUSTON SQUARE (III, B 2) and KING'S CROSS & ST PANCRAS (III, A 3), all on the Circle and Metropolitan lines; MARYLEBONE (II, C 1) and REGENT'S PARK (II, C 3), on the Bakerloo line; WARREN STREET (III, B 1) and EUSTON (III, A 2), on the Northern line. Edgware Road is also on the Bakerloo and District lines; Baker Street on the Bakerloo line; and King's Cross & St Pancras on the Northern and Piccadilly lines. — MOTOR-BUSES Nos. 6, 7, 8, 15, 16, 36, and 60 in Edgware Road; Nos. 1, 18, 27, 30, and 176 in Marylebone Road; Nos. 2, 13, 23, 30, 59, 74, 113, 153, and 159 in Baker Street; Nos. 14, 18, 30, 73, 77, and 196 in Euston Road (the two last from Woburn Place to King's Cross only). For other buses to Marble Arch, see Routes 9, 12, 14; in Tottenham Court Road, see Route 18; in Woburn Place, see Route 19; to King's Cross, see Routes 22, 29; to the Angel, see Routes 29, 30.

ADMISSION to MADAME TUSSAUD'S WAXWORKS, daily (including Good Friday) 10 to 7 (Monday–Friday in winter to 6; 4/-, children 2/-); to LONDON PLANETARIUM, Monday–Friday at 11, 12.15, 3, 4.15, and 7, Saturdays and Sundays at 3, 4.15, 5.30, 6.30, and 8 (4/-), children's presentations on Saturdays at 11 and 12.15 (2/-); combined ticket for Madame

Tussaud's and London Planetarium, 6/- (children 3/-); to BLINDIANA MUSEUM, Monday–Friday 9.30 to 5.30 (free; closed Bank Holidays); to WELLCOME HISTORICAL MEDICAL MUSEUM, Monday–Friday 10 to 5 (free; closed Bank Holidays).

Great Cumberland Place, starting opposite the Marble Arch (Route 14), runs north to BRYANSTON SQUARE (II, D 1, 2), which preserves many façades of about 1810. MONTAGU SQUARE, farther east, was likewise built about 1810, and Anthony Trollope, the novelist, lived in 1873–80 at No. 39, on the west side. At the north-west corner a new building was erected in 1957 by Yorke, Rosenberg, and Mardale for the JEWS COLLEGE, founded in 1856 to train rabbis and ministers for Jewish congregations in Britain, and now a world centre of Jewish scholarship. From Bryanston Square, Wyndham Place faces north to the semi-circular portico of ST MARY'S CHURCH, built in 1823 by Sir Robert Smirke. YORK STREET, behind the church, preserves a row of early-19th-century shops (Nos. 78–94); from its west end Seymour Place leads north to Marylebone Road.

MARYLEBONE ROAD (II, D 1–III, B 1), constructed in 1754–6, traverses the borough of St Marylebone, which stretches from Regent's Park as far south as Oxford Street and takes its name from the church of 'St Mary on the bourne' or stream (*i.e.* the Tyburn, long since vanished).

MARYLEBONE GRAMMAR SCHOOL, opposite Seymour Place, founded in 1792 as the Philological School, is housed in typical Victorian buildings of 1856. The western part of Marylebone Road, leading through a humble district to Edgware Road (p. 473), is of little interest. In Cosway Street, on the right, is the large CHRIST CHURCH, a rather forbidding classical structure by Philip Hardwick (1822). On the left, in Harcourt Street, is the SWEDISH CHURCH, a lofty Gothic building of 1910, well restored in 1956.

Marylebone Road, running east, broadens out into a boulevard beyond Enford Street. On the left is an ornate late-Victorian building (formerly the Hotel Great Central) and behind this is MARYLEBONE STATION (II, B, C 1), opened in 1899, a smaller terminus of the Western Region, used also by the London Midland Region. The road, lined for the most part by commercial buildings and large blocks of 'mansions', passes ST MARYLEBONE TOWN HALL, built in 1914–20, and the more restrained Public Library (1938), both by Sir Edwin Cooper. CASTROL HOUSE, the 16-

storey 'egg box' opposite, was designed by Gollins, Melvin, Ward and Partners, and completed in 1959. The upper part of Gloucester Place, alongside, leads to DORSET SQUARE, with unspoiled terraces of the early 19th century. A plaque was unveiled in 1957 on No. 1, at the south-east corner, to 'commemorate the deeds of the men and women of the Free French Forces and their British comrades who left from this house on special missions to enemy-occupied France'.

The main road crosses BAKER STREET (II, C, D 2), a busy street running north to Regent's Park (Route 17) and south to Portman Square (Route 14). It was laid out about 1790, but the surviving houses of this time (south of Marylebone Road) have been disguised by their conversion into shops. In one of them (No. 120) William Pitt lived in 1803–4, his niece, the eccentric Lady Hester Stanhope, keeping house for him. The fabulous 'Sherlock Holmes' also had rooms in Baker Street. In CHILTERN COURT, the huge block of flats at the junction with Marylebone Road, Arnold Bennett, the novelist, died in 1931 (at No. 97). It stands above BAKER STREET STATION (II, C 2), the original terminus of the Bakerloo Railway, the oldest 'tube' in London, which was opened in 1906 from here to Waterloo. The station is now also a starting-point of the Metropolitan trains.

Marylebone Road goes on east past MADAME TUSSAUD'S (II, C 2), the famous waxworks exhibition first established in Paris by Marie Tussaud, a Swiss who began by modelling the victims of the French Revolution. She opened her museum in the Strand in 1802 and transferred it in 1835 to Baker Street, where she died in 1850. Moved to its present site in 1884, the exhibition was reconstructed (after a fire) in 1928. It contains a wide range of wax models of the famous and the infamous, past and present, and tableaux of notable events. The Chamber of Horrors, with models and relics of notorious criminals, is not suitable for children. The adjoining LONDON PLANETARIUM, the only one in Britain, opened in 1958, shows the night sky in both hemispheres or at different periods of history.

Opposite YORK GATE, a characteristic example of the Regency style associated with John Nash (1822), forming an approach to Regent's Park, is ST MARYLEBONE PARISH CHURCH (II, C 3), an imposing building by Thomas Hardwick (1813–17) with a large classical portico. The chancel was rebuilt in 1885 in an early baroque style by Thomas Harris. Robert Browning was married to Elizabeth Barrett in 1846 in this church, an event commemorated by a window in the north aisle. The bronze medallion of the poet on the west wall is by Gustave Natorp, an American artist (1887); in the other aisle is a tablet to Richard Cosway, the miniaturist, who died in 1821 in Marylebone.

On the left, just beyond the church, is the ROYAL ACADEMY OF MUSIC, founded in 1822, in a building by Sir Ernest George (1911); the contemporary Duke's Hall next to it is used for concerts. Opposite begins MARYLEBONE HIGH STREET (II, C, D 3), the nucleus of the old village, but retaining nothing of its original character except its narrow winding shape.

A house on the west corner, unhappily demolished in 1958, was the home in 1839–51 of Charles Dickens, who was visited here by H. W. Longfellow, the American poet, in 1841. *The Old Curiosity Shop, Barnaby Rudge, Martin Chuzzlewit*, the *Christmas Carol*, and *David Copperfield* were all written here. *Dombey and Son*, though mostly written during a sojourn in Switzerland, draws many of its scenes from this neighbourhood; the church in which Paul Dombey was christened and Mr Dombey married has been identified as St Marylebone.

On the west of the High Street stood the former parish church, called MARYLEBONE CHAPEL after the new church was completed. The chapel, rebuilt in 1741 and seriously damaged by bombing, was demolished in 1949 and the site is now a formal garden. An obelisk marks the grave of Charles Wesley (d. 1788), the hymn-writer, and his nephew, Samuel Wesley (d. 1837), the composer, and a tablet on the wall opposite records famous persons connected with the church and its predecessor.

ULSTER PLACE, on the left of Marylebone Road, is a range of good Regency building by Nash (about 1824). Beyond this the road has PARK CRESCENT (II, C 3) on its right, leading to Portland Place (see Route 15), and on its left is PARK SQUARE, also by Nash (1823–4), but rather heavier in its detail. The north side of the square is traversed by the Outer Circle (Route 17). A little farther on is HOLY TRINITY CHURCH (III, B 1), by Sir John Soane (1825), the interior of which was reconstructed in 1956 as the headquarters of the Society for Promoting Christian Knowledge, a body founded in 1698. Visitors are admitted to services and for private prayer. The crypt was the headquarters of Penguin Books when they started in 1935.

The church stands opposite the entrances to GREAT PORTLAND STREET, which runs south to Oxford Street (compare Route 14). On the left are the ROYAL NATIONAL ORTHOPÆDIC HOSPITAL, founded in 1838, now containing also the Wellcome Museum of Orthopædics, established in 1956, and the ROYAL NATIONAL INSTITUTE FOR THE BLIND, founded in 1868, with another relevant museum. On the other side of the road, farther on, is the CENTRAL SYNAGOGUE, destroyed by bombing but rebuilt in 1958.

In Osnaburgh Street, east of Holy Trinity Church, is ST SAVIOUR'S HOSPITAL, built in 1852 by Butterfield to house a sisterhood founded by Dr E. B. Pusey in 1845. The first building to be opened in England as a religious foundation since the Reformation, the hospital has been run since 1947 by an Anglican nursing order. The chapel contains elaborately carved oak stalls and choir screen formerly in the Charterhouse at Buxheim (Bavaria) and re-erected here about 1880. This splendid early-17th-century woodwork, with numerous figures of saints, prophets, etc., is the most outstanding example of carving in the baroque style to be found in England.

Marylebone Road is prolonged beyond Great Portland Street station by EUSTON ROAD (III, B 1–A 3), at first a purely commercial thoroughfare running through a poorer quarter. Conway Street, on the right, leads to FITZROY SQUARE, which has some notable houses. The east side was built in 1790–4 by Robert Adam, but the north and west sides are later (1825–9).

George Bernard Shaw lived at No. 29 in 1887–98, when he was music and dramatic critic of various papers. Samuel Morse, the pioneer of electric telegraphy, and C. R. Leslie, the artist, lived at No. 141 CLEVELAND STREET (to the west) when they came from America in 1811, and John Flaxman, the sculptor, died in 1826 at No. 7 GREENWELL STREET (formerly Buckingham Street), close by. On the south-east corner of the square is the fine Y.M.C.A. INDIAN STUDENTS' UNION building and hostel (by Ralph Tubbs, 1953), and in GRAFTON WAY, which leads east to Gower Street, No. 58 was the residence for a time of Francisco de Miranda (d. 1816), the Spanish-American adventurer, who was visited here in 1810 by Simon Bolivar, the liberator. Octavia Hill, the social reformer and a founder of the National Trust, died in 1912 at No. 8 FITZROY STREET, south of the square.

Euston Road broadens out beyond Warren Street station, where it crosses the junction of Tottenham Court Road, on the right, and Hampstead Road. From Euston Square station, Gower Street leads south to the University of London and the British Museum (see Route 18). Beyond is the WELLCOME FOUNDATION (III, B 2), a flourishing scientific research institution established in 1913 by Sir Henry Wellcome (d. 1936), occupying a large building of 1932 by Septimus Warwick.

On the second floor is the HISTORICAL MEDICAL MUSEUM, a unique collection illustrating the history of medicine and allied sciences since the earliest times, with an ethnographical section showing the reaction of primitive peoples to illness. On the landing outside is a fine bronze of Edward Jenner, the discoverer of vaccination (1796), by Monteverde. Special exhibitions (changed from time to time) of historical and scientific interest are held on the ground floor, and here also is the MUSEUM OF MEDICAL SCIENCE, an ingeniously arranged display, devoted especially to tropical diseases, but accessible only to medical men, students, and research workers. The valuable library of 250,000 volumes, on the third floor, is also available to these for reference.

Opposite EUSTON SQUARE (1805), named after the Suffolk estate of the Fitzroy family who owned it, is FRIENDS' HOUSE (III, B 2), built in 1927 (by Hubert Lidbetter) as the head-offices of the Society of Friends. The library contains a fine collection of Quaker literature, including the journal of George Fox, the founder, and documents concerning the foundation of Pennsylvania by William Penn. A statue by Marochetti of Robert Stephenson (d. 1859), the civil engineer, stands at the beginning of the approach to EUSTON STATION (III, A 2), the oldest terminus in London (1835–49) and one of the principal stations of the London Midland Region, laid out by Robert Stephenson. In the entrance hall is a statue of his father, George Stephenson (d. 1848), who built the first public railway. The station is now being rebuilt and the work is to be completed by 1966.

At the corner of Upper Woburn Place, which bears right for Tavistock Square (Route 19), is ST PANCRAS CHURCH (III, B 2), built in a Grecian style in 1819–22 by W. and H. W. Inwood, who were inspired by the temple of Erechtheus and other buildings at Athens. The octagonal tower is modelled on the Tower of the Winds, and the church has an impressive classical portico. On either side at the east end are curious extensions with caryatids in terracotta (by Rossi) imitated from the Erechtheion. The successful interior, finely restored in 1953, is a plain rectangle with the addition of an apse remarkable for its huge scagliola columns. The unusual pulpit is contemporary. The ELIZABETH GARRETT ANDERSON HOSPITAL, on the other side of Euston Road, was founded in 1866 and is one of the only two hospitals in London managed entirely by women.

The enormous St Pancras Station (III, A 3), the other chief terminus of the London Midland Region, was built in 1868–74 by Sir George Gilbert Scott and displays the romantic spirit of the Victorians in its most effusive manner. Its great façade embodies details from French and Italian Gothic architecture, and it has a soaring clock-tower 300 ft high; the west tower rises to 270 ft. The vault over the platforms behind (by W. H. Barlow), severely functional in comparison, has a length of 690 ft and an exceptional span of over 240 ft. Opposite the station is St Pancras Town Hall, by A. J. Thomas (1937).

Pancras Road, starting on the east of St Pancras Station, leads under the railway to St Pancras Old Church, largely rebuilt in 1848, but retaining a few 12th–13th-century details. John Christian Bach (d. 1782), the composer, and John Flaxman (d. 1826), the sculptor, were buried in the churchyard (now a public garden), which contains a remarkable mausoleum designed by Sir John Soane for his wife (1815), in which the architect himself was buried in 1837. Beyond the church, Crowndale Road runs west past the Working Men's College, established in 1854 in Bloomsbury by F. D. Maurice and moved here in 1905. The Royal Veterinary College, in a street on the right before this, was founded in 1791 and is now affiliated to London University. From the junction of Crowndale Road and Camden High Street (with Mornington Crescent underground station), Hampstead Road leads south to the upper end of Tottenham Court Road (see above). George Cruikshank, the illustrator of Dickens, died in 1878 at No. 263, and Dickens himself went to school in 1824–6 at No. 247, probably the original of 'Salem House' in *David Copperfield.*

Euston Road ends at King's Cross Station (III, A 3), the main terminus of the Eastern Region, with a frontage designed by Lewis Cubitt (1852) and much praised for its fitness for purpose in comparison with St Pancras station. The tower (120 ft high) contains a clock which adorned the Crystal Palace during the 1851 Exhibition.

King's Cross, a bustling centre of traffic, takes its name from a monument to George IV which stood here until 1845. Gray's Inn Road turns south to Holborn (see Route 22), while Pentonville Road (IV, A 1, 2) goes on east to Islington (Route 31), passing in less than ½-mile St James's Church, built in 1787 and altered in 1920. Joseph Grimaldi (d. 1837), the famous clown, is buried in the churchyard. In Rodney Street, on the east, James Mill, the Utilitarian philosopher, lived in 1805–10 at No. 13, where his son, John Stuart Mill, the philosopher, was born in 1806.

REGENT'S PARK

17 Regent's Park and Neighbourhood

Plan I, A 1–II, B 3

STATIONS: BAKER STREET (Plan II, C 2) on the Bakerloo, Circle, and
Metropolitan lines; REGENT'S PARK (II, C 3) and ST JOHN'S WOOD
(½ m. NW. of Hanover Gate; beyond II, A 1), on the Bakerloo line; GREAT
PORTLAND STREET (III, B, C 1), on the Circle and Metropolitan lines;
CAMDEN TOWN (½ m. NE. of Gloucester Gate; beyond I, A 3), on the
Northern line. — MOTOR-BUSES in Marylebone Road and Baker Street,
see Route 16; Nos. 2, 13, 59, 74, 113, 153, and 159 in Park Road (W. of the
park); No. 74 in Prince Albert Road (N.); Nos. 3, 53, and 276 in Albany
Street (E.).

REGENT'S PARK is open daily until dusk. — MOTOR-CARS are allowed
on the Outer Circle (speed limit 30 m.p.h.), on the Inner Circle only if
calling at a house.

ADMISSION to the LORD'S CRICKET MUSEUM, weekdays 10.30 to
close of play (winter, Monday–Friday 10 to 4; 6d); to the ZOOLOGICAL
GARDENS, see p. 464; to CECIL SHARP HOUSE, Monday–Friday 9.30 to
5.30, first Saturday in month 9.30 to 12.30 (free).

REFRESHMENTS in Queen Mary's Gardens in summer. — BANDS
play at the Bandstand (S. of the Zoo) on Sundays, late May to early September, 7 to 8.30 p.m. — BOATING on the lake (boats for hire at the NW. end,
near which there is a motor-boat pond for children).

REGENT'S PARK, one of the largest open spaces in London,
with an area of 472 acres (including Primrose Hill, on the north),
was originally Marylebone Park, a royal hunting-ground until
the time of the Commonwealth. It reverted to the Crown in 1811
and was laid out afresh after 1812 by John Nash for the Prince
Regent, after whom it was named and who contemplated taking
one of the country villas to be built here. At the same time Nash
also built Regent Street as part of a 'royal mile' connecting the
park with the prince's house in St James's (compare p. 122) and
began the series of classic terraces, in the style now known as
Regency, which enclose the park on all sides but the north. The
first of these terraces, whose grandiose façades conceal unpreten-
ous residences, was built in 1820 and the scheme was complete by
1827, several of the terraces being designed by Decimus Burton.
Considerably damaged in the Second World War, they have been
restored and in some cases are in use as government offices. Only
a few of the intended villas were in fact built in the park, and in
1838 it was thrown open to the public.

180

The park is surrounded by a carriage-drive, over 2¾ miles long, called the Outer Circle. Roads on the south and east connect this with the Inner Circle, nearly ¾-mile long (see p. 183), which encloses the beautiful Queen Mary's Gardens, containing the Open Air Theatre. On the west of the Inner Circle is an attractive boating lake of 22 acres, and on the north of the park are the Zoological Gardens, reached by the Outer Circle or by the Broad Walk, an avenue stretching north from Park Square (p. 176).

The OUTER CIRCLE may be reached from Marylebone Road, which runs a little south of the park, by York Gate (Route 16) or by the upper section of Baker Street, leading to Park Road (see below) and to the CLARENCE GATE (II, B 2). Inside the park the carriage-drive bears to the left, passing SUSSEX PLACE, one of the most dignified of Nash's terraces (1822). A new building for the ROYAL COLLEGE OF OBSTETRICIANS was opened close by in 1960. Farther on is HANOVER TERRACE, also of 1822, and ultra-classical in style. H. G. Wells, the novelist, died in 1946 at No. 13.

The road on the left beyond this, opposite a path leading to the boating-lake, returns to Park Road at HANOVER GATE, with a lodge built by Nash. At a divergence of ways beyond the Regent's Canal is ST JOHN'S WOOD CHAPEL (II, A 1), a pleasant little Regency church by Thomas Hardwick (1813); J. S. Cotman (d. 1842), the landscape-painter, is buried in the church-yard. From the chapel, the centre of a favoured residential district, Welling-ton Road goes on north-west towards St John's Wood station (nearly ½-mile) and Hampstead; and Prince Albert Road runs north-east to Primrose Hill and Camden Town. In St John's Wood Road, which descends south-west to Maida Vale (Edgware Road), is the main entrance to LORD'S CRICKET GROUND, the headquarters of the Marylebone Cricket Club (M.C.C.), the governing body of the English summer game since 1788, and the county ground of Middlesex. Thomas Lord (d. 1832) opened his first ground in Dorset Square in 1787, but in 1814 he removed to the present ground, bringing with him the original turf. The gateway (1923) is a memorial to the immortal Dr W. G. Grace (d. 1915); the old racket court contains a museum of interest to cricket enthusiasts.

The Outer Circle passes (on the right) WINFIELD HOUSE, built in 1936 and presented to the United States Government in 1946 as a residence for the American Ambassador. The house stands on the site of St Dunstan's Lodge, in which St Dunstan's Hostel for blinded ex-servicemen (now at Brighton) was founded in 1915. The road is now followed on the left by the REGENT'S CANAL, a branch of the Grand Union Canal, opened in 1820 to connect the Grand Junction Canal at Paddington with the Thames at Wapping. Macclesfield Bridge (1816) crosses the canal to Prince Albert Road (for Primrose Hill), and farther on the Outer Circle passes the main entrance to the **Zoological Gardens.** Beyond this on the left are the offices of the ZOOLOGICAL SOCIETY OF LONDON, founded in 1826; on the right is the northern entrance to the Broad Walk (see below).

The Broad Walk is extended northward over Prince Albert Road ts REGENT'S PARK ROAD, in which Henry Handel Richardson, the Australian novelist, lived in 1910–34 at No. 90 (to the left). The road ascendo along the side of PRIMROSE HILL, an open space the top of which (219 ft) affords a wonderful view over London. No. 2 Regent's Park Road, in the other direction, is CECIL SHARP HOUSE, the headquarters of the English Folk Dance and Song Society, named in honour of Cecil Sharp (1859–1924), a pioneer in the collection of folk music. Built in 1929 by H. M. Fletcher, it was rebuilt in 1951 after war damage.

The drive turns south, passing GLOUCESTER GATE, another classical terrace by Nash (1827). Just beyond this is ST KATHARINE'S CHAPEL (I, A, B 3), built in 1829 in a Gothic style to the designs of Ambrose Poynter.

This was formerly the chapel of the St Katharine's Royal Hospital, estab˜ lished in 1148 by Matilda, wife of King Stephen, near the Tower, and the oldest surviving ecclesiastical foundation in England. In 1825, when the St Katharine Docks were excavated, the hospital was removed to Regent's Park, but in 1950 it returned to the East End of London. The chapel, well restored in 1952 after war damage, is now the church of the Danish community in London. It has a notable coffered ceiling, good modern fittings, and wooden figures of Moses and St John the Baptist by C. G. Cibber, the Danish sculptor (1696), brought from the old Danish church at Limehouse. Below the windows are 39 shields of arms of the queens of England from Matilda to Queen Mary, recalling that in 1273 the patronage of St Katharine's Hospital was reserved by Eleanor, wife of Henry III, for the queens of England. The chapel is opened for visitors by the caretaker, who lives at St Katharine's Hall (adjoining on the north), now a social centre of the Danes in London. In the garden on the south side of the chapel is a copy of the famous Rune stone at Jelling (Denmark).

The Outer Circle goes past more Regency terraces, of which the most notable is CUMBERLAND TERRACE (1826; converted into flats, 1962). Chester Road, on the right, leads to the Inner Circle, crossing the BROAD WALK, the southern part of which is lined with beautiful flower gardens and is noted for its chestnuts, best seen when in blossom. Opposite the south-east corner of the part is a building by Denys Lasdun for the ROYAL COLLEGE OF PHYSICIANS (see p. 99), to be completed in 1963. At the south end of the Broad Walk is PARK SQUARE (Route 16), from which the Outer Circle runs west via YORK TERRACE, designed by Decimus Burton (1821), and YORK GATE (II, B 2–C 3; see below), then turns north-west by CORNWALL TERRACE (also by Burton) back to Clarence Gate.

From York Gate a road leads north over an arm of the lake to the INNER CIRCLE. On the left is BEDFORD COLLEGE for women, founded in 1849 (in Bedford Square) to provide a liberal education in secular subjects, and now a school of the University of London, with faculties of arts, science, and economics. The buildings, by Basil Champneys (1913), with a library (130,000 volumes) by Sidney R. J. Smith, were extended in 1931 by Maxwell Ayrton. The parts damaged by bombing in 1941 were rebuilt by Ayrton and reopened in 1950. THE HOLME, a villa of about 1819 by Decimus Burton near the left arm of the Inner Circle, is now part of the college.

A gate opposite the road from York Gate admits to QUEEN MARY'S GARDENS (II, A, B2), filling the space within the Inner Circle. Leased by the Royal Botanic Society from 1840 until 1932, these are perhaps the most beautiful public grounds in London, with their delightful rose and other gardens, and a water-lily pond. On the north-west side is the charming OPEN AIR THEATRE, instituted in 1933 (compare p. 68).

18 From Piccadilly Circus to Euston (Soho, Bloomsbury)

Plan III, F 2–III, A 2

STATIONS: PICCADILLY CIRCUS (Plan III, F 2), on the Bakerloo and Piccadilly lines; TOTTENHAM COURT ROAD (III, D 2), on the Central and Northern lines; GOODGE STREET (III, C 2; for London University) and EUSTON (III, A 2), on the Northern line; EUSTON SQUARE (III, B 2), on the Circle and Metropolitan lines. — MOTOR-BUSES Nos. 14, 19, 22, and 38 in Shaftesbury Avenue; Nos. 1, 24, 29, 39, 127, 134 and 176 in Charing Cross Road; Nos. 1, 14, 24, 29, 39, 73, 127, 134, and 176 in Tottenham Court Road (northbound only) and Gower Street (southbound only). Other buses to Piccadilly Circus, see Routes 7, 15; in Euston Road, see Route 16.

ADMISSION to the HOUSE OF ST BARNABAS, Mondays 10.30 to 12, Thursdays 2.30 to 4.15 (or by appointment; gratuity); to the BRITISH MUSEUM, see p. 315; to the BUILDING CENTRE, Monday–Friday 9.30 to 5, Saturdays 9.30 to 1 (free; closed on Bank Holidays); to UNIVERSITY COLLEGE (Flaxman Gallery and Flinders Petrie Egyptology Collection), on written application to the secretary.

For PICCADILLY CIRCUS, see Route 7. The shortest route thence to Euston Road taken by the motor-buses runs via Shaftesbury Avenue, Charing Cross Road and its continuation Tottenham Court Road (an alternative route is via Shaftesbury Avenue, Bloomsbury Way, and Southampton Row; compare Route 19). SHAFTESBURY AVENUE (III, F 2–D 3), cut in 1886 through a humble quarter to connect Piccadilly with Holborn, skirts Soho (see below) on the south, and is otherwise best known for its shops and theatres.

On the left are the LYRIC THEATRE (1888), at which Eleanore Duse, the great Italian actress, made her first London appearance in 1893, the APOLLO THEATRE (1901), the GLOBE THEATRE (1906), and the QUEEN'S THEATRE, built in 1907, but reconstructed (by Bryan Westwood) after war damage and reopened in 1959. WINGATE HOUSE, on the same side farther up, designed by Sir John Burnet, Tait, and Partners (1958), has a car park on the first floor and a cinema below ground. For CAMBRIDGE CIRCUS, where Charing Cross Road is crossed, and the continuation thence to New Oxford Street, see Route 19.

In GERRARD STREET, which runs south of Shaftesbury Avenue beyond Wardour Street, Edmund Burke lodged in 1787–8 at No. 37 (altered) and John Dryden, the dramatist, lived at No. 43 (largely rebuilt) from 1686 until his death in 1700. Dr Johnson and Sir Joshua Reynolds founded their famous 'Literary Club' in 1764 in this street at the 'Turk's Head', a tavern long since vanished. Mr Jaggers, in *Great Expectations*, had a 'rather stately' house on the south side.

A route of greater interest than the main road threads the congested and rather squalid streets of SOHO, which extends north to Oxford Street and became the chief foreign quarter of London after the revocation of the Edict of Nantes (1685) caused thousands of French Protestant refugees to flee across the Channel. Soho is noted for its numerous foreign shops and restaurants and for its cosmopolitan atmosphere; the inhabitants include a large proportion of French, Italian, and Swiss, with a sprinkling of many other nationalities.

From GLASSHOUSE STREET, which leaves Piccadilly Circus

on the north (between Regent Street and Shaftesbury Avenue), Sherwood Street ascends on the right, passing the PICCADILLY THEATRE (1928), towards GOLDEN SQUARE (III, E 1), once a fashionable address, but now the London home of the woollen cloth trade. No. 11, at the south-east corner, has a fine carved doorway of the late 18th century. The statue, in the centre of the square, of George II in Roman costume (1753) is by John van Nost.

BEAK STREET, farther north, where Canaletto, the Venetian painter, lodged in 1749–51 at No. 41 (now a shop), ends on the east at Lexington Street. This extends left to BROADWICK STREET, in which William Blake, poet and artist, was born at No. 28 (now No. 74, a signwriter's shop) in 1757. To the right this street leads to Berwick Street, which with Rupert Street, farther south, is the scene of the lively BERWICK MARKET. Kemp House here (by Riches and Blythin, 1961) is the first example of 'mixed development' in central London, with shops and offices, and flats in a 170-ft-high tower block. Other streets go on to WARDOUR STREET, now the centre of the film industry in London, running south to Shaftesbury Avenue and passing the tower of 1806 (by S. P. Cockerell), practically all that survives of the church of ST ANNE'S, SOHO (III, E 2), gutted by bombing. On the tower are memorials to William Hazlitt (see below), the essayist, buried 'on the north side of this ground', and to Theodore, king of Corsica (who died in 1756 in poverty in Soho), with an epitaph by Horace Walpole.

Leading east on the north side of the tower is OLD COMPTON STREET, one of the most characteristic streets of Soho, with many foreign restaurants. From it DEAN STREET runs north, passing (on the left) MEARD STREET, which has a row of good if modest houses of 1732. In Dean Street, No. 28 was the birthplace of Joseph Nollekens, the sculptor, in 1737, but has been much altered since; No. 88, a stationer's, preserves a late-18th-century shop front.

Carlisle Street, on the right of Dean Street, admits to SOHO SQUARE (III, D, E 2), laid out in the reign of Charles II, of whom there is a statue in the gardens. His natural son, the Duke of Monmouth, who owned a mansion here, chose 'Soho' as his watchword at the Battle of Sedgemoor (1685). In the 18th century the square became one of the most favoured places of residence in London, and after Sir Joseph Banks came to live here in 1777 it was the centre for scientific gatherings, the first meeting of the Royal Institution being held here. The houses have almost wholly been rebuilt since that time, but No. 36, on the west side, and No. 21A, on the east, are good survivals. On the north side is a FRENCH PROTESTANT CHURCH, built in terracotta by Sir Aston Webb (1893), with a carved tympanum of 1950 in memory of Edward VI 'who by his charter of 1550 granted asylum to the Huguenots from France'. The Roman Catholic ST PATRICK'S CHURCH, on the east side, was opened in 1792 and rebuilt, in a classical style, in 1893.

In FRITH STREET, which leads south from the square to Shaftesbury Avenue, William Hazlitt died in 1830 at No. 6, one of a pair of 18th-century houses, and J. L. Baird gave his first demonstration of television in 1926 at No. 22. GREEK STREET, the parallel street on the east and likewise noted for its foreign restaurants, is named after the colony of Greeks who settled here. De Quincey lodged in poor circumstances at No. 61 in 1802, after running away from Manchester Grammar School.

On the east corner of Greek Street and Soho Square is the HOUSE OF ST BARNABAS, a charity founded in 1846 to help the destitute and homeless poor in London, and occupying a mid-18th-century mansion with an interior (restored after war damage) notable for its carved woodwork, rococo plasterwork, and staircase with a wrought-iron balustrade. The French Gothic chapel was designed in 1863.

From the square, Soho Street goes north to Oxford Street (Route 14) and Sutton Row east to CHARING CROSS ROAD (compare Route 19), which it reaches just below ST GILES CIRCUS (III, D 2). Hence St Giles High Street bears sharp right for the church of St Giles-in-the-Fields (Route 23), while TOTTEN-HAM COURT ROAD (III, D 2–B 1), noted for its furniture-dealers, goes on northward to Euston Road, skirting the district of BLOOMSBURY, with its many squares, mostly developed in the early 18th century. At first an aristocratic quarter, it became in the late 19th century an intellectual and literary centre, but is now better known as the home of the British Museum and the growing University of London. In GREAT RUSSELL STREET, on the right of Tottenham Court Road, is the large London Central building (by Rowland Plumbe, 1912) of the YOUNG MEN'S CHRISTIAN ASSOCIATION, founded in 1844 by Sir George Williams (d. 1905) as a club and recreation centre in which young men could also seek to improve themselves spiritually. The Y.M.C.A. now numbers over 4 million members representing 80 nationalities. The National Council for England, Wales, and Ireland has its offices here. Farther east, on the other side, are the central club of the similar YOUNG WOMEN'S CHRISTIAN ASSOCIATION established in 1887 by the amalgamation of two organizations, both started in 1855, and occupying a building by Sir Edwin Lutyens (1931); and the headquarters and training college (by David du R. Aberdeen, 1956) of the TRADES UNION CONGRESS, a voluntary association of trades unions established in 1866 and now numbering 183 unions with over $8\frac{1}{4}$ million members. In the forecourt is a striking war-memorial sculpture, by Sir Jacob Epstein (1958).

Great Russell Street goes on past the main entrance of the **British Museum,** while Bloomsbury Street, on the left, leads to BEDFORD SQUARE (III, D 2), the finest of the squares of Bloomsbury, surviving quite unspoiled. It was built about 1775, probably by Thomas Leverton, and named after the landowner, the Duke of Bedford; the middle houses of the ranges on each side are good examples of the style made popular by the brothers Adam.

No. 51, on the south side, is the FRENCH CONSULATE and No. 48 the INSTITUTE OF BUILDERS (1834). The Earl of Oxford and Asquith (d. 1928), the Liberal statesman, lived in 1921-4 at No. 44. Nos. 34-6, on the west, house the ARCHITECTURAL ASSOCIATION, incorporated in 1847, and Nos. 26-7, on the north, the NATIONAL COUNCIL OF SOCIAL SERVICE. No. 22 was the home of Sir Johnston Forbes-Robertson (d. 1937), the actor, and No. 21 is the ROYAL ANTHROPOLOGICAL INSTITUTE, established in 1843. At No. 11, in the north-east corner, Henry Cavendish, the natural philosopher, lived from 1786 until his death in 1810; at No. 2 Gower Street (see below), next door, Millicent Fawcett, a champion of women's rights, died in 1929. No. 6, a large house on the east side, was the residence in 1798-1815 of the Earl of Eldon, Lord Chancellor, and is now the headquarters of the CENTRAL COUNCIL OF PHYSICAL RECREATION.

From the north-east angle of the square, MONTAGUE PLACE leads right to Russell Square (Route 19), passing the north entrance of the British Museum, and GOWER STREET (III, B,

C 2), a long thoroughfare with regular if uninspired terraces of 1796 and after, runs northward to Euston Road. In Store Street, on the left, is the BUILDING CENTRE, opened in 1931 as a 'permanent exhibition and information service for all interested in building'. Excellent temporary exhibitions of architecture and allied subjects are also held here.

At the corner of Gower Street and Keppel Street is the LONDON SCHOOL OF HYGIENE AND TROPICAL MEDICINE, founded in 1924, incorporating the London School of Tropical Medicine established in 1899 and admitted as part of London University in 1905. The school, which has faculties of medicine and science, and about 300 students, is in a fine building by P. Morley Horder and O. Verner Rees (1929). Farther on in Gower Street is the ROYAL ACADEMY OF DRAMATIC ART, founded in 1904 by Sir Herbert Beerbohm Tree, the actor-manager, and occupying a building of 1931. The Vanbrugh Theatre, the private theatre of the academy, with an entrance in Malet Street (see below), was named in honour of the sister-actresses Irene and Violet Vanbrugh. Designed by Alister MacDonald, it was opened in 1954. William de Morgan, potter and novelist, was born in 1839 at No. 69 Gower Street, the continuation of which is described below.

Keppel Street leads to the main entrance (in Malet Street) of the UNIVERSITY OF LONDON (III, C 2, 3), founded by royal charter in 1836 as a purely examining organization, and consisting mainly of a number of federated schools and colleges. In 1878 it became the first university in Britain to admit women as candidates for degrees, on equal terms with men, but it was created a teaching university only in 1900. Many of its departments are now being brought together in new buildings begun in 1933.

The university, the last to be established in any great European capital, was constituted to grant academic degrees without religious bias, at first to students of University College, King's College, and certain other institutions which became affiliated, but after 1858 to all students without restriction. In 1900 it was reorganized as a teaching body, the instruction being given in the schools and colleges already existing. The Chancellor is H.M. Queen Elizabeth, the Queen Mother, and the Vice-Chancellor is Dr P. S. Noble. Under statutes made in 1926, London University is governed by the Senate, which controls all academic matters, and the Court, which controls the finances; the Senate includes the heads of the principal schools and eighteen members elected by Convocation, which comprises graduates of the university who have attained the age of twenty-one (approximately 50,000) and acts also as an advisory body.

The university has faculties of theology, arts (including architecture), laws, music, medicine, science, engineering, and economics (including sociology, etc.), and awards degrees in philosophy. Students attending the affiliated schools and institutes (which have their own governing bodies) are registered as 'internal students', while those presenting themselves for examination only are known as 'external students'. Other institutions are not part of the organization, but have teachers 'recognized' by the university. The total number of teachers is about 2,000, of internal students more than 25,000.

The schools of the university include *Bedford College* (p. 182), *Birkbeck College* (see below), *Imperial College of Science & Technology* (p. 150), *King's College* (p. 212), *London School of Economics* (p. 217), *London School of Hygiene & Tropical Medicine* (see above), *New College* (Hampstead), *Queen Elizabeth College* (p. 155), *Queen Mary College* (p. 481), *Richmond College* (Richmond, Surrey), *Royal Holloway College* (near Egham, Surrey), *Royal Veterinary College* (p. 179), *School of Dental Surgery* (p. 198), *School of Oriental & African Studies* (see below), *School of Pharmacy* (p. 220), *University College* (see below), *Westfield College* (Hampstead), and *Wye College* (near Ashford, Kent). Of these Bedford College, Royal Holloway College, and Westfield College are for women undergraduates only. In addition, there are medical schools attached to the principal hospitals (compare p. 267), while specialist institutes established by the university include the *Courtauld Institute of Art* (p. 165), *Institutes of Advanced Legal Studies* (p. 195), *Archæology* and *Classical Studies* (p. 196), *Commonwealth Studies* (p. 195), *Education* (see below), *Germanic Languages & Literatures* (p. 195), and *Historical Research* (see below), the *Lister Institute of Preventive Medicine* (p. 139), the *School of Slavonic & East European Studies* (see below), and the *Warburg Institute* (p. 195).

The principal building of the university, designed by Charles Holden with a massive tower 210 ft high, is the SENATE HOUSE. This contains the administrative offices and the University Library, which holds over 800,000 volumes and 4,000 current periodicals and includes special collections of Elizabethan literature, economics, and music; and houses also the SCHOOL OF SLAVONIC AND EAST EUROPEAN STUDIES (founded 1933), the INSTITUTE OF HISTORICAL RESEARCH (founded 1921), and (on the north) the INSTITUTE OF EDUCATION, established in 1932 for the training of teachers in south-east England. To the north of this building is BIRKBECK COLLEGE, founded in 1823 as a scientific and technical institute, and admitted to the university in 1920. It has about 1,500 students (all evening or part-time), catered for in buildings opened in 1951. The SCHOOL OF

ORIENTAL AND AFRICAN STUDIES, to the east of this, was founded in 1916 and moved to a new building here in 1941–4; it has about 620 students, and faculties of arts and laws. To the north of Birkbeck College, and entered from Malet Street, is the STUDENTS' UNION building, opened in 1955, with a dining-hall, library, gymnasium, etc. All these three buildings were likewise designed by Charles Holden.

COLLEGE HALL (1931), on the other side of Malet Street, is a hall of residence for women students. Some institutes of the university are accommodated in Russell Square (Route 19), while other schools and departments will be housed in this area as space becomes available.

Malet Street ends on the north at TORRINGTON PLACE, which leads to the right towards Gordon Square (Route 19) and left to Tottenham Court Road.

In Malet Place, the continuation of Malet Street, are a new building (by H. O. Corfiato, 1960) for the FACULTY OF ENGINEERING of London University, and the NATIONAL CENTRAL LIBRARY, established in 1933 for the exchange of books among public and official libraries throughout the British Isles. It is able to draw on over 21 million books in practically all the chief libraries.

In Tottenham Court Road, almost facing Torrington Place, stood WHITEFIELD'S TABERNACLE, a chapel built originally in 1756 by George Whitefield (d. 1770), the evangelist, but destroyed by bombing in 1945. A new memorial chapel, designed by Edward C. Butler, was completed in 1958. The shop, nearly opposite, of MESSRS HEAL, the furniture-dealers, by Messrs Smith and Brewer (1937), is one of the most successful commercial buildings in London. Goodge Street station is a little to the south.

Torrington Place crosses Gower Street (compare p. 187), which leads northward past the ROYAL NATIONAL INSTITUTE FOR THE DEAF (established 1911) and the entrance to UNIVERSITY COLLEGE (III, B 2), founded in 1826 through the efforts of Lord Brougham, Thomas Campbell, James Mill, and other lovers of religious toleration for the purpose of providing, on a non-sectarian basis, 'at a moderate expense the means of education in literature, science and art'. Incorporated in the University of London in 1907, the college provides courses in the faculties of arts, laws, science, engineering, and economics, and in medical sciences, and has about 3,800 students. The main building, in a classical style by William Wilkins (1828), has a fine Corinthian portico approached by flights of steps. Considerable extensions and additions have been made from time to time, and restoration from severe war damage was completed in 1954.

Beneath the dome, recast by T. L. Donaldson in 1848 and restored in 1952, is the FLAXMAN GALLERY, containing models by John Flaxman (d. 1826), the sculptor, bought in 1858 by public subscription. In the ground-floor galleries on either side are drawings by Flaxman, and (on the south) the 'Marmor Homericum', a design in marble showing Homeric subjects by Baron Triqueti (1865), presented by George Grote, the historian. Interested visitors may also see the clothed skeleton of Jeremy Bentham (d. 1832), preserved (in the South Corridor) under the terms of his will, and the EGYPTOLOGY COLLECTION formed by Sir Flinders Petrie (d. 1942). Incorporated in the college are the SLADE SCHOOL OF FINE ART, established in 1871 by the bequest of Sir Felix Slade (d. 1868), the art-collector; the GALTON LABORATORY, set up by Sir Francis Galton (d. 1911), the founder of eugenics; the BARTLETT SCHOOL OF ARCHITECTURE, in a building provided by Sir Herbert H. Bartlett (d. 1921); and the SCHOOL OF LIBRARIANSHIP AND ARCHIVES. Sir William Jenner, Lord Lister, the economists Walter Bagehot and W. S. Jevons, and Sir William Ramsay, the chemist, were all teachers at the college; Alexander Graham Bell, the inventor of the telephone, worked as an undergraduate here; and Sir Ambrose Fleming was professor of electrical technology for forty-one years (1885–1926). Walter Sickert, Sir William Orpen, and Augustus John were students at the Slade School. In the south wing is the new building (by Sir Albert Richardson, 1954) housing the valuable MOCATTA LIBRARY AND MUSEUM of the Jewish Historical Society, presented to the college in 1906 and built up again after its destruction in the war. The fine GUSTAVE TUCK LECTURE THEATRE here is also by Richardson. A wall monument in Gower Street to Richard Trevithick (d. 1833) recalls that 'close to this place' he built the first railway on which a steam locomotive drew carriages for passengers (1808).

Opposite the college in Gower Street is UNIVERSITY COLLEGE HOSPITAL, founded in 1833 and rebuilt in 1897–1906 by Alfred Waterhouse, with a new wing of 1936 on the west, and a noted Medical School (1907) to the south. Grafton Way, starting north of the hospital, leads across Tottenham Court Road to Fitzroy Square (Route 16), while Gower Street goes on to EUSTON ROAD (III, B 2).

19 From Charing Cross to Euston via Holborn

Plan III, F 3–III, A 2

STATIONS: TRAFALGAR SQUARE (Plan III, F 3), on the Bakerloo line; STRAND (III, F 3), on the Northern line; LEICESTER SQUARE

(III, F 2, 3), on the Northern and Piccadilly lines; TOTTENHAM COURT ROAD (III, D 2), on the Central and Northern lines; HOLBORN (IV, D 1), on the Central and Piccadilly lines; RUSSELL SQUARE (III, C 3), on the Piccadilly line; EUSTON SQUARE (III, B 2), on the Circle and Metropolitan lines; EUSTON (III, A 2), on the Northern line. — MOTOR-BUSES Nos. 1, 24, 29, 39, 134, and 176 in the lower part of Charing Cross Road; Nos. 19, 22, and 38 in the upper parts of Charing Cross Road (northbound only) and Shaftesbury Avenue (southbound only); Nos. 7, 8, 19, 22, 23, 25, 32, and 38 in Bloomsbury Way (eastbound only) and High Holborn (westbound only); Nos. 68, 77, 188, and 196 in Southampton Row and Woburn Place. Other buses to Trafalgar Square, see Routes 2, 6, 21; in Euston Road, see Route 16.

ADMISSION to the NATIONAL PORTRAIT GALLERY, see p. 367; to POLLOCK'S TOY MUSEUM, weekdays 10 to 5 (free); to the PERCIVAL DAVID FOUNDATION OF CHINESE ART, Monday 2 to 5, Tuesday–Friday 10.30 to 5, Saturday 10.30 to 1 (free; closed on Bank Holidays, for the first two weeks in September, and on 24–31 December); to DR WILLIAMS'S LIBRARY, Monday–Friday 10 to 5, Saturday 10 to 1 (free); to the JEWISH MUSEUM, Monday–Thursday 2.30 to 5, Friday and Sunday 10.30 to 12.45 (free; closed on Jewish holy days); to the COURTAULD INSTITUTE GALLERIES, weekdays 10 to 5, Sundays 2 to 5 (free).

For CHARING CROSS and TRAFALGAR SQUARE, see Route 1. Opening off the north-east angle of the square, between St Martin-in-the-Fields and the National Gallery, is ST MARTIN'S PLACE, No. 6 in which is a survival of about 1830. In the centre of the road is a monument by Sir George Frampton (1920) to Edith Cavell, the nurse who was shot by the Germans at Brussels in 1915. On the left is the **National Portrait Gallery**, and on the north side of this is a statue of Sir Henry Irving (d. 1905), the actor, occupying approximately the site of the 'Old Curiosity Shop' immortalized by Dickens. Hence the short Irving Street leads to Leicester Square (Route 20). On the other side, near the foot of Charing Cross Road, are the WESTMINSTER CITY HALL (1890) and the GARRICK THEATRE (1889).

CHARING CROSS ROAD (III, F 3–D 2), an unprepossessing thoroughfare opened in 1887 and well known for its second-hand booksellers, runs north to St Giles Circus, at the junction of Oxford Street and Tottenham Court Road. On the right is WYNDHAM'S THEATRE (1899), just beyond which Cranbourn Street (Route 20) is crossed. In CAMBRIDGE CIRCUS, where Shaftesbury Avenue crosses (see below), is the PALACE THEATRE, built in 1891 as the English Opera House, and farther on are the PHOENIX THEATRE (1930), and the ST MARTIN'S SCHOOL OF ART, founded in 1854 and occupying a good modern building of 1936.

St Martin's Lane (III, E, F 3), an older and more interesting street, also known for its theatres, starts from the north-east corner of St Martin's Place. The Coliseum Theatre, on the right, opened in 1904, is one of London's largest theatres and was the first in the world to have a revolving stage. On the left are the Duke of York's Theatre (1892) and the New Theatre (1903), and on the other side of the road between these opens Goodwin's Court, containing a complete row of shops of the late 18th century. A tablet almost opposite the New Theatre recalls that the Chippendales had their furniture workshop near this site (1753–1813). Beyond the junction of Cranbourn Street, Long Acre, and Garrick Street (see Route 20) extends Upper St Martin's Lane, on the left of which rises the huge Thorn House (1960), designed by Sir Basil Spence, with an abstract bronze sculpture by Geoffrey Clarke on its flat wall.

In West Street, which leads beyond this to Cambridge Circus, are the St Martin's Theatre (1916) and the Ambassadors Theatre (1913), and adjoining this is the former St Giles's Mission Church, built originally in 1700 as a chapel for Huguenot refugees, but much altered later in the 18th century for the Methodists. John and Charles Wesley (from 1743), George Whitefield, and John Fletcher all preached here.

Upper St Martin's Lane is prolonged by Monmouth Street. At No. 44 is Pollock's Toy Museum, an exhibition of toys and dolls of many countries and periods, as well as toy theatres and early experiments in moving pictures. The street crosses Seven Dials (III, E 3), the junction of seven dingy streets and once notorious as the centre of a thieves' quarter; it takes its name from a column with seven dials which stood here until 1773 and is now at Weybridge (Surrey). On the right is the Cambridge Theatre, a notable modern building of 1930. Monmouth Street joins Shaftesbury Avenue, coming from Cambridge Circus (see above). To the left in this street are the Saville Theatre, another fine modern building (1931), decorated on the front by a bas-relief, and (on the other side) the French Hospital, founded in 1867 and occupying a building of 1899.

Shaftesbury Avenue, leaving St Giles High Street with its church on the left and High Holborn on the right (see Route 23), goes on past the Shaftesbury Theatre (built in 1911 and until recently the Princes Theatre) to reach New Oxford Street. Coptic Street, opposite the junction, is an approach to the **British Museum** (compare Route 18), while BLOOMSBURY WAY (formerly Hart Street) inclines to the right to Bloomsbury Square and Southampton Row (Route 22), passing ST GEORGE'S, BLOOMSBURY (III, D 3), a fine building of 1720–31 by Nicholas Hawksmoor, a pupil of Wren, now serving as the church of London University. Square in plan and in the classical style favoured by Hawksmoor, it has a grand display of Corinthian columns inside and out; the stepped spire, inspired by Pliny's description of the tomb of Mausolus at Halicarnassus (compare p. 319), is topped by an incongruous statue of George I that was a butt for the wits of the period.

BLOOMSBURY SQUARE (III, D 3), once a fashionable address, was laid out in 1661 by Thomas Wriothesley, fourth Earl of Southampton, and was the first open space in London to be called a 'square'. The original mansions of this time have all disappeared, but houses on the north side by James Burton (1800–14) have survived. The gardens were planted about 1800 by Humphry Repton; at the north end is a statue of Charles James Fox (d. 1806), the politician, by Westmacott.

Southampton Place, which runs south to High Holborn, has good houses of about 1750, in one of which (No. 17) Cardinal Newman spent part of his early life. No. 45 Bloomsbury Square, at the corner of the Place, was the town house of the Earls of Chesterfield; No. 2, farther west, is the COLLEGE OF PRECEPTORS (1889), an institute granting diplomas to teachers; and No. 6, on the west side, was the home of Isaac D'Israeli (d. 1848), father of Lord Beaconsfield. Nos. 16–17 are occupied by the PHARMACEUTICAL SOCIETY of Great Britain, founded in 1841. At the north-east corner stood the house of the Earl of Mansfield, Lord Chief Justice, burned in 1780 by the Gordon Rioters, as described by Dickens in *Barnaby Rudge.*

Great Russell Street leads west from the square to the main entrance of the British Museum, while BEDFORD PLACE, well built (like Montague Street farther west) by James Burton after 1800, runs north to the large RUSSELL SQUARE (III, C 3), which began to be laid out by him about the same time and became a favourite residence of merchants and professional men. On the south side of the gardens (in which entertainments are given in

summer) is an elaborate monument by Westmacott to the fifth
Duke of Bedford (d. 1805), the landowner.

The Imperial and Russell Hotels, on the east side, are examples of the
ostentatious style beloved by the late Victorians. No. 30, on the west (by
Sir John J. Burnet, 1915), is the ROYAL INSTITUTE OF CHEMISTRY
(founded 1877), with a seated figure of Joseph Priestley (d. 1804) over the
entrance in an approach to the Senate House of LONDON UNIVERSITY
(see Route 18). Nos. 25–9, among the few surviving houses by Burton in
the square (about 1814), now contain the INSTITUTES OF ADVANCED
LEGAL STUDIES (founded in 1948), OF COMMONWEALTH STUDIES
(1949), and OF GERMANIC LANGUAGES AND LITERATURES (1950), all
branches of the university. Sir Samuel Romilly (d. 1818), the law reformer,
lived at No. 21, on the north side; the large block of government offices
on this side includes the PAYMASTER GENERAL'S OFFICE, formed in
1835 and moved here from Whitehall. Readers of Thackeray's *Vanity Fair*
will recall that the Osbornes and Sedleys occupied houses in this square.

BEDFORD WAY, with uniform houses of 1814–17 by James
Burton, leads north from the square to Tavistock Square (see
below), while to the north-west is the narrow WOBURN SQUARE
(III, C 2, 3), built in 1828. CHRIST CHURCH here was designed
by Lewis Vulliamy in 1833 and contains an altarpiece (with
paintings by Burne-Jones) in memory of Christina Rossetti, the
poet, who died in 1894 at No. 30 Torrington Square, farther west,
now largely built over by London University. At the north-west
corner of Woburn Square is a building by Charles Holden (1958),
shared by the WARBURG INSTITUTE, founded in 1944 for
'research on the character and history of the classical tradition'
(and part of the university), and the COURTAULD INSTITUTE
GALLERIES, with an outstanding collection of paintings and
other works of art bequeathed by Samuel Courtauld (see p. 166)
and Lord Lee of Fareham, including some fine 18th-century
furniture and a splendid selection of the French Impressionists
and Post-Impressionists.

To the north of Woburn Square is GORDON SQUARE (III,
B, C 2), laid out by Thomas Cubitt about 1820, but mostly rebuilt
at various times. At its south-west angle is the imposing
CATHOLIC APOSTOLIC CHURCH, built in 1853 by Raphael
Brandon for a sect (known also as 'Irvingites') that had its origin
in the teaching of Edward Irving (d. 1834), the Scottish divine.
Next to it is UNIVERSITY HALL, opened in 1848 as a hall of

residence for Unitarians studying at University College, and now housing DR WILLIAMS'S LIBRARY of philosophy, theology, and the history of Nonconformity, founded in 1716 under the bequest of Daniel Williams, the Presbyterian minister. No. 53, at the south-east corner of the square, contains the PERCIVAL DAVID FOUNDATION OF CHINESE ART, comprising the unrivalled collection of ceramics made by Sir Percival David and given by him in 1950, together with his library dealing with Chinese art and culture, to the University of London.

The collection consists of about 1,500 pieces covering the Sung, Yüan, Ming and Ch'ing dynasties (from A.D. 960 onwards), some of which came from the former Imperial Collection in Peking and are inscribed with poems. etc., from the brush of the Emperor Ch'ien Lung (1735–95). Notable also are the 'blue and white' porcelain of Ching-tê-chên, and representative enamel decoration of the Ch'êng Hua period.

A building of 1958 on the north side of Gordon Square houses the INSTITUTES OF ARCHÆOLOGY (founded 1937) and of CLASSICAL STUDIES (1953) of the University.

Farther east is TAVISTOCK SQUARE (III, B 2, 3), also by Cubitt, a range of whose building (1826) survives on the west. In Woburn House, built in 1932, on the north side, is a thriving Jewish Communal Centre which accommodates also the JEWISH MUSEUM (entered from Upper Woburn Place), containing an interesting assembly of antiquities and of domestic and ritual art. Opposite on the east is the large building (by Sir Edwin Lutyens, 1925) of the BRITISH MEDICAL ASSOCIATION, established in 1832. The fountain memorial in the courtyard, by James Woodford and S. Rowland Pierce, was dedicated in 1954 to British medical men and women who died in the Second World War.

Woburn House occupies the site of Tavistock House, where Dickens lived in 1851–60, writing *Bleak House*, *Hard Times*, *Little Dorrit*, the *Tale of Two Cities*, and part of *Great Expectations*. A description of the Dickens household has been left by Hans Andersen, who visited the novelist here in 1857. Tavistock House South, adjoining the B.M.A. building, contains the head office of the ROTARY INTERNATIONAL. The first Rotary Club was formed in 1905 in Chicago (in 1911 in Britain), and there are now 431,000 Rotarians in ninety-nine countries. In the south-east corner of the square is a memorial by Lutyens to Dame Louisa Aldrich-Blake (d. 1925), the surgeon. WOBURN PLACE goes on thence to Russell Square (see above), while Tavistock Place runs east towards Regent Square (Route 22).

UPPER WOBURN PLACE, leading north from Tavistock Square, passes the end of WOBURN WALK, with its picturesque early-19th-century shop fronts. W. B. Yeats, the poet, lived at No. 5 here in 1895–1919. Upper Woburn Place reaches EUSTON ROAD beside St Pancras Church (see Route 16).

20 From Piccadilly Circus to Fleet Street via Covent Garden

Plan III, F 2–IV, E 2

STATIONS: PICCADILLY CIRCUS (Plan III, F 2), LEICESTER SQUARE (III, F 2, 3), COVENT GARDEN (III, E 3), HOLBORN (IV, D 1), and ALDWYCH (IV, E 1), all on the Piccadilly line; CHANCERY LANE (IV, D 2), on the Central line. Piccadilly Circus is also on the Bakerloo line, Leicester Square on the Northern line, and Holborn on the Central line. — MOTOR-BUSES to Piccadilly Circus, see Routes 7, 15, 18; to Charing Cross Road, see Route 19; to the Strand and Fleet Street, see Route 21; to Kingsway, see Route 22; to Chancery Lane, see Route 24.

ADMISSION to SIR JOHN SOANE'S MUSEUM, Tuesday–Saturday 10 to 5 (free; closed Sundays, Mondays, and in August; guide lectures on Saturdays at 2.30); to the ROYAL COLLEGE OF SURGEONS MUSEUM weekdays 10 to 5 (Saturdays to 1), on written application to the secretary (closed in August); to LINCOLN'S INN (Halls, Library, and Chapel) on application at the Porter's Lodge, Chancery Lane (best on Saturdays and Sundays or during vacation; gratuity); to the PUBLIC RECORD OFFICE MUSEUM, Monday–Friday 1 to 4 (free; closed on Bank Holidays).

For PICCADILLY CIRCUS, see Route 7. COVENTRY STREET, extending Piccadilly eastward from the upper end of the Haymarket, leads past the PRINCE OF WALES THEATRE (first opened in 1884), and the large headquarters of the AUTOMOBILE ASSOCIATION, which was founded in 1905 and now caters for over 2 million members. The building (extended in 1959) stands on the west side of LEICESTER SQUARE (III, F 2), named after the second Earl of Leicester, who built a house near by in 1637 (pulled down in 1790). The square, laid out about 1665 and once a favourite resort of duellists, was converted in 1874 into a public garden, an oasis in London's traffic, by Baron Grant, the company promoter. The marble statue of William Shakespeare, in the centre, is a copy of that in Westminster Abbey; around the garden are busts of Reynolds, Newton, Hogarth, and John

Hunter, all of whom lived in or near the square, which is now best known for its large cinemas.

The square was called by Thomas Pennant the 'pouting-place of princes', for in 1718 George II, when Prince of Wales, moved to Leicester House on quarrelling with his father, and in 1741 Frederick, Prince of Wales (son of George II), did the same. On the south side, beside the road leading to St Martin's Place and Trafalgar Square (Route 19), is the ROYAL DENTAL HOSPITAL, founded in 1858, with a school of dental surgery attached to London University.

In Leicester Place, north-east of the square, is the church of NOTRE DAME DE FRANCE, a circular building acquired by French Roman Catholics in 1865, bombed in 1940, and reconstructed in a fine modern style in 1955 by H. O. Corfiato. The circular wall is in fact a survival from an 18th-century 'panorama'. Over the entrance is a striking sculpture of the Virgin and Child, by Saupique; above the altar is a rich Aubusson tapestry woven by a Benedictine monk; and in the Lady Chapel are murals by Jean Cocteau (1959). Farther up is the PRINCE CHARLES THEATRE, designed by Carl Fisher and opened in 1962, with seats for 500 and a roof garden open to the public.

Coventry Street is prolonged eastward beyond Leicester Square by CRANBOURN STREET, which crosses Charing Cross Road (Route 19) at the former HIPPODROME THEATRE (1900), close to Leicester Square station. It meets St Martin's Lane at the junction of several streets, in one of which, Great Newport Street (on the left), is the NEW ARTS THEATRE, the best-known theatre club in London, first founded in 1927. The modern building faced with black tiles next to it occupies the site of a house in which Sir Joshua Reynolds lived in 1753–61. LONG ACRE (III, E 3), which continues Cranbourn Street towards Bow Street (see below), was a favoured address in the 17th century: Oliver Cromwell and John Dryden had houses here. Later it was given over to coach-builders, but it is now absorbed in the wholesale fruit trade of Covent Garden.

Garrick Street, which starts to the right of Long Acre, takes its name from the GARRICK CLUB (No. 15), founded in 1831 and favoured by the dramatic and literary professions. Its collection of theatrical paintings is said to be the best in Britain. From the farther end of the street Bedford Street descends to the Strand (Route 21), while KING STREET bears left to Covent Garden. A passage on the right of this street admits to the 'actors' church' of ST PAUL'S, COVENT GARDEN (III, E, F 3), a curious barn-like building, but the 'handsomest barn in Europe' in the words of its designer, Inigo Jones (1633). Rebuilt to the original design by Thomas Hardwick in 1798, after a fire, it has a portico at the east end, though the entrance is actually at the other end. A silver casket on the south wall contains the ashes of Dame Ellen Terry (d. 1928), the actress. Near by is a memorial to Charles Macklin (d. 1797), the actor, and on the north wall are others to John Bellamy (d. 1794), founder of the Whig Club, and Dr Thomas Arne (d. 1778), the composer of *Rule Britannia* (all are buried here).

The vaults and precincts of the church are said to contain the remains of more famous people than any other church in London, excepting Westminster Abbey and St Paul's Cathedral. Among these are Samuel Butler (d. 1680), the author of *Hudibras*; Sir Peter Lely (d. 1680), the artist; William Wycherley (d. 1715), the dramatist; Grinling Gibbons (d. 1721), the woodcarver; and Thomas Girtin (d. 1802), the water-colourist. Most of the gravestones, however, were moved when the churchyard was levelled. J. M. W. Turner, born in 1775 in Maiden Lane (house demolished), was baptized in this church.

A gate on the north side of the church gives access to COVENT GARDEN MARKET (III, E 3), the principal market in London for vegetables, fruit, and flowers. Though painfully congested, it presents a picturesque and lively scene when business is in full swing, particularly in the early morning and when the spring flowers are displayed. The market is most animated at about 6 a.m. and the main work of the day is over by midday; in the late afternoon and evening it seems unnaturally quiet. The fruit and vegetable market mostly occupies the northern half; the flower market is in the southern half.

The name of the place was originally Convent Garden, from an old garden of the monks of Westminster Abbey which stretched from Long Acre to the Strand. After the Dissolution the site was claimed by the Crown and in 1552 it was sold to the first Earl of Bedford, who built himself a house facing the Strand. In 1631–5 the area behind this was laid out for the fourth Earl as a select residential quarter by Inigo Jones. The central square was enclosed on two sides by terraces with arcades (miscalled 'piazzas'); these have now all vanished, though the eastern block on the north side has been recast in a style approaching the original. The south side of the square was formed by the gardens of Bedford House, the west side largely by St Paul's Church (see above). In 1661 the Duke of Bedford established a small market here under royal charter, the original of the present market, which was sold in 1913 by a later Duke and again in 1918 for £2½ million (the annual value of the site in 1552 had been about 6 guineas).

The older market buildings in the centre of the square were designed by Charles Fowler in 1831–3. On the north-west corner, at the beginning of King Street, is a late-17th-century house (much altered), the home after 1696 of Admiral Lord Orford (d. 1727) and later famous as Evans's Supper Rooms, the entertainments at which were visited by the Newcomes in Thackeray's novel. The east portico of St Paul's Church (p. 198), with its large Tuscan columns preserving Inigo Jones's design, was used as a background by Shaw in the first scene of *Pygmalion*. David Garrick, the actor, lived in 1750–72 at No. 27 SOUTHAMPTON STREET, which descends from the flower market to the Strand (Route 21).

RUSSELL STREET, east of the market, was well known in the late 17th and 18th centuries for its coffee-houses, frequented by Dryden, Pope, Swift, Fielding, Smollett, Johnson, and other literary lions. Boswell first met Johnson in 1763 at No. 8, then a bookshop, but considerably altered since. Russell Street leads past the north front of the Drury Lane Theatre (see Route 22), crossing, before this, the junction of Wellington Street, which descends to the Strand, and BOW STREET, running north 'in the shape of a bent bow'. On the left in this street is the ROYAL OPERA HOUSE (III, E 3), better known as the COVENT GARDEN THEATRE, the principal home of grand opera and ballet in London. The huge building, by Edward M. Barry (1856–8), has seats for about 2,000 and is well known for its excellent acoustics. Under the impressive Corinthian portico are a sculptured frieze and panels by Flaxman and Rossi salved from the previous theatre.

The theatre is the third on the site. At the first, built in 1732 by John Rich, the 'father of English pantomime', and burned down in 1808, Handel's *Samson* (1744) and all his later oratorios were produced. The second, built in 1809 and burned down in turn in 1856, became the chief opera-house in England. At one or other of the theatres have appeared David Garrick, Peg Woffington, Mrs Siddons, the Kembles, the Keans, and William Charles Macready, while the innumerable famous singers who have been heard here include Jenny Lind and Dame Nellie Melba. Adjacent to the theatre on the south is the glass-domed floral hall of Covent Garden Market, at present used as a store.

Opposite the theatre is BOW STREET POLICE COURT, built in 1881 and the chief of the fourteen Metropolitan police courts. The first courthouse was opened in 1748, with Henry Fielding and his blind half-brother, Sir John Fielding, as the magistrates. The novelist wrote part of *Tom Jones* while living in Sir John's house close by, burned down in the Gordon Riots (1780). The 'Bow Street Runners' (nicknamed 'Robin Redbreasts' from their scarlet waistcoats) were the predecessors of the present-day detective force. The colonnaded building in LONG ACRE facing the north end of Bow Street (now a publishing office) incorporates the Queen's Theatre, where in 1867 Henry Irving and Ellen Terry acted together for the first time.

Long Acre runs west to St Martin's Lane (see above) and in the other direction to Drury Lane, beyond which it is continued by GREAT QUEEN STREET, built about 1640 and named in honour of Henrietta Maria, queen of Charles I. Once a fashionable street, it still retains a few of its fine old houses (above more recent shop-fronts). On the right is the imposing FREEMASONS' HALL, the headquarters of the United Grand Lodge of England, rebuilt in 1927–33 as a war memorial to masons by H. V. Ashley and Winton Newman. The massive central tower rises to 200 ft above the pavement.

Great Queen Street is extended beyond the broad Kingsway (Route 22) by the short Remnant Street, which ends at the north-west angle of LINCOLN'S INN FIELDS (IV, D, E 1), the largest square in central London. The gardens, with their noble plane-trees and their tennis-courts, etc., are a favourite lunch-time promenade for city workers.

Before their enclosure in 1735 the 'fields' were the haunt of thieves and duellists, and an occasional place of execution. The north walk is named CANADA WALK to commemorate the setting up in the square of the Royal Canadian Air Force headquarters in 1940, and a memorial maple-tree, the gift of the City of Ottawa, was planted in 1945. Farther west in this walk is a memorial (with bronze figures by R. R. Goulden) to Margaret MacDonald (wife of the prime minister), who died in 1911 at No. 3 Lincoln's Inn Fields.

On the north side of the square, at No. 13, is SIR JOHN SOANE'S MUSEUM (IV, D 1), the private collection of antiquities and works of art gathered together by Sir John Soane (1753–1837), the architect, in the house he designed for himself in 1812 and where he lived until his death. He had previously lived next door at No. 12, which he designed in 1792, and these houses, together with No. 14, likewise by Soane, make a balanced composition. The collections have been left as far as possible as the architect arranged them, and features of the museum are the ingenious arrangements for enhancing the effect of space by the use of mirrors and for increasing the room available in the picture gallery by means of hinged shutters. Soane, a bold follower of the classical tradition, exercised a great influence on architecture, and the museum remains a valuable record of the taste of his time.

On the right of the entrance hall are the Dining Room and Library, thrown into one, with Soane's furniture and many of his books, and a portrait of the architect at the age of seventy-five, by Lawrence. Beyond the small Study and Dressing Room, containing antique marbles, etc., is a corridor which leads right to the Picture Room. This is chiefly notable for the two famous series of paintings by William Hogarth: *The Election*, four scenes executed in 1754–7, and *The Rake's Progress*, a series of eight painted in 1735 (beginning in the bottom left-hand corner). They are superb examples of the robust humour and harmonious composition of Hogarth. Also here are landscapes by Turner, Callcott, and others, 18th-century architectural drawings by Piranesi and Clérisseau, and large pictorial drawings of Soane's own compositions. A stair close by leads down to the 'Crypt', with the Monk's Parlour (left), described as a 'Gothick fantasy', and the Sepulchral Chamber, which contains the remarkable sarcophagus of Seti I, king of Egypt about 1370 B.C. and father of Rameses the Great. This was discovered in 1817 and purchased by Soane for £2,000 after it had been declined by the British Museum. Made from a monolithic block of alabaster, it is ornamented inside and out by scenes and texts from the 'Book of the Gates', while inside, on the bottom, is a figure of the goddess Nut into whose keeping the deceased king was committed. Recesses around the chamber contain Roman funerary urns and other antiquities, and models by the sculptors Flaxman and Banks.

On the ground floor a colonnade, above which is a gallery with models of Soane's buildings (shown on application to the curator), leads to the central Dome, a kind of 'grotto of antiquities' with original sculptures and casts, the former including a bust of Soane by Chantrey. The New Picture Room at the end (replacing the architect's study) and the adjacent ante-room were added in 1889, and contain sculptures, and paintings by Watteau and Canaletto (three fine Venetian scenes). The Breakfast Room, reached from the ante-room, has a shallow domed ceiling, and terracotta busts by Flaxman on the black marble mantelpiece.

The staircase ascends, passing the Shakespeare Niche (with a model of the poet's bust at Stratford), to the Drawing Rooms, the principal rooms of the house in Soane's time, now arranged to contain his collection of architectural books and over 30,000 drawings, ranging from the Elizabethan plans of John Thorpe to work by Wren, Chambers, Robert Adam, and Soane himself. These and the books may be consulted on application to the curator, Sir John Summerson.

The varied doorways of Nos. 15, 16, and 26, on the north side of Lincoln's Inn Fields, are worth notice. POWIS HOUSE, on the west side (No. 66), is a well-restored brick mansion of 1686 built for the first Duke of Newcastle; No. 65 is a house of 1772 by Thomas Leverton. Nos. 59–60, built about 1640 for the Earl of Lindsey, comprise a fine mansion designed most probably by Inigo Jones, while Nos. 57–8 were built in the same style in the 18th century by Henry Joynes. No. 60 was the residence in 1790–1807 of Spencer Perceval, the prime minister, and No. 58, the home in 1834–56 of John Forster, the biographer of Dickens, is described as the abode of Mr Tulkinghorn in *Bleak House*. Nell Gwyn lived in lodgings here while an actress and here her first son, later the Duke of St Albans, was born. From the south end of this range Sardinia Street (see Route 22) leads back to Kingsway, while Portsmouth Street runs south towards the Strand.

On the south side of the square are the research centre (1960) of the IMPERIAL CANCER RESEARCH FUND and the large building, with a pronounced Ionic portico, of the ROYAL COLLEGE OF SURGEONS (IV, E 1), rebuilt in 1835 by Sir Charles Barry, but much altered since. The college, founded in 1800, contains a museum that was the finest of its kind in the world before the war, but unfortunately suffered greatly from bombing. Its nucleus is the fine collection of anatomical preparations formed by John Hunter (d. 1793) and presented to the college in 1799, and new collections have been added as a result of a gift from the Wellcome Trustees. A handsome building on the west (by Alner W. Hall), completed in 1957, houses the NUFFIELD COLLEGE OF SURGICAL SCIENCES. The last building on this side is the LAND REGISTRY, established in 1862, in a characteristic Victorian building.

The archway at the south-east corner of the Fields admits to LINCOLN'S INN (IV, D 1, 2), one of the four great Inns of Court (compare p. 231), with its main entrance in Chancery Lane (see below). The quiet precincts are freely accessible to the public (except on Ascension Day).

Lincoln's Inn may have taken its name from Henry de Lacy, Earl of Lincoln (d. 1311), who had a house not far away in Holborn. His crest of a lion appears in the society's arms and he was probably an early patron. Later in the 14th century, however, the inn occupied a site in Holborn that belonged to Thomas de Lincoln, described as the King's Serjeant. Between 1412 and 1422 (when the existing records begin) the society moved to its present site, where it took over the town house of the bishops of Chichester, built after 1227 by Ralph Nevill, also chancellor of England, from whom Chancery Lane (formerly 'Chancellor's Lane') derived its name. The rolls of the inn contain many famous names, among which may be mentioned Sir Thomas More, John Donne, William Penn, Horace Walpole, William Pitt, George Canning, Cardinal Newman, Disraeli, and Gladstone.

On the left of the west entrance is the NEW HALL AND LIBRARY, a building in the Tudor Gothic style by Philip Hardwick (1845). The hall is decorated with a huge mural painting, 45 ft high, by G. F. Watts ('Justice, a Hemicycle of Lawgivers'), completed in 1859 and restored in 1955. The library, founded in 1497, is the oldest in London and comprises the most complete collection of law-books in England (80,000 volumes). On the north-east are the gardens, open to the public on Monday–Friday (12 to 2.30), and beyond are the attractive STONE BUILDINGS, a classical range by Sir Robert Taylor (1756) mainly occupied by practising barristers.

NEW SQUARE, south of the road through the inn, is a charming and well-preserved quadrangle of the late 17th century, now mainly occupied by solicitors. Dickens, at the age of fourteen, served as a clerk in a solicitor's office here for a short time. On the north of the gardens is a fine ironwork gate dated 1863. Farther east are the picturesque OLD BUILDINGS, dating mainly from the 16th and early 17th centuries. An archway opens to a small courtyard, on the west side of which is the OLD HALL, built in 1491, extended on the south by one bay in 1624, and carefully restored in 1928. It has a fine open roof, a painting by Hogarth of St Paul before Felix, and a carved oak screen attributed to Inigo Jones. The hall served as the Court of Chancery from 1737 until 1883, and the case of Jarndyce v. Jarndyce (in *Bleak House*) was heard here. The CHAPEL, on the north of the courtyard, was built in a Gothic style by Inigo Jones (1620–3), but was restored in 1685 by Wren and lengthened westward in 1883, and has been otherwise repaired. The foundation stone was laid by John Donne, the poet, who also preached the first sermon here. The chapel has old oak pews, an 18th-century pulpit, and 17th-century Flemish glass (by Bernard van Linge), restored after being shattered by a Zeppelin bomb in 1915. The east window contains the arms of treasurers from 1680 to 1908. In the open crypt or undercroft below, long used (like the Temple Church) as a meeting-place for barristers and their clients, is buried John Thurloe (d. 1668), Cromwell's secretary of state, who had chambers in Old Buildings in 1646–59. On the east side of the courtyard is the noble GATE-HOUSE, facing Chancery Lane and bearing the arms of Sir Thomas Lovell, who built it in 1518. It was restored in 1957. Below the archway is the porter's lodge, and rooms above are said to have been occupied by Oliver Cromwell as a law student.

CHANCERY LANE, with the offices of stationers, patent agents, and others connected with the law, runs north to High Holborn (see Route 23) and south to Fleet Street. In Carey Street, on the right in this direction, No. 60 is a fine house of the mid 18th century. On the left, just beyond the street, is the PUBLIC RE-CORD OFFICE (IV, E 2), an elaborate building in a Tudor Gothic style, begun in 1851 by Sir James Pennethorne and completed in 1902 by Sir John Taylor. This is the chief repository for the national archives and legal records, brought together from various courts of law and government departments, and it con-tains also a small museum where a selection of documents of exceptional interest is displayed.

During the office hours (9.30 to 5, Saturday to 1) the Search Rooms, containing records from the Norman Conquest onward, are open to the public. Records more than fifty years old are generally open to inspection by holders of students' tickets, obtainable on written application to the secre-tary, and photographic copies of records are obtainable. The Keeper of the Records was until recently the Master of the Rolls, a judge who ranks im-mediately below the Lord Chief Justice.

The museum, renovated in 1956, is entered on the left under the archway. It occupies the exact site of a chapel of a house founded in 1232 by Henry III for converted Jews, but assigned in 1377 by Edward III to the Keeper (later the Master) of the Rolls, who adapted it for his private use. The chapel was pulled down in 1896 to make way for the present buildings, but the 13th-century chancel arch, which came to light then, has been re-erected against a wall beyond the archway (on the right). The museum preserves three monuments in their original positions on the north wall: on the left, to Richard Alington (d. 1561) and his wife; in the centre, to Edward, Lord Bruce of Kinloss (d. 1611), Master of the Rolls; and on the right, to Dr John Yong (d. 1516), another Master, a splendid Renaissance work confidently attributed to Torrigiani. The windows contain heraldic glass, mostly modern, showing the arms of Keepers and Masters of the Rolls.

Of the many famous documents on view, only a few can be mentioned. A case against the north wall contains the two vellum volumes of *Domesday Book*, the most important exhibit, a statistical survey of thirty-four counties of England made by order of William the Conqueror (1086). Case I: Medieval letters and charters, the earliest dated 1254. Cases II, III: 16th-century letters, etc., including letter from Cardinal Wolsey asking Henry VIII's forgiveness (1529); and view of Kirk o' Field, Edinburgh, illustrating Lord Darnley's murder (1567). Cases IV, V: 17th-century letters, etc.; anonymous letter to Lord Monteagle warning him of the Gunpowder Plot, and confessions signed by Guy Fawkes (1605). Cases VI, VII: 18th–19th-century letters, etc., including one from Napoleon to George III. Case VIII: Magna Carta in its final form as issued by Henry III (1225; compare p. 334); letters patent of Edward I confirming the charter, and the first enrolment of the charter in Chancery (1297). Case IX: Plea Rolls, the earliest dated 1194. Case X: Exchequer Rolls, including the earliest surviving Pipe Roll (1129–30), on which the accounts of revenue collected by the sheriffs were entered. Case XI: Painted wooden coffer made for documents concerning the Peace of Calais (1360). Case XII: 'Olive Branch' Petition to George III from Congress (1775), with the signatures of John Adams, Benjamin Franklin, and others; map made by George Washington (1753–4), and letter of his to his 'great and good friend' George III (1795); and other documents concerning the United States. Case XIII: Commonwealth documents; letter from Livingstone reporting his meeting with Stanley (1871). Cases XIV–XVI: Royal Autographs, the earliest of the Black Prince (1370); coronation roll of Queen Elizabeth II, showing the oath signed by Her Majesty (1953).

Next to Case A, which contains Charter and Patent Rolls of King John, etc., is the iron-bound chest in which the Domesday volumes were kept in the Chapter House of Westminster Abbey. Case B: Medieval Charters, the earliest of William Rufus (1094). Case C: Great Seals of Elizabeth I, James I, and Victoria, and other official seals. Case D: Papal Bulls, etc., including bull of Pope Clement VII confirming Henry VIII as 'Defender of the Faith' (1524); letters patent of John Baliol signifying his sworn allegiance to Edward I (1292). Cases E, F: Exchequer Books and two Royal Surveys, the illuminated 'abbreviatio' of Domesday Book (early 13th century) and Henry VIII's 'Valor Ecclesiasticus' (1535). Cases G, H: Seals attached to the Barons' letter to Pope Boniface VIII (1301); tallies used for keeping accounts; dies and bindings. Cases J, K: Account books of Henry VII and Elizabeth of York, etc. Case L: Letters of musicians, painters, architects, engineers, and scientists. Cases M, N: Parliament and the Law; earliest surviving parliamentary writ (1275); illuminated book of statutes (1327–1460); gaol book delivered by Judge Jeffreys at the 'Bloody Assizes' (1685). Cases O, P: The Navy; Black Book of the Admiralty (15th century); despatches from Lieut. Bligh relating to the Mutiny of the *Bounty* (1789); log-book of the *Victory*, describing the Battle of Trafalgar (1805). Case Q: The Army; indentures for the pay of Welsh men-at-arms drawn up for Henry V (1415); Marlborough's despatch from the Battle of Blenheim (1704) and Wellington's from Waterloo (1815). Cases R, S: Treaties with Portugal (1386), France (1527), and Spain (1605). Case T: 'Scrap of Paper' guaranteeing the neutrality of Belgium (1839), and other modern treaties. Cases U–Y: Literature: letter of about 1222, one of the earliest extant paper documents in Europe; the Abingdon Indulgence, the earliest specimen of printing in England (1476); warrant authorizing the King's Players (including Shakespeare) to perform at the Globe Theatre (1603); signature of Shakespeare (1612); Bunyan's application for a preaching licence (1672); letters of Sir Philip Sidney, Spenser, Ben Jonson, Bacon, Milton, Boswell, Scott, and other men of letters, and the only known copy of a poem by Shelley (1812). In the corridor is one of the medieval bells of the Rolls Chapel.

Opposite the Record Office is the classical building (by Lewis Vulliamy, 1832) of the LAW SOCIETY, founded in 1827 and controlling the education and examination of articled clerks in England and Wales and the admission of solicitors. It has about 18,000 members and a library of over 60,000 volumes. Chancery Lane ends at FLEET STREET near Temple Bar; thence to Charing Cross, see below; to St Paul's Cathedral and the Bank, see Route 24.

21 From Charing Cross to Fleet Street via the Strand

Plan III, F 3–IV, E 2

STATIONS: TRAFALGAR SQUARE (Plan III, F 3), on the Bakerloo line; STRAND (III, F 3), on the Northern line; ALDWYCH (IV, E 1), on the Piccadilly line. — MOTOR-BUSES Nos. 1, 6, 9, 11, 13, 15, 60, 77, and 176 in the Strand (eastbound buses follow Aldwych); Nos. 1 and 176 cross Waterloo Bridge and No. 77 turns up Kingsway. For other buses to Charing Cross, see Routes 2, 6, and 19.

ADMISSION to the ROYAL SOCIETY OF ARTS (Hall), weekdays on application (after 9.30), when not in use; to the QUEEN'S CHAPEL OF THE SAVOY, Monday–Friday 10 to 4 (in winter to 3), Saturday 10 to 1

(Service on Sunday at 11.15, except in August and September); to the 'ROMAN' BATH, weekdays 10 to 12.30 (1/-); to AUSTRALIA HOUSE, Monday–Friday 9 to 5.15; to the LAW COURTS, see p. 214.

For CHARING CROSS and TRAFALGAR SQUARE, see Route 1. The STRAND (III, F 3–IV, E 2), which runs eastward from the square, was so named because it skirted the bank of the Thames, but this has receded in the course of time and is now hidden by intervening buildings. In Tudor and Stewart times the road was bordered by aristocratic mansions whose gardens sloped down to the river. It is still, as then, the principal thoroughfare between the West End and the City, and in consequence is one of the busiest streets in London, apart from its many shops, hotels, and theatres. CHARING CROSS STATION (III, F 3), on the right, is a terminus of the Southern Region, built in 1864 (for the South Eastern Railway Company) by Sir John Hawkshaw; the large hotel above it was designed by E. M. Barry. In the station yard stands an 'Eleanor Cross' (a memorial, though not a copy, of the one that stood at Charing Cross), likewise designed by Barry (1865).

In the north-west corner of the yard is an entrance to the Strand underground station. The Southern Region station occupies the site of Hungerford Market and Hungerford Stairs, which descended beside the blacking factory in which Charles Dickens worked as a boy. CRAVEN STREET and Villiers Street, on either side of the station, go down towards the Victoria Embankment (Route 26) and Charing Cross underground station. Heinrich Heine, the German poet, lodged at No. 32 Craven Street in 1827, and Benjamin Franklin, the American statesman, scientist, and author, lived in 1757–62 and 1764–72 at No. 36, now the head-offices of the British Society for International Understanding, founded in 1939, and various Anglo-American societies. VILLIERS STREET, like Buckingham Street, parallel on the east, is named after George Villiers, Duke of Buckingham, who rebuilt York House on this site (compare p. 246). Rudyard Kipling made his first London home (in 1889–91) at No. 43 Villiers Street. Samuel Pepys lived in 1679–85 at No. 12 BUCKINGHAM STREET (much altered since), and the painters William Etty (in 1824–49) and Clarkson Stanfield (in 1826–31) at No. 14. Pepys occupied a previous house on this site in 1685–1700, and others associated with this once-favoured district include Robert Harley, Earl of Oxford, the statesman, Sir Richard Steele, Henry Fielding, and David Hume. Dickens lived at No. 15 Buckingham Street, where also Miss Betsey Trotwood took rooms for David Copperfield, but this house has been rebuilt. Nos. 17 and 18, however, are good houses with notable doorways.

JOHN ADAM STREET, which runs east from Villiers Street and parallel to the Strand, traverses a region formerly known as THE ADELPHI (Greek 'adelphoi', brothers) from the four brothers Adam, who laid it out in 1768–74. The character of the neighbourhood has been destroyed by modern building, but a delightful example of the work of Robert Adam survives in No. 8 John Adam Street, built in 1772–4 and occupied by the ROYAL SOCIETY OF ARTS (III, F 3), founded in 1754 for the promotion of science in art, manufactures, and commerce. The fine hall is decorated with six large mural paintings by James Barry (1777–83) illustrating the progress of civilization. Next to it is the MINISTRY OF PENSIONS and National Insurance, in a modern building, and opposite is the huge Adelphi, a grandiose block of offices built in 1938. It takes the place of Adelphi Terrace, the forefront of the Adam design and the residence of David Garrick, the actor (who died here in 1779), Thomas Hardy, and Bernard Shaw. In ROBERT STREET, close by, Nos. 1–3 (possibly to be demolished) were occupied at one time or another by Robert Adam (d. 1792), Thomas Hood, John Galsworthy, and Sir James Barrie. ADAM STREET, in which No. 7 retains the original decorative scheme of the Adams, leads back from the east end of the Adelphi to the Strand.

VILLIERS HOUSE, on the south side of the Strand beyond Villiers Street, was built partly over the pavement to allow the road to be widened (1960). Opposite is COUTTS' BANK, the bank of the royal family, founded in 1692 and moved here in 1904. Beyond this, but lying back from the corner of Agar Street, is the CHARING CROSS HOSPITAL (III, F 3), established in 1818 and rebuilt in 1831 by Decimus Burton; the medical school on the north, now part of London University, was founded in 1821. On the other side of the Strand is a glimpse of the north front (by Sir Aston Webb, 1927) of the Royal Society of Arts building (see above). On the north of the Strand are the NEW ZEALAND GOVERNMENT OFFICES (to be moved to the Haymarket, p. 130); the shop of Messrs Peter Robinson's opposite is a successful example of recent commercial architecture. Beyond this, Adam Street (see above) goes off on the right.

On the north side of the Strand are the ADELPHI THEATRE, built originally in 1806 but reconstructed in 1930, and the VAUDE-VILLE THEATRE, opened in 1870 and rebuilt in 1926. Nearly opposite this is the huge SHELL-MEX HOUSE, better seen from the Embankment (Route 26). Southampton Street, on the opposite side of the Strand, leads to Covent Garden Market (see Route 20). On the right of the Strand are the SAVOY HOTEL, entered from a forecourt, and the SAVOY THEATRE (rebuilt in 1929), at which most of the Gilbert and Sullivan operas were produced from 1881 onwards under the direction of Richard D'Oyly Carte.

Savoy Street, on the same side farther on, descends to the Victoria Embankment (Route 26), passing the QUEEN'S CHAPEL OF THE SAVOY (IV, F 1), built in 1505 in the late-Perpendicular fashion and largely rebuilt in the same style after a fire in 1864. The private chapel of the ruling monarch as Duke of Lancaster, it has been since 1937 also the Chapel of the Royal Victorian Order, the youngest order of chivalry in Britain (1896), of which the Queen is sovereign. At the west end are the royal pews, and on the panelling at the sides are small copper plates emblazoned with the arms of the members of the order. The window over the door displays the arms of masters and chaplains of the Savoy and others connected with the chapel, including Gavin Douglas (d. 1522), the poet, bishop of Dunkeld, who is buried here.

The window next to this is in memory of Richard D'Oyly Carte (d. 1901; see above), while a window in the opposite wall with heraldic glass by Joan Howson (1956) commemorates Queen Mary (d. 1953). The window over the altar, designed in part by George VI, has heraldic glass relating to the Royal Victorian Order, and other windows were inserted in memory of the King and the Duke of Kent (d. 1942).

The chapel stands on part of the site of the Savoy Palace, built by Henry III and granted in 1246 to Peter, Count of Savoy, his wife's uncle. Subsequently it passed to John of Gaunt, Duke of Lancaster, whose son Henry IV annexed the Lancastrian estates (including the manor of the Savoy) to the Crown (1399). King John of France, taken prisoner in 1356 at the Battle of Poitiers, died in the palace in 1364, and Geoffrey Chaucer, the poet, is thought to have been married here (in 1366 or before). John Wyclif, the propagator of the Reformation, preached here under the patronage of John of Gaunt. Burned down during the Peasants' Rising of 1381, the palace was rebuilt by Henry VII in 1505 as a hospital, but of this only the chapel has survived. The Independents drew up their 'Confession of Faith' here during the Commonwealth (1658), and the important Savoy Conference on the revision of the Prayer Book took place here in 1661. Samuel Pepys has described several visits to hear the sermons of Thomas Fuller, author of *The Worthies of England*, who died in 1661 after being seized with a fever in the chapel. The ancient ceremony of beating the bounds of the Liberty of the Savoy takes place annually on or near 20 July (after a service in the chapel at 10.20 a.m.).

In SAVOY HILL, below the chapel, the British Broadcasting Company (see below) opened their well-known studio in 1923. Their successor, the BBC, incorporated in 1927, remained here until 1931.

LANCASTER PLACE (IV, F 1), on the right beyond the Savoy, runs past the west front of Somerset House to Waterloo Bridge (Route 25), while WELLINGTON STREET ascends on the left to Bow Street and the Covent Garden Theatre.

In this street is the LYCEUM THEATRE (now a dance-hall), at which Sir Henry Irving experienced many of his greatest triumphs. He began his long connexion with the theatre in 1871 and took over the management in 1878, with Ellen Terry as his leading lady, a partnership that lasted until Irving's death in 1905. At No. 26, on the corner of Tavistock Street, Dickens edited his weekly journal, *All the Year Round* (1859–60), in which the *Tale of Two Cities*, *Great Expectations*, and *The Uncommercial Traveller* appeared.

The crescent of ALDWYCH (IV, E 1), followed by all eastbound traffic, bears to the left for Kingsway (see Route 22). The former Gaiety Theatre, at the corner, has been replaced by a new building (by Adams, Holden, and Pearson; 1960) for the English Electric Company. Beyond, in the Strand, is MARCONI HOUSE, in which the Marconi Wireless Telegraphy Company set up the first public broadcasting station in Britain in May 1922. In November it was taken over by the British Broadcasting Company, who, however, moved in 1923 to Savoy Hill (see above).

On the other side of the Strand is the classical north front of SOMERSET HOUSE (IV, E, F 1), a vast quadrangular building erected by Sir William Chambers in 1776–86, with additional wings on the east (by Smirke, 1835) and west (by Sir J. Pennethorne, 1856). Its principal façade is on the south, facing the Thames (see p. 247). In the quadrangle is a notable bronze fountain-group by John Bacon the elder (1778).

Somerset House occupies the site of a palace begun for himself in 1547 by the Duke of Somerset, Lord Protector of Edward VI, but still unfinished at his execution in 1552, when it passed to the Crown. Elizabeth I occupied the palace for part of the reign of her sister Mary, and it later became the residence of the queens of James I and Charles I and II. Inigo Jones, the architect, is believed to have died here in 1652, and Oliver Cromwell lay in state here in 1658. In the present building rooms were occupied at first by the Admiralty (to which some of the decorations in the quadrangle refer), the Royal Academy, the Royal Society, and the Society of Antiquaries.

The building is now mainly occupied by public offices. In the north wing is the GENERAL REGISTER OFFICE for the registration of births, marriages, and deaths, an office thought to have been established in 1522 by Thomas Cromwell, though it was not until 1836 that a system of civil registration was instituted. The west wing is occupied by the BOARD OF INLAND REVENUE, inaugurated in 1849 and dealing mainly with death duties, stamps, and taxes. In the south wing is the PROBATE AND DIVORCE REGISTRY, containing a register of wills and testaments dating back to 1382. During office hours (Monday–Friday 10 to 4) any will may be inspected for a fee of 2/- (1/- for a registered copy). Among the many interesting wills kept here are those of Shakespeare, William Penn, Sir Isaac Newton, Dr Johnson, Lord Nelson, the Duke of Wellington, and Charles Dickens.

The east wing of Somerset House is partly occupied by KING'S COLLEGE, which has a separate entrance in the Strand. Founded in 1829, primarily for members of the Church of England, it was incorporated in 1910 in the University of London. It provides courses in the faculties of arts, laws, science, and engineering, and in medicine, and has a library of about 200,000 volumes. A separate theological department was established in 1846 with the object of training candidates for holy orders in the Church of England.

In the middle of the Strand here rises the charming little baroque church of ST MARY-LE-STRAND (IV, E 1), a masterpiece of James Gibbs (1714–17), beautifully proportioned and with a graceful steeple and an unusual coffered ceiling to the nave. This was the first of the 'Fifty Churches' designed by the order of Queen Anne. Prince Charles Edward Stewart, the 'Young Pretender', a Roman Catholic, is claimed to have been secretly received into the Church of England here in 1750. The most famous rector of the previous church on this site was Thomas Becket, archbishop of Canterbury.

At No. 5 STRAND LANE, an alley starting on the right opposite the east end of the church, is the so-called ROMAN BATH (N.T.), a brick bath or possibly reservoir of unknown date, probably Tudor, but certainly not Roman, as is now generally recognized. Measuring 15 ft 6 in. long, it is fed by a spring with a rate of flow of about 2,000 gallons a day. Here also is a second bath or reservoir perhaps installed by Thomas Howard, Earl of Arundel, Surrey, and Norfolk (d. 1646), whose town house stood near by and is, like that of Robert Devereux, Earl of Essex (d. 1601), remembered in the names of the neighbouring streets (compare below).

To the north of St Mary's towers the huge BUSH HOUSE, whose main entrance faces Kingsway (see Route 22). Farther east is the imposing AUSTRALIA HOUSE (IV, E 1), built in 1911–18 by A. Marshall Mackenzie and A. G. R. Mackenzie as the headquarters in London of the Commonwealth of Australia. Flanking the entrance are groups representing Exploration and Agriculture, and above the cornice are the Horses of the Sun, by Mackennal. The interior, embellished with Australian wood and marble, contains a reference library open to visitors. In the middle of the roadway where the Strand is re-joined by Aldwych is the national memorial to W. E. Gladstone, by Sir Hamo Thornycroft (1905), showing the statesman robed as Chancellor of the Exchequer, with groups at the foot representing Brotherhood, Education, Aspiration, and Courage.

In the roadway to the east stands the church of ST CLEMENT DANES (IV, E 1), built in 1680–1 by Sir Christopher Wren, gutted by bombing in 1941, but beautifully restored in 1958 by W. A. S. Lloyd in its original style as the headquarters church of the Royal Air Force. The steeple (115 ft high), added by Gibbs in 1719, happily escaped damage, though the 17th-century bells of the famous peal ('Oranges and lemons, say the bells of St Clement's') were all cracked by falling to the ground. They were recast in 1957 from the old metal by Messrs Mears and Stainbank, who in 1588 cast the sanctus bell, the only one that escaped injury.

Let into the floor are the 735 crests, carved in Welsh slate, of all the units in the R.A.F., and rolls of honour contain the names of 125,000 men and women of the R.A.F. and associated services who died in the World Wars. On the piers are the crests of the R.A.F. Commands. The pulpit was pieced together from fragments, salvaged from the bombing, of the original, attributed to Grinling Gibbons. The reredos was painted by Ruskin Spear; the stained glass windows in the sanctuary are by Carl Edwards. The organ was subscribed for by members of the United States Air Forces. Under the west gallery is a United States Air Force shrine, and let into the floor here are the crests of the Commonwealth air forces. The Crypt, constructed in 1691 and now converted into a chapel, has an altar and sanctuary given by the Royal Netherlands Air Force and a fine black marble font, the gift of the Royal Norwegian Air Force. A stone in the floor at the head of the staircase commemorates pilots of the R.A.F. who trained in Georgia in 1941–2.

A previous church on this site is said to have derived its name from a settlement of Danes here before the Norman Conquest, and to have been the burial-place of Harold I (Harold Harefoot; d. 1040) and other Danish leaders. Oranges and lemons are again distributed among the children of the former parish after a special service held in March. Dr Samuel Johnson (d. 1784), who worshipped regularly in the church, is commemorated by a statue (by Percy Fitzgerald, 1910) outside the east end.

CLEMENT'S INN, north of the church, survives in name only as one of the nine Inns of Chancery (compare p. 225). Justice Shallow, in Shakespeare's *Henry IV*, Part II, was 'once of Clement's Inn'. No. 3 was the headquarters of the Women's Social and Political Union (the Suffragette Movement), founded by Emmeline Pankhurst in 1903. ESSEX STREET, on the right beyond the church, was laid out on the grounds of Essex House in 1675, but has been rebuilt since. Henry Fielding and other lawyers lived here. Prince Charles Edward Stewart stayed in this street in 1750, and Dr Johnson established a club here in 1783. ESSEX HALL, destroyed in 1944 and rebuilt (by Kenneth Tayler) in 1958, is the headquarters of the Unitarian and Free Christian Churches and stands on the site of the original Unitarian church, established in 1774.

On the north of the Strand just beyond rises the elaborate Gothic edifice of the LAW COURTS (IV, E 1, 2), officially the ROYAL COURTS OF JUSTICE, the central office of the Supreme Court of Judicature for England and Wales, established in 1873. This rambling and unrealistic pile of buildings, with a frontage of 514 ft to the Strand, was begun in 1874 by G. E. Street and completed in 1882 after the architect's death by Sir Arthur Blomfield and A. E. Street. The lofty Central Hall (no general admission), 238 ft long and 80 ft high, has a mosaic floor by Street and statues of the architect (d. 1881), of Sir William Blackstone (d. 1780), presented by the American Bar Association in 1924, and of Lord Russell of Killowen (d. 1890). The various courts, entered by way of the hall, number thirty in all, serving the Court of Appeal and the three divisions of Chancery, Queen's Bench, and Probate, Divorce and Admiralty. When the courts are sitting (Monday–Friday 10 to 4.15, during the legal terms), the public is admitted to the galleries, approached on either side of the main entrance.

The entrances for the judges, barristers, and solicitors are in Carey Street, on the north, and here also is the Bankruptcy Court. On or about 23 October the historic ceremony of paying Quit Rents (to which visitors are admitted) takes place at the Law Courts. The payment is for the rent of two pieces of land whose whereabouts have been forgotten: the 'Moors' in Shropshire and the 'Forge' at St Clement Danes. For the first the Corporation of London offers two faggots cut with a bill-hook and a hatchet, and for the second six horse-shoes and sixty-one nails, and the rents are collected by the Queen's Remembrancer on behalf of the Crown.

The shop of Messrs Twining's, the tea merchants, opposite the main entrance of the Law Courts, is probably the smallest in London. Near the east end of the Law Courts and the foot of

Chancery Lane is the ineffectual TEMPLE BAR MEMORIAL, denoting the end of the Strand and the beginning of Fleet Street, as well as the boundary between Westminster and the City. Designed by J. E. Boehm and set up in 1880, with statues of Queen Victoria and Edward VII (as Prince of Wales) on either side and a bronze 'griffin' (by C. B. Birch), the unofficial badge of the City, on the top, it marks the site of Temple Bar, a triple gateway built by Wren in 1672, taken down in 1878, and erected ten years later at Theobald's Park (Herts).

A gateway of one kind or another marking the entrance to the City is thought to have stood on this spot as early as the 12th century. On spikes at the top the heads of executed traitors and felons were exposed, while Titus Oates (in 1685) and Daniel Defoe (1703) were among those stood in the pillory here. When the sovereign visits the City on state occasions the custom (dating back to the reign of Elizabeth I, if not earlier) of 'asking permission' to pass Temple Bar is still observed. The sovereign is met here by the Lord Mayor of London, who surrenders the Sword of State; this is immediately returned to him and is henceforth carried before the Queen as a symbol that he is responsible for her protection in the City.

For FLEET STREET, and thence to St Paul's Cathedral and the Bank, see Route 24; for CHANCERY LANE, etc., see Route 20.

22 From the Strand to King's Cross via Kingsway and Coram's Fields

Plan IV, E I–III, A 3

STATIONS: ALDWYCH (Plan IV, E 1), on the Piccadilly line; HOLBORN (IV, D 1), on the Central and Piccadilly lines; CHANCERY LANE (IV, D 2), on the Central line; RUSSELL SQUARE (III, C 3), on the Piccadilly line; KING'S CROSS & ST PANCRAS (III, A 3), on the Circle, Metropolitan, Northern, and Piccadilly lines. — MOTOR-BUSES Nos. 68, 77, 170, 172, 188, and 196 in Kingsway; Nos. 68, 77, 188, and 196 in Southampton Row; Nos. 5, 19, 38, 170, and 172 in Theobalds Road; Nos. 17, 18, 45, and 168 in Gray's Inn Road. For buses in the Strand and Aldwych, see Route 21; in New Oxford Street and High Holborn, see Route 23; to King's Cross, see Routes 16, 29.

ADMISSION to INDIA HOUSE, Monday–Thursday 9 to 5.30, Friday 9 to 5; to DICKENS HOUSE, weekdays (except Bank Holidays) 10 to 12.30 and 2 to 5 (1/-); to the FOUNDLING HOSPITAL (Offices), Mondays (except Bank Holidays) and Fridays 10 to 12 and 2 to 4 (or by arrangement; free).

From Charing Cross to Lancaster Place, the approach to

Waterloo Bridge, see Route 21. ALDWYCH, which curves to the north from the Strand at this point, is said to take its name from an old settlement ('ald wic') of the Danes in this neighbourhood (compare p. 213). Catherine Street, the first street on the left, leads past the DUCHESS THEATRE (1929) and the main entrance of the DRURY LANE THEATRE (IV, E 1; officially the Theatre Royal, Drury Lane), one of the largest (3,000 seats) and most famous theatres in London, long noted for spectacular drama and pantomime, but now better known for musical comedy. The theatre, the fourth on this site, was built in 1809–12 by Benjamin Wyatt; the massive Ionic colonnade in Russell Street on the north was added by Samuel Beazley in 1832 and the auditorium was reconstructed in 1922, but Wyatt's vestibule, rotunda, and staircases remain intact and are the only interior parts of a Georgian theatre surviving in London.

In the foyer is a statue of Shakespeare by John Cheere (d. 1787), while the rotunda beyond contains statues of Edmund Kean (as Hamlet), Michael Balfe, the composer, David Garrick, and Shakespeare, and a plaque with a portrait of Sir Henry Irving, 'from the dramatic artistes of Italy'. The first theatre on the site was built in 1663 for Thomas Killigrew and the 'King's Company', and Nell Gwyn, said to have been born in an alley off Drury Lane, traditionally sold oranges here before she became an actress. It was rebuilt in 1674 (after a fire) by Wren, and John Dryden became its principal playwright. The theatre, restored in 1775 for Garrick (after being damaged in a riot), was rebuilt again in 1791–4 by Henry Holland for R. B. Sheridan, and burned down in 1809. Garrick's management began in 1746 with a prologue by Dr Johnson that included the famous line, 'We that live to please must please to live'. Sheridan was manager from 1776 until 1816 and produced his delightful comedies here, and others connected with Drury Lane were Colley Cibber, Charles Macklin, John Kemble, Sarah Siddons, and Edmund Kean (who made his first appearance in London here). The prologue for the opening of the present building was written by Lord Byron.

Russell Street (see Route 20) leads west from the theatre to Bow Street and Covent Garden. On the north side are the FORTUNE THEATRE (1924) and an alley admitting to the CROWN COURT CHURCH of Scotland, opened in 1718 and rebuilt in 1909.

On the north-west side of the wide crescent of Aldwych are the STRAND THEATRE and the ALDWYCH THEATRE, with the Waldorf Hotel between them, a single composite design of 1905, and on the other side of the road is INDIA HOUSE (IV, E 1), the office of the High Commissioner for the Republic of India, built in 1928–30 by Sir Herbert Baker. The interior, decorated in the Indian style with carving and paintings by artists of that country, includes a reference library, reading room, and cinema (films on Monday–Friday at 3, Saturday at 11.30). Facing up Kingsway is BUSH HOUSE, a massive block of office buildings completed in 1931 to the designs of Messrs Helmle, Corbett, and Harrison of New York, and named after Irving T. Bush, the American business executive. Over the main entrance is a colossal sculpture, 'Youth' (by Malvina Hoffman, 1925), 'to the friendship of English speaking peoples'.

Aldwych makes a wide sweep down again to the Strand (Route 21), with a good view of St Clement Danes. In Houghton Street, on the left, is the LONDON SCHOOL OF ECONOMICS, founded in 1895 and now a branch of London University. It has faculties of arts (in certain spheres), laws, and economics and political science. The present buildings date from 1902 and 1920–8. Attached to the school is the British Library of Political and Economic Science, established in 1896 and now the largest of its kind in the world, comprising over 350,000 volumes and about 400,000 tracts and pamphlets.

KINGSWAY (IV, D, E 1), a fine boulevard 100 ft wide opened in 1906, runs northward from Aldwych to High Holborn and Southampton Row, lined mainly by large office buildings. The tram subway nearly ¾-mile long beneath the street, connecting the Embankment with Southampton Row, was closed in 1952, when London's last tram ran, but is being converted (1963) into a road underpass for northbound traffic. On the west side of Kingsway is the chief sales department of the STATIONERY OFFICE (compare p. 227). TELEVISION HOUSE, at the east corner, now the headquarters of the London commercial television programme contractors, was the principal office of the Royal Air Force in 1919–55. The site of the Stoll Theatre, farther up, is occupied by an office building, by Lewis Solomon, Kaye, and Partners (1960), with the ROYALTY THEATRE in its basement.

The theatre is entered from Portugal Street, on the south side, which leads to CLARE MARKET, formerly notorious as a thieves' quarter, and PORTSMOUTH STREET, a quaint 16th-century antique shop which claims to be the original of Dickens' 'Old Curiosity Shop' (but see p. 192). Sardinia Street, on the right of Kingsway farther north, leading to Lincoln's Inn Fields (Route 20), takes its name from a chapel of the Sardinian embassy (see below). On the north side of the street is the PUBLIC TRUSTEE OFFICE, a government office opened in 1906 and rehoused in 1916.

The KINGSWAY HALL, on the west side of Kingsway, is the headquarters of the Methodist West London Mission and is used for services, lectures, and concerts. Beyond it Great Queen Street leads left to Drury Lane and Long Acre (Route 20). On the right in Kingsway is the Roman Catholic church of SS. ANSELM AND CECILIA, built in 1909 by Frederick Walters to take the place of the Sardinian chapel, the first building to be burned in the 'No Popery' riots of 1780. HOLY TRINITY CHURCH (IV, D 1), on the left, built in 1910 by Sir John Belcher and J. J. Joass, stands on the site of the house in which Mary Lamb killed her mother in a fit of insanity in 1796.

Kingsway is prolonged beyond High Holborn (with Holborn station; Route 23) by SOUTHAMPTON ROW (III, C, D 3), which goes on to Russell Square (Route 19). On the right are the BAPTIST CHURCH HOUSE (1903), with a statue of John Bunyan at the Eagle Street angle, and the CENTRAL SCHOOL OF ARTS AND CRAFTS of the L.C.C. (by W. E. Riley, 1908; with a large new extension on the north, 1962). The huge ADASTRAL HOUSE (1948–50), in Theobalds Road, to the right, became in 1955 the headquarters of the Air Ministry, who brought with them the name of their previous home in Kingsway, adapted from the R.A.F. motto, *Per ardua ad astra*.

A new road on the right, near the beginning of Theobalds Road, admits to RED LION SQUARE (IV, D 1), laid out in 1684 by Nicholas Barbon, a notorious speculative builder, but almost entirely rebuilt since. No. 17, on the south side, was occupied by D. G. Rossetti in 1851 and by William Morris and Edward Burne-Jones in 1856–9. At the north-east angle is CONWAY HALL (1929), the headquarters of the South Place Ethical Society, a liberal religious body founded originally in 1793. Princeton Street leads east from the square to BEDFORD ROW (IV, C, D 1), an exceptionally wide street with characteristic examples of early-18th-century architecture. Well restored after bomb damage, it is mainly occupied by solicitors and accountants. The street is extended north beyond Theobalds Road by GREAT JAMES STREET, with unspoiled terraces of about 1720–30, and this by Millman Street to Guilford Street (see below).

At No. 22 THEOBALDS ROAD, east of Great James Street,

Benjamin Disraeli was born in 1804. Farther on is the HOLBORN CENTRAL LIBRARY (1960). The line of the road is continued eastward beyond Gray's Inn Road by Clerkenwell Road (passing near St John's Gate and Church, Route 29) and Old Street, which ends at Shoreditch (Route 32), but the route follows JOHN STREET, starting opposite the gardens of Gray's Inn. This street, which has rows of houses of about 1760, is prolonged by DOUGHTY STREET, in which Sydney Smith, the clerical wit, lived in 1803–6 at No. 14.

No. 48 Doughty Street, now called the DICKENS HOUSE (IV, C 1), was the home of Charles Dickens from March 1837 until late in 1839, and is the only residence of the novelist to have survived intact structurally. Here the *Pickwick Papers* were completed, *Oliver Twist* and *Nicholas Nickleby* written, and *Barnaby Rudge* started (though the last did not begin to appear in print until 1841). Mary Hogarth, Dickens' sister-in-law, died in this house in 1837, and here his daughters Mamie and Kate were born. The house was purchased in 1924 by the Dickens Fellowship and now contains a wealth of portraits, illustrations, autograph letters, and furniture and relics of Dickens, as well as the most complete library in the world appertaining to the novelist. In the basement is the 'Dingley Dell' kitchen, a reproduction of that in which the Pickwickians made merry.

LONDON HOUSE, at the corner of Doughty Street and Guilford Street, was designed by Sir Herbert Baker in 1937 (and extended in 1948) as a hall of residence for men students from the Commonwealth. Doughty Street ends at MECKLENBURGH SQUARE, the east side of which (damaged by bombing) was built as a formal design by Joseph Kay about 1812, while GUILFORD STREET runs west past the end of Millman Street (compare above).

GREAT ORMOND STREET, which leads west from Millman Street, has several good houses of the early 18th century. No. 23 (a later building) was the home of John Howard, the prison reformer, from 1777 until his death in 1790. On the north side is the HOSPITAL FOR SICK CHILDREN (IV, C 1), the first and perhaps the largest hospital of its kind, founded in 1852 by Dr Charles West, and occupying buildings of 1872–90, with a new wing on the north in memory of Viscount Southwood (d. 1946), the newspaper proprietor, a former chairman of the hospital. The large bronze figures of SS. Nicholas and Christopher, by Gilbert Ledward (1952–5), are intended for new buildings to be designed by Easton and Robertson. At the west end of the street is the LONDON HOMŒOPATHIC HOSPITAL (1895), with an extension of 1909 in QUEEN SQUARE (III, C 3), probably named after Queen Anne, though the lead statue in the garden may well represent Mary II, Caroline, or Charlotte. F. D. Maurice, the theologian who established the Working Men's College near by (now at Camden Town), lived in 1846–56 at No. 21, at the north-west corner. At the north-east corner is the NATIONAL HOSPITAL for Nervous Diseases, founded in 1859 and to be rebuilt; at the south end are the ITALIAN HOSPITAL (1899) and the church of ST GEORGE THE MARTYR, built in 1706–23 and restored in 1952. A footway from the south-west corner of the square goes on to Southampton Row.

Guilford Street skirts the south side of CORAM'S FIELDS (III, B 3–IV, B 1), a large playground laid out over the grounds of the FOUNDLING HOSPITAL. The hospital was established in 1739 by Captain Thomas Coram (d. 1751) for the care of destitute children, and enjoyed the support of the composer Handel and the painter Hogarth, who persuaded artists to give works for sale to raise funds for the charity. Dickens, in *Little Dorrit*, made Tattycoram a 'foundling'. The hospital was moved in 1926 to Redhill (Surrey), then to Berkhamsted (Herts), where it is now the Thomas Coram School, but the offices remain, in a new building of 1937 on the north side of Brunswick Square, west of the fields. In the handsome Court Room here, an exact copy of the original, much of the old woodwork and plaster-work has been installed, and this room and the Picture Gallery contain fine paintings by Hogarth (Captain Coram, etc.), Kneller, Reynolds, and Millais, a cartoon by Raphael, and sculpture by Roubiliac. Other mementoes include Hogarth's punch bowl, the keyboard of Handel's organ, and the original score of *Messiah*.

BRUNSWICK SQUARE (III, B 3) was laid out with Mecklenburgh Square, on the other side of the fields, as a balanced composition by S. P. Cockerell (1790), and still retains some of its original houses. The large new SCHOOL OF PHARMACY (founded in 1842) of London University, next to the Foundling Hospital offices, was begun in 1939, to designs by Herbert J. Rowse, and completed in 1960. West from the square, Bernard Street leads to Russell Square station, and CORAM STREET, in which Thackeray lived at No. 13 in 1837–42, to Woburn Place (Route 19).

John Ruskin was born in 1819 at No. 54 HUNTER STREET,

which runs north from Brunswick Square, passing the SCHOOL OF MEDICINE of the Royal Free Hospital, a school of London University founded in 1874. The street ends at Tavistock Place, leading west to Tavistock Square (see Route 19) and east to REGENT SQUARE (III, B 3), of which only the south side survives from the Regency.

The PRESBYTERIAN CHURCH (of England), on this side, was designed in 1824 by Sir William Tite, who apparently received the inspiration for the north front from York Minster. The church (gutted by bombing) was built for Edward Irving, the Scottish Presbyterian minister, and here took place the 'speaking with unknown tongues', as described by his friend Carlyle, before Irving's expulsion for his heterodox views in 1832. The Presbyterian Church House close by was erected in 1955–7 by Maxwell Ayrton and Courtenay Theobald. On the east side of the square is ST PETER'S CHURCH, built in 1824–6 by W. and H. W. Inwood in a Grecian style less satisfying than their parish church of St Pancras. It was likewise severely damaged by bombing and still awaits restoration.

Sidmouth Street runs east from Regent Square to GRAY'S INN ROAD (IV, A 1–D 2), a long dismal thoroughfare leading southward to Holborn. In this direction is the ROYAL FREE HOSPITAL, founded in 1828 and occupying classical buildings first opened in 1842 as the Light Horse Volunteer Barracks, and extended several times since. The EASTMAN DENTAL HOSPITAL adjoining (by Burnet, Tait and Lorne, 1929) was the gift of an American citizen.

In AMPTON STREET, the extension of Sidmouth Street, the Carlyles lodged for nearly four months in 1831–2 at No. 33 (then No. 4). The northward end of Gray's Inn Road is at KING'S CROSS (Route 16).

23 From St Giles Circus to St Paul's Cathedral via Holborn

Plan III, D 2–IV, E 3

STATIONS: TOTTENHAM COURT ROAD (Plan III, D 2), HOLBORN (IV, D 1), CHANCERY LANE (IV, D 2), and ST PAUL'S (IV, E 3), all on the Central line. Tottenham Court Road is also on the Northern line (Charing Cross section) and Holborn on the Piccadilly line. HOLBORN VIADUCT (IV, D 3) is a terminus of the Southern Region. — MOTOR-BUSES Nos. 7, 8, 22, 23, 25, and 32 all ply from St Giles Circus to the Bank; No. 171 in Chancery Lane (northbound) and New Fetter Lane (southbound);

Nos. 17, 18, 45, 168, and 171 in Gray's Inn Road; Nos. 17, 45, and 168 in Shoe Lane (northbound) and Farringdon Street (southbound), for Ludgate Circus. For other buses to St Giles Circus, see Routes 14, 18; for buses in Shaftesbury Avenue, High Holborn, and Bloomsbury Way, see Route 19; in Kingsway and Southampton Row, see Route 22; in Cheapside and St Martin's-le-Grand, see Route 29.

ADMISSION to the PATENT OFFICE LIBRARY, Monday–Friday 10 to 9 (the office itself closes at 4), Saturday 10 to 1 (free); to GRAY'S INN HALL, CHAPEL, AND LIBRARY, usually on written application to the Under-Treasurer (to the gardens, see p. 224); to ST SEPULCHRE'S CHURCH, Monday–Friday 8 to 4 (Saturdays to 3.30); to ST ANDREW'S, HOLBORN, Monday–Friday 8 to 5; to the CENTRAL CRIMINAL COURT, on Saturdays at 11, on other weekdays when the court is not sitting at 11 and 3 (free; to the public galleries, see p. 228); to the GENERAL POST OFFICE, Monday–Thursday, 10 to 7.30 (visit takes about $2\frac{1}{2}$ hours), to the CENTRAL TELEGRAPH OFFICE, Monday–Friday, at 2, both on application to the Regional Director, London Postal Region, EC1 (three weeks' notice advisable; no children admitted).

For ST GILES CIRCUS, where Oxford Street meets Tottenham Court Road and Charing Cross Road, see Route 14. NEW OXFORD STREET (III, D 2, 3), which extends Oxford Street eastward to join High Holborn, was cut through a slum quarter in 1847. ST GILES HIGH STREET, the older and more interesting thoroughfare, starting south-east of the circus, leads to the beginning of High Holborn. It passes the church of ST GILES-IN-THE-FIELDS (III, E 3), rebuilt in 1731–3 by Henry Flitcroft, with a noble baroque steeple 150 ft high. The church is the third on the site, the first having been a royal foundation of Matilda, queen of Henry I (1101). The fine interior, well restored in 1953, has columns of Tuscan red marble and a decorative stucco barrel vault. The original wrought-iron altar rails have been replaced and the Regency font brought back.

At this font Clara Allegra Byron, daughter of Lord Byron and Miss Clairmont, was baptized in 1818, and Shelley had his two children baptized (possibly on the same day), three days before he left England for the last time. In the north-west corner of the church is a tombstone to the memory of George Chapman (d. 1634), translator of Homer, and on the north wall is a memorial tablet to Andrew Marvell (d. 1678). Both poets are buried in the church, as are Lord Herbert (d. 1648), the poet, and James Shirley (d. 1666), the dramatist. In the vestibule is a monument erected in 1930 to John Flaxman (d. 1826), with a sculpture by his own hand.

The gateway on the west side of the churchyard has a curious relief of the

Day of Judgement in the tympanum, dating from 1687. Opposite the south-east corner of the church is the restored table-tomb of Richard Penderel, 'unparallel'd Pendrell' (d. 1672), who helped Charles II to escape after the Battle of Worcester. The inscription (original in the church) is worth reading. Sir John Oldcastle, the Lollard leader and supposed original of Shakespeare's Falstaff, was 'hung and burnt hanging' in St Giles's Fields in 1417. The Great Plague of London (1665) began in this area, later spreading to the City.

The huge ST GILES COURT, north of the High Street, accommodates branches of the Ministry of Aviation and other government departments. HIGH HOLBORN (III, D 3–IV, D 2) starts beyond Shaftesbury Avenue (Route 19) and passes south of the Shaftesbury Theatre. In Endell Street, on the right, is the SWISS PROTESTANT CHURCH, founded in 1762 and rebuilt in 1854; services are held on Sunday in French (in German at St Mary Woolnoth). Beyond the WESTMINSTER OPHTHALMIC HOSPITAL, founded in 1816 by George Guthrie, the military surgeon, and rehoused in 1928, Drury Lane (Route 20) diverges on the right, and farther on is the HOLBORN TOWN HALL, a flamboyant building of 1906 by Warwick and Hall.

High Holborn, joined on the left by New Oxford Street, goes on to cross the north end of Kingsway (Route 22). Little and Great Turnstile, two passages on the right farther on, lead to Lincoln's Inn Fields and the Soane Museum (Route 20). Between the passages are the heavily ornate buildings of the PEARL ASSURANCE COMPANY, erected in 1914–30 and extended in 1956–62. On the left rises the 16-storey STATE HOUSE, by Trehearne and Norman Preston and Partners (1960), the main offices of the DEPARTMENT OF SCIENTIFIC AND INDUSTRIAL RESEARCH, established in 1916. In a courtyard is a huge abstract bronze, 'Meridian' (15 ft high and weighing 4 tons), by Barbara Hepworth. CHANCERY LANE (Route 20) bears to the right farther on for Lincoln's Inn and Fleet Street. In Southampton Buildings, the next turning on the right, is the PATENT OFFICE (IV, D 2), a department of the Board of Trade which grants patents for new inventions and registers designs and trade-marks. The library of over 380,000 volumes includes the finest collection of scientific and technical works in England. The office is adjoined on the east by the gardens of Staple Inn (see below).

On the north side of High Holborn (at No. 21) is a late-17th-century entrance gateway to GRAY'S INN (IV, C 1–D 2), one of the four Inns of Court (compare p. 231), known to have existed as a school of law in the 14th century, and named after the landowners, the Lords de Gray. Many of the buildings were greatly damaged by bombing. The Library, rebuilt by Sir Edward Maufe (1958), is on the east side of South Square, which contains a statue (by F. W. Pomeroy, 1912) of Francis Bacon, the philosopher and statesman, who was treasurer of the inn and retained his chambers here from 1576 until his death in 1626. On the north side of the square is the fine Hall, built in 1556–60, bombed in 1941, and rebuilt in 1951 largely in its original style, though with an additional oriel window, the gift of the American Bar Association. The late-16th-century carved screen and 16th–17th-century heraldic glass survived the bombing and have been replaced, and plaques on the walls bear the arms of treasurers since 1775. Shakespeare's *Comedy of Errors* was first acted in the hall in 1594, and the Court of Exchequer met here in the 18th century. To the north of this range of building is the delightful late-17th-century Gray's Inn Square (restored after war damage), from which there are exits to Gray's Inn Road. The contemporary Chapel, on the south, altered about 1840, was gutted by bombing but restored in 1960. To the west are the charming Gardens, laid out about 1600, where Pepys and Addison walked, the 'best gardens of the Inns of Court' (Charles Lamb). The older of the catalpa trees here is reputed to have been planted by Bacon from slips brought home from America by Sir Walter Raleigh. The gardens are open from Monday to Friday in June–July (12 to 2) and August–September (9.30 to 5).

Famous members of the inn include Sir Nicholas Bacon, the statesman, father of Francis Bacon; Sir William Gascoigne, the Chief Justice who is credited with committing the Prince of Wales (later Henry V) to prison; Thomas Cromwell, the minister of Henry VIII; Lord Burghley and Sir Francis Walsingham, the Elizabethan statesmen; Archbishop Laud; John Bradshaw, the regicide; Sir Samuel Romilly, the legal reformer, who occupied chambers at No. 6 Gray's Inn Square in 1778–91; Lord Macaulay, the historian; and Lord Birkenhead, the Conservative statesman.

High Holborn ends at the foot of Gray's Inn Road, and HOLBORN (IV, D 2) begins here. This broad thoroughfare takes its name from the 'Hole Bourne', the upper part of the Fleet River (compare p. 230), which flowed through a deep hollow or valley. Stone obelisks on either side of the road (Holborn Bars) mark the entrance to the City of London. Opposite is STAPLE INN, with its picturesque half-timbered façade of overhanging gables, built in 1586 and the only survival of Elizabethan domestic architecture in London, restored in 1937.

The inn, reputed to have been in the 14th century a hostel of the wool merchants ('merchants of the staple'), became in the reign of Henry V (1413–22) one of the nine Inns of Chancery in London. These were subordinate to the Inns of Court (compare p. 231) and the custom was for students of law to enter an inn of chancery before passing on to an inn of court, but since the 18th century they have had no connexion with the law and have mostly disappeared or been rebuilt. Staple Inn was arranged round two courtyards, erected in 1545–89 and largely rebuilt in the 18th century. In 1886, after it had ceased to be an inn of chancery, it was acquired by the Prudential Assurance Company, who later leased it to the INSTITUTE OF ACTUARIES, founded in 1848. Devastated in 1944 by a flying-bomb, the inn was largely restored in its former style by 1954. The Hall, on the south side of the first court, was rebuilt in 1955 incorporating material salved from the bombed 16th-century hall. Dr Johnson occupied No. 2 in the court in 1759–60, when he is said to have written *Rasselas* in the evenings of a week to pay for his mother's funeral. Mr Grewgious, in *Edwin Drood*, had chambers in the second court, which has only partially been rebuilt.

In the roadway is the ROYAL FUSILIERS WAR MEMORIAL (City of London Regiment), by Albert Toft (1922), and to the left are the offices of the PRUDENTIAL ASSURANCE COMPANY, grandiose Gothic buildings in red brick by Alfred Waterhouse (1879). Under the arch to the inner court is a bust (by Percy Fitzgerald) of Charles Dickens, who lived in 1834–7 (and began the *Pickwick Papers*) at Furnival's Inn, a former inn of chancery on this site. On the south side of Holborn is the entrance to the former MERCERS' SCHOOL, founded in 1447 but closed in 1959. The hall was the Tudor hall of Barnard's Inn (another inn of chancery), where Pip and Herbert Pocket shared rooms, in *Great Expectations*. Beyond Fetter Lane and the tall offices of the *Daily Mirror* group (by Anderson, Forster, and Wilcox; 1961), remarkable for the use of colour, is HOLBORN CIRCUS (IV, D 2), with an inferior equestrian statue of Prince Albert (1874).

St Andrew Street, to the right here, descends to St Bride Street (for Ludgate Circus). On the north of the circus begins HATTON GARDEN, well known as the street of diamond merchants. Giuseppe Mazzini, the Italian patriot, lived in exile at No. 5 (which has a bas-relief portrait) in 1841–2, while inspiring his young countrymen in their struggle for political freedom.

Charterhouse Street runs north-east from Holborn Circus towards Smithfield and Charterhouse (Route 29). On the left at the outset is ELY PLACE (IV, D 2), a private cul-de-sac, lined by charming late-18th-century houses with 'Adam' doorways. Still outside the jurisdiction of the police, it is watched over day and night by a beadle who before the war called the hours from 10 p.m. to 5 a.m. The street derives its name from a town house of the bishops of Ely (pulled down in 1772), in which John of Gaunt died in 1399. The famous garden, referred to in *Richard III* (iii, 4), was granted in 1576 to Sir Christopher Hatton, Lord Chancellor of Elizabeth I, for the annual rent of £10, ten loads of hay, and a red rose plucked at midsummer. The only survival from the bishop's house is ELY CHAPEL, called ST ETHELDREDA'S CHURCH since it was purchased in 1874 by the Roman Catholics (the first pre-Reformation church in England to be so returned). Built about 1290, it is a masterpiece of the Geometrical or early Decorated style, restored in 1935 by Sir Giles G. Scott and again in 1952 after damage to its fine chestnut roof. The splendid windows at the east and west ends show interesting tracery: the east window has striking new glass by Joseph E. Nuttgens (1953); the west window is claimed to be the largest in London. Notable also are the carved corbels for statues, with crocketed gables above, between the side windows The moulded doorway on the south-west is the original entrance from the palace, and the little cloister on this side is planted with fig-trees. Below the church is a large crypt or undercroft, built in 1251 incorporating the stout walls of a much older structure, probably of Romano-British origin. The wooden piers here were introduced during a restoration in 1875.

HOLBORN VIADUCT (IV, D 2, 3), about ¼-mile long, was built in 1867–9 by William Haywood over the valley of the 'Hole Bourne' to connect Holborn Circus with Newgate Street. On the right is ST ANDREW'S CHURCH, rebuilt in 1686–7 by Wren (who in 1704 refaced and heightened the medieval tower), but bombed in 1941 and restored in 1961 in its former style by Lord Mottistone, who also designed the tomb of Captain Thomas Coram (see p. 220). The font, pulpit, and organ were originally in the Foundling Hospital.

The salvaged registers record the burial of Thomas Chatterton, the youthful poet (who poisoned himself at his lodgings at No. 39 Brooke Street, since rebuilt), and the baptism in 1817 (at the age of 12) of Benjamin Disraeli, born into the Jewish communion. William Hazlitt was married in 1808 in

the church, Charles Lamb being the best man and his sister Mary the brides-
maid.

The CITY TEMPLE just beyond, a Congregational church opened in 1874 under Dr Joseph Parker, the famous preacher, was destroyed in an air-raid in 1941. Rebuilt in 1958 to the designs of Lord Mottistone and Paul Paget, but embodying the façade of the old building, it has seats for 1,400 and a theatre beneath seating 800 people. ATLANTIC HOUSE, opposite, is the headquarters (1951) of H. M. STATIONERY OFFICE, the government printing and publishing organization, established in 1786.

Beyond the middle section of the viaduct, which bridges Farringdon Street (Route 24; reached by steps), is the HOLBORN VIADUCT STATION (IV, D 3) of the Southern Region, rebuilt in 1962 by Ronald Ward and Partners. On the left farther on is ST SEPULCHRE'S CHURCH, properly the Church of the Holy Sepulchre, the largest of the City churches, a foundation of the 12th-century Crusaders rebuilt in the 15th century and greatly repaired in 1670–7 by Wren, after damage in the Great Fire. The medieval tower and three-storey fan-vaulted porch have survived, but the church was restored, in poor fashion, in 1878 and again in much better shape in 1950. Near the west end of the south aisle is a wall tablet (a copy of the original) to Captain John Smith (d. 1631), 'sometime Governour of Virginia and Admiral of New England', who was rescued by Pocahontas, the Indian chieftain's daughter. He is buried near the east end of the aisle, which is now the memorial chapel of the Royal Fusiliers, a regiment raised in 1685. The east window here contains heraldic glass (1952) by Gerald Smith, who also designed the east window of the chancel (1949). The two pulpits, the font, and the fine altarpiece all date from the 17th century.

The north chapel was dedicated in 1955 as the musicians' memorial chapel and has new panelled walls and a book of remembrance. A window of 1946 (by Gerald Smith) on the north commemorates Sir Henry Wood (d. 1943), founder of the Promenade Concerts, who deputized for the organist here at the age of twelve, and whose ashes are buried below. Another window, by Brian Thomas (1962), commemorates Dame Nellie Melba (1862–1931), the Australian opera singer.

The church is well known for its musical activities, and special services are held, e.g. on St Cecilia's Day (22 November). At the west end of the north aisle is a bell of 1605 which used to be rung at midnight outside the condemned cell at Newgate Prison (see below) before an execution. Here also is a charred oak beam from the prison chapel, burned in 1780. Until the late 18th century a nosegay was presented to every condemned criminal as he passed St Sepulchre's on his way to Tyburn, and it remained the custom to toll the church bells for each execution until 1890.

Giltspur Street, east of the church, leads to St Bartholomew's Hospital and Church (Route 29). On the other side of the road is the CENTRAL CRIMINAL COURT (IV, D, E 3), popularly called the OLD BAILEY from the street at whose corner it stands. Built in 1902–7 by E. W. Mountford (and restored after heavy war damage), it embodies some stones from the notorious Newgate Prison which stood on this site. The copper dome, 195 ft above the ground, is surmounted by a large bronze figure of Justice (not blindfolded as is usually the case), by F. W. Pomeroy.

This is the chief court for crimes committed in London, Middlesex, and the neighbouring parts of Kent, Surrey, and Essex. When the courts are sitting (Monday–Friday at 10.30 and 2, except in August) the public is admitted to the galleries, entered from Newgate Street. On the first two days of each session the judges carry posies of flowers and sweet herbs are strewn round the courts, a survival from the time when these were necessary to overcome the noxious smells from the prison. The main hall is decorated with frescoes by G. Moira (1954) and contains a statue (by Drury, 1913) of Elizabeth Fry (see below).

NEWGATE PRISON, the principal prison of London from the 13th century, began to be rebuilt in 1770, but was fired during the Gordon Riots (1780) and not finally completed until 1782. Public executions, previously carried out at Tyburn (p. 165), took place in front of the prison from 1783 to 1867, and then within its walls until 1901. Among famous prisoners who were confined at Newgate were William Penn, the Quaker; Titus Oates, the perjurer; Daniel Defoe (in 1702–4); Jonathan Wild, hanged in 1725 (compare Fielding's novel); and Lord George Gordon, leader of the Gordon Rioters, who died of gaol fever in 1793. The appalling conditions in the prison were greatly alleviated through the efforts of Mrs Elizabeth Fry (d. 1845), and the prison was pulled down in 1902.

In Old Bailey, which descends to Ludgate Hill, Milton's *Tenure of Kings and Magistrates*, a defence of the execution of Charles I, and other political writings were burned by the common hangman in 1660.

The line of Holborn is continued by NEWGATE STREET (IV, D, E 3), named from one of the City gates (demolished in 1767). WARWICK LANE, on the right, passing CUTLERS' HALL (1887), with its terracotta frieze by George Tinworth, leads to

Stationers' Hall and Ludgate Hill (see Route 24). On the other side of the road is the fine steeple of CHRIST CHURCH, built by Wren in 1677–91. The church, burnt out in 1941 and since demolished, stood on the site of the choir of a great church of the Franciscans, used after the Dissolution by the boys of Christ's Hospital (see below).

In King Edward Street, beyond the church, are the principal entrances to the GENERAL POST OFFICE (IV, D 3; the 'G.P.O.'). On the left, in the King Edward Building, completed in 1910, is the London Chief Office (always open for postal business), the counter of which is over 150 ft long. Opposite on the east is the General Post Office North, the headquarters building (1895) of the Postmaster-General (an office created by Oliver Cromwell in 1657), and between the buildings is a statue of Sir Rowland Hill (d. 1879), who introduced the penny post in 1840. On the north of the headquarters building is the Postmen's Park (see p. 265), and on the south, connected by a flying bridge, is the General Post Office West (1873), largely occupied by the CENTRAL TELEGRAPH OFFICE (severely damaged by bombing).

Visitors may also see the unique POST OFFICE RAILWAY, 6½ miles long, which runs underground from Whitechapel to Paddington, via Liverpool Street Station, the King Edward Building and Mount Pleasant (p. 270). Electrically driven and automatically controlled, the trains transmit about 40,000 mailbags a day at a speed of 35 m.p.h. The railway was completed in 1928 and carries about 40 trains an hour during the rush hours. Under the loading-yard of the G.P.O., west of the King Edward Building, visitors are shown a well-preserved bastion of the Roman wall.

The King Edward Building occupies part of the site of a monastery of the Franciscans, or Grey Friars, established here early in the 14th century. The conventual buildings were replaced after the Dissolution by Christ's Hospital, the famous 'Bluecoat School', founded in 1552 by Edward VI and moved in 1902 to Sussex.

Newgate Street is joined by the street of St Martin's-le-Grand (Route 29) opposite St Paul's underground station. PANYER ALLEY, to the right of this, was named from its having been inhabited by basketmakers. A relief of 1688 showing a boy seated on a pannier, and supposed to mark the highest ground in the City, has been removed until this sadly devastated area is rebuilt. Cheapside (Route 29) goes on eastward to the Bank, while ST

PAUL'S CHURCHYARD (IV, E 3), the road that encloses St Paul's Cathedral, opens on the right.

24 From Fleet Street to St Paul's Cathedral (The Temple)

Plan IV, E 2–IV, E 3

STATIONS: ALDWYCH (Plan IV, E 1), on the Piccadilly line; ST PAUL'S (IV, E 3), on the Central line; TEMPLE (IV, F 1), BLACKFRIARS (IV, E 3), and MANSION HOUSE (V, E 1), on the Circle and District lines. Blackfriars is also a terminus of the Southern Region. — MOTOR-BUSES Nos. 4, 6, 9, 11, 13, and 15 in Fleet Street and Ludgate Hill, passing St Paul's Cathedral; No. 18 in Shoe Lane (from Holborn) and Ludgate Hill. For other buses in Shoe Lane, and in Farringdon Street, see Route 23; in Chancery Lane and Fetter Lane (New Fetter Lane), see Route 23; in New Bridge Street, see Route 26.

ADMISSION to MIDDLE TEMPLE HALL and INNER TEMPLE HALL. Monday–Friday 10 to 12 and 3 to 4.30, Saturday (daily in August and September) 10 to 4.30 (free); to the TEMPLE CHURCH, daily 10 to 1 and 2 to 5; to PRINCE HENRY'S ROOM, weekdays 1.45 to 5 (Saturday to 4.30; free); to ST DUNSTAN-IN-THE-WEST, Monday–Friday 7.30 to 5.30 (Saturdays to 12); to DR JOHNSON'S HOUSE, weekdays (except Bank Holidays) 10.30 to 5 (October–April to 4.30; 2/-); to ST BRIDE'S CHURCH, weekdays 9 to 5.30, Sundays 10.15 to 7.30 (crypt, weekdays to 5); to ST MARTIN-WITHIN-LUDGATE, Monday–Friday 11 to 3; to STATIONERS' HALL, usually on written application to the Clerk.

From Charing Cross via the Strand to Temple Bar, the beginning of FLEET STREET (IV, E 2, 3), see Route 21. The street, mentioned as early as the 13th century, takes its name from the Fleet River, which rises at Hampstead and flows down the valley from Holborn to enter the Thames at Blackfriars Bridge. The stream was covered over in 1765 and is now conveyed through a sewer under Farringdon Street and New Bridge Street. Fleet Street, universally famous as the 'street of ink', contains the publishing offices of most of the national newspapers and the London offices of many of the larger provincial newspapers; it is invariably congested and animated, and as it slopes steeply down to Ludgate Circus the street affords one of the most striking views of St Paul's Cathedral.

Fleet Street has been associated with printing since about 1500, when Wynkyn de Worde, the assistant of William Caxton, set up his press 'in Fletestrete at the signe of the Swane'. The newspapers are mostly printed in the narrow streets, courts, and alleys that cluster round Fleet Street, particularly on the south side. This neighbourhood is busiest between 9 p.m. and midnight, when most of the daily papers are printed, in time to catch the night trains from the London termini to the provinces. 'Late London' editions, however, continue to be printed until about 4 a.m., after which the presses are silent until the first editions of the evening papers are called for. These appear at about 10 a.m. and new editions continue to be published throughout the day until 6 p.m. or later. Visitors can often arrange to see the papers being printed, on written application to one or other of the newspaper offices.

On the south side of Fleet Street, at No. 1, opposite the Temple Bar Memorial, is CHILD'S BANK (now amalgamated with Messrs Glyn, Mills), established in 1671 and perhaps the oldest bank in London. Charles II, the Duke of Marlborough, Prince Rupert, Nell Gwyn, Pepys, and Dryden were among the early customers of the bank, which is generally agreed to be the original of Tellson's Bank in Dickens' *Tale of Two Cities*.

A gateway just beyond, built in 1684 by Roger North, admits to MIDDLE TEMPLE LANE, which descends to the Victoria Embankment and bisects THE TEMPLE (IV, E 2), a name which covers both the Inner and the Middle Temple, two of the great Inns of Court. [For the continuation of Fleet Street, see p. 235.]

The Temple was originally the headquarters in England of the Knights Templars, an order of military crusaders founded in 1119 at Jerusalem with the object of protecting the Holy Sepulchre and recovering Palestine from the Saracens. They were established in Holborn about 1130 and moved here in the reign of Henry II (1154–89). In 1312, on the dissolution of the order, the Temple passed to the Crown and in 1324 it was granted to the Knights Hospitallers of St John, who in the reign of Edward III leased it to a number of professors of the common law. These shortly began to take in students to reside with them, thus establishing the beginnings of the legal community that has persisted at the Temple ever since. The Temple is first known to be mentioned as an Inn of Court in 1449; at the Dissolution of the Monasteries (1540) it reverted to the Crown, but in 1608 the two societies were confirmed in their possessions by James I.

The four INNS OF COURT (Lincoln's Inn and Gray's Inn are the others) originated in the reign of Edward I, by which time the clergy no longer practised in the courts of justice, their place being taken by professional students of law. By long custom the inns enjoy the exclusive privilege of admitting law students to practise as advocates in the courts of England and Wales. Students may pursue their legal studies elsewhere, but they must pass the examinations of one of the inns and must 'keep terms' (usually twelve) by dining in hall a certain number of days in each term before they can be 'called to the Bar', after which they are entitled to plead for others in a court of law. Barristers remain outside the bar (originally the division in hall between the senior members, called 'benchers', and the barristers) until they are elected Queen's Counsellors, when they 'take silk'. *i.e.* don silk gowns (other barristers wear 'stuff' gowns). Women have been called to the Bar since 1922. The four inns remain independent of each other, and each is governed by its 'benchers' under the presidency (usually honorary) of a 'treasurer'.

The Inner and Middle Temple were named from their proximity to the City and in relation to the Outer Temple. This last, however, was never more than a piece of land that belonged to the Templars and later became the site of Essex House, the mansion of the Earl of Essex, favourite of Elizabeth I. The name is now given to an office building in the Strand. Buildings belonging to the Inner Temple bear the device of the Winged Horse, those of the Middle Temple bear the Lamb and Flag. The buildings of both inns suffered severely from bombing during the war, but they have now largely been restored, mostly in their original styles. The secluded precincts are accessible to the public, except on Ascension Day.

The buildings of the Middle Temple lie mainly to the west of Middle Temple Lane. On the right, about half-way down, is MIDDLE TEMPLE HALL, with a noble assembly chamber, over 100 ft long, opened by Elizabeth I in 1576. It was considerably damaged by bombing, but has been restored using the original materials as far as possible. The elaborate double hammerbeam roof is one of the most splendid in England; the walls are covered with panelling bearing the arms of Readers of the Inn since 1597. At the east end is a heavily carved oak screen with doors added in 1671, and on the dais are portraits of Charles I and other monarchs. The serving table is said to have been made from the timbers of Drake's ship, the *Golden Hind*. Shakespeare's own company is believed to have acted in *Twelfth Night* in this hall on 2 February 1602.

The many famous members of the Middle Temple include Sir Walter Raleigh; John Pym, the Parliamentarian; the Earl of Clarendon, the Royalist statesman and historian; John Evelyn; William Congreve; Henry Fielding; Sir William Blackstone, the famous jurist; Edmund Burke; William Cowper; R. B. Sheridan; the Earl of Eldon, Lord Chancellor; Thomas Moore, the Irish poet; Thomas De Quincey; and W. M. Thackeray. Oliver Goldsmith, though not a member, lived at No. 2 Brick Court (since rebuilt) from 1768 until his death in 1774, during which time Blackstone, who occupied the rooms below, often complained of the noise made by his 'revelling neighbour'.

FOUNTAIN COURT, on the north of Middle Temple Hall, was the trysting place of Ruth Pinch with her brother Tom (in *Martin Chuzzlewit*). From the fountain steps lead down to Garden Court, beyond which a gate opens towards the Embankment. On the right of Middle Temple Lane, farther down, is the new building, by Sir Edward Maufe (1958), of the MIDDLE TEMPLE LIBRARY, which grew out of a bequest of Robert Ashley (d. 1641), a barrister, and now contains over 80,000 volumes (including the most comprehensive collection of American legal textbooks and law reports in Britain). Some 65,000 volumes were lost when the old library (which stood farther west) was bombed. Between the old and new libraries, and bounded on the south by the Embankment, are the MIDDLE TEMPLE GARDENS (no admission).

An opening on the east of Middle Temple Lane opposite Brick Court admits to PUMP COURT, the north and west sides of which survive from about 1680, while the south side with the ranges of building beyond were rebuilt in 1949–51 after war damage. The east side is now enclosed by an arcade, to the south-east of which rises INNER TEMPLE HALL, destroyed by bombing in 1941 and newly built in 1952–5 by Sir Hubert Worthington, who adopted a modified Georgian style. It has a marble floor (heated from underneath) and windows containing heraldic glass by Hugh Easton that includes the arms of former benchers of the inn who have become Lord Chancellors. The vaulted chamber called the buttery at the west end, with the crypt below, survives from the 14th century. The INNER TEMPLE LIBRARY, to the east, founded before 1507 but destroyed in the bombing, was rebuilt in 1958 by Sir Hubert Worthington and now holds over 90,000 books.

Among famous members of the Inner Temple are John Hampden, the statesman; William Wycherley; the notorious Judge Jeffreys; Lord Chancellor Thurlow; James Boswell; and the historian, Henry Hallam.

Farther east is KING'S BENCH WALK, with delightful chambers Nos. 4–6 of which were built in the late 17th century. Mitre Court, on the north side, opens to Fleet Street, and a gate on the east admits to Bouverie Street (see below). To the southwest are Paper Buildings, built in 1848, and beyond are the large INNER TEMPLE GARDENS (no admission), fronting the Embankment. The fountain-figure of a child here is in memory of Charles Lamb, the essayist, who was born in 1775 in Crown Office Row (facing the gardens on the north, but recast after war damage) and who lived in the Temple until 1817. In one or other of the Temple Gardens were traditionally plucked the white and red roses that became the badges of the Houses of York and Lancaster (compare *Henry VI*, Part I, ii, 4).

To the north of Inner Temple Hall is the TEMPLE CHURCH (IV, E 2), which serves both inns of court and is exempt from episcopal jurisdiction. It consists of a circular nave (the 'Round'), completed in 1185 on the model of the Church of the Holy Sepulchre at Jerusalem and one of the only four medieval round churches surviving in England, and a large chancel (the 'Oblong'), a splendid example of the Early English style, added in 1240. The church, drastically renovated in 1840, was very badly damaged in 1941, but the fan-vaulted chancel, with its wide nave and aisles, and triplets of lancet windows, was carefully restored by Walter H. Godfrey in 1954, when the reredos of 1682 (by Sir Christopher Wren) was brought back and new clustered columns of Purbeck marble were introduced. In the south aisle are the old double piscina and a fine medieval effigy of a bishop; through a panel of glass let into the floor at the west end can be seen the grave-slab of John Selden (d. 1654), the great jurist and antiquary, who is buried in the 13th-century undercroft below. The round church, which has an elaborate doorway in the late-Norman style, protected by a porch, was rededicated, after its restoration by W. H. Godfrey, in 1958. The Purbeck marble for the clustered columns (which have richly carved capitals) and for the shafts of the excellent triforium arcading was obtained from the original quarries. Almost all of the fine 12th–13th-century military effigies of Associates of the Temple in the nave were severely damaged in the bombing, but have been carefully repaired (1961).

Lawyers used to await their clients in the 'Round', each occupying a particular place like the merchants on the Stock Exchange. Charles Lamb was baptized in the church in 1775. On the north, in the former churchyard, a stone slab marks the approximate whereabouts of the grave of Oliver Goldsmith. To the north-east is the MASTER'S HOUSE, the residence of the incumbent of the church; attributed to Wren, it was destroyed in 1941 but has been rebuilt in its former style.

INNER TEMPLE LANE leads north from the church porch to Fleet Street, which it reaches through a gateway opposite Chancery Lane (Route 20). Above the gate is a restored timbered building of 1610–11 with an overhanging upper storey. PRINCE HENRY'S ROOM, on the first floor, with its original 17th-century plaster ceiling and carved oak panelling, is supposed to have been the council chamber of the Duchy of Cornwall under Prince Henry, the elder son of James I. Farther on is the *Cock Tavern*, built in 1887 to replace the 16th-century tavern, frequented by Tennyson and Dickens, which stood on the other side of the road. It preserves some of the fittings of its predecessor, including the gilded sign of the cock carved by Grinling Gibbons of which there is a copy outside.

On the north side of Fleet Street is the octagonal church of ST DUNSTAN-IN-THE-WEST (IV, E 2), of 13th-century foundation, but rebuilt in 1829–33 by John Shaw and repaired in 1950. The noble tower has an open-work lantern inspired by that of All Saints' Pavement at York. Over the east or vestry porch is a contemporary statue of Elizabeth I (1586) and inside are figures of 'King Lud' and his sons, all of which were brought from Ludgate when it was demolished. The clock of 1671 with its 'striking jacks', removed when the former church was pulled down, was returned in 1936.

The north bay of the octagon serves as the chancel and has a window by Gerald Smith replacing one destroyed in 1940. The north-west window (by Kempe) shows Izaak Walton, the angler, a vestryman of the church in 1629–44, and the subjects of his *Lives*. The *Compleat Angler* was first published in St Dunstan's churchyard in 1653. Thomas White, the founder of Sion College, was vicar here in 1575–1624 and was followed by John Donne, the poet, vicar until his death in 1631.

FETTER LANE (IV, D, E 2), on the left farther on, leading to Holborn, is said to derive its name from the 'faitours' or vagrants that once infested it, but more likely takes it from a colony of 'feutriers' or felt-makers. Clifford's Inn, a block of flats on its west side, occupies the site of the oldest of the inns of chancery (compare p. 225). Opposite the lane is Mitre Court, admitting to the Inner Temple (see above), and just beyond on the same side opens SERJEANTS' INN, originally one of the two independent societies of serjeants-at-law ('servientes ad legem'), the highest order of barristers, dissolved in 1877. Now an insurance building, the north side was partly restored (after war damage) in 1955 in a style intended to maintain its traditional character.

On the north side of Fleet Street are numerous little courts and alleys noted for their literary associations, though wholely rebuilt in recent years. CRANE COURT was the headquarters of the Royal Society in 1710–80 and later the home of the Philosophical Society, before whom Coleridge gave his famous lectures on Shakespeare (1810–13). Dr Johnson lived in JOHNSON'S COURT (not called after him) in 1765–76 and then in BOLT COURT, farther on, until his death in 1784. Goldsmith is said to have written the *Vicar of Wakefield* in Wine Office Court (see below), at No. 6 (since vanished).

Johnson's Court, reached under the wing of No. 166 Fleet Street, gives access to GOUGH SQUARE, on the west side of which rises DR JOHNSON'S HOUSE (IV, E 2), the charming late-17th-century building in which the great lexicographer lived from 1748 to 1759 and where his wife Tetty died in 1752. The famous *Dictionary* (published in 1755) was compiled here and *The Rambler*, which appeared twice weekly for two years, was written, as were the earlier numbers of *The Idler*. The kitchen, the old staircase and panelling, and the quaint cupboards are worth inspection, but the most interesting room is the attic, where Johnson laboured at the dictionary, assisted by six amanuenses. The house contains the chair and other relics of Johnson, engravings and autograph letters, and an early edition of the dictionary. In WINE OFFICE COURT, on the left of Fleet Street farther east, is the *Old Cheshire Cheese*, a delightful old tavern, rebuilt in 1667, which claims to have been frequented by Johnson, Boswell, and Goldsmith (though it is not mentioned by Boswell).

BOUVERIE STREET and WHITEFRIARS STREET, with the offices of *Punch* and other well-known papers, lead south from Fleet Street to the Embankment. The latter street takes its name from a monastery of Carmelites or White Friars, founded about 1241 and dissolved in 1538. The privilege of sanctuary attached to the precincts of the monastery survived until 1697 and in consequence it became the haunt of lawless characters (under the name of Alsatia; compare Scott's *The Fortunes of Nigel*).

On the north side of Fleet Street are the huge offices (by Elcock and Sutcliffe, 1930) of the *Daily Telegraph*, the first London daily penny paper, founded in 1855, and farther down is the prominent

Daily Express office (by Ellis and Clarke, 1931), with its facing of black tiles. Opposite this is the headquarters of *Reuter's*, the famous international news agency, established as a world-wide service in 1858.

Beside this opens an entrance to ST BRIDE'S CHURCH (IV, E 2), dedicated to Bridget, a 6th-century Irish saint, and the 'parish church of the Press'. First mentioned in the 12th century and rebuilt in 1670–84 by Wren, it was burnt out in an air-raid in 1940, except for the beautiful steeple of 1701, called by W. E. Henley a 'madrigal in stone'. This was originally 234 ft high, but after it was struck by lightning in 1764 it was reconstructed 8 ft shorter, though still the loftiest of the City's steeples. The church was restored in 1956–7 by W. Godfrey Allen in a style following closely the original intentions of Wren (one of his most handsome designs), but with a fresco (by Glyn Jones) on the flat east wall of the sanctuary to give it the appearance of an apse. In front of this is a carved oak reredos (a memorial to the Pilgrim Fathers and in particular to Governor Winslow, who was an apprentice printer in Fleet Street), and the graceful font of 1615, saved from the bombing, has been replaced. Samuel Pepys, born in 1633 in Salisbury Court close by (on the site of the *White Swan*), was baptized in this font. The statues of St Bride and St Paul (1957) are the work of David McFall.

Samuel Richardson (d. 1761), the novelist, who had a printing business in Salisbury Square, to the west, is buried in the church, while Wynkyn de Worde (d. about 1534), the early printer, and Richard Lovelace (d. 1658), the Cavalier poet, were buried in the previous church. Excavations below the building in 1952–6 have revealed the lower parts of a sequence of earlier churches, the oldest possibly, though not certainly, Saxon and incorporating Roman material. Beneath the churchyard and partly underlying the church, remains were discovered in 1952 of a Roman building, the earliest known in London outside the City wall. A museum containing the excavated remains has been opened in the crypt and may be seen on application to the verger.

Fleet Street finishes at LUDGATE CIRCUS (IV, E 3), on the north-west side of which is a tablet to Edgar Wallace (d. 1932), the crime-novelist and journalist. New Bridge Street (Route 26) leads south from the circus to Blackfriars Bridge, and FARRINGDON STREET, following the course of the Fleet River, runs north towards Holborn and Clerkenwell.

On the right in this street is the CONGREGATIONAL MEMORIAL HALL, a large Gothic building of 1874 commemorating the 'fidelity to conscience' shown by the ministers ejected in 1662 from the Church of England under the Act of Uniformity of Charles II. It stands partly on the site of the FLEET PRISON, a notorious debtors' prison that is depicted in Hogarth's *Rake's Progress* and described in Dickens' *Pickwick Papers*. William Penn was among those unfortunate enough to be incarcerated here. The prison, rebuilt after the Great Fire of 1666 and again after its destruction in the Gordon Riots (1780), was finally demolished in 1846. Farringdon Street passes under Holborn Viaduct (Route 23) and is prolonged beyond Charterhouse Street by Farringdon Road, leading towards King's Cross (compare Route 29).

LUDGATE HILL (IV, E 3), a short but busy thoroughfare, ascends briskly from Ludgate Circus to St Paul's Cathedral. The large HILLGATE HOUSE, beyond the railway, designed by Theo H. Birks (1962), is partly occupied by the Board of Trade. There is a good 'surprise' view of St Bride's steeple before Old Bailey (see Route 23) bears left for Newgate Street and Smithfield. Farther up, adjoining the site of Ludgate, one of the City gates (pulled down in 1760), is the church of ST MARTIN-WITHIN-LUDGATE, rebuilt by Wren in 1677–87 and now pleasantly restored. It has notable doorways and a font of 1673 with a Greek palindromic inscription, and is secluded from the noisy street by vestibules between which rises the tower, with an elegant spire forming an effective foil to the twin towers of St Paul's.

An alley on the left farther up leads to STATIONERS' HALL (IV, E 3), the hall of the Stationers' and Newspaper Makers' Company, founded in 1403 and incorporated in 1557 (the newspaper makers were first included in the title in 1933). The company, long restricted to those engaged in printing, publishing, and allied trades, maintained a monopoly of printing during the latter part of the 16th century, and until the passing of the Copyright Bill of 1911 every work published in Britain had to be registered at Stationers' Hall. The registers, which date from the foundation of the company, are of the highest interest and contain such entries as the First Folio of Shakespeare (1623), Milton's *Paradise Lost* (1667), and Dr Johnson's Dictionary (1755). Rebuilt in 1670 after the Great Fire, the Hall was given a new east front in 1800 by Robert Mylne and extended by a wing on the north-east in 1887. The great hall, restored after war damage, has a fine 17th-century screen and oak panelling; the Court Room, also badly damaged by bombing, was rebuilt in its former style in 1956.

Ave Maria Lane, leaving Ludgate Hill farther east, is continued by Warwick Lane (see Route 23) to Holborn, skirting an area sadly devastated in the Great Fire of 29 December 1940, but now being rebuilt (1963). A gateway on the left admits to AMEN COURT, a quiet precinct containing the houses, partly of the 17th century, of the Canons Residentiary of St Paul's. The Rev. Richard Harris Barham, author of the *Ingoldsby Legends*, died in 1845 at No. 1. Farther up on the same side is WARWICK SQUARE, in which Amen House, a publisher's office, is a restored building of the late 17th century. A passage beside it leads to steps (descending to Old Bailey) at the foot of which a section of the old City wall can be seen to the left.

Ludgate Hill ends at ST PAUL'S CHURCHYARD (IV, E 3), the road that surrounds St Paul's Cathedral. The southward arm, passing Dean's Court, with the Deanery (p. 389), is extended by Cannon Street (for London Bridge and the Bank, see Route 25).

25 From St Paul's Cathedral to the Bank or London Bridge

Plan IV, E 3–V, F 2

STATIONS: ST PAUL'S (Plan IV, E 3), on the Central line; MANSION HOUSE (V, E 1), CANNON STREET (V, F 1), and MONUMENT (V, F 2), all on the Circle and District lines; LONDON BRIDGE (IX, E 2), on the Northern line. The Monument station is connected by an escalator with the Bank station (compare Route 28); Cannon Street and London Bridge are termini also of the Southern Region. — MOTOR-BUSES Nos. 6, 9, 11, 13, 15, and 18 in the west part of Cannon Street; No. 13 only passes Cannon Street Station; and Nos. 7, 8A, 10, 13, 21, 35, 40, 43, 47, 133, and 257 across London Bridge. For buses in Queen Victoria Street, see Route 26; across Southwark Bridge, see Route 27; in King William Street and Gracechurch Street, see Route 34.

ADMISSION to ST MARY ABCHURCH, Monday–Friday 8 to 3.30; to the MONUMENT, weekdays 9 to 6 (to 4 in October–March), Sundays 2 to 6 in May–September only (6*d*); to FISHMONGERS' HALL, usually on written application (free).

To ST PAUL'S CHURCHYARD from Holborn via Newgate Street, see Route 23; from Fleet Street via Ludgate Hill, see Route 24; for the route from St Paul's to the Bank via Cheapside, see Route 29. CANNON STREET (IV, E 3–V, F 2), the shortest way from St Paul's to London Bridge or the Tower, runs eastward from the south side of the cathedral. The west part was constructed in 1854; the older section beyond Walbrook was formerly Candlewick Street, the street of the wax-chandlers. The whole street is now lined by large new blocks of office building. ST PAUL'S GARDEN, a formal garden on the left, marks the site of

Cordwainers' Hall (*i.e.* shoemakers', from Cordovan leather), burned down in 1941. On the north is ST AUGUSTINE'S CHURCH, built by Wren in 1680–7 and likewise severely damaged by bombing. R. H. Barham, author of the *Ingoldsby Legends*, was rector here in 1842–5. Only the tower is to be preserved under the new plan for St Paul's precincts. To the east of the garden rises GATEWAY HOUSE, a dignified office building designed by Messrs Trehearne and Norman Preston & Partners and completed in 1956. The south front has been recessed so as not to impede the view of St Paul's from Cannon Street. In the main vestibule is a stone from a foot-postern of 1663, formerly part of the City gateway to Aldgate. On the right farther on new buildings to the designs of Sir Albert Richardson were completed in 1959 for the *Financial Times*. While excavating for the foundations, slight remains of two timber huts of the Saxon period (about A.D. 900) were discovered.

Cannon Street crosses Queen Victoria Street, which leads right to Blackfriars Bridge and left to the Bank (see Route 26). At the corner is the entrance to the Mansion House underground station, and to the left is the church of St Mary Aldermary. QUEEN STREET (V, E, F 1), farther east, runs north to Cheapside (Route 29) and south to Southwark Bridge (Route 26). At the corner is the LONDON CHAMBER OF COMMERCE, founded in 1881 and moved here in 1934, and below in Queen Street is a notable late-18th-century house (No. 28), one of the few surviving in the City. College Hill, the next turning on the right of Cannon Street, takes its name from a college established here in 1422 by Richard Whittington (see p. 254). It crosses Cloak Lane, in which are the headquarters of the City of London Special Constabulary.

DOWGATE HILL, the next side-street, contains TALLOW CHANDLERS' HALL (No. 4), largely remodelled about 1880, and SKINNERS' HALL (No. 8), rebuilt after the Great Fire of 1666, but with a façade of about 1790 and later alterations. The restored hall is decorated with large panel paintings commissioned in 1902 from Sir Frank Brangwyn, while a fine staircase of about 1670 ascends to the 17th-century Court Room, panelled with fragrant Virginian cedar. The Skinners' Company, which alternates in precedence with the Merchant Taylors' (see p. 15), has met on this site at least since 1295. Lower down is DYERS' HALL (No. 10), built in 1840, but altered since.

CANNON STREET STATION (V, F 1), a terminus of the Southern Region, was built in 1866, the main block being designed as a hotel by Edward M. Barry. A partial reconstruction of the station was begun in 1955.

Opposite formerly stood ST SWITHUN'S CHURCH, rebuilt by Wren in 1677–87, but altered in 1869, gutted by bombing in 1941, and demolished in 1958. The dedication to Swithun or Swithin, bishop of Winchester in 852–62, may have implied a Saxon foundation. John Dryden, the poet, was married in the previous church in 1663. Built into a niche of the south wall was the LONDON STONE, of unknown origin, though claimed by Camden and later writers to have been the Milliarium of Roman London from which distances were measured. In Shakespeare's *Henry VI*, Part II (iv, 6), the rebel Jack Cade strikes the stone with his staff, exclaiming 'Now is Mortimer lord of this City' (1450). Originally much larger, the stone formerly stood on the other side of the street and it was set up here in 1798. Temporarily in the Guildhall Museum (p. 260), the stone will be incorporated in an office building to be erected here. In St Swithin's Lane, to the east, is FOUNDERS' HALL (No. 13), rebuilt in 1877.

Abchurch Lane, farther on to the left, passes the church of ST MARY ABCHURCH, rebuilt by Wren in 1681–7 with an internal dome painted about 1708 most probably by Sir James Thornhill, painter of the dome of St Paul's. Seriously damaged in 1940, this was restored in 1953; the splendid reredos by Grinling Gibbons (1686), the largest in the City, has likewise been restored, the canopied pulpit and other fine woodwork have been brought back, and the church was reopened for worship in 1957. The 14th-century crypt of the original church, revealed by the bombing, has been opened up.

Cannon Street ends at a busy junction of roads from which King William Street leads north-west to the Bank (Route 34), Gracechurch Street north-east to Bishopsgate (Route 32), and Eastcheap east towards the Tower (Route 34). KING WILLIAM STREET also runs south to London Bridge, passing the end of the street, on the left, in which rises THE MONUMENT (V, F 2), the 'loftiest isolated stone column in the world', a prominent fluted Doric column, 202 ft high, designed by Sir Christopher Wren in collaboration with Robert Hooke. It was erected in 1671–7 to commemorate the Great Fire of London, which broke out on

2 September 1666 at a point in Pudding Lane said to be exactly 202 ft east of the column. The fire, which raged for five days, destroyed about 460 streets with some 89 churches and more than 13,000 houses, devastating 436 acres of the City. A further inscription on the pedestal, ascribing the fire to the 'Popish faction', was removed in 1831. The relief on the west side of the pedestal is by C. G. Cibber, the Danish sculptor; the top of the column is surmounted by an urn with a gilt flaming ball, 42 ft high. The platform, reached by an internal spiral staircase with 311 steps, commands an impressive view over the City and the river.

King William Street crosses Thames Street (Route 27) by a viaduct. On the right, at the approach to London Bridge, is FISHMONGERS' HALL (V, F 2), one of the noblest of the halls of the City livery companies, rebuilt in 1832–4 by Henry Roberts.

The Fishmongers' Company, one of the oldest and wealthiest of the twelve great livery companies, and fourth in order of precedence (compare p. 15), was already in existence before 1154 and received its first charter from Edward I. The hall, originally built on this site in 1504, was the first of the City halls to catch alight during the Great Fire of 1666, and was again the first to be set on fire in the air-raids of September, 1940. The interior, finely restored in 1951 by Austen Hall, contains a beautifully embroidered 15th–16th-century pall, a wooden statue of Sir William Walworth, Mayor in 1374 and a Prime Warden of the company, and the dagger with which he slew the rebel Wat Tyler in 1381. The paintings include two fine portraits by Romney, charming river scenes by Samuel Scott and others, and a delightful study in tempera of Queen Elizabeth II (1955) by Pietro Annigoni. ADELAIDE HOUSE, on the other side of the bridge approach, is a huge block of shipping offices by Sir John J. Burnet (1924).

LONDON BRIDGE (V, F 2), the oldest and most famous of all the bridges across the Thames, connects the City with Southwark, and until 1749 was the only bridge over the river. The present rather prosaic structure of five granite arches, 928 ft long and with a central span of 152 ft, was begun in 1824 by John Rennie and completed in 1831 by his sons, Sir John and George Rennie. The width was increased from 54 ft to 63 ft in 1902–4, by which time the cost, including the approaches, had come to over £2½ million.

It seems likely that the Romans would build a bridge across the river near this point to their settlement on the north bank, though no evidence for one has been found. The first known bridge, of timber, was erected in the time of King Edgar (973–5); the first stone bridge, built to the order of Henry II, was begun in 1176 by Peter, chaplain of St Mary Colechurch in Cheapside, and not completed until 1209. It stood a little downstream from the present bridge, opposite the church of St Magnus the Martyr (compare p. 255). Houses and shops came to be built on either side of the roadway, with a chapel in the middle dedicated to St Thomas of Canterbury. The bridge had nineteen narrow arches, which made the passage by river dangerous, and at each end were fortified gates, on the spikes of which it became the custom to expose the heads of traitors. The houses were pulled down about 1760, when the bridge was widened, and the bridge itself was finally demolished in 1832.

The bridge is the highest point on the Thames that can be reached by ships of any size. The reach below is known as the POOL OF LONDON, while that above was named the KING'S REACH in 1935. The view downstream, interesting for its shipping, includes the White Tower and Tower Bridge, with the heights of Greenwich beyond and the Custom House and the Port of London Authority Offices to the left. Upstream there is a fine panorama encompassing Shell-Mex House, Somerset House, and other buildings lining the river, the large Unilever House with the steeples of St Dunstan-in-the-West and St Bride's to the right of it, and the dome of St Paul's over Cannon Street Station.

Near the south end of the bridge are **Southwark Cathedral** and the approach to LONDON BRIDGE STATION (see Route 35).

26 From Westminster Bridge to London Bridge and the Bank

Plan VIII, B 3–V, E 1

STATIONS: WESTMINSTER (Plan VIII, B 3), CHARING CROSS (VIII, A 3), TEMPLE (IV, F 1), BLACKFRIARS (IV, E 3), and MANSION HOUSE (V, E 1), all on the Circle and District lines; BANK (V, E 1), see Route 28. Charing Cross is also on the Bakerloo and Northern lines; and Blackfriars is a terminus of the Southern Region. — MOTOR-BUSES Nos. 12, 53, 76, 109, 153, 155, 163, 168, 170, 172, 177, 184, and 276 across Westminster Bridge; Nos. 109, 155, 168, 177, and 184 along Victoria Embankment to Blackfriars Bridge (also No. 163 to Horse Guards Avenue only, and Nos. 170 and 172 to Temple Place); Nos. 1, 4A, 6A, 60, 68, 171, 176, 188, and 196 across Waterloo Bridge; Nos. 4, 17, 45, 63, 76, 109, 141, 155, 177, and 184 across Blackfriars Bridge; Nos. 4, 17, 45, 63, 141, and 168 in New Bridge Street; No. 76 in Queen Victoria Street from Blackfriars Bridge to the Bank (also Nos. 6, 9, 11, and 15 from Cannon Street to the Bank).

ADMISSION to HENRY VIII's WINE CELLAR, Easter–mid-December, on Saturday afternoons on application to the Secretary (Dept. A. S. 8L), Ministry of Public Building and Works, Lambeth Bridge House, SE1; to the *Discovery*, daily 1 to 4.45 (free); to APOTHECARIES' HALL, occasionally, on application to the Clerk; to the BRITISH & FOREIGN BIBLE SOCIETY, Monday–Friday 9.30 to 5.30 (free); to ELECTRA HOUSE, weekdays, except Friday, 10 to 7; to the FARADAY BUILDING, Monday-to Friday 10 to 12, 2 to 4, and 6 to 8, Saturdays 6 to 8 only, both on application to the Regional Director, London Postal Region (see p. 222); to the COLLEGE OF ARMS, see p. 251; to ST MARY ALDERMARY, Monday–Friday 8 to 5.

WESTMINSTER BRIDGE (VIII, B 3), reached from Parliament Square (Route 3) by the short Bridge Street, is a graceful cast-iron structure, 810 ft long, built in 1854–62 by Thomas Page, and crossing the Thames from Westminster to Lambeth. It replaces the earlier stone bridge of 1749 (the first to be built over the river after London Bridge), the prospect from which inspired Wordsworth's famous sonnet, 'Earth has not anything to show more fair', written in 1802.

The view today, still as inspiring, includes the long river façade of the Houses of Parliament, with the new Vickers skyscraper rising beyond, and St Thomas's Hospital and Lambeth Palace on the opposite bank. Below the bridge on the right bank is the London County Hall, with the huge new Shell building beyond, and St Paul's Cathedral and the Royal Festival Hall to the left. The Law Courts and Somerset House are seen above the Charing Cross Railway Bridge, with Shell-Mex House and other large buildings standing above the Embankment gardens.

At the Westminster end of the bridge is a large bronze group of Boudicca (Boadicea) in her chariot, by Thomas Thornycroft (1902). Thence the VICTORIA EMBANKMENT (VIII, B 3–IV, F 2), built in 1864–70 by Sir Joseph Bazalgette, makes a wide sweep following the left bank of the river as far as Blackfriars Bridge, a distance of over a mile and a quarter. Its construction involved the reclamation of an area regularly covered by the tide and the provision of a protecting wall 8 ft thick. The broad roadway, lined for the most part with attractive gardens, affords the shortest, most convenient, and pleasantest route from Westminster to the City.

On the right, just below the bridge, is WESTMINSTER PIER, the chief starting-point of the river steamers. On the other side of the road is NEW SCOTLAND YARD (VIII, B 3), the headquarters of the Metropolitan Police, in a building by R. Norman Shaw (1891) with a modern extension on the north. Beyond this rises a colossal block of government offices, by E. Vincent Harris (1957), now the head-office of the BOARD OF TRADE, but shared with the Air Ministry and probably to become the headquarters of the projected new unified Ministry of Defence. The main entrance, flanked by grotesque sculptures, is on the north side, in Horse Guards Avenue. Under the building is HENRY VIII's WINE CELLAR, one of the few surviving parts of Whitehall Palace (compare p. 103), a vaulted chamber, 56 ft long, which had to be moved when the foundations were constructed. In the garden on the river side of the building is QUEEN MARY'S TERRACE, part of the river quay with a flight of steps, built in front of the palace in 1691 by Wren for Mary II, and rediscovered in 1939.

In front of the building are statues of General Gordon (d. 1885), and Lord Trenchard (d. 1956), the first Marshal of the Royal Air Force, by William McMillan (1961). On the Embankment is the ROYAL AIR FORCE MEMORIAL, by Sir Reginald Blomfield and Sir W. Reid Dick (1923). In the garden north of Horse Guards Avenue are statues of William Tyndale (d. 1536), translator of the New Testament, by Boehm (1884); of Sir Bartle Frere (d. 1884), the first High Commissioner for South Africa; and of Sir James Outram (d. 1863), the 'Bayard of India'. In front of the garden is a bust of Samuel Plimsoll (d. 1898), the social reformer and 'seamen's friend', and behind rises WHITEHALL COURT, a huge edifice designed by Alfred Waterhouse (1887) and containing suites of apartments and the NATIONAL LIBERAL CLUB, founded in 1882. On the wall of the Embankment opposite Northumberland Avenue is a monument to Sir Joseph Bazalgette (d. 1891).

The broad NORTHUMBERLAND AVENUE (VIII, A 3), starting north of the garden, leads west to Charing Cross (Route 1). It took its name from Northumberland House here, the town mansion of the Dukes of Northumberland, pulled down in 1874. On the right is the PLAYHOUSE THEATRE (1907), now used by the BBC, beside which Craven Street (Route 21) ascends to the Strand. In Whitehall Place, leading left to Whitehall (Route 2), is the MINISTRY OF AGRICULTURE AND FISHERIES, in a building of 1935. On the right in the avenue is the ROYAL COMMONWEALTH SOCIETY, founded in 1868 as the Royal Colonial Institute and now numbering 30,000 members. The library (introduction from a Fellow necessary) contains over 250,000 volumes, specializing in Commonwealth subjects. The building, restored in 1957 after bomb damage, has rooms panelled in woods from many parts of the Commonwealth.

The Victoria Embankment passes under CHARING CROSS RAILWAY BRIDGE, erected in 1863–6 to replace the Hungerford Suspension Bridge, parts of which were used for the Clifton Suspension Bridge over the Avon at Bristol. The separate footway alongside on the north (giving access to Waterloo Station) is still known as HUNGERFORD BRIDGE. Beyond the bridge is the CHARING CROSS PIER (VIII, A 3) of the river steamers, and opposite this is the Charing Cross underground station. From Villiers Street, starting on the other side of this, there is an entrance to the Charing Cross Station of the Southern Region (see Route 21).

The course of the river now bends sharply from north to east. Across it there is a fine view of the South Bank Gardens and the Royal Festival Hall, with the monstrous Shell building to the right, while ahead is Waterloo Bridge with the dome of St Paul's rising above it. To the left is a delightful section of the VICTORIA EMBANKMENT GARDENS (III, F 3–IV, F 1), above which soar three huge modern buildings, the Adelphi (p. 209) to the left, the Savoy Hotel to the right, and in the centre SHELL-MEX HOUSE, opened in 1933, with a tower rising to over 200 ft and containing the largest clock in London. It is now the headquarters of the MINISTRY OF AVIATION. In the west corner of the gardens is the charming YORK WATER GATE, sculptured by Nicholas Stone and the only surviving part of York House, begun in 1625 for the Duke of Buckingham, the favourite of James I and Charles I, on the site of a mansion of the archbishops of York, the birthplace in 1561 of Francis Bacon. The position of the gate indicates the former extent of the river.

In the gardens are a refreshment place and a bandstand, and an open-air art exhibition is usually held early in summer. There is a small memorial to the IMPERIAL CAMEL CORPS (1921); statues of Robert Burns (d. 1796), a fine work by Sir John Steell (1884); Sir Wilfrid Lawson (d. 1906), the temperance advocate; and Robert Raikes (d. 1811), the founder in 1780 of Sunday schools; a wall-fountain to Henry Fawcett (d. 1884), the blind statesman; and a bust of Sir Arthur Sullivan (d. 1900), the composer, with a line by Sir William S. Gilbert (d. 1911), who is himself commemorated by a bronze medallion near Charing Cross Pier.

On the right of the Embankment rises CLEOPATRA'S NEEDLE (IV, F 1), an obelisk of pink granite 68 ft 6 in. high and weighing 180 tons. It has not the slightest connexion with Cleopatra, but was one of a pair erected about 1500 B.C. by Thothmes III at Heliopolis, the ancient Egyptian centre of sun-worship on the edge of the Nile delta. Presented to Britain in 1819 by Mohammed Ali, the Egyptian viceroy, it was brought to London and set up here in 1878. The inscriptions on the sides record the deeds of Thothmes III and of Rameses II (the Great), who acquired the obelisks in the 13th century B.C. The companion obelisk is now in Central Park, New York. The bronze sphinxes flanking the base, designed by George Vulliamy, have been left as scarred by a bomb in 1917.

Opposite the needle is the BELGIAN WAR MEMORIAL, by Sir Reginald Blomfield, with sculptures by Victor Rousseau, erected by the people of Belgium in 1920 in gratitude for British aid in 1914–18. In Savoy Place, farther on to the left, is the INSTITUTION OF ELECTRICAL ENGINEERS, founded in 1871. Savoy Street, just beyond this, ascends past the Savoy Chapel (Route 21) to the Strand.

The Embankment passes under WATERLOO BRIDGE (IV, F 1), the newest of London's bridges, designed by Sir Giles Gilbert Scott and completed in 1939, though not opened officially until 1945. Built of steel and concrete in a clean functional style, it has five graceful arches each about 240 ft wide. Replacing the famous bridge completed in 1817 by John Rennie, it crosses the river to the South Bank Gardens and Waterloo Station (Route 36). On the right beyond the bridge is the floating station of the RIVER THAMES POLICE, while to the left rises the noble south façade, nearly 600 ft long, of SOMERSET HOUSE (see Route 21). The terrace is raised 50 ft above the level of the roadway, and the lower arcade originally stood in the river, the middle arch forming a water-gate. At the corner of TEMPLE PLACE, where the buses for the Strand and Aldwych bear to the left, is a statue of Isambard Brunel (d. 1859), the civil engineer. Moored in the river here is H.M.S. *Discovery*, the polar research ship of Captain R. F. Scott, now recruiting headquarters for the Royal Navy and Royal Marines. Visitors are allowed to see Captain Scott's cabin, containing many relics of Antarctic voyages.

Farther downstream are the *Wellington*, once a naval sloop, now serving as the livery hall of the Honourable Company of Master Mariners, and the *President* and *Chrysanthemum*, training ships of the London Division of the Royal Naval Volunteer Reserve.

In the garden east of the Temple Station are statues of W. E. Forster (d. 1886), the Liberal statesman who secured the passing of the Education Act, and John Stuart Mill (d. 1873), the philosopher and economist. Behind is ELECTRA HOUSE, the head-office of Cable and Wireless Services, with a telegraph station (open always). In the parapet of the Embankment is a memorial to W. T. Stead (d. 1912), the journalist, and farther east is the SUBMARINE WAR MEMORIAL for both wars.

The Embankment now skirts the TEMPLE GARDENS (IV, E, F 2; see Route 24), on the wall of which is a tablet marking the boundary of the City. Beyond Middle Temple Lane a fine view opens of Inner Temple Hall and other new buildings, while ahead Blackfriars Bridge is seen, with a huge power-station rising beyond it. On the left farther on is SION COLLEGE, founded under the bequest of Dr Thomas White (d. 1624) for the Anglican clergy of London and neighbourhood, and housed in Gothic buildings by Sir Arthur Blomfield (1886). The theological library of over 100,000 volumes includes many rare printed books and manuscripts of interest and beauty. The CITY OF LONDON SCHOOL (850 boys), just beyond, was established in 1834 in succession to a foundation of 1442 by John Carpenter, a town clerk of London, for 'foure poore men's children'. The new buildings (by Davis and Emanuel) opened here in 1883 have been several times extended.

Noted Old Citizens include Sir John Seeley, the historian; Sir William Henry Perkin, the discoverer of aniline dyes; Lord Oxford and Asquith, the statesman; Bramwell Booth of the Salvation Army; Sir Frederick Gowland Hopkins, a pioneer in the discovery of vitamins; and C. E. Montague, the journalist and author. In John Carpenter Street, starting west of the school, is the GUILDHALL SCHOOL OF MUSIC AND DRAMA of the City Corporation (1880), and adjoining this on the west, in Carmelite Street, is the CITY OF LONDON SCHOOL FOR GIRLS (1894; 400 pupils).

The Victoria Embankment finishes at BLACKFRIARS BRIDGE (IV, F 3), which crosses the river for Southwark and Bankside (Route 36). It was rebuilt in 1865–9 by Joseph Cubitt and widened in 1908. An underpass beneath the bridge approach, emerging in Queen Victoria Street (see below), was begun in 1962. During the excavations, part of the hull of a wooden ship of unknown date was discovered. Opposite the approach, with a distinctive curved façade, is the large UNILEVER HOUSE, designed by J. L. Simpson and Sir John Burnet and opened in 1932. The statuary at the ends is by Sir W. Reid Dick, the mermaid and merman over the side entrances are by Gilbert Ledward. From in front there is a good 'surprise' view of the dome and towers of St Paul's.

NEW BRIDGE STREET (IV, E 3) leads north from the bridge approach to Ludgate Circus (Route 24). No. 14, on the left, now the CHARTERED INSTITUTE OF SECRETARIES (founded 1891), but probably to be rebuilt, stands on part of the site of the medieval palace of BRIDEWELL, named from a well near by dedicated to St Bride or Bridget (p. 237). Rebuilt in 1523 by Henry VIII, it was granted by Edward VI to the City to house the Royal Bridewell Hospital founded in 1553. This subsequently became a place of detention and correction for vagrants and immoral women. The present building (1802) incorporates the original court room of the hospital. ST BRIDGET'S HOUSE, in Bridewell Place, behind, is a fine modern office building of 1951. In Bride Lane, farther north, is the ST BRIDE FOUNDATION INSTITUTE, established in 1894, mainly for printers.

QUEEN VICTORIA STREET (IV, E 3–V, E 1), opened in 1871 to connect the Embankment and Blackfriars Bridge with the Bank, runs eastward from the foot of New Bridge Street, passing the main entrance to the BLACKFRIARS STATION of the Southern Region.

The district it cuts through at first was named from a monastery of the Dominicans or Black Friars founded in the 13th century and laid waste at the Dissolution. Black Friars Lane, on the left beyond the railway bridge, ascends past APOTHECARIES' HALL (No. 12), a building partly of 1670, partly of 1786, enclosing a quiet courtyard. The society, one of the City livery companies, separated from the Grocers' Company and incorporated in 1617, is still an examining body in medicine and surgery. The charming interior includes a hall and court room with 17th-century panelling, a bust of Gideon de Laune (apothecary to Anne of Denmark), and portraits of James I, Charles I, and the surgeon, John Hunter (the last a sketch by Reynolds). John Keats became a licentiate of the society in 1816. The name of PLAYHOUSE YARD, just below the hall, recalls the Blackfriars Playhouse, first opened in 1576 and reopened in 1596 by James Burbage, the friend of Shakespeare (who had a house near by and probably played here).

Queen Victoria Street keeps to the left from Upper Thames Street (Route 27), which follows the course of the river. On the left is the office of THE TIMES (IV, E 3), founded in 1785 by John Walter as the *Daily Universal Register* and given its present title in 1788. Since 1922 it has been managed by a trust set up to ensure its political independence. The printing office is behind, in PRINTING HOUSE SQUARE, so called from the King's Printing House established here in the 17th century from which was published in 1665 the first issue of the *London Gazette*, the official government newspaper. John Walter II installed here in 1814 the first steam printing press in England. The whole of the offices are being rebuilt on a new plan (1963).

Farther up on the same side as *The Times* office is the church of St Andrew-by-the-Wardrobe, rebuilt by Wren in 1685–95, gutted by bombing in 1940, and restored in 1961. Its name was derived from the proximity of the King's Great Wardrobe or storehouse established by Edward III. Next to it is the headquarters (1868) of the British and Foreign Bible Society, founded in 1804 'to encourage a wider circulation of the Holy Scriptures, without note or comment'. Since its inception it has published or circulated the whole or parts of the Bible in 865 different languages and distributed about 660 million copies. The library contains an unrivalled collection of versions of the Scriptures, including rare editions of early English, Hebrew, Greek, and other Bibles. The lofty Faraday Building beyond, completed in 1933, is the G.P.O.'s London station for long-distance telephone services, both at home and overseas.

An opening on the right admits to St Benet's Church (see Route 27). On the other side of the road just above is the College of Arms (IV, E 3), sometimes called the Heralds' Office, the official authority in England, Wales, Northern Ireland, and the Commonwealth in all matters appertaining to armorial bearings and pedigrees. It received its first charter from Richard III in 1484; its present charter was granted by Mary Tudor in 1555, two years after it had acquired Derby Place, the town house of the Earls of Derby. This mansion, burned down in the Great Fire, was rebuilt in brick in 1671–7, under the direction of Francis Sandford, the Lancaster Herald, and is one of the few surviving secular buildings erected immediately after the fire. It was restored in 1953–6, when the fine 18th-century wrought-iron entrance gates (previously at Goodrich Court, Herefordshire) were given by an American benefactor.

The library of the college is the most extensive of its kind in the world, while the heraldic and genealogical records and collections are unparalleled. The corporation comprises three Kings of Arms (Garter, who presides, Clarenceux, and Norroy & Ulster), assisted by six Heralds (York, Richmond, Windsor, Somerset, Lancaster, and Chester) and four Pursuivants (Portcullis, Rouge Dragon, Rouge Croix, and Bluemantle). The chief functions of these officers of arms are to assist the Earl Marshal in arranging certain State ceremonies, such as coronations, royal proclamations, and the opening of Parliament, and to confirm and preserve pedigrees and armorial bearings. The office of Earl Marshal has been hereditary in the person of the Duke of Norfolk since 1672. Though he is not a member of the corporation, that body cannot act in any important matter without his approval. Members of the public who have particular questions to ask may visit the college between 10 and 4 on Monday–Friday (10 and 1 on Saturdays), and arrangements can sometimes be made for showing the college to parties, after these hours (on application to the Secretary). The college contains fine woodwork by William Emmett, whose brother Maurice erected the building and may also have had a hand in its design. A Museum of Heraldry is to be built on an adjoining site.

On the right are the international headquarters, begun in 1962, of the SALVATION ARMY, founded by William Booth in the East End of London in 1865. Higher up, on the left, is the church of ST NICHOLAS COLE ABBEY, rebuilt by Wren in 1671–81, burnt out in 1941, and restored in 1962. The name was formerly 'Cold Abbey', probably from 'Cold Harbour' (a shelter for travellers). It bears the weathervane, a fine sailing-ship model, of the vanished church of St Michael Queenhithe (1677). Also on the left, farther on, is the solitary brick tower of ST MILDRED'S CHURCH, the smallest of Wren's churches (1681–7), which was destroyed by bombing in 1941. The poet Shelley was married here to Mary Wollstonecraft Godwin in 1816. In Great Trinity Lane, which diverges to the right, is BEAVER HOUSE, the head-office (1926) of the Hudson's Bay Company, founded in 1670 by Prince Rupert to trade in furs with the North American Indians and still the most important Canadian fur company.

Queen Victoria Street crosses Cannon Street (Route 25) and Queen Street, the latter leading north to Cheapside, beyond which can be seen the south façade of Guildhall (Route 30). On the left is the church of ST MARY ALDERMARY, so named, according to Stow, because 'elder than any church of St Marie in the Citie'. First mentioned in the 11th century, it was rebuilt by Wren in 1681–2, incorporating some part of the 16th-century walls. Of the tower, 135 ft high, completed in 1629, the upper stage was refashioned in 1711 by Wren. Rebuilt under a bequest made by Henry Rogers on the condition that the church be a copy of the previous building, it is the finest of Wren's few excursions into the

Gothic style. The plaster fan-vaulting, repaired after war damage, is particularly remarkable. The pulpit and west doorway have been attributed to Grinling Gibbons, and a sword-rest (dated 1682) against a pier of the south arcade is also said to be his. New stained-glass windows have been inserted to the designs of Crawford and Lee, that at the west end commemorating the defence of London against air attack in 1939–45.

John Milton married his third wife, Elizabeth Minshull, in the church in 1663. The St Antholin Lectures, established in 1559 at a church of that name near by (pulled down in 1875), are now given here (Wednesdays in January at 1.5).

On the right of Queen Victoria Street is the colossal BUCKLERS-BURY HOUSE, a block of offices designed by O. Campbell-Jones and completed in 1962. It stands over the site of the Roman TEMPLE OF MITHRAS, revealed in 1954 during excavations for the foundations of the building and laid bare under the direction of W. F. Grimes, then director of the London Museum. The remains have been rebuilt in the forecourt of the adjacent Temple Court and are accessible to visitors. The temple, which was in use from about A.D. 90 to 350, was on the plan of a basilica, about 60 ft long by 20 ft broad. The entrance, at the east end, led directly into the nave, which was separated on either side from narrow aisles by arcades of circular columns, the bases of which survive, supported by sleeper walls. The west end, a raised sanctuary terminating in a triple apse, lay on the bank of the Walbrook.

The basilica was an architectural form used originally for pagan temples, but adopted also for the earliest Christian churches. The important discoveries within the temple made clear that it had been dedicated to the worship of Mithras, a sun-god of Persian provenance, whose cult was introduced to Rome from Asia Minor. The god came to be worshipped throughout the Roman Empire in the 1st–3rd centuries and specially venerated by soldiers, officials, and merchants. Mithraism, in fact, was a personal religion for men only, with progressive grades of initiation, to which admission could be gained only through a series of rigorous ordeals. The beautiful head of Mithras and other finds from the site are on view in the Guildhall Museum at present in the Royal Exchange (p. 259).

Queen Victoria Street is joined by Poultry immediately before reaching the open space in front of the BANK OF ENGLAND (Route 28).

27 From Blackfriars Bridge to the Tower via Thames Street

Plan IV, F 3–V, F 3

STATIONS: BLACKFRIARS (Plan IV, E 3), MANSION HOUSE (V, E 1), CANNON STREET (V, F 1), MONUMENT (V, F 2), and TOWER HILL (V, F 3), all on the Circle and District lines. — MOTOR-BUSES Nos. 18, 95, 149, and 182 across Southwark Bridge; in Queen Victoria Street, see Route 26; in Cannon Street and across London Bridge, see Route 25; to the Tower, see Route 34.

ADMISSION to ST BENET'S CHURCH, Monday–Friday 12 to 3; to VINTNER'S HALL, usually on written application (free); to ST MAGNUS THE MARTYR, Tuesday–Saturday 11.30 to 4.

UPPER THAMES STREET (IV, E 3–V, F 2), branching to the right from Queen Victoria Street north of BLACKFRIARS STATION (see Route 26), runs east at no great distance from the river. It is a narrow and usually congested thoroughfare from which alleys go down to wharves on the Thames. The street is being severed near the outset by the approach to the Blackfriars underpass (see p. 248), but the two sections will be connected by a subway. The part of the street beyond this, appropriated by the paper-making trade, traverses the site of Baynard's Castle, built originally by Ralph Baynard, a follower of William the Conqueror, but rebuilt about 1428 by Humphrey, Duke of Gloucester, and destroyed in the Great Fire. On the right, at Puddle Dock, is the MERMAID THEATRE (IV, F 3), built to an unusual design by Elidir Davies and opened in 1959. The theatre, the first to be erected in London since the war and in the City since the 16th century, is the inspiration of Bernard Miles, the actor. It has a restaurant in the foyer and other unusual features.

On the left, farther east, is ST BENET'S CHURCH, a pleasant little church rebuilt by Wren 1677–85 and used by Welsh Episcopalians since 1879. The exterior has good brickwork and carved festoons over the windows; the interior is notable for its carved woodwork (galleries, altar-table, etc.). Henry Fielding, the novelist, was married here to his second wife in 1747, and Inigo Jones (d. 1652), the architect, was buried in the previous church. Farther on is the fine tower (all that remains) of ST MARY SOMERSET, built by Wren about 1694 and topped by curious obelisks and urns. The body of the church was pulled down in

1871. On the right beyond is QUEENHITHE DOCK, first mentioned in 899 and the site of the earliest fish-market in London.

On the left, in Little Trinity Lane, is the PAINTER-STATIONERS' HALL, rebuilt in 1668 and much altered in 1880 (new wing) and 1915; and in Garlick Hill, to the east, is the church of ST JAMES GARLICKHITHE, built in 1674–87 by Wren and restored in 1959 after war damage. It has a charming steeple resembling those of St Stephen Walbrook and St Michael, Paternoster Royal. The interior has good woodwork, iron hat-racks and sword-rests, etc., but is still closed. Garlick Hill and the neighbouring streets are given over to the wholesale fur trade.

On the right in Upper Thames Street is VINTNER'S HALL (V, F 1), rebuilt in 1671 after the Fire, which, however, spared its court room of about 1450, panelled in the 17th century. The exterior of the building was remodelled in 1908–10. The Vintners' Company, one of the twelve great City livery companies, was incorporated in 1437, and possesses rich 15th–16th-century tapestries, a painting of St Martin of Tours, possibly by Rubens, and fine collections of plate and 18th-century English wine-glasses.

The company enjoys the royal prerogative (with the Dyers' Company) of keeping swans on the Thames, and in July each year a voyage is made up river from above Blackfriars Bridge to Henley for the purpose of counting and marking swans ('swan upping'). Geoffrey Chaucer, whose father was a vintner, was probably born (about 1340) in the Vintry, as the neighbourhood was formerly called.

Upper Thames Street crosses Queen Street, which ascends on the left to Cannon Street and in the other direction leads to SOUTHWARK BRIDGE (V, F 1), rebuilt in 1913–21 by Sir Ernest George. Richard Whittington (d. 1423) four times Mayor of London, had a house in College Hill, farther on (compare p. 240), and was buried in the church of ST MICHAEL, PATERNOSTER ROYAL, one part of whose name comes from the paternosters or rosaries made near by, while the 'royal' shows the connexion of the district with La Réole, the centre of a wine-producing region near Bordeaux. The church was rebuilt in 1686–94 by Wren and the steeple added in 1713, but it was shattered by flying-bombs in 1944 and awaits restoration. Beyond Dowgate Hill the roadway passes under the large CANNON STREET STATION (see Route 25). Excavations in 1955 for a new building in Arthur Street, beyond, revealed the tessellated floor and a hypocaust of a Roman building of the 1st–3rd century.

Upper Thames Street passes Fishmongers' Hall (Route 25) and goes under LONDON BRIDGE (reached by steps), beyond which it is continued by LOWER THAMES STREET (V, F 2–IX, D 3), largely utilized as an extension of the Billingsgate fishmarket and best seen (or otherwise avoided) in the early morning. On the left Fish Street Hill ascends to the Monument (Route 25); on the river side is the church of ST MAGNUS THE MARTYR, rebuilt in 1671–87 by Wren, with one of his very finest steeples, 185 ft high, added in 1705. After 1760 the passage beneath this formed part of the footway to Old London Bridge. The interior, restored in 1951 after war damage, has a handsome organ, by Abraham Jordan (1712), and other good woodwork. Henry Yevele (d. 1400), architect of the nave of Westminster Abbey, was buried in the previous church, while Miles Coverdale (d. 1569), publisher of the first complete English Bible (1535), was rector in 1563–6 and is buried here. The dedication is something of a mystery; it may be to Magnus of Orkney, canonized in 1135, though the church was already in existence in the 11th century.

Farther east is BILLINGSGATE MARKET (V, F 2), the principal market in London for fish of all kinds, named after a river gate in the City wall and that in turn probably from a Saxon family.

A wharf here, perhaps the oldest on the Thames, has been in use from Saxon times. A free fishmarket was established by statute in 1699, but until the early 18th century it was used also for coal, corn, and provisions. The market, rebuilt in 1874 by Sir Horace Jones, and extended in 1961, is the scene of intense activity from about 5 a.m. The fish-porters wear curious 'leather hats' actually made of leather and wood, with flat tops and wide brims. These hats enable each to carry about a hundredweight of fish on his head. The hats were formerly known as 'bobbing hats', bobbing being the charge made by a porter to carry fish from the wholesaler to the retailer. The reputation of Billingsgate for vituperative language has passed into the realm of history.

Opposite the market, at the foot of St Mary-at-Hill, below the site of the Coal Exchange (demolished in 1963) a Roman hypocaust for heating a small bathing chamber has been preserved. WATERMEN'S HALL, on the left in St Mary-at-Hill, has a late-18th-century front.

Adjoining the fishmarket is the CUSTOM HOUSE (V, F 2) of the Board of Customs and Excise (compare p. 296), built in

1813–17 by David Laing, though the centre portion was recast in 1826–8 by Sir Robert Smirke. It has an impressive frontage, 490 ft long, towards the Thames (best seen from London Bridge). A custom house has stood on or near this site since the 14th century. St Dunstan's Hill, opposite, ascends to the church of ST DUNSTAN-IN-THE-EAST, with a tower and lantern-steeple by Wren (1698) perhaps inspired by that of Newcastle Cathedral. The church, of Saxon origin, was rebuilt in 1817–21 by David Laing, but it was gutted by bombing in 1941 and is not to be rebuilt.

Lower Thames Street ends at the foot of TOWER HILL (Route 34), near the entrances to Tower Pier and the **Tower of London.**

28 The Bank of England and its Neighbourhood

Plan V, E 1, 2

STATION: BANK (Plan V, E 1), on the Central and Northern lines, and the terminus of the Waterloo and City line of the Southern Region, is connected by escalator with Monument station (V, F 2), on the Circle and District lines. — MOTOR-BUSES in Queen Victoria Street, see Route 26; in Cheapside, see Route 29; in Princes Street, see Route 30; in Threadneedle Street, see Route 32; in Cornhill, see Route 33; in King William Street, see Route 34.

ADMISSION to the MANSION HOUSE, on Saturday afternoons on written application to the Lord Mayor's secretary (free); to ST STEPHEN, WALBROOK, daily 8 to midnight; to the ROYAL EXCHANGE (Guildhall Museum), weekdays (except Bank Holidays) 10 to 5 (free); to the STOCK EXCHANGE (Public Gallery), Monday–Friday 10.30 to 3 (free); to DRAPERS' HALL, usually on written application (free).

The triangular open space familiarly known as 'the Bank' is the commercial pulse of the City of London and one of the most congested points in the metropolis. From it radiate seven important streets, and it is estimated that some 500 motor-buses pass it during the business day. On the north side rises the Bank of England, on the east is the Royal Exchange, and to the south-west is the Mansion House. Under the centre of the cross-roads is the BANK STATION, reached from the pavements on all sides by subways, and connected to the terminal platforms of the Waterloo and City railway by a 'travolator', completed in 1960 and running at 180 ft per minute. The Mansion House station is nearly ¼-mile south-west, at the junction of Cannon Street and Queen Victoria Street.

The BANK OF ENGLAND (V, E 1, 2), the premier bank of the world, is a huge building seven storeys high, with three further storeys below the ground, and covers an area of over four acres. It is bounded by Princes Street (on the west), Lothbury (north), Bartholomew Lane (east), and Threadneedle Street (south). Over the main entrance are sculptures by Sir Charles Wheeler; in the pediment of the lofty portico can be seen the 'Old Lady of Threadneedle Street', a popular nickname for the Bank. The oldest part of the building is the massive external blank wall, relieved by fluted mock-Corinthian columns, the work of Sir John Soane, appointed architect of the Bank in 1788. The Lothbury façade was begun in 1795, the Threadneedle Street frontage in 1825, and the Bank was completed in 1833. The buildings within the wall were reconstructed in 1924–39 by Sir Herbert Baker, who, however, retained the Court Room, designed by Sir Robert Taylor, and several interiors by Soane. Only the entrance hall is accessible to visitors, but from this can be seen the central courtyard (on the site of the burial-ground of a vanished church) containing sculptures of Charles Montague (d. 1715; see below), and Lord Norman, governor in 1920–44, the latter by Wheeler.

The idea for a national bank was first mooted by William Paterson, a wealthy City merchant, but the bill for its establishment was introduced by Charles Montague, later Earl of Halifax, who was rewarded with the chancellorship of the exchequer. Incorporated by Royal Charter in 1694, it was the first joint stock bank in England (and the only one until 1834), its original capital being £1,200,000. In 1946 the capital stock, then amounting to £14,553,000, was transferred to the Treasury. The Bank of England is the Government's banker and is the only bank in England and Wales with the right of issuing paper money, the profits on which are paid to the Exchequer. It manages the National Debt, administers the Exchange Control Regulations, and acts as the banker of British banks and of most overseas banks, though no new commercial business is now undertaken. It is controlled by a governor, a deputy governor, and sixteen directors appointed by the sovereign for a limited term of years. The vaults of the Bank hold the nation's gold reserve. Since 1780, when it was threatened in the Gordon Riots, the Bank has been protected nightly (from 6 p.m.) by a detachment of the Brigade of Guards. The gate-keepers and messengers have long-tailed pink coats and scarlet waistcoats, said to be modelled on the livery of the first governor's servants.

To the south-east of the Bank, near the junction of Queen Victoria Street and Poultry, is the MANSION HOUSE (V, E 1), the official residence of the Lord Mayor of London, a classical building by George Dance the Elder (1739–53), rather spoiled by its shallow Corinthian portico. The tympanum is filled with allegorical reliefs by Sir Robert Taylor.

The mayoralty was established in 1191 or 1192 after the recognition by Prince John of the corporate unity of the citizens of London. The first mayor was Henry FitzAilwyn, who held office for twenty-one years, but in 1215 a new charter was granted by John (now king) under which the mayor was to be elected annually. The same individual, however, was not debarred from holding office more than once, the most famous instance being that of 'Dick' Whittington, four times mayor (in 1397, 1398, 1406, and 1419). The phrase 'Lord Mayor' is first found (in English) in 1414 and became general from the early 16th century onwards. The Lord Mayor for the ensuing year is now chosen on Michaelmas Day (29 September) from two Aldermen who have served as Sheriff (compare p. 273) and who are nominated by the Liverymen of the City guilds. He is installed on the Friday preceding the second Saturday in November, and on the Saturday rides in the State coach of 1756 to the Law Courts, where he is received by the Lord Chief Justice, part of a popular pageant (the Lord Mayor's Show) that dates back to the 14th century, when the Mayor rode to Westminster to present himself to the sovereign.

Visitors enter the Mansion House (see p. 256) on the west by the door in Walbrook. The principal room is the Egyptian Hall, 90 ft long, used for banquets, receptions, and similar functions, and said to be modelled on the hall of that name described by Vitruvius though by no means Egyptian in style. Other rooms shown are the Conference Room, with a notable stucco ceiling; the Salon, which has good 19th-century tapestries and a Waterford glass chandelier with 8,000 pieces; the Drawing Rooms, containing portraits by Lely and Kneller; and the small Court of Justice, which has cells beneath. The corporation plate includes notable 16th–18th-century pieces.

WALBROOK, the short street leading south from the Mansion House to Cannon Street Station, lies a little to the east of the course of a stream of that name navigable in medieval times but now conveyed through a sewer. The church of ST STEPHEN, WALBROOK, immediately behind the Mansion House, has an interior that is one of the masterpieces of Sir Christopher Wren (1672–7). The beautiful circular dome, 63 ft high, carried by eight arches supported on Corinthian columns, was wrecked by bombs in 1941, but finely restored in 1954. The stone font with its carved wood cover, the fine carved pulpit and elaborate sounding-board, and the altar-rails are of Wren's time, but the combined organ and doorcase at the west end were introduced in 1765. On the north wall is a painting of the Martyrdom of St Stephen by the American artist, Benjamin West.

Of the first church, built about 1100 on the west side of the Walbrook, Henry Chichele, afterwards archbishop of Canterbury, was rector in 1396–7; it was rebuilt on its present site in 1429–39. John Dunstable (d. 1453), the 'father of English harmony', and Sir John Vanbrugh (d. 1726), the architect and playwright, were buried here.

To the south-east of the Bank, in the angle between Threadneedle Street and Cornhill, is the ROYAL EXCHANGE (V, E 2), the third building of its kind on this site. The first exchange, founded in 1565 by Sir Thomas Gresham, was destroyed in the Great Fire, and the second was burned down in 1838. The present building, erected in 1842–4 by Sir William Tite, is a classical structure with a Corinthian portico, approached by a broad flight of steps from which it is the custom to proclaim a new sovereign. The group in the tympanum, by Sir Richard Westmacott, depicts Commerce with the charter of the Exchange, attended by the Lord Mayor, British merchants, and representatives of foreign nations. In front of the building are an equestrian statue of the Duke of Wellington, by Chantrey (1844), and a war memorial by Sir Aston Webb (with figures by Alfred Drury; 1920) to Londoners who served in the armed forces in 1914–19 and 1939–45. The campanile, rising to 180 ft on the east side of the Exchange, has a statue of Sir Thomas Gresham on one face and is surmounted by a gilded vane (perhaps the original) shaped like a grasshopper, the crest of Gresham.

The interior of the building is occupied by the Royal Exchange Assurance Company (founded 1720) and exchange business has not been transacted since 1939. The large central court, in a Renaissance style, has a pavement of Turkish honestone, a survival from Gresham's exchange. The panels of the wall arcades carry large paintings, mostly of episodes in the history of London, by Lord Leighton, Frank O. Salisbury, Stanhope Forbes, Sir Frank Brangwyn, and others (1897–1922). At the corners of the court are statues of Elizabeth I (by M. L. Watson), Charles II (by John Spiller), Queen Victoria (by Sir Hamo Thornycroft), and

Prince Albert (by J. G. Lough), and a striking bust of Abraham Lincoln (1930), carved from Indiana limestone by Andrew O'Connor, the American sculptor.

The court has been since 1955 the temporary home of the GUILDHALL MUSEUM (founded in 1826), a display of whose fine collections has been arranged in two groups, the Roman antiquities round the outside of the court itself and those of Saxon and later London in the outer passage or ambulatory. The most notable of the objects is the marble head of the sun-god Mithras, wearing a Phrygian cap and once probably part of a large group showing the god killing a bull, found in the Roman temple west of Walbrook (see p. 252). The following are the principal exhibits on view.

Roman Antiquities. West side of court (left of the entrance): bronze statuary, pottery, etc. North side: portions of columns from the temple of Mithras and other finds from the site; model of the Mithraic temple; marble head, probably of Minerva and of the 2nd century; marble group of Bacchus and his companions (probably 4th century), etc.; head of Mithras (see above); marble head of Serapis, the Graeco-Egyptian god of the under-world, with a corn-measure on his head (2nd century); large marble hand (2nd century), perhaps of Mithras; marble figure of Mercury (2nd century); recent finds from Walbrook. East side: Samian and other Roman pottery found in London. South side: complete wooden ladder over 15 ft long, pair of well-preserved leather trunks, and other finds from a 1st-century well on the site of the Bank of London & South America, Queen Street, excavated in 1953–5; Roman glassware; the 'Austalis tile', an inscribed brick found in Warwick Lane near the City Wall; figurines in bronze, terra-cotta, etc.; building materials and fragments of tessellated pavements; shoes, sandals, and toilet articles. West side: statue of a warrior found in a bastion of the wall near Bishopsgate, and other Roman sculpture.

Saxon and Later Antiquities. North side: figure of St Christopher found built into the Tudor wall, two large heraldic fragments of the Eleanor Cross on Cheapside (erected about 1294 and destroyed in 1643), part of a robed figur (probably a bishop; 12th century), 14th-century headless female statue found in 1956 on the site of the church of the Minoresses (p. 290), and other medieval sculpture; bronze head reliquary of about 1550 from northern Italy found in the Thames at Wapping, pilgrim signs and badges, and other reli-gious objects; medieval dress and ornament; 14th–15th-century swords and daggers; polychrome jugs and other pottery; Saxon weapons, etc.; and a remarkable 11th-century Viking tombstone with a Runic inscription, found in St Paul's Churchyard in 1852. East side: stone slab of 1681 formerly on No. 25 Pudding Lane ascribing the origin of the Great Fire to a Roman Catholic conspiracy; the fine Spencer collection of gloves, from the 15th to the 19th centuries. South side: 16th–18th-century Bellarmine jugs, tankards, etc.; pottery finds from a refuse pit (about 1490–1525) on the site of Gateway House, Cannon Street; 16th–17th-century knives and spoons; 16th–19th-century clay tobacco pipes found in excavations in the City; 16th–17th-century dress, including characteristic woollen Tudor caps; 17th–18th-century slip-ware; glazed tiles, mostly 16th century, one with a portrait of Elizabeth I; 16th–18th-century glass, English 'Delft-ware', etc.; 18th-century whipping-post and manacles from Newgate Prison (to the left); model of the state barge built in 1807 for the Lord Mayor; and a varied collection of old shop and tavern signs. In the south-west corner is a MUSEUM OF LEATHERCRAFT, with excellent examples of leather work from Roman times to the present day, including medieval caskets, leather bottles, etc., and saddles made for Queen Victoria and the Prince Consort.

In the open space behind the Royal Exchange are a seated bronze figure of George Peabody (d. 1869), the American merchant and philanthropist, and a charming bronze group of Maternity by Dalou (1878).

Hidden away in the angle between Threadneedle Street and Throgmorton Street, on the north, is the STOCK EXCHANGE (V, E 2), the institution for the buying and selling of stocks and shares, founded in 1773. The present building, colloquially 'the House', was opened in 1802, reconstructed in 1853 and enlarged in 1884. The original entrance is in Capel Court, off Bartholomew Lane, east of the Bank, but the principal entrances are now in Throgmorton Street and here also (at No. 8) is the entrance to the public gallery overlooking 'the floor', where visitors can see the exchange in operation. Adjoining the gallery is a cinema where a film is shown six times a day (Monday–Friday, 10.30 to 2.30).

The London Stock Exchange is owned by a private company, with about 3,600 members, governed by a council of thirty-six, one-third of whom are elected every year by ballot. Members are elected on the nomination of a retiring member, pay an entrance fee of 600 guineas and an annual subscription of 100 guineas. They are required to find three sureties of £500 each for the first four years and must purchase at least three shares in the Stock Exchange company. Applicants who have served for four years as clerks are usually admitted if they pay half the fee and subscription and find only two sureties. Members are divided into 'jobbers', or dealers, and 'brokers'. The former, as a rule, deal only with other members, confining their activities to particular classes of securities; the broker acts as intermediary between the jobber and the public, buying and selling on commission. Bargains are made 'on the nod', no documents being signed and no written pledges being given; members who cannot comply with their bargains, however, are 'hammered'. Speculators who buy anticipating a rise in prices are called 'bulls', while those who sell believing they will fall are known as 'bears'. The Stock Exchange Official List, published daily, is compiled from the day's transactions. After closing hours (3.30 p.m.) an animated 'street market' in securities is carried on in Throgmorton Street and the neighbouring courts.

Also in Throgmorton Street (No. 28) is DRAPERS' HALL, rebuilt after the Great Fire, but largely reconstructed in 1866 by Herbert Williams, who gave it a new front, and restored in 1949 after war damage. The hall contains valuable plate, including the Elizabethan Lambard Cup (1578), and some notable portraits, one by Zucchero supposed to represent Mary, Queen of Scots, and James I. In the gardens is a mulberry-tree, believed to have been planted during the reign of James I. The company, which ranks third in order of civic precedence among the City livery companies, was incorporated in 1364. In Austin Friars, starting to the east at the junction of Old Broad Street, is the DUTCH CHURCH (V, E 2), originally the nave of an Augustinian friary founded in 1253 and granted in 1550 by Edward VI to Dutch and other foreign Protestant refugees. This building, which became the church of the Dutch community in London, was completely destroyed by a bomb in 1940, and a fine new church, designed by Arthur Bailey, was built on part of the site in 1950–4. It has a large west window with stained-glass by Max Nauta of Amsterdam telling the story of the churches, and other windows by Hugh Easton and William Wilson.

OLD BROAD STREET (V, D, E 2) runs north past the east end of London Wall (Route 31) to Broad Street and Liverpool Street Stations (Route 32). At No. 13, on the right, is the NATIONAL BANK, founded in 1835; No. 19, next to it, is the CITY OF LONDON CLUB, built in 1832 by Philip Hardwick and occupying the site of the South Sea Company's office, where Charles Lamb was a clerk in 1789–92.

29 From the Bank to King's Cross via Cheapside and Smithfield

Plan V, E 1–III, A 3

STATIONS: BANK (Plan V, E 1), see Route 28; ST PAUL'S (IV, E 3), on the Central line; ALDERSGATE (IV, C 3), FARRINGDON (IV, C 2), and KING'S CROSS & ST PANCRAS (III, A 3), on the Circle and Metropolitan lines. King's Cross is also on the Piccadilly and Northern lines. — MOTOR-BUSES Nos. 7, 8, 22, 23, 25, and 32 in Poultry and Cheapside; No. 4 in Aldersgate Street; No. 141 in London Wall (from Aldersgate Street to Moorgate); No. 279 in St John Street; Nos. 63, 143, and 221 in Farringdon Road and King's Cross Road; Nos. 5 and 170 in Clerkenwell Road; Nos. 19, 38, 171, and 172 in Rosebery Avenue.

ADMISSION to BOW CHURCH (Crypt) Monday–Friday 9 to 6; to ST BOTOLPH ALDERSGATE Monday–Friday 12 to 3; to ST BARTHOLOMEW THE GREAT, daily 7.45 to dusk; to ST JOHN'S GATE and ST JOHN'S CHURCH, usually on written application to the Curator of the Museum at

St John's Gate (free); to MOUNT PLEASANT POST OFFICE, on application as for the G.P.O. (p. 222), Monday–Thursday 2.30 to 4 and 5.30 to 7.30, Friday 2.30 to 4 only (visit takes about 2 hours).

POULTRY (V, E 1), a short street named from its medieval occupation by poulterers, runs west from the Mansion House (Route 28), leaving Queen Victoria Street on the left. On the right, at the corner of Princes Street, is the old Union Bank branch of the NATIONAL PROVINCIAL BANK (by Sir Edwin Cooper, 1931) and next to it is the ornate head-office of the MIDLAND BANK (founded in 1836), by Messrs Gotch and Saunders with Sir Edwin Lutyens (1925–8).

The name of OLD JEWRY, farther on, recalls that this was the quarter occupied by the Jews before their expulsion by Edward I in 1290. No. 26, rebuilt in 1930 round a quiet courtyard by Sydney Perks, is the headquarters of the CITY OF LONDON POLICE. A few restored Georgian houses survive in FREDERICKS PLACE, opening on the left before this.

Poultry is extended beyond Bucklersbury by CHEAPSIDE (IV, E 3–V, E 1), once known as the Chepe or West Chepe (from the Old English 'ceap', to barter) and in the Middle Ages the chief market of London. The names of side-streets probably indicate the positions of the various traders' stalls. BECKET HOUSE, on the right, designed by Noel Clifton and completed in 1958, incorporates a new MERCERS' HALL, replacing that on the same site destroyed by bombing in 1941.

The Mercers' Company, first mentioned as a fraternity in the 12th century and incorporated in 1393, is the richest of the City livery companies and the first in order of civic precedence. The hall stood on the site of a hospital of St Thomas of Acon, founded about 1190 by the sister of Thomas Becket, traditionally on the site of the house where the archbishop was born about 1118. The hospital was placed under the patronage of the Mercers, and after the Dissolution its chapel became the chapel of the company. Under the floor an early-16th-century recumbent figure of the dead Christ, of outstanding beauty, was discovered in 1954 (it has been transferred to the Guildhall Museum). Sir Thomas Gresham, the founder of the Royal Exchange, was a member of the company, which possesses some valuable plate.

The tower of ST OLAVE'S JEWRY, in Ironmonger Lane, on the north, is the only survival of a Wren church built in 1670–9 and pulled down in 1888. Under the offices of Messrs Peat, Marwick, Mitchell and Co. (No. 11) is a Roman pavement (usually shown to visitors on application).

King Street and Queen Street, named after Charles II and his

consort, lead respectively right to Guildhall (Route 30) and left to
Southwark Bridge (Route 27). On the left beyond the road
junction rises the famous steeple of BOW CHURCH (V, E 1;
properly St Mary-le-Bow), a beautiful campanile 221 ft high,
designed by Sir Christopher Wren and completed in 1683, with a
spire surmounted by a weathervane in the form of a griffin nearly
9 ft long. The church itself, rebuilt by Wren in 1670–83, was
severely damaged by bombing in 1941, but is being restored
(1963) to the designs of Laurence King. It stands above an early-
Norman crypt (approached from Bow Lane) of about 1080–90
(the oldest ecclesiastical work in London, except the Tower
chapel). This is supposed to have given the medieval church its
name of St Maria-de-Arcubus because it was the first in London
to be built on arches (or bows) of stone. The crypt, restored in its
original style as far as possible, incorporates some Roman brick
and has aisles separated from the nave by monolithic columns. Its
south aisle, converted into a chapel, has a fine glass screen by
John Hayward.

The church was at one time the chief 'peculiar' in the City, coming
directly under the jurisdiction of the archbishop of Canterbury. The Court
of Arches, the principal ecclesiastical court, named from the church, was
held here at least as early as 1272 (but now sits in the Sanctuary at Westminster). True Londoners, or 'cockneys', are those born within the sound
of Bow Bells. The bells in the old story that called back Dick Whittington
to be 'Lord Mayor of London' perished in the Great Fire; fragments of
their successors, similarly destroyed in 1941, are incorporated in twelve
new bells, rung for the first time in 1961.

In the former churchyard, on the west, is a statue of Captain John Smith
(see p. 227), a replica of one in Jamestown (Virginia), unveiled in 1960. Sir
Thomas More, the statesman, was born in 1478 in Milk Street, on the right
beyond the church, and John Milton, the poet, son of a scrivener, in 1608
in Bread Street, nearly opposite, but both birthplaces have disappeared.

In Wood Street, on the right, north of Cheapside, is an old plane-
tree protected in the leases of adjacent buildings and believed to
be that in which the thrush sang loud in Wordsworth's *Poor Susan*.
SADDLERS' HALL, on the same side, was destroyed by fire in
the war, but a new hall (by L. Sylvester Sullivan) just off Cheapside
was opened in 1958. The company, claiming to be the oldest of the
City livery companies, is believed to have received a charter from
Edward I. Foster Lane, just beyond, contains ST VEDAST'S

CHURCH, the only church in England (apart from Tathwell in Lincs) dedicated to this saint, who was bishop of Arras and died in 540. Rebuilt by Wren in 1670–3, it was sadly bombed in 1940, but restoration (by S. Dykes Bower) began in 1955. The graceful steeple, one of Wren's finest (1697), escaped destruction, as did an unusual colonnade on the north, leading to former parochial school (1691), seen from Priest's Court. Robert Herrick, the poet, son of a goldsmith of Cheapside, was baptized in 1591 in the previous church here. Additional buildings for the BANK OF ENGLAND, in a modified Georgian style by Victor Heal, are being erected (1963) on the south side of Cheapside and will be adorned with sculptures by Sir Charles Wheeler.

At the head of Cheapside, St Paul's Churchyard opens to the left, with a fine view of the cathedral. Newgate Street (Route 23) keeps on to Holborn, while ST MARTIN'S-LE-GRAND (IV, D, E 3) leads to the right past the General Post Office (p. 229). This short street takes its name from a college of secular canons established before the Norman Conquest and demolished in 1548. The site of this is partly occupied by the building (No. 16; by Leo S. Sullivan, 1927) of Messrs Courtauld. Just beyond Gresham Street (Route 30) is the site of Aldersgate ('Aldred's Gate'), pulled down in 1761. The church of ST BOTOLPH ALDERSGATE is one of three (originally four) churches dedicated to the 7th-century Saxon saint and standing by City gates of London. It escaped the Great Fire, but was rebuilt in 1754 and the interior recast in 1788. New stained-glass windows by M. C. Farrar-Bell of historical subjects were dedicated in the south aisle in 1955. The churchyard, on the south, has been converted into the secluded little POSTMEN'S PARK, with a statue of Sir Robert Peel (d. 1850) and a cloister given by G. F. Watts (1880) containing tablets recording acts of heroism in everyday life.

Aldersgate Street goes on to Clerkenwell Road and Old Street (compare Route 30), but the route bears left beyond St Botolph's, following LITTLE BRITAIN, in which Mr Jaggers had his forbidding office in *Great Expectations*. The name is said by Stow to be taken from a house of the Duke of Brittany. The narrow street turns sharply right, passing St Bartholomew's Hospital, and ends at WEST SMITHFIELD (*i.e.* 'smooth field'), a large open space that was once a tournament ground outside the City walls, and is now best known for its meat market.

From the reign of Henry I (1100–35) until 1840 the great St Bartholomew's Fair was held here around Bartholomew Tide (24 August). The most important cloth fair in England (lasting three days) during the later Middle Ages, when the country's wealth expanded with its growing exports of wool and cloth, it became from the 16th century a pleasure fair lasting a fortnight, with dramatic and other entertainments (compare Ben Jonson's *Bartholomew Fair*). Smithfield was also the principal horse and cattle market from about 1150 until 1855, and in the 12th century it became the chief place of execution. Sir William Wallace (see below) and Anne Askew (p. 274) are among those who suffered here, and in the reign of Mary Tudor no fewer than 270 Protestants were burned at the stake. Wat Tyler, the rebel leader, was slain here in 1381 by Sir William Walworth, the mayor, in the presence of Richard II.

To the south-east of Smithfield are the extensive buildings of ST BARTHOLOMEW'S HOSPITAL (IV, D 3), the oldest hospital in London on its original site, founded in 1123, together with an Augustinian priory (see below), by Rahere, a courtier of Henry I, as the result of a pilgrimage to Rome. On the outer wall are memorials to Sir William Wallace, the Scottish patriot, executed here in 1305 (unveiled in 1956), and to several of the Protestant martyrs (see above). The hospital was refounded by Henry VIII in 1546 after the suppression of the priory. The fine gatehouse, with a statue of the king, was erected in 1702; the Great Hall and other buildings in the quadrangle are to the designs of James Gibbs (1730–4), while later additions (from 1808) were made by Thomas Hardwick. Yet further additions were made between 1878 and 1923. Within the gates to the left (visitors admitted) is the small church of ST BARTHOLOMEW THE LESS, of medieval origin, but largely rebuilt (except for the 15th-century tower) in 1823 by Hardwick, who preserved the octagonal form of the previous church of 1789 by the younger Dance. It was restored in 1950, when new memorial windows by Hugh Easton were inserted. In the floor of the vestibule is a brass of 1439 to William Markeby and his wife. Inigo Jones, the architect (see below), was christened in the medieval church in 1573.

The Great Hall (no general admission), farther east, is a noble work by Gibbs with a gilded and decorated ceiling, and the so-called Charter window of the 17th century showing Henry VIII presenting a document to the Lord

Mayor. It contains portraits by Reynolds, Lawrence, and others, and on the staircase are two large paintings by Hogarth given in 1737 by the artist to the hospital, of which he became a governor.

William Harvey, the discoverer of the circulation of the blood, was chief physician of the hospital in 1609–43. The famous medical college ('Bart's'), the oldest in London, was founded in 1662, and John Abernethy was lecturer here from 1791 until 1815, when he was elected principal surgeon of the hospital. The college, now affiliated to the University of London, has faculties of medicine and certain branches of science, a valuable library, and a museum of 12,000 anatomical specimens. It is partly housed in new buildings close to the Charterhouse (see Route 30).

GILTSPUR STREET leads from the south corner of Smithfield to the junction of Holborn Viaduct and Newgate Street (Route 23). In Cock Lane, on the right, is a gilt figure of a naked boy marking PYE CORNER, where the Great Fire of 1666, which started at Pudding Lane, is popularly (but incorrectly) supposed to have stopped.

On the east side of Smithfield is the entrance to the Norman church of ST BARTHOLOMEW THE GREAT (IV, D 3), the oldest in London (after the chapel in the Tower) and the most interesting. The present building consists of little more than the choir of the great priory-church founded in 1123 for Augustinian canons (compare above). The churchyard occupies the site of the nave, and the 13th-century entrance gate (restored in 1932) was originally the west entrance to the south aisle. Above the gateway is an Elizabethan house with a half-timbered front (1595), revealed in 1915 by the explosion of a Zeppelin bomb loosening the tiles that concealed it. At the Reformation most of the church and the conventual buildings were destroyed or alienated. There survives, apart from Rahere's choir and vaulted ambulatories, the crossing and one bay of the nave, built before 1170; the transepts, shortened by Sir Aston Webb, who began a successful restoration in 1863; and the Lady Chapel, of 14th-century origin.

The choir has massive piers and round arches in the mature Romanesque style; the triforium is also Norman work, but the clerestory was rebuilt early in the 15th century. On the south side the triforium is broken by a lovely oriel introduced by Prior William Bolton (1506–32) and formerly communicating with the prior's house. It bears his rebus, a bolt (or arrow) piercing a tun. The apsidal east end of the choir, with its attenuated columns, was built in 1863–85 by Webb, but probably recaptures the style of the original apse, demolished in the 15th century in favour of a square end. On the north side of the sanctuary is the beautiful canopied tomb (late 15th or early 16th century) with an effigy of the founder (d. 1143), a prebendary of St Paul's Cathedral and the first prior of St Bartholomew's. The South Transept contains the 15th-century font (the only medieval font in the City) at which William Hogarth (see below) was baptized. In the South Ambulatory is the alabaster tomb of Sir Walter Mildmay (d. 1589), founder of Emmanuel College, Cambridge, and Chancellor of the Exchequer under Elizabeth I. The Lady Chapel, divided from the east end of the choir by a fine modern iron screen, was largely rebuilt after 1885. In the 18th century it was used as a printing office and Benjamin Franklin was employed here (1725). Below it is a small Crypt, probably once a charnel-house. In the North Ambulatory are the entrances to former chapels; the North Transept, restored in 1893 after long occupation by a blacksmith's forge, is separated from the crossing by a 15th-century stone screen.

A Norman doorway with 15th-century wooden doors, west of the south transept, opens to the east walk of the Cloisters (key with the verger), built about 1405 but largely reconstructed in its original style in 1905–28. Arches in the east wall indicate the entrance to the vanished chapter-house. On Good Friday, in continuance of a custom begun in 1686, twenty-one poor widows each receive a new sixpence at St Bartholomew's. The money (now supplemented by gifts of hot-cross buns and a proportion of the collection at the service) is laid out on a tombstone in the churchyard. The painter Hogarth was born in 1697 in BARTHOLOMEW CLOSE, south-west of the church, and Milton went into hiding here for a time after the Restoration in 1660. Inigo Jones was the son of a clothworker of CLOTH FAIR, north of the church, which preserves a charming house of about 1640 (No. 41), one of the very few surviving in the City from before the Great Fire.

On the north side of Smithfield is the large CENTRAL MEAT MARKET (IV, C, D 3), built in 1886 by Sir Horace Jones and covering about 10 acres with an extension on the west towards Farringdon Road. The market is at its busiest between 5 and 9 o'clock in the morning, and there are sections for poultry (rebuilt in 1962 after a fire), provisions, etc. Long Lane leads to the right for Aldersgate Station, while the roadway through the middle of the market from Smithfield gives access to Charterhouse Street, running west to Holborn (Route 23) and east to Charterhouse Square (p. 277), and to ST JOHN STREET, which goes on north to Islington (see Route 30).

St John's Lane, branching to the left, is spanned by ST JOHN'S GATE (IV, C 3), once the main entrance to an influential priory of the Order of the Hospital of St John of Jerusalem, better known as the Knights Hospitallers, an order of chivalry founded late in the 11th century at Jerusalem. Its headquarters were later moved to the island of Rhodes and then to Malta (1530–1798). The priory, built about 1148, soon after the establishment of the order in England, was burned down by Wat Tyler's rebels (1381) and the gatehouse was rebuilt in 1504 by Prior Thomas Docwra.

After the suppression of the order in England the priory buildings were appropriated by the Crown (1559), and by the 19th century they had become the 'Old Jerusalem Tavern'. The order was revived in 1831, and in 1873 the English members purchased St John's Gate, practically all that survived of the priory, and began to develop the ambulance work for which they are now best known. In 1888 they were established as the Venerable Order of the Hospital of St John of Jerusalem, an entirely British royal order of chivalry.

The room over the gate was once occupied by Edward Cave, the founder in 1731 of the *Gentleman's Magazine*, to which Johnson and Garrick contributed. Now known as the Council Chamber, it contains interesting relics of the Knights Hospitallers. The annexe on the south-east of the gateway was added in 1903 by J. Oldrid Scott. On the north side of the gatehouse are the arms of the order and Prior Docwra.

ST JOHN'S SQUARE, cut through by Clerkenwell Road, occupies the site of the courtyard of the priory. On its north-east side is ST JOHN'S CHURCH (IV, C 3), rebuilt in 1721–3 on the site of the priory church consecrated in 1185. Parts of the choir walls were incorporated in the 18th-century building; the original church had a round nave (as usual with the Order of St John) the outline of which is marked on the ground in the Square. In 1931 the church reverted to the order, but it was very severely damaged in 1941 by incendiary bombs. Rebuilding was completed in 1958 to designs by Lord Mottistone. The 15th-century altar-paintings, given by Grand Prior John Weston to commemorate the order's victory at the siege of Rhodes, were looted from the church at the Dissolution but rediscovered in 1915. Below the chancel survives the original Crypt, the three west bays of which are pure Norman work of about 1140, while the two east bays and the side chapels were completed about 1170.

CLERKENWELL ROAD (IV, C 1–3; pronounced 'Clark-') leads west across Farringdon Road to Gray's Inn Road (Route 22). On the west side of Clerkenwell Green (opening on the right) is the former MIDDLESEX SESSIONS HOUSE, a classical building of 1782, much altered and now used as offices. On a slope to the north rises ST JAMES'S CHURCH (IV, C 2), the parish church of Clerkenwell, built in 1788–92 by James Carr and renovated in 1882 by Blomfield. The baroque steeple was rebuilt in its former style in 1849.

FARRINGDON ROAD, the continuation of Farringdon Street (compare Route 24), goes on north-west from Clerkenwell Road, crossing Rosebery Avenue. In Pine Street, a parallel street on the right just before the crossing, is the excellent FINSBURY HEALTH CENTRE, a fine example of modern architecture by Lubetkin and Tecton (1938). Beyond the crossing, at Mount Pleasant, is the huge PARCEL POST OFFICE (IV, B 1, 2), built in 1900–34 and damaged in 1943. It is the largest of its kind in the world, with 9½ acres of floor space, and about a million parcels are handled every week. Visitors are shown the Sorting Offices and the Post Office Railway (see p. 229). Lloyd Baker Street, on the right at the beginning of King's Cross Road, ascends to LLOYD SQUARE, on three sides of which are unusual semi-detached houses of 1819. King's Cross Road joins Pentonville Road a little east of KING'S CROSS STATION; thence to Euston, etc., and to the Angel at Islington, see Route 16.

ROSEBERY AVENUE, starting from Clerkenwell Road near Gray's Inn Road, was cut through a squalid district and leads north-east to St John Street (Route 30) short of the Angel. It passes FINSBURY TOWN HALL (by C. Evans Vaughan, 1895) and the offices (1920) of the METROPOLITAN WATER BOARD, incorporating a room, with notable wood-carving and plasterwork, from the Water House of 1693. The fine Research Building to the north-east was added by Howard Robertson in 1938. The surrounding reservoirs are on the site of the New River Head, the end of the water-supply brought to London from the Lea Valley by Sir Hugh Myddelton in 1613. Opposite are large new blocks of flats (by Lubetkin and Tecton) characteristic of the borough of Finsbury, and just beyond is the SADLER'S WELLS THEATRE (IV, A 2), rebuilt in 1931 by Frank Marcham as a home of popular opera in north London, under the management of Lilian Baylis (see p. 212). Its ballet company has achieved an international reputation under the direction of Ninette de Valois. The previous theatre was built by Thomas Sadler, who in 1683 discovered an old well in the garden of his house and developed it as a popular 'spa'. At this theatre Grimaldi, the famous clown, played in 1818–28, and Samuel Phelps produced thirty-four of Shakespeare's plays in 1844–63.

30 From the Bank to the Angel (Islington) via Guildhall and the Charterhouse

Plan V, E 1–IV, A 2

STATIONS: BANK (Plan V, E 1), see Route 28; ST PAUL'S (IV, E 3), on the Central line; ALDERSGATE (IV, C 3), on the Circle and Metropolitan lines; ANGEL (IV, A 2), on the Northern line. — MOTOR-BUSES Nos. 9, 11, 21, 43, 76, and 133 in Princes Street; No. 4 in Aldersgate Street and Goswell Road; No. 277 in Goswell Road and No. 279 in St John Street (both from Smithfield); in Cheapside, see Route 29; others to the Angel, see Routes 16, 29.

ADMISSION to ST MARGARET LOTHBURY, Monday–Friday 8 to 5, Sundays 10 to 5; to ST LAWRENCE JEWRY, Monday–Friday 8 to 6, Saturdays 8 to 5, Sundays 2 to 5; to GUILDHALL, Great Hall, weekdays 10 to 5, Sundays and Bank Holidays in May–September 2 to 5 (free); Art Gallery, weekdays 10 to 5, and Library, weekdays 9.30 to 5 (free; both closed on Bank Holidays); to GOLDSMITHS' HALL, usually on written application (free); to the CHARTERHOUSE, on Saturdays (parties only) by previous arrangement with the Registrar (2/6, devoted to the Charterhouse Mission at Southwark).

From the open space fronting the Mansion House (Route 28), PRINCES STREET (V, E 1) runs north-west, with the Bank of England on its right. On the left are entrances to GROCERS' HALL, the fourth on this site, completed in 1892 and restored after its partial demolition by a flying-bomb in 1944. The guild of 'pepperers', the forerunners of the grocers, first heard of in 1180, lapsed in the reign of Edward III, but was revived as a fraternity in 1345 and received its first charter as the Grocers' Company in 1428. The company is the second in precedence of the twelve great City livery companies.

In Lothbury, on the north side of the Bank, is the church of ST MARGARET LOTHBURY, rebuilt in 1686–95 by Wren and containing an unusual 17th-century chancel screen, probably of Hanseatic origin. In the north aisle is a bronze bust of Sir Peter le Maire (d. 1631), perhaps by Hubert le Sueur; and in the south aisle (now a chapel) is the charming font, attributed to Grinling Gibbons.

In a niche of the wall opposite the church is a statue of Sir John Soane (d. 1837), architect of the Bank. No. 41 Lothbury is the head-office (1929) of the WESTMINSTER BANK, founded in 1834. The street is extended eastward by Throgmorton Street, passing the main entrances to the Stock Exchange (Route 28).

GRESHAM STREET (V, D, E 1), starting opposite Lothbury at the foot of Moorgate (Route 31), leads west to Aldersgate Street. On the right, at the junction of Basinghall Street, is GRESHAM COLLEGE, established in 1579 under a bequest of Sir Thomas Gresham, the founder of the Royal Exchange, for the delivery of free public lectures in Latin and English in divinity, astronomy, music, geometry, physic, law, and rhetoric, the last three under the auspices of the Mercers' Company. The lectures, begun in 1597, are now all given in English between mid-October and mid-June (Monday–Thursday at 5.30). The present college, by Dendy Watney, was built in 1913. Farther on, at the corner of King Street, is the church of ST LAWRENCE JEWRY, rebuilt by Wren in 1670–87, but gutted by bombing in 1940, and restored in 1954–7, largely in its former style, by Cecil Brown. The classical tower and spire, rebuilt to their old design, are surmounted by the original weathervane in the form of a gridiron, recalling the martyrdom of St Lawrence. In the nave and the Commonwealth chapel are stained-glass windows by Christopher Webb, and the reredos has a painting by the restorer. A new vicarage has been provided in the north-west corner of the church, which is the official church of the City Corporation. The retiring Lord Mayor attends service here before the election of his successor on Michaelmas Day.

The Spital Sermon, preached originally at the priory of St Mary Spital (p. 291), and at Christ Church (Newgate Street) before its destruction, is now given here on the second Wednesday after Easter, when the Lord Mayor and Aldermen attend in state.

King Street ends on the north in the yard of GUILDHALL (V, D, E 1), the Hall of the Corporation of the City of London, rebuilt in the early 15th century, but given a new south front in the Gothick fashion in 1789 by George Dance the younger, and altered and extended at various other times.

Guildhall, the seat of municipal government in the City and the principal place of civic assembly, replaces an earlier hall of great but unknown age which stood farther west in Aldermanbury. The present hall was built in 1411–25, and of this period there survives the porch of the gatehouse, part of the Great Hall and a double crypt. The building was seriously damaged in the Great Fire of 1666, but was immediately repaired, perhaps by Wren. Further rebuildings and restorations were carried out, particularly by Sir

Horace Jones (1864–84) and by Sydney Perks, who rebuilt the east wing (1909). Guildhall was injured again during the great fire of 29 December 1940, but was partly restored by Sir Giles Gilbert Scott in 1954.

Visitors are admitted to the Court of Common Council which meets in Guildhall on alternate Thursdays at 1 p.m.

High over the porch is the coat-of-arms of the City, with its motto, 'Domine dirige nos' ('Lord, direct us'). The porch, which retains its fine 15th-century vaulting, leads direct into the GREAT HALL, the principal chamber, 152 ft long, 49½ ft wide, and 89 ft high. Though preserving part of its original walls, it was largely rebuilt after the Great Fire, and considerably restored in 1864–6 by Sir Horace Jones, who gave it a new timber roof. This roof, destroyed in 1940, has been reconstructed by Sir Giles Scott, but he has provided stone arches with a flat panelled ceiling between, giving an effect of extra height. He has also introduced new panelling at the ends of the hall, and new stained-glass windows whose design incorporates scrolls bearing the names and dates of 663 Mayors and Lord Mayors. Around the cornice are painted shields of the livery companies, and embroidered banners with the arms of the twelve 'great' companies were hung here in 1957.

The large monuments by the north wall commemorate Lord Nelson (by James Smith, with an inscription by Sheridan), the Duke of Wellington (by John Bell), and the Earl of Chatham (by John Bacon the elder; inscription attributed to Burke); those on the south wall are to William Pitt (by J. G. Bubb; inscription by Canning) and William Beckford, Lord Mayor in 1762 and 1769 (by F. J. Moore). The inscription on this last, said to have been a speech made by Beckford to George III, is worth reading. At the west end is a new timber screen and gallery, above which are recent figures of Gog and Magog, carved in limestone by David Evans, replacing the 18th-century figures lost in the bombing and themselves said to be inspired by effigies carried in medieval pageants. To the right of the screen is a fine bronze seated statue of Sir Winston Churchill (1959), by the Yugoslav sculptor, Oscar Nemon; to the left survives an unusual 15th-century window.

The hall is used for municipal and public meetings, and for civic receptions and banquets, among the most notable being those given to visiting royalty and State officials. On Midsummer Day (24 June) the 'Common Hall' of the mayor and aldermen with the liverymen of the City guilds is held here, a colourful ceremony at which the Sheriffs for the ensuing year are elected (visitors usually admitted on previous application). On the second Saturday in November the new Lord Mayor, elected to office here on the preceding day, gives a banquet to members of the Cabinet and other important citizens. The hall was formerly used for important trials, and Anne Askew, the Protestant martyr (1546), Henry Howard, the poet Earl of Surrey (1547), Lady Jane Grey, and Archbishop Cranmer (both in 1554) were among those condemned here. The Council Chamber, the Aldermen's Court Room and other rooms north of the Great Hall were destroyed in 1940 and have not yet been restored.

Beneath the hall is a magnificent early-15th-century CRYPT (restored in 1961), part of the original building. It is divided by a wall into two sections, the eastern of which, nearly 77 ft long, has six clustered columns of Purbeck marble supporting a groined vault with carved bosses. The western section was much restored after the Great Fire.

On the east of Guildhall Yard is the GUILDHALL ART GALLERY, temporarily repaired after war damage. Established in 1886 on the site of the Guildhall Chapel (demolished in 1822), its large collection (only part of which can be shown) consists mainly of British paintings of the 19th century. Loan exhibitions of the work of London art societies are held frequently. Opposite the gallery to the south is the IRISH CHAMBER (1825), the headquarters of the Honourable the Irish Society, incorporated in 1613 to manage the estates allotted to the corporation after the plantation of Ulster in 1609. In Guildhall Buildings, the adjacent street, is the MAYOR'S AND CITY OF LONDON COURT (1893) and on the west side of Guildhall Yard are the JUSTICE ROOM and other offices, in a building put up in 1823 for the Courts of Queen's Bench and Common Pleas, discontinued in 1883 when new Law Courts were opened in the Strand.

A corridor opening on the east of the porch, with paintings of events in the City's history, gives access to the GUILDHALL LIBRARY, founded originally in 1425 and re-established in 1828. On the left of the landing, which has statues by Arnold Quelling of Charles II and Sir John Cutler (d. 1693), a City merchant and benefactor, is the Newspaper Room, and to the right is the useful Commercial Reference Room, with directories and periodicals. Between these is the Principal Library, a spacious hall of 1872 in the Tudor Gothic style, to which readers are admitted on signing their names. It contains about 135,000 volumes (though it lost many in the bombing) and is particularly notable for its works on every aspect of London; it also has numerous MSS. and an unrivalled collection of London prints.

Among the many valuable possessions may be noted Ralph or Radulph Agas's plan of Elizabethan London (about 1591); the deed of purchase of a house in Blackfriars bearing Shakespeare's signature (1613); the first, second, and fourth folios of Shakespeare's plays; a MS. volume of French chronicles (1399); the Great Chronicle of London, used by John Stow, the Elizabethan topographer; an illuminated English missal of the early 15th century from St Botolph Aldersgate; and a remarkable modern MS. register (in four volumes) containing representations of the monuments, coats-of-arms, etc., in the City churches. The timber ceiling of the library bears the arms of fourteen of the City livery companies.

On the east side of the Commercial Reference Room is another landing to the left of which opens the East Lobby, containing a fine assembly of old clocks, watches, and chronometers, the property of the Clockmakers' Company. From the landing a staircase, with three 17th-century figures of English monarchs by Nicholas Stone, from the Guildhall chapel, descends to the Basinghall Street entrance.

The interesting antiquities of the Guildhall Museum are temporarily housed in the Royal Exchange (Route 28).

To the west of Guildhall is ALDERMANBURY, a street named from a 'bury' or court of an alderman and leading north from Gresham Street. It passes the church of ST MARY ALDERMANBURY, rebuilt by Wren in 1680–7, but not improved by a restoration of 1863 and bombed out in 1940. The walls and tower are probably to be re-erected at Fulton University (Missouri). John Milton was married in the previous church to his second wife (1656) and Judge Jeffreys was buried under the altar (1689). In the churchyard is a 19th-century monument to John Heming and Henry Condell, Shakespeare's fellow-actors and editors of the First Folio (1623). In Aldermanbury, farther north, are the CHARTERED INSURANCE INSTITUTE (1934) and BREWERS' HALL, rebuilt in 1960 by Sir Hubert Worthington and T. W. Sutcliffe.

Gresham Street continues west past Wood Lane (see below), on the corner of which is GARRARD HOUSE, a large block of offices designed by Arthur S. Ash (1956). It incorporates HABERDASHERS' HALL (entrance in Staining Lane), the third on the site, the first (built in 1448) having been burned down in the Great Fire and the second destroyed during the war. The company is one of the twelve senior livery companies. On the right farther on is the church of ST ANNE AND ST AGNES, a small but attractive building by Wren (1676–87), damaged in 1940 and still closed. At the corner of Foster Lane, to the left, is GOLDSMITHS' HALL (V, D 1), an elaborate building in the Renaissance style by Philip Hardwick (1835).

The rich interior contains some notable portraits and a very fine collection of plate. The company, ranking fifth in order of precedence among the great livery companies, was incorporated in 1327 and still has the duty of assaying and stamping precious metals, its hall-mark being the leopard's head. The 'Trial of the Pyx', *i.e.* the testing of the coinage issued from the Royal Mint, has been the prerogative of the company since medieval times, and the test is still carried out every March, samples of coins, each value in its own box (called a 'pyx'), being sent to the hall for the purpose.

The route turns right into St Martin's-le-Grand, joining Route 29, then follows ALDERSGATE STREET (IV, C, D 3) past St Botolph's Church. On the right begins ROUTE 11, a new road cut through to Moorgate (Route 31) and opened in 1959. It traverses an area that was sadly devastated by the bombing but is now largely covered by massive blocks of offices.

The new road crosses WOOD STREET, which leads south to Gresham Street (see above) and Cheapside; on the right, in Oat Lane, is PEWTERERS' HALL, built in 1960 to the designs of David Evelyn Nye and Partners. The court room contains oak panelling and fittings salved from the bombed hall in Lime Street. ['Route 11' is to be extended west to Newgate Street (Route 23) and east via London Wall and Camomile Street (Route 31).]

Wood Street leads north past the end of LONDON WALL (V, D 1, 2), a street running inside the line of the old City wall. A section of the wall, showing Roman and medieval work, can be seen in the former churchyard of ST ALPHEGE (now a public garden). In the south-east corner of St Giles' churchyard (see below) is a large bastion that stood at an angle of the City wall, and to the south of this two further bastions have been revealed by the bombing. The wall connecting these bastions and that skirting St Alphege's churchyard formed the west and north boundaries of a ROMAN FORT dating from the 1st century A.D. and hence older than the City wall itself. Its existence was discovered only in 1950, on the clearance of bomb damage. Wood Street crosses the centre of the fort (following more or less a Roman predecessor), and the junction of this street with London Wall marks the probable site of Cripplegate (perhaps from the Old English 'crepelgeat', a covered way).

Wood Street ends at Fore Street, to the left in which is the large church of ST GILES CRIPPLEGATE (V, D 1), rebuilt after a fire in 1545 and altered several times since, badly damaged (except for the 15th-century tower, heightened in 1683) in the first air-raid on London, and restored in 1959. Oliver Cromwell was married in this church in 1620; and among those buried here are John Foxe (d. 1587), author of the *Book of Martyrs*; Sir Martin Frobisher (d. 1594), the explorer; John Speed (d. 1629), the map-maker; and John Milton (d. 1674), whose supposed burial-place is marked by a stone west of the chancel. Lancelot Andrewes, one of the translators of the Bible, was vicar of St Giles' in 1589–1605. ROMAN HOUSE, east of the church, covers the spot where the first bomb fell on London, at 12.15 a.m. on 25 August 1940.

St Giles Cripplegate is being incorporated in the BARBICAN SCHEME, an elaborate plan for the area north of 'Route 11'. At a cost of £20 million, it provides for large blocks of offices, flats, and schools, as well as shopping centres, an arts centre, and other amenities. The first building was started in 1962; the tallest will be a skyscraper, 35 storeys and nearly 400 ft high, to be built for the British Petroleum Company.

At No. 35, on the right of Aldersgate Street, is the entrance to IRONMONGERS' HALL, by Sydney Tatchell (1925). The company is the smallest of the twelve great livery companies. Farther on is ALDERSGATE STATION, from which Long Lane runs west to Smithfield (Route 29) and Barbican east towards Finsbury Square (Route 31).

Barbican actually ends at the junction of Redcross Street, leading south to St Giles Cripplegate (see above), and Golden Lane, which runs north to Old Street, passing CRIPPLEGATE INSTITUTE, founded in 1894, and the large BOWATER HOUSE, a block of flats of striking design by Chamberlin, Powell, and Bon (1960).

The short Carthusian Street, on the left beyond Aldersgate Station, leads to Charterhouse Square. On the north side of this is the CHARTERHOUSE (IV, C 3), one of the most interesting institutions on the fringe of the City, founded in the 14th century as a Carthusian priory, but re-established in 1611 by Thomas Sutton as a school and a hospital for poor gentlemen. The buildings, mostly of the 16th century, were greatly damaged by incendiary bombs in 1941, but have been carefully restored in their former style by Lord Mottistone and Paul Paget (1956).

The priory, founded in 1371 by Sir Walter de Manny, a distinguished soldier who fought under Edward III, owed allegiance to the great French monastery of the Grande-Chartreuse, of which name Charterhouse is a corruption. After its suppression in 1537 the buildings were granted to Lord North, who in 1545 constructed himself a mansion out of them. This passed to John Dudley, Duke of Northumberland (beheaded in 1553), and later to Thomas Howard, Duke of Norfolk (executed in 1572), who made considerable alterations. Elizabeth I was entertained here, as was James I after his arrival from Scotland in 1603 for his coronation. By this time the property had passed to another Thomas Howard, later Earl of Suffolk, but in 1611 he sold it for £13,000 to Thomas Sutton, a wealthy coal-owner, who established a hospital for eighty poor 'brethren' and a school for forty poor boys.

The school, which grew into one of the foremost public schools in England, was transferred in 1872 to Godalming in Surrey. W. M. Thackeray, who was a pupil, has described the Charterhouse (under the name of Grey-friars) in *The Newcomes*, Colonel Newcome being both an ex-pupil of the school and a poor brother. In 1875 the Merchant Taylors' School, founded in 1561, was accommodated here, but in 1933 this school moved in turn, to Moor Park (Herts). The Master's Court and neighbouring buildings were gravely damaged during an air-raid in 1941; the first stage of the restoration, however, was completed in 1951, when thirteen brethren returned from temporary quarters at Godalming. Owing to a decline in the revenues of the charity the number of these will probably never rise much above forty. The brethren must be bachelors or widowers over sixty years of age and members of the Church of England.

The modernized 15th-century Gatehouse gives access to the MASTER'S COURT, where restoration after war damage has revealed the old stone walls, parts of which belonged to the monastic church, on the east. This was pulled down by Lord North to make way for his house, but in 1947 the lead coffin of the founder, Sir Walter de Manny (d. 1372), was found near the site of the altar. The present CHAPEL, farther north-east, was formerly the chapter-house of the priory, and the south and east walls survive from the 14th century. The ante-chapel was added in 1512 as the lay-brothers' choir; the north arcade and aisle were built in 1614 and the outer aisle in 1824. The chapel has a notable pulpit and screen, and contains the ornate tomb of Thomas Sutton (d. 1611), by Bernard Jansen, with a fine effigy by Nicholas Stone, and monuments by Chantrey to Lord Ellenborough (d. 1818) and by Flaxman to Dr Raine (d. 1811), headmaster of the school. A small fragment of the tomb of Sir Walter de Manny is also preserved.

On the north of the Master's Court is the magnificent GREAT HALL, erected in the 16th century by Lord North, largely with stonework from the monastic buildings. Restored after war damage, it is again used as a dining hall by the brethren. It has a lovely 16th-century fireplace and screen, and a 17th-century gallery, and incorporates the original hammerbeams of the roof. Next to it is the 17th-century LIBRARY, and above this is the GREAT CHAMBER, one of the finest Elizabethan rooms in England before the bombing, and now restored to its former splendour, with a rich gilded plaster ceiling, an elaborate fireplace, and handsome Flemish tapestries. On the site of Brooke Hall, to the north-east of the court, a new muniment room has been erected; the 16th-century WASH HOUSE COURT, to the west, has been rebuilt after war damage to provide new quarters for the brethren. To the north-east of this is the GREAT CLOISTER, originally surrounded by the cells of the monks, but later occupied by both Charterhouse and Merchant Taylors' Schools.

ST BARTHOLOMEW'S MEDICAL COLLEGE (see p. 267) is partly accommodated in new buildings by Messrs Easton and Robertson begun in 1949 and approached from Rutland Place, on the north-east side of Charterhouse Square.

Aldersgate Street is prolonged by GOSWELL ROAD (IV, A–C 3), which passes the junction of Clerkenwell Road (leading west to St John's Square, Route 29), and Old Street, running east across City Road to Shoreditch (see Route 31). In King Square, a little to the right of Goswell Road, is ST BARNABAS'S CHURCH, built in 1826 by Thomas Hardwick and pleasantly restored after war damage. To the left of the road is Northampton Square, with the NORTHAMPTON COLLEGE OF ADVANCED TECHNOLOGY, built in 1896 (as the Northampton Polytechnic) by E. W. Mountford, but extended several times since. Its main front is skirted by ST JOHN STREET (IV, A 2–D 3), leading north from Smithfield to the Angel at Islington and passing the end of Rosebery Avenue (Route 29). Chadwell Street, on the left beyond this, leads to the well-built MYDDELTON SQUARE (1827), in the centre of which is the Gothic ST MARK'S CHURCH, erected in 1828 by W. C. Mylne but damaged during the war. Goswell Road joins City Road just before it reaches the ANGEL (see Route 31).

31   From the Bank to the Angel via Moorgate

Plan V, E 1–IV, A 2

STATIONS: BANK (Plan V, E 1), see Route 28; MOORGATE (V, D 1), on the Circle, Metropolitan, and Northern lines; OLD STREET (V, B 2), and ANGEL (IV, A 2), on the Northern line. — MOTOR-BUSES in Moorgate: Nos. 9, 11, and 133 to London Wall and Broad Street Station; No. 21 to Finsbury Square; No. 76 to Old Street; No. 43 to City Road and the Angel. No. 141 from London Wall to Old Street; Nos. 104, 214, and 239 from Finsbury Square to the Angel (Nos. 5, 170, and 243 traverse Old Street).

ADMISSION to WESLEY'S HOUSE weekdays 10 to 1 and 2 to 4 (1/–; to the Chapel, daily, 10 to dusk); to BUNHILL FIELDS, 7.30 to 7 or dusk, Sundays 12.30 to 6.30 (September–March, 1 to 4; free).

From the BANK to the north end of Princes Street, see Route 30. MOORGATE (V, E 1–D 2), a busy thoroughfare lined by banks and insurance offices, goes on northward. Great Swan Alley, on the right, gives access to the INSTITUTE OF CHARTERED ACCOUNTANTS, founded in 1880, with a decorative hall built in 1893 by Sir

John Belcher and extended in 1930. The reliefs on the front are by Sir Hamo Thornycroft and Harry Bates. Moorgate crosses LONDON WALL, which runs west to join the new thoroughfare of 'Route 11' (see Route 30) and east to Old Broad Street. On the left, at the head of Coleman Street, is ARMOURERS' AND BRASIERS' HALL, first erected about 1450, but rebuilt in 1840 by J. H. Good, junior, and beyond is the 20-storey ST ALPHAGE HOUSE, the tallest of the new office buildings in this neighbourhood (1961).

In the east branch is CARPENTERS' HALL (V, D 2), dating from 1876–80, though the Carpenters, among the wealthiest of the City livery companies, have occupied this site for over 500 years. The hall was destroyed by bombs in 1941, but rebuilding began in 1956 (when also a commemoration stone was unveiled) and was completed in 1960. Near the junction with Old Broad Street (Route 28) is the church of ALL HALLOWS, LONDON WALL, rebuilt in 1765–7 by George Dance the younger, severely damaged in the war and restored in its original style in 1962. A short section of the City wall bounds the churchyard, on the west.

Immediately beyond London Wall stood the old Moor Gate, one of the City gates, pulled down in 1762. The name, like Finsbury, which lies beyond it, preserves the memory of the moor or fen which lay outside the City wall until it was drained in the 16th century. John Keats, the poet, was born in 1795 at the sign of the 'Swan and Hoop' in Moorgate, then occupied as livery stables in which his father was an ostler (No. 85, on the left, now stands on the site). On the right is the CITY OF LONDON COLLEGE, founded in 1848, and moved here after its building in Ropemaker Street (to the north-west) was burned down in 1940. It is primarily for those intending to take up careers in commerce, and Sidney Webb, the Fabian sociologist, was a student here. Farther on opens the oval FINSBURY CIRCUS, its centre a shady oasis with mulberry and other trees.

Beyond South Place, Moorgate is extended by the short Finsbury Pavement to FINSBURY SQUARE (V, C 2), laid out in 1777–90 but preserving only a few of its original houses (on the east side), now overshadowed by great blocks of commercial building. The square was the first place where gas was employed for public lighting. The long CITY ROAD runs north from the square, passing the entrance to the parade-ground and headquarters of the

HONOURABLE ARTILLERY COMPANY of the City of London (V, C 1, 2), the oldest military body in Britain.

The first origins of the company are unknown, but it was incorporated in 1537 by Henry VIII as the Guild or Fraternity of St George and from it were chosen the officers of the City Trained Bands. Milton, Wren, and Pepys are among the famous men who have served in its ranks. The company has been established on its present ground since 1642; the centre block of its headquarters (Armoury House) dates from 1735, but extensions were made in 1828 (the wings) and in 1857 (the fortress-like front). Since 1660 the captain-general has usually been either the Sovereign or the Prince of Wales. The H.A.C., though a territorial regiment, provided many officers for the regular army in the two World Wars. It takes precedence after the regular army and is one of the few regiments privileged to march through the City with 'bayonets fixed, drums beating, and colours flying'. The H.A.C. also fires all salutes from the Tower of London and claims the right of furnishing a guard of honour when royalty visits the city, and it provides a company of pikemen and musketeers as a bodyguard to the Lord Mayor on ceremonial occasions. The Ancient and Honourable Artillery of Boston, the oldest military body in the United States, was founded in 1638 by Captain Robert Keayne and other emigrant members of the H.A.C.

On the other side of City Road (No. 47) is WESLEY'S HOUSE (V, C 2), a characteristic house of about 1770, the home of John Wesley (1703–91) for the last years of his life. Among the rooms shown are Wesley's study, the bedroom where he died, and the small adjoining room used by him for private prayer. These contain much of his furniture, and his books and many personal mementoes. Next to the house on the north is WESLEY'S CHAPEL, the 'cathedral of Methodism', opened by the founder in 1778 and rebuilt in 1899 after a fire. John Wesley is buried in the little graveyard behind the chapel and commemorated by a statue (by J. A. Acton, 1891) in front. A library of nearly 5,000 volumes on the history of Methodism was opened in the crypt in 1959 and is administered by the Wesley Historical Society, formed in 1893.

Opposite is the entrance to BUNHILL FIELDS (V, B 1–C 2), the chief burial-place of the Nonconformists from 1685, but disused since 1852. Its name is said to be a corruption of 'bone-hill', so called from its being the repository for the bones disinterred from the charnel-house of St Paul's by Protector Somerset in 1547. On the right of the main walk are the altar-tomb of Isaac Watts (d. 1748), the hymn-writer, and the graves of Daniel

Defoe (d. 1731), with an obelisk erected in 1870 by boys and girls of England, and William Blake (d. 1827), 20 yds north-west of Defoe. On the left is the tomb of John Bunyan (d. 1688), with an effigy of 1862 by E. C. Papworth; and about 50 yds west of this is the grave of Susannah Wesley (d. 1742), mother of John Wesley.

Defoe died in lodgings in Ropemaker Street, in an area west of Moorgate laid waste by bombing that affected also Bunhill Row, west of the cemetery, where John Milton lived from 1662 until his death in 1674, completing *Paradise Lost* (1664) and writing *Paradise Regained* (1671). The area is to be rebuilt under the Barbican plan (see p. 276). In Roscoe Street, on the left of Bunhill Row near its north end, is the former FRIENDS' BURIAL GROUND, opened in 1661 and converted into a garden in 1952. George Fox (d. 1691), founder of the Society of Friends, was buried here.

OLD STREET (IV, C 3–V, B 3) runs west to Goswell Road (Route 30) and east across City Road to Shoreditch (Route 32). The CITY OF LONDON MATERNITY HOSPITAL, at the junction with City Road, is the oldest hospital of its kind in the country, founded in 1750, but rebuilt in the 19th century and much damaged by bombing. Next to it on the west is a large building erected in 1782–4 by the younger Dance as a hospital for the insane, partly reconstructed in 1920, and occupied by the printing works of the Bank of England until 1959.

City Road, bearing left from East Road (for Highgate, etc.), runs north-west to Islington, passing the ROYAL LONDON OPHTHALMIC HOSPITAL, the earliest in Britain (1804), rehoused in 1899. Opposite the point where the road is joined by Goswell Road are DUNCAN TERRACE and Colebrooke Row, two long streets with fair, if decayed, terraces of the late 18th century, facing each other across a garden on the site of the New River (now carried underground). Charles Lamb lived in 1823–7 in a cottage (No. 64) at the farther end of Duncan Terrace. City Road ends at the ANGEL (IV, A 2), a restaurant on the site of a famous coaching inn, from which Pentonville Road goes on to King's Cross (see Route 16).

32 From the Bank to Shoreditch via Bishopsgate

Plan V, E 2–V, A 3

STATIONS: BANK (Plan V, E 1), see Route 28; LIVERPOOL STREET (V, D 2), on the Central, Circle, and Metropolitan lines. — MOTOR-BUSES Nos. 6, 8, and 22 in Threadneedle Street; Nos. 6, 8, 22, 35, 47, 78, 149, and 257 in Bishopsgate and Shoreditch High Street (Nos. 35, 47, and 257 from Gracechurch Street; No. 78 in Middlesex Street and Houndsditch, to and from Aldgate; No. 8 turns into Bethnal Green Road).

ADMISSION to St HELEN'S CHURCH, Monday–Friday 8.30 to 4, Sundays 9.30 to 1; to St ETHELBURGA'S CHURCH, Monday–Friday 8 to

5; to St Botolph Bishopsgate, 8 to 6 (Saturdays and Sundays to 1); to Bishopsgate Institute (Library), weekdays 10 to 5.30 (Saturday to 12.30); to the Geffrye Museum, Tuesday–Saturday 10 to 5, Sundays 2 to 5 (free; closed on Mondays and Christmas Day).

From the Bank the route, skirting the north side of the Royal Exchange (Route 28), follows the quaintly-named Thread-needle Street (V, E 2), almost wholly given over to banking. On the left opens Old Broad Street, leading to Throgmorton Street and the Stock Exchange (see Route 28). On the right (at No. 30) is the entrance to Merchant Taylors' Hall, the largest of the City livery companies' halls, dating originally from 1345, but partly rebuilt after the Great Fire. Completely gutted by bombing in 1940, it was restored in 1959 to the designs of Sir Albert Richardson. The company, the largest in the number of liveries of the twelve great companies (see p. 15), received its earliest known charter in 1327.

Threadneedle Street ends at Bishopsgate (V, E 2–C 3), starting on the south at the east end of Cornhill, from which it is extended by Gracechurch Street towards London Bridge (see Route 34). On the left is the head-office of the National Pro-vincial Bank (founded 1833), a classical building by John Gibson (1866). Gresham House, just beyond, occupies the site of the residence of Sir Thomas Gresham (see below), founder of the Royal Exchange and Gresham College.

Great St Helen's, opening on the right, admits to St Helen's Church (V, E 2), one of the largest and finest of the old London churches, often called the 'Westminster Abbey of the City' from the number and interest of its monuments to City dignitaries. The church, dedicated to the Empress Helena (d. 327), mother of Constantine the Great, may be of Saxon foundation, but its first known mention is in the mid 12th century. It became the church of a Benedictine nunnery founded about 1212, and in consequence has two parallel naves, that on the north used by the nuns (mostly daughters of City merchants) and that on the south by the parish-ioners. The church dates mainly from the 13th century, but the single arcade, which has clustered piers and lofty arches, was recast in 1475. A south transept, with a double chapel on the east having niches for statues, was added about 1374.

The entrance on the west to the parochial choir is through a fine 17th-century doorcase, and there is an even finer doorcase covering a door dated 1633 on the south side. On the south wall is the excellent monument (recoloured) of Sir John Spencer (d. 1608). The pulpit is Jacobean work, and in the chancel is an unusual wooden sword-rest of 1665, perhaps the oldest in the City. On the north of the chancel is the finest monument in the church, the canopied tomb of Sir William Pickering (d. 1574), ambassador to France, and on the south is the table-tomb with effigies of Sir John Crosby (d. 1475), builder of Crosby Hall, and his first wife. The south chapels contain the table-tomb of John Otteswich (about 1400) and other monuments brought from St Martin Outwich in Threadneedle Street, pulled down in 1874. In the nuns' choir are the table-tombs of Sir Thomas Gresham (d. 1579; see above) and Sir Julius Caesar (d. 1636), Master of the Rolls and Chancellor of the Exchequer to James I, the latter carved by Nicholas Stone.

On the east wall here is a monument to Sir Andrew Judd (d. 1558), the founder of Tonbridge School, and on the north wall is a 16th-century Easter Sepulchre, the apertures below which allowed a view of the altar from the sacristy. Blocked squints and a doorway and a wall-stairway (perhaps the night stairs) formerly opened to the conventual buildings on the north side of the church. The foundations of these and of the Norman or Saxon church were discovered during excavations in St Helen's Place in 1922.

In St Helen's Place farther north, is LEATHERSELLERS' HALL, rebuilt in 1878 and extended by the addition of a court room, etc., in 1926. The hall was seriously damaged by fire in an air-raid in 1941, but was again rebuilt (by Kenneth Peacock) in 1960. The Leathersellers, first mentioned in the 14th century and incorporated in 1444, are among the wealthiest of the City livery companies.

The small ST ETHELBURGA'S CHURCH, abutting on Bishopsgate north of St Helen's Place, is one of the oldest in London, though much restored from time to time. The dedication to Ethelburga, abbess of Barking and sister of St Erconwald, bishop of London in 675, may imply a Saxon foundation. The church was rebuilt about 1430, but practically the only work of this time is in the arcade and the west gable, above which rises a quaint belfry. Three windows in the nave (by Leonard Walker, 1928–30) commemorate Henry Hudson (d. 1611), who made his Communion here in 1607 with his crew before setting out on his first voyage in search of the North-West Passage. In the chancel are panels of 17th-century heraldic glass. The parish of St Ethelburga is the smallest in London (3 acres).

The site of the Bishop's Gate (demolished in 1760) is at the junction with Camomile Street and Wormwood Street. Just beyond is the church of St Botolph Bishopsgate (compare p. 265), rebuilt in 1725–9 by James Gold and altered internally in the 19th century. In the south aisle is the roll of honour of the London Rifle Brigade. Edward Alleyn, the actor and founder of Dulwich College, was baptized in the previous church (1566) and John Keats, the poet, in the present building (1795). In the churchyard, on the west, is the former church school, a quaint building of 1861 with figures of a boy and girl in Coade stone.

Houndsditch, on the right, and Middlesex Street, farther on, lead to Aldgate High Street (see Route 33). Liverpool Street, on the left, passes the main entrance to the large Liverpool Street Station (V, D 2, 3), a terminus of the Eastern Region, built in 1875 over a burial-ground used as a plague pit in 1665. Adjacent on the west is Broad Street Station (V, D 2), a terminus of the London Midland Region. On the right in Bishopsgate is the Bishopsgate Institute, opened in 1894. Concerts, organ recitals, and lectures are given, and the reference library includes over 6,000 volumes on the history and topography of London. In the main corridor is a selection from the institute's worthy collection of prints and water-colours of old London.

Bishopsgate is extended by the short Norton Folgate to Shoreditch High Street (V, B, C 3), an unattractive commercial thoroughfare. Great Eastern Street, on the left, leads to Old Street (see below), while Commercial Street, starting opposite, runs south-east to Whitechapel High Street (see Route 33). On the same side, a little farther on, is Bethnal Green Road, leading towards the Bethnal Green Museum and Victoria Park. At the junction of Shoreditch High Street with Hackney Road is St Leonard's Church (V, B 3), the parish church of Shoreditch, founded as early as 900 and rebuilt in 1736–40 by George Dance the elder. It was seriously damaged by bombing, though the portico, with Tuscan columns, and the imposing steeple, 192 ft high, remained intact. In the churchyard, pleasantly laid out as a garden, are the old stocks and whipping-post; the former verger's house, to the south-west, dates from 1735. James Burbage (d. 1597) and his son Richard (d. 1619; the friend of Shakespeare), who are buried in the church, built the first theatre in London in 1576 in Curtain

Road, west of the High Street (tablet on Nos. 86–8). In 1598, owing to a difficulty over the lease, The Theatre, as it was called, was pulled down overnight and the materials taken to Southwark to build the Globe Theatre (see p. 313).

OLD STREET, starting west of the church, leads across City Road (Route 31) to Goswell Road, from which it is prolonged by Clerkenwell Road and Theobalds Road to Holborn, a useful if uninteresting cross-route. At the outset it passes SHOREDITCH TOWN HALL, built in 1866 by C. A. Long and enlarged in 1902. Pitfield Street, on the right farther on, passes the SHOREDITCH TECHNICAL INSTITUTE, in the former Haberdashers' Almshouses, built in 1825 by D. R. Roper.

Over ¼-mile north of Shoreditch church, in Kingsland Road, is the interesting GEFFRYE MUSEUM (V, A 3), occupying the charming Ironmongers' Almshouses, built round a spacious forecourt about 1715 under a bequest of Sir Robert Geffrye, a master of the Ironmongers' Company and Lord Mayor of London in 1685–6. At the time of their erection the almshouses were in rural surroundings, but by the beginning of the present century they had become absorbed in an industrial quarter. In 1912 new almshouses were built at Mottingham (Kent) and the property was taken over by the L.C.C., who opened it as a museum in 1914. Above the entrance is a copy of a statue of Sir Robert Geffrye (d. 1704; the original is at Mottingham). The entrance hall was originally the almshouse chapel, and the rooms, mostly arranged chronologically, contain a fascinating collection of furniture and woodwork, from Elizabethan times to the present day, with panelling, doorways, staircases, etc., from old London houses. In the north wing are children's workrooms and in the south wing a lecture room. The museum, situated in a cabinet-making district, is designed partly to assist students, who may use the reference library and seek technical advice from the staff.

33 **From the Bank to Aldgate via Cornhill, returning via Fenchurch Street**

Plan V, E 1–V, E 3

STATIONS: BANK (Plan V, E 1), see Route 28; ALDGATE (V, E 3), on the Circle and Metropolitan lines; ALDGATE EAST (beyond V, E 3), on the District and Metropolitan lines; MONUMENT (V, F 2), on the Circle and District lines, connected to the Bank by escalator. — MOTOR-BUSES Nos. 15, 23, 25, and 32 in Cornhill and Leadenhall Street, and Nos. 10 and 40 in Fenchurch Street (all these continue along Aldgate High Street); Nos. 8A, 35, and 47 in Gracechurch Street; Nos. 42 and 78 in the Minories and Mansell Street (to and from Tower Bridge); No. 78 in Middlesex Street and Houndsditch (to and from Bishopsgate).

ADMISSION to ST MICHAEL'S CORNHILL, Monday–Friday 8.30 to 6; to ST PETER'S CORNHILL, Monday–Friday 8.30 to 5; to LLOYD's, by introduction from a member only; to St ANDREW UNDERSHAFT, Monday–Friday 10 to 3, Sundays 10 to 1; to St KATHARINE CREECHURCH, Monday–Friday 9.30 to 5; to St BOTOLPH ALDGATE, Monday–Friday, 8 to 6; to St OLAVE'S CHURCH, Monday–Friday 10 to 3, Saturdays 2 to 5; to St EDMUND THE KING, Monday–Friday 9 to 6.

CORNHILL (V, E 1, 2), a busy centre of commerce named from a former grain-market, leads east from the Bank, passing the Royal Exchange (Route 28) on its south side. Thomas Gray, the poet, was born in 1716 in the house whose site is occupied by No. 39. On the same side is St MICHAEL'S CORNHILL, a church of Saxon foundation, rebuilt by Wren in 1670–7 and greatly restored by Sir Gilbert Scott in 1857–60. The handsome Gothic tower, 130 ft high, with delicately carved pinnacles, was added in 1715–22 by a pupil of Wren, either William Dickenson or Nicholas Hawksmoor. The bench-ends, carved about 1850 by W. Gibbs Rogers, are worth notice. The first London coffee-house was opened in St Michael's Alley, close by, in 1652.

Farther on is St PETER'S CORNHILL, long thought to be the earliest church in London, on the strength of an old brass tablet in the vestry claiming it to have been founded in A.D. 179 by 'Lucius, the first Christian king of this land, than called Britaine'. The church, rebuilt by Wren in 1677–87, has an Italianate brick tower and an unusual chancel-screen, the only one known to be erected by Wren and still in its place. Memorial windows to the Fifth Army (1916–18) and the Royal Tank Regiment were dedicated in 1960. The organ was originally built by Father Smith, but the manual on which Mendelssohn played in 1840 is preserved in the vestry. George Borrow, the author, was married in this church in 1840.

Cornhill ends at the point from which Bishopsgate leads north, passing Threadneedle Street (Route 32), and Gracechurch Street runs south towards London Bridge (see Route 34). It is extended eastward by LEADENHALL STREET (V, E 2, 3), the chief centre of the shipping industry. An opening on the right gives access to LEADENHALL MARKET, rebuilt in 1881 and dealing mainly in meat, game, and provisions. This site, occupied as a market since the 14th century, was the centre of Roman London, and remains of a basilica, or town hall, and other administrative buildings were brought to light in 1881. Farther on to the right is the huge building (1925–8) designed by Sir Edwin Cooper for LLOYD'S (V, E 2). A new and even larger building, by Terence Heysham, was erected in 1952–7 on the other side of Lime Street.

Lloyd's is an association of underwriters (over 5,000 members) incorporated in 1871 for the promotion of marine insurance and the diffusion of shipping intelligence. It grew out of a gathering of merchants at the coffee-house kept in 1688 in Tower Street and later in Lombard Street by Edward Lloyd, who posted up shipping information for the benefit of his patrons. These customers formed their own committee in 1771, and in 1774 took rooms at the Royal Exchange. In 1811 a trust deed was adopted giving Lloyd's a 'constitution' and since 1911 all kinds of insurance (except long-term life assurance) have been undertaken. Lloyd's maintain some 1,500 agents in every part of the world who send in a ceaseless flow of marine information. *Lloyd's News*, a single sheet giving shipping information, was first published in 1696 (but ran for nine months only); *Lloyd's List and Shipping Gazette*, started in 1734, is still published.

The Underwriting Room, in the fine new building, is an elegant chamber 340 ft long with the caller's rostrum near the centre. Bad news is signalled by one stroke and good news by two strokes on the Lutine Bell, salvaged from a frigate of that name which sank in 1799 while carrying a cargo of gold specie valued at £1,400,000 and insured at Lloyd's. The Nelson Room holds many relics of the great admiral, together with his portrait by Lemuel Abbott and the log-book of the *Euryalus*, his signal-frigate at Trafalgar, containing the only record of his famous message. The ceiling and fittings in the Committee Room, with decoration by Robert Adam and Thomas Carter, were brought from the beautiful 18th-century dining-room at Bowood, Wilts (part of a wing demolished in 1955). At the outer corners of the new building are carved panels symbolizing Air, Sea, Fire, and Land, by James Woodford. The former underwriting room, familiarly known as 'The Room', in the older building, is a handsome chamber 160 ft square.

The older building of Lloyd's stands on the site (from 1726) of East India House, where Charles Lamb, James Mill, and John Stuart Mill were clerks in the employment of the East India Company, chartered by Elizabeth I in 1600 and dissolved in 1858.

At the foot of St Mary Axe, on the left, is the church of ST ANDREW UNDERSHAFT, rebuilt in 1520–32, except for the lower part of the tower (15th century), and given a new east gable in 1876. The name is apparently derived from a maypole shaft, taller than the church, which until 1517 was set up each May Day outside it. Notable are the door with its knocker in the tower, the beautiful 17th-century pulpit and the font by Nicholas Stone (1631). The fine nave ceiling was rebuilt in 1950 using the old bosses. Of the several excellent monuments the most interesting is that at the east end of the north aisle to John Stow (d. 1605), author of the *Survey of London* (1598), an alabaster tomb by Nicholas Johnson. The quill in Stow's hand is renewed by the Lord Mayor at a service held annually in April. The monument on the north wall to Sir Hugh Hamersley, Lord Mayor in 1627, is remarkable for the finely sculptured figures of the attendants; that in the chancel to Sir Thomas Offley, Lord Mayor in 1556, is by Gerard Johnson. Hans Holbein, the painter, lived in the parish, as recorded by a tablet in the south aisle, and he may have died here (of the plague, 1543). The west window contains heraldic glass and royal portraits, partly of the 17th century.

At No. 26 St Mary Axe is the BALTIC EXCHANGE (V, E3), rebuilt in 1903 and enlarged in 1956, the headquarters of merchants and shipping brokers who deal in grain, timber, coal, oil, and other floating cargoes. It was formed by the amalgamation of two exchanges, one of which arose from the 'Virginia and Baltick' coffee-house, and hence it has nothing specifically to do with the Baltic.

Farther on in Leadenhall Street is ST KATHARINE CREE-CHURCH, *i.e.* Christchurch (from an Augustinian priory of that name founded in 1108). The tower dates from 1504, but the body of the church was rebuilt in 1628–31 and consecrated by William Laud, then bishop of London, the 'Popish' character of the service later being cited against him at his trial. At the south-west angle is a pier of the previous church, now projecting only 3 ft above the floor, the level of which has risen some 15 ft in the rebuilding. The 17th-century plaster ceiling has bosses with the arms of the chief City livery companies. The font bears the arms of Sir John Gayer, Lord Mayor in 1646, whose escape from a lion in Arabia is commemorated by the 'Lion Sermon' given annually on 16 October. In the south aisle is a fine monument to Sir Nicholas Throckmorton (d. 1571), ambassador to France, after whom Throgmorton Street is named. In a case on the north of the altar are the Prayer Book and Bible of Archbishop Laud; the upper part of the east window has early-18th-century glass in the form of a Catherine wheel. An extensive restoration was completed in 1962.

Leadenhall Street is joined by Fenchurch Street (see p. 291) at the quaint ALDGATE PUMP, a 'draught' (draft) on which was long a facetious expression for a worthless bill. Near the corner of Duke's Place stood (until 1760) the Ald Gate, the easternmost of the City gates, the house above which was leased by Geoffrey Chaucer in 1374. Hence ALDGATE HIGH STREET (V, E 3) runs east through a distinctively Jewish quarter, the beginning of the 'East End' of London.

In Duke's Place are the elementary and secondary schools of the SIR JOHN CASS FOUNDATION, established in 1710 for poor children by Alderman Sir John Cass (d. 1718), and the GREAT SYNAGOGUE, the Jewish cathedral of London, built in 1790 but much altered and very badly damaged during the war. The SPANISH AND PORTUGUESE SYNAGOGUE, entered from No. 12 Bevis Marks (the continuation of Duke's Place), is the oldest synagogue in England, founded in Creechurch Lane in 1657 and rebuilt here in 1701. JEWRY STREET, running south from Aldgate to Crutched Friars (see below), contains the SIR JOHN CASS COLLEGE, a technical institute founded in 1898 with funds provided by the estates of the Sir John Cass Foundation, and housed in a building erected in 1902 (by A. W. Cooksey) and extended in 1934 (by Verner O. Rees). Now 'recognized' by the University of London, it has faculties of science and engineering (metallurgy).

HOUNDSDITCH, which runs north-west to Bishopsgate, is the centre of Jewish brokers and dealers, and the scene of an animated street-market on Sunday mornings. At its foot is the church of ST BOTOLPH ALDGATE (V, E 3), founded in 1125 and rebuilt in 1741–4 by George Dance the elder, with a prominent steeple. The interior was much altered in the late 19th century, and the south end has been restored after being hit by a bomb in 1941. The lectern, given in 1943, is made of oak from the roof of Guildhall, destroyed in 1940. In the vestry (not usually shown) is preserved a mummified head said to be that of the Duke of Suffolk (father of Lady Jane Grey), beheaded in 1554. J. S. Cotman, the landscape-painter, was a churchwarden here, and William Symington (d. 1831), a pioneer of steam navigation, is buried in the churchyard.

The MINORIES (pronounced 'Minneries'), an unattractive street leading south from Aldgate High Street to Tower Hill (Route 34), takes its name from a vanished convent of Minoresses or nuns of St Clare (founded in 1294). On the right farther on is the ALDGATE COACH STATION of the Green Line services, opposite Aldgate underground station.

The *Hoop and Grapes*, on the right of Aldgate High Street, is a quaint old tavern of the 17th century. MIDDLESEX STREET, on the left, leading to Liverpool Street Station (Route 32), is better known under its popular name of Petticoat Lane. The cosmopolitan street-market held here on Sunday mornings is one of the more curious sights of London. Aldgate High Street is prolonged from this point by WHITECHAPEL HIGH STREET to penetrate the mainly Jewish district of Whitechapel.

Commercial Road, diverging on the right, is a long thoroughfare giving access to the London Docks, while COMMERCIAL STREET, starting opposite, leads northward to Shoreditch (Route 32). On the right in this street is TOYNBEE HALL, the first of the Universities Settlements, an adult education centre founded in 1884 by Canon Samuel Barnett and named in honour of Arnold Toynbee (d. 1883), the economist and reformer, who worked in Whitechapel from 1875. The buildings, by E. Hoole, were much damaged in the war, though the hall, with murals by Archibald Ziegler, survived. Farther on in Commercial Street is CHRIST CHURCH (V, D 3), the parish church of Spitalfields, now a manufacturing district. It belonged in medieval times to the priory of St Mary Spital, founded in 1197 but long since disappeared. The church, with its heavy portico and wide tower, is a characteristic work of Nicholas Hawksmoor (1723–9), and has a good 18th-century pulpit and a monument of 1794 by Flaxman. Beyond to the left is the large SPITALFIELDS MARKET, the principal East End market for fruit and vegetables, founded in 1682 and rebuilt in 1928.

In Whitechapel High Street, adjoining Aldgate East Station, is the WHITECHAPEL ART GALLERY, a building well in advance of its time (1899), by C. H. Townsend. Loan exhibitions of unusual interest are held at frequent intervals.

FENCHURCH STREET (V, E 2, 3), running south-west at first from Aldgate Pump (see above), contains the offices of many shipping companies. On the left is LLOYD'S REGISTER OF SHIPPING, in a decorative building of 1901 by T. E. Collcutt.

This society, which has no connexion with Lloyd's (see above), was founded in 1760 for the classification of merchant ships in accordance with their strength and cargo-carrying capacity. A committee of merchants, ship-owners, and underwriters supervises the construction of new ships and fixes the load-lines of merchant vessels, while a staff of ship and engine surveyors is maintained in all the chief ports of the world. *Lloyd's Register*, issued annually, gives the particulars of all ships carrying merchandise, British and foreign, of 100 tons or upwards in deadweight. The highest class for iron and steel ships is 100 A 1 and for wooden ships A 1, a symbol that has become a guarantee of good faith in the shipping world ('A 1 at Lloyd's').

Railway Place, on the same side farther west, gives access to
FENCHURCH STREET STATION (V, E, F 3), a terminus of the
Eastern Region used also by the London Midland Region for its
services to Tilbury and Southend. At the corner of Mark Lane,
just beyond, is the war memorial building (by Ronald Ward),
erected in 1955–7, of the INSTITUTE OF MARINE ENGINEERS,
founded in 1889.

On the right in MARK LANE, which leads south to Great Tower Street
(see Route 34), is the restored 15th-century tower of ALL HALLOWS
STAINING. The church was demolished in 1870, but two years later a
12th-century crypt chapel, from the hermitage of St James-on-the-Wall,
near Cripplegate, was re-erected here by the Clothworkers' Company. In
Hart Street, starting opposite the huge Dunster House (occupied by shipping companies), is ST OLAVE'S CHURCH (V, F 3), dedicated to King
Olaf, the patron-saint of Norway, after his martyrdom in 1030, mostly
rebuilt in 1450, but sadly wrecked by bombing in 1941. From this ordeal
only the tower, heightened in 1732, the vaulted 12th-century crypt and the
panelled vestry of 1662 (on the south) escaped. The church was reopened
after its restoration (retaining some of the fire-blackened stones) in 1954.
On the north of the chancel is a delightful bust of Elizabeth Pepys (d. 1669),
sculptured by John Bushnell and erected by her husband Samuel Pepys (d.
1703), who was a regular worshipper here from the time he became secretary
at the Navy Office (see below). Both Pepys and his wife are buried in the
vault beneath the chancel, and the diarist is commemorated by a bust of
1884 on the wall of the south aisle (above the Navy Officers' gallery where
he had his pew) and an annual service in May. The east window contains
striking glass (a war memorial) by A. E. Buss (1954), and other windows by
the same artist show the arms of the Port of London Authority, the Clothworkers' Company, and the Corn Exchange. The south aisle is the chapel of
the corporation of Trinity House, who attend a service here every Trinity
Monday. The finely-carved pulpit (possibly by Gibbons) and the altar-rails
date from the 17th century and the communion-table from the 18th
century. The skulls above the churchyard gate (1658) in Seething Lane are
referred to by Dickens as 'St Ghastly Grim' in *The Uncommercial Traveller*.
Pepys lived in Seething Lane from 1660, when he obtained his secretaryship,
but later moved into the Navy Office in CRUTCHED FRIARS (*i.e.* 'Crossed
Friars', from a vanished friary of the Holy Cross), the continuation of Hart
Street. No. 42 in this street (now the Toc H Women's Association) is an
excellent residence of the early 18th century.

MINCING LANE, farther west, said by Stow to be named
from the 'minchens' or nuns of St Helen's (Bishopsgate), is the
centre of the colonial tea and wine trades. At the corner of
Fenchurch Street a new CLOTHWORKERS' HALL was opened in

1958; the first hall of the company, built in 1482, perished in the Great Fire and the third hall, opened in 1860, was destroyed in an air-raid in 1941. The Clothworkers, one of the twelve great livery companies, were incorporated in 1528, and possess a loving-cup presented by Samuel Pepys, who was Master in 1677. Opposite Mincing Lane is FOUNTAIN HOUSE, a 14-storey office sky-scraper, designed by W. H. Rogers and Sir Howard Robertson and erected in 1956–8. Rood Lane, on the left farther on, leads to St Margaret Pattens church in Eastcheap (Route 34).

At the corner of Fenchurch Street and Gracechurch Street (Route 34) is the Overseas Branch of the MIDLAND BANK (1962), believed to be the largest foreign banking unit in the world. Fenchurch Street is continued by LOMBARD STREET (V, E 2), the banking and financial centre of London since the Middle Ages. It takes its name from the Lombard merchants from northern Italy who settled here as early as the 12th century and established themselves as money-lenders after the expulsion of the Jews. Some of the numerous banks in the street hang out signs in the medieval fashion. No. 54 is BARCLAY'S BANK, founded in 1896; No. 67 is GLYN, MILLS (founded 1753), the only sur-viving private bank in the London Clearing House (see below); No. 68 is the London office of MARTIN'S BANK (founded 1563), the oldest in England; and No. 71 is LLOYD'S BANK (founded 1865), occupying a building by Sir John J. Burnet (1930).

PLOUGH COURT, on the south side of the street, is believed to have been in 1688 the birthplace of Alexander Pope, the poet. On the north side is the church of ST EDMUND THE KING, dedicated to the king of East Anglia martyred by the Danes in 870, rebuilt in 1670–9 by Wren, and restored after being hit by a bomb in 1917. It has an unusual steeple and good woodwork (pulpit, font cover, etc.). Joseph Addison, the author, was married in this church in 1716 to the Dowager Countess of Warwick. In Post Office Court, to the left farther on, is the LONDON BANKERS' CLEARING HOUSE, established in 1770 and rebuilt in 1951.

This is an institution through which the claims on each other of certain banks (called 'clearing banks') during each day can be compared and the difference settled by means of a cheque on the Bank of England (compare

p. 257). The total amount in cheques and bills that changes hands in the course of an average day approaches £700 million. The clearing banks are Barclay's, Lloyd's, the Midland, the National Provincial, and the Westminster (the 'big five'), together with Coutts & Co, the District, Glyn, Mills, Martin's, the National, and Williams Deacon's. The influential INSTITUTE OF BANKERS, founded in 1879, is housed in the same building.

Lombard Street skirts the north side of St Mary Woolnoth church to join King William Street just short of the BANK (see below).

34 From the Bank to London Bridge or to the Tower and Tower Bridge

Plan V, E 1–IX, E 3

STATIONS: BANK (Plan V, E 1), see Route 28; MONUMENT (V, F 2; escalator connexion to the Bank) and TOWER HILL (V, F 3), on the Circle and District lines. — MOTOR-BUSES Nos. 7, 8, 21, 43, and 133 in King William Street; 8A, 35, 47, and 257 in Gracechurch Street; Nos. 42 and 78 in the Minories and Mansell Street, and across Tower Bridge; Nos. 47 and 70 in Tooley Street; across London Bridge, see Route 25; in Fenchurch Street, see Route 33.

ADMISSION to ST MARY WOOLNOTH, weekdays 9.30 to 5.30; to ST CLEMENT'S EASTCHEAP, Monday–Friday 10 to 4; to ST MARY-AT-HILL, Monday–Friday 12 to 2; to ST MARGARET PATTENS, Monday–Friday 10 to 4.45; to ALL HALLOWS BY THE TOWER, weekdays 8 to 6, Sundays 8 to 12.30 and 2 to 6.30; to the TOWER, see p. 405; to TRINITY HOUSE, Saturdays at 2.30 on written application to the Secretary (parties only); to the ROYAL MINT, see p. 299.

KING WILLIAM STREET (V, E 1–F 2), named after William IV, runs south-east from the BANK (Route 28) to London Bridge. On the left, at the beginning of Lombard Street (Route 33), is the church of ST MARY WOOLNOTH (a name of uncertain origin), the most original work of Nicholas Hawksmoor, a pupil of Wren, built in 1716–27 with a rugged west front having an oblong tower from which rise unusual square turrets. The striking entrance leads into a rich interior, square in plan and with groups of triple Corinthian columns at each corner. The church has a good reredos in the form of a baldacchino, fine ironwork altar-rails, and a carved pulpit with an unusual canopy; against the walls have been set the former fronts of the galleries. On the north wall is a tablet to John Newton (d. 1807), the evangelist, joint author with

Cowper of the *Olney Hymns*. He was rector of St Mary Woolnoth from 1779 until his death, but his remains were later removed to Olney (Bucks). There is a tablet on the south wall to Edward Lloyd (d. 1713), the coffee-house proprietor (see p. 288). The church is used on Sundays by the Swiss Church (compare p. 223) for their services in German.

In Clement's Lane, on the left farther on, is ST CLEMENT'S EAST-CHEAP, a church rebuilt by Wren in 1683–7, but restored internally in 1872 by Butterfield and again in 1933 by Sir Ninian Comper. It contains notable 17th-century woodwork (font cover, pulpit with canopy, and reredos), and tablets commemorate Thomas Fuller (d. 1661), the historian, who lectured here from 1647; John Pearson (d. 1686), later bishop of Chester, who gave his celebrated *Exposition of the Creed* here; and Brian Walton (d. 1661), compiler of the Polyglot Bible and likewise bishop of Chester, who was rector of St Martin Orgars (since pulled down) from 1628.

King William Street reaches an irregular open space formed by the junction of Cannon Street, leading west to St Paul's (Route 25), Gracechurch Street, running north-east to Bishopsgate (Route 32), and Eastcheap, which leads east towards the Tower. On the south is the entrance to the MONUMENT STATION (V, F 2), from one side of which King William Street goes to LONDON BRIDGE (see Route 25), while a little to the east Fish Street Hill descends to the Monument (Route 25) and St Magnus the Martyr church (Route 27). Gracechurch Street derives its name from the vanished St Benet Gracechurch ('grass church', probably because it stood in a grassy plot), while EASTCHEAP (V, F 2) was so called to distinguish it from Cheapside (compare Route 29). In Lovat Lane, on the right, is an entrance to ST MARY-AT-HILL, a medieval church only partly destroyed in the Great Fire. The east end and the interior were rebuilt by Wren in 1670–6, but the old west end and tower survived until 1780 and the north and south walls until about 1830. The organ-case, font, reredos, and box-pews (among the few old pews in the City) all date from the 17th century, but the pulpit and reading-desk and the carvings on the gallery were added in 1849 by W. Gibbs Rogers. Edward Young, author of *Night Thoughts*, was married here in 1731 and Wilson Carlile, founder of the Church Army, was rector from 1891 to 1926. According to Stow, Thomas Becket was at some time 'parson' here. In St Mary-at-Hill, the lane on the east, are a fine projecting clock and a quaint passage on the south with a skull and crossbones over the entrance.

The church of ST MARGARET PATTENS, on the left near the beginning of Great Tower Street, is named, according to Stow, from the pattens (clogs with iron rings on the soles for keeping shoes out of the mud) formerly made in the adjoining Rood Lane (two pairs are preserved in a case on the south wall). The church, founded in 1067, was rebuilt in 1684–9 by Wren, with a simple but effective spire, 199 ft high. At the west end are two canopied pews (unique in London), one of which bears the monogram 'CW 1686', most probably that of the architect himself. The alabaster font has been attributed to Grinling Gibbons. The north gallery was converted into conference rooms and a rest centre for clergy when the church was renovated in 1956.

In Harp Lane, on the right farther on, is BAKERS' HALL (by Trehearne and Norman Preston and Partners, 1960), the fourth hall to stand on this site. The first was built in 1506 and the previous hall was bombed in 1940.

MARK LANE (originally 'Mart'), leading on the left to Fenchurch Street (see Route 33), is the centre of the grain trade. King's Beam House, at the corner, is the huge headquarters (1956) of the BOARD OF CUSTOMS AND EXCISE. The Commissioners of Customs, first appointed by Charles II in 1671, were previously accommodated in Lower Thames Street (Route 27); the Excise Department was divorced from the Inland Revenue Department in 1909. The CORN EXCHANGE, on the right in Mark Lane, founded originally in 1750 and rebuilt in 1880, was seriously damaged in 1941 and reopened in 1953. The principal market is held on Mondays from 12 to 3.

GREAT TOWER STREET goes on to Tower Hill (see below), while Byward Street leads left past Tower Hill Station to Trinity Square. In the angle between the streets is the ancient church of ALL HALLOWS BARKING BY THE TOWER (V, F 3), founded as early as about 675, mostly rebuilt in the 13th–15th centuries, and sadly damaged by bombing in 1940. The north aisle was reopened for service in 1949, and the other work of restoration (by Lord Mottistone and Paul Paget) completed in 1957. The name 'Barking' refers to the early possession of the church by the Abbey of Barking, in Essex. Remains of a 7th-century arch can be seen in the lower part of the tower, which escaped the bombing, and during the clearance of damage parts of a Saxon cross of the 11th century were brought to light. The brick tower, erected in 1658, is the only example in London of church building surviving from the Commonwealth; from it Samuel Pepys viewed the devastation caused by the Great Fire (Diary: 5 September 1666). A handsome new steeple was added in 1959. Above the north porch, built on in 1884 by J. L. Pearson, are statues of St Ethelburga, the first abbess of Barking, and Bishop Lancelot Andrewes, who was born in the parish and baptized here (1555). William Penn, the founder of Pennsylvania, born on Tower Hill, was also baptized in the church (1644); and here John Quincy Adams, sixth President of the United States, was married in 1797.

Since 1922 All Hallows has been the guild church of Toc H (compare below). The 'Lamp of Maintenance', from which all other Toc H lamps are lit, is kept on the 15th-century altar-tomb at the east end of the North Aisle, and the ashes of many members of the organization are deposited in the vault. Also in the north aisle are a war-memorial effigy of Alfred Forster (son of the governor-general of Australia), by Cecil Thomas (1926), and part of a 15th-century Flemish triptych (the centre panel is missing) apparently ordered by Sir Robert Tate, Lord Mayor in 1488. In the Nave are 18th-century sword-rests and a pulpit of about 1670 from the demolished church of St Swithun in Cannon Street. The South Aisle, now the Mariners' Chapel, has a 16th-century Spanish crucifix. Under the east end is an interesting 14th-century Crypt, opened out in 1926 and reserved for private prayer, and adjoining this is a small 17th-century vault. A Memorial Chapel constructed beneath the chancel contains the crusading altar originally in Richard I's castle at Athlit in north Palestine. In a new Baptistry at the west end can be seen the Saxon arch mentioned above and a font of 1944 carved from a piece of the Rock of Gibraltar, with an exquisite cover attributed to Grinling Gibbons (saved from the bombing). The church has much heraldic glass, and an extensive series of 14th–17th-century brasses (the finest collection in London).

The sculpture on the east gable of the church, showing the Toc H lamp, is also by Cecil Thomas. The terrace below this, constructed in 1951 overlooking Tower Hill, affords a characteristic view of the Tower.

No. 15 Trinity Square, north-east of the church, is the headquarters of Toc H, an organization for Christian fellowship founded originally at Poperinghe (Belgium) by the Rev. Neville Talbot and the Rev. P. B. Clayton, long vicar of All Hallows, and named Talbot House (the initials of which are 'Toc H' in the army signaller's old alphabet) in memory of Lieut. Gilbert Talbot, killed in action in 1915.

TOWER HILL (V, F 3), the broad open space on the west side of the **Tower of London** (p. 405), is a place of great historic interest, the principal scene of the execution of traitors confined in the Tower. No less than seventy-five are known to have suffered here, from Sir Simon Burley, the supporter of Richard II (1388), to Simon Fraser, Lord Lovat (1747). The site of the scaffold is marked by a square of pavement, a memorial to the Earl of Kilmarnock and Lord Balmerino, the Jacobites (beheaded in 1746), in the garden of TRINITY SQUARE, on the north-east side. Here also are the striking MERCHANT SEAMEN'S WAR MEMORIALS to men of the Merchant Navy, the fishing fleets, and the lighthouse and pilotage services who lost their lives in the two World Wars. That on the south, designed by Sir Edwin Lutyens (1928), commemorates the 12,000 of the mercantile marine who died in 1914–18. The second memorial, unveiled in 1955, was designed by Sir Edward Maufe (with sculptures by Sir Charles Wheeler) in memory of nearly 24,000 merchant seamen who died in 1939–45 and have no grave but the sea.

On the north-west side of Trinity Square rises the ornate and massive building of the PORT OF LONDON AUTHORITY (V, F 3), designed by Sir Edwin Cooper and completed in 1922, with a prominent tower 170 ft high. The over-large sculptures are by Albert Hodge (on the tower) and C. L. J. Domen.

The Port of London extends officially from a point just below Teddington Lock to the Nore Lightship in the estuary of the Thames, a distance of about 69 miles. Commercially the port begins at London Bridge, and it includes the five great dock systems covering an area of 4,246 acres (of which 722 acres are water) and extending from the St Katharine Docks (see below) to the outlying Tilbury Docks, 26 miles below London Bridge. The total annual tonnage of ships entering and leaving this, the greatest port in the world, is nearly 60 millions, and the tonnage of imported and exported goods nearly 50 millions. Since 1909 the whole of this system has been under the control of the Port of London Authority, consisting of twenty-eight members (ten appointed by the authority, and eighteen elected by payers of port-dues, wharfingers, and owners of rivercraft) and an appointed chairman and vice-chairman.

TRINITY HOUSE (V, F 3), on the north side of Trinity Square, was rebuilt in 1793–5 by Samuel Wyatt for the 'Guild, Fraternity, or Brotherhood of the Trinity', already a body of some importance when it was granted its first charter by Henry VIII in 1514. The building, severely damaged from the air in 1940, was well restored and extended in 1953. On the front are the arms of the corporation and medallions of George III and Queen Charlotte.

The corporation comprises a Master (at present the Duke of Gloucester), a Deputy Master, and about twenty Elder Brethren (usually including several heads of state and chiefs of the armed forces), as well as a much larger number of Younger Brethren. Trinity House is entrusted with the duty of erecting and maintaining lighthouses, lightships, and other sea-marks; it is the chief pilotage authority in Great Britain, and it attends to the relief of aged and distressed master mariners. Until 1874 Masters of the Navy were examined by the Elder Brethren, and these still sit with the judges of the Admiralty division in deciding marine causes in the High Court of Justice.

In the Front Hall are models of ships (including the first lightship, 1796) and lead statues of Captain Richard Maples (d. 1680), by Jasper Latham (the oldest by a British sculptor), and Captain Robert Sandes, deputy master in 1719-21, by Scheemakers. The Court Room, upstairs, is hung with royal portraits by Sir William Beechey and others. The new extension, on the east, contains the Library, used also as a banqueting hall.

Several sections of the old CITY WALL have been disclosed in this neighbourhood. Adjoining Tower Hill, east of Trinity Square, can be seen an impressive stretch of the medieval wall, incorporating re-used Roman material and standing fully 20 ft in height, with some remains of the parapet and sentry walk. In a modern wall close by (and approached on its west side from Trinity Place) is a copy of a Roman funerary inscription of about A.D. 65 found near this spot (original in the British Museum). A further stretch of wall is preserved in the basement of the Toc H club at No. 42 Trinity Square; visitors are usually admitted by courtesy of the Warden (but not on Saturdays and Sundays, or after 6 p.m.). A third section, about 110 ft long and 32 ft high, is being incorporated in the basement of a new office building in Cooper's Row, just to the north, and will be accessible when the building is completed in 1963.

To the north-east of the Tower is the ROYAL MINT (V, F 3), built in 1808-11 by James Johnson and Robert Smirke and enlarged in 1882, but to be rebuilt, though the Regency offices will be retained. Before 1809 the Mint was housed in the Tower. Here are struck the coins of the realm, of several colonies and of various European countries, the Great Seals of the kingdom, and many naval and military medals.

The coins minted are of gold (sovereigns), silver (for Maundy Money only; see p. 442), cupro-nickel (75 per cent copper and 25 per cent nickel, for 'silver' coins), nickel-brass (3d pieces) and bronze (other 'copper' coins). The Mint is open on Monday–Friday (except Bank Holidays) from 9.20 to 2.50 (Monday and Thursday to 5), but admission is obtainable by order only, application for which must be made to the Deputy Master, giving six weeks' notice of the intended visit. Visitors are shown the extremely interesting processes of coining and the museum of coins (from the Roman era onwards) medieval and modern seals, etc. The official head of the Mint is the Chancellor of the Exchequer, who in 1870 took over the mastership, an office held in 1699–1727 by Sir Isaac Newton and in 1850–5 by Sir John Herschel. The 'trial of the pyx' of all coins minted here is still carried out at Goldsmiths' Hall (see p. 276).

Tower Bridge Approach, skirting the east side of the Tower, leads south from the Mint to TOWER BRIDGE (IX, E 3), the farthest downsteam of the bridges over the Thames, as well as the best known and most distinctive. Built in 1886–94 at a cost of £800,000 (£1½ million, including the approaches), it was designed by Sir Horace Jones and Sir John Wolfe Barry. The bridge is about 800 ft long between the abutment towers and 200 ft between the massive Gothic towers that rise from the river and are connected near the top by a footway (permanently closed) which stands 142 ft above high-water level. The central span of the carriage-way, reaching 29½ ft above high-water, consists of twin bascules or drawbridges, each weighing about 1,000 tons, which can be raised hydraulically in a minute and a half to allow the passage of large vessels – an operation that takes place a dozen or more times a day, and has been accomplished (without a single failure) more than 340,000 times since the bridge was built. It is estimated that over 10,000 vehicles cross the bridge daily; the speed-limit varies from 10 to 20 m.p.h.

Immediately below the bridge, on the north bank of the river, are the ST KATHARINE DOCKS, the farthest upstream of the Docks, constructed in 1825–8. With the adjacent (and larger) LONDON DOCKS, they have an area of 127 acres (45 acres water). The warehouses beside the Tower Bridge Approach, designed by Thomas Telford, the engineer, contain an assortment of wool, tea, wines, tinned goods, rubber, hides, ivory, marble, spices, and perfumes.

On the south side of the river is the borough of BERMONDSEY, partly inhabited by leatherworkers, though an area is occupied by docks. Tower Bridge Road leads south across TOOLEY STREET (a corruption of St Olave's Street), the main east-to-west thoroughfare. A little west of the junction is a memorial bust of Ernest Bevin (d. 1951), the Labour states-man, and north-west of this is ST OLAVE'S AND ST SAVIOUR'S GRAMMAR SCHOOL (IX, E 3), formed by the amalgamation (in 1899) of two schools founded in 1561 and 1562 respectively. Robert Harvard, a butcher of Bermondsey, was a governor of St Saviour's School, and his son John, the founder of Harvard University, almost certainly attended it. The handsome buildings of 1896 are by E. W. Mountford. Duke Street Hill bears left near the west end of Tooley Street to reach the Borough High Street beside the approach to London Bridge Station (see below).

For the continuation of Tower Bridge Road to Bermondsey Church and the Old Kent Road, see p. 303.

35 From London Bridge to Lambeth Bridge via St George's Circus

Plan IX, D 2–VIII, D 3

STATIONS: LONDON BRIDGE (Plan IX, E 2), BOROUGH (IX, F 1), and ELEPHANT & CASTLE (IX, D 3), all on the Northern line; the Elephant & Castle is also the terminus of the Bakerloo line, on which LAMBETH NORTH (IX, C 2) is the nearest station to Lambeth Palace and Bridge. London Bridge, Elephant & Castle, and VAUXHALL (VIII, F 3) have stations on the Southern Region. — MOTOR-BUSES across London Bridge, see Route 25; No. 10 from London Bridge to Lambeth Bridge; also Nos. 21, 35, 40, and 133 in Borough High Street; No. 44 in Borough Road; and Nos. 3, 44, 59, and 159 in Lambeth Road to Lambeth Bridge. Nos. 44, 77, 168, 170, and 276 ply along the Albert Embankment.

ADMISSION to SOUTHWARK CATHEDRAL, see p. 394; to the IMPERIAL WAR MUSEUM, see p. 346; to LAMBETH PALACE, usually on Saturday afternoons (conducted parties), by arrangement with the Chaplain.

FOR LONDON BRIDGE, see Route 25. The BOROUGH HIGH STREET (IX, E 2–F 1), which runs southward from the Bridge, is the beginning of one of the great highways of England, the main approach to the Continent, as it has been since the Middle Ages. Kings and statesmen, prelates, ambassadors, and armies set out along this road, not to mention the bulk of the pilgrims bound for the shrine of St Thomas Becket at Canterbury (as related by Chaucer in the *Canterbury Tales*). The hostelries that lined the street in those and in the later coaching days, however, survive only in the names of yards.

On the west at the end of London Bridge are NANCY'S STEPS, claimed to be those immortalized by Dickens in *Oliver Twist*. On the left are the approaches to Tooley Street (Route 34) and to LONDON BRIDGE STATION (IX, E 2), the first station to be opened in London (in connexion with the London and Greenwich Railway, 1836) and now a terminus of the Southern Region. Rebuilt in 1851 by an unknown architect, it has been much damaged by bombing. On the west side of the High Street rises

Southwark Cathedral, with an approach to Bankside south of the churchyard (see Route 36).

St Thomas Street, on the left beyond the railway, leads past ST THOMAS'S CHURCH, built in 1703 as the chapel of St Thomas's Hospital (moved in 1868 to Lambeth) and now used as the chapter-house of Southwark Cathedral. Adjoining are two fine houses (one with an elaborate doorway) of the same period, originally the treasurer's apartments of the hospital, and next to these are plainer houses of the late 18th century. On the right just beyond is GUY'S HOSPITAL (IX, E 1, 2), founded in 1721 by Thomas Guy, a City bookseller who made a fortune from South Sea stock. The older part, opened in 1725, is built round a forecourt and two inner quadrangles (partly damaged by bombing), and the iron gates and railings of the entrance are the originals. In the forecourt is a statue by Scheemakers of the founder (d. 1724), who is commemorated also by a very fine marble statue by John Bacon the elder in the chapel, in the west wing, which was completed in 1780. The sculpture on the centre wing is also by Bacon. In one of the quadrangles (to which visitors are usually admitted) is an alcove from old London Bridge (1760), and in the other a statue of Lord Nuffield by Maurice Lambert (1949). Large buildings at the back were put up at various times after 1853. John Keats was a student in 1814–16 at the medical school, established about 1769 and now affiliated to London University. Remains of a Roman boat were discovered when digging the foundations for a new surgical block in 1959.

On the right in the Borough High Street is the BOROUGH MARKET, claiming to be the oldest municipal fruit and vegetable market in London, the successor of a market held on London Bridge in the 13th century and moved to its present site in 1756. In a courtyard on the left is the picturesque GEORGE INN (N.T.), the last remaining galleried tavern in London, rebuilt in 1677 after a fire which laid Southwark waste. In the 18th and early 19th centuries it became well known as a coaching terminus, and it is mentioned in Dickens' *Little Dorrit*, but the north wing was demolished in 1889.

White Hart Yard, opposite the junction with Southwark Street (an uninteresting thoroughfare leading towards Blackfriars Bridge, see Route 36), occupies the site of the White Hart Inn, referred to in Shakespeare's *Henry VI* and Dickens' *Pickwick Papers*; and a little beyond is Talbot Yard, on the site of the TABARD INN, the most famous of the hostelries, from which Chaucer's Canterbury pilgrims set out on their celebrated journey. Nos. 50–2 and 68–70, on the right in the High Street, are notable old houses.

On this side of the street stood the notorious MARSHALSEA PRISON, first heard of in the 14th century and moved farther south in 1813. Edmund Bonner, bishop of London, the adherent of Mary Tudor, died here in 1569. Adjoining it on the south was the KING'S BENCH, so called because prisoners committed by the Court of the King's Bench were incarcerated here. This is the prison to which Judge Gascoigne is said (without foundation) to have committed the Prince of Wales (later Henry V). Tobias Smollett and John Wilkes were among the many famous prisoners confined here, as was Mr Micawber in *David Copperfield*, something having failed to 'turn up'. In 1758 the prison was moved to Newington Causeway and used also for debtors, some of whom were permitted to live in lodgings close by (see Dickens' *Nicholas Nickleby*). The King's Bench was burned in 1780 during the Gordon Riots (compare *Barnaby Rudge*) and finally closed in 1860, when imprisonment for debt was abolished. The White Lion Prison, farther south, the Surrey county gaol from the 16th century, later became the site of the NEW MARSHALSEA PRISON (closed in 1849), where 'Roderick Random' and Dickens' father (in 1824) were confined for debt, and 'Little Dorrit' was born and brought up. The county gaol was established from 1798 until 1879 in HORSEMONGER LANE (now Union Street) and here Leigh Hunt was committed in 1812 for two years for libelling the Prince Regent as 'a fat Adonis of fifty'.

Great Dover Street (leading to the Old Kent Road) branches left from the Borough High Street by the classical church of ST GEORGE THE MARTYR (IX, F 1), rebuilt in 1734–6 (on the site of a Norman church) by John Price and restored in 1952 after its damage by bombing. Bishop Bonner (see above) and many others who died in the neighbouring prisons were buried here. General Monck was married here in 1652 and 'Little Dorrit' was both christened and married here. In LANT STREET, on the right, Dickens lodged while his father was in the New Marshalsea (see above); the house has gone, but others of the same period survive on the north side. Trinity Street, on the left farther on, leads to HOLY TRINITY CHURCH (by Francis Bedford, 1824), repaired after war damage, but now closed and probably to be demolished. In front of the church, which stands in a pleasant Georgian square, is a 14th-century statue formerly in Westminster Hall and supposed (with no certainty) to represent King Alfred. At its south end the Borough High Street divides into two.

NEWINGTON CAUSEWAY, the left branch, leads past the LONDON SESSIONS HOUSE (1921; restored in 1958) to the ELEPHANT AND CASTLE (IX, D 3), the junction of six busy thoroughfares named from a tavern now pulled down. In Newington Butts, going on south-west to Kennington Park, is the METROPOLITAN TABERNACLE, built in 1861 for Charles Haddon

Spurgeon (d. 1892), the Baptist preacher, and rebuilt after a fire in 1898. It was completely gutted by bombing, but again rebuilt in 1959. St George's Road runs westward to Westminster Bridge Road (see below) and London Road north-west to St George's Circus. The area round the Elephant and Castle, greatly devastated by bombing, is being entirely rebuilt (1963) to a new and ambitious plan. The huge Alexander Fleming House is to be the headquarters of the Ministry of Health.

Walworth Road runs south-east from the Elephant and Castle, passing the SOUTHWARK TOWN HALL (1866). The adjoining Central Library contains also the CUMING MUSEUM (well restored in 1959 after war damage), devoted largely to the history of Southwark, but including also relics of Michael Faraday, the pioneer of electro-magnetism, who was born in 1791 at Newington. The ROBERT BROWNING SETTLEMENT, in Browning Street, on the left farther on, houses a collection of memorials of the poet (shown to visitors on application). Yet farther on, in Liverpool Grove, is ST PETER'S CHURCH, built in 1823 by Sir John Soane, damaged internally in the war, but now restored and in use again.

The New Kent Road leads east from the 'Elephant' to the OLD KENT ROAD (compare above), long known as the resort of costermongers. Hence Tower Bridge Road goes on to BERMONDSEY SQUARE, where a celebrated 'rag fair' (transferred from the Caledonian Market, Islington) takes place every Friday (at 10 a.m.). Just to the north is ST MARY MAGDALEN, the parish church of Bermondsey, where the costermongers' harvest festival, attended by the 'Pearly King' and 'Queen', is often held, about the end of September. The church, founded in 1290, was rebuilt in 1691 incorporating the 15th-century tower; it has good contemporary woodwork (organ case, galleries, pulpit, and reredos) and preserves some carved 12th-century capitals from Bermondsey Abbey, a flourishing house of Cluniac monks established on this site in 1082. Catherine of Valois, the widow of Henry V, died in the abbey in 1437 and Elizabeth Woodville, widow of Edward IV, in 1492. To the north-west of the church, and reached from Long Lane, is the important LEATHER MARKET, opened in 1833. Tower Bridge Road continues past the LEATHERSELLERS' COLLEGE (No. 176) and the church of ST JOHN HORSELYDOWN (built in 1732, probably by John James, but gutted by bombing), a little beyond which it crosses Tooley Street (p. 300).

BOROUGH ROAD leads right from the Borough High Street to ST GEORGE'S CIRCUS (IX, C 2, 3), another important traffic point, from which Blackfriars Road runs north to Blackfriars Bridge (Route 36) and Westminster Bridge Road west to the County Hall and Westminster Bridge (compare below), while Waterloo Road, bearing right from this in a few yards, goes past the Old Vic (Route 36) to Waterloo Bridge. LAMBETH ROAD (IX, C 2–D 1) runs south-west to Lambeth Palace and Bridge.

At its junction with St George's Road is ST GEORGE'S CATHEDRAL, the principal church of the Roman Catholic diocese of Southwark, built in 1840–8 in a Gothic style by A. W. Pugin and severely damaged during an air-raid in 1941. Restoration to the designs of Romilly B. Craze was completed in 1958.

On the opposite corner is a milestone in the form of an obelisk erected in 1771 in honour of the mayoralty of Brass Crosby and moved here in 1905 from St George's Circus. Lambeth Road passes the entrance to the **Imperial War Museum,** in the surviving part of the former Bethlem Hospital. The grounds, purchased in 1926 by Lord Rothermere, have been converted into the GERALDINE MARY HARMSWORTH PARK in memory of his mother. Lambeth Road retains some Georgian houses, in one of which (No. 100) Admiral Bligh of the *Bounty* was born in 1754.

Lambeth Road crosses KENNINGTON ROAD, which ends on the north at Westminster Bridge Road. At the junction here stood CHRIST CHURCH (IX, C 2), a united Congregational and Baptist church, built in 1876 as the successor to the old Surrey Chapel in Blackfriars Road where Rowland Hill (d. 1833) was minister. Only the spire, erected mainly with American contributions as a memorial to Abraham Lincoln (and ringed with the stars and stripes) survived the bombing, but a new church has been incorporated in a large office block (1960). To the east in Westminster Bridge Road (No. 61) is MORLEY COLLEGE, founded in 1885 for working men and women, and moved in 1924 to a building enlarged in 1937 and restored in 1958 after extensive war damage.

On the right of Lambeth Road, farther west, is MORTON PLACE, a humble terrace where Emma Cons and Lilian Baylis, founders of the Old Vic, lived at No. 6. China Walk, on the left of the road, leads to LAMBETH WALK (IX, D 1), well known for its street-market and now made famous by a song and dance.

WALNUT TREE WALK, on its left, has some good late-18th-century houses, while No. 8 BOLWELL STREET, farther on, was the birthplace in 1842 of Sir Arthur Sullivan. Lambeth Walk ends on the south at Black Prince Road, which leads right to the Albert Embankment (see below).

Lambeth Road goes on westward to LAMBETH BRIDGE (Route 3). On the right here is ST MARY'S CHURCH (IX, D 1), the parish church of Lambeth, of ancient foundation, but rebuilt in 1851 by Philip Hardwick, except for the 15th-century tower. On the north chancel wall is a 16th-century brass of a lady, and on either side of the sanctuary are the fine Tudor Gothic table-tombs, with canopies, of Hugh Peyntwin (d. 1504), archdeacon of Canterbury (on the north), and John Mompesson (d. 1524), master of the registry to the archbishop. The east window, restored after war damage, has stained-glass by Francis Stephens (1953).

The small 'Pedlar's Window' in the south chapel commemorates the tradition of a bequest to the parish of the 'Pedlar's Acre', which was valued at 2/8 a year, but brought in £81,000 when it was sold to the L.C.C. in 1910 as part of the site for the new County Hall. Elias Ashmole (d. 1692), founder of the Ashmolean Museum at Oxford, Cuthbert Tunstall (d. 1559), bishop of London and Durham, and several archbishops are buried in the church; and in the churchyard (on the east) are the tombs of Admiral William Bligh (d. 1817) and the naturalist, John Tradescant (d. 1638).

On the left of the church is the entrance to LAMBETH PALACE (IX, D 1), the London residence of the archbishops of Canterbury for 750 years. The buildings were begun by Archbishop Hubert Walter (1193–1205), though Stephen Langton (1207–28) was the first archbishop to live here. The palace has been extensively altered and added to by many of his successors, but it still retains to a large extent its medieval atmosphere.

The palace occupies the site of a Saxon manor house that seems to have belonged before the Conquest to the sister of Edward the Confessor. The manor, given by William the Conqueror to the Benedictine monks of Rochester, was acquired about 1190 by Archbishop Baldwin, whose successor began the palace. This was attacked in 1381 by Wat Tyler's rebels, who forced Archbishop Simon of Sudbury to seek refuge in the Tower of London. The palace has now been restored after the heavy damage it received from the air in 1941. The Lambeth Conference of Anglican bishops under the presidency of the archbishop of Canterbury, instituted in 1867, is now held every ten years (last in 1958), with over 300 representatives from Britain, the Commonwealth, and the United States. The Library (entered from Lambeth Palace Road) is open to students and accredited readers on application to the Librarian.

The entrance is through a fine Tudor gateway of red brick, usually called MORTON'S TOWER after Cardinal Morton, who built it in 1490 and had his audience chamber over the vaulted archway. Thence visitors turn to the right into the courtyard, in the centre of which is a memorial to Archbishop Lord Davidson (d. 1930). The residential part of the palace, forming a Gothic wing on the north, was added in 1828–33 by Edward Blore for

Archbishop Howley. The fig-trees on the west of the courtyard are believed to have stemmed from those planted in the 16th century by Cardinal Pole. Behind them rises the GREAT HALL, a noble chamber 93 ft long, of medieval origin but greatly damaged during the Commonwealth and rebuilt after 1660 by Archbishop William Juxon, whose arms are over the door inside. The magnificent hammerbeam roof, 70 ft in height, in a Gothic style resembling that of Westminster Hall, has been carefully restored after war damage. The windows contain panels and shields of 16th–17th-century glass. The hall, the scene of the Lambeth Conferences, houses part of the valuable Library built up round the collection bequeathed to the see in 1610 by Archbishop Bancroft. The many treasures include beautiful illuminated MSS., the medieval registers of archbishops, and early printed books, including a Latin grammar prepared in 1540 for the young Prince Edward.

A corridor on the site of the medieval cloisters leads to the CRYPT below the chapel, the oldest part of the palace, a vaulted chamber with Purbeck marble pillars built about 1200, probably by Archbishop Walter. From an ante-chamber (formerly called the Post Room) on the floor above, an exquisite 13th-century doorway, resembling that of the chapter-house of Westminster Abbey, admits to the CHAPEL, built by Archbishop Boniface (1245–73) but much restored and unhappily gutted in the bombing, from which only parts of the 17th-century gallery and bench-ends survived. Rebuilt in its former style by Lord Mottistone and Paul Paget, the chapel was rededicated in 1955. The new stained-glass windows, by Edwards and Powell, are likewise in the style of their forerunners, inserted by Matthew Parker (d. 1575), archbishop under Elizabeth I, who is buried in the sanctuary. The second trial of John Wyclif, the reformer (1378), was held in the chapel, in which also many English bishops have been consecrated. The former Post Room, which contains a richly carved 17th-century screen with the arms of Archbishop Laud, is in the LOLLARDS' TOWER, built as a water-tower by Archbishop Chichele (1414–43), and named from the supposition that the Lollards, followers of Wyclif, were imprisoned here. Opening off the staircase on the north is a turret called the 'Lollards' Prison'. Adjoining the tower on the south is the smaller LAUD'S TOWER, added about 1635 by that archbishop. Hence another corridor leads to the GUARD CHAMBER, rebuilt by Blore, who, however, retained the unusual 14th-century timber roof. Around the walls are many fine portraits of archbishops, including works by Holbein (Archbishop Warham), Van Dyck (Archbishop Laud), Kneller, Hogarth, Reynolds, Romney, Lawrence, and Sargent.

The ALBERT EMBANKMENT (VIII, D 3–F 3) runs south from Lambeth Bridge to Vauxhall Station, following the bank of the Thames at first. At the corner is the large LAMBETH BRIDGE HOUSE, the head-office of the Ministry of Public Building and Works, and farther on are the headquarters of the LONDON FIRE BRIGADE, established in 1866 as the Metropolitan Fire Brigade, and moved to new buildings here (by E. P. Wheeler) in 1937. During the Second World War the brigade was considerably augmented and incorporated in the National Fire Service, but in 1948 it was returned to the L.C.C., who had first assumed control in 1889. The force, which numbers over 2000, maintains sixty-one stations (including three on the river) and responds to some 28,000 calls during the year. Of other characteristic examples of modern commercial architecture on the embankment, the NATIONAL DOCK LABOUR BOARD was designed by Frederick Gibberd and opened in 1956. Across the river are seen the Tate Gallery and the lofty new Vickers building, and upstream are Vauxhall Bridge and the huge Battersea power-station. The Albert Embankment turns away from the river, crossing the site of Vauxhall Gardens, a celebrated pleasure resort which flourished from 1661 until 1859 and is described in Thackeray's *Vanity Fair*. From the end of the street Bridgefoot leads right to VAUXHALL BRIDGE (Route 3), while Harleyford Road, bearing right from Kennington Lane, runs south-east towards Kennington Park, rounding The Oval (see p. 490).

36 From Lambeth Bridge to London Bridge via Waterloo and Bankside

Plan VIII, D 3–IX, D 2

STATIONS: LAMBETH NORTH (Plan IX, C 2), on the Bakerloo line; WATERLOO (IX, B 1), on the Bakerloo line and the Northern line (Charing Cross branch); and LONDON BRIDGE (IX, E 2), on the Northern line (Bank branch). Waterloo and London Bridge are served also by the Southern Region, and the former is the terminus of the short Waterloo & City Railway to the Bank. — MOTOR-BUSES Nos. 46, 149, 168, 170, and 276 in Lambeth Palace Road; Nos. 46, 76, 149, and 171 in York Road; Nos. 70, 76, and 149 in Stamford Street; and No. 70 in Southwark Street (to London Bridge). Nos. 12, 53, 109, 153, 155, 163, 171–2, 176, and 184 in Westminster Bridge Road; Nos. 1, 60, 68, 171, 176, 188, and 196 across

Waterloo Bridge to Waterloo Station; Nos. 4, 17, 45, 63, 109, 141, 155, 177, and 184 in Blackfriars Road; No. 44 in Southwark Bridge Road (to London Bridge Station). For buses across Westminster Bridge and Blackfriars Bridge, see Route 26; across Southwark Bridge, see Route 27.

ADMISSION to the LONDON COUNTY HALL, Saturdays 1.30 to 4.30 (free; also Bank Holidays in summer 10.30 to 12 and 1.30 to 3.30).

For the shortest route between Lambeth Bridge and London Bridge, see Route 35, above. The route described below follows the river as far as is practicable.

From LAMBETH BRIDGE (Route 3), Lambeth Palace Road runs northward, skirting the wall of the archbishop of Canterbury's palace (see Route 35) and passing behind St Thomas's Hospital. Paris Street, on the right, leads to ARCHBISHOP'S PARK, part of the palace grounds opened to the public in 1900. The ALBERT EMBANKMENT (VIII, C, D 3), following the river, is a broad footwalk constructed by Sir Joseph Bazalgette in 1866–9 and leading to Westminster Bridge. It affords a fine view of the Houses of Parliament on the opposite bank, with the towers of Westminster Abbey behind. ST THOMAS'S HOSPITAL (IX, C 1), founded at Southwark in 1552, is the successor of a hospital established by the Augustinians there in 1173 and dedicated to St Thomas Becket. The dedication was changed by Edward VI to St Thomas the Apostle, and the hospital was moved in 1868 to new buildings here, which were damaged by bombing. An entirely new hospital, to the designs of W. Fowler Howitt, was begun in 1963. The associated medical school, part of London University, is to be incorporated in the buildings.

On the north side of the approach to Westminster Bridge (Route 26) rises the LONDON COUNTY HALL (IX, B 1), the imposing headquarters of the London County Council, designed by Ralph Knott (with the assistance of W. E. Riley, the council's architect) in a free Renaissance style. Begun in 1912, the building, opened in 1922 and finally completed in 1933, has nine floors and about 1500 rooms. Constructed partly on ground recovered from the river, the foundations, covering about 6½ acres, are supported by a concrete raft 5 ft thick. The exterior, faced with Portland stone, has sculptures by Ernest Cole and A. F. Hardiman. Its most notable features are the steep-pitched roofs and the curved colonnade in the centre of the river façade, which is 750 ft long.

The total cost, including the embankment and terrace (open to the public), has amounted to over £3½ million. The central part of a new extension, to the designs of E. P. Wheeler and F. R. Hiorns (with Sir Giles G. Scott as consultant), was opened in 1939; a new wing on the north was completed in 1957 and the south block in 1963.

The London County Council, constituted under an act of 1888, consists of 126 councillors (elected by the ratepayers for three years) and 21 aldermen (co-opted by the councillors for six years), presided over by a chairman, who is himself usually (though not necessarily) an elected member or alderman. The council, the ruling authority for the County of London (see p. 14), controls (or shares control with the borough councils in) such matters as education, public health, the care of children and other welfare services, housing and street improvements, main drainage, the fire service, and the maintenance of parks and open spaces, historic buildings, etc. The meetings of the county council, on alternate Tuesdays at 3 p.m., are open to the public.

The visitors' entrance is in Belvedere Road, on the east of the main building, through bronze doors displaying the council's coat-of-arms. The Entrance Hall and the Ceremonial Staircase, ascending to the first floor, are decorated with Italian, Belgian, and Ashburton marbles, and the numerous committee rooms are panelled in English oak. Among the rooms shown are the Conference Hall, a fine elliptical chamber at the north end; the Voting Lobbies, decorated with Indian laurel; the handsome octagonal Council Chamber, with monolithic columns of veine dorée, a marble quarried in the Italian Alps; the Members' Reading Room, affording a view of the terrace and colonnade; the Members' Library, devoted mainly to London topography and local government (see below; from the adjacent corridor there is a view of the members' courtyard above the main record room); and the Members' Waiting Room, containing an 18th-century fireplace removed from No. 59 Lincoln's Inn Fields. A room in the east wing contains an exhibition of the work of the L.C.C. (open weekdays 9 to 5; Saturday to 12). The excellent library is accessible to students on weekdays (9.30 to 5, Saturdays to 12.30) on application to the Clerk of the Council, but the fine collection of London prints, water-colours, etc., is not yet on view.

A Roman boat of the 3rd century, discovered in 1910 during the excavations for the foundations of the hall, was presented to the London Museum. In York Road, which skirts the newer building on the east and leads to Waterloo Station (see below), is the GENERAL LYING-IN HOSPITAL, built in 1828 by Henry Harrison.

The area to the north of the County Hall, extending to Waterloo Bridge and now known as the SOUTH BANK (IX, A, B 1), was the site of the Festival of Britain held in 1951. The embankment has been laid out as a promenade and gardens. To the east of Belvedere Road rises the SHELL CENTRE, two vast ranges of office building, covering about 7½ acres, completed in 1962 for the Shell International Petroleum Company and including an enormous skyscraper, 26 storeys and 351 ft high, designed by Sir Howard Robertson. In the main courtyard is a towering bronze fountain, 30 ft high, by Franta Belsky, and at the top of the building is a public viewing gallery from which there extends a widespread panorama of London and the Thames in both directions.

On the north side of the Charing Cross railway bridge (see p. 245) is the ROYAL FESTIVAL HALL (IX, A 1), the most successful example of modern architecture in London, designed by Sir Robert H. Matthew and Sir Leonard Martin for the L.C.C. and opened in 1951. The main concert hall, praiseworthy for its decorative scheme and its acoustics (declared the finest in the world), has seats for 3400 and a platform that will accommodate a choir of 250. The splendid organ, completed in 1954, was built by Messrs Harrison and Harrison of Durham, with Ralph Downes, the organist, as consultant. The hall is effectively insulated against the noise of passing trains. The building, which is of reinforced concrete faced with Portland stone, contains also a recital room (seating about 200), a restaurant commanding a fine view across the river, and many novel features. The river frontage is now being enlarged to contain the main entrance, another restaurant, etc., to be completed in 1964.

A plan is afoot to build a new National Theatre (replacing the Old Vic; see below) and a new opera house (to replace Sadler's Wells; p. 270) on the south side of the railway bridge; and a new small concert hall, recital room, and art gallery between the Festival Hall and Waterloo Bridge. Under the southern arch abutment of the bridge is the NATIONAL FILM THEATRE (compare p. 71), first opened in 1951 but rebuilt here in 1957. Designed by the architects of the L.C.C., the theatre is capable of seating 500.

On the other side of York Road rises WATERLOO STATION (IX, B 1, 2), a principal terminus of the Southern Region and the largest station in Britain, first opened in 1848 by the London and South Western Railway Company and rebuilt in 1907–22. The main entrance, on the north-west, with sculptured groups, is by J. R. Scott.

The monumental lion (1837) beside the main approach to the station was formerly the trade-mark of a brewery which stood on the South Bank. Its principal interest is that it is made of Coade stone, an artificial stone practically impervious to weather, first manufactured by Richard Holt in 1722 and developed commercially in her factory at Lambeth by Eleanor Coade after about 1769. The stone, a kind of terracotta, was extensively used for the decoration of London buildings in the late 18th and early 19th centuries, but the secret of its composition has now been lost.

WATERLOO ROAD (IX, A 1–C 2) leads south-east from Waterloo Bridge (Route 26) to St George's Circus (Route 35), passing an entrance to Waterloo Station. On the left before this is ST JOHN'S CHURCH, a classical building by Francis Bedford (1824), damaged by bombing in 1940 but restored in 1951 as the 'Festival Church'.

Beyond the railway is the UNION JACK CLUB for soldiers, sailors, and airmen, opened in 1907, and farther on, at the corner of The Cut, is the OLD VIC (IX, B 2), officially the Royal Victoria Theatre, famous for its productions of Shakespeare. Founded in 1816 as the Royal Coburg Theatre, it was at first notorious for melodrama; its name was changed in 1833 and in 1880 it was remodelled and taken over by Emma Cons, who made it a home for opera and classical plays at popular prices. After the death of Miss Cons in 1912 the work was ably carried on by her niece, Lilian Baylis (d. 1937), who in 1914 formed a permanent Shakespearian company but after the rebuilding of Sadler's Wells (p. 270) the opera productions were transferred there. The Old Vic suffered considerable bomb damage in the war, when the company was transferred to the New Theatre, but it returned to its old home in 1950. The theatre is to be taken over by the new National Theatre organization in 1963. THE CUT, which leads eastward to Blackfriars Road (see below), is extended on the west by LOWER MARSH, with its animated street market.

STAMFORD STREET (IX, A 1, 2), which leaves Waterloo Road north of St John's Church, retains some formal late-Georgian terraces (Nos. 63–89 and 95–121). Also on the right are a building erected in 1820 as a school for Irish children, and the UNITARIAN CHAPEL, founded in 1666 and rebuilt in 1823 in a severe Greek style. Stamford Street ends at BLACKFRIARS ROAD (IX, A 3–C 3), which connects Blackfriars Bridge (Route 26) with St George's Circus.

A little to the right is CHRIST CHURCH, rebuilt in 1738 but set on fire from the air in 1941. Subsequently demolished except for the chancel, added in 1900, it was again rebuilt in 1959. PARIS GARDEN, the street on the west, occupies the site of the 14th-century manor house of Robert de Paris; the manor later became a fashionable amusement place and the Swan Theatre, at which Shakespeare was employed, stood here from 1595 until 1633.

SOUTHWARK STREET, a long dismal thoroughfare, continues from Stamford Street to the Borough High Street (Route 35), crossing Southwark Bridge Road and passing St Christopher House, the large new offices (1960) of the MINISTRY OF TRANSPORT. In Great Guildford Street (on the right before Southwark Bridge Road) is DUTHY HALL, where a Shakespeare festival is held annually in April.

A more interesting route turns to the left beyond the railway into Hopton Street, passing the pleasant HOPTON ALMSHOUSES, built in 1752 and restored after war damage, and a quaint little house of the early 18th century (No. 61). On the right at the end is the beginning of BANKSIDE (IX, A 3–D 1), which skirts the huge Bankside power-station (designed by Sir Giles G. Scott and completed in 1953), then keeps close to the river, with a splendid view of the dome and towers of St Paul's, surrounded by the City spires (though these are being increasingly obscured by large new blocks of office building). The street, though now mostly lined by warehouses, traverses historic ground, the site of amusement gardens and theatres in the 16th–17th centuries. BEAR GARDENS and ROSE ALLEY, narrow openings just before Southwark Bridge (Route 27), which Bankside passes under, recall the Hope Theatre (built in 1583) on a former bear-garden, and the Rose Theatre (opened by Philip Henslowe in 1587), where Shakespeare is believed to have played. From the picturesque old *Anchor Inn*, Bankend turns inland. In the branch of PARK STREET to the right, a tablet has been affixed to the wall of Messrs Barclay, Perkins brewery close to the site of the GLOBE THEATRE ('this wooden O'), erected by Richard and Cuthbert Burbage late in 1598 (or early in 1599) and burned down in 1613. Shakespeare acted here until 1612 with the King's Company, and here *Hamlet* (1602), *Othello* (1604), *Macbeth* (1606), *King Lear* (1606), and others of his plays were produced.

The other branch of Park Street turns south-east towards the junction of Southwark Street and the Borough High Street. CLINK STREET goes on eastward from Bankend, passing under the Cannon Street Railway Bridge (by Sir John Hawkshaw, 1866) and hemmed in by lofty warehouses. Among these, though not visible from outside, are the scanty remains of WIN-CHESTER PALACE, a 13th-century house of the bishops of Winchester (whose diocese included south London), occupied by them until 1649, but mostly burned down in 1814. Attached to the palace was the Liberty of the Clink, a manor outside the jurisdiction of the City and later, because of this, the chief pleasure quarter of London, with theatres, bear-gardens, and 'stews' (brothels). The Clink Prison, in which Bishops Bradford and Hooper, the opponents of Mary Tudor, were confined, survives only in the name of Clink Street and the expression 'the clink' for imprisonment.

The ravine-like street goes on past ST MARY OVERIE'S DOCK (where parishioners of St Saviour's were entitled to land goods free of toll) to Cathedral Street, which skirts the west side of Southwark Cathedral. A foot-passage on the south side of the churchyard leads out to the BOROUGH HIGH STREET (IX, E 1), opposite the approach to London Bridge Station (Route 35).

PLACES OF INTEREST

BRITISH MUSEUM Plan III, C, D 3

STATIONS: TOTTENHAM COURT ROAD, ¼-m. SW., on the Central and Northern lines; HOLBORN, ¼-m. SE., on the Central and Piccadilly lines; GOODGE STREET, ½-m. NW., on the Northern line; and RUSSELL SQUARE, ¼-m. NE., on the Piccadilly line. — MOTOR-BUSES in Tottenham Court Road, see Route 18; in New Oxford Street, see Route 23; in Bloomsbury Way and Southampton Row, see Route 19.

ADMISSION weekdays 10 to 5; Sundays 2.30 to 6 (free). Closed on Good Friday and Christmas Day. — LECTURE TOURS on weekdays at 11.30 and 3, starting in the Entrance Hall. — REFRESHMENT ROOM, approached from the Mausoleum Room (see Ground Floor plan), open weekdays 10.30 to 4.30 (Tuesdays and Thursdays also 6 to 7.30).

The READING ROOM is open from 9 to 5 on weekdays (to 9 on Tuesdays and Thursdays), except Good Friday, Christmas Day, and Boxing Day, and the week beginning with the first Monday in May, to subscribers to the National Art-Collections Fund (see p. 64) and to holders of tickets (free), for which application in writing to the Director, together with a letter of recommendation from a person of recognized position, should be made at least two days in advance. Application slips for books not on the shelves cannot be handed in after 4.15 (8 on Tuesdays and Thursdays). The Students' Rooms of the Departments of MANUSCRIPTS (weekdays 10 to 4.45), of ORIENTAL PRINTED BOOKS AND MANUSCRIPTS (Monday–Friday 10 to 5, Saturdays 10 to 1), and of PRINTS AND DRAWINGS (Monday–Friday 10 to 4, Saturdays 10 to 1), and the Map Room (weekdays 9.30 to 4.30) and the State Paper Room (weekdays 9.30 to 4.30; to 9 on Tuesdays and Thursdays) in the Department of PRINTED BOOKS are all open under similar conditions. The Department of COINS AND MEDALS is open to students and scholars on weekdays 10 to 4.30.

The BRITISH MUSEUM, comprising the national museum of archaeology and ethnography and the national library, is the largest and richest of its kind in the world. Built in 1823–52 to the designs of Sir Robert Smirke, it is situated in Bloomsbury, in the angle between Tottenham Court Road and New Oxford Street. The main entrance is on the south side, from Great Russell Street, but there is another entrance on the north, in Montague Place, to the King Edward VII Building, added in 1907–14 by Sir John J. Burnet. The main façade, 370 ft long, is in a severe classical style, with heavy projecting wings and a rather ponderous colonnade of forty-four Ionic columns. The pediment above the entrance portico has allegorical sculptures by Sir Richard Westmacott.

The museum was founded in 1753, its nucleus being the Cottonian Library of state-papers and other manuscripts, collected by Sir Robert Cotton (d. 1631) and presented to the nation in 1702. To this were added the natural history collection, antiquities, and works of art bequeathed to the nation for £20,000 by Sir Hans Sloane (d. 1753) and the collection of manuscripts formed by Robert Harley, first Earl of Oxford (d. 1724), and his son, and bought for £10,000. Montague House in Bloomsbury was purchased in 1755, after a public lottery had raised £300,000, the Royal Library presented by George II was incorporated in 1757, and the collections were opened to the public in 1759. By gift, bequest, and purchase the museum grew rapidly, and in the early 19th century new buildings had to be provided to accommodate the Egyptian sculptures, the Townley Marbles, and the Elgin Marbles. With the gift by George IV in 1823 of the splendid library collected by his father, Montague House proved quite inadequate, and a new and larger building was begun on the same site by Robert Smirke. The first wing completed was the fine gallery called the King's Library (1826) and the classical south front was finished in 1852. The building, however, was already too small, partly owing to the growth of the library, and in 1857 the famous domed Reading Room was constructed by Sydney Smirke to a plan by Sir Anthony Panizzi, the principal librarian, in what had been the interior courtyard. With the acquisition of the Grenville Library and the material from excavations in Assyria and Asia Minor, accommodation once more became a problem, and in 1881 the natural history collections were transferred to their present home in South Kensington. New wings were added on the south-east and south-west in 1882–4, and in 1914 the fine King Edward VII Building was opened on the north side. The North Library was reconstructed in 1937, and finally a new gallery on the west, the gift of Lord Duveen, was built in 1938 for the magnificent sculptures of the Parthenon; damaged by bombing, the gallery was restored only in 1961.

The vast treasures of the museum cannot be absorbed in a single visit; visitors with limited time at their disposal are advised to begin with the KING EDWARD VII GALLERY (p. 329), where a selection representative of the scope and riches of the collections is displayed. The gallery is reached by a staircase or adjacent lift from the north entrance in Montague Place, or by turning right from the main vestibule through the King's Library to a staircase and bridge which give access to the east end of the gallery (see plan). Visitors may then descend to the ground floor of the main building to see the Greek, Roman, Egyptian, and Assyrian sculptures (in the west wing) and the Printed Books and Manuscripts (east wing).

The main doorway opens direct into a large vestibule or ENTRANCE HALL. On the left is the approach to the collection of Greek and Roman sculptures, and beyond is the main staircase, ascending to the Prehistoric Rooms, the Eastern and Ethnographical Galleries, etc., with the cloakroom to the left of it. Opposite the staircase is the entrance to the exhibition of Books

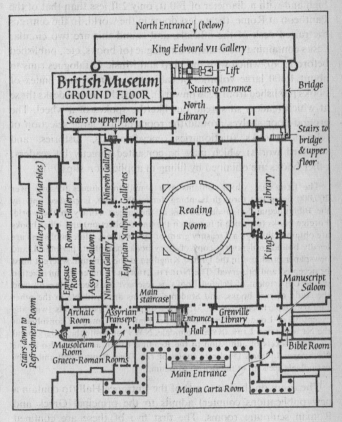

and Manuscripts, and straight ahead is the Reading Room. Flanking the entrance to this are sculptures of the 2nd–3rd centuries A.D. from the great Buddhist shrine at Amaravati, in southern India (on the left), and a colossal Buddha of A.D. 585 and other Chinese sculpture.

The READING ROOM is open to ticket holders only, but visitors are often allowed to see it from the entrance on application to the superintendent at the enquiry office. The huge circular hall, accommodating about 450 readers, is covered by a dome 106 ft high and with a diameter of 140 ft, only 2 ft less than that of the Pantheon at Rome, the widest dome in the world. In the centre is the raised desk of the officials, and round this are two circular desks containing the General Catalogue (of books, etc., published before 1956), which with the Map and Music Catalogues runs to about 1,400 large volumes (a cabinet contains a card index of books published from 1956 onward). From the central desks those at which readers sit spread out like the spokes of a wheel. The ground-floor shelves around the room hold a large selection of reference books (dictionaries, encyclopedias, histories, and standard works) which may be consulted directly by readers; other books are obtained by filling in application slips.

The LIBRARY, which contains over 6 million volumes (despite over 200,000 being lost through bombing during the war), is rivalled only by the Bibliothèque Nationale at Paris as the largest library in the world. Foreign books (of which it has much the finest collection) and older books are obtained through a Treasury grant or by donation, while publishers are legally bound to deposit a copy of every book, pamphlet, periodical, and newspaper produced in the United Kingdom at the museum, where it must be accepted and preserved. The NORTH LIBRARY, under the jurisdiction of the Department of Printed Books, is reserved for special research and the study of rare books, and Students' Rooms are available in the other Library Departments (see p. 315). Newspapers and periodicals (with the exception of London newspapers earlier than 1801) may be consulted at the NEWSPAPER LIBRARY at Colindale, NW9 (opposite the underground station); tickets of admission to the Reading Room are valid also at the Newspaper Library. Duplicate copies of *The Times* (from 1809) and a few periodicals are kept at the British Museum.

The room on the left (west) of the Entrance Hall (to contain a new publications counter) admits to the principal Greek and Roman sculpture rooms. The first five of these are confined mainly to Greek sculptures of the archaic and classical periods (down to about 320 B.C.). The FIRST GRAECO-ROMAN ROOM contains copies and imitations of Greek sculptures, mostly executed in Italy under the Roman Empire. In the SECOND GRAECO-ROMAN ROOM is a beautiful statue of the goddess

Demeter, of about 330 B.C., from Cnidus, a Dorian city on the south-west coast of Asia Minor. The MAUSOLEUM ROOM is devoted to sculptures from the tomb built at Halicarnassus for Mausolus (d. 353 B.C.), a prince of Caria in Asia Minor, by his wife Artemisia, and one of the seven wonders of the ancient world. On the walls is a sculptured frieze portraying a battle between Greeks and Amazons, and at the farther end is a heroic statue, probably of Mausolus himself.

On the right is the ARCHAIC ROOM, containing columns and other fragments from the miscalled Treasury of Atreus at Mycenae (in reality a royal tomb of about 1330 B.C.) and Greek sculpture of the 5th–6th centuries B.C. from Asia Minor, notably the marble reliefs from the 'Harpy Tomb' and the frieze of cocks and hens, both of about 500, from Xanthos in Lycia; the Strangford 'Apollo', a statue of a young man of about 490 in the Dorian style, from Lemnos or Anaphe; and the seated figures and lions of the 6th century from the temple of Apollo at Branchidae, near Miletus. Beyond the GREEK ANTE-ROOM, containing small heads and statuettes dating from the 6th century B.C. to the 2nd century A.D., is the EPHESUS ROOM, which holds remains of sculptured columns from the great temple in honour of Artemis at Ephesus ('Diana of the Ephesians'; see the *Acts of the Apostles*, XIX), a centre of the Ionian Greeks in Asia Minor, rebuilt after 356 B.C. and another of the seven wonders of the world. At the south end of the room are figures of the 4th century B.C. and later; at the north end are sculptured tombstones and votive reliefs, including the Apotheosis of Homer, a white marble relief of about 210 B.C. signed by Archelaus of Priene, found at Bovillae on the Appian Way near Rome.

Beyond is the ROMAN GALLERY (to be arranged in 1963), containing statues and portrait busts of Roman emperors, etc., as well as sarcophagi, grave reliefs, and other sculpture, including some found in Britain. At the north end is a lovely caryatid (the figure of a woman serving as a pillar) from the 5th-century temple of Erechtheus on the Acropolis (see below).

A door on the left of the gallery gives access to the DUVEEN GALLERY, opened in 1962 expressly to display the famous ELGIN MARBLES. These are named after the seventh Earl of

Elgin, ambassador at Constantinople, who in 1801–3 collected them and brought them to England at a cost of £75,000, and sold them to the government in 1816 for less than half that sum. The collection includes remains of the temple of Erechtheus and other buildings in Athens, but by far the most important part consists of the superb sculptures from the Parthenon or temple of the Athena Parthenos (*i.e.* the Virgin), the patron goddess of the city.

The temple, which crowned the rocky hill of the Acropolis, was built between 447 and 432 B.C., at a time when Athens was flourishing under the brilliant leadership of Pericles. The principal architect was Ictinus and the decorations were most probably executed under the supervision of the great sculptor Pheidias. A statue of Athena, 40 ft high, made of gold and ivory by Pheidias, was raised in the temple, which remained dedicated to the goddess until about A.D. 450, after which it was converted for Christian worship. At the fall of Athens to the Turks in 1458 it became a Mohammedan mosque. In 1687 the Parthenon was gravely damaged by an explosion during the siege of Athens by the Venetians, and after the restoration of the city to the Turks in 1688 it suffered further injury. A series of drawings made in 1674 by a French draughtsman, however, have served as a valuable record of the sculptures before their damage.

Models, drawings, and photographs in the South Slip Room, left of the entrance to the gallery, illustrate the history and structure of the Parthenon. The sculptures, generally agreed to be the finest in the world, consist of the Pediment Groups, which filled the east and west gables of the temple and each contained more than twenty statues ranging from just over life-size to 11ft in height; the Metopes, square panels in high relief set into the outside of the building above the colonnade; and the Frieze, a band of low relief over 500 ft long which ran round the outer walls of the inner chamber.

Around the walls of the central part of the gallery is the FRIEZE, which portrays the procession up to the Acropolis at the end of the Panathenaic Festival, the greatest of all Athenian festivals. The representation started at the south-west corner of the building with a parade of horsemen, which increases in numbers and artistic virility as it moves towards the left (mostly from the north frieze); the leading horsemen (on slab XXIV, at the north-east angle of the room) are particularly notable. The procession is joined by chariots and citizens, by animals being led to sacrifice (south frieze), and by girls carrying vessels for use in sacrifice, and magistrates and other officials, and culminates in the presentation of a sacred peplos or robe to the image of Athena (Nos. 34–6, east frieze; almost facing the door).

In the raised alcove at the north end of the gallery are the sculptures from the EAST PEDIMENT group, symbolizing the Birth of Athena, who is supposed to have sprung from the head of Zeus in complete armour and fully grown. The remains of the group begin on the left with a fragment of Helios, the sun-god, who rises from the sea in his four-horse chariot at daybreak, and ends with one of the horses of Selene, goddess of the moon, sinking into the waves. The male figure facing the surviving horse of Helios is probably either Heracles, a hero famous for his strength, or Dionysus, the youthful god of wine; the two seated female figures to the right of him are Demeter, the goddess of the grain-bearing earth, and her daughter Persephone, while the maiden apparently running towards them is most likely Hebe, the cup-bearer of the gods. The identity of the three other figures has not been definitely agreed on.

In the alcove at the south end of the gallery are the sculptures of the WEST PEDIMENT, which represent the contest between Athena and Poseidon, ruler of the sea, for Attica, the country containing Athens. The object of the contest was to produce the gift most useful to man: Poseidon struck the ground with his trident and a horse appeared, but Athena caused the first olive to grow and was awarded the verdict by the gods. The surviving sculptures have been considerably mutilated; the fine figure in the left angle, however, is recognized as Kephisus or Ilissus, a river god of Athens, and the figures on either side of the centre are Hermes and Iris, the supporters of Athena and Poseidon. To the right of Iris is the driver of Poseidon's chariot, while the figure to the extreme right was probably a sea-nymph.

On the walls of the alcoves are fifteen of the original ninety-two METOPES that alternated with the triglyphs (tablets ornamented with three vertical bands) on the outside of the Parthenon. Forty-one still survive in a decayed condition on the temple and one is in the Louvre at Paris. The museum's panels depict the lively battle between the Lapiths, a mythical Thessalian people, and the Centaurs, half horses and half men, who had attempted to carry off the bride of Peirithous, the Lapith king, and other women from the wedding feast. The myth, a favourite subject in Greek art, represents the triumph of civilization over barbarism.

To the east of the Greek and Roman rooms are the EGYPTIAN ANTIQUITIES, which are mostly arranged chronologically, starting at the north end of the main gallery. The NORTH GALLERY contains statues of Senusret III, a king of the 12th Dynasty (about 2000 B.C.), and remains from earlier dynasties, but the most notable sculptures are those of the 18th Dynasty, mainly from Thebes, on the upper Nile, which became the capital of the New Empire about 1600 B.C. They include the colossal red granite head and the arm of a statue, probably of Thothmes III (about 1450 B.C.), and two seated statues and three huge heads of Amenhetep III (about 1400 B.C.), whose name is inscribed on a pair of red granite lions. The CENTRAL SALOON is devoted to sculptures of the New Kingdom (1600–1000 B.C.), among them the black granite sarcophagus of Merimes, who was viceroy of Nubia under Amenhetep III, and two red granite statues of Rameses II (about 1250 B.C.), whose names and titles are inscribed on two monolithic columns. The colossal green granite scarab of about 550 B.C. is an emblem of the sun-god and was a symbol of creative power among the Egyptians. The SOUTH GALLERY contains monuments from the later dynasties. Near the centre is the 'Rosetta Stone', a slab of black basalt dated 195 B.C., inscribed with a trilingual decree – twice in Egyptian (first in hieroglyphs, the classical writing of the priests, and again in demotic or secular characters) and once in a Greek translation. The stone, which was found near Rosetta, in the Nile delta, in 1798, gave scholars the key, through the Greek, to the Egyptian language.

Parallel to the Egyptian galleries on the west are the ASSYRIAN ANTIQUITIES, displaying the vigorous art of the northern part of the old Babylonian kingdom. The NINEVEH GALLERY, at the north end, contains reliefs from the palace built at Nineveh, the capital of Assyria, by Sennacherib (705–681 B.C.); the adjoining NIMROUD CENTRAL SALOON holds sculptures mostly of the time of Shalmaneser III (858–28 B.C.). The NIMROUD GALLERY, on the south, contains sculptures from the palace of Ashurnasir-pal II (883–59 B.C.) at Calah (the modern Nimroud or

Nimrud), including wall reliefs of battles and hunting scenes. On the right opens the ASSYRIAN SALOON, which has sculptures of the time of Tiglath-pileser III (746–28 B.C.), Sennacherib, and his grandson, Ashur-bani-pal (668–about 630 B.C.), including a series of lively reliefs showing the lion hunts of Ashur-bani-pal. The ASSYRIAN TRANSEPT, at the south end of the Egyptian galleries, contains the colossal winged and human-headed bulls that stood at the entrances to the palace of Sargon II (722–05 B.C.), the father of Sennacherib, at Khorsabad, near Nineveh, and man-headed lions from the doorways of Ashur-nasir-pal's palace, as well as slabs portraying Sargon II and other sculpture. The black obelisk here records the exploits of Shalmaneser III.

Mummies and smaller Egyptian objects are exhibited on the upper floor (p. 327), reached by the staircase to the north of the Egyptian sculpture galleries.

In the east wing of the building is the museum's unrivalled collection of PRINTED BOOKS AND MANUSCRIPTS. The wall-cases in the first room hold the GRENVILLE LIBRARY of over 20,000 volumes bequeathed by the Rt Hon. Thomas Grenville (d. 1846). The centre cases contain a fine collection of beautiful illuminated manuscripts of the 10th–16th centuries, mostly of English, Flemish, French, and Italian origin. They include Bibles, psalters, books of hours, breviaries, etc., notable being a Winchester Psalter of about 1060, Bede's Life of St Cuthbert (of the 12th century, from Durham Cathedral), a Latin Bible from the abbey of St Mihiel (13th century), and the St Aethelwold Benedictional formerly at Chatsworth (Derbyshire).

The MANUSCRIPT SALOON beyond contains numerous manuscripts of outstanding literary and historical interest.

Only a few of the treasures can be mentioned. Cases C–F and X, on the right of the entrance, contain English Literary Autographs; in Case F is the *Booke of Sir Thomas More*, believed to be partly in Shakespeare's handwriting. Case B, on the right, holds a 15th-century illuminated French manuscript of Froissart's Chronicle. Cases A and V: Historical Autographs, including letters and documents of Nelson, Wellington, General Gordon, Mary, Queen of Scots, and many other famous persons. Case W contains Chronicles of England, the most notable of which are a late-8th-century manuscript of Bede's *Ecclesiastical History*, an 11th-century manuscript of the *Anglo-Saxon Chronicle*, and the History of Matthew Paris (d. 1259), a monk of St Albans. Case U: Early-12th-century illuminated copy of the

Commentary on the Apocalypse by Beatus, an 8th-century Spanish theologian and geographer. Case T: Medieval charters; on left is the Bosworth Psalter, probably written at St Augustine's Abbey, Canterbury, in the late 10th century. Case S: Medieval English Manuscripts, notably the unique MS. of *Beowulf* (about A.D. 1000) and an early-15th-century MS. of Chaucer's *Canterbury Tales*. At the end of the room are two cases containing Seals and Monastic Records.

Case R contains Miscellaneous Manuscripts, including *Sumer Is Icumen In*, the oldest piece of music extant with English words, composed at Reading Abbey in the 13th century; and documents concerning the Antarctic Expedition of Captain Scott (1910–12). Case Q: Early Medieval Biblical Manuscripts written in England. Case Q: Nelson's memorandum on naval tactics at Trafalgar (1805). Case P: The Alcuin Bible, a 9th-century copy of a Latin Bible revised in 796–801 by Alcuin of York, abbot of Tours. Case N: Early and Medieval Bindings. Case M: 15th-century books of Heraldry, a 14th–15th-century Greek copy of the Geography of Ptolemy (about A.D. 90–168), and an Anglo-Saxon map of the world of about A.D. 1000. Case K: The Wyclif Bible, the first to be written in English (about 1380). Case Y: Greek Papyri, including the unique MSS. of the Odes of Bacchylides, and the *Constitution of Athens* of Aristotle. Case Z: Latin Manuscripts, among them commentaries on the Book of Job by Pope Gregory the Great (8th century). Case J: Greek and Latin Biblical Manuscripts. Case I: Greek Manuscripts, and Royal Books, including the prayer book of Lady Jane Grey. Case H: Foreign Literary Autographs, notably sketch-books of Leonardo da Vinci and Dürer. Case G: Musical Manuscripts.

In the MAGNA CARTA ROOM, opening off the Manuscript Saloon, on the right, are shown some of the museum's most famous treasures: the *Codex Sinaiticus*, a 4th-century Greek manuscript of the Bible, purchased from the Soviet Government in 1933 for £100,000; the *Codex Alexandrinus*, a 5th-century Greek manuscript of the Bible; and the Lindisfarne Gospels, an exquisite illuminated manuscript believed to have been written about A.D. 700 by Eadfrith, bishop of Lindisfarne. Of the first importance also are a Bull of Pope Innocent III accepting the grant by King John of the kingdoms of England and Ireland to the Holy Roman Church (1214), the original articles of the Barons accepted by John as the basis of Magna Carta (1215), and two of the four surviving original copies of the Great Charter itself. Other cases contain a deed of mortgage bearing the signature of William Shakespeare (1613) and two original Log-Books of the *Victory*, Nelson's flagship at the battle of Trafalgar.

The BIBLE ROOM, on the right at the end of the Manuscript

Saloon, contains manuscripts and printed Bibles, illustrating the history of the Scriptures in Britain, and including the first printed English Bible (by Miles Coverdale, 1535).

On the left of the Central Saloon is the KING'S LIBRARY, a fine hall built to house the magnificent library of George III, the 65,000 volumes of which are in the cases ranged round the walls. The floor cases are used frequently for temporary exhibitions of books and manuscripts drawn from the museum's vast riches; otherwise they contain a fine selection of Oriental Manuscripts and early Printed Books. Notable among these are the Gutenberg Bible, printed about 1454, the first printed edition of Chaucer (1478), a first edition of Cranmer's Bible (1540), and the first folio edition of Shakespeare's plays (1623). In the centre of the hall is a statue of Shakespeare by Roubiliac (1758), bequeathed to the museum by the actor David Garrick, and at the north end are first editions of famous books and interesting collections of Postage Stamps.

The staircase beyond ascends to the upper Egyptian Rooms, the Ethnographical Gallery and the bridge to the King Edward VII Gallery. On its walls are mosaic pavements excavated from Roman buildings in Britain.

From the west side of the Entrance Hall the main staircase ascends to the UPPER FLOOR. On the right of a corridor containing Roman sepulchral tablets, etc., found in Britain is the temporary STONE AGE ROOM, which has Palaeolithic carvings and engravings, mostly from France, and stone tools from Mount Carmel and other well-known sites. To the west is the GREEK AND ROMAN TERRACOTTA ROOM, with Greek, Roman, and Etruscan terracottas and bronzes, and beyond this opens the delightful room devoted to GREEK AND ROMAN LIFE, containing also the museum's collections of classical jewellery, silver, and glass. Farther west is the Department of COINS AND MEDALS (compare p. 315), housing a million coins of all ages and countries.

The main corridor leads to a room (to be rebuilt) devoted to PREHISTORY AND ROMAN BRITAIN. Cases here hold further remains of the Roman occupation of Britain, including a fine Iron Age mirror found at Desborough (Northants), bronze wine vessels of the 4th–5th centuries B.C. from Lorraine, marble busts of the 2nd century from the Roman villa at Lullingstone (Kent), excavated in 1949, and late Roman glass vessels found at Burgh Castle (Suffolk). Other cases contain early Iron Age metalwork and part of the Snettisham Treasure, a hoard of pre-Roman coins and metalwork found near Sandringham (Norfolk). Of the several fine Roman helmets here, one was found in the Thames at Waterloo Bridge. Around the room is ranged a selection of prehistoric and Roman relics mainly found in Britain, among the most notable exhibits being the Neolithic pottery, the Bronze Age weapons, etc., including trumpets from Ireland and shields from Wales (all on the left), and the Celtic shield boss of about 200 B.C. found in the Thames at Wandsworth, the fine bronze shields of the early Iron Age from the Witham (Lincs) and the Thames near Battersea, and the beautiful MILDENHALL TREASURE, a 4th-century Roman silver hoard from Mildenhall (Suffolk), ploughed up in 1942, including a large embossed dish of exquisite craftsmanship. [Some of these objects may be seen in a temporary room to the right of the Chinese and Japanese Room (see below) until the rebuilding is complete.]

The next room is the ASIATIC SALOON, which contains rich collections of Islamic pottery, glassware, metalwork, ivories, etc. (notable are the Turkish faience and the enamelled glass mosque-lamps), textiles and antiquities from Central Asia (including paintings, etc., from Tibet), and weapons, textiles, ivories, wood carvings, etc., from Indonesia, Indo-China, Burma, and Ceylon, among them a remarkable gilt-bronze figure of the 9th or 10th century from Ceylon. The INDIAN ROOM, which follows, has a fine assembly of Buddhist sculpture and bronzes, intricately carved, including the base of a column from a 9th-century Jain temple (north India) and a slab of the 2nd century, carved on both sides, and other sculpture from the Amaravati shrine. Here also are seals and other antiquities from the Indus Valley (3rd millennium B.C.), a gold reliquary of the 1st century A.D. from a Buddhist shrine, etc. At the end is the CHINESE AND JAPANESE ROOM, containing characteristic antiquities and artistic objects from the Far East. Notable are the bronze, jade, and pottery of the T'ang and earlier periods from China, funerary vases, etc., from Japan and Korea, and exotic 18th–19th-century armour and beautiful collections of small ivories and lacquer work from Japan.

On the north of the Asiatic Saloon opens the long ETHNO-GRAPHICAL GALLERY, dealing with the life and culture of the primitive peoples of Africa, America, and the Pacific. It is divided into five bays, arranged according to geographical regions. The

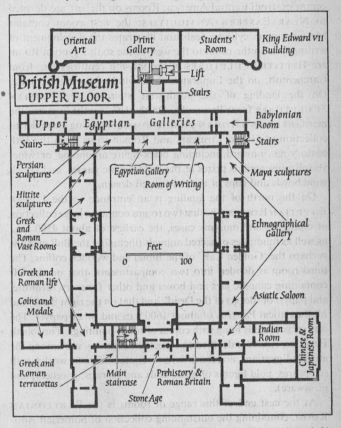

first bay covers Ancient Central and South America (on the left) and Mexico, the West Indies, and North America (right), the second and third bays are confined to the Pacific Islands, Australia, and New Zealand, the fourth bay to Central Africa, and the fifth bay to Modern America and Greenland (left) and South and East

Africa (right). Many of the most interesting exhibits are arranged down the centre of the gallery.

Beyond the gallery is the upper landing of the north-east staircase, which has a selection of MAYA SCULPTURE of the 4th–10th centuries, from Central America. Rooms on the left are devoted to NEAR EASTERN ANTIQUITIES; the first room contains Mesopotamian cylinder seals and illustrates the development of writing, and in the room to the west of the sixth Egyptian Room are HITTITE SCULPTURES of the 9th–8th centuries B.C. from Carchemish, on the Euphrates, the capital of the later empire. On the landing of the north-west staircase are PERSIAN SCULPTURES from Persepolis. On the left (south) here are the new GREEK AND ROMAN VASE ROOMS, containing a wonderful collection of Greek, Etruscan, and Roman vases from the 10th century B.C. onward, including black-figure amphorae or wine-vessels presented as prizes at the Panathenaic games, and Greek wine bowls and cups of the red-figured design.

On the north of the landing is an entrance to the UPPER EGYPTIAN ROOMS. The first two rooms contain a large collection of mummies and mummy cases, the earliest of about 4500 B.C., as well as mummies of sacred animals (including the Bull of Apis, perhaps the 'Golden Calf' of the Bible) and wooden coffins. The third room is divided into two compartments, that on the left containing canopic jars and boxes and other funerary furniture, and papyri of 'Books of the Dead', and that on the right the Rhind Mathematical Papyrus of about 1600 B.C. and other papyri. The central passage is hung with copies of tomb-paintings. The fourth Egyptian Room is devoted to objects in everyday use among the ancient Egyptians, and the fifth room contains artistic work (small sculptures, gold figures of gods, seals and scarabs, jewellery, and glassware).

At the east end of this range of rooms is the BABYLONIAN ROOM, containing the outstanding collection of Sumerian Antiquities from Ur of the Chaldees, dating from about 3500–1500 B.C. and largely excavated in 1919–34 by Sir Leonard Woolley. Among the many beautiful and interesting objects may be mentioned the reconstructed harp and silver lyre (in the wall case) and a shell and lapis-lazuli mosaic showing a Sumerian king in peace and war. On the east wall is a copper relief of a lion-headed eagle. Also in this room are early painted pottery, seals, tools, and weapons from western Asia and Babylonian writing tablets with cuneiform inscriptions.

From the Fourth Egyptian Room a corridor leads north to the KING EDWARD VII BUILDING, where a staircase goes up to the exhibition of Prints and Drawings and down to the King Edward VII Gallery. The corridor contains Coptic sculpture and remarkable mummy-portraits of the Roman period in Egypt.

The collection of PRINTS AND DRAWINGS, one of the largest and finest in the world, includes water-colours, woodcuts, engravings, and etchings. It is representative of every European school from the 15th century onward, and is particularly rich in British works. Only a small selection can be put on view in the gallery (the bulk of the collection is kept in the Students' Room, at the east end); changes are frequent, and special exhibitions are held from time to time. The west end of the gallery is devoted to an exhibition of ORIENTAL ART, changed regularly to illustrate the range and variety of the collections, which cover almost every aspect of Eastern art and are especially rich in Chinese and Japanese painting and Buddhist objects, and Persian and Indian miniatures.

The KING EDWARD VII GALLERY, on the lower floor of the building, is arranged to display a variety of the museum's most interesting and valuable possessions, and almost every object on view is worthy of detailed study. For the approaches to the gallery, see p. 316. Changes in the arrangement of the gallery are made from time to time, and the principal exhibits usually on view are grouped below according to provenance and period.

ETHNOGRAPHICAL COLLECTIONS of artistic interest from Africa, America, and Central Asia (east bay of gallery). Particularly notable are the wood carvings, ivories, and cast bronzes from Benin (West Africa) and the Congo, the Afro-Portuguese ivories, and from Mexico the ceremonial turquoise mosaic objects and a skull fashioned out of rock crystal, probably of the Aztec period.

ORIENTAL ANTIQUITIES (east section of main gallery; east end): Chinese pottery, porcelain, bronzes, silver, ivories, and jade from early times down to the Sung, Ming, and Ch'ing dynasties (including pottery, grave figures, and the figure of a lady, T'ang or earlier; ritual bronze vessels; and chariot fittings from Chin Ts'un, of the 4th century B.C.); Korean and Japanese porcelain and pottery, including Tea Ceremony pottery.

GREEK AND ROMAN ANTIQUITIES (east section of gallery; west end): Greek pottery, a fine selection, including examples of white ground red figure, and black figure ware; Greek and Phoenician perfume-pots and toilet vessels (7th–6th centuries B.C.); Greek, Etruscan, and Roman bronzes, ivories, amber, and pottery figures; fine Minoan, Mycenaean, and Etruscan jewellery; Greek and Italic terracottas; Greek and Roman glass gold and silver work, coins and medals, arms and armour, etc.; Etruscan wall-paintings; and Etruscan and Roman vases, coins, and pottery; Silver treasure of the late 4th century A.D. from the Esquiline Hill at Rome; Marble sarcophagus of the late 3rd century, probably from Italy, depicting the story of Jonah; Bronze heads of Apollo (about 460 B.C.; a beautiful sculpture formerly in the Duke of Devonshire's collections at Chatsworth) and of Hypnos, the god of sleep (Greek; late 4th century B.C.), of a Greek goddess, perhaps Aphrodite (2nd century B.C.), Sophocles (3rd century B.C.), and Augustus (d. A.D. 14); and the PORTLAND VASE, a Roman work of the 2nd century B.C. in the Greek style, consisting of two layers of opaque glass, the white which forms the design being cut away to reveal the blue background. It was smashed by an insane person in 1845, but has been carefully repaired.

BRITISH AND MEDIEVAL ANTIQUITIES (west section of gallery; east end). The antiquities from Britain include a gravestone of about A.D. 500 from Ivybridge (Devon) with inscriptions in Latin and Ogham characters; Stone from Trecastle (near Brecon) with Latin and Ogham characters; 9th-century cross-shaft with vine-scroll ornament from Sheffield; Anglo-Saxon art of Britain and Ireland, a fine selection including hanging-bowls from Saxon graves, the Franks Casket of carved whale's bone (Northumbrian, about A.D. 700), and the 10th-century Crosier of Kells; interesting and beautiful objects worked in gold, bronze, and enamel from the SUTTON HOO SHIP-BURIAL, the relics of an East Anglian chieftain of about A.D. 660, including his weapons, armour, and jewellery (Bay X); Viking grave-slab found in the City of London (11th century); Late-Saxon and medieval pottery; Religious art of the 10th–17th centuries; Set of 12th-century chessmen made in walrus ivory in the Isle of Lewis; 13th-century mosaic tile pavement from Byland Abbey (Yorks); Wall-paintings of about 1356 from St Stephen's Chapel in the Palace of Westminster; and English medieval arms and armour (notably the immense sword of state of Edward V when Prince of Wales).

Among the Medieval Antiquities are Early Christian pottery, ivories, silver, bronzes, tapestries, and glassware, including the Lycurgus Cup, a beautiful glass vessel of the 4th century; Late-antique and Byzantine jewellery and silver (compare p. 421), notably a 4th-century treasure from Carthage; Byzantine ivories and bronzes of the 7th–13th centuries; Early Germanic pottery, jewellery, etc., and Viking antiquities of the 4th–11th centuries; the remarkable 9th-century Lothar crystal; an exquisite little casket, German work of about 1200 with ivory panels illustrating the legend of Tristram and Iseult; Medieval jewellery and secular art; and the splendid ROYAL GOLD CUP of the kings of France and England, probably made in Paris in 1380 for the Duc de Berry and decorated with translucent enamels (Bay XXI).

LATER COLLECTIONS (west section of gallery; west end) include part of a hoard of 16th–17th-century jewellery, from Cheapside, the major portion of which is in the London Museum; 15th–16th-century Renaissance sculpture; Seals, coins, and medals, notably the Armada Medal struck for Elizabeth I (1589); Gems and cameos of the 15th–19th centuries; Abyssinian, Russian, and Jewish antiquities (17th–19th centuries); English and Continental pewter and silversmiths' work; English and Continental pottery and porcelain, including a fine selection of Italian majolica, Spanish and other earthenware (Delft, etc.), Lambeth 'Delft', English slip-ware, Bow porcelain, Staffordshire salt-glaze, and Wedgwood ware (medallions, etc.); and relics of famous persons. Here also is a fascinating assembly of CLOCKS AND WATCHES of the 15th–19th centuries, chiefly from the Ilbert Collection, including a clock shaped like a ship, made by Hans Schlottheim of Augsburg about 1580 for the Emperor Rudolph II; an ornate standing clock, with figures that move and strike the chimes, made in 1589 at Strasbourg, it is believed for Pope Sixtus V; a clock made in 1676 by Thomas Tompion, the most famous of British clock makers, for the Royal Observatory; long-case clocks made by Tompion and A. Fromanteel (the latter one of the first to use the 'bob'-pendulum); and a remarkable rolling-ball clock to the design of Sir William Congreve (about 1810).

The cases in the west bay contain the WADDESDON BEQUEST of Baron Rothschild (d. 1898), of Waddesdon Manor (Bucks). This fine bequest consists mainly of miscellaneous works of art of European origin of the 15th–17th centuries (pendants, cups, vases, caskets, enamels, etc.).

The staircase from the central entrance to the gallery descends to the NORTH ENTRANCE LOBBY, in which is displayed a selection of globes and maps, including Christopher Saxton's atlas of England and Wales (1579).

CHELSEA HOSPITAL Plan VII, F 2

STATION: SLOANE SQUARE, about ¼-m. NE., on the Circle and District lines. — MOTOR-BUSES No. 39 in Royal Hospital Road, on the N.; Nos. 11, 46, and 137 in Lower Sloane Street, to the NE.

ADMISSION to the MUSEUM and GROUNDS (free) and to the CHAPEL and GREAT HALL (gratuities expected), weekdays 10 to 12 and 2 to dusk (Sundays 2 to dusk only); to the COUNCIL CHAMBER, Saturdays 2 to 4 (in summer), and after the Parade Service on Sundays. — SERVICES in the chapel on Sundays at 8.30, 11 (Parade Service), and 11.45; visitors are admitted, but seats are often filled early.

THE ROYAL HOSPITAL, Chelsea, more familiarly known as Chelsea Hospital, is an institution for veteran and invalid soldiers founded in 1682 by Charles II. The establishment of a standing army during the Commonwealth had made the provision of a hospital, rather than a system of pensions or poor relief, imperative; the inspiration for the idea, however, came from the Hôtel des Invalides in Paris (founded by Louis XIV in 1670), and not from the king's mistress, Nell Gwyn, as was long popularly supposed. The buildings, mainly of brick, were designed by Sir Christopher Wren and consist of three ranges enclosing a quadrangle open towards the river Thames, with wings extending on the east and west. Here the in-pensioners, who at present number about 400, are lodged, boarded, and clothed; invalid pensioners are cared for in the recently-built infirmary, which has about 80 beds.

Built on the site of an unsuccessful theological college founded by James I in 1609, the hospital owes its inception largely to Sir Stephen Fox, the former paymaster-general, who contributed the bulk of the funds and undertook the responsibility for its management. The scheme was supported by John Evelyn, the diarist, and the site was chosen by Wren. The buildings were first opened in 1692, when nearly 500 pensioners were admitted, armed, clothed, and organized under a Governor and other officers. Under William III nearly one-third of the extensive hospital grounds was granted to the Earl of Ranelagh, the treasurer. Some alterations and additions to the buildings were made by Robert Adam in 1765–82 and again later by Sir John Soane, but the main block has remained practically unchanged. The hospital was struck by bombs several times during the war, when the fatal casualties included one centenarian pensioner.

The pensioners wear a uniform dating from the Duke of Marlborough's time: scarlet frock coats in the summer and dark blue overcoats in the winter. Forage caps are normally worn, but these are exchanged for three-cornered cocked hats on special occasions, such as Oak Apple Day (29 May), when the pensioners receive double rations in honour of their founder's birthday. Military duties are now practically confined to attendance at church and pay parades. Pensioners must be of good character and at least 65 years of age, unless they are unable to earn their own living, when they must be 55 (younger only if disabled during their term of service). On entering the hospital they surrender their out-pensions, but in return are provided with board, accommodation, and clothing, a daily ration of beer or tobacco, and, if necessary, a small weekly allowance. Each year before Christmas the pensioners are presented with a large cake by Australian comrades.

The usual entrance is from Royal Hospital Road by the LONDON GATE, on the north-east. On the left is the OLD BURIAL GROUND, consecrated in 1691 and closed in 1855. Dr Charles Burney (d. 1814), organist of the hospital from 1783 until his death, is buried here. The buildings on the east of the road, apart from the guardhouses of Wren, were mainly designed by Sir John Soane (1819) and include the Secretary's Office, with a

MUSEUM containing an interesting collection illustrating the history of the Royal Hospital, its pensioners and staff. Opposite the Office is the LIGHT HORSE COURT, named from the old cavalrymen who formerly occupied the southern of the two projecting wings added by Wren in 1688. The northern wing, comprising officers' quarters, was destroyed by bombing in 1945, but is to be rebuilt. In the centre of the court is a well-head protected by a fine wrought-iron cage with a lantern.

A passage at the north end of the main east range admits to the delightful FIGURE COURT, the central quadrangle, in the middle of which is a fine bronze statue of Charles II in Roman costume, by Grinling Gibbons. This is decorated with oak boughs on Oak Apple Day to commemorate the escape of the king from the Parliamentarians after the Battle of Worcester (1651) by hiding in an oak-tree. The north range of building is adorned with a cupola, and on the side facing the Figure Court has a large Doric portico flanked by low colonnades with pairs of columns. Between this portico and the main entrance, with its original massive doors, is an octagonal VESTIBULE, steps on either side of which ascend to the Chapel, on the east, and the Great Hall. In both of these visitors are shown round by pensioners.

The CHAPEL, which has panelled walls and a barrel vault, was completed by Wren in 1687 and has survived almost untouched since, except for the addition in 1920 of carved choir stalls, arranged unusually in the centre on either side of the nave. The older carving (including the fine reredos and altar-rails) is by William Emmett and William Morgan, the plasterwork by Henry Margetts. The spirited painting of the Resurrection, in the dome of the apse, is by Sebastiano Ricci (an Italian who lived in England about 1710–15) and was last restored in 1948. The notable plate bears the hall-mark for 1687–8; the altar cross was made to harmonize with it by Leslie Durbin (1953).

The panelled GREAT HALL, again serving its original purpose as a dining-hall, has royal portraits and copies of flags captured in 1793–1815 in France and the Netherlands and in 1812–15 from the Americans (the originals are preserved in the hospital). Over the dais at the west end is a large mural painting of Charles II on horseback, begun by Antonio Verrio but completed by Henry

Cooke; and on the tables are six 'blackjacks', great leather jugs from which beer was formerly served. The Duke of Wellington lay in state in this hall before his burial in St Paul's (1852).

In the main east and west ranges are the quarters of the pensioners, occupying the whole of the four floors. Each floor in both ranges is divided into two galleries or Long Wards, containing twenty-six berths or cubicles, one for each pensioner. Visitors may be shown these on application to the Adjutant. At the south end of the east range is the GOVERNOR'S HOUSE, which includes a council chamber beautifully decorated by Wren, with additions by Robert Adam, and hung with fine portraits by Van Dyck (Charles I and his family), Lely (Charles II), Kneller (William III), and others. From the SOUTH TERRACE, between the ends of the ranges, there is a good prospect of the hospital and the gardens stretching down to the Embankment in which the annual Chelsea Flower Show is held (compare Route 8). The guns displayed below the terrace include a battery captured at Waterloo.

The COLLEGE COURT, formerly the Infirmary Court, on the west of the hospital, is similar in design to the eastern court. Its northern wing has been converted into recreation rooms and a pensioners' club. The buildings on the farther side of the west road (which leads to the Chelsea Gate) are mainly by Soane (1809–22), but his Infirmary, which lay behind the Stable Yard, was destroyed in 1941 by a land mine, with much loss of life. Near the south end of the road is a greenhouse or orangery built by Vanbrugh about 1725 for Sir Robert Walpole. The house behind, built by Thomas Leverton, a pupil of Adam, has since been enlarged and converted into officers' quarters.

Entered from the east road of the hospital and now included in its grounds are the RANELAGH GARDENS (open to visitors), which formed part of the estate of the Earl of Ranelagh (d. 1712), and afterwards became a fashionable place of entertainment. The gardens were laid out afresh about 1860, and of the Rotunda and other 18th-century buildings no trace remains. On the north side of Royal Hospital Road is a large open space known as BURTON'S COURT (now a playing-field), on the farther side of which is the old main entrance to the hospital, with notable wrought-iron gates. The avenue across the court was intended as the beginning of a grand avenue leading direct to Kensington Palace.

HOUSES OF PARLIAMENT Plan VIII, C 3

STATION: WESTMINSTER, to the N., on the Circle and District lines. — MOTOR-BUSES in Whitehall, see Route 2; in Victoria Street, see Route 4;

along Millbank, see Route 3; across Westminster Bridge and along the Victoria Embankment, see Route 26.

ADMISSION to the Houses of Parliament and Westminster Hall on Saturdays, Easter Monday and Tuesday, Whit Monday and Tuesday, and each Monday and Tuesday in August, by the public entrance adjacent to the Victoria Tower, from 10 to 5 (free; no entrance after 4.30). Visitors may accompany the official guides, but will find it more leisurely to walk round by themselves. Westminster Hall is open also on weekdays (except Good Friday and Christmas Day) from 10 until one hour before the House of Commons meets (see below), from 10 to 4 (Saturdays to 5) when the House is not sitting, and the entrance is then by the north door of the hall. Visitors may also be conducted round the Houses of Parliament under the escort of a member, in which case they generally see parts of the building not accessible to the ordinary visitor. 'Tea on the Terrace' with a member is a favoured social occasion.

The HOUSE OF COMMONS normally meets on Monday–Thursday at 2.30 p.m. and on Friday at 11 a.m. Visitors are admitted to the gallery (reached via St Stephen's Porch), by order from a member, between 2.30 and 3 (11 and 11.30 on Fridays), or on application at the Admission Order Office in St Stephen's Hall after 4.15 (Friday after 11.30) until the house rises (see p. 343). In the latter case there is often some delay, and Commonwealth and foreign visitors will find it preferable to apply to their representatives in London for an introduction. The HOUSE OF LORDS usually meets on Tuesdays and Wednesdays at 2.30 and on Thursdays at 3 p.m. Visitors must await outside St Stephen's Porch (Old Palace Yard side; or in Westminster Hall during inclement weather) and are admitted to the Strangers' Gallery (limited accommodation) at 2.40 (Thursdays at 4.10). They are also admitted by permits obtainable from a member or officer of either house, and when the House of Lords is sitting as a Court of Appeal (usually in the morning).

The HOUSES OF PARLIAMENT, officially the New Palace of Westminster, the seat of the supreme legislature in Great Britain and Northern Ireland, is a rambling but dignified pile of buildings in an elaborate late-Gothic style, bordering the river Thames and close to Westminster Bridge. Designed by Sir Charles Barry (who was assisted in the details by A. W. Pugin), it was begun in 1840 and the first parliament here was opened by Queen Victoria in 1852. After the death of the architect in 1860 the work was continued under the direction of his son, Edward M. Barry, and finally completed in 1888. The stone used for the exterior was magnesian limestone from Anston, in Yorkshire, but it has failed to stand up to the exacting London climate and is constantly in need of repair. The building, which cost over £3 million, covers an area of about 8 acres and has 11 courtyards, 100 staircases, over 1000 apartments, and about 2 miles of passages. Besides the House of Commons, in the northern part, and the House of Lords, in the southern part, it contains innumerable offices, committee rooms, libraries, dining-rooms, etc., as well as the residences of the Speaker of the House of Commons, the Serjeant at Arms, and other officers, and incorporates Westminster Hall and the crypt of St Stephen's Chapel, practically the only parts of the former royal palace to survive the fire which destroyed the previous building.

At the south-west corner of the building rises the VICTORIA TOWER, completed in 1858, the largest and loftiest square tower in the world, with 75-ft sides and reaching 336 ft to the tops of the pinnacles. The archway, 50 ft high, below the tower is that through which the sovereign enters on the State opening of Parliament (generally the second week in November). Adjacent is the usual visitors' entrance, and in the richly decorated façade fronting Old Palace Yard is the ornate porch of the Peers' Entrance. The CENTRAL SPIRE, which has an open lantern serving as the mouth of a ventilating shaft, rises to 300 ft above the ground. On the north of Old Palace Yard is ST STEPHEN'S PORCH, recast by J. L. Pearson in 1888, and farther north is WESTMINSTER HALL, the only remaining part of the medieval building (except St Stephen's Crypt and the Jewel Tower). The north front of the hall (likewise altered by Pearson) faces NEW PALACE YARD, in which is the members' entrance to the House of Commons. The façade of the main building is embellished with niches containing statues of English monarchs, and the north side of the yard is shaded by old catalpa-trees.

At the north end of the building stands the splendid CLOCK TOWER, the finial above the lantern of which rises to 320 ft. A light in the tower by night and a flag on the Victoria Tower by day indicate that the House of Commons is sitting. The clock, famous for the accuracy of its time-keeping, has four dials each 23 ft in diameter, with figures 2 ft high and hands 14 and 9 ft long. The pendulum, which beats once every two seconds, is 13 ft long and weighs 685 lb. The hours are struck on the great bell of 'Big Ben' (a name often misapplied to the clock or even the tower),

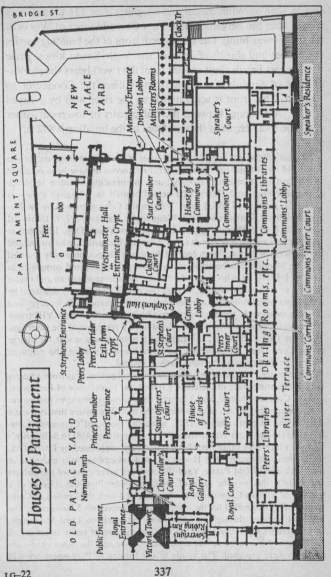

cast in 1858 at Whitechapel and weighing over 13½ tons. It was named after Sir Benjamin Hall, First Commissioner of Works at the time it was hung. The short north front of the building carries the statues and shields-of-arms of the Anglo-Saxon kings, while the fine east façade (best viewed from the river) bears the shields-of-arms of English sovereigns from William the Conqueror to Victoria. This front is separated from the river wall by a paved terrace, 700 ft long, between the noble pairs of towers at either end. The total length of the east front of the building is 872 ft.

As their official title suggests, the Houses of Parliament stand on the site of the old royal Palace of Westminster, first known to have been occupied by Edward the Confessor (1042–66) and the principal London residence of the sovereign until Henry VIII helped himself to Whitehall Palace in 1529. The palace was added to by William the Conqueror and by his successor William Rufus, who built Westminster Hall in 1097–9. Henry III gave a feast to 6,000 poor people here on New Year's Day, 1236, but in 1299 the hall was largely rebuilt (after a fire) by Richard II, who introduced the magnificent hammerbeam roof. St Stephen's Chapel, originally founded by King Stephen, was begun anew by Edward I in 1292 and completed in 1346 by Edward III, who founded a college, consisting of a dean and twelve canons, in connexion with it. In 1512 the palace was gravely damaged by a fire from which only Westminster Hall and the chapel with its crypt and cloisters escaped. It was never entirely rebuilt, and after Henry VIII transferred his loyalties to Whitehall it ceased to be a residence of the sovereign. The New Palace, however, still ranks as a royal palace, under the charge of the Lord Great Chamberlain, an office hereditary since the reign of Henry I in the family of De Vere, Earls of Oxford.

Westminster Hall, as the great hall of the royal palace, was from an early date the meeting-place of the Great Council, the predecessor of Parliament and the Courts of Justice, and it became the custom to proclaim parliament here, though few in fact actually met in the hall. The palace first became a regular seat of parliament in 1547, when the House of Commons transferred its sittings from Westminster Abbey (compare p. 458) to St Stephen's Chapel, which (like other free chapels) had been suppressed by Edward VI. From the 16th century the House of Lords assembled in a chamber at the south end of Old Palace Yard (formerly an inner court of the palace) and in 1605 this was the scene of the Gunpowder Plot, the attempt of a number of Roman Catholics to blow up James I with the Lords and Commons as they assembled for the opening of Parliament on 5 November. The plot was revealed through an anonymous letter sent to Lord Monteagle, and the cellars were searched; Guy Fawkes, discovered ready to set fire to the barrels of gunpowder, was captured. Fawkes and the other chief conspirators were executed. The vaults of the Houses of Parliament are still formally searched by Yeomen of the Guard each year before the State opening of the session by the sovereign.

In 1834 the palace was burned to the ground, with the exception of Westminster Hall, the chapel crypt, part of the cloisters, and the Jewel Tower (p. 108). A new building for the legislature was decided on and in 1836 the design of Charles Barry was selected from ninety-seven entered in open competition. The river wall, built of Aberdeen granite, was completed in 1840, the Lords moved into their new home in 1847, and the building was officially opened with the occupation of the new House of Commons in 1852. The buildings were damaged on fourteen occasions during the Second World War, the most serious attack, on 10 May 1941, resulting in the destruction of the House of Commons. A new chamber, designed by Sir Giles Gilbert Scott in keeping with the older work, was opened in 1950.

Under the Victoria Tower the sovereign is met by the high officers of state at the official opening of Parliament. Visitors, entering by an adjacent door, follow the route of the procession up the ROYAL STAIRCASE, which leads to the NORMAN PORCH, so called from the intention to embellish it with statues of Norman sovereigns and frescoes illustrating that period of history. The carved and groined vault is supported by a clustered central pillar. On the right is the entrance to the QUEEN'S ROBING ROOM, 54 ft long, the first of several handsome rooms finely decorated in the style of the period. It was adapted as the meeting-place of the Lords in 1941–51. On the walls is a series of frescoes by William Dyce of episodes from the Legend of King Arthur, illustrative of the spirit of chivalry, while around the room runs an oak dado with a series of carved panels, by H. H. Armstead, also depicting Arthurian legends. The ceiling, likewise panelled, is decorated with the badges of the sovereigns of England; the fireplace of variegated marble and the metalwork of the doors are also worthy of note. At the farther end, beneath a rich canopy, is a chair of state of Queen Victoria.

The next room entered is the ROYAL GALLERY, an imposing hall 110 ft long, with an elaborate ceiling. Around the frieze are the shields-of-arms of the monarchs of England and Scotland, and on the long walls are two huge frescoes by Daniel Maclise: the Death of Nelson (on the left) and the Meeting of Wellington and Blücher after Waterloo, executed in 1858–65. The bronze-gilt statues of English monarchs from Alfred to Queen Anne are by J. B. Philip, and the portraits of more recent sovereigns and their consorts include Queen Victoria and Prince Albert by Winterhalter, Edward VII and Queen Alexandra by Sir Luke Fildes, and George V and Queen Mary by Sir William Llewellyn. In an alcove near the south end is the war memorial, by John Tweed, to peers and officers of the House of Lords and their sons who fell in the two World Wars. The gallery contains a model of the old Westminster Palace at the time of Henry VIII.

Beyond is the PRINCE'S CHAMBER, an ante-room to the House of Lords, with dark panelling, probably in the manner of its medieval forerunner. In the wainscoting are portraits of the Tudor monarchs and their royal and noble relatives, and below these are twelve bronze bas-reliefs by William Theed of events in their reigns. Opposite the entrance is a white marble statue by John Gibson of Queen Victoria, enthroned between Justice and Clemency.

Doors on either side admit to the HOUSE OF LORDS, a noble Gothic hall, 80 ft long, elaborately decorated by A. W. Pugin. On either side are the red leather benches of the peers, who at present number about 920, and at the south end, raised on a dais and covered by a richly carved and gilded canopy, is the ornate throne of the queen. When the sovereign is a king, a second throne, slightly lower, stands on the right for his consort. At the opening of Parliament this space contains the state chair of the Duke of Edinburgh, while the compartment on the left was designed for that of the Prince of Wales. In front of the throne is the Woolsack, a plain ottoman stuffed with wool from the British countries and the Commonwealth, occupied during the sitting of the House by the Lord Chancellor, who is its president, with the mace behind him. The woolsack, which by tradition has stood in the house since the time of Edward III, is a reminder of the days when the wealth of England depended to a great extent on its thriving wool trade. The two smaller woolsacks beyond the Chancellor's woolsack are occupied by the judges at the opening of Parliament, and in front of them is the Table of the House, in which motions for discussion are placed ('tabled'). At the north end of the chamber is the Bar, where lawsuits on final appeal are pleaded (see below) and where the Commons, headed by their Speaker, attend on ceremonial occasions. Above the north entrance is the Reporters'

Gallery, with the Strangers' Gallery behind; and above the throne on either side are galleries for Distinguished Visitors.

The six recesses behind the galleries are decorated with frescoes that are notable as the first examples of large wall-paintings by British artists. Those on the south, of events in British history, are by C. W. Cope and William Dyce; those at the north end, by Daniel Maclise and J. C. Horsley, symbolize Justice, Religion, and Chivalry. The windows on either side, restored after war damage, contain stained glass by Carl Edwards showing the armorial bearings of peers from 1360 to 1900, while the niches around the chamber are filled with statues of the barons who extorted Magna Carta from King John. The chamber was used by the House of Commons (compare below) in 1941–50.

Compared with the House of Commons, procedure in the House of Lords is relatively simple and sittings are rarely lengthy. After prayers (conducted by a bishop) and a few questions, the house goes on to the examination of a bill or (if a member has 'moved for papers') to a debate on a topical subject or a matter of policy. Divisions are infrequent, but on these occasions the peers file into the lobbies on either side, where they record a vote of 'Content' or 'Not Content'. The House of Lords is also the final Court of Appeal for all courts in Great Britain and Northern Ireland.

Beyond the House of Lords, and entered through solid brass gates, is the PEERS' LOBBY, a square chamber with a pavement of fine encaustic tiles. Over the four doors are painted the arms of the six royal lines of England (Saxon, Norman, Plantagenet, Tudor, Stewart, and Hanoverian) with the initial letters of each carved below, and above the south door are the royal arms and motto, and the coats of arms of England, Scotland, and Ireland. The door on the west leads to the Peers' Robing Room, while that on the east gives access to the House of Lords' Library, but these parts of the palace are not normally shown to visitors.

The PEERS' CORRIDOR, painted with eight frescoes by C. W. Cope of episodes in the Stewart and Commonwealth periods, leads north to the CENTRAL LOBBY, an elaborately decorated octagonal vestibule, 60 ft across and 75 ft high, with a vaulted stone ceiling that supports the central spire of the palace. The spaces between the embossed ribs of the vault are filled with Venetian glass mosaics showing royal emblems. Over the doors are mosaics of the British patron saints, SS. George and David, designed by Sir Edward Poynter and executed by Salviati (1870–98), and SS. Andrew and Patrick, designed by R. Anning Bell and executed by Gertrude Martin (1923–4). The niches round the doors and windows contain statues of the Plantagenet sovereigns and their consorts, and on pedestals are statues of Victorian statesmen. In the pavement of encaustic tiles is the text, in Latin from the Vulgate, 'Except the Lord keep the house, they labour in vain that build it'.

The Central Lobby marks the division between the precincts of the Lords and those of the Commons. Any visitor who has business with a member when Parliament is sitting is admitted to the lobby, where he fills in a 'card' and hands it to one of the policemen on duty.

The COMMONS' CORRIDOR, which has eight paintings by E. M. Ward of incidents in the Commonwealth and Restoration periods, runs north to the COMMONS' LOBBY, a square Gothic chamber with statues of 20th-century statesmen. The door on the east gives access to the House of Commons' Library, etc. (no general admission). On the north is the CHURCHILL ARCH, made from stones damaged in the fire of 1941 and erected here at the suggestion of Sir Winston Churchill in memory of those who 'kept the bridge' during the dark days of the War.

The door beyond the arch admits to the HOUSE OF COMMONS, completely destroyed by fire in the air-raid of 10 May 1941, and rebuilt in a free adaptation of the late-Gothic style by Sir Giles Gilbert Scott. The new chamber, begun in 1948 and opened in 1950, has the same floor length as the old (68 ft), but is longer above the gallery level (now 103 ft). At the north end is the chair of black bean wood (the gift of Australia) of the Speaker, who presides over the House, and in front of it is the Table, of Canadian oak, on which the mace rests while the House is sitting (when the House is 'in Committee', however, the mace is placed under the table and the Speaker vacates his chair). The despatch boxes were presented by New Zealand, the three clerks' chairs by South Africa, and the Serjeant at Arms' chair by Ceylon, and many of the other furnishings are gifts also from the Commonwealth; the woodwork around the chamber is of oak from Shropshire. On either side of the 'floor' of the House are the green hide benches of the members, with seats for 437 (as before), though there are now 630 members. The party in office occupies the benches to the right of the Speaker, the front bench being reserved for cabinet ministers and the Prime Minister taking the seat opposite the despatch box. Facing are the seats of the opposition, whose leaders likewise occupy the front benches. On the floor before the benches are two red lines (by tradition two sword-lengths apart) across which members must not step while in debate. On the back of the Speaker's chair is a bag in which petitions to Parliament are placed; above it is the Press Gallery and at the other end of the chamber is the Public Gallery. The coats of arms below the galleries are those of members of the House who lost their lives in the two World Wars.

The House is opened each day with a procession in which the Speaker (in his traditional dress of knee breeches and long black gown) is preceded by a messenger (wearing a House of Commons badge, dating from 1755) and the Serjeant at Arms, who carries the mace (the symbol of authority), and is followed by his train-bearer, chaplain, and secretary. On Monday–Thursday, after prayers (read by the chaplain) and 'questions' addressed to ministers, public business begins about 3.30 and consists of the presentation of bills and the moving of motions, followed by the 'Orders of the Day', which include the discussion of public bills and certain motions. Visitors should obtain a copy of the official guide containing the procedure and the agenda of the day's business, from a messenger. If a division is taken, members voting 'aye' file out behind the Speaker's chair into the lobby on his right, while those voting 'no' pass out at the other end of the chamber to the lobby on his left, where they are counted in each case by two members called 'tellers'. The Speaker (unlike the Chancellor in the House of Lords) cannot vote. Business is normally suspended by order at 10 p.m. and a debate of a general nature on a 'motion for the adjournment' then takes place for half an hour, after which the house rises. The sitting of the House may be extended after the 10 o'clock order, however, for business of a special character (financial bills, etc.). Friday is generally devoted to private members' bills; questions are not usually asked, and the house rises at about 4.30 p.m.

In the No Lobby are three volumes of the journals of the house open to show the record of significant events in parliamentary history: the Commons' protestation of their rights and privileges torn out by James I (1621), the attempted arrest by Charles I in the House of the five members he had impeached of high treason (1642), and the forcible expelling of the Rump Parliament by Oliver Cromwell (1653).

The return is made to the Central Lobby, where the door on the right (west) admits to ST STEPHEN'S HALL, a lofty vaulted chamber, 95 ft long, on the exact site of the royal chapel of St Stephen, and the meeting-place of the House of Commons from

1547 until the fire of 1834. The name 'St Stephen's' is still sometimes used as a synonym for the House of Commons. Over the
doors are large mosaics by R. Anning Bell and Gertrude Martin
relating to the original founding of the chapel by King Stephen
(east end) and the completion of its rebuilding by Edward III.
In niches at the angles of the hall are statues of the Norman and
Plantagenet kings and queens, and pedestals support statues of
British statesmen of the 17th–19th centuries. The windows contain
the arms of Parliamentary cities and boroughs, and the panels
below them hold paintings, unveiled in 1927, depicting the Building of Britain (877–1707).

Steps lead down to ST STEPHEN'S PORCH, which discloses an
impressive view along the length of Westminster Hall. The large
window on the left formerly closed the south end of the hall, but
it was set back in its present position by Barry. The stained glass
of service badges and armorial bearings or monograms of
members, by Sir Ninian Comper (1953), together with the sculptured frieze below, by Sir Bertram Mackennal (1922), form the
war memorials to members and officers of both Houses of Parliament.

WESTMINSTER HALL, the oldest and chief survival of the
medieval palace of Westminster, is a noble and beautiful hall
nearly 240 ft long, 68 ft wide, and 92 ft high to the centre of the
roof. Built originally in 1097–9 by William II, it was practically
rebuilt by Richard II in 1394–9. The architect was Henry Yevele,
who designed the naves of Westminster Abbey and Canterbury
Cathedral; the splendid hammerbeam roof of twelve bays, the
finest of its kind in the world, was largely the work of Hugh Her-
land, master-carpenter to Edward III. The oak is believed to have
come from Wadhurst, in Sussex, and the delightful angels which
form the ends of the beams were carved by Robert Grassington.
The lantern was redesigned in 1822 on a smaller scale by Sir John
Soane, and the roof, which has the largest unsupported span in
the country, was completely restored in 1914–23, using timber
from the original source, to overcome the ravages of the death-
watch beetle. Four bays of the roof greatly damaged in 1941 have
again been restored. In niches and window recesses of the south
and east walls are late-14th-century statues of kings, and below the

windows is a string-course displaying the chained-hart badge of Richard II.

The chief courts of English law sat in the hall from the late 13th century until 1825 and then in new adjoining buildings until 1882, when the new Courts of Justice were opened in the Strand. The 19th-century buildings were then pulled down and the west front restored by J. L. Pearson.

The hall has witnessed many grave and stirring events in English history. Sir William Wallace, the Scottish patriot, was condemned to death in the old hall in 1305, and here Edward II was forced to abdicate in 1327. One of the first events to take place in the new hall of Richard II was, oddly enough, the deposition of that king in 1399 in favour of Henry IV. The hall has been the scene of many important state trials, and among those condemned to death here have been Perkin Warbeck (1498), Sir Thomas More and Bishop Fisher (1535), Lord Protector Somerset (1551), the Earl of Essex (1601), Guy Fawkes and seven of his fellow conspirators (1606), and the Earl of Strafford (1641). The most memorable event was perhaps the condemnation of Charles I in 1649, and a tablet on the steps (actually constructed by Barry) marks approximately the place where the king sat during his trial. Oliver Cromwell was installed as Lord Protector here in 1653, and in 1661, after his body had been exhumed from Westminster Abbey, his head was set up on a pole on the roof of the hall, where it remained until 1684. Titus Oates, the conspirator, was convicted of perjury in the hall in 1685, and here in 1688 the seven bishops who refused to proclaim the declaration of indulgence of James II were acquitted by a jury. The Earl of Derwentwater and others who revolted in 1715 were condemned here, as were Lord Lovat and the Jacobite lords of 1745. Warren Hastings was here acquitted of the charge of impeachment after a trial extending over seven years (1788–95). The last public trial in the hall was that of Viscount Melville in 1806 for the corrupt administration of navy funds. Feasts preceding their coronations were given in the hall by kings from Stephen to George IV, and until the time of James II it was the custom for the monarch to proceed by river from the Tower for the occasion. Several recent sovereigns and their consorts lay in state in the hall.

From the south-east angle of Westminster Hall a staircase descends to ST STEPHEN'S CRYPT or the chapel of St Mary Undercroft. This was in fact the crypt of St Stephen's Chapel; completed in 1327, it escaped the fire of 1834. It was rather too elaborately painted and gilded in 1868 by E. M. Barry, but the clustered columns of Purbeck marble, the fine early lierne vault, and the carved bosses depicting the martyrdoms of saints are interesting. The chapel is used for marriages of M.P.s (of whatever persuasion) and the christenings of their children. Another staircase leads up from the west end to Old Palace Yard.

St Stephen's Cloisters, to the east of Westminster Hall, are now used as a cloakroom by members and are not generally accessible to visitors. Built in 1526–9, they are remarkable for their fan-vaulted ceiling, rivalling that of Henry VII's Chapel in Westminster Abbey. An oratory opening from the west walk contains a richly-carved mahogany table used in the House of Commons from about 1730 until 1834. The south and east sides of the cloisters, severely damaged in 1940, have been finely restored in their former style.

IMPERIAL WAR MUSEUM Plan IX, D 2

Stations: Lambeth North, ⅓-m. NW., on the Bakerloo line Elephant & Castle, nearly ½-m. E., on the Bakerloo and Northern lines. — Motor-Buses in Lambeth Road, see Route 35; Nos. 3, 59, 109, 155, 159, 163, and 172 in Kennington Road (W. of the museum); Nos. 12, 53, 153, 171, 177, and 184 in St George's Road (E. of the museum). No. 10 from Victoria Station and Nos. 10 and 44 from London Bridge Station pass the museum entrance.

Admission weekdays 10 to 6; Sundays 2 to 6 (free). Closed on Good Friday and Christmas Day. The Library and other reference sections (see below) are open on Monday–Friday 10 to 5.

The Imperial War Museum, established after the First World War and transferred to its present building at Lambeth in 1936, records and illustrates in every aspect all the campaigns in which the armed forces of Britain and the Commonwealth have been engaged since August 1914. Apart from typical examples of the actual material and equipment used by the Royal Navy, the Army, the Royal Air Force, and other services, the museum contains numerous models, paintings, and sculptures, and relics of famous war leaders. In addition, it has valuable reference sections of books, maps, photographs, films, etc., accessible to students.

The creation of a national war museum was approved by the War Cabinet in 1917 and the museum was first opened in 1920 at the Crystal Palace. It was housed in part of the Imperial Institute at South Kensington from 1924 until 1935, and in the following year it was removed to its present home in what was originally the central portion of the Bethlem Royal Hospital for the insane, designed in 1812–15 by James Lewis and given its imposing portico and lofty dome in 1846 by Sydney Smirke. The hospital was transferred to new buildings near Croydon (Surrey) in 1930 and the wings of the old building were subsequently demolished, with the result that the dome now looks top heavy. The building suffered considerable damage from bombing but new galleries are brought into use as they are restored. Only a proportion of the museum's possessions can be displayed, and in consequence the disposition of the exhibits is liable to be altered. The museum also arranges special temporary exhibitions designed to develop particular themes or mark notable occasions.

From the Entrance Hall a staircase descends to the large Centre Gallery, which is divided into three sections where most of the larger exhibits can be seen. The corridors running east and west of the Entrance Hall give access to a series of smaller rooms, mostly devoted to special exhibits, and lead to the Picture Galleries in each wing.

WARFARE AT SEA is illustrated by a fine collection of models of naval and merchant ships, submarines, and transport and landing craft which have taken part in war at sea since 1914. Also exhibited are an actual German one-man submarine and an Italian 'human torpedo', both used in the Second World War, the first German magnetic mine recovered intact by the British in 1939, and the gun which Boy Jack Cornwell was firing when he won the Victoria Cross at the Battle of Jutland in 1916. The collection also includes naval uniform and battleship badges; arms, equipment, etc., of the Royal Marines; and models of the landing at Walcheren (Holland) and the 'Mulberry' harbour prefabricated for the invasion of Normandy, in 1944.

WARFARE ON LAND is shown by the extensive display of field, machine, and anti-aircraft guns, and other ordnance and small arms, models of the battlefields of 1914–18, equipment used in the trenches in the First World War, a French Renault light tank of 1918, and models of other armoured fighting vehicles of both wars, and the 'home-made' rifles used by the Mau Mau in Central Africa. The 13-pounder gun which fired the first British round in France in August 1914 is shown near the naval gun from H.M.S. *Lance* which fired Britain's opening shot at sea in the same month.

AIR WARFARE from its origins to the present day is demonstrated by a comprehensive collection of aircraft models showing most of the main types used by the combatant powers since 1914. The aircraft in the museum's collection include several which took part in the First World War, a Spitfire that flew in the defence of London during the Battle of Britain, and German military aircraft (Heinkel 162 and Messerschmitt 163B). Other exhibits include cockpit sections of a Lancaster bomber, a Typhoon fighter, and a Japanese 'Zeke', a German V1 flying-bomb on part of its launching-ramp, and a German V2 rocket.

Special sections are devoted to the Home Guard, Civil Defence, and the Fire Service; the Fleet Air Arm and the Air-Sea Rescue Service; the part played by women in the two World Wars; a fine display of the uniforms of Britain, her allies, and her enemies in both wars; British and foreign decorations and medals; and a variety of equipment ranging from aero-engines to escape devices evolved by prisoners of war. Models, maps, photographs, etc., showing the campaigns and battles of the Second World War, include relief maps made for Sir Winston Churchill. Among the many personal relics and souvenirs are the uniforms of Field-Marshals Earl Haig and Viscount Montgomery and Admiral of the Fleet Earl Mountbatten.

The PICTURE GALLERIES contain a selection of the museum's 9,000 paintings, drawings, and prints, a remarkable record of the two World Wars as they affected all who were engaged in them. They are the work of the leading British artists, the majority of whom were employed by the government for this purpose. There are important groups of paintings by Sir William Orpen, Sir John Lavery, John S. Sargent, C. R. W. Nevinson, Wyndham Lewis, Paul Nash, Dame Laura Knight, and others; drawings by Muirhead Bone, James McBey, Eric Kennington, John Piper, Vivian Pitchforth, Feliks Topolski, etc.; and sculpture by Sir Jacob Epstein (notably a fine head of Sir Winston Churchill), Sir Charles Wheeler, and others. The landing above the south staircase has panels of Shipbuilding on the Clyde, by Stanley Spencer, and paintings illustrating the Peace Conferences of 1919, and the staircase is hung with portraits of military leaders in the Second World War.

Any painting or sculpture not on view may usually be seen on advance application to the Keeper of the Art Department. The REFERENCE LIBRARY comprises a unique collection of over 90,000 books, periodicals, and works in manuscript, in many languages, dealing with the World Wars, not only in their military aspect, but also from the social, economic, and political points of view. The Dome, originally designed as a chapel, is now being refitted (1963) as a reading room. The Film Library contains thousands of miles of cinematograph films and the Photographic Library has some 3 million photographs, both official and unofficial, from allied and enemy sources.

KENSINGTON PALACE AND THE LONDON MUSEUM Plan VI, A 1

STATIONS: QUEENSWAY, nearly ½-m. N., on the Central line; BAYS-WATER, over ½-m. N., NOTTING HILL GATE, over ½-m. NW., and HIGH STREET, KENSINGTON, ¾-m. SW., all on the Circle and District lines. Notting Hill Gate is also on the Central line. — MOTOR-BUSES in Kensington Road, see Route 11; in Bayswater Road, see Route 12.

ADMISSION to the STATE APARTMENTS and the LONDON MUSEUM, weekdays 10 to 6 (October–February to 4); Sundays ¦from 2 (free). Closed on Good Friday, Christmas Eve, and Christmas Day.

KENSINGTON PALACE, which stands on the extreme west side of Kensington Gardens (Route 12), was the principal private residence of the sovereign from 1689 until 1760 and the birthplace of Queen Victoria. Partly rebuilt as a country house for William III by Sir Christopher Wren, it was added to by William Kent to make a more palatial residence for George I. The palace may be approached by the drive leading south from the Orme Square Gate in Bayswater Road, or from the Palace Gate in Kensington Road by the Broad Walk. The State Apartments, on the first floor, were reopened to the public, after extensive restoration, in 1956. Rooms on the ground floor and in the basement are the home of the LONDON MUSEUM, illustrating the history and social life of the capital from the earliest times. Only a comparatively small part of the collections can be displayed here, but material not on view is made available to students and interested visitors, as far as possible, on application to the Director.

Originally named Nottingham House, the palace was built after 1661 by Lord Chancellor Finch, later the first Earl of Nottingham. In 1689 it was purchased from the second Earl by William III, who employed Wren to make many alterations and additions; the south wing, completed by about 1695, is the most notable surviving part of his work. The palace was further enlarged by Kent in 1718–26 for George I, and it remained the sovereign's chief residence until the death of George II here in 1760. Mary II (1694), William III (1702), and Queen Anne (1714) also died here, and Princess Victoria, born in the palace in 1819, lived here until the day in 1837 when she was roused from her bed in the early hours to hear the news of her accession. Queen Mary, the wife of George V, was likewise born in the palace (1867), which except for the State Apartments and the rooms taken by the London Museum is now occupied by relatives of the royal family and aristocratic pensioners of the Crown.

The STATE APARTMENTS, entered at the north-east corner of the building, include some simple but skilful rooms by Wren and other more ostentatious rooms by Kent, in which are hung numerous portraits by Kneller and other 18th-century artists, from the royal collection. The rooms in which Queen Victoria lived before her accession contain numerous mementoes of her, assembled by Queen Mary, as well as furniture and small works of art from the collection of Queen Mary herself. In addition there are royal costumes on view from the excellent collection of the London Museum.

The QUEEN'S STAIRCASE, designed by Wren about 1690, ascends to the QUEEN'S GALLERY, which is panelled in oak and has two fine carved and gilded mirrors on the chimney-pieces. The small rooms beyond were used as private apartments by Mary II and Anne: the QUEEN'S CLOSET and the QUEEN'S DINING ROOM, which preserves its original panelling, contain relics of later queens. The QUEEN'S PRIVY CHAMBER, beyond, contains portraits by Lely, and an elaborate writing-desk of the late 17th century forms a striking centrepiece in the QUEEN'S BEDROOM, the adjacent chamber. The QUEEN'S DRAWING ROOM, farther on, is the first of the rooms decorated by Kent (1724); the windows face across the Clock Court to Wren's charming gate-tower in the west wing. The CUPOLA ROOM, on the left, has a coved ceiling painted to simulate a coffered dome, niches with gilded statuary (probably Italian), and a fine bas-relief by Rysbrack depicting a Roman marriage, over the fireplace. In the centre is a remarkable clock, the 'Temple of the Four Monarchies', made about 1730 for the Princess of Wales, mother of George III, with scenes on its four sides showing rulers of Assyria, Persia, Greece, and Rome. The KING'S DRAWING ROOM, which affords a view of Kensington Gardens, contains several paintings by Benjamin West and the Coronation robes of George V and Queen Mary (1911). The KING'S PRIVY CHAMBER, on the left, and QUEEN VICTORIA'S BEDROOM, on the right, were altered in the early 19th century and now contain many mementoes of the queen, to which have been added some of the treasures gathered by Queen Mary. It was from the Bedroom that the young Princess Victoria was called to learn of the death of William

IV and of her own accession. In the ANTE-ROOM beyond are toys and the doll's house of the princess, and in the NURSERY a piano that belonged to the Prince Consort.

KING WILLIAM'S GALLERY, 96 ft long, on the south side of the palace, was designed by Wren (1694) and has contemporary wood-carving, probably by Grinling Gibbons, and a ceiling painted in 1725 by Kent ('Adventures of Ulysses'). On the walls is a fine selection of paintings of London of the 18th and early 19th centuries (by Samuel Scott and others), and above the marble chimney-piece is a map of north-west Europe showing the king's possessions (painted in 1694 by Richard Norden), with a compass whose pointer is operated by a wind-vane on the roof. A short passage on the right at the end admits to the KING'S STAIR-CASE, partly by Wren, but with an iron balustrade by Jean Tijou and walls painted to represent a gallery by Kent. The PRESENCE CHAMBER on the right, the last room visited, has a ceiling painted in the 'antique' fashion by Kent, a fine overmantel carved in lime-wood by Grinling Gibbons, and historical paintings ('Death of General Wolfe', etc.) by Benjamin West. Beyond is the Queen's Drawing Room (already visited), from which the staircase at the north end is regained.

The approach to the palace passing the entrance to the State Apartments leads to the rooms occupied by the LONDON MUSEUM.

The museum, founded in 1911 by Viscounts Esher and Harcourt, was in fact first accommodated in the State Apartments at the palace. In 1914 it was moved to Lancaster House, but in 1951 it returned on a long lease to the former apartments of Princess Beatrice. Remains of a Roman boat found in 1910 with 3rd-century coins, etc., on the site of the London County Hall, and other large exhibits, are still kept at Lancaster House (see p. 127).

The collections are mostly arranged chronologically, though some rooms are set apart for special subjects. The arrangement begins in the Basement, in the north-east corner, reached from Room 21 (left of the Entrance Hall) by a stairway opening on the left. Room 1, devoted to PREHISTORIC LONDON, contains implements and weapons of the Stone, Bronze, and Iron Ages, from the Thames and the gravel terraces on which much of London is built. Especially remarkable are the Neolithic and Iron

Age objects from Heathrow (the site of London Airport), leaf-shaped swords and other weapons and tools of the late Bronze Age, and bronze scabbards, fine horse-bits, chariot fittings, and a bronze-mounted oak tankard, all dating from the early Iron Age. Room 2, confined to ROMAN LONDON, contains notable pottery, including a jug of the late 1st century found at Southwark and inscribed with the name *Londini*, perhaps the earliest occurrence of this name. Here also are good examples of bronzework, glassware, and leather-work (sandals); a Mithraic relief of the 2nd century, found near Walbrook (compare p. 258); figures of Cautopates, a river god (from Walbrook; probably 2nd century); a fine carved sarcophagus from Englefield Green (Surrey); and a tessellated pavement found 20 ft below the ground, near the Mansion House. Reconstructed views show the Roman city at various stages of development.

Room 3 holds a small selection (changed from time to time) of the museum's outstanding collection of PRINTS AND DRAWINGS of old London. Rooms 4 and 5 are confined to the THEATRE, with stage costumes, etc., and mementoes of David Garrick and other actors. Room 7, devoted to PARLIAMENT and the LAW, contains an 18th-century Speaker's chair from the House of Commons, and relics of Pitt, Wellington, Gladstone, and other statesmen, and of the Suffragette Movement.

Room 8 covers the SAXON AND VIKING periods. Spears and scramasaxes, the large knives from which the Saxons are believed to have been named; fine brooches, etc., from Saxon cemeteries on the outskirts of London; axes, spearheads, and other Viking weapons and horse-equipment; chessmen and counters found in various parts of London; and a large hand-bell of bronze-coated iron, found in the Thames at Mortlake. Room 9 is devoted to the MIDDLE AGES, with an outstanding collection of pottery, as well as horse furniture, fine leather-work, weapons, tools, and implements, metal and wooden vessels and figures, domestic appliances, jewellery, and pilgrim signs. Notable are a 15th-century Gothic cupboard, and an oak cradle from Chepstow Castle, traditionally that of Henry V, but in fact not earlier than the 15th century. Room 10, entered through a late-15th-century door frame from the church of St Ethelburga-within-Bishopsgate, has three interesting models of 16th-century London.

Room 11 contains dolls and dolls' houses of the 18th and 19th centuries, a 17th-century rocking horse, 18th–19th-century games and toys, and London 'street pennyworths' of the early part of the present century. In Room 12 is the ROYAL COLLECTION, which includes the robes worn at the coronations of Queen Victoria (1838), Edward VII (1902), and George VI (1937); costumes of Princess Charlotte (daughter of George IV), Victoria, Queen Alexandra, and Queen Mary; a 17th-century Italian cradle and a swing-cot (1840) used for all the children of Queen Victoria; dolls dressed by the queen as a child; and Queen Mary's dolls' house and other possessions. There are models of the State coach built in 1762 (see p. 119) and of Westminster Abbey during the coronation of George VI.

Stairs (with 17th–19th-century paintings of London) reascend to the Ground Floor. Room 13, on the right, is devoted to the TUDOR PERIOD, with typical Elizabethan clothing of the courtier and the merchant; a painted wooden portrait head of Elizabeth I; a copper plate engraved with part of the earliest known map of London (about 1558); the steelyard of Sir Thomas Gresham (1579); two steel 'close helmets' made in Henry VIII's royal armoury at Greenwich; pottery, domestic articles, and metalwork; and a splendid hoard of jewellery discovered in Cheapside in 1912 and thought to be the stock of a Jacobean jeweller. The fine models here are of 16th–17th-century London, and an illuminated model in Room 14, beyond, depicts vividly the Great Fire of 1666.

Rooms 15 and 16 relate to the STEWART AND COMMONWEALTH Periods. In the first room are costumes and clothing of the time; leather 'blackjacks' or beer-jugs, and other articles of leather, pewter, and wood; a jewel-case of about 1620; Lambeth 'Delft ware' and majolica, introduced into England by Flemish immigrants; the silk vest, etc., worn by Charles I on the scaffold, the death-mask of Cromwell, and relics of the Civil War; pikemen's armour, swords made at Hounslow, and armour made at Greenwich about 1630 and worn by John Dymoke as the hereditary king's champion at the coronation of George III (1761). Room 14A, on the left, contains relics of the Great Plague and the Great Fire. In Room 16 are a silver-gilt cup made to celebrate the launching of H.M.S. *London*, the ship presented (reluctantly) in 1670 to Charles II by the merchants of London; an inlaid chessboard, with ivory pieces for chess, draughts, and backgammon, given to Samuel Pepys by James II; a sedan chair of about 1700;

a model of a Frost Fair on the Thames; a carved pinewood chimney-piece of about 1650; a set of virginals by James White (1656); and 17th-century London pottery (Lambeth 'Delft' and Fulham stoneware), pewter, silver, and 'Venetian' and other glassware. In Room 17 is a striking contemporary painting of the Great Fire of 1666 by a Dutch artist.

Rooms 17–20 are mostly devoted to the 18TH CENTURY. The first room has a pianoforte of the period; domestic bygones; articles of glass, horn, wood, and pottery; fine watches and jewellery; and pistols and small swords. In Room 19, on the left, are a Georgian shop-front from High Holborn and early shop signs; while Room 18, to the right of this, contains a London bedroom of about 1740, with the bed in which James Stewart, the 'Old Pretender', was born (1688). Room 20 has a fine selection of costumes of the late 18th and early 19th centuries; a grand piano made in 1817 for Princess Charlotte; beautiful Bow and Chelsea porcelain, and Battersea enamels; London flint glass of the 18th century; and silver-gilt church plate from St Martin-in-the-Fields.

The 19TH CENTURY and later collections are contained in Rooms 21–22. In the first room are a bicycle of 1870 and a 'penny-farthing' of about 1880; firemen's uniform and equipment; furnishings shown at the Great Exhibition of 1851; a 19th-century telephone and other instruments; models of trams and buses, and of the traffic in Piccadilly about 1875; etc. Room 22 contains 19th-century costumes, accessories, and personal ornaments, and paintings of social life in Victorian and Edwardian London.

Recent acquisitions are displayed in the ENTRANCE HALL, which also contains a remarkable musical clock by G. Pike (about 1760).

NATIONAL GALLERY Plan III, F 2, 3

STATIONS: TRAFALGAR SQUARE, on the Bakerloo line; STRAND, to the E., on the Northern line (Charing Cross section). — MOTOR-BUSES to Trafalgar Square, compare Route 1.

ADMISSION weekdays 10 to 6; Sundays 2 to 6 (free). Closed on Good Friday, Christmas Eve, and Christmas Day. — LECTURE TOURS on Wednesdays at 1 p.m., Thursdays at 3, and Saturdays at 2.30 (each lecture is usually devoted to one room or artist); Discussion Group on Tuesdays at 5.30, in the Lecture Room in the Basement. — RESTAURANT in the Basement, open 10 to 2 and 3 to 5.

The NATIONAL GALLERY, comprising one of the richest and most extensive collections of paintings in the world, stands on a terrace overlooking the north side of Trafalgar Square. The older and central portion, with a Grecian portico incorporating columns brought from Carlton House, was designed by William Wilkins and built in 1834–7. The façade, 460 ft long, is too low for the elevation of the building, and the design has been criticized also for its ineffective dome and 'pepper-box' turrets. The view from the portico, however, over Trafalgar Square and down Whitehall to the Houses of Parliament, is one of the finest in London. The collection admirably covers all schools and periods of painting, but is especially notable for its representation of the Italian schools of the 15th–16th centuries. The British school is also well represented, though in this case the national collections are shared with the Tate Gallery, where also the 20th-century European paintings and sculptures will be found. The National Gallery now possesses over 4,500 paintings; only about one-third of these can be displayed, but any picture not on view may usually be seen on written application to the Keeper. The room-to-room arrangement is by the national schools, an order followed in the description below; only the most important works can be mentioned, though almost every picture merits detailed examination.

The National Gallery was founded in 1824 through the purchase by the government of the collection of John Julius Angerstein. The thirty-eight paintings, including five by Claude and the six of Hogarth's 'Mariage à la Mode' series, were first exhibited at Angerstein's house at No. 100 Pall Mall. Other paintings were soon acquired, notably Titian's 'Bacchus and Ariadne', Rubens' 'Château de Steen', and Canaletto's 'The Stonemason's Yard', and in 1838 the collection was moved to its present home. Though the first director (Sir Charles Eastlake) was appointed in 1855, the National Gallery had to share its limited quarters with the Royal Academy until 1868. As the collection grew rapidly by purchase, gift, and bequest, further accommodation was needed, and extensions were made in 1876 (the Dome and neighbouring rooms), in 1887 (the central rooms), in 1927 (to house the Mond Bequest), and in 1929 (the Duveen Room). Among the principal bequests have been those of J. M. W. Turner (of his own works; 1851), Wynn Ellis (1876), George Salting (1910), Sir Hugh Lane (p. 366), and Ludwig Mond (1924). A number of masterpieces, including the Rokeby 'Venus' of Velazquez, Holbein's 'Duchess of Milan', Tintoretto's 'Morosini',

Rubens' 'Watering Place', and the Leonardo cartoon (see below) have been acquired with the assistance of the National Art-Collections Fund.

On the left of the ENTRANCE HALL is the cloakroom, where umbrellas, etc., must be given up, and farther left is the bookstall, while to the right is a counter where various reproductions of the paintings may be obtained. Staircases ascend from the hall to vestibules whose floors are decorated with mosaics by Boris Anrep showing contemporary figures. The British schools are displayed in the north-east part of the building, the French and Spanish schools in the south-east, the Dutch and Flemish in the north, and the Italian mainly in the centre and west. The paintings are listed below in alphabetical order of artists, as changes are made from time to time in the arrangement of the rooms.

The Vestibules usually contain some of the recent acquisitions and a representative selection of other works, both British and foreign. On the south wall, above the foot of the staircase, is *Tintoretto*'s large 'Christ washing Peter's feet'. The cartoon of 'The Virgin and Child with St John the Baptist and St Anne' by *Leonardo da Vinci*, purchased from the Royal Academy in 1962 for £800,000, mainly raised by public subscription, is at present being restored (1963).

In the centre of Room II is the exquisite WILTON DIPTYCH, purchased for £90,000. Its subject is Richard II presented to the Virgin and Child by his patron saints, SS. John the Baptist, Edward the Confessor, and Edmund, king and martyr, and on the back are the arms and badge of Richard. This is generally agreed to be a French work of the late 14th century (about 1395), though Dr Joan Evans considers it possibly by an English painter.

BRITISH SCHOOL (Rooms XV and XVI; see plan). 17th–18th centuries: *Arthur Devis* (d. 1787), 'Lady in a Park'; *Thomas Gainsborough* (d. 1788), 'Cornard Wood', 'The Watering Place', 'The Morning Walk', 'Mr and Mrs Robert Andrews', 'Dr Ralph Schomberg', 'Mrs Siddons', a famous study, and 'The Painter's Daughters', several delightful portraits at varying ages; *William Hogarth* (d. 1764), 'Mariage à la Mode', a series of six satirical paintings in the artist's well-known manner, and 'The Shrimp Girl'; *John Hoppner* (d. 1810), 'Sir George Beaumont', an instigator of the founding of the National Gallery; *Sir Peter Lely* (d. 1680), 'Frans van Helmont'; *Sir Joshua Reynolds* (d. 1792),

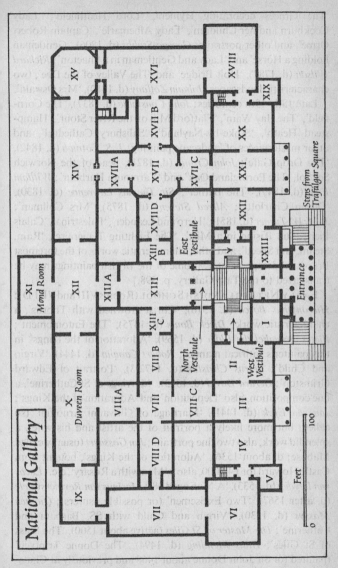

National Gallery

XV, XVI, XVIII, XIX, XVII B, XX, XVII A, XVII, XVII C, XXI, XIV, XXII, XIII B, XIII A, XXIII, XI Mond Room, XII, XIII, XIII C, East Vestibule, Entrance, X Duveen Room, VIII A, VIII, VIII B, VIII C, North Vestibule, West Vestibule, I, II, III, IX, VIII D, VII, IV, V, VI

Steps from Trafalgar Square

100

Feet

0

'The Graces decorating Hymen', 'Lord Heathfield', 'Lady Cockburn and her Children', 'Lady Albemarle', 'Captain Robert Orme', and other portraits; *George Stubbs* (d. 1806), 'Gentleman holding a Horse' and 'Lady and Gentleman in a Phaeton'; *Richard Wilson* (d. 1782), 'Holt Bridge' and 'The Valley of the Dee', two characteristic landscapes; *Johann Zoffany* (d. 1810), 'Mrs Oswald'.

Late 18th–19th centuries: *John Constable* (d. 1837), 'The Corn-field', 'The Hay Wain', 'Flatford Mill on the River Stour', 'Hampstead Heath', 'Stoke-by-Nayland', 'Salisbury Cathedral', and other masterpieces of landscape painting; *J. S. Cotman* (d. 1842), 'The Drop Gate'; *John Crome* (d. 1821), head of the Norwich School, 'The Poringland Oak' and 'Yarmouth Harbour'; *William Etty* (d. 1849), 'The Bather'; *Sir Thomas Lawrence* (d. 1830), 'Queen Charlotte'; *Alfred Stevens* (d. 1875), 'Mrs Collman'; *J. M. W. Turner* (d. 1851), 'Hero and Leander', 'Palestrina', 'Calais Pier', 'Sun Rising in a Mist', 'The Fighting Téméraire', 'Rain, Steam, and Speed', and other characteristic works of the foremost British landscape painter. [Some of the British paintings may be transferred to the Tate Gallery, p. 398.]

EARLY NETHERLANDISH SCHOOL (Rooms VIII and VIII D): *Hieronymus Bosch* (d. 1516), 'Christ crowned with Thorns', a characteristic work; *Dirck Bouts* (d. 1475), 'The Entombment'; *Pieter Brueghel the Elder* (d. 1569), 'Adoration of the Kings' in this painter's satirical manner; *Robert Campin* (d. 1444), 'Virgin and Child'; *Petrus Christus* (d. 1472/3), 'Portrait of Edward Grimston'; *Gerard David* (d. 1523), 'Marriage of St Catherine', a fine composition, also 'Deposition' and 'Adoration of the Kings'; *Jan van Eyck* (d. 1441), 'Marriage of Giovanni Arnolfini' (so called, but more likely a portrait of the artist and his wife), a splendid work, also two fine portraits; *Jan Gossaert* (usually called Mabuse; d. about 1536), 'Adoration of the Kings', bought from Castle Howard for £40,000, also a 'Man with a Rosary', etc.; *Lucas van Leyden* (d. 1533), 'A Man aged 38'; *Marinus van Reymerswaele* (d. after 1567), 'Two Excisemen' (or possibly usurers); *Quinten Massys* (d. 1530), 'Virgin and Child with SS. Barbara and Catherine'; *The Master of St Giles* (active about 1500), 'The Mass of St Giles'; *Hans Memling* (d. 1494), 'The Donne Triptych' (painted for Sir John Donne about 1468 and previously at Chatsworth), 'Young Man at Prayer', etc.; *Roger van der Weyden* (d. 1464), 'The Magdalen Reading' and 'Portrait of a Lady'.

EARLY GERMAN SCHOOL (Room IX): *Albrecht Altdorfer* (d. 1538), 'Landscape with a Footbridge'; *Hans Baldung* (d. 1545), 'Portrait of a Senator' and 'Pietà'; *Lucas Cranach the Elder* (d. 1553), 'Portrait of a Young Lady', etc.; *Albrecht Dürer* (d. 1528), 'The Artist's Father'; *Hans Holbein the Younger* (d. 1543), who settled in England in 1527 and became court painter to Henry VIII in 1536, 'The Ambassadors', painted in 1533 (on the floor between them is an elongated skull), and 'Christina of Denmark, Duchess of Milan', painted in 1538 when she was sixteen and Henry VIII was considering her as a bride; *Stefan Lochner* (d. 1451), 'Three Saints'; *The Master of Liesborn* (late 15th century), 'St Dorothy' and 'St Margaret'; *The Master of Werden* (15th century), 'Conversion and Mass of St Hubert'; *Michael Pacher* (d. 1498), a Tyrolese painter, 'Virgin and Child', a charming small work.

ITALIAN SCHOOLS (Rooms I–VII, VIII A–C, XIII, XIII A–C, XVII, and XVII A–D). Gothic Schools (Sienese, etc.): *Fra Angelico* (d. 1455), 'Christ in Glory', the predella of the altarpiece of San Domenico di Fiesole, a masterpiece painted about 1430 and including 266 figures; *Duccio di Buoninsegna* (d. about 1319), 'Virgin and Child with Saints', a triptych, 'The Annunciation', etc.; *Giotto* (d. 1337), 'Pentecost', attributed to this early master; *Giovanni di Paolo* (d. about 1482), 'Scenes from the Life of St John the Baptist', four predella panels; *Lorenzo Monaco* (d. 1422 or later), 'Coronation of the Virgin, with Saints', a triptych; *Margarito of Arezzo* (active about 1260), 'Virgin and Child enthroned'; *Masolino* (d. about 1447), 'A Pope and St Matthias' and 'SS. John the Baptist and Jerome', two panels of an altarpiece; *Matteo di Giovanni* (d. 1495), 'Madonna of the Girdle' and 'St Sebastian'; *Nardo di Cione* (d. 1365), 'Three Saints'; *Orcagna* (d. about 1368), 'Coronation of the Virgin', three large panels, and many smaller works, possibly by followers; *Stefano di Giovanni* (called Sassetta; d. 1450), 'Scenes from the Life of St Francis', a polyptych; *Ugolino da Siena* (active about 1327), 'The Betrayal, Deposition, and Resurrection of Christ'.

Florentine School (15th–16th centuries): *Fra Bartolommeo* (d. 1517), 'Adoration of the Child' and 'Virgin and Child with St

John'; *Alessandro Botticelli* (d. 1510), 'Mars and Venus', 'Adoration of the Magi', 'Mystic Nativity', and 'Life and Miracles of St Zenobius'; *Angelo Bronzino* (d. 1572), 'Holy Family' and 'Venus, Cupid, Folly, and Time'; *Piero di Cosimo* (d. after 1515), 'Mythological Subject' (perhaps the Death of Procris) and 'Battle of the Centaurs and Lapiths' (compare p. 321); *Lorenzo di Credi* (d. 1537), two fine 'Madonnas'; *Domenico Ghirlandaio* (d. 1494), 'Portrait of a Girl', probably from his studio; *Benozzo Gozzoli* (d. 1497), 'Virgin and Child among Angels and Saints'.

Leonardo da Vinci (d. 1519), 'The Virgin of the Rocks', a beautiful later version of the subject in the Louvre, and 'Virgin and Child with St John the Baptist and St Anne' (cartoon; see p. 356); *Filippino Lippi* (d. 1504; son of Filippo), 'Virgin and Child with Saints', 'Adoration of the Magi', etc.; *Filippo Lippi* (d. 1469), 'The Annunciation' and 'Seven Saints'; *Masaccio* (d. 1428), 'Virgin and Child'; *Michelangelo* (d. 1564), 'The Entombment' and 'Virgin and Child with St John and Angels', two magnificent if unfinished works; *Antonio Pollaiuolo* (d. 1498), 'The Martyrdom of St Sebastian', a masterpiece of Florentine figure painting, and 'Apollo and Daphne', small but excellent; *Andrea del Sarto* (d. 1531), 'Virgin and Child with St Elizabeth' and 'Portrait of a Sculptor'; *Andrea del Solario* (d. 1524), 'Giovanni Longono' and 'Portrait of a Man'; *Paolo Uccello* (d. 1475), 'The Rout of San Romano' (in 1432, of the Sienese by the Florentines) and 'St George and the Dragon', an important and remarkable acquisition; *Domenico Veneziano* (d. 1461), 'Heads of Saints'; *Andrea del Verrocchio* (d. 1488), 'Virgin and Child with Angels' (possibly by a follower), and 'Tobias and the Angel', of the School of Verrocchio.

Venetian School (15th–16th centuries): *Gentile Bellini* (d. 1507), 'Man with a pair of Dividers' and 'The Sultan Mehmet II'; *Giovanni Bellini* (d. 1516), 'Doge Leonardo Loredan', 'Madonna of the Meadow', 'Madonna of the Pomegranate', and 'Pietà', four masterly works; 'The Agony in the Garden', and 'The Circumcision'; and 'Assassination of St Peter Martyr', from the School of Giovanni Bellini; *Vittore Carpaccio* (d. about 1526), 'Adoration of the Magi' and 'Embarkation of St Ursula'; *Vincenzo Catena* (d. 1531), 'St Jerome in his Study', 'Virgin and Child with St John', and 'Warrior adoring the Infant Christ'; *G. B. Cima* (d. 1517/18), 'Madonnas', 'St Jerome in a Landscape', etc.; *Carlo Crivelli* (d. 1493), 'The Demidoff Altarpiece', with thirteen panels, 'The Annunciation', the artist's acknowledged masterpiece, 'Virgin and Child Enthroned', etc.; *Giorgione* (d. 1510), 'Adoration of the Magi' and 'Sunset Landscape with SS. George and Anthony', also 'Il Tramonte', attributed to Giorgione; *Antonello da Messina* (d. 1479), 'Salvator Mundi', 'Crucifixion', 'St Jerome in his Study', and 'Portrait of a Man'; *Alvise Vivarini* (d. about 1503), 'Virgin and Child'; *Antonio Vivarini* (d. 1476), 'Saints'; *Bartolommeo Vivarini* (d. about 1499), 'Virgin and Child with Saints'.

Schools of Lombardy (Milanese, etc.; 15th–early 16th centuries): *Ambrogio Bergognone* (d. 1523), 'Virgin and Child' and 'Scenes from the Passion'; *Boltraffio* (d. 1516), 'Virgin and Child'; *Bramantino* (d. 1536), 'Adoration of the Magi'; *Gaudenzio Ferrari* (d. 1546), 'The Annunciation', two panels; *Vincenzo Foppa* (d. 1515/6), 'Adoration of the Magi', a splendid work; *Bernardino Luini* (d. 1532), 'Christ Teaching' and 'Virgin and Child with St John', rich in colour; *Pisanello* (d. about 1455), 'Vision of St Eustace'; *Ambrogio Preda* (d. after 1508), 'Angels', etc.

Other Northern Schools (Bologna, Ferrara, Verona, etc.): *Antonio Correggio* (d. 1534), 'Venus, Mercury, and Cupid', etc.; *Francesco del Cossa* (d. about 1477), 'St Vincent Ferrer'; *Lorenzo Costa* (d. 1535), 'A Concert'; *Dosso Dossi* (d. 1541), 'Adoration of the Magi'; *Francesco Francia* (d. 1517/18), 'Virgin and Child with Saints, etc.', an altarpiece; *Garofalo* (d. 1559), 'Sacrifice to Ceres'; *Liberale da Verona* (d. about 1529), 'The Death of Dido'; *Gerolamo dai Libri* (d. 1556), 'Virgin and Child with St Anne'; *Andrea Mantegna* (d. 1506), 'Virgin and Child with the Magdalen and St John the Baptist', 'The Agony in the Garden', and 'The Triumph of Scipio', in monochrome; *Bartolommeo Montagna* (d. 1523), 'SS. John the Baptist, Zeno, and Catherine of Alexandria'; *Paolo Morando* (d. 1522), 'St Roch and the Angel', part of a triptych; *Francesco Morone* (d. 1529), 'Virgin and Child'; *Cosimo Tura* (d. 1495), 'Virgin and Child', 'Allegorical Figure', and 'St Jerome'; *Marco Zoppo* (d. about 1478), 'The Dead Christ', small but good.

Central Italian Schools (15th–16th centuries): *Piero della Francesca* (d. 1492), 'The Baptism of Christ', 'The Nativity', and

'St Michael and the Dragon'; *Pietro Perugino* (d. 1523), 'Virgin and Child, with SS. Raphael and Michael', a triptych; *Pintoricchio* (d. 1513), 'St Catherine of Alexandria', 'Return of Odysseus', etc.; *Raphael* (d. 1520), 'St Catherine of Alexandria', 'Madonna of the Tower', 'Virgin and Child' (called the 'Ansidei Madonna'), 'Crucifixion', and other works of this serene master; *Luca Signorelli* (d. 1523), 'Holy Family', 'The Triumph of Chastity', 'Virgin and Child with Saints and Angels', and 'Coriolanus persuaded to spare Rome'.

Later 16th-century Venetian School: *Bonifazio* (d. 1553), 'Virgin and Child with Saints'; *Paris Bordone* (d. 1570), 'Portrait of a Lady'; *Lorenzo Lotto* (d. 1556), 'Lucretia', 'Family Group', etc.; *Moretto* (d. 1555), 'St Bernardino of Siena', and other saints, etc.; *G. B. Moroni* (d. 1578), 'Italian Nobleman' and other portraits; *Palma Vecchio* (d. 1528), 'Portrait of a Poet' and 'Flora'; *Sebastiano del Piombo* (d. 1547), 'Holy Family' and 'Salome'; *Girolamo Romani* (called Il Romanino; d. 1566), 'Virgin and Child' and 'The Nativity', a polyptych; *Tintoretto* (d. 1594), 'Vincenzo Morosini', 'St George and the Dragon', and 'The Origin of the Milky Way', notable examples of this master; *Titian* (d. 1576), 'Venus and Adonis', 'Bacchus and Ariadne', 'Noli me Tangere', 'Man in a Blue Sleeve' (once supposed to be Ariosto), 'The Vendramin Family', 'Caterina Cornaro', and other masterpieces by this great artist; *Paolo Veronese* (d. 1588), the last of the great Venetians, 'The Adoration of the Magi', 'The Family of Darius before Alexander', two large-scale compositions, 'The Vision of St Helena', 'The Magdalen laying aside her Jewels', and four paintings from a ceiling decoration ('Happy Union', 'Respect', 'Scorn', and 'Unfaithfulness').

17th-century Italian Schools: *Caravaggio* (d. 1609), 'The Supper at Emmaus', and 'Salome with the Head of St John the Baptist' (painted in Malta); *Annibale Carracci* (d. 1609), 'Landscape with Figures' and 'Pietà'; *Bernardo Cavallino* (d. 1654), 'The Finding of Moses'; *Luca Giordano* (d. 1705), 'Martyrdom of St Januarius'; *Guercino* (d. 1666), 'The Incredulity of St Thomas'; *Jan Liss* (or Lys; d. 1629), 'Mercury and Argus' and 'Judith and Holofernes'; *Guido Reni* (d. 1642), 'Adoration of the Shepherds by Night', a large altarpiece, 'Susannah and the Elders', 'Ecce Homo', etc.;

Salvator Rosa (d. 1673), 'Self Portrait' and 'Landscape with Tobias and the Angel'; *Sassoferrato* (d. 1685), 'Virgin and Child'; *Bernardo Strozzi* (d. 1644), 'Allegorical Figure of Fame'; *Domenico Zampieri* (called Domenichino; d. 1641), 'Landscapes with Figures'.

18th-century Venetian School: *Antonio Canaletto* (d. 1768), 'The Stonemason's Yard', 'View on the Grand Canal', 'The Scuola di San Rocco', 'The Bucentaur at the Piazzetta', and 'Regatta on the Grand Canal', also 'Eton College' and 'Interior of the Rotunda at Ranelagh', examples of his work in England (1747–54); *Francesco Guardi* (d. 1793), 'Santa Maria della Salute', 'The Doge's Palace', 'The Piazza San Marco', and other delightful scenes by this master; *Pietro Longhi* (d. 1785), 'Masked Visitors at a Menagerie', etc.; *G. A. Pellegrini* (d. 1741), 'Rebecca at the Well'; *G. B. Pittoni* (d. 1767), 'Nativity' (the figure of the Almighty had been painted out); *G. B. Tiepolo* (d. 1754), 'The Trinity appearing to St Clement', 'The Deposition', and other fine works. Also *Pompeo Batoni* (worked in Rome; d. 1787), 'Time destroying Beauty' and 'Mr Scott of Banks Fee'.

DUTCH SCHOOL (Rooms X–XI): *Hendrik Avercamp* (d. after 1663), 'Winter Scene'; *Jan van de Capelle* (d. about 1679), 'River Scenes'; *Aelbert Cuyp* (d. 1691), 'Portrait of a Man', and "The Large Dort" and other characteristic landscapes with cattle; *Karel Dujardin* (d. 1678), 'Portrait of a Young Man' (perhaps the artist); *Jan van Goyen* (d. 1656), 'Winter Scene'; *Frans Hals* (d. 1666), 'Family Group in a Landscape', 'Man with a Glove', 'Lady with a Fan', and other fine portraits; *Bartholomeus van der Helst* (d. 1670), Portraits; *Meindert Hobbema* (d. 1709), 'The Avenue at Middelharnis', 'The Path through the Wood', and other notable landscapes; *Gerard Honthorst* (d. 1656), 'Christ before the High Priest' and 'St Sebastian'; *Pieter de Hooch* (d. about 1683), Dutch Courtyards and Interiors; *Michiel Mierevelt* (d. 1641), 'Portrait of a Lady'; *Aert van der Neer* (d. 1677), 'Canal Scene'; *Jacob van Ruisdael* (d. 1682), 'Landscape', an exceptionally fine work; *Gerard Terborch* (d. 1681), 'The Peace of Munster' (1648), 'The Guitar Lesson', etc.; *Willem Van de Velde* (the Younger; d. 1707), 'Coast Scene'; *Jan Vermeer* (d. 1675), 'Ladies at the Virginals'; *Jan Wynants* (d. 1682), 'Landscape with Figures and Animals'; and many small landscapes, seascapes, and genre works by these artists and by Jan Both, Gerard Dou, Nicolaes Maes, Gabriel Metsu, Isaak and Adriaen van Ostade, Paul Potter, Salomon van Ruysdael, Jan Steen, and Adriaen Van de Velde.

Room XI (the Mond Room) contains the gallery's superb collection of paintings by REMBRANDT VAN RIJN (d. 1669), notable among which are the 'Portrait of a Man on Horseback' (a large and magnificent work acquired in 1960), 'An Old Man in an Armchair' (from the Duke of Devonshire's collection at Chatsworth, Derbyshire), 'A Jewish Merchant', 'A Capuchin Friar', 'A Jewish Rabbi', 'An Old Man as St Paul', two 'Self Portraits' (1640 and 1660), 'Burgomaster Trip and his Wife', 'Saskia as Flora', 'A Woman Bathing', 'The Adoration of the Shepherds', and 'The Woman taken in Adultery'. Other works here, by pupils or followers of Rembrandt, include: *Gerbrandt van den Eeckhout* (d. 1674), 'The Wine Contract'; *Carel Fabritius* (d. 1654), 'Man in a Fur Cap'; *Philips Koninck* (d. 1688), two fine Landscapes; and *Nicholas Maes* (d. 1693), 'Card Players'.

FLEMISH SCHOOL: Room XIV contains many examples illustrating every aspect of the work of *Peter Paul Rubens* (d. 1640) and his pupil, *Anthony Van Dyck* (d. 1641). Rubens was in England as envoy to Charles I in 1629–30, when he painted 'Peace and War', and Van Dyck, invited to this country in 1632 by the king, became the court painter and died in London. Both painters received knighthoods, Rubens for the ceiling of Whitehall Palace (compare p. 103). Among the many splendid works by Rubens are 'The Château de Steen', a brilliant landscape, 'Le Chapeau de Poil' (often miscalled the Chapeau de Paille), 'The Watering Place', 'The Adoration of the Magi', and 'Rape of the Sabines', 'The Brazen Serpent', and 'The Judgement of Paris', three rich canvases of his late period. Van Dyck is represented by 'Charles I on Horseback', a large and thoughtful study, 'George and Francis Villiers', 'Portrait of an Artist', an early work, 'Portrait of a Lady and Child', 'Il Marchese Cattaneo and his Lady', and 'The Abbé Scaglia adoring the Virgin'. The 'First Earl of Denbigh' is also attributed to this artist, and 'The Triumph of Silenus' is a combined work of Rubens and Van Dyck. Also in this room are: *Jacob Jordaens* (d. 1678), 'Portrait of a Man and a Woman' (previously at Chatsworth), and two groups of the 'Holy Family' in his characteristic 'peasant' style; and *David Teniers the Younger* (d. 1690), two fine Village Scenes.

SPANISH SCHOOL (Room XVIII): *Goya* (d. 1828), two characteristic Portraits; *El Greco* (d. 1614), 'Christ expelling the Traders from the Temple', 'The Agony in the Garden', two masterpieces, and 'The Adoration of the Name of Jesus', an enchanting sketch for a painting in the Escorial near Madrid; *Morales* (d. about 1586), 'Virgin and Child'; *Murillo* (d. 1682), 'The Two Trinities', 'Self Portrait', and 'Peasant Boy'; *Ribera* (d. 1652), 'The Dead Christ'; *Velazquez* (d. 1660), 'The Rokeby Venus', slashed by militant suffragettes in 1914, 'Christ in the House of Martha', 'Christ after the Flagellation', 'St John on Patmos', and 'Philip IV', a full-length portrait and a brilliant later bust-portrait; *Zurbaran* (d. about 1664), 'St Francis' and 'St Margaret'.

FRENCH SCHOOL (Rooms XIX–XXIII). 17th century: *Philippe de Champaigne* (d. 1674), 'The Dream of St Joseph', a large altarpiece, and 'Cardinal Richelieu'; *Claude Lorraine* (d. 1682), 'Marriage of Isaac and Rebecca', 'Embarkation of St Ursula', and other magnificent examples of his classical landscapes; *Gaspard Dughet* (d. 1675), Landscapes; *Louis Le Nain* (d. 1648), 'Adoration of the Shepherds'; *Eustache Le Sueur* (d. 1655), 'St Paul at Ephesus'; *Francisque Millet* (d. 1679), 'Mountain Landscape'; *Nicolas Poussin* (d. 1665), 'Adoration of the Shepherds' (formerly owned by Reynolds), 'Cephalus and Aurora', 'The Annunciation', 'The Adoration of the Golden Calf', 'Landscape with a Snake', and other examples of this master; *Simon Vouet* (d. 1649), 'Ceres'.

18th century: *Boucher* (d. 1770), 'Pan and Syrinx'; *Chardin* (d. 1779), 'The Lesson' and 'The House of Cards'; *Fragonard* (d. 1806), 'Interior Scene'; *Lancret* (d. 1743), 'The Ages of Man'; *Nattier* (d. 1766), 'Manon Balletti' and 'Man in Armour'; *Perronneau* (d. 1783), 'Girl with a Kitten', a pastel; *Quentin de la Tour* (d. 1788), 'Portrait of Henry Dawkins', pastel; *Watteau* (d. 1721), 'La Gamme d'Amour'.

Earlier 19th century: *Corot* (d. 1875), *'Avignon from the West' (see below), 'Dardagny', 'La Charrette, Souvenir de Saintry', and other landscapes; *Courbet* (d. 1877), *'Snowstorm' and 'Still

Life'; *Daumier* (d. 1879), *'Don Quixote and Sancho Panza';
Delacroix (d. 1863), 'Baron Schwiter' and 'Ovid among the
Scythians'; *Géricault* (d. 1824), 'Horse frightened by Lightning';
Ingres (d. 1867), 'M. de Norvins' and 'Madame Moitessier'.

Later 19th century (Impressionists and Post-Impressionists):
Boudin (d. 1898), 'Harbour at Trouville', and other landscapes;
Cézanne (d. 1906), 'Cézanne Chauve', 'La Vieille au Chapelet',
'Aix, Paysage Rocheux', and other characteristic Provençal
landscapes; *Degas* (d. 1917), 'Après le Bain', 'Danseuses', 'La
Coiffure', 'Lola at the Cirque Fernando', etc.; *Fantin-Latour* (d.
1904), 'Roses'; *Gauguin* (d. 1903), 'Bouquet de Fleurs'; *Manet* (d.
1883), *'Eva Gonzales', 'La Servante de Bocks', 'Concert at the
Tuileries' (with portraits of Baudelaire, Fantin-Latour, Gautier,
and Offenbach), and 'The Firing Party', two fragments from a
large canvas, 'The Execution of the Emperor Maximilian';
Monet (d. 1926), 'La Plage de Trouville', 'Le Bassin aux Nymph-
éas', 'Vétheuil; Sunshine and Snow', and 'L'Inondation; Bords de
l'Epte' (a snow scene); *Berthe Morisot* (d. 1895), 'Jour d'Été';
Pissarro (d. 1903), 'Springtime at Louveciennes', 'Côte des Bœufs',
'The Louvre, Snowy Morning' and 'The Boulevard Montmartre at
Night'; *Renoir* (d. 1919), *'Les Parapluies', 'La Source', 'La
Première Sortie', 'Portrait of Misia Sert', 'Danseuses', and 'Cradle
Rock, Guernsey'; *Seurat* (d. 1891), 'Une Baignade, Asnières';
Sisley (d. 1899), 'L'Abreuvoir de Marly'; *Toulouse-Lautrec* (d.
1901), 'Femme assise dans un Jardin'; *Van Gogh* (d. 1890),
'Landscape with Cypress Trees', 'Sunflowers', and 'L'Herbage
aux Papillons'.

*The paintings (nearly all of the French school) bequeathed by Sir Hugh
Lane in 1917 have been the subject of a lengthy dispute arising out of his will.
They have been divided into two groups, to be shown alternately at the
National Gallery and in Dublin, an exchange being made every five years
(from 1961). The group being seen first in Dublin includes Corot's 'Avignon
from the West', Renoir's 'Les Parapluies', and Manet's 'Eva Gonzales',
while the second group contains Manet's 'Concert at the Tuileries'.

National PORTRAIT GALLERY Plan III, F 3

STATIONS: TRAFALGAR SQUARE, to the S., on the Bakerloo line;
STRAND, to the SE., on the Northern line; LEICESTER SQUARE, to the

N., on the Northern and Piccadilly lines. — MOTOR-BUSES to Trafalgar Square, compare Route 1; in Charing Cross Road, see Route 19.

ADMISSION Monday–Friday 10 to 5; Saturdays 10 to 6; Sundays and Boxing Day 2 to 6 (free). Closed on Good Friday, Christmas Eve, and Christmas Day. — LECTURES on Saturdays at 3.15 in October–March.

The NATIONAL PORTRAIT GALLERY adjoins the National Gallery on its north-east side and is entered from St Martin's Place, which leads north from Trafalgar Square. The collection was founded in 1856 with the object of illustrating British history, literature, arts, and science by means of portraits of the most eminent men and women. The Italianate building, erected mostly at the charge of W. H. Alexander, was designed by Ewan Christian and completed in 1896, and an extension, the gift of Lord Duveen, was opened in 1933.

The collection now numbers about 4,000 paintings, sculptures, and drawings, representing nearly 3,000 persons. Apart from those of the royal family (and a few other notable exceptions) no portrait is admitted until its subject has been dead for ten years. Though the avowed aim of the gallery is 'to look to the celebrity of the person represented, rather than to the merit of the artist', there are good examples of the work of Lely, Kneller, Reynolds, Romney, Lawrence, Millais, G. F. Watts, and other leading artists. Only about one-third of the collection is on view, but any portrait in storage can usually be shown on request. The portraits are hung more or less in chronological order, starting on the Second Floor.

From the Vestibule, where umbrellas, etc., must be left, stairs go up to a landing from which a lift ascends to the SECOND FLOOR. On the landing here are 16th–17th-century copies of portraits of medieval kings, and here and on the adjoining staircase are electrotypes taken from effigies on royal and noble tombs. Henry III is the earliest representation, and others are of Edward II and III, the Black Prince, Richard II, Henry IV, Henry VII, Elizabeth I, and Mary, Queen of Scots.

Room 7, opening off the landing, is devoted to the TUDOR PERIOD, with portraits of Henry VII (1485–1509), believed to be the oldest from life in the gallery (1505); Henry VIII (1509–47) and his first two queens, Catherine of Aragon and Anne Boleyn; Edward VI (1547–53) as Prince of Wales; Mary I (1553–8); Mary, Queen of Scots (1542–87), and her son James I at the age of eight. Elizabeth I (1558–1603) is shown in two portraits, one of about 1572 and the other of 1592 depicting her standing on a map of

England and celebrated by a sonnet. Here also are Cardinal Wolsey and Thomas Cromwell, the advisers of Henry VIII; Thomas Cranmer, the Protestant martyr; Cardinal Pole, the last Roman Catholic archbishop; Sir Francis Walsingham, Lord Burghley, and his son Robert Cecil, Earl of Salisbury, the counsellors of Elizabeth; her favourites the Earl of Leicester and the Earl of Essex; Sir Thomas Gresham, the founder of the Royal Exchange; and such men of action as Sir Philip Sidney, Sir Richard Grenville, and Sir Walter Raleigh. At the end of the room is a large group of Sir Thomas More, the statesman and author of *Utopia*, with his family and descendants; and in the centre is a curious perspective portrait of Edward VI (1546), on the back of which are hung engravings of Sir Francis Drake and William Shakespeare (by Droeshout, from an early folio). The so-called 'Chandos' Shakespeare, also in this room, is now considered only doubtfully to represent the poet. Beside the opening to Room 8 is a remarkable portrait of Sir Henry Unton, with scenes from his life forming a background.

Room 8 is confined to the STEWART PERIOD. On the left are James I (1603–25; by Mytens), his queen Anne of Denmark, and his favourite the Duke of Buckingham; Ben Jonson, the poet; Inigo Jones, the architect; and Francis Bacon, the statesman and philosopher, robed as Lord Chancellor. Opposite are Charles I (1625–49; also by Mytens); his consort, Henrietta Maria; his supporters, Archbishop Laud and the Earl of Strafford; and his nephew Prince Rupert, the Cavalier general. At the west end are Oliver Cromwell (by R. Walker) and his general, Henry Ireton. In Room 9 are John Locke and Thomas Hobbes, the philosophers; Sir Godfrey Kneller and Sir Peter Lely (both self-portraits); Sir Christopher Wren (by Kneller); Sir Isaac Newton; John Dryden; John Milton (as a young man); Samuel Pepys; John Bunyan; and Isaak Walton, the angler.

Room 10 contains portraits of Charles II (1660–85); his queen, Catherine of Braganza; three of his mistresses, Nell Gwyn and the Duchesses of Portsmouth and Cleveland; his statesmen, the Duke of Albemarle and the Earl of Clarendon; and the members of the notorious 'Cabal' ministry (Clifford, Ashley, Buckingham, Arlington, and Lauderdale). Here also are James II (1685–8; by

Kneller) and his two wives; his opponent, the Duke of Monmouth; the infamous Judge Jeffreys; and the seven bishops whom the king committed to the Tower in 1688. In Room 11 are William III (1688–1702) and Mary II (1688–94); Queen Anne (1702–14) and her consort Prince George of Denmark; James Stewart, the 'Old Pretender', and his sister, as children (by Largillière); Robert Harley, Earl of Oxford, the Tory statesman; and the Duke of Marlborough (an equestrian portrait by Kneller) and his redoubtable Duchess.

Room 3 (left of Room 10) and Room 2 contain portraits of members of the KIT-CAT CLUB, a political and literary circle of the Whig party that flourished during the first twenty years of the 18th century. The forty-two portraits, all painted by Sir Godfrey Kneller, include Joseph Addison, Sir Richard Steele, William Congreve, Sir John Vanbrugh, Sir Robert Walpole, and the Duke of Newcastle.

Room 1. 18TH-CENTURY ARTS AND SCIENCE: Jonathan Swift, Alexander Pope, and others of the great Augustans; Bishop Berkeley, the philosopher; Samuel Richardson and Tobias Smollett, the novelists; George Frederick Handel (by Hudson); Isaac Watts, the hymn-writer; Peg Woffington, the actress; 'Beau' Nash, the arbiter of fashion; William Hogarth (by himself); and Sir Hans Sloane, the physician. This room also contains five notable busts by Roubiliac: of himself, in marble; terracottas of Handel, Pope, and Hogarth; and a remarkable coloured plaster bust of Colley Cibber, the actor.

Room 6 (opening off Room 7). 18TH-CENTURY STATESMEN AND MEN OF ACTION: George I (1714–27); George II (1727–60) and Queen Caroline of Anspach; George III (1760–1820) and Queen Charlotte; Prince Charles Edward Stewart, the 'Young Pretender', his brother Cardinal York, the 'last of the Stewarts', and his opponent the Duke of Cumberland; Lord Chesterfield (by Ramsay); Admiral Vernon and Stringer Lawrence (both by Gainsborough); Admiral Lord Anson; General Wolfe, the hero of Quebec; and William Pitt, Earl of Chatham; also a terracotta bust of Sir Robert Walpole, by Rysbrack.

In Room 5 are John Wesley, the founder of Methodism; Robert Adam, the architect; Sir Richard Arkwright, the inventor of a 'spinning-jenny'; Richard Wilson, Allan Ramsay, and Joseph Wright of Derby (all self-portraits); Thomas Gray and William Cowper, the poets; and Horace Walpole, statesman and man of letters. The most interesting portraits, however, are those of Dr Johnson and his circle, including David Garrick, James Boswell, Oliver Goldsmith, and Dr Charles Burney, the historian of music, all painted by Sir Joshua Reynolds, who is himself represented by a self-portrait as a young man. Room 4. MEN OF ACTION AND EMPIRE-BUILDERS: Captain Cook, the explorer; Admirals Rodney, Hood, and Duncan; Admiral Lord Nelson (by L. F. Abbott); Lady Hamilton (by Romney); Sir Stamford Raffles, Lord Clive, and Warren Hastings.

On the west landing, reached from Room 3, are busts of 18th–19th-century statesmen, authors, etc., among them Charles James Fox and Laurence Sterne, both by Nollekens. The rooms beyond mostly contain portraits of 19TH-CENTURY STATESMEN AND MEN OF ACTION. Room 12: Sir John Moore (by Lawrence); William Pitt the Younger addressing the House of Commons (1793), a large canvas; and a portrait of Pitt (by Hoppner); Edmund Burke, the opponent of the French Revolution; Sir William Blackstone, the great jurist; Benjamin Franklin and George Washington; and the Duke of Wellington. Room 13: George IV (1820–30) and Caroline of Brunswick; William IV (1830–7) and Queen Adelaide; the 'grand old' Duke of York (by Wilkie); the prime ministers Lord Liverpool and George Canning (both by Lawrence); Jeremy Bentham, the economist; and William Cobbett, the reformer; also a large group of the House of Lords discussing the Bill to Divorce Queen Caroline (1820), by Sir George Hayter. Room 14: Earl Grey, promoter of the Reform Bill; Sir Charles Napier and other Indian generals; David Livingstone and Sir John Franklin, the explorers; and William Wilberforce, the abolitionist (a fine unfinished portrait by Lawrence).

Room 15: Lord Lawrence of India (by Watts); Richard Cobden and John Bright, the advocates of Free Trade; and Sidney Herbert, the Crimean War minister. In the centre of the south wall is a large group by Sir George Hayter of the first Meeting of the House of Commons after the Reform Bill of 1832, with 375 figures. On the west wall is Queen Victoria (1837–1901), in her coronation robes (by Hayter), surrounded by nine of her prime ministers, including Lord Melbourne, Sir Robert Peel, Lord Palmerston, W. E. Gladstone, and Benjamin Disraeli (these two by Millais), Lord Derby, and Lord Aberdeen. On the north wall are Prince Albert (d. 1861); Henry Fawcett, the blind statesman; Lord Macaulay, the historian; Cardinals Newman and Manning; General Booth of the Salvation Army; Octavia Hill, the reformer (by Sargent); and Cecil Rhodes, the South African statesman.

From the west landing stairs descend to the FIRST FLOOR. Halfway down are busts of Lord Lister, the surgeon (by Brock), and Florence Nightingale (by Steell). Room 24, on the left, contains sculptures, including a bust of Thomas Carlyle by Boehm, the life mask of John Keats, a cast for a life mask of William Blake, and cases of small medallions. The rooms beyond are devoted to 19TH-CENTURY ARTS AND SCIENCE. Room 25: John Hunter, the surgeon; Edward Jenner, the discoverer of vaccination; Sir Joseph Banks, the naturalist; Matthew Boulton and James Watt, the engineers; George Romney (a self-portrait); Sarah Siddons, the actress; R. B. Sheridan, the playwright; Robert Burns; and Edward Gibbon. Among the writers in Room 26 are Leigh Hunt, the essayist; Thomas Moore, the Irish poet; S. T. Coleridge; Charles Lamb (by Hazlitt); Sir Walter Scott (in his study); William Wordsworth (by B. R. Haydon); Lord Byron, in Albanian costume; and P. B. Shelley (the only authentic portrait). Here also are Sir Humphry Davy and Michael Faraday, the chemists; George Stephenson, the engineer; Sir Thomas Lawrence and John Constable, the painters; and Sir John Soane, the architect.

Room 27: Sir John Millais and D. G. Rossetti (both by Watts); John Ruskin; George Borrow; the Brontë sisters (by their brother); W. M. Thackeray and Anthony Trollope (both by Samuel Laurence); Charles Dickens (by Maclise); and Matthew Arnold, Lord Tennyson, and A. C. Swinburne (all by Watts). Room 28: Charles Darwin, T. H. Huxley (both by Collier), and other men of science; Samuel Butler; Robert and Elizabeth Barrett Browning; Thomas Carlyle (by Millais); G. F. Watts (by himself); Herbert Spencer, the philosopher; William Morris, the craftsman and visionary (by Watts); and Sir Edward Burne-Jones.

In the corridor are drawings of Sir John Herschel, the astronomer, Madame Tussaud, and the sporting Marquess of Queensberry; watercolours of Elizabeth Farren, later Countess of Derby, and Mrs Sarah Siddons, by Downman; the guardsman-balloonist Colonel Burnaby (by Tissot); and busts of Sir Walter Scott (by Chantrey), George Stephenson, the engineer, and others. Room 18, the corridor leading east from the landing, contains a large painting of the Convention of the Anti-Slavery Society (1840), by B. R. Haydon. On the walls are drawings, etc., of authors and artists, including Jane Austen (a small sketch by her sister), William Hazlitt, John Keats (a pencil study by his friend Charles Brown), the landscape painters, Turner, Constable, and Cotman, and Sir Francis Chantrey (in chalk).

Room 19, on the right, contains a group of the Private View of the Old Masters Exhibition at the Royal Academy (1888), with leading artists and patrons of the day. In Room 22, opposite, are pastels by George Richmond of Ruskin, as a young man, Harriet Martineau, Charlotte Brontë, Elizabeth Gaskell, the churchman John Keble, etc., as well as a self-portrait and a charming water-colour of Swinburne as a child. Other portraits are of Christina Rossetti and her mother (by D. G. Rossetti), George Eliot, and Arthur Hugh Clough. Room 23, to the left, is used as a Lecture Room.

On the walls of Room 17, the continuation of the corridor, are further drawings, etc., of authors, including Sir Arthur Conan Doyle (with 'Sherlock Holmes'), Lewis Carroll, Charlotte M. Yonge (by Richmond), Rupert Brooke, W. B. Yeats (an etching by Augustus John), Lawrence of Arabia (drawing by John), and George Moore (pastel by Henry Tonks); and examples of the illustrators and caricaturists (Roger Fry, by Max Beerbohm, etc.). The corridor also contains busts of artists and authors, including bronzes of Thomas Hardy (by Thornycroft) and W. E. Henley (by Rodin).

Room 16, at the end of the corridor, holds portraits of J. L. Baird, the inventor of television; Lord Baden-Powell, the founder of the Boy Scouts; and Sir Henry Wood, the founder of the Promenade Concerts, and Dame Ethel Smyth and other composers; and bronzes of Sir Jacob Epstein (by himself), Sir Edward Elgar, Sir Thomas Beecham, and Dr Ralph Vaughan Williams. Room 21, on the left, is reserved for recent acquisitions. On the staircase ascending to the Second Floor are drawings and small paintings; among the subjects are Dr Thomas Arne, composer of *Rule, Britannia*, and Allan Ramsay (a fine self-portrait in red chalk).

To the right of Room 16 a staircase descends to the ROYAL LANDING, which has portraits of Queen Victoria, Edward VII (1901–10), and Queen Alexandra; groups of George V (1910–36) and Queen Mary with their two eldest children (by Sir John Lavery) and of George VI (1936–52) and his family (by Sir James Gunn); and a bust of Queen Victoria, by Chantrey. Rooms 29–31, opening on the south, are mainly devoted to MODERN ART AND LITERATURE. Room 29: George Meredith (by Watts), R. L.

Stevenson (by Richmond), Henry James (by Sargent), Rudyard Kipling, and Thomas Hardy; Sir William Gilbert and Sir Arthur Sullivan; Sir Henry Irving, and Ellen Terry, at the age of 17 (by Watts); Sir Oliver Lodge, etc.; and a bronze of Joseph Conrad by Epstein. Room 30: P. Wilson Steer (by Sickert) and Walter Sickert (by Steer); Sir Max Beerbohm (by Sir William Nicholson); Sir Matthew Smith (self-portrait); Aubrey Beardsley; and other artists. Room 31: G. K. Chesterton, Hilaire Belloc, and Maurice Baring (a group by Sir James Gunn); James Joyce, D. H. Lawrence, and Virginia Woolf; Beatrice Webb, the Fabian socialist; and bronzes by Epstein of Bernard Shaw, W. B. Yeats, and W. H. Davies, the poet-tramp (a fine head).

The staircase goes on down to the Ground Floor, where the room on the right contains portraits of Field-Marshal Lord Roberts and Lord Grey of Fallodon, the Liberal statesman; busts of General Gordon, Lord Wolseley (by Boehm), and Cecil Rhodes; and cases of fine miniatures, including Elizabeth I, Sir Walter Raleigh, and the Earl of Leicester, all by Nicholas Hilliard. Through the openings on the right can be seen two large groups of the Naval and Military Commanders of the First World War.

To the left of these is another group of Empire Statesmen of the period, among them Lloyd George and the young Winston Churchill. This is best seen from the BASEMENT (reached from the Vestibule), which also contains a bust of Ramsay Macdonald, by Epstein, and portraits of 20th-century Statesmen and War Leaders, including Lord Milner, Joseph Chamberlain, Lord Kitchener, Stanley Baldwin, Lloyd George (by Orpen), Ernest Bevin, and others, and of such pioneers as Sir Ernest Shackleton and Captain R. F. Scott, the Antarctic explorers, and Sir John William Alcock, who first flew across the Atlantic.

NATURAL HISTORY MUSEUM Plan VI, C 2, 3

STATION: SOUTH KENSINGTON, nearly ⅓-m. SE., on the Circle, District, and Piccadilly lines. — MOTOR-BUSES in Brompton Road and Cromwell Road, see Route 10; in Kensington Road, see Route 11.

ADMISSION weekdays 10 to 6; Sundays 2.30 to 6 (free). Closed on Good Friday and Christmas Day. — LECTURE TOURS on weekdays at 3, starting from the Central Hall; special lectures and films from time to time in the Lecture Hall. — RESTAURANT (unlic.) on the First Floor.

The NATURAL HISTORY MUSEUM, one of the group of interesting museums at South Kensington, is reached from Cromwell Road, west of the Victoria and Albert Museum, and housed in a vast Romanesque palace designed by Alfred Waterhouse and erected in 1873–80. The south front of this has a length of 675 ft and it is flanked by symmetrical towers 192 ft high. The building is faced throughout with terracotta slabs bearing series of animals moulded in relief. In addition to the public galleries, which cover nearly 4 acres of floor-space, the museum includes an important Reference Library and very extensive Study Collections, usually accessible to students and research workers on application to the Director.

The museum was built up round the scientific collections of Sir Hans Sloane, purchased for the nation after his death in 1753 to form part of the nucleus of the British Museum (see p. 316). To this was added the large botanical collection bequeathed in 1820 by Sir Joseph Banks, and in 1856, at the suggestion of Sir Richard Owen, the first director, the museum was divided into its present five departments of Zoology, Entomology, Palaeontology, Mineralogy, and Botany. The collections were removed from Bloomsbury and opened here in 1881, and in 1962 the Natural History Museum became independent of the parent museum. The galleries suffered considerable damage during the war, when most of the botanical exhibits were lost, but this and sections of other departments are being reopened as the collections are built up and restoration completed.

The entrance through an ornate Romanesque portal leads direct into the CENTRAL HALL, 170 ft long and 72 ft high, with moulded terracotta decorations. On either side are statues of Charles Darwin (d. 1882), behind which is the Children's Centre, and of Thomas Henry Huxley (d. 1895). In the centre of the hall is a display representing the five departments of the museum (see above); behind this are examples of such larger mammals as hippopotami, rhinoceroses, and elephants, including an African bush elephant, 11 ft 4 in. high, and farther on are other mammals (gorilla, polar bear, etc.). The bays on either side of the hall contain special displays illustrating evolution, selection, and genetics (east side); fishes, including the coelacanth, and other vertebrates; and the evolution of man.

The NORTH HALL, behind the grand staircase, is partly devoted to an exhibition showing organisms of importance (chiefly in a harmful manner) to man. Cases illustrate the damage done by rats and mice, and by noxious insects; pests and diseases of cultivated plants; and insect pests and the diseases caused by them; as well as examples of mimicry and the biology of water supply. Here also are exhibits of British trees and crystals of minerals of commercial importance. Against the staircase wall is a section of a Wellingtonia, or Big Tree of California, cut down in 1892, by which time it had attained a height of 276 ft and a girth of 49 ft. The 1,335 rings of annual growth indicate that it started life in A.D. 557.

From the North Hall, a passage with specimens of further mammals (reindeer, grey seal, etc.), original natural-history drawings, and an exhibit of modern taxidermy, leads to the NORTH BLOCK, completed in 1959, but not open to the public. It contains a general library (with map and reading rooms, etc.) and a splendid lecture theatre, but is mainly taken up by the museum's vast reference and study collection of mammal specimens, occupying eleven floors.

The east wing of the ground floor is devoted to the extensive FOSSIL COLLECTION, mostly arranged zoologically. On the left is an introductory case; the first bay on the right deals with fossil men, their tools and weapons, with a case devoted to the notorious 'Piltdown Man'. In the second bay are fossils from the London area. The long main gallery contains the larger mammals, including a giant lemur from Madagascar; a sabre-toothed 'tiger' from California, U.S.A.; skulls of primitive elephants; a mastodon from Missouri, U.S.A.; a Hippidium or short-legged mountain horse from South America; a 'straight-tusked elephant' nearly 13 ft high found near Chatham (Kent); the giant Irish deer, which had antlers sometimes over 11 ft in span; and two skulls and a cast of the Arsinoitherium from Egypt. The pavilion at the end contains skeletons of extinct marsupials from Australia; the glyptodon, a huge armadillo-like mammal from South America; the megatherium and other giant sloths; and fossil birds, including the archaeopteryx from Bavaria, the earliest-known bird, and wingless moas from New Zealand.

The corridor extending on the north of the main gallery contains a fine collection of Extinct Reptiles. Notable are the pariasaur, a massive herbivorous reptile from South Africa; the ophthalmosaur, a large-eyed swimming reptile; and great sea-lizards, the ichthyosaurs and plesiosaurs, the first of which were discovered at Lyme Regis (Dorset) in 1811 by Mary Anning. The first gallery running north is devoted to Fossil Plants, including the earliest known land plants and fine specimens from the Coal Measures; the second gallery contains Fossil Invertebrates, starting with protozoa, the simplest of all animals. The next gallery open (beyond the Geological Library) contains remains of dinosaurs, the largest of the prehistoric land animals. Among these are iguanodons found in England and Belgium, and a model of a diplodocus, based on a skeleton, 84 ft 9 in. long and 11 ft 5 in. high, in the Carnegie Museum at Pittsburgh, U.S.A. The last gallery on this side contains Fossil Fishes, with dioramas illustrating their evolution.

In the west wing, left of the entrance, is the excellent BIRD GALLERY, newly opened in 1951 after reconstruction. The first bays on the south side, designed as an introduction to the study of birds, include a skeleton and model of the flightless Dodo of Mauritius, which became extinct in the 17th century. In the other bays birds are grouped according to families, and include some beautiful humming birds from Central America. The pavilion at the farther end shows British birds, partly in their native habitat. Parallel to the Bird Gallery is a corridor devoted to corals, sponges, and protozoa. The first gallery opening on the north is the FISH GALLERY, which has models of a whale shark (34 ft long), a basking shark (30 ft long), and other large fish. On the right is a small gallery confined to arachnida (scorpions and spiders); on the left comes the ARTHROPOD GALLERY, containing a small part of the museum's fine collection of insects, as well as crustacea (lobsters, crabs, etc.). The REPTILE GALLERY, with crocodiles, tortoises and turtles, lizards, snakes, and amphibians, opens on the north to the WHALE HALL, containing skeletons of the blue or rorqual whale, the largest of living mammals (82 ft long; with a model of one 91 ft long); sperm whale (60 ft), the largest of the toothed whales; right whale (60 ft); and Californian grey whale (44 ft). Beyond the Reptile Gallery is the STARFISH GALLERY, containing also sea urchins, worms, and molluscs, together with a cast of a giant squid stranded on the Yorkshire coast in 1925. At the north end is a case of lovely corals from the Great Barrier Reef of Australia. Lastly comes the LECTURE HALL, where films are frequently shown (especially during school holidays) in connexion with the lecture tours.

From the Central Hall the grand staircase, on the landing of which is a statue of Sir Richard Owen (d. 1892), ascends to the FIRST FLOOR. Cases on the east balcony are devoted to comparative anatomy, with skeletons of a man, horse, and baboon. On the west and south balconies is a selection of mammals, including the Alaskan moose, the largest species of deer, and the primitive egg-laying platypus and echidna (or ant-eater) of Australia. The MAMMAL GALLERY, in the west wing, still only partly open, displays European mammals, including the principal British species, and (temporarily) some African mammals, such as the giraffe and its relative the okapi (discovered only in 1901) from the Belgian Congo, and the small forest elephant from West Africa. At the farther end is the fine Rowland Ward Pavilion, showing groups of African mammals in their natural habitat.

On the south and east balconies are meteorites, including one which fell in the Argentine and weighs over ½-ton; stalactites and stalagmites; fluorescent minerals; marbles and other ornamental stones; and a large crystal of calcite illustrating its double refractive properties. The MINERAL GALLERY, in the east wing, contains a remarkable collection of specimens of minerals, rocks, and meteorites. The wall cases on the left of the entrance illustrate crystal structure; those on the right demonstrate the identification of minerals by X-rays, in which much work has been done in recent years. Cases on the right near the door (2a–f) hold a fine selection of gold, platinum, and precious stones, notable being the 'Colenso Diamond' of 133 carats, presented to the museum by Ruskin. Cases 2g, h contain radioactive minerals, 1e, f (to the left) new minerals and new acquisitions, and 1g, h natural glasses. The window case here has ore minerals with new uses. In the centre of the gallery are the asbestos purse of Benjamin Franklin and a table-top inlaid with antique marbles from the Appian Way, Rome. Case 10c, farther on, holds models of famous diamonds, including the 'Cullinan' (3,106 carats) and the 'Koh-i-Noor' (800 carats). At the east end (not accessible at present) is an iron meteorite weighing $3\frac{1}{2}$ tons which was found in 1854 near Melbourne.

A staircase from the balconies leads to the SECOND FLOOR, on which stands a marble statue by Chantrey of Sir Joseph Banks (d. 1820). The galleries here were badly damaged during the war, but a new BOTANICAL GALLERY was opened in the east wing in 1963.

ST PAUL'S CATHEDRAL Plan IV, E 3

STATIONS: ST PAUL'S, to the NE., on the Central line; MANSION HOUSE, $\frac{1}{4}$-m. SE., on the Circle and District lines. — MOTOR-BUSES Nos. 4, 6, 9, 11, 13, 15, 18, and 141 all pass the cathedral on the S. side; Nos. 7, 8, 22, 23, 25, and 32 pass the entrance to St Paul's Churchyard on the NE.

ADMISSION daily from 7.45 a.m. to 7 p.m. (to 5 in October–March), but visitors are requested not to walk about during Service, which begins on Sunday at 8, 10.30, and 11.30 a.m. and 3.15 and 6.30 p.m., and on weekdays at 8 and 10 a.m. and 4 p.m. (Wednesday and Friday at 12.30 also). — Tickets for the CRYPT (6d), open on weekdays 10.45 to 3.30 (to 5.30 in April, 6 in May and September, and 6.30 in June–August) are obtainable in the South Transept; for the LIBRARY, WHISPERING GALLERY, and STONE GALLERY (1/-) at the E. end of the South Aisle; for the GOLDEN GALLERY (1/-) at the Stone Gallery; and for the BALL (1/-) at the Golden Gallery. The Library and Galleries are open at the same times as the Crypt.

ST PAUL'S CATHEDRAL, the seat of the bishopric of London and the 'parish church of the British Commonwealth', stands in a commanding position at the top of Ludgate Hill, the spiritual heart of the City of London, as the Bank is its commercial centre. The largest as well as the most famous of the City's churches, it stands on the site of the great medieval church of 'Old St Paul's', burned down in the Great Fire of 1666. Built of Portland stone, now much darkened by the London climate, the new church was begun in 1675, opened for service in 1697, and finally completed in 1710. It is the masterpiece of Sir Christopher Wren (1632–1723), a beautiful and harmonious Renaissance building with twin baroque towers rising above the dignified west façade and dominated by its famous dome, the largest in the world after St Peter's at Rome. The cathedral is 515 ft long outside and 180 ft wide across the west front; internally, it is 463 ft long and $227\frac{1}{2}$ ft wide across the transepts. The nave, 180 ft long, is the widest of any Anglican church in England (125 ft, including the aisles) and

92½ ft high to the vault. The dome is 112 ft in diameter, and the height from the floor of the church to the top of the cross is 365 ft. The west towers are each 212½ ft high. The area of the church (87,400 sq. ft) is the greatest of any cathedral in England (though it will be surpassed by Liverpool when that cathedral is complete).

The earliest recorded church on this historic site was endowed by Ethelbert, the first Christian king of Kent, and here Mellitus was consecrated bishop of the East Saxons by St Augustine in 604. His cathedral, rebuilt in stone between 675 and 685 by the saintly Bishop Erconwald, was burned down by Viking raiders in the 9th century. It was raised again in 962, but was destroyed by a fire that swept through the City in 1087, and a new church on a larger and more elaborate plan was begun by the Norman Bishop Maurice. Though the work was delayed by another fire in 1136, the choir was in use by 1148 and the steeple completed in 1221. King John submitted himself to the Papal Legate here in 1213, pledging his kingdom to pay an annual tribute to Rome. By this time the choir was considered inadequate; it was rebuilt by 1240 and later extended eastwards, and in 1315 the church was given a lofty new spire of wood covered with lead, which reached a height of at least 480 ft (and possibly much higher). St Paul's, now attached to a college of secular canons, was the longest cathedral in England (596 ft) and one of the largest in Europe. Here in 1377 John Wyclif, the reformer, was tried for heresy, and in 1527 William Tyndale's translation of the New Testament was publicly burned. Prince Arthur, the elder brother of Henry VIII, was married in the cathedral to Catherine of Aragon in 1501. In the 14th–15th centuries the great church had increased in splendour, but by the middle of the 16th century it began to be seriously neglected: Henry VIII removed many of its treasures. Lord Protector Somerset demolished the north cloister to provide stones for his new palace in the Strand, and the nave began to be used as a place of business ('Paul's Walk'). In 1561 the great spire was struck by lightning and brought down, causing a fire that damaged much of the church, and though a restoration was undertaken in 1627–42, when Inigo Jones partly rebuilt the west end and added a fine new portico, the church was again in a sadly ruinous state when it was almost completely destroyed in the Great Fire of 1666.

At first it was thought that the cathedral could be repaired (the ruined nave was patched up and used for service until 1673), but Sir Christopher Wren, Surveyor General of the Works under Charles II, persuaded the Commissioners to accept his plan for a completely new church. He gathered round him some of the finest craftsmen of the time: Nicholas Hawksmoor as clerk of the works, Thomas and Edward Strong as master-masons, Grinling Gibbons and Jonathan Maine as wood-carvers, Jean Tijou as ironworker, and Francis Bird and Caius Gabriel Cibber as sculptors. The first stone was laid in 1675, the choir was opened for service in 1697, and the last stone was placed in position in 1710. Wren had originally planned the church in the form of a Greek cross (one having four equal arms), with a large central dome supported by eight massive pillars, but in response to the demands of the Court party, who hoped for the return of Roman Catholicism, it was given a longer nave and side chapels. Wren had to face much adverse criticism both during and after the completion of the church; his salary was withheld with the object of making him finish the building more rapidly, and in 1718 he was dismissed from his post as surveyor. After his death, however, he was buried in the crypt, where many other famous men have since been interred, some of them commemorated by memorials (not always in the best taste) in the cathedral.

St Paul's was miraculously spared during the great fire of 29 December 1940, which devastated a great area around it. During the whole of the war it was guarded by a devoted band of voluntary firewatchers, whose courage and promptness on many occasions saved it from the fate of Old St Paul's. In 1941, however, it received direct hits from high-explosive bombs which wrecked the high altar and the north transept and destroyed most of the glass, now all replaced by clear glass. — Special Services are held in the cathedral and music performed on certain occasions (see pp. 90–2).

The cathedral was once so notoriously hemmed in by buildings that it was difficult to obtain a good general impression of the exterior. The open spaces created by aerial bombardment, however, revealed many splendid and sometimes unusual prospects, and the new buildings that have been erected in the vicinity have been designed to allow some of these vistas to remain. The church as a whole is remarkable for the relationship between the Gothic plan of the structure and the classical Renaissance details. The exterior columns and coupled pilasters consist of two orders, the lower Corinthian, the upper Composite. On the north and south sides of the nave and choir aisles the upper part is little more than a screen masking the flying buttresses that help to support the clerestory of the nave. The stone balustrade along the top was one of the features introduced against the wishes of the architect, who declared that 'ladies think nothing well without an edging'. The arms of the transepts are each terminated by a semi-circular portico, the pediment above which contains (on the north) the royal arms of the Stewarts, by Grinling Gibbons, and (on the south) a Phoenix, with the inscription 'Resurgam', by C. G. Cibber. The phoenix characterizes the rise of the new St Paul's from the ashes of the old; the inscription recalls the story that when the position of the dome had been decided, a labourer was

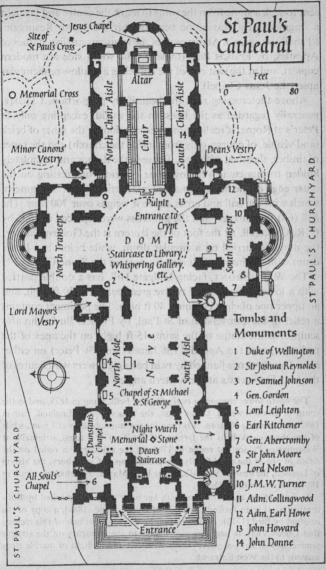

St Paul's Cathedral

Jesus Chapel

Site of St Paul's Cross

Altar

Memorial Cross

North Choir Aisle

Choir

South Choir Aisle

Minor Canons' Vestry

Dean's Vestry

Feet
0   80

North Transept

South Transept

Pulpit

Entrance to Crypt

D O M E

Staircase to Library, Whispering Gallery, etc.

Lord Mayor's Vestry

ST PAUL'S CHURCHYARD

North Aisle

N a v e

South Aisle

Chapel of St Michael & St George

St Dunstan's Chapel

Night Watch Memorial Stone

Dean's Staircase

All Souls' Chapel

ST PAUL'S CHURCHYARD

Entrance

Tombs and Monuments

1 Duke of Wellington
2 Sir Joshua Reynolds
3 Dr Samuel Johnson
4 Gen. Gordon
5 Lord Leighton
6 Earl Kitchener
7 Gen. Abercromby
8 Sir John Moore
9 Lord Nelson
10 J.M.W. Turner
11 Adm. Collingwood
12 Adm. Earl Howe
13 John Howard
14 John Donne

sent to seek a stone from the ruins to mark the centre and brought a fragment of a gravestone bearing only the word 'Resurgam' ('I shall rise again'). Above each of the transepts are five statues of Apostles, by Francis Bird (those on the south side are modern copies), and at the east end of the church is a shallow semicircular apse (the Jesus Chapel).

Above the crossing rises the beautifully proportioned DOME, generally regarded as the finest in the world, excepting only St Peter's at Rome. It really comprises two domes, the inner of brick (and visible, of course, only from inside the church) and the outer of timber, sheathed with lead. Between the domes and completely hidden from view is a hollow cone of brickwork resting on the outer edge of the inner dome and supporting a graceful lantern, which with the ball and cross above it weighs over 700 tons. The ball (6 ft in diameter) and the gilt cross were replaced in 1821 by C. R. Cockerell. At the foot of the lantern is the Golden Gallery; the dome is carried on a circular drum, while below is a larger drum with Corinthian columns supporting the Stone Gallery.

The WEST FRONT, facing Ludgate Hill, has a double portico with a lower colonnade of twelve great columns, 50 ft high, and an upper one of eight columns, 40 ft high. The pediment contains a relief of the Conversion of St Paul, by Francis Bird, who also sculptured the statue of the saint, 15 ft high, on the apex of the pediment, and the Apostles (St James? and St Peter) on either side. The portico is flanked by twin baroque towers with figures of the four Evangelists at the western angles.

The north tower contains a peal of twelve bells, hung in 1878, and in the south or clock tower is 'Great Paul', the largest bell in England, cast in 1882 and weighing 16¾ tons. It is rung for five minutes daily at 1 p.m., while of the three clock bells the largest, 'Great Tom' (5½ tons), originally at Westminster Palace but recast in 1709 for the cathedral, is tolled on the death of one of the royal family, the archbishop of Canterbury, the bishop of London, the dean of St Paul's, or the Lord Mayor. The clock was built in 1893 by John Smith of Derby.

In front of the cathedral (and with her back to it, as remarked by 18th-century wits) is an ineffectual statue of Queen Anne (1886), a copy of the original by Bird (1712). An inscription in the pavement behind this records that Queen Victoria here returned thanks to the Almighty on the sixtieth anniversary of her accession (1897). Thence a broad flight of marble steps ascends to the West Entrance.

The INTERIOR shows even more clearly the contrast between the Gothic plan of the church and the classical details. The nave has massive rectangular piers with pilasters on the inner face carried up to the barrel vault, which in each bay is intercepted by a small dome. The aisles, which also have shallow domes, are lower than the nave, a fact not evident from outside the church, as already inferred, and the triforium space above contains the Library and other rooms. The triforium has consequently a blank wall to the nave, the upper part of which is lit by a single large window in each bay of the clerestory.

Visitors are recommended first to walk up the NAVE to the dome space to enjoy the spacious dignity of the cathedral. At the west end are two bronze candelabra by Henry Pegram (1897) and a memorial slab in the floor to the Night Watch that guarded St Paul's during the war. Under the third arch of the north arcade is a colossal monument to the Duke of Wellington (d. 1852), the principal work of Alfred Stevens, begun in 1856 but still unfinished at his death in 1875. The equestrian statue of the duke was added in 1912 to the designs of Stevens by John Tweed. A bronze effigy of Wellington rests on a large sarcophagus, with a marble canopy over it and allegorical sculptures above the pediments. On the east piers of the nave are paintings by G. F. Watts: 'Time, Death and Judgement' (on the north) and 'Peace and Goodwill'.

The great DOME, the inner face of which rises 218 ft above the floor, is supported by eight massive double piers with Corinthian capitals, themselves buttressed at the angles of the crossing by four supports so huge that they contain space in their interiors for vestries and the library staircase. In the spandrels below the Whispering Gallery are mosaics executed by Antonio Salviati and representing (from the north) SS. Matthew and John (designed by G. F. Watts), SS. Mark and Luke (by W. E. F. Britten), and Isaiah, Jeremiah, Ezekiel, and Daniel (all by Alfred Stevens). In the quarter-domes below the arches are mosaics of the Crucifixion, the Entombment, the Resurrection, and the Ascension, by Sir William Richmond (d. 1921). In niches above the Whispering Gallery are statues of the Fathers of the Church, while the surface of the dome itself is decorated with eight large paintings in grisaille of scenes in the life of St Paul, by Sir James Thornhill (1715–21).

At the north angles of the dome space, beside the entrances to the transept aisles, are statues of Sir Joshua Reynolds (d. 1792), by John Flaxman, and Dr Samuel Johnson (d. 1784), in a Roman toga, by John Bacon the elder. The NORTH TRANSEPT, badly damaged in 1941 by a bomb which fell through into the crypt below, bringing down the famous inscription to Wren (see below), was rededicated after its restoration in 1962, and now contains a small chapel. Among the memorials that survived in the transept are those to Admiral Lord Rodney (d. 1792), by J. C. F. Rossi, and Sir Arthur Sullivan (d. 1900), with a bronze relief by Sir W. Goscombe John.

In the first recess of the NORTH AISLE are Two Angels at the Gate of Death, by Marochetti, in memory of Viscount Melbourne (d. 1848), the prime minister, and his brother. On the wall beyond is a bust of Earl Roberts (d. 1914), by Tweed, and in the next recess (opposite the Wellington monument) is the sarcophagus of General Gordon (d. 1885), with a bronze effigy by Boehm. The last recess on this side contains the cenotaph of Lord Leighton (d. 1896), the painter, with a bronze figure by Sir Thomas Brock. Beyond is ST DUNSTAN'S CHAPEL (reserved for private prayer), with a 17th-century oak screen by Jonathan Maine and a mosaic by Salviati. At the end of the aisle, beneath the north-west tower, is ALL SOULS' CHAPEL, converted in 1925 into a memorial chapel to Field-Marshal Earl Kitchener (d. 1916). The white marble effigy, the figures of SS. Michael and George, and the altar, with a Pietà, were all sculptured by Sir W. Reid Dick. Behind the grille on the north wall are rolls of honour of Royal Engineers, including Dominion and Indian corps, who fell in the two World Wars.

The south-west tower (usually closed) contains the DEAN'S STAIRCASE, built by William Kempster, with an ironwork balustrade by Jean Tijou. Next to it is the CHAPEL OF ST MICHAEL AND ST GEORGE, an order instituted in 1818 to reward distinguished service in the foreign affairs of the Empire. Above the stalls of the Knights Grand Cross (G.C.M.G.) hang their banners. The oak throne at the west end commemorates Lord

Forrest (d. 1918), the first Australian peer; the screen between the chapel and the aisle was carved by Jonathan Maine. The memorials in the SOUTH AISLE are of little interest, but on a pier of the south arcade is Holman Hunt's 'Light of the World', a replica of his painting at Keble College, Oxford. At the east end of the aisle is the entrance to the staircase ascending to the Library and Galleries (see below).

The west aisle of the SOUTH TRANSEPT, now used as the Baptistery, contains monuments to General Sir Ralph Abercromby (d. 1801), by Westmacott, and Sir John Moore of Corunna (d. 1809), by John Bacon the younger. To the left of the latter is a bronze memorial by Princess Louise to the 4,300 of the Colonial Troops who fell in the South African War. In the main bay is a monument to Admiral Lord Nelson (d. 1805), a fine work by Flaxman with figures on the pedestal typifying the North Sea, the Baltic, the Nile, and the Mediterranean. In the east transept aisle are monuments to J. M. W. Turner (d. 1851), a statue by Patrick Macdowell; Admiral Lord Collingwood (d. 1810), by Westmacott; Admiral Earl Howe (d. 1799), by Flaxman; and Lord Heathfield (d. 1790), the defender of Gibraltar, by Rossi. Under the arch is a monument to Sir Henry Lawrence (d. 1857), the defender of Lucknow, by J. G. Lough, and facing this is the entrance to the Crypt (see below). At the angle of the dome space is a statue of John Howard (d. 1790), the prison reformer, by the younger John Bacon, the first memorial to be admitted to the new St Paul's.

The SOUTH CHOIR AISLE, entered through fine ironwork gates by the French craftsman Jean Tijou, contains monuments to Dean Milman (d. 1868), by F. J. Williamson; Archbishop Frederick Temple (d. 1902), by F. W. Pomeroy; and various bishops. In a niche of the south wall is the unusual monument of John Donne (d. 1631), poet and Dean of St Paul's, a delicately sculptured figure in a shroud, by Nicholas Stone. This was practically the only monument of Old St Paul's to survive the Great Fire. The JESUS CHAPEL, occupying the apse at the east end of the church, was severely damaged by bombing, but has been restored more in keeping with the original intentions of Wren. Consecrated in 1958, this is Britain's memorial to its American allies who lost their lives in military operations based on this country, and it

LG–25   385

contains a roll of honour of 28,000 names. The chapel has new windows by Brian Thomas and a new altar-rail designed by S.E. Dykes Bower and made at Mortlake, in Surrey.

The CHOIR is enclosed by a low screen made from the original wrought-iron altar-rails by Tijou. On the right is the pulpit of variegated marble, and on either side of the choir are the two parts of the Organ case, richly carved by Grinling Gibbons. The organ, originally built by Father Smith (1697), was reconstructed in 1930 by Henry Willis and Sons. The beautifully carved Choir Stalls are also the work of Gibbons; especially notable are the oblong panels below the canopy, with foliage exquisitely carved in pear-wood. The reredos, damaged beyond repair by bombing, was replaced in 1958 by a new High Altar of marble with a carved oak baldacchino to the designs of W. Godfrey Allen and S. E. Dykes Bower. This is Britain's memorial to more than 324,000 men and women of the Commonwealth who lost their lives in the two World Wars.

The vaulting and walls of the choir are decorated with glass mosaics, designed by Sir William Richmond, the details of which are difficult to make out in ordinary light. Those in the saucer-domes represent (from the west) the Creation of the Beasts, Birds, and Fishes, while the dome of the great eastern apse shows Christ in Majesty, with recording angels on either side.

The CRYPT, entered from the South Transept, extends under the entire cathedral and contains the graves of many famous men. To the right in the South Choir Aisle, at the foot of the staircase, is a bust of Sir John Macdonald (d. 1891), premier of Canada. The second recess contains the tomb of John Rennie (d. 1821), the engineer, and a monument to Sir Edwin Landseer (d. 1873), the painter. In the third recess is the tomb of Sir Christopher Wren (d. 1723) and above it the original tombstone with the famous epitaph, 'Lector, si monumentum requiris, circumspice' ('Reader, if you seek his monument, look around'). This bay is known as the 'Painters' Corner' from the many graves of artists, who include Lord Leighton, Benjamin West (d. 1820), Sir Thomas Lawrence (d. 1830), Sir John Millais (d. 1896), J. M. W. Turner, and Sir Joshua Reynolds. Close by are memorials to Sir Anthony Van Dyck (d. 1641) and William Blake (d. 1827).

The chapel at the east end of the nave, occupying the site of the medieval parish church of St Faith, was redesigned by Lord Mottistone and dedicated in 1960 to the use of the Order of the British Empire, instituted by George V in 1917. In the nave, to the north-east, are the graves of Sir Hubert Parry (d. 1918) and Sir Arthur Sullivan, the composers; and on the walls on the north side are a relief of the Redemption, by J. S. Sargent (d. 1925), memorials to John Constable (d. 1837) and P. Wilson Steer (d. 1942), the artists, and a tablet to Sir Alexander Fleming (d. 1955), the discoverer of penicillin, whose ashes are buried near by. The ashes of Sir Max Beerbohm and Walter de la Mare, both of whom died in 1956, are also buried here, and they are commemorated by plaques on a pier to the south.

The west portion of the crypt contains the huge sarcophagus of the Duke of Wellington, made from a block of Cornish porphyry and resting on a granite base. Farther on to the left are memorials to the Air Transport Auxiliary in 1939–45 and to Florence Nightingale (d. 1910). Below the centre of the dome is the imposing tomb of Admiral Lord Nelson, in which his body is preserved in spirit (the only one so preserved in the cathedral). The tomb consists of a coffin made from the mainmast of the French flagship *L'Orient*, in a 16th-century marble sarcophagus designed by Benedetto da Rovezzano and intended first for Cardinal Wolsey and later for Henry VIII, but occupied by neither.

The recesses to the south contain the tombs of Admirals Lord Beatty (d. 1936), Lord Jellicoe (d. 1935), and Lord Collingwood, Nelson's successor, and of Lord Napier of Magdala (d. 1890) and a tablet to Admiral Lord Keyes (d. 1945). To the north are the graves of Field-Marshals Viscount Wolseley (d. 1913), Sir Henry Wilson (d. 1922), and Earl Roberts, and of the Earl of Northesk (d. 1831), third in command at Trafalgar, and a bust of Lawrence of Arabia (d. 1935). In the next bay to the left are a memorial to W. E. Henley (d. 1903), the poet, with a fine bust by Rodin, and a bust (after Houdon) of George Washington, presented in 1921 by the American people. On the wall close to this is a tablet to Pilot-Officer William Fiske, who lost his life while flying with the R.A.F. in the Battle of Britain, 'an American citizen who died that England might live'. In the opposite bay are busts of Sir Stafford Cripps (d. 1952), the Labour minister, by Sir Jacob Epstein, and R. J. Seddon (d. 1906), prime minister of New Zealand, and memorials to W. M. Hughes (d. 1952), prime minister of Australia, and other Colonial statesmen. The nave contains wall monuents to Charles Reade (d. 1884), the novelist; Sir Walter Besant (d. 1901), the historian of London; R. H. Barham (d. 1845), author of the *Ingoldsby Legends* and a minor canon of St Paul's; Prebendary Wilson Carlile (d. 1942), founder of the Church Army (all on the left); and Sir George Williams (d. 1905), founder of the Y.M.C.A. Farther on are some mutilated monuments from Old St Paul's, and a Bible placed here in 1947 in tribute to Sir Winston Churchill. At the west end of the crypt is the ornate funeral car, weighing 18 tons, in which the body of the Duke of Wellington was brought from Chelsea Hospital to St Paul's in 1852. It was partly made from cannon captured at Waterloo and bears the names of his victories.

The Upper Parts of the cathedral are approached by the staircase opening off the South Aisle. An easy climb of 143 steps leads to the SOUTH TRIFORIUM GALLERY, which has plans, sketches, etc., of the successive churches, architectural fragments, and other relics. At the west end is the LIBRARY, notable for its carved woodwork and containing a good collection of manuscripts, books, autographs, etc., the nucleus of which was formed by a bequest of Bishop Compton (1714). The medieval collections were destroyed in the Great Fire or scattered during the Commonwealth. The WEST GALLERY, affording a striking view of the interior of the cathedral, admits to the TROPHY ROOM, on the north side, with Wren's models and various designs for St Paul's and relics relating to the history of the church.

From the entrance to the Triforium a flight of 116 steps ascends to the WHISPERING GALLERY, at the foot of the drum supporting the inner dome and 100 ft above the floor of the cathedral, of which it offers an unusual survey. It is also the best place from which to see Thornhill's paintings on the dome. The gallery derives its name from the fact that words whispered against the wall on one side are distinctly audible near the wall on the opposite side, 107 ft away in a straight line. A further climb of 117 steps leads out to the STONE GALLERY, at the base of the outer dome and commanding an extensive prospect over London, most of whose famous buildings are in view, while an increasing number of new buildings are springing up all round. To the south can be seen the high-lying television mast at Crystal Palace.

An even more impressive view is obtained from the GOLDEN GALLERY, at the foot of the lantern surmounting the outer dome, and 166 steps higher by a winding staircase between the domes. Thence a further ascent leads into the BALL at the top of the lantern (limited view), 627 steps from the floor of the church.

The churchyard around the cathedral, laid out as a public garden, is still enclosed by railings made of iron smelted at Lamberhurst, in the Kentish Weald. On the south side of the nave are some fragments of the medieval cloisters and chapter house, destroyed in the Great Fire. To the north of the choir a memorial with a figure of St Paul, by Mackennal (1910), marks the approximate site of Paul's Cross, a famous open-air pulpit, taken down by Parliament in 1643. Here the Pope's condemnation of Martin Luther was proclaimed in the presence of Cardinal Wolsey.

On the north-west of the street around the cathedral (also called St Paul's Churchyard) is the CHAPTER HOUSE, a charming brick building by Wren (1712–14), altered in the 19th century. Gutted by bombing in 1940, it was restored to Wren's original design in 1957. Dean's Court, starting south-west of the cathedral, leads past the DEANERY, another delightful work by Wren, built about 1670. The adjoining CHOIR HOUSE, with the choristers' school (entered from Carter Lane) was erected in 1874. An entirely new plan for the precincts of the cathedral, drawn up by Sir William Holford, was approved in 1956.

SCIENCE & GEOLOGICAL MUSEUMS Plan VI, C3

STATION: SOUTH KENSINGTON, nearly ¼-m. S., on the Circle, District, and Piccadilly lines, reached by a subway entered in Exhibition Road north of the Science Museum. — MOTOR-BUSES in Brompton Road and Cromwell Road, see Route 10; in Kensington Road, see Route 11.

ADMISSION to both museums, weekdays 10 to 6; Sundays 2.30 to 6 (free). Closed on Good Friday and Christmas Day. The museums are connected by a covered gallery at first floor level. — LECTURES in the Science Museum on Tuesdays, Thursdays, and Saturdays at 3.15 in the galleries or the Lecture Theatre (reached from Gallery 5); in the Geological Museum on Tuesdays–Thursdays and Saturdays at 3 in the Lecture Room. — The SCIENCE LIBRARY is open on weekdays (except Bank Holidays) from 10 to 5.30, by reader's ticket (obtainable on application at the Library or, in writing, to the Director). The GEOLOGICAL LIBRARY is open (free) on weekdays, 10 to 5.

The SCIENCE MUSEUM and the GEOLOGICAL MUSEUM are adjoining museums in Exhibition Road, South Kensington, close to the Natural History Museum. The Science Museum, established in 1856, occupies a large building by Sir Richard Allison which will eventually be extended as far as Queen's Gate; the first part, the Eastern Block, was completed in 1928. The museum, covering almost every aspect of science in its application to technology and industry, comprises an unparalleled assembly of machines, industrial plant, and scientific instruments, including many working models and examples of original and historic apparatus. The museum is of great educational value and even the unscientific visitor will find it of much interest. Changes in the arrangement described below will be made when the Centre Block, now under construction, is completed, probably in 1963.

The Museum of Practical Geology (p. 393) is the headquarters of the Geological Survey of Great Britain, the oldest in the world, founded in 1835. The collections were first opened in 1837 and were moved in 1935 to a handsome building here by John H. Markham.

In the VESTIBULE of the Science Museum are a statue in terracotta of Galileo Galilei (d. 1642), the Italian scientist, and a model of the Foucault Pendulum, devised in 1851 to demonstrate the rotation of the Earth on its own axis. GALLERY 1, on the right, is devoted to Air and Sea Navigation.

A staircase to the left of the Vestibule descends to the interesting CHILDREN'S GALLERY in the basement, designed as an introduction to the main branches of physical science. Models, dioramas, and working demonstrations show the development of transport by land, sea, and air; methods of communication; sources of mechanical power; the measurement of time, etc. Other sections here illustrate the development of lighting and fire-making, and of mining, including an excellent reconstruction of a modern mine; and there are interiors showing a flint-worker's shop, a nail-maker's forge, and a wheelwright's shop.

From the Vestibule steps descend to the EAST HALL, which contains most of the larger exhibits illustrating the development of motive power. Among the notable and historic machinery are an atmospheric beam engine from Pentrich Colliery, Derbyshire (1791); two rotative engines, of 1788 and 1797, by James Watt; the high-pressure vertical steam engine and boiler of Richard Trevithick (1803); the steam turbine and dynamo invented by Sir Charles Parsons (1884); and the first diesel engine to be made in Britain (by Rudolf Diesel, 1897). Models include windmills at Sprowston (Norfolk) and Cranbrook (Kent), the Pelton wheel (for utilizing the power of waterfalls), Newcomen's atmospheric pumping engine (1740), and Smeaton's mine pumping engine (1772). GALLERY 2, on the left, demonstrates animal, water, and wind power, with models of horse-gears, waterwheels, and wind-mills, and steam boilers and turbines.

GALLERY 3, on the right of the hall, devoted to stationary steam engines, includes models made by Watt in 1765 for his experiments on steam, engines designed by him in partnership with Boulton, and models of beam and horizontal engines. GALLERY 4 is confined to railway locomotives and rolling stock, with many working models, some of which are arranged to show their internal construction. Here also are William Hedley's 'Puffing Billy', the oldest locomotive in the world (1813), George Stephenson's 'Rocket' (1829), and Timothy Hackworth's 'Sans Pareil' (1829); and near these is a case with memorials of Stephenson. Drawings, photographs, etc., show the development of railway construction and operation. In an alcove on the north of this gallery is a reproduction of James Watt's workshop at Heathfield Hall, near Birmingham. GALLERY 5, at the west end of the hall, contains hot air, gas, and oil engines, including the Parsons axial-flow turbo-blower of 1901, and illustrates the evolution of the mechanically-propelled road vehicle from the steam carriages of Cugnot (1770) and Murdock (about 1784), of which there are models, to the petrol-driven motor-car (Benz, 1888; etc.) and motor-cycle (Wolfmüller, 1894), and the Rover gas-turbine car, the first in the world (1950). GALLERY 4A, opening to the right (with an exit to Imperial Institute Road), shows the development of the bicycle from the Hobby Horse of 1818 and the Michaux 'Boneshaker' of about 1867.

On the west of Gallery 5 are the LECTURE HALL and a lift to the upper floors; opposite the lift-gate is a room reserved for special exhibitions. GALLERY 6, farther west, is devoted to Electric Power, with a reproduction of Faraday's original experiment in the continuous generation of electricity (1831), models of early hydro-electric power-stations (the first designed by Edison in New York, 1881), Parsons' original turbo-generator installed at Ackton Hall colliery (Yorkshire) in 1900, and models of the power-station at Castle Donington (Leicestershire), the largest in Britain when it was built (1956). At the farther end is a working million-volt impulse generator.

The FIRST FLOOR is mainly occupied by the smaller exhibits relating to industry and engineering. Gallery 21: Mechanical Engineering (the original model of the first steam hammer, early machine tools, a model of a 19th-century workshop, etc.); Telegraphy and Telephony. Gallery 22: Iron and Steel (a Bessemer convector of 1865, etc.). Gallery 23: Radio Communication, Radar, and Television, including J. L. Baird's first transmitter (1926). Gallery 24: Textile Machinery; Arkwright's hand spinning wheel and other machines (1769–80), copies of Hargraves' spinning-jenny (1767) and Crompton's mule (1779). Gallery 25: Typewriting, Printing (wooden hand press of about 1700 compared with later presses that may be operated by visitors), Paper Making, and Non-Ferrous Metals. Gallery 26 (to the west): Agricultural Implements and Machinery, including a working combine harvester; and Gas Manufacture.

The SECOND FLOOR has an outstanding collection of models of ships of all kinds. Gallery 41: Merchant Steamers and Motor-Ships (the paddle steamers *Sirius* and *Great Western* that made the first crossings of the Atlantic under power, 1838; the *Great Britain*, 1843, the first screw steamer to cross the Atlantic), and Warships (H.M.S. *Warrior*, the first sea-going ironclad, 1861; etc.), submarines, and landing-craft of the Second World War. Gallery 42: Sailing Ships, including an early Egyptian boat, a Viking galley, the *Santa Maria* of Christopher Columbus, an Elizabethan galleon, and Nelson's famous flagship, the *Victory*. Gallery 43: Yachts, fishing vessels, and other small craft. Gallery 44: Marine Engines, among them Symington's 'atmospheric' engine of 1788, and Turbines (model for Parsons' *Turbinia*, the first turbine-driven vessel), Boilers, Propellors, and Steering Gear. Gallery 45: Weights and Measures; Timepieces, including 14th-century clock mechanism from Wells Cathedral. Gallery 46 (to the west): Industrial Chemistry.

The THIRD FLOOR is confined mostly to physics and allied subjects. Gallery 61: Magnetism and Electricity (cylinder frictional machine used by Joseph Priestley; original hydro-electric machine constructed by Sir W. G. Armstrong); Electron Physics (tube designed by Crookes for his researches on cathode rays, and that used by J. J. Thomson in the discovery of the electron, 1897); and Acoustics (Edison's original phonograph). Gallery 62: Meteorological, Heat, and Thermal Instruments (Joule's original apparatus, 1843). Gallery 63: Map-Making and Surveying; Atomic Physics, including part of the apparatus with which Cockcroft and Walton 'split the atom' (1932), and a model of the first atomic pile at Harwell (Berkshire). Gallery 64: Astronomy (copies of early telescopes made by Galileo and Newton; instruments made by Sir William Herschel; and a working star projector); Mathematics (early calculating devices, etc.), continued in Gallery 65, which also contains Optical Instruments and Microscopes (a large and fine collection, including one made in 1675 for Robert Hooke) and illustrates Geophysics. Gallery 66 (to the west): Pure Chemistry (apparatus of John Dalton, Sir William Ramsay, and others), Photography (two of the earliest impressions, made by Niepce in 1826–7; early daguerrotype apparatus; etc.) and Cinematography (apparatus of Le Prince, Edison, and Paul, and examples of the pioneer work of Eadweard Muybridge and William Friese-Greene). Here also are the scientific instruments used for the instruction of the children of George III.

The fine AERONAUTICAL COLLECTION, to be opened on the third

floor of the new Centre Block, includes a model of Montgolfier's hot-air balloon (1783); a reproduction of the first model glider (1804) of Sir George Cayley, a pioneer of aviation; the model for the first projected aeroplane, made by Henson and Stringfellow (1843); the original glider used successfully in 1895 by Otto Lilienthal; and a replica of the aeroplane built by the Wright brothers in 1903, the first power-driven heavier-than-air machine to make a sustained flight carrying a man. Among later aircraft are the Roe triplane (1909), the J.A.P.-Harding monoplane (1910), the Fokker monoplane (1916), the Vickers-Vimy aeroplane in which Alcock and Brown made the first non-stop Transatlantic flight (1919), the De Havilland 'Gipsy Moth' flown by Amy Johnson to Australia (1930), and the Supermarine seaplane which won the Schneider Trophy for Britain in 1931. A case contains models, etc., of the experiments in aeronautics of Leonardo da Vinci, and other exhibits include Frost's 'Ornithopter', a curious but unsuccessful machine with flapping wings (1902), Professor Piccard's stratosphere gondola (1932), and a wide range of aero engines, including examples of the latest jet engines. Exhibits of the Second World War include the Gloster-Whittle aircraft (the first successful jet-propelled machine; 1941), a German rotating-wing kite (1943), and a V1 flying-bomb, shown in section to disclose its mechanism. Here also is the Rolls-Royce 'Flying Bedstead', the first jet-propelled machine to take off vertically (1952). A series of over a hundred scale models illustrates the development of aircraft up to the modern civil airliner.

The SCIENCE LIBRARY, reached from an entrance on the south side of Imperial Institute Road, comprises about 450,000 volumes and about 25,000 periodicals covering every important branch of pure and applied science (except medicine).

The collections of the GEOLOGICAL MUSEUM are displayed in a large hall with two galleries above. From the Entrance Hall, decorated with British ornamental stones, steps lead up through an arch of beautiful British marbles to the MAIN HALL. Facing the entrance is a rotating globe, 6 ft in diameter, showing the geology of the Earth. In the centre of the hall are cases containing a splendid collection of precious and ornamental stones. Fronting these is a fountain of granite from Aberdeenshire, and notable also are the vases of Siberian aventurine quartz, Derbyshire fluorspar or 'blue john', alabaster, and Cornish serpentine. At the sides are dioramas of landscapes illustrating geological features, and at the end is a copy of the Farnese Hercules in Portland stone. The south-east bay covers the geology of the London district and the Thames Valley, that on the north-east is devoted to South-East England. Other bays deal with the Hampshire Basin, rock structures and metamorphic rocks, volcanoes, and ceramics and geology (on the north side); glaciers and early man, coal, marine action, rivers and lakes, weathering, and earth structure (on the south). Special temporary exhibits are arranged from time to time in the Main Hall.

The First Floor Gallery is confined mainly to the REGIONAL GEOLOGY OF BRITAIN. At the east end are an illuminated column showing the duration of the geological periods and a record of the chief events, and (in the bays) a comprehensive collection of British fossils. The Second Floor Gallery is devoted to ECONOMIC MINERALOGY, with interesting maps and dioramas, and a section exhibiting British minerals (south-east bay).

The GEOLOGICAL LIBRARY, on the north-west side (ground floor), contains some 62,000 books and 27,000 maps, as well as numerous pamphlets and periodicals.

SOUTHWARK CATHEDRAL Plan IX, E 1

STATION: LONDON BRIDGE, 200 yds E., on the Northern line and a terminus of the Southern Region. — MOTOR-BUSES across London Bridge, see Route 25; in Borough High Street and Southwark Street, see Route 35.

ADMISSION daily until dusk. Services on Sundays at 8.30, 10.15, and 11 a.m., and 3 and 6.30 p.m.; on weekdays at 7.30, 8, and 5.15 (choral, except on Wednesday; 5 on Saturday).

SOUTHWARK CATHEDRAL, officially the collegiate and cathedral church of St Saviour and St Mary Overy, is the mother church of the diocese of Southwark, which was created in 1905 and includes most of south London and much of east Surrey. Though often altered and restored, and given a new nave in the late 19th century, the church remains, after Westminster Abbey, the most impressive Gothic building in London. It has associations with Shakespeare and other Elizabethan players of Bankside and with John Harvard, the founder of Harvard University. The cathedral stands near the southern approach to London Bridge, its noble tower a familiar object in views across the river from the City.

The first church on this site was founded, according to tradition, by a community of nuns who settled here about A.D. 606. The dedication until 1540 was to St Mary Overy or Overie, a suffix that has been the subject of much controversy based on no definite evidence. The most probable of the numerous conjectures is that it means 'over the river' (i.e. from the

City). In 852, presumably after the nuns had left Southwark, a college of priests declaring allegiance to no particular order was established by St Swithun, bishop of Winchester. This later became a priory for canons regular of the Augustinian order, who in 1106 erected a large church in the Norman style of which some traces survive. The priory enjoyed the patronage of the bishops of Winchester, who built a diocesan palace near by. The Norman church was burned down in 1206, and the new building that rose in its place under Peter des Roches, bishop of Winchester, was the first in London to be constructed in the Gothic style. Of this church there survives the crossing, with the lower part of the central tower, the choir with its ambulatories, and the retro-choir. The transepts were added early in the 14th century, but the south transept was recast about 1420 by Cardinal Beaufort. The 13th-century nave, partly rebuilt in 1469, when it was given a timber roof, was declared to be in a dangerous state by 1830. Demolished in 1839, it was replaced at first by an ineffectual 'preaching place' and in 1890-7 by a more satisfactory Gothic nave to the designs of Sir Arthur Blomfield.

The church continued to be the property of the Augustinians until 1540, when the priory was dissolved. A small parish church had been built adjoining the priory church on the south, but at the dissolution the parishioners took over the larger church, whose dedication they changed to St Saviour, the name of the suppressed abbey of Bermondsey. The church remained in the diocese of Winchester until 1877, when south London was transferred to that of Rochester (under one of whose bishops, Dr Thorold, the nave was rebuilt), but in 1905 the diocese of Rochester was divided, so that Southwark became an independent see, with St Saviour's as its cathedral.

Almost the only notable feature of the exterior of the cathedral is the fine TOWER, 163 ft high, the lower part of which was built in the early 13th century, while the two upper stages were raised in 1520 (the pinnacles, however, are later). The oldest of the peal of twelve bells dates from 1735. On the south of the choir can be seen some of the paving stones of the old parish church, demolished in 1822.

The Cathedral is entered by the SOUTH TRANSEPT, rebuilt about 1420 by Cardinal Beaufort (half-brother of Henry IV), whose niece, Joan Beaufort, was married to James I of Scotland in the church in 1423. The arms of the cardinal are carved on the pillar to the north of the door. Opposite is a memorial to John Bingham (d. 1625), one of the 'bargainers' who bought the church for the parish in 1612 (it had been rented only since 1540), and below this is a small monument to William Emerson (d. 1575), supposed to be an ancestor of R. W. Emerson, the American essayist. The transepts have no triforium and are otherwise simpler than the choir in architectural form, confirming the fact that the canons completed their church only after overcoming financial difficulties. The unsatisfactory vaulting was raised in 1830, and the large gable windows are both 19th-century insertions.

The NAVE of seven bays, rebuilt in 1890–7 by Sir Arthur Blomfield, follows the medieval choir closely in style (see below). At the west end of the south aisle is a section of 13th-century arcading; the marble font close by, designed by G. F. Bodley, has an elaborate wooden Gothic cover, 13 ft high, by Walter Hare. A case near the south door contains Roman and medieval pottery, tiles, etc., found during restorations of the church. At the west end of the north aisle are two relics from the Norman church; a round-headed doorway and a recess that was once probably part of a tomb. In front of this is a 'memento mori' of a monk, probably from the tomb of one of the canons, and against the west wall are preserved some of the 150 richly-carved and coloured bosses that formed part of the 15th-century roof. In the north aisle is the tomb of John Gower, the friend of Chaucer, with the head of the effigy resting on his three best-known works. The poet lived and died (in 1408) in the precincts of the priory. In the south aisle is a memorial to William Shakespeare (1912), with a recumbent alabaster figure by Henry McCarthy and a relief depicting Southwark during the poet's time. The stained-glass window above, by Christopher Webb (1954), shows numerous figures from the plays.

The early-13th-century CHOIR of five bays contains the oldest Gothic work in London. It has massive piers with detached shafts, the inner three of which are carried up to the springing of the vault ribs. The vault itself was remade in the early 19th century, though the bosses are perhaps original. The triforium has an arcaded wall-passage with free-standing columns (the first of its kind in England), and shows interesting detail. The clerestory also has a wall-passage, with a stepped triplet arch, and a single lancet window in each bay. The choir stalls were designed by Blomfield, the bishop's throne and the stalls for the suffragan bishops (north of the sanctuary) are by Bodley and Hare. In the floor between the stalls are slabs commemorating the dramatists, John Fletcher (d.

1625) and Philip Massinger (d. 1639), and Edmund Shakespeare (d. 1607), 'a player', youngest brother of the poet; all are buried in the church, but their graves are unidentified. The splendid altar-screen, in the Perpendicular style, was erected in 1520 by Richard Fox, bishop of Winchester. Mutilated in 1703, it was restored in 1830, when the cornice of angels was added, and in 1912 the niches (divided horizontally by charming rows of angels) were filled with statues mostly representing persons connected with the church or diocese. A new altarpiece was introduced in 1929 by Sir Ninian Comper, who also gilded the lower part of the screen and designed the glass in the 19th-century east window.

The massive piers of the CROSSING are part of the early-13th-century building. Those on the south have clustered shafts that are carried down almost to the floor, but on the north these are stopped at a platform about 12 ft from the floor, perhaps to allow for a screen enclosing the NORTH TRANSEPT, completed early in the 14th century. On the west wall here is an unusual and much-repaired memorial, by Nicholas Stone (1633), to the Austin family, and below it is an elaborately carved muniment chest of 1588. On the north wall are a blocked aumbry; a wooden sword-rest of 1674 with the arms of the City and Southwark; the tomb of Lyonell Lockyer (d. 1672), a quack doctor of the time of Charles II (the inscription is worth reading); and a good bust of Richard Blisse (d. 1703). On the east of the transept opens the Chapel of St John the Evangelist, called the HARVARD CHAPEL since it was re-built in 1907 (by C. R. Blomfield) in memory of John Harvard, the founder of Harvard University, Massachusetts, who was born in the parish (1607) and baptized in the church. The east window, painted by the American artist, John La Farge, was presented by Joseph H. Choate, the United States ambassador, in 1905 and restored in 1948 after war damage. The chapel is entered through two much-restored Norman arches; and on the left of the altar is a Norman shaft, discovered during the rebuilding.

The NORTH AMBULATORY or choir aisle is approached through an unusual moulded arch. On the left are a 16th-century studded doorway and a memorial to John Trehearne (d. 1618), 'gentleman portar' to James I. Farther east are two recessed tombs, perhaps of priors; the second now contains a fine wooden effigy of a cross-legged knight of about 1290, possibly one of the De Warennes who were benefactors of the priory. On the south side is the characteristic Jacobean tomb of Alderman Richard Humble (d. 1616). At the east end of the church is the delightful LADY CHAPEL, properly a retro-choir, as the original Lady Chapel, farther east, was pulled down in 1830. It consists of four parallel aisles of equal height, separated by graceful clustered columns supporting a low vault and ending in chapels with groups of triple lancets. Here in 1555 Stephen Gardiner, bishop of Winchester, and Edmund Bonner, bishop of London, presided at the courts at which Bishops Hooper and Ferrar and other Marian martyrs were condemned to the stake. The chapel was well restored in 1832–5. On the west side can be seen the tracery of openings blocked by the 16th-century screen. In the north wall is a window by C. E. Kempe with figures of St Thomas Becket, Charles I, and Archbishop Laud; the second chapel from the north contains a beautifully carved 17th-century altar-table (covered, but shown by a verger). In the SOUTH AMBULATORY is seen the fine tomb of Lancelot Andrewes (d. 1626), bishop of Winchester, with a new canopy (1919) replacing that destroyed by fire in 1676, and the arms of dioceses and cathedrals that he served. Next to it is the tomb of Edward Stuart Talbot (d. 1934), the first bishop of Southwark, with a gilded effigy by Cecil Thomas.

A window on the south side contains a panel of Elizabethan glass, the only old glass in the church. Below the arch to the South Transept are Roman tesserae dug up in the churchyard. The quaint inscription on the brass (to the right) of Susanna Barford, who died in 1652 at the age of ten, is worth reading.

TATE GALLERY Plan VIII, E 3

STATIONS: WESTMINSTER, ¾-m. N., on the Circle and District lines; VAUXHALL, ½-m. SE., on the Southern Region. — MOTOR-BUSES along Millbank and in Vauxhall Bridge Road, see below and Route 3.

ADMISSION weekdays 10 to 6; Sundays and Boxing Day 2 to 6 (free). Closed on Good Friday, Christmas Eve, and Christmas Day. — LECTURE TOURS on Tuesdays, Thursdays, and Saturdays, at 3 p.m. — LICENSED RESTAURANT, with delightful murals by Rex Whistler (1928), in the Basement.

The TATE GALLERY accommodates the greater part of the national collection of British painting, as well as the national collections of modern foreign painting (mainly from France) and of modern sculpture. It owes its establishment largely to the munificence of Sir Henry Tate, the sugar refiner, who commissioned the building and gave his own collection of sixty-five paintings. The gallery, designed by Sidney R. J. Smith in a modified classical style and opened in 1897, stands on Millbank, facing the Thames, between Lambeth and Vauxhall Bridges. It is most conveniently reached by motor-bus from Parliament Square (passing the gallery) or from Victoria Station to Vauxhall Bridge, a few minutes' walk from the entrance. As only about one-sixth of the large and growing collection can be displayed at any one time, changes in the arrangement are frequent. The British paintings, though shared with the National Gallery, include almost every important artist since the 17th century. Among the foreign paintings are good selections of the French Impressionists and Post-Impressionists, while the sculpture, if less complete, includes notable works by Rodin, Maillol, and other masters.

The idea of a national collection of British art was first mooted by Sir Francis Chantrey, the sculptor, who in 1841 bequeathed his fortune to the Royal Academy for that purpose. Many further bequests were made and eventually Sir Henry Tate (d. 1899) offered to build a gallery, a site for which was found on ground previously occupied by the Millbank Penitentiary, a model prison opened in 1816 in accordance with the ideals of Jeremy Bentham, the legal reformer, and pulled down in 1893. New galleries and a sculpture hall were added in 1899 by the founder, and in 1910 further galleries were built (through the generosity of Sir Joseph Duveen) to house the bequest of a great number of his own paintings, drawings, and sketches by J. M. W. Turner (compare p. 355). In 1926 Lord Duveen (son of Sir Joseph) provided for new galleries (one of which was to house the works of the American artist, J. S. Sargent) and in 1937 an enlarged sculpture gallery was opened at his expense. Works purchased under the Chantrey Bequest, which now realizes about £3,000 annually, are presented to the Tate. In 1961 most of the better-known French Impressionist and Post-Impressionist paintings were transferred to the National Gallery.

To the north of the entrance is a statue of Sir John Millais (d. 1896), by Sir Thomas Brock. Steps ascend to a Vestibule, where umbrellas, etc., must be left. Beyond is the CENTRAL HALL, with the bookstall, and here and in the fine SCULPTURE GALLERY is a representative selection of British and foreign sculpture. This usually includes a number of the following works, some of which, however, will be found in the picture galleries. *Rodin*, 'Le Baiser' (marble), 'St John the Baptist', 'The Age of Bronze', and other splendid bronzes; *Reg. Butler*, 'Woman' and 'Girl'; *Carpeux*, 'H. J. and Mrs Turner'; *César*, 'The Man of Saint-Denis'; *Dalou*, 'Alphonse Legros' and 'La Paysanne'; *Degas*, 'La Petite Danseuse' and other bronzes of dancers; *Frank Dobson*, 'Susannah', 'Truth', 'Head of Sir Osbert Sitwell' (in brass); *Epstein*, 'The Visitation', 'Somerset Maugham', 'Professor Einstein', etc.; *Gaudier-Brzeska*, 'La Chanteuse Triste' and 'Horace Brodzky'; *Eric Gill*, 'Mankind' and 'Prospero and Ariel'; *Barbara Hepworth*, 'Bicentric Form'; *Eric Kennington*, 'Effigy of T. E. Lawrence'; *Kršinic*, 'Study of a Girl'; *Maurice Lambert*, 'Swan'; *Arnold Machin*, 'Spring' (terracotta); *Maillol*, 'The Three Nymphs', 'Torso', and 'Woman with a Necklace'; *Manzù*, 'Susanna' and 'Cardinal'; *Marini*, 'Cavaliere'; *Meštrovič*, 'Head of the Artist', 'Strahinič Ban' (14th-century Serbian hero), and 'Woman with a Guitar'; *Carl Milles*, 'Folke Filbyter'; *Henry Moore*, 'Family Group', 'King and Queen', and 'Recumbent Figure'; *Nimptsch*, 'Reclining Woman'; *Renoir*, 'La Laveuse' and 'Venus Victrix'; *Alfred Stevens*, Casts for the Wellington monument in St Paul's Cathedral (see p. 383); *J. Havard Thomas*, 'Cassandra', 'Lycidas', 'Thyrsis', 'Cardinal Manning'; *G. F. Watts*, 'Clytie' and 'Daphne'; *Derwent Wood*, 'Torso'; *Zadkine*, 'Venus'.

On the walls are usually hung some of the gallery's larger paintings: *J. S. Copley*, 'The Siege of Gibraltar'; *Augustus John*, 'Galway', a cartoon; *Stanley Spencer*, 'Resurrection (1926)' and 'Resurrection (1950)'; *G. F. Watts*, 'A Story from Boccaccio'; *Ethel Walker*, 'Nausicaa' and 'Zones of Love and Hate'.

The BRITISH PAINTINGS are arranged, for the most part chronologically, on the left (west) of the gallery. EARLY PORTRAIT PAINTING (Room I): *John Bettes*, 'Man in a Black Cap' (the earliest work in the gallery, 1545); *William Dobson* (d. 1646), 'Endymion Porter'; *Marc Gheeraerdts* (d. 1635), 'Lady Anne and Lady Elizabeth Pope'; *George Gower* (d. about 1596), 'Sir Thomas and Lady Kytson'; *Cornelius Johnson* (d. 1664), 'Cornelia Veth'; *Sir Godfrey Kneller* (d. 1723), 'The Angel appearing to Tobit', a remarkable early work, 'First Marquess of Tweeddale', etc.; *Sir Peter Lely* (d. 1680), 'Girl feeding a Parrot' and 'Two Ladies of the Lake Family'; *Daniel Mytens* (d. before 1648), 'James, third Marquess of Hamilton'; *Paul van Somer* (d. 1622), 'Elizabeth Grey, Countess of Kent'; *John Michael Wright* (d. about 1700), 'Sir Neill O'Neill'.

Room II is devoted to a collection of paintings, drawings, and water-colours by WILLIAM BLAKE (d. 1827), the poet-mystic, including illustrations to Dante's *Divine Comedy*, and other characteristic works. The mosaic floor, by Boris Anrep (1923), was inspired by Blake's *Marriage of Heaven and Hell*.

18TH-CENTURY PAINTING (Rooms III and IV): *Francis Cotes* (d. 1770), 'Paul Sandby'; *Arthur Devis* (d. 1787), 'The James Family'; *Thomas Gainsborough* (d. 1788), 'James Baillie and Family', 'Landscape at Sunset', 'Lord Kilmorey', 'Margaret Gainsborough' (his elder daughter), 'Musidora', 'View of Dedham', etc.; *Francis Hayman* (d. 1776), 'Wrestling Scene from *As You Like It*'; *Joseph Highmore* (d. 1780), Illustrations to Richardson's *Pamela*; *William Hogarth* (d. 1764), 'Bishop Hoadly', 'Calais Gate (the Roast Beef of Old England)', 'The Graham Children', 'Lavinia Fenton', 'Scene from *The Beggar's Opera*', 'Self Portrait', etc.; *Thomas Hudson* (d. 1779), 'Mrs Collier'; *William Marlow* (d. 1813), 'Capriccio: St Paul's and a Venetian Canal'; *George Morland* (d. 1804), 'Stable Interior', etc.; *John Opie* (d. 1807), 'A Peasant's Family'; *Allan Ramsay* (d. 1784), 'Portrait of a Man'; *Sir Joshua Reynolds* (d. 1792), 'Admiral Keppel', 'Francis and Susannah Beckford', 'Lady Bamfylde', 'Lord Ligonier', and other portraits, and 'Heads of Angels' and 'The Age of Innocence', two favourite pictures; *George Romney* (d. 1802), 'Jacob Morland of Capplethwaite' and 'Mr and Mrs William Lindow'; *Samuel Scott* (d. 1772), 'Admiral Anson's Action off Cape Finisterre'; *George Stubbs* (d. 1806), 'Mares and Foals in a Landscape'; *Sir James Thornhill* (d. 1734), 'Sketch for a Ceiling Decoration; *Richard Wilson* (d. 1782), 'Lake Avernus', 'Llyn-y-Cau, Cader Idris', 'The Thames near Twickenham', and other landscapes; *John Wootton* (d. 1765), 'Members of the Beaufort Hunt'; *Joseph Wright* (of Derby; d. 1797), 'An Experiment with the Air-Pump' and 'Sir Brooke Boothby'; *Johann*

Zoffany (d. 1810), 'Charles Macklin as Shylock', 'Florentine Fruit Stall', etc.

EARLY 19TH-CENTURY PAINTING (Room XVII, right of Room IV): *R. P. Bonington* (d. 1828), 'Column of St Mark at Venice'; *J. S. Copley* (d. 1815), 'The Death of Major Peirson'; *David Cox* (d. 1859), 'The Welsh Funeral'; *John Crome* (d. 1821), 'Slate Quarries' and 'Mousehold Heath'; *William Etty* (d. 1849), 'Hero and Leander'; *Henry Fuseli* (d. 1825; a Swiss admirer of Blake), 'Unidentified Subject'; *Andrew Geddes* (d. 1844), 'Mrs Greatorex'; *B. R. Haydon* (d. 1846), 'Punch, or May Day' and 'Chairing the Member'; *Sir Edwin Landseer* (d. 1873), 'The Duchess of Abercorn' and 'Lake Scene'; *Sir Thomas Lawrence* (d. 1830), 'Mrs Siddons', and other portraits; *C. R. Leslie* (d. 1859), 'Uncle Toby and Widow Wadman'; *John Linnell* (d. 1882), 'Kensington Sand Quarry'; *John Martin* (d. 1854), 'Biblical Scene'; *James Ward* (d. 1859), 'Gordale Scar', a large romantic canvas, and 'The Deer Stealer'; *Benjamin West* (d. 1820), 'Cleombrotus ordered into Banishment' and 'Lady Beauchamp-Proctor'; *Sir David Wilkie* (d. 1841), 'The Blind Fiddler' and 'Village Festival'.

In Room V are delightful and characteristic landscapes by JOHN CONSTABLE (d. 1837), 'Marine Parade and Old Chain Pier, Brighton' (1827), 'Salisbury', 'The Valley Farm', 'Dedham Mill', 'Hadleigh Castle', 'Hampstead Heath', 'Trees near Hampstead Church', etc.; also portraits of 'Dr and Mrs Andrew'.

Rooms VI–X contain an unsurpassed range of paintings by J. M. W. TURNER (d. 1851), the majority bequeathed by the artist. The many splendid landscapes include the early 'Buttermere', 'The Arch of Titus and the Campo Vaccino at Rome', 'The Bay of Baiae', 'Frosty Morning', 'Hero and Leander', 'London from Greenwich', 'The Old Chain Pier, Brighton', 'Petworth Park' (Sussex), 'Phryne going to the Bath as Venus', 'Richmond Hill' (Surrey), 'A Ship Aground', 'The Shipwreck', 'Spithead', and 'The Tenth Plague of Egypt'; also a Portrait of the Artist at the age of about twenty-three. Room X usually contains a selection of watercolours by Turner and relics from his studio.

THE PRE-RAPHAELITES (Room XI, beyond Room VII): *Ford Madox Brown* (d. 1893), 'Chaucer at the Court of Edward

III', 'Christ washing Peter's Feet', 'Lear and Cordelia'; *Sir Edward Burne-Jones* (d. 1898), 'The Golden Stairs' and 'King Cophetua and the Beggar Maid'; *William Dyce* (d. 1864), 'St John leading the Virgin from the Tomb'; *Arthur Hughes* (d. 1915), 'The Eve of St Agnes' and 'April Love'; *Holman Hunt* (d. 1910), 'Claudio and Isabella' and 'Strayed Sheep'; *Sir John Millais* (d. 1896), 'Christ at the House of His Parents' (often called 'The Carpenter's Shop', painted when the artist was twenty), 'The Boyhood of Raleigh', 'Ophelia', 'The Order of Release'; *William Morris* (d. 1896), 'La Belle Iseult'; *D. G. Rossetti* (d. 1882), 'Beata Beatrix' and 'The Girlhood of the Virgin'; *Henry Wallis* (d. 1916), 'The Death of Chatterton'.

LATE VICTORIAN PAINTING (Rooms XII and XIV): *Richard Dadd* (d. 1887), 'The Flight out of Egypt'; *Augustus Egg* (d. 1863), 'Past and Present'; *Sir Luke Fildes* (d. 1927), 'The Doctor'; *Stanhope Forbes* (d. 1948), 'The Death of the Bride'; *W. P. Frith* (d. 1909), 'Derby Day'; *R. B. Martineau* (d. 1869), 'Kit's Writing Lesson' and 'The Last Day in the Old Home'; *Sir W. Q. Orchardson* (d. 1910), 'The First Cloud'; *Sir Edward Poynter* (d. 1919), 'A Visit to Aesculapius'; *David Roberts* (d. 1864), 'A Cathedral Porch'; *Alfred Stevens* (d. 1875), 'Samuel Pegler' and other portraits, and self-portrait at the age of fourteen; *G. F. Watts* (d. 1904), 'Eve Tempted', 'Eve Repentant', 'Hope', and 'Psyche'.

Also in Room XIV are works by JOHN S. SARGENT (d. 1925), the American painter, who was born in Florence in 1856 and settled first in Paris and later in London: 'Carnation, Lily, Lily, Rose', 'Ellen Terry as Lady Macbeth', 'Lord Ribblesdale', 'The Misses Hunter', 'Claude Monet Painting', 'Mont Blanc', and a series of Portraits of the Wertheimer Family.

From the south side of this room a staircase goes down to the BASE-MENT, where the rooms (XXVII–XXXV) are confined to Modern Foreign Paintings (see p. 405).

Room XIII (and part of Room XIV) is given over to JAMES MCNEILL WHISTLER (d. 1903), the American artist who lived in Chelsea from 1857, and to his contemporaries and followers. Paintings by *Whistler* include 'The Little White Girl', 'Miss Cecily

Alexander', 'Valparaiso', two 'Nocturnes', and 'Three Figures, Pink and Grey'. *Aubrey Beardsley* (d. 1898), 'Caprice' and 'The Front at Hove'; *Charles Condor* (d. 1909), 'Springtime' and 'Windy Day, Brighton'; *Walter Greaves* (d. 1930), 'Battersea Reach', 'Hammersmith Bridge', 'Self Portrait', etc.; *Gwen John* (d. 1939), 'Portrait of Dorelia'; *Ambrose McEvoy* (d. 1927), 'Euphemia' and 'The Ferry'; *Sir William Orpen* (d. 1931), 'The Mirror'; *James Pryde* (d. 1941), 'The Doctor' and 'The Grave'; *Charles Ricketts* (d. 1931), 'Deposition from the Cross'; *Sir William Rothenstein* (d. 1945), 'The Doll's House'; *Walter Sickert* (d. 1942), 'Ennui', 'George Moore', and 'The Interior of St Mark's, Venice'; *P. Wilson Steer* (d. 1942), 'Mrs Cyprian Williams and her daughters', 'Chepstow Castle', 'The Toilet of Venus', and 'Walberswick Pier'; *Henry Tonks* (d. 1937), 'An Evening in the Vale'.

20TH-CENTURY BRITISH PAINTINGS (Room XV, entered from Room V, and the adjoining annexe): *Augustus John* (d. 1961), 'Llyn Treweryn', 'Madame Suggia', 'Sir Matthew Smith', 'Smiling Woman', 'W. B. Yeats', and other fine works; *Wyndham Lewis* (d. 1957), 'Edith Sitwell' and 'Ezra Pound'; *Stanley Spencer* (d. 1959), 'Apple Gatherers', 'Christ Bearing the Cross', 'Self Portrait', 'Swan Upping'; and works by the Camden Town group (Mark Gertler, Harold Gilman, Charles Ginner, Spencer Gore, and others), and by Sir Winston Churchill, Duncan Grant, Henry Lamb ('Lytton Strachey'), John and Paul Nash, Sir Matthew Smith, Edward Wadsworth, and Christopher Wood. Some of these may be found in Rooms XXI–XXIV, east of the Central Hall, which are usually given over to CONTEMPORARY BRITISH PAINTING and contain works by the former Euston Road school (Sir William Coldstream, Rodrigo Moynihan, Victor Pasmore, etc.) and by Francis Bacon, Ivon Hitchens, David Jones, Henry Moore, Ben Nicholson, John Piper, Ceri Richards, Graham Sutherland ('Somerset Maugham'), and other living painters.

Rooms XVIII–XX, east of the Sculpture Hall, are reserved for the special exhibitions held frequently at the gallery.

THE IMPRESSIONISTS AND POST-IMPRESSIONISTS (Rooms XXIX–XXX, in the Basement, see above): *Bonnard* (d. 1947), 'La Table', 'The Window', etc.; *Cézanne* (d. 1906), 'The Gardener', and characteristic Provençal landscapes; *Degas* (d. 1917), 'Carlo Pellegrini', 'La Toilette', etc.; *Fantin-Latour* (d. 1904), 'Mr and Mrs Edwards'; *Forain* (d. 1931), 'Girl Bathing' and 'Le Prétoire'; *Gauguin* (d. 1903), 'Harvesting' and other paintings done in Brittany and Tahiti; *Manet* (d. 1883), 'Madame Manet with a Cat'; *Modigliani* (d. 1920), 'Peasant Boy' and 'Portrait of a Girl'; *Monet* (d. 1926), 'Dans le Parc' and 'Les Peupliers'; *Pissarro* (d. 1903), 'Haymaking', 'Self Portrait', etc.; *Henri Rousseau* (le Douanier; d. 1910), 'Flowers'; *Seurat* (d. 1891), 'La Poudreuse'; *Sisley* (d. 1899), 'Bridge at Sèvres'; *Toulouse-Lautrec* (d. 1901), 'Les Deux Amies'; *Utrillo* (d. 1955), 'Montmartre', 'Place du Tertre', 'Porte St-Martin'; *Van Gogh* (d. 1890), 'Field at Arles', 'View at Auvers', 'The Yellow Chair'; *Vuillard* (d. 1940), 'Seated Woman', and 'The Mantelpiece'.

CONTEMPORARY FOREIGN PAINTING (Room XXVII, etc., in the Basement), includes works by Georges Braque (the co-founder with Picasso of Cubism), Marc Chagall, Paul Delvaux, André Derain ('The Pool of London' and 'Portrait of Matisse'), Raoul Dufy, Juan Gris, Paul Klee, Oskar Kokoschka, Fernand Léger, André Masson, Henri Matisse (d. 1954; 'Standing Model', 'Portrait of Derain', etc.), Edvard Munch ('The Sick Child'), Pablo Picasso (b. 1881; 'Flowers', and a series of figures showing the development of his style), Georges Rouault ('La Mariée', etc.), Maurice Vlaminck ('La Carouge'), and others. The gallery has also a growing collection of contemporary American paintings.

TOWER OF LONDON Plan V, F 3

STATION: TOWER HILL, to the NW., on the Circle and District lines. — MOTOR-BUSES Nos. 42 and 78 in the Minories and across Tower Bridge; in Fenchurch Street, etc., see Route 33; across London Bridge, see Route 25.

ADMISSION on weekdays from 10 to 5.30 (May to early October), 4.30 (mid-March to April) or 4 (early October to mid-March); on Sundays from 2 to 5 in May–mid-October (1/6; servicemen in uniform free). Closed on Good Friday and Christmas Day. Tickets cover admission to the Bloody Tower, the Beauchamp Tower, and the White Tower (with the armouries). The Byward, Salt, Broad Arrow, Constable, and Martin Towers may also be seen on application to the warder at the Byward Tower, who conducts parties starting at 11 a.m. and 2 and 3 p.m. Tickets for admission to the CROWN JEWELS (daily; 1/-) are obtainable at the entrance to the Wakefield Tower. The CHAPEL OF ST PETER is usually shown on application to a warder on duty (except between 12 and 2 each weekday, and after

3 on Saturdays). Visitors are also admitted (without ticket) to the services held in the chapel on Sundays at 8.15 and 11.15. — RESTAURANT (licensed) adjoining the ticket-office.

The TOWER OF LONDON, one of the most imposing fortresses in England, as well as the most interesting and best known, stands on the north bank of the Thames a little below London Bridge. Begun by William the Conqueror with the triple object of protecting the city, overawing its citizens, and controlling the approaches to London by river, it has been altered and added to by many succeeding monarchs. Built originally within the south-east angle of the City walls, its boundaries were extended eastward beyond the walls in the 12th century, and it now forms a separate Liberty with an overall area of 18 acres. The Tower has been in its time a citadel, a royal palace, and a state prison; it is still an arsenal maintained by a garrison, and in the World Wars it was again used as a prison. Though often attacked and besieged, it has never been captured.

The exceptional interest of the Tower depends partly on its close association with many events in English history, partly on the excellence of its medieval fortifications. In the centre rises the Norman keep or White Tower, largely the work of the Conqueror, with a chapel that shows the oldest ecclesiastical architecture in London. The tower is surrounded by the large Inner Ward, enclosed by a massive wall flanked with thirteen towers, and this is surrounded in turn by the narrow Outer Ward, protected by a second wall with six towers facing the river and two (formerly three) bastions on the north front. A broad moat (now dry) encircles the fortifications, which can be approached only at the south-west angle, as in medieval times, when they were defended by two outer or barbican towers commanding a series of drawbridges.

The commander of the Tower is a high-ranking army officer who bears the title of 'Constable of the Royal Palace and Fortress of London'. He is seconded by a Lieutenant, but neither of these officers now resides in the Tower and their duties are performed in the main by the Major and Resident Governor. This officer is supported (apart from the garrison) by the Yeomen Warders, a body of about forty ex-servicemen, specially selected, who will

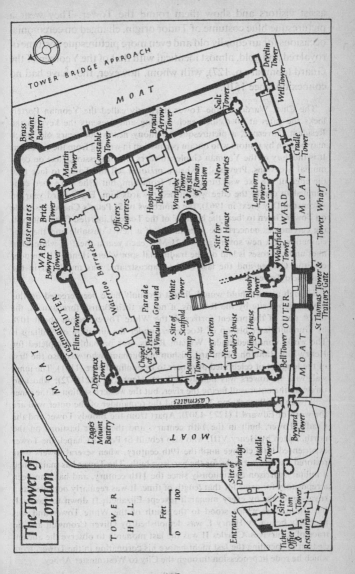

The Tower of London

TOWER BRIDGE APPROACH

MOAT

Brass Mount Battery

Casemates

Martin Tower

Brick Tower

Constable Tower

Broad Arrow Tower

Salt Tower

Well Tower

Devlin Tower

WARD

Bowyer Tower

Officers' Quarters

Hospital Block

Wardrobe Tower on site of Roman bastion

New Armouries

Lanthorn Tower

Cradle Tower

OUTER

MOAT

WARD

Flint Tower

Waterloo Barracks

White Tower

Parade

Site for Jewel House

Tower Wharf

Casemates

Devereux Tower

Tower Green

Site of Scaffold

Wakefield Tower

St Thomas's Tower & Traitors' Gate

Chapel of St Peter ad Vincula

Beauchamp Tower

Yeoman Gaoler's House

King's House

Bloody Tower

OUTER

MOAT

MOAT

Legge's Mount Battery

Casemates

Bell Tower

Byward Tower

Middle Tower

Site of Drawbridge

MOAT

TOWER HILL

Feet

0   100

Entrance

Ticket Office

Site of Lion Tower

Restaurant

407

assist visitors and show them round the Tower. They wear a picturesque blue costume of Tudor origin, changed on ceremonial occasions for an equally old and even more picturesque costume of royal red and gold, almost identical with that of the Yeomen of the Guard (compare p. 127), with whom, however, they have had no connexion since 1510.

The Chief Warder of the Tower (formerly called the Yeoman Porter) locks the gates at 10 o'clock each evening and presents the keys to the Resident Governor, a picturesque ceremony nearly 700 years old which may be seen by visitors who obtain permission in writing from the governor. It is the duty of the Yeoman Gaoler to carry the processional axe on ceremonial occasions. Previously, when a prisoner left the Tower to face trial the edge of the axe was turned away from him, but if he were then condemned to death, the edge was turned towards him. Every third year on Ascension Day (next in 1963), the choirboys of St Peter's Chapel assemble on Tower Green to 'beat the bounds' of the Tower Liberties. Other interesting ceremonies concern the installation of a new Constable and the proclamation of a new sovereign. On 21 May each year a sheaf of white Eton lilies and red roses is laid on the traditional spot where Henry VI, founder of Eton College and the last of the Lancastrians, was murdered in the Wakefield Tower.

Though a stronghold would almost certainly have been erected on this advantageous site by the Romans, if not by their British forerunners, the oldest part of the present fortress is the White Tower, begun about 1078 by Gundulf, later bishop of Rochester, under the direction of William I. The work, continued under William Rufus, was probably completed for Henry I by Ranulph Flambard, bishop of Durham, who was also the first of the long list of celebrated prisoners to be confined here (1101). The inner wall with its towers was mainly built by Henry III (1216–72), who also threw up the outer wall facing the river, but the western section of the inner wall, with the Beauchamp Tower, and the remainder of the outer wall are the work of Edward I (1272–1307). Apart from the Bloody Tower and the Cradle Tower, built in the 14th century, and the outer bastions on the north, added by Henry VIII, who also rebuilt St Peter's Chapel, the Tower experienced little change until the 19th century, when several towers were restored and the barracks for the garrison built. The Tower has maintained a military garrison continuously since the 11th century, and has also been a repository for arms for that length of time. It was regularly occupied as a royal residence by every monarch (except Elizabeth I) down to James I, but the palace, which stood to the south of the White Tower and was probably begun by Henry I, was demolished by Oliver Cromwell and no trace of it survives. Charles II was the last monarch to observe the ancient custom of spending the last night before his coronation in the Tower, from which he rode in procession through the City to Westminster Abbey.

In its function of royal fortress and state prison, the Tower has been intimately connected with the gloomier side of English history. Sir William Wallace (beheaded in 1305), David II of Scotland (1346–57), and King John of France (1356–60) were all imprisoned here during the wars with France and Scotland. Richard II signed his abdication in the Tower (1399) and James I of Scotland was kept here in 1406–7, the first part of his long imprisonment. Charles, Duke of Orleans, and other prisoners taken at Agincourt (1415) were also confined here. Henry VI (1471) and the Duke of Clarence, brother of Edward IV (1478), were murdered in the Tower, as were Edward V and his brother the Duke of York, the 'little princes in the Tower' (1483). Henry VIII was married in the Tower to Catherine of Aragon (1509), and Anne Boleyn, her successor, was executed here in 1536, as was Catherine Howard, Henry's fifth queen, in 1542. Others who suffered during the bluff king's reign were Sir Thomas More and Bishop John Fisher, both beheaded in 1535; Thomas Cromwell, Earl of Essex, the royal favourite (1540); the Countess of Salisbury, the last of the Plantagenets (1541); and Henry Howard, the poet Earl of Surrey (1547). Lord Protector Somerset was imprisoned here by Edward VI, and subsequently executed (1552). The many victims of Mary Tudor include Lady Jane Grey, who spent her nine days' reign here, her husband Lord Guildford Dudley, and her father the Duke of Suffolk, all beheaded in 1554; and Archbishop Cranmer and Bishops Ridley and Latimer (all burned at Oxford in 1553). Princess Elizabeth was closely confined here for two months by her sister in 1554, and in the same year the Tower was subjected to its last siege, by Sir Thomas Wyatt (afterwards beheaded) and his Men of Kent.

The roll of famous prisoners continued under Elizabeth, with the Duke of Norfolk, executed in 1572 for intriguing on behalf of Mary, Queen of Scots; the Earl of Northumberland, found stabbed in 1585; and the Earl of Essex, the queen's favourite, beheaded in 1601. Sir Walter Raleigh was imprisoned three times in the Tower, in 1592, in 1603–16, and in 1618, before his execution at Westminster, and in 1605–6 Guy Fawkes and his fellow conspirators were likewise confined here. Among other illustrious prisoners of the 17th century were the Earl of Strafford and Archbishop Laud (beheaded in 1641 and 1645); George Monck, Duke of Albemarle (1644–7); General John Lambert and other regicides (1660–1); William Penn, the Quaker (1668–9); Samuel Pepys (1679–80), on an unsuccessful charge of complicity in the Titus Oates plot; Algernon Sidney, charged with being implicated in the Rye House plot and beheaded in 1683; and the Duke of Monmouth, the opponent of James II, beheaded in 1685. The infamous Judge Jeffreys died in the Bloody Tower in 1689. Among the last prisoners who passed through the Tower to their execution were the Jacobites, the Earl of Derwentwater (1716) and Simon Fraser, Lord Lovat (1747), the last man to be beheaded in England. Later prisoners include John Wilkes, the Radical politician (1768), Lord George Gordon, who organized the 'No Popery' riots (1780), and Rudolf Hess (1941), while several spies were shot here during the World Wars.

The only entrance to the Tower is at the south-west angle, from the lower part of Tower Hill, where so many of those confined in the fortress met their doom (compare Route 34). On the right inside the modern gate are the ticket-office and refreshment room, on the site of the Lion Tower, where the royal menagerie was lodged from the 14th century until 1834. The tower was defended on the north by an outer moat (now filled in), crossed by a causeway with a drawbridge built in 1278 and now partly recovered. The approach to the main fortifications, taking a sharp turn to the left (to the confusion of attackers), passes over the site of a second drawbridge to the MIDDLE TOWER, built by Edward I (d. 1307), but refaced in the 19th century. Beyond it a causeway replacing a third drawbridge crosses the wide MOAT, dug out by Richard I and drained in 1843. On the farther side rises the BYWARD TOWER, built by Edward I and altered later in the 14th century. On each side of the archway are guardrooms, and in the rooms above can be seen the machinery for the portcullis, a plain 16th-century screen, and a remarkable 14th-century mural painting of the Crucifixion, discovered in 1953.

The Byward (i.e. 'password') Tower admits to the OUTER WARD, between the two lines of walls. On the left is the BELL TOWER, built by Richard I about 1190, but altered in the 13th century. This was the prison of Bishop Fisher, Sir Thomas More, Princess Elizabeth, and the Duke of Monmouth, and curfew is still rung nightly just before 9 p.m. or dusk. Along the top of the rampart leading north to the Beauchamp Tower is 'Princess Elizabeth's Walk'; the late-12th-century wall on the east of the tower encloses the King's House. On the right farther east is ST THOMAS'S TOWER, a turreted structure built by Henry III about 1242 and containing an oratory dedicated to St Thomas of Canterbury. Below it is the famous TRAITORS' GATE, with an arch 60 ft wide, formerly the entrance from the river, through which passed many traitors and others opposed to the royal power, after being brought by water from Westminster. Opposite is the Bloody Tower (see below), the gateway below which, the only entrance to the INNER WARD in the Middle Ages, was built by Henry III and still retains its portcullis in working order.

On the right (east) of the gate inside the Inner Ward is the entrance to the massive WAKEFIELD TOWER, likewise the work of Henry III. A vaulted chamber on the ground floor, where Henry VI is believed to have been murdered (1471), contains the heavily-guarded CROWN JEWELS or Regalia. Practically all the regalia of the English monarchy was sold or melted down during the Commonwealth, and though some of it was recovered at the Restoration (1660), most of the present regalia dates from after that time. The oldest crown is *St Edward's Crown*, named from King Edward the Confessor and weighing nearly 5 lb. It was made of gold for the coronation of Charles II (1661) and is still used for the actual coronation ceremony. It is changed immediately after for the lighter *Imperial State Crown*, made for Queen Victoria's coronation (1838) and used also when the sovereign appears at the Opening of Parliament and other State functions. Its gold frame is set with over 3,000 diamonds and other precious stones, including the large uncut ruby given to the Black Prince in 1367 by Pedro the Cruel of Castile and worn by Henry V in his coronet at the Battle of Agincourt, and one of the two 'Stars of Africa' cut from the 'Cullinan' diamond, the largest ever found, presented to Edward VII in 1907. The *Imperial Indian Crown*, with an emerald of 34 carats and over 6,000 diamonds, was worn by George V at the Delhi Durbar in 1911. The *Crown of Queen Elizabeth* (consort of George VI), also made in 1911, is set with the famous 'Koh-i-Noor' diamond of 108 carats presented to Queen Victoria in 1850 by the army of the Punjab. The oldest *Queen Consort's Crown* is that made for Mary of Modena, consort of James II (1685), for whom also the gold *Diadem* or circlet was made. Other crowns are those of Queen Mary (consort of George V) and the Prince of Wales (son of George II; 1728), and the Small Crown of Queen Victoria (1870).

The larger of the *Orbs* (the King's Orb) was made for Charles II, the smaller (the Queen's Orb) for Mary II. *St Edward's Staff*, made of gold and 4 ft 7 in. long, is surmounted by an orb and was also fashioned for Charles II. The *Royal Sceptre* is surmounted by a cross and adorned with gems, including the larger of the 'Stars of Africa' (530 carats), the largest cut diamond in the world. The *Sovereign's Sceptre with the Dove*, also called the Rod of Equity, is held in the sovereign's left hand at the coronation. The *Queen's*

Sceptre with the Cross (used by all queens consort at coronations) and the *Ivory Sceptre*, with a dove of white onyx, were both made for Mary of Modena, and the *Queen's Sceptre with the Dove* for Mary II. The *Anointing Spoon*, made in the late 12th century, perhaps for the coronation of King John (1199), and the *Ampulla*, a vessel (shaped like an eagle) to contain the oil for the anointing, probably of the time of Henry IV (1399–1413), are the only survivals of the medieval regalia, but both were restored for the coronation of Charles II. The jewelled *Sword of State* was made for George IV's coronation (1821).

Other regalia include the *Bracelets* worn at the coronation as emblems of sovereignty (two pairs made for Charles II and one pair presented by the Commonwealth for the coronation of Queen Elizabeth II) and the *Golden Spurs of St George*, an emblem of chivalry, likewise made for Charles II. Also displayed is a fine selection of royal plate, of which the *Queen Elizabeth Salt* (1572–3) is the oldest piece. The *Exeter Salt*, shaped like a tower, was given to Charles II by the city of Exeter, and the *Wine Fountain* to the same monarch by the corporation of Plymouth. There are *Maces of Serjeants-at-Arms* of the time of Charles II and James II, and a late-17th-century alms-dish used on Maundy Thursday (compare p. 442).

The side cases contain other maces, the 'Curtana', or Sword of Mercy, the State Sword used at the opening of Parliament, the Swords of Spiritual Justice (with a blunt point) and Temporal Justice (with a sharp point), the insignia of the Orders of Knighthood, and decorations for valour.

The Wakefield Tower contained the public records from 1360 until 1856. The adjoining Great Hall, where Anne Boleyn stood trial in 1536, was pulled down during the Commonwealth. A private entrance stairway, built about 1230 for Henry III, was discovered during excavations adjoining the Wake-field Tower in 1958.

In front of the Wakefield Tower rises the impressive White Tower (see below), approached by a flight of steps. A terrace starting from the top of the steps leads back to the BLOODY TOWER, built during the reign of Richard II and given this name at least as early as 1597. A room on the second floor is said to be that in which the Little Princes were smothered in 1483 at the instigation of Richard III. Archbishop Cranmer and the Protestant bishops were also confined in the tower, and through the small window on the north side Archbishop Laud stretched his hands to bless the Earl of Strafford on his way to the scaffold. Sir Walter Raleigh spent the thirteen years of his second imprisonment here, writing the *History of the World* and taking the air on the terrace along the rampart to the west.

This rampart runs behind the KING'S HOUSE (now sometimes called the Queen's House), a picturesque timber-framed dwelling built during the reign of Henry VIII (1509–47) and extended on the east in the 17th century. It is now the residence of the governor and is not accessible to the public.

In a small room in the west wing Anne Boleyn was incarcerated for the last days of her life, and in the council chamber (in the south wing) Guy Fawkes and his confederates were examined in 1605. The Scottish Jacobite lords were confined in this house (then the residence of the lieutenant) and it was from the doorway here in 1716 that Lord Nithsdale escaped, in the dress of his wife's maid, on the night before he was to have been beheaded. The King's House is adjoined on the north by the YEOMAN GAOLER'S HOUSE, rebuilt in the early 17th century. Lady Jane Grey was imprisoned here in 1554 and on the morning of her own execution saw the headless body of her husband brought back from Tower Hill. Rudolf Hess was kept here after landing in Scotland on his abortive mission in 1941.

The west part of the Inner Ward, bounded on the north by the royal chapel, is known as TOWER GREEN. The ravens always to be seen here are perhaps a relic of the menagerie kept in the Lion Tower; they are protected by the Crown under the care of a Raven Master and a special allowance is made for food. Their disappearance is held to presage the fall of the White Tower and the British Empire. A brass plate on the northward part of the green marks the SITE OF THE SCAFFOLD, reserved for those of royal or noble blood. Here were executed Anne Boleyn (1536) and Catherine Howard (1542), the wives of Henry VIII, the aged Countess of Salisbury (1541), Viscountess Rochford (1542), Lady Jane Grey (1554), and the Earl of Essex (1601). All fell by the axe, except Anne Boleyn, who was beheaded with a sword. Lord Hastings was executed near by in 1483 by the order of the Duke of Gloucester (later Richard III), but most other condemned prisoners met their end on Tower Hill.

On the west of the green rises the BEAUCHAMP TOWER (pronounced 'Beecham'), a semicircular three-storeyed bastion built about 1300 and named after Thomas Beauchamp, Earl of Warwick, imprisoned here in 1397–9 by Richard II. The walls of the room on the first floor are covered with inscriptions carved or scratched by prisoners, some of which, however, have been brought from other parts of the Tower.

The inscription over the fireplace was carved by Philip Howard, Earl of Arundel, who was confined here in 1585 and died in custody ten years later; No. 14, on the right of the fireplace, is an elaborate carving by John Dudley (d. 1554), who was imprisoned here with his father, the Duke of Northumberland, and his four brothers, Ambrose, Earl of Warwick (represented by a wreath of roses), Robert, Earl of Leicester (oak leaves, from *robur*, an oak), Guildford, husband of Lady Jane Grey (gillyflowers), and Henry (honeysuckle). The single word 'Jane' on the north side of the room (No. 48) is supposed to refer to the unfortunate Lady Jane Grey. Cases in the room contain Roman tiles, medieval pottery, etc., found in the Tower.

The CHAPEL OF ST PETER AD VINCULA, north of the green, was founded probably in the reign of Henry I (1100–35) and owes its name to its being consecrated on the festival of 'St Peter in Chains'. It was rebuilt in the late 13th century, was almost completely reconstructed after a fire in 1512 and has been much repaired since. Before the altar are buried Anne Boleyn and Catherine Howard, with the Duke of Northumberland and the Duke of Somerset, 'two dukes between two queens . . . all four beheaded', in the words of Stow. Here also are interred Lady Jane Grey and her husband, the Earl of Essex, and the Duke of Monmouth, and in the crypt lie Bishop Fisher, Sir Thomas More (whose head, however, is at Canterbury), and the Jacobite lords executed in 1746–7. Other illustrious victims of the headsman's axe lie in unmarked graves in the chapel or the burial-ground (now part of the green; 'no sadder spot on earth', says Macaulay). The font of the chapel is Tudor work; the organ was built originally in 1699 by Father Smith; the altar frontal is of cloth used at the coronation of Queen Elizabeth II and divided among the royal chapels. In the north aisle is the splendid monument of the Duke of Exeter (d. 1447), formerly in St Katharine's Chapel, Regent's Park, but moved here in 1950.

To the east of Tower Green rises the imposing WHITE TOWER, the oldest part of the whole stronghold and named from its being built originally of white Caen stone from Normandy. Begun about 1078 for William the Conqueror by Gundulf, afterwards bishop of Rochester and architect of that cathedral, it was completed about 1100 for Henry I. The tower, a characteristic Norman keep, is roughly rectangular in plan, measuring about 118 ft (from east to west) by 107 ft; of four storeys, it has walls varying from 11 to 15 ft in thickness and extends 90 ft from the floor to the battlements. The corner turrets, which differ from each other in design, are capped by curious cupolas added in the 17th century, when also the exterior was restored by Wren, who replaced the Norman windows (except four on the south side) with others of a classical nature. The original entrance was on the south side, and at first-floor level (as usual in Norman keeps), approached by a staircase (now vanished) under which the bones of two boys, conjectured to be the Little Princes, were discovered in 1674. The present-day approach is through a door reached by an outside staircase on the north-east. The interior, little changed and still conveying the atmosphere of a grim Norman fortress, is interesting for its ancient chapel and its extensive collection of arms and armour.

The RECORD ROOM, on the first or Gun Floor, contains relics of famous soldiers, including swords and the telescope of the Duke of Wellington, the jacket he wore as Constable of the Tower, the cloak on which Wolfe died at Quebec (1759), and the original draft of Kitchener's Appeal to the Nation (1915). Two carved figures, called 'Gin' and 'Beer', were brought from the buttery of Greenwich Palace in the 17th century. Here also are parts of the State barge of the Master General of the Ordnance, models and drawings of the Tower, etc. To the south of the room is the CRYPT of St John's Chapel, containing instruments of punishment and torture, an execution axe of about 1660, and the block used in 1747 for Lord Lovat, the Jacobite. In the tiny cell opening from the crypt Sir Walter Raleigh is supposed to have spent his last imprisonment. The SMALL ARMS ROOM, occupying the western half of this floor, illustrates the development of fire-arms (matchlocks, flintlocks, pistols, sporting guns, etc.); the percussion-lock, some early examples of which are shown, was invented in the Tower by the Rev. Alexander Forsyth (d. 1843). Two of the decorated cannon here were made for the Duke of Gloucester, the young son of Queen Anne, two were brought from Paris in 1815, and the other, an elaborate bronze cannon of Italian make, was captured by the French at Malta in 1798 and shortly after by the British. Here also are the horse furniture of William III and two kettle-drums taken at Blenheim (1704).

A staircase from the Small Arms Room ascends to the second or Banqueting Floor. In the south-east angle is the CHAPEL OF ST JOHN, the oldest church in London (about 1080), a beautiful example of mature Norman architecture, consisting of a nave of four bays with aisles and a clerestory, covered by a barrel vault, and an apse opening by five stilted arches to an ambulatory. The nave arcades have plain arches and massive round piers with square capitals, some of which are carved with an early T-shaped figure. The gallery behind the clerestory is a continuation of the wall passage at the third-floor level. The old glass in the windows was part of Horace Walpole's collection at Strawberry Hill. In former times aspirants to the knighthood of the Bath kept their vigil here throughout the night before their investiture. Mary I was married by proxy in the chapel to Philip of Spain (1554), and Archbishop Simon of Sudbury was dragged from the altar to his execution on Tower Hill in 1381 by Wat Tyler's rebels.

On the north of the chapel is the SWORD ROOM, which has a notable collection of swords and similar weapons from the early Middle Ages to the 19th century. The two long-bows salved from the *Mary Rose*, sunk by the French in 1545, are almost the only ones to survive from medieval times. The room retains its original fireplace, and garderobes or latrines in the thickness of the wall. The WEAPON ROOM, on the west, formerly the Banqueting Hall, has a fine collection of staff-weapons, maces, axes, spears, etc., and notable Scottish weapons of the 16th–18th centuries. The figures on horseback portray a cuirassier and trooper of the Civil War, and at the farther end of the room is displayed pikemen's armour of 1620–30.

A staircase at the north-west angle goes up to the third or Council Floor, remarkable for its magnificent display of arms and armour. The first room, formerly the Council Chamber and now called the HORSE ARMOURY, contains a series of figures, mounted and on foot, showing the development of armour from the 15th century to the time of Charles I. Near the entrance is the 15th-century Brocas Helm, considered to be the finest tilting-helmet in existence. Cases contain decorated armour, including the enriched breast-plates, etc., of the Venetian garrison at Rhodes, and helmets, the earliest a bascinet of the 14th century from Churburg. Much of the armour in the TUDOR ROOM was made in the royal armouries established at Greenwich by Henry VIII. It includes foot armour made for the king himself and weigh-ing 94 lb., and the armour of Robert Dudley, Earl of Leicester, and other famous Elizabethans. The equestrian 'Burgundian Bard' armour, beauti-fully engraved, the splendid body armour made at Augsburg, and the helmet with curious ram's horns were all presented to Henry VIII by the Emperor Maximilian. Another suit of armour for horse and man was made for the king later in life. Near the exit is a suit of armour for a man nearly 7 ft tall, and other notable exhibits include a huge lance used by the Duke of Suffolk, father of Lady Jane Grey. A case on the left contains a spiked club with three pistol-barrels called 'Henry VIII's walking-stick'; and a case at the farther end of the room holds the gilt armour presented to Charles I by the City of London (but of French make), and armour of Prince Henry, son of James I, and of Charles I and II when princes, and that of James II, a late example of the craft.

A stairway from the north-east of the Tudor Room descends to the so-called Dungeons in the Basement. The MORTAR ROOM, the first room entered, contains several interesting pieces of ordnance, among them a gun from the *Royal George*, which sank at Spithead in 1782 with over 800 on board. At the south end is the SUB-CRYPT of St John's Chapel, entered by an archway popularly but quite erroneously regarded as the cell where Guy Fawkes was confined while being subjected to torture. The CANNON ROOM, on the west, has English and foreign guns, starting with some salved from the *Mary Rose* (see above), and a Norman well 40 ft deep.

Hence the exit is made to the Parade Ground, on the north side of which are the WATERLOO BARRACKS, built in 1845 and now the headquarters of the Royal Fusiliers (City of London Regiment), formed in 1685. To the east of the Parade Ground are the officers' quarters, of the same date, and south of these are the Hospital Block and a late-17th-century brick building, restored in 1959 to house the NEW ARMOURIES. The collections (opened in 1961) mainly cover the 18th and 19th centuries and include a fine assembly of firearms, as well as Oriental armour and weapons.

On the ground floor are Oriental and African exhibits, including the only suit of elephant armour in Britain, probably a trophy won at the Battle of Plassey in 1757 and brought home by Lord Clive. On either side are complete suits of armour for rider and horse, one of the 18th century from India, the other a fine 19th-century example from Tibet, probably worn against British troops and captured by Colonel Younghusband in 1904. Other armour is on loan from the royal collections. The first floor is given over to European firearms, with many highly ornamental royal and imperial weapons, and a series of British service muskets and rifles dating from 1680 to 1914. On the second floor is a display of uniforms and swords, among them uniforms of the Duke of Connaught, a Scottish uniform of Sir Ian Hamilton, and the swords of Lord Roberts, Lord Wolseley, and Lord Kitchener.

Near the south-east angle of the White Tower are the slight remains of the 12th-century WARDROBE TOWER, adjoined by a section of the lower courses of the 2nd-century City wall, and one of its bastions, added later. A further length of the wall was uncovered in 1955, built of Kentish ragstone bonded with brick. It extends south towards the LANTHORN TOWER (rebuilt in the 19th century), whose predecessor probably occupied the site of a tower at the south-east corner of the Roman city, while the Wakefield, Bell, and Middle Towers may well stand on the foundations of bastions of the Roman river-wall.

A modern breach between the Lanthorn Tower and the Salt Tower gives access to the Outer Ward, which may be explored to the east and north. The 13th-century SALT TOWER, at the south-east angle, has many inscriptions and carvings of prisoners, including a figure cut in 1561 for casting horoscopes. Farther north are the BROAD ARROW TOWER, which (like the wall) is of the 13th century, and the CONSTABLE TOWER, rebuilt in the 19th century; and at the north-east angle is the MARTIN TOWER (13th century, but modernized), the scene of the daring attempt by Colonel Blood in 1671 to carry off the Crown and other regalia. Farther west (but not visited) is the 13th-century BOWYER TOWER, where the Duke of Clarence is supposed to have been drowned in a butt of malmsey wine in 1478 at the instigation of his brother the Duke of Gloucester, and at the north-west angle is the DEVEREUX TOWER, where the Earl of Essex was confined. The corner bastions on the north of the outer wall were constructed by Henry VIII, and a similar bastion between these, added in the 19th century, was destroyed by a bomb in 1940.

An opening in the wall to the east of the Traitors' Gate gives access to the TOWER WHARF, commanding a view of the river with its shipping and of Tower Bridge. It was originally constructed (before 1228) with soil from the moat and supports a number of 18th–19th-century cannon. The Honourable Artillery Company fires a salute of 62 guns here on the anniversaries of the birth, accession, and coronation of the sovereign, and one of 41 guns on the birth of a prince or princess and other royal occasions.

VICTORIA AND ALBERT MUSEUM Plan VI, C 3

STATION: SOUTH KENSINGTON, nearly ¼-m. SW., on the Circle, District, and Piccadilly lines, reached by a subway starting near Gallery 21 (NW. side; see plan). — MOTOR-BUSES in Brompton Road and Cromwell Road, see Route 10; in Kensington Road, see Route 11.

ADMISSION weekdays 10 to 6; Sundays 2.30 to 6 (free). Closed on Good Friday and Christmas Day. — LECTURE TOURS on Tuesdays and Thursdays at 1.15, on Saturdays at 3 p.m. Evening lectures on Wednesdays at 6.15 in winter (October–March) in the Lecture Theatre, approached from Exhibition Road. — RESTAURANT (licensed) and self-service café in Room 39, open daily until 5.30. — CONCERTS, see p. 72.

The LIBRARY is open from 10 to 6, the PRINT ROOM from 10 to 4.50, on weekdays (except Bank Holidays), to subscribers to the National Art-Collections Fund (see p. 64) and to holders of tickets (free), obtainable under the same conditions as readers' tickets for the British Museum (p. 315). The TEXTILE STUDY ROOMS are open without obligation on Monday–Friday 10 to 5, Saturdays 10 to 1.

The VICTORIA AND ALBERT MUSEUM, at South Kensington, is the national museum of fine and applied art of all countries and periods. It comprises also the national collections of sculpture (except modern sculpture), water-colours, and miniatures, and the national library of art. The museum has an impressive Renaissance façade designed by Sir Aston Webb and completed in 1909. Over the main entrance in Cromwell Road, on the south, are statues of Queen Victoria and Prince Albert, by Alfred Drury, and flanking it are others by Goscombe John of Edward VII and Queen Alexandra. There is a second entrance in Exhibition Road, on the west; and the niches between the windows on both fronts are occupied by statues of famous British artists and craftsmen. The great central tower, 185 ft high, has a lantern in the shape of an Imperial Crown surmounted by a figure of Fame.

Even the most cursory survey of this vast treasure house will occupy at least a full day, and successive visits are essential to gain a satisfactory knowledge of its contents. The exhibits are arranged in two separate groups: the Primary Collections, in which masterpieces of all the arts are brought together by style, period, or nationality, and the Study Collections, in which the exhibits are grouped within the various classes of sculpture, ceramics, painting, metalwork, etc. In the description below, the Primary Collections are dealt with first.

The museum, colloquially the 'V. and A.', grew out of the Museum of Manufactures established at Marlborough House in 1852 under the inspiration of the Prince Consort and Sir Henry Cole. It included objects bought at the Great Exhibition of 1851 and collections of the Government School of Design that had been set up in 1837. The original intention was the 'application of fine art to objects of utility', but the museum soon extended its ideals and changed its name to the Museum of Ornamental Art. In 1857, under the inspiration of Prince Albert (who aimed to establish a cultural centre out of the profits of the Great Exhibition), it was moved to its present site and its name again changed, to the South Kensington Museum. Gifts and bequests were heaped on the museum and these with government grants enabled it to expand greatly beyond its original plan, so that its buildings, though frequently added to, became quite inadequate. In 1891 a competition was held for the design of additional buildings facing Cromwell Road and Exhibition Road. It was won by Sir Aston Webb and in 1899 the foundation stone was laid (her last major engagement) by Queen Victoria, who directed that the title be changed once more. When the museum was reopened in 1909 the scientific collections were transferred to the Science Museum.

Facing the MAIN VESTIBULE (where cases, parcels, etc., must be given up) is Room 49, reserved for RECENT ACQUISITIONS, and beyond this and the corridor is Room 43, containing the Primary Collection of EARLY MEDIEVAL ART, a superb assembly of many treasures. It is divided into three sections, the first covering Late Antique and Early Christian Art, which developed from the art of Greece and Rome and flourished throughout Europe and the Near East from the late 2nd to the 7th century, and was adapted by the Christian church after A.D. 313; especially notable are the small but beautiful ivory diptychs. The second section deals with Byzantine Art and Christian Art under Islam, illustrating the expansion of the Byzantine style of the Near East from the 8th to the 15th century and its influence on Europe, and the contemporary style that developed in Persia under the Sassanian dynasty (3rd–8th centuries). Among the many fine works by Byzantine inspiration are a 9th-century cross-reliquary made in Italy, the 10th-century Veroli casket, made of ivory and carved with mythological scenes, a unique late-11th-century statuette of the Virgin and Child, and a 12th-century gilt-bronze triptych of the Virgin and Child enthroned.

The third section is devoted to Early Medieval Art in Western Europe, from the fall of the Roman Empire (4th century) until the early 13th century. Of the first period is the stone cross-shaft of the late 7th or early 8th century from Easby Abbey (Yorkshire); of the second, or Carolingian, period (early 9th to mid 10th century) are the Sion Gospels, with a cover of gold cloisonné and precious stones (French or German work), and the 9th-century North German ivory book-cover. The third period (mid 10th to mid 11th century), influenced by Byzantine art, is represented by the rare situla or holy-water bucket from Milan. The fourth period witnessed the development of the Romanesque style, well known in England; among the notable works may be mentioned the splendid early-12th-century relief in whalebone of the Adoration of the Magi, a leaf from a 12th-century psalter, the Gloucester candlestick of about 1110, and a crozier-head in ivory, of about 1180 (all English work); and the 12th-century Eltenberg reliquary, in the shape of a church, from the Rhineland; a 12th-century French triptych, of enamel on gilt-copper, previously at Alton Towers (Staffordshire); and a 13th-century reliquary of the True Cross, in gilt copper and enamel, from the School of Meuse. Near the end of

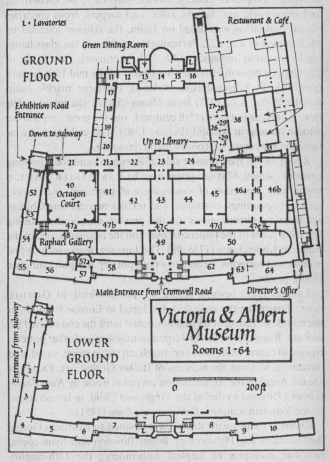

the room are a late-Romanesque stone window from a house near Gisors (northern France) and 12th–13th-century carved columns and capitals from Italy, France, and Spain; and on the right wall is a 12th-century limestone relief from Barcelona showing SS. Philip, Jude, and Bartholomew.

Room 42, to the left, is devoted to ISLAMIC ART, with outstanding examples of pottery, ivories, glassware, wood-carvings, and metalwork, and velvets, silks, and carpets, from countries whose civilization was based on Islam, the religion founded by Mohammed in A.D. 622. Particularly notable are the glass hanging-lamps from mosques (12th–13th centuries), the 'Luck of Edenhall', a beautiful Syrian glass beaker of the mid 13th century previously at Edenhall (Cumberland), the large marble basin dated 676 (*i.e.* A.D. 1277) from Hama (Syria), the inlaid pulpit from a mosque in Cairo (15th century), and the great carpet from a tomb-mosque at Ardabil (Persia; 1540). The collection is continued in the corridor (Room 47B) on the south.

Room 44 (on the opposite side of Room 43) and the adjoining corridor (Room 47A) are given over to FAR EASTERN ART, a magnificent collection of stoneware and porcelain, metalwork, sculpture, paintings, costumes, and textiles representing Chinese art from prehistoric times to the present day, and including beautiful robes of the Imperial Court and the lacquer throne of the Emperor Ch'ien Lung (1736–95). The Japanese works include fine armour and weapons, lacquered wood, pottery and porcelain, and colour-prints.

Rooms 22–5, beyond Room 43, are confined to GOTHIC ART, illustrating the style that developed in Europe from about the middle of 12th century and flourished until the end of the 15th century. Room 22 (on the left) contains majolica and other pottery, ivories, etc., and madonnas and angels carved in stone, wood, and terracotta, showing the richness of Italian Gothic Art. Examples are the Angel of the Annunciation carved in wood by *Nino Pisano* (about 1350) and a relief of the Virgin and Child, in Istrian stone, by the Venetian sculptor, *Bartolommeo Buon* (1451).

Room 23 (which with Room 24 is devoted to Northern Gothic Art) contains the 14th-century Butler-Bowdon and Syon copes, two fine examples of English embroidery; the 14th-century German Hildesheim cope; and (in the cases) the Reichenau crozier (1351); an early-14th-century diptych of Christ blessing the Virgin and Child, English work in ivory; and the 14th-century Ramsey censer, in silver-gilt, an excellent specimen of English metalwork. The stained-glass windows on the north side include a fine example of about 1400 from Winchester College chapel. Room 24 contains a 15th-century French Angel of the Annunciation, in painted oak; a reliquary believed to have contained the relics of St Boniface (15th-century South German work); and a late-15th-century 'palmesel' or wooden figure of Christ on the ass, for use in the Palm Sunday procession in south Germany. On the right are a late-14th-century limestone altarpiece from Sutton Valence (Kent); a 15th-century English oak figure of St Anne, from Bude Castle (Cornwall); and other statues, altarpieces, etc. In the cases are the delicate ivory Soissons diptych, French work of the late 13th century; an early-14th-century ivory statuette of the Virgin and Child, also French; the late-14th-century Studley Bowl, English work in silver-gilt, chased and enamelled; a 14th–15th-century altar cross from Basle Cathedral; and the silver-gilt Merode Cup, French or Flemish craftsmanship of the early 15th century.

Room 25 (Spanish Gothic Art) contains a processional cross of about 1400, silver and gilt on wood, from Barcelona, and the large retable or altarpiece of the same period from the church of St George at Valencia, with scenes from the life of the saint.

The stairway on the right, with 15th–17th-century Spanish carpets, ascends to the Library (p. 435). The walls of Rooms 32 and 33, east of Room 25, are hung with Persian, Turkish, and other carpets, and two 16th-century tapestry maps of Warwickshire and Worcestershire. To the left is the corridor giving access to the Restaurant; Room 46, on the right, contains the museum's extensive collection of CASTS of famous sculpture. Room 45, on the south of Room 24, is used for temporary exhibitions.

Rooms 26–9: LATE GOTHIC AND EARLY RENAISSANCE ART, with sculpture, woodwork, metalwork, and textiles, mainly from France, Germany, and the Netherlands, showing the decline of the Gothic style and the advent of the Renaissance. Notable in Room 26 are the St Hubert crosier, Flemish work of the mid 16th century; the English Campion cup, of engraved silver-gilt (1500); the German Agate cup of about 1500; the Burghley Nef, a salt-cellar in the form of a ship (French; 1482–3); and the Louis XII triptych of about 1500, in Limoges enamel, with portraits of the king and his wife, Anne of Brittany. Rooms 27 and 28 are given over mainly to German Late-Gothic Art of the early 16th century, including beautiful carved figures in wood by *Veit Stoss* and *Tilman Riemenschneider*, 'honestone' reliefs, and three stained-glass windows and two carved and painted limewood altarpieces, one showing the legend of St Margaret. Room 29 contains a painted and gilded stone altarpiece of about 1535 from the neighbourhood of Troyes (France), and 15th–16th-century English, Flemish, Italian, and Spanish copes and palls. Room 29A, south of this, has examples of Renaissance art from Spain, notably the wrought-iron screen from Avila and the effigies of a grandee and his wife.

Room 38, entered from Room 29, contains a rich assembly of GOTHIC TAPESTRIES, mostly of the 15th–16th centuries and of Flemish provenance. One depicting the Story of Troy was made in 1472 by Pasquier Grenier of Tournai for the magistrates of Bruges to present to Charles the Bold, Duke of Burgundy, and came from the castle of the Chevalier Bayard, near Grenoble. The three large 'Triumphs' illustrate Petrarch's allegorical poem *I Trionfi* and were woven in Brussels in 1507. The four large and magnificent 'Hunting Tapestries', woven between 1425 and 1450, probably at Tournai, were previously in the possession of the Duke of Devonshire at Chatsworth (Derbyshire).

Rooms 11–20: ITALIAN RENAISSANCE ART, starting in Room 16 (entered from Room 27), an exceptionally fine selection showing well the spirited revival of art that began in Italy in the 15th century. Room 16 contains a splendid collection of carved and gilded marriage chests ('cassoni') and chest-fronts; a lovely relief of the Adoration of the Shepherds, in polychrome terracotta, by *Luca della Robbia*; two fine kneeling angels in enamelled terracotta by *Andrea della Robbia*; early Renaissance sculptures by *Michelozzo* and others; and processional crosses and other fine silver-gilt work. In Room 15 are some of the masterpieces of Italian sculpture in the museum: Christ delivering the keys to St Peter, a marble relief, and a Virgin and Child in gilded terracotta, both by *Donatello*; a marble relief of the Virgin and Child with angels, by *Agostino di Duccio*; and a bust of Giovanni Chellini, by *Antonio Rossellino*. The sandstone doorway on the north side is from the palace at Gubbio of Federigo da Montefeltro, Duke of Urbino. Room 14 contains a fine series of enamelled terracotta sculptures by *Luca della Robbia* (d. 1482), his nephew *Andrea*, and the latter's son, *Giovanni*. Of particular note are the arms of René of Anjou and the twelve roundels of the Labours of the Months, by Luca, and two Madonnas in relief by Andrea. In the centre of the room is a tiled pavement in majolica (tin-glazed earthenware) from the Palazzo Petrucci at Siena. Room 13 is devoted to Florentine and Paduan sculpture, including two outstanding reliefs by *Donatello*, the Flagellation and the Crucifixion (in terracotta) and the Lamentation over the Dead Christ (in bronze); a marble relief of the Dead Christ supported by Angels, attributed to Donatello; a fine Lamentation by *Bellano*, a disciple of his; and a Pietà in bronze ascribed to *Giovanni Minelli*. On the north of this room is the GREEN DINING ROOM, designed, decorated, and furnished by William Morris, Philip Webb, and Edward Burne-Jones.

Room 12 contains painted 'cassoni', cases of bronze statuettes by *Bertoldo*, *L'Antico*, *Riccio*, and others; a fine chimney-piece by *Desiderio da Settignano*; the carved tomb of Santa Giustina, made before 1476; and cases of medals by *Pisanello*, *Matteo de' Pasti*, and others. In Room 11 are later examples of *Della Robbia* ware, notably two altarpieces by Andrea and Giovanni, and Andrea's attractive Boy with the Bagpipes, works which inspired the design of the adjacent staircase. Room 17, on the left, has a painted ceiling of about 1500 from Cremona, with figures of Apollo and the Muses, and contains a remarkable oratory of walnut, with carved and inlaid decoration, a rare example of north Italian church furniture of about 1500. Here also are a pair of marquetry doorways from the ducal palace at Gubbio, and early-16th-century furniture and majolica. Room 18 is mostly devoted to Florentine and Sienese sculpture of the later 15th century, including a delightful marble relief of the Virgin and Child by *Desiderio da Settignano* and the lovely Virgin with the laughing Child, in terracotta, of *Antonio Rossellino*; Scenes from the Life of St Francis, terracotta studies by *Benedetto da Majano* for reliefs on the pulpit of Santa Croce in Florence (1474–5); the Allegory of Discord, a stucco study for a bronze relief by *Francesco di Giorgio Martini*; a Virgin and Child in marble by *Domenico Rosselli*;

and a striking terracotta Bust of St Mary Magdalen, by *Giovanni Rustici*. Also here is a Ferrarese tapestry with the figure of St Antoninus. Room 19 contains sculpture from Northern Italy: Venetian works by *Antonio Bregno* (Annunciation), *Pietro Lombardi* (an enchanting Christ Child), *Tullio Lombardi* (Head of Faith), etc., and Milanese sculptures by *Amadeo* (Dead Christ supported by Angels) and *Cristoforo Mantegazza* (Lamentation); also a tempera painting of the Virgin and Child, by *Carlo Crivelli*, and the famous Martelli mirror of bronze encrusted with gold and silver (15-century Mantuan work). Cases hold Venetian glass and North Italian metalwork. In Room 20 are works by *Andrea del Verrocchio*, the great Florentine master: a sketch-model for the monument of Cardinal Niccolo Forteguerri in the cathedral at Pistoia (1476), and a terracotta statuette of St Jerome; a fine gilt-wax group of the Deposition by *Jacopo Sansovino*, probably for the use of Perugino and other painters; an early-16th-century bust of Henry VII, in painted and gilded terracotta, by *Torrigiani* (compare p. 452); marble statuettes and reliefs by the Milanese sculptor, *Agostino Busti*, called Il Bambaia; and a remarkable pearwood altarpiece and predella of the early 16th century from Piacenza.

Rooms 21A (beyond Room 20) and 21 (right): CONTINENTAL ART OF THE 16TH CENTURY, mostly in the style now known as Mannerist. In Room 21A are an elaborate marble altarpiece by *Andrea Ferrucci*, from San Girolamo at Fiesole (1490–5); a fresco in the style of *Bernardino Luini* from Santa Maria della Passione at Milan; and stained-glass windows of the 16th century, one from the cathedral at Cortona, by *Guillaume de Marcillat*. Among the objects in the cases are a crystal altar-cross and candlesticks made by *Valerio Belli* of Vicenza for Francis I of France. In the centre of Room 21 is the celebrated Samson slaying a Philistine, a marble group by *Giovanni da Bologna* (about 1565), purchased in 1953 from Hovingham Hall (Yorkshire) for £25,000. Also in this room are a Cupid formerly attributed to Michelangelo but probably by *Vincenzo Danti*; a bust of Pope Sixtus V in giltbronze by *Bastiano Torrigiani*; a Head of Cosimo I, Grand-Duke of Tuscany, in porphyry on serpentine, by *Francesco del Tadda*; and a small model in red wax of a Slave, a sketch for the tomb of

Pope Julius II, by *Michelangelo*. The cases hold beautiful bronze statuettes by *Alessandro Vittoria, Giovanni da Bologna*, and others; metalwork, including examples of Milanese damascening; and terracotta sketch-models.

In an alcove formed at the north end of the Octagon Court has been placed *Giovanni Bernini*'s splendid Neptune and a Triton (about 1620), which stood n the garden of the Villa Montalto at Rome and later belonged to Reynolds.

At the west end of Room 21 is the stair to the EXHIBITION ROAD VESTIBULE, beside which other stairs go down to the underground subway and to Rooms 1–5 on the Lower Ground Floor, devoted to CONTINENTAL ART OF 1570–1825, arranged to show the decorative taste of the period, which covers the transformation from the late-Renaissance style to the baroque. Rooms 1A and 1B contain 16th–17th-century Flemish and other tapestries, 16th-century French and Italian furniture, a virginal bearing the arms of the Duke of Cleves, probably made at Antwerp and dated 1568, and a splendid astronomical globe with a clock, in gilt-copper and silver, made at Augsburg in 1584. In Room 1C are 17th-century Italian tapestries with scenes from Tasso's epic, *Gerusalemme Liberata*, and four magnificent 17th-century marble busts by the Italian sculptors, *Giovanni Bernini, Alessandro Algardi, Carlo Marcellini*, and *G. B. Foggini*. In the centre is a Dying Achilles, by *Veyrier* (1683). One spinet was made by *Annibale Rossi* of Milan (1577) and another, of about 1600, is decorated with scenes from Ovid's *Metamorphoses*. The cases hold ivories and terracottas, ebony and silverware, and beautiful ceramics (Nevers and Delft ware, Italian majolica and faience, and a Spanish talavera bowl).

The small Room 2 contains a fine bust of Charles II by *Honore Pelle* (1684) and a French ebony and marquetry cabinet of the mid 17th century. The objects in Room 3 are almost all of the 17th century. In the first part are a French tapestry after designs by *Simon Vouet*, a Flemish tapestry woven at the Oudenarde factory, a monumental Dutch clock, and a Dutch monstrance in silver gilt. In the centre is a panelled room of the late 17th century brought from a farmhouse near Alençon (Normandy), believed to have been a hunting-lodge of Henri IV. The farther section is confined to religious art of the Counter-Reformation, with French and

Italian vestments, altar-frontals, and metalwork, and a characteristic Virgin of the Sorrows, a head in painted wood by *Pedro de Mena* (d. 1688). Room 4 contains five Flemish tapestries of the Seasons (about 1700), and sculptures by *Canova* (Sleeping Nymph, in marble) and *L.-S. Adam* (Louis XV as Apollo, in terracotta).

Room 5, on the left, devoted to the 18th century, contains the boudoir of Madame de Sérilly, from Paris, and a panelled room, probably Italian (both of about 1780). At the nearer end are cases of glassware and exquisite Meissen porcelain; in the centre is a group in ivory and walnut, the Judgement of Solomon, south German work of the early part of the century; and at the farther end are a French harpsichord in the 'Chinese' style, dated 1786, and a fireplace of steel ornamented with brass and copper-gilt, made in the Russian Imperial Arms factory. The sculptures in the room include marbles by *J. Saly* (Young Girl) and *J.-A. Houdon* (Voltaire in Old Age), a bronze by *J.-B. Pigalle* (Jean-Rodolphe Perronet), and terracottas by *J.-B. Lemoyne* (Comtesse de Feuquières) and *Claude-Michel*, called Clodion (Cupid and Psyche).

Rooms 6–7, beyond, contain the JONES COLLECTION, an outstanding assembly of works of art bequeathed in 1882. Mainly French and of the 17th and 18th centuries, the collection forms in effect an extension of the previous Continental galleries. It comprises beautiful furniture; paintings by Boucher, Lancret, Pater, etc.; porcelain from Sèvres, Vincennes, and Chelsea; sculpture, clocks, snuff-boxes, etc. The English paintings include works by Lely, Gilbert Jackson, William Etty, Landseer, and others. The 18th-century Gobelins tapestries of the Story of Jason, designed by J.-F. de Troy, were purchased in 1951. The staircase at the end of Room 7 ascends to the Main Vestibule.

By passing through Room 49 again and turning left in the corridor (Room 47) the magnificent Primary Collection of INDIAN ART will be reached. In the principal gallery (Room 41) are cases of Mughal jade and crystal carvings, etc., and (in the centre) a splendid Mughal carpet, made probably at Lahore about 1640 and presented to the East India Company. The bays contain a fine selection of Indian miniature paintings, ranging from the enchanting Rajput and Mughal works of the 16th–18th centuries to Hindu paintings down to the 19th century from the Punjab Hills of northern India. On the walls are hung carpets, bedspreads, embroideries, and temple-hangings, many of great beauty. The first part of the adjoining corridor (ROOM 47B) holds Gandhara and other early sculpture, bronzes, etc. (from the 3rd millennium B.C. onward); in the western sections (ROOM 47A) are furniture (inlaid tables and cabinets, etc.), bedspreads and hangings, ivories (including a set of chessmen of about 1790 from Bengal, one side of which represents troops of the East India Company and the other of an Indian army), and paintings done by British artists in India. A curiosity is the large wooden model of a tiger mauling a British officer, made about 1790 for Tippoo Sahib, the notorious ruler of Mysore. Inside is a small organ which produces sounds imitating the groans of the unfortunate victim.

As the space available allows for the display of only a relatively small proportion of the treasures of the Indian collection, rooms for the study of paintings and textiles have been arranged in the museum (north of Room 28).

In Room 48, south of the corridor, are hung the celebrated RAPHAEL CARTOONS, seven of a set of ten commissioned by Pope Leo X as designs for tapestries, and executed by Raphael in 1515–16. The cartoons, painted in sized colours on paper and depicting scenes in the lives of SS. Peter and Paul, are among the finest examples of mature Renaissance art; they were purchased in 1623 for Prince Charles (later Charles I) at a cost of £300 and are now the property of H.M. the Queen. The tapestries, woven in Brussels for the Sistine Chapel of the Vatican, are now in the picture gallery there. The room also contains a 17th-century tapestry, woven at Mortlake (Surrey) from one of the cartoons and lent by the Duke of Buccleuch. The large Octagon Court (Room 40), north of the corridor, holds a fine series of COSTUMES, mostly English, of the 16th–20th centuries, as well as costume dolls, English and Continental fans, and contemporary fashion plates. Also in the court are a panelled room of about 1620 from Haynes Grange (Bedfordshire) and part of the dining-room at Drakelowe Hall (Derbyshire), painted in 1793 by Paul Sandby.

From Room 21 (north of the Octagon Court) the ascending staircase leads to Rooms 52–8, covering ENGLISH FURNITURE AND DECORATIVE ARTS OF 1500–1750. The first rooms are confined to the Tudors and early Stewarts. Room 52 contains panelling from houses at Waltham Abbey (Essex) and Exeter (late 16th century); Queen Elizabeth's virginal, dating from about 1570; a carved and inlaid bedstead of 1593 from Moreton Corbet, near Shrewsbury; and the 'Great Bed of Ware', a celebrated carved and painted Elizabethan bed. 12 ft square, mentioned in 1596 and referred to by Shakespeare and Ben Jonson. Here also are notable silver-gilt plate, including the Mostyn Salt, bearing the hall-mark of London (1586–7), and the Vyvyan Salt (London, 1592–3); and bookbindings with the arms of Henry VIII and James I. In the centre is a panelled room of about 1575 from Sizergh Castle (Westmorland), Rooms 53 and 54 include notable table carpets and other embroidery of the late 16th and early 17th centuries; oak panelling and the plaster ceiling from the state room of the Old Palace at Bromley-by-Bow, completed in 1606 for James I, and the Mucklow Cup of silver-mounted pearwood (1620).

Room 55 and Room 57A (farther on) contain a superb collection of PORTRAIT MINIATURES, arranged chronologically. In the first room are delightful works by Hans Holbein the Younger (d. 1543), Nicholas Hilliard (d. 1619; the foremost British miniaturist), Isaac Oliver (d. 1617), Peter Oliver (d. 1647; his son), and Samuel Cooper (d. 1672) and other 17th-century artists. One case holds foreign miniatures. In Room 57A are later miniatures, from 1750 onward, by Richard Cosway (d. 1821) and others.

Room 56, continuing the English Decorative Art, covers the Restoration and William and Mary periods (1660–1700). It includes a panelled room of 1686–8 from Clifford's Inn; the Stoning of St Stephen, a relief in lime and lancewood by Grinling Gibbons; two fine late-17th-century bedsteads; clocks and watches, glassware, earthenware, silver, etc.; and notable furniture, including an elaborate japanned cabinet and mirror, and examples of the newly introduced marquetry. Rooms 57 and 58 deal with the Queen Anne and early Georgian periods (1700–50). The latter contains three typical rooms: one of about 1730, panelled in pinewood, from Hatton Garden; the music room from Norfolk House, St James's Square (about 1756); and a panelled room of about 1755 from Great George Street, Westminster. The furniture, which shows the advent of the rococo style, includes side-tables designed by James Moore and by the architect Henry

Flitcroft, and a looking-glass by William Kent. Joseph High-more's illustrations to Richardson's *Pamela* are part of a series others of which are at the Tate Gallery.

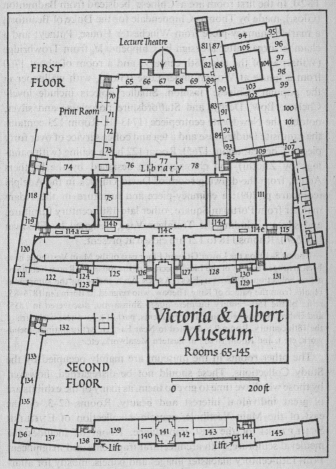

The adjoining staircase ascends to the First Floor, where the landing (Room 126) displays a selection of ENGLISH SCULPTURE of the 17th–18th centuries, with portrait busts by

Rysbrack, Peter Scheemakers, Wilton, Nollekens, and others, and terracotta statuettes for monuments. Rooms 120–5 are devoted to ENGLISH FURNITURE AND DECORATIVE ARTS OF 1750–1820. In the first room are a 'Chinese' bedstead from Badminton (Glos.), made by Thomas Chippendale for the Duke of Beaufort; a marble chimney-piece from Winchester House, Putney; and a chamber-organ after a design by Chippendale, from Trowbridge (Wilts); all of the mid 18th century; and a room of about 1760 from a house at Wotton-under-Edge (Glos.), with wallpaper in the popular 'Chinese' fashion. Smaller objects include lovely Chelsea, Bow, Derby, and Staffordshire porcelain; and silver, notably the Newdegate centrepiece (1743–4). Room 123 contains the exquisite Dudley vase and a tea and coffee service of over forty pieces (Chelsea; about 1765). Room 122 has a ceiling (with paintings by Zucchi) and chimney-piece designed by the brothers Adam, from the drawing room of David Garrick in the Adelphi (compare p. 209); a chimney-piece and furniture in the Adam manner from Portman Square; other late-18th-century furniture; and silver, including the Trafalgar Vase, designed by Flaxman (1805–6). Rooms 118 to 121 are closed at present.

Rooms 8–10, on the Lower Ground Floor east of the Main Vestibule, have been arranged as part of the Indian section of the museum. Room 8 contains a fine collection of SOUTH-EAST ASIAN ART, including the sumptuous regalia from the palace of King Thebaw, who reigned in Burma in 1876–85; relics of the 15th-century Burmese queen Shinsawbu, discovered in 1855; and elaborately carved musical instruments, part of a Javanese orchestra of the 18th century. Room 9 is devoted to Near Eastern Art (paintings, metalwork, etc.), and Room 10 to Far Eastern Metalwork, etc.

The other rooms in the museum are mainly occupied by the Study Collections. These should not be disregarded, however, by those who have time to give to them, as many of the exhibits are of great individual interest and beauty. Rooms 62–3, on the east of the Main Vestibule, contain a collection of ENGLISH SCULPTURE of the first importance. Room 62 includes the medieval sculpture, with architectural fragments and magnificent 14th–15th-century alabaster images and panels, mostly for altarpieces and originally painted and gilded. The next room has a carved marble fireplace with a wood and plaster over-mantel of about 1750 from Northumberland House, near Charing Cross;

portraits in wax, bronzes, etc.; and a fine series of portrait busts extending in date from the 17th to the early 19th century, with characteristic examples by Le Sueur (Charles I), John Nost the Younger (George III), Rysbrack, Roubiliac, Nollekens, Wilton, Chantrey, and Thomas Banks. The eastern half of Room 62 has European, Near Eastern, and Latin-American carvings in ivory; Room 64 holds Italian bronzes, medals, and plaquettes.

The large Room 50, on the north, is devoted to CONTINENTAL ARCHITECTURE AND SCULPTURE, including the larger objects from the Primary Collections for which no space can be found elsewhere. The western part of the room contains architectural details and sculptures of the 15th–18th centuries, chiefly from Central and Northern Italy. Particularly notable are the great doorway of 1515 from Ghedi (Brescia) and the monument of about 1435 to the Marquis Spinetta Malaspina from Verona, both on the south wall. At the west end is a carved and painted limewood altarpiece of the late 15th century, from Tyrol. At the east end is a large and handsome rood-screen in marble and alabaster from Bois-le-Duc (1613); the figure of St Peter on the left is by Nicholas Stone, who worked in Holland for a time.

The eastern part of the gallery is mainly confined to the Italian Renaissance, with carved doorways, chimney-pieces, fountains, well-heads, tombstones, etc. On the left in the first section are two doorways in slate from the workshop of *Giovanni Gaggini* (d. 1517) at Genoa; in the centre are well-heads of Verona marble; and on the right are a chimney-piece of about 1500 from Padua, carved with hunting scenes; the balcony of the Palazzo Pola at Treviso (in Istrian stone; after 1492); and the monument to Gabriele Moro (d. 1546), from Venice. The second section contains the singing-gallery from Santa Maria Novella at Florence, designed after 1490 by *Baccio d'Agnolo*, on the north wall; and a large mosaic (Nativity of the Virgin) of the late 14th century from Orvieto; the arch of an altar, possibly by *Giuliano da Majano* (d. 1490); and a fountain attributed to *Benedetto da Rovezzano* (d. 1552); all on the south wall. Smaller works include enamelled terracottas, such as the striking Head of Christ by *Giovanni della Robbia*, and the Lamentation by *G. F. Gonelli* (north wall; early 17th century). The eastern apse of the gallery is filled with the tribune of Santa Chiara, Florence, built in 1493 by *Giuliano da Sangallo.*

Rooms 127–30 on the First Floor and 133–45 on the Second Floor are given over to the rich and extensive Study Collection of CERAMICS. Rooms 127–8 contain French earthenware and porcelain of the 16th–19th centuries; 129–30, Chinese glassware, jade carvings, etc., and Japanese netsuke and lacquer-work; 133, Islamic pottery of the Near East; 134–5, Italian and other European tin-glazed earthenware; 136, German stoneware and faience; 137, English earthenware and stoneware, a fine selection, and Continental peasant pottery; 138, Renaissance enamels from France and Italy; 139–40, English pottery, porcelain, and enamels, mainly of the 18th century, from the Schreiber collection; 141, Northern European tiles and tilework; 142, German, Spanish, and Italian porcelain and enamels; and 143–5, Far Eastern pottery and porcelain. Room 131 holds the collection of GLASSWARE, and Room 132, at the north-west end, illustrates THEATRE ART, with interesting models and other exhibits, changed from time to time.

The adjoining staircase descends to the First Floor, where Room 74 is devoted to the ART OF THE BOOK. The first section contains beautiful illuminated manuscripts, 16th-century printed writing manuals, and notable modern manuscripts; the next, printed and illustrated books, and book-bindings; and the third, books and manuscripts of literary interest, type design, etc. A case at the end contains the manuscript of Dickens' *Tale of Two Cities* and the author's desk and pen-case. The eastern bay of the room shows methods of etching, engraving, and lithography. Room 75, on the right, illustrates the History of the Museum. The long corridor beyond (Room 114) contains an exceptionally comprehensive collection of IRONWORK. Rooms 70–3, on the left of Room 74, contain an exhibition of engraving, illustration, and design.

Rooms 65–9 are given over to DOMESTIC SILVER, British work in the first three rooms and Continental work in the others. Notable pieces are the Pusey Horn, of about 1450, the Howard Grace Cup (1525), and the earliest known teapot (1670) and coffee-pot (1682); the mace of St Andrew's church, Holborn (1694); and an engraved silver table-top, French work of about 1700. Rooms 81–4 and 87–93 are devoted to METALWORK: Room 81 (left) to Pewter and Lead; Room 82, Sheffield Plate; Room 89, which follows, to English church plate from the Middle Ages to the early 19th century; Room 83, Continental silver church plate; Room 84, Brass and bronzework; Room 93 (left), Watches and metal-cased clocks; Rooms 91–2, Jewellery, rings, and gold snuff-boxes, another very fine collection; Rooms 88A and 90, European arms and armour; and Room 88, Near Eastern metalwork. Room 87 contains a selection of FOREIGN PAINTINGS, including a remarkable late-15th-century Martyrdom of St Ursula from Cologne.

Rooms 103–6, on the First Floor, reached from Room 90 (see above), contain a representative selection of PAINTINGS from the Sheepshanks, Ionides, and other valuable bequests, including Italian and Dutch masters

(Louis Le Nain, Nardo di Cione, Tintoretto, Rembrandt, G. B. Tiepolo, etc.), but richest in 19th-century French and 18th–19th-century British works, with many paintings, drawings, and sketches by John Constable (d. 1837).

The LIBRARY (Rooms 76–8), the largest and finest art library in the world, contains over 250,000 books, pamphlets, and periodicals, covering every aspect of fine and applied art, and an extensive collection of photographs. It also houses the Dyce and Forster Libraries, which include the correspondence of Garrick, several novels in manuscript of Dickens, etc. The TEXTILE STUDY ROOMS, on the north-east side of the building and entered from Room 107, at the top of the staircase, hold many fine examples of European and Far Eastern woven fabrics, embroideries, etc., including splendid Chinese court robes and silken tapestry pictures. On the landing is a full-size coloured photographic copy of the Bayeux Tapestry.

WALLACE COLLECTION Plan II, D 2

STATIONS: BOND STREET, ½-m. SE., on the Central line; BAKER STREET, ½-m. NW., on the Bakerloo, Circle, and Metropolitan lines. — MOTOR-BUSES in Baker Street, see Route 16; in Wigmore Street and Oxford Street, see Route 14.

ADMISSION weekdays 10 to 5; Sundays 2 to 5 (free). Closed on Good Friday, Christmas Eve, and Christmas Day.

The WALLACE COLLECTION, the finest as well as the largest collection of works of art of all kinds presented to any nation by a private individual, was formed mainly by the third and fourth Marquesses of Hertford and the latter's son, Sir Richard Wallace. It was bequeathed by Lady Wallace in 1897 and is maintained in Hertford House, the residence of the Marquesses and Sir Richard, an 18th-century mansion on the north side of Manchester Square, in the angle between Baker Street and Wigmore Street, a little north of Oxford Street. The collection is especially valuable for its 17th–18th-century French paintings, furniture, sculpture, and porcelain, but is remarkable, too, for its European and Oriental arms and armour, its fine gallery of English, Flemish, Dutch, Spanish, and Italian paintings, and its Renaissance terracottas and bronzes, Italian majolica, and other smaller objects of ornamental art. The treasures receive added distinction by being set out as in a private residence.

The collection, begun by the first and second Marquesses of Hertford, was considerably enlarged by the third Marquess (d. 1842), who has been brilliantly pilloried as Lord Steyne by Thackeray in *Vanity Fair*. The main part, however, was formed by the fourth Marquess (d. 1870), who resided for most of his life in Paris and was a connoisseur of 18th-century French art. The collection passed to his son, Sir Richard Wallace (d. 1890), who greatly augmented it by the addition of the armouries and the medieval and Renaissance works, and after the Franco-Prussian War (1871) transferred a large part of it to London. He reopened Manchester House (built in 1776–8 for the fourth Duke of Manchester and later the London residence of the Marquesses of Hertford), renamed it Hertford House in their honour, and extended it northward to contain his now priceless collection. This was bequeathed to the nation by his widow on condition that a home be found for it in central London. The freehold of Hertford House was purchased, and the collection was made accessible to the public in 1900.

From the ENTRANCE HALL, which contains a portrait of George IV by Sir Thomas Lawrence, the GRAND STAIRCASE ascends to the First Floor, where the more important objects in the collection are displayed. The marble staircase has a balustrade of wrought-iron and gilt-bronze made for Louis XV's Cabinet des Medailles in Paris, now part of the Bibliothèque Nationale. On the first landing is a marble bust of Louis XIV, by Coysevox, and on the upper landing are French marble sculptures and French and Italian bronzes of the 18th century. The fine paintings by François Boucher (the Rising and the Setting of the Sun, etc.) were designs for tapestries and once in the possession of Madame de Pompadour.

Room XII, on the left of the landing, contains notable Sèvres porcelain, as well as cabinets, clocks, chairs, etc., of the periods of Louis XV (1715–74) and Louis XVI (1774–92). On the walls are hung characteristic views of 18th-century Venice by Antonio Canaletto and Francesco Guardi. Rooms XIII and XIV, beyond, are devoted to Dutch and Flemish paintings of the 17th century, with notable works by Rembrandt (including a fine portrait of the artist), J. A. Backer, M. J. Mierevelt, A. van der Neer, J. van Noordt, and Cornelis de Vos; and A. Brouwer, N. Maes, G. Metsu, A. van Ostade, Jan Steen, D. Teniers the Younger, and Gerard Terborch. Room XV, which follows, contains 17th-century Dutch landscape and seascapes, including works by Aelbert Cuyp, M. Hobbema, I. van Ostade, J. van Ruisdael, and W. Van de Velde the younger.

The large PICTURE GALLERY (Room XVI) contains the most important paintings in the collection. Among the masterpieces usually on view here are: *Philippe de Champaigne*, 'The Annunciation'; *Claude*, 'Italian Landscape'; *A. Cuyp*, 'River Scene at Dordrecht'; *Gainsborough*, 'Mrs Robinson' ('Perdita', the mistress of George IV) and 'Miss Haverfield'; *Frans Hals*, 'The Laughing Cavalier', the best-known picture in the collection; *Hobbema*, 'Stormy Landscape'; *Pieter de Hooch*, two fine Dutch interiors; *Murillo*, 'Holy Family'; *Poussin*, 'Dance to the Music of Time'; *Rembrandt*, 'The Artist's Son, Titus', 'The Centurion Cornelius', and 'Jean Pellicorne with his son, and his wife with his daughter'; *Reynolds*, 'Miss Bowles', 'Mrs Hoare and her Son', 'Nelly O'Brien', 'The Strawberry Girl', etc.; *Romney*, 'Perdita Robinson', a fine study; *Rubens*, 'Isabelle Brandt', his first wife, 'Christ on the Cross', 'Christ's Charge to Peter', 'The Holy Family', and 'The Rainbow Landscape'; *J. van Ruisdael*, 'Rocky Landscape'; *Titian*, 'Perseus and Andromeda', painted in 1554 for Philip II of Spain; *Van Dyck*, 'Philippe le Roy and his wife, Marie de Raet' and 'Young Italian Nobleman'; *Velazquez*, 'Don Baltasar Carlos' and 'Lady with a Fan'; and *Watteau*, 'Fête in a Park' and 'Halt during the Chase'. The furniture includes a handsome bureau by J.-H. Riesener and two fine commodes, by Gaudreau and Caffieri and by Crescent.

Room XVII, entered from the west end of the gallery, contains 19th-century French paintings, including a number of small but detailed works by Meissonier, and others by Corot, Decamps, Delacroix, Géricault, Prud'hon, and Théodore Rousseau. A table in the centre holds Renaissance and other jewellery. Room XVIII is devoted to 18th-century French art: on the walls is a delightful series of romantic pastoral scenes ('fêtes champêtres' and 'conversations galantes') by Watteau, Pater, Lancret, Boucher, and Fragonard, and portraits by Nattier, Greuze, and Mme Vigée Le Brun, and cases in the centre hold a rich collection of snuff-boxes and bonbonnières. Three secretaires by Riesener are known to have belonged to Marie Antoinette. In Room XIX are the so-called marriage commode of Marie Antoinette, by Dubois, and a portrait of Mme de Pompadour by Boucher, as well as four other panels painted by him. Room XX contains further French furniture, including a writing-table and cartonnier in green lacquer and bronze by Dubois that belonged to Catherine the

Great of Russia. Over the fireplace is another portrait of 'Perdita' Robinson, by Reynolds, and on the walls are landscapes by R. P. Bonington.

A passage, with cases of turquoise-blue porcelain from the Sèvres factory, leads left to Room XXI, which contains exquisite 'bleu de roi' Sèvres porcelain, a monumental clock attributed to Boulle, and paintings by Desportes, Lancret, Pater, and others. Room XXII, the last room entered on this floor, has further Sèvres porcelain, and cases of metalwork, miniatures, and relics of the French royal house. On the walls are 18th-century French paintings.

The descent is made again to the GROUND FLOOR. Rooms I and II, a large combined room on the east side of the Entrance Hall, contain cases of Sèvres porcelain and 18th-century French furniture, including chairs covered with Beauvais tapestry and a large ebony and marquetry wardrobe believed to be by Boulle. Among the paintings are portraits by Hoppner ('George IV as Prince of Wales'), Lawrence ('Miss Siddons', and 'The Countess of Blessington'), and Largillière ('Louis XIV and his heirs'). Room III is devoted to the late Middle Ages and the Renaissance. Cases contain a fine collection of Italian majolica, as well as bronzes, enamels, ivories, and boxwood carvings – the last including a beautifully carved miniature shrine, Flemish work of about 1500 – and exquisite illuminations done on vellum. On the walls are paintings by Bronzino and Memling, alabaster reliefs from England (15th century) and Denmark (16th century), and a noble head of Christ, carved in marble by Torrigiani. Room IV continues the medieval and Renaissance collections, with fine Limoges enamels of the 15th–16th centuries, bronze medals, ivories, metalwork, and wax miniatures. Notable are the 7th-century Bell of St Mura, from Ireland, and the 15th-century Horn of St Hubert, in the first of the centre cases, and the astronomical clock of gilt-copper made at Augsburg in the 16th century, in the second case. Other cases contain 16th–17th-century Continental earthenware and Venetian glass, and the paintings include works by Philippe de Champaigne ('Adoration of the Shepherds') and Rigaud ('Cardinal Fleury'), and a portrait of Mary, Queen of Scots, after François Clouet.

A corridor (with cases of 16th-century Italian majolica) gives access to Rooms V–VII, which contain the superb collection of EUROPEAN ARMS AND ARMOUR, arranged for the most part in chronological order (beginning in Room VII). Notable pieces are the equestrian armour made at Nuremberg in 1532–6 and bearing the arms of the Palatinate (Room V), the war harness for man and horse made about 1475–85 for the Von Freyberg family of Upper Bavaria, and a richly decorated shield with the arms of Diane de Poitiers (both in Room VI). Room VIII (beyond Room VII) has a notable collection of ORIENTAL ARMS AND ARMOUR, mostly of the 17th–19th centuries, and paintings of Oriental scenes by 19th-century French artists.

The FOUNDERS' ROOM, or Old Board Room, in the south-west corner, contains a large early-18th-century French wardrobe incorporating a clock by P. Gaudron. Here also are busts of the fourth Marquess of Hertford, Sir Richard Wallace, and Lady Wallace, and family and other portraits by Reynolds and Sully. Room IX, beyond, has a case of Chinese celadon vases with French mounts, further Venetian views by Canaletto and Guardi, and a portrait of George III by Allan Ramsay. A passage to the left, hung with fine water-colours by Bonington and Turner, leads to Room X, which has notable French furniture, Italian and other terracottas, and paintings of the Italian schools by Cima, Luini, Andrea del Sarto, and Sassoferrato, and others attributed to Foppa and Titian. Room XI, behind the Grand Staircase, contains Spanish and Italian paintings of the 17th century, including several important works by Murillo, and a very fine collection of miniatures, showing the work of Holbein (portrait of himself), Isaac Oliver and Richard Cosway, Lanfransen (or Lavreince) and P.-A. Hall, the Swedish artists, and E. G. Isabey (Napoleon, Wellington, and others).

The offices of the NATIONAL ART-COLLECTIONS FUND (see p. 64) are in the basement at Hertford House.

WESTMINSTER ABBEY Plan VIII, C 3

STATIONS: WESTMINSTER, Bridge Street, to the NE., and ST JAMES'S PARK, Broadway, to the W., both on the Circle and District lines. —

MOTOR-BUSES Nos. 3, 11, 24, 29, 39, 59, 76, 77, 88, 127, 134, and 159 all pass the abbey.

ADMISSION daily from 8 a.m. to 7 p.m. (6 in October–March), but on Sundays only the nave and transepts are open. Services are held on Sunday at 8, 10.30, and 11.30 a.m. and 3 and 6.30 p.m.; on weekdays at 8, 9 (for the boys of Westminster School), 10, and 5 (Saturdays at 3). The hours available for an extended visit on weekdays are therefore from about 11 a.m. until 4.45 p.m. (Saturdays 2.45). On Ash Wednesday, Good Friday, and Christmas Day the abbey is open for service only. — The AMBULATORY and CHOIR CHAPELS are open on Mondays, Wednesdays, and Thursdays, 9.45 to 4; Tuesdays and Fridays 10.45 to 4; Saturdays 9.45 to 2.15 and 3.45 to 5 (1/-; Mondays free); visitors must obtain tickets from a verger at the south gate of the Ambulatory (near the Poets' Corner). — The CHAPTER HOUSE and the CHAMBER OF THE PYX are open on weekdays from 10.30 to 6.30 (to 4 in October–February; free), and the NORMAN UNDERCROFT, with the abbey museum, on weekdays from 10.30 to 4.30 (to 4 in winter; 6d); all are closed on Good Friday and Christmas Day.

The usual ENTRANCE to the abbey is from Broad Sanctuary by the West Door, but there are other entrances from Parliament Square to the North Transept, and from Old Palace Yard (facing the Houses of Parliament) to the South Transept (Poets' Corner). The Chapter House, the Chamber of the Pyx and the Norman Undercroft may also be approached from Dean's Yard by the South Cloister.

WESTMINSTER ABBEY, officially the Collegiate Church of St Peter, is the premier church of England not of cathedral status. Refounded in the 11th century by Edward the Confessor, it has been the scene of the coronation of the English sovereigns from that of William the Conqueror in 1066 to Elizabeth II in 1953, and most of the English kings from Henry III to George II, with their consorts, are buried here. No church is more intimately connected with English history (the Chapter House, for instance, was the meeting place of early parliaments), and interment within the abbey walls has for centuries been considered the most fitting honour that a nation can bestow on its illustrious sons. The abbey is crowded with monuments, some to persons long since forgotten and others of doubtful artistic value. Many of the monuments are to men who are buried elsewhere, and as a whole they tend to distract attention from the architecture of the abbey itself, for apart from the splendid chapel added at the east end by Henry VII and the twin west towers raised in the 18th century, the church is the purest example in the country of the Early English style. The abbey is 513 ft long, including Henry VII's Chapel, 75 ft wide across the nave and aisles and 200 ft across the transepts; the nave, 102 ft high to the vault, is the loftiest Gothic nave in England (York Minster 99½ ft). The height of the western towers is 225 ft.

Westminster Abbey is not the seat of a bishop, neither is it a parish church. It is a 'royal peculiar', a distinction shared only with St George's Chapel in Windsor Castle. The abbey is under the jurisdiction of a Dean and Chapter who are subject only to the sovereign, and neither the Archbishop of Canterbury nor the Bishop of London has any authority over its affairs.

The abbey occupies a site once known as Thorney Island, a tract of low ground surrounded by water and first utilized by the Romans. Here, according to tradition, a church was built by Sebert, king of the East Saxons, and consecrated in 616 by Mellitus, the first bishop of London. The first authentic church is that of a Benedictine abbey founded before 750 and known as 'Westminster' (*i.e.* 'west monastery') from its position in relation to the City of London. The abbey was rebuilt on a larger scale some time after his accession in 1042 by Edward the Confessor, and the church, which followed a Norman plan, was consecrated by him in 1065, shortly before his death. In 1163 the Confessor was canonized and his remains transferred to the place of honour behind the high altar. A Lady Chapel was added at the east end in 1220 by Henry III, but in 1245 the king determined to rebuild the entire church on a more magnificent scale in honour of St Edward. The architect was Henry of Reims, who adopted the French style of the time, especially in the arrangement of polygonal chapels radiating from the ambulatory, and by 1269, when the church was rededicated, it was completed as far as the fourth bay of the nave. Henry III was buried in the church in 1272 and from this time (until the 19th century) it became the royal burial place. In 1298 the domestic buildings of the abbey were largely destroyed by fire, and the existing remains date from the 13th–14th centuries, except for the Norman work surviving in the Chamber of the Pyx and the near-by Undercroft.

The western part of the Norman nave was left standing until 1376, when it was rebuilt in the style of the remainder of the church by Henry Yevele, the architect of the nave of Canterbury Cathedral. The work was largely completed by 1388, except for the nave vaulting, raised by Abbot Islip in 1506. The Henry V Chantry was added in 1441, but in 1503 the Lady Chapel was demolished in favour of a splendid new chapel intended by Henry VII as the burial place of the saintly Henry VI, whose canonization he hoped to secure. But the king's body was never transferred from Windsor and in 1509 the chapel (completed in 1519) became the resting-place of Henry VII himself. In 1532 Abbot Islip was buried in the chantry chapel he had built for himself off the north ambulatory.

At the Reformation the abbey suffered the same fate as other religious establishments. In 1540 it became the seat of a bishopric, which lasted, however, only for ten years. The monks returned under the Catholic Mary Tudor, but they were removed again by Elizabeth I, who in 1561 placed the abbey under an independent Dean and Chapter (originally twelve prebendaries, but now five canons residentiary), who still govern it today. The renewal of the outer stonework, begun by Sir Christopher Wren in 1688, has gone on practically ever since, so that the exterior is by no means a faithful copy of the medieval church. The incongruous west towers, with the gable between them, were raised by Nicholas Hawksmoor, a pupil of Wren, in 1739, and Henry VII's Chapel was refaced by James Wyatt in 1822. The façade of the north transept was completely recast by Sir Gilbert Scott and J. L. Pearson in 1875–92, and the west front and south transept restored by J. T. Micklethwaite after 1898. The central tower intended by Wren, however, has never been built. A further very extensive restoration of the fabric, at an estimated cost of £1 million (for which an appeal was launched in 1953), is now going forward under the cathedral architect, S. E. Dykes Bower.

The annual distribution of the ROYAL MAUNDY, a ceremony dating from the reign of Edward III, takes place (usually) in the abbey at noon on Maundy Thursday, i.e. the Thursday before Easter. Purses of money, specially minted (formerly also clothing and food), are distributed by the sovereign, attended by the Lord High Almoner, to as many poor elderly men and as many poor elderly women as the sovereign has lived years. The service includes traditional anthems, etc.; parts of the abbey are reserved for the occasion and tickets may be obtained at the Royal Almonry Office, Buckingham Palace, S W 1. The name 'Maundy' is probably derived from the first word of the antiphon, 'Mandatum novum do vobis' (John xiii, 34), with which the ceremony begins, though possibly from the baskets ('maunds') of bread formerly carried on the attendants' heads. — Services are also held in the abbey before the opening of the Law Courts (in October) and on other special occasions.

Entering by the great WEST DOOR the visitor will be impressed by the striking beauty of the interior of the church, an effect owed to a great extent to the harmony of its proportions. The nave is divided from the aisles by arcades of acutely pointed arches supported by circular piers round each of which are grouped eight attached shafts, the shaft on the nave side in every case being carried up to form a rib of the lofty fan vault. Above the arcade runs the triforium, with its beautiful tracery and series of small carved heads, and higher still is the spacious clerestory. The recent cleaning of the stonework and the gilding of the roof bosses and ribs has enhanced the beauty of the great church.

It is as well to survey the architecture of the church as a whole before studying the numerous monuments (some of the older of

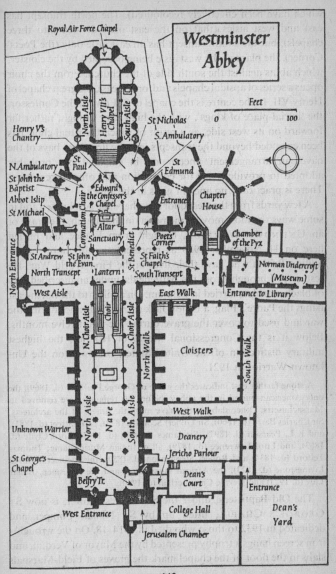

Royal Air Force Chapel

Westminster Abbey

Feet

0   100

North Aisle

Henry VII's Chapel

South Aisle

St Nicholas

S. Ambulatory

Henry V's Chantry

St Paul

N. Ambulatory

St John the Baptist

Abbot Islip

St Michael

Edward the Confessor's Chapel

Coronation Chair

Altar

Sanctuary

St Edmund

Entrance

Chapter House

Entrance

Poets' Corner

Chamber of the Pyx

St Andrew

St John the Evan.

North Transept

Lantern

St Benedict

St Faith's Chapel

South Transept

Norman Undercroft (Museum)

North Entrance

West Aisle

East Walk

Entrance to Library

N. Choir Aisle

Choir

S. Choir Aisle

North Walk

Cloisters

South Walk

North Aisle

Nave

South Aisle

West Walk

Unknown Warrior

St George's Chapel

Deanery

Jericho Parlour

Belfry Tr.

Dean's Court

Entrance

West Entrance

College Hall

Dean's Yard

Jerusalem Chamber

which have been effectively recoloured). The north transept has east and west aisles (that on the east once divided into three chapels), but the south transept has an east aisle only (the Poets' Corner), the place of the west aisle being occupied by the cloister, which abuts against the south side of the church. From the choir opens a series of apsidal chapels and, on the east, the great chapel of Henry VII. In the centre is the chapel of St Edward the Confessor, the 'burial-place of kings', with the high altar brought rather far forward on its west side, as a result of which the ritual choir has been extended beyond the transepts into the first three bays of the nave, an arrangement uncommon in England but probably adopted to provide space for coronation and other ceremonies. There is practically no ancient glass in the abbey.

A few yards from the west door is perhaps the best known and in some ways the most moving memorial in the church, the grave of an UNKNOWN WARRIOR, brought from France and buried here on 11 November 1920 as representative of more than a million British who gave their lives in the First World War. He rests in soil brought from the battlefields, under an inscribed slab of black marble quarried in Belgium. On a pillar to the north-east hangs the Padre's Flag, a Union Jack carried in France during the war and used to cover the grave during the first twelve months. Below it is the Congressional Medal of Honour, the highest military distinction of the United States, bestowed on the Unknown Warrior in 1921.

A stone farther east indicates the grave of George Peabody (d. 1869), the only American buried in the abbey, before his remains were removed to Massachusetts. Other slabs in the nave mark the graves of the architects, Sir Charles Barry (d. 1860), Sir Gilbert Scott (d. 1878), G. E. Street (d. 1881), and J. L. Pearson (d. 1897); Sir James Outram (d. 1863), Lord Clyde (d. 1863), and Lord Lawrence (d. 1879), all of Indian Mutiny fame; Thomas Telford (d. 1834) and Robert Stephenson (d. 1859), the engineers; David Livingstone (d. 1873), the African missionary; and the statesmen, Bonar Law (d. 1923) and Neville Chamberlain (d. 1940).

The Old Baptistery, under the South-West Tower, is now ST GEORGE'S CHAPEL, fitted up by Sir Ninian Comper and dedicated in 1932 to those who died in 1914–18. On the wrought-iron screen hangs a trophy presented by the Mayor of Verdun, and slabs in the floor of the chapel mark the graves of Field-Marshals

Viscount Plumer (d. 1932) and Viscount Allenby (d. 1936). A case to the right of the entrance contains memorial books with the names of civilians killed in 1939–45, and above this is a tablet in memory of President Franklin D. Roosevelt (d. 1945). On a pillar to the left is a contemporary portrait of Richard II (1377–99), the oldest known portrait of an English monarch.

All the monuments in the nave aisles date from after the Reformation. In the floor at the west end of the SOUTH AISLE is a stone in memory of Lord Baden-Powell (d. 1941), the founder of the Boy Scouts. On the south wall is the Abbot's Pew, a small oak gallery erected in the 16th century by Abbot Islip and communicating with the adjoining house (now the Deanery) built by him. Below is a monument to William Congreve (d. 1729), the dramatist, by Francis Bird, and in the third bay beyond the cloister door one to Major John André, hanged in 1780 during the American War as a spy; the bas-relief below, designed by Robert Adam and carved by Peter van Gelder, shows George Washington receiving his vain petition for a soldier's death. This and the next bay contain fine 13th-century shields-of-arms. In front of the choir screen (1848) are a pair of bronze candelabra, each 6 ft high and 7 ft wide, by Benno Elkan, representing the Old and New Testaments and presented anonymously in 1939.

The south aisle is extended by the SOUTH CHOIR AISLE. On the left are the characteristic Elizabethan monument of Thomas Owen (d. 1598), with his effigy in alabaster still showing traces of painting, and a tablet to William Tyndale (d. 1536), translator of the Bible. Farther on is the fine marble monument with effigy of William Thynne (d. 1584). On the right (second bay) are monuments to Dr Isaac Watts (d. 1748), the hymn-writer, John Wesley (d. 1791) and Charles Wesley (d. 1788); all are buried elsewhere. On either side of the over-elaborate monument to Admiral Sir Cloudsley Shovel (d. 1707) are memorials to Lord Clive of India (d. 1774) and Admiral Blake (d. 1657), and above is a bust by Rysbrack of Sir Godfrey Kneller (d. 1723), the only painter commemorated in the abbey. The door in the next bay admits to the east walk of the cloisters.

Above the central space between the ritual choir and the sanctuary rises the LANTERN, the roof of which was destroyed by bombing in 1941. From this space there are good views of the great rose windows in the transepts: that on the north was designed by Sir James Thornhill (1722) but altered in the restoration of Scott and Pearson; the window on the south, the largest of its kind in England, was reglazed in 1902. The SANCTUARY, within the altar-rails, is the impressive setting of coronations; it has a mosaic pavement (usually covered by a carpet) executed by a Roman artist in 1268 for Abbot Ware. On the north are the three finest medieval tombs in the abbey: that on the east is of Edmund Crouchback (d. 1296), Earl of Lancaster, second son of Henry III and founder of the house of Lancaster, and next to this is the tomb of his cousin, Aymer de Valence (d. 1324), Earl of Pembroke. Around the tombs are finely sculptured 'weepers' or statuettes of relatives, while the canopies bear the figures of the earls on horseback. The other and smallest tomb is that of Aveline, Countess of Lancaster (d. 1273), wife of Edmund Crouchback. The Altar and Reredos, designed by Sir Gilbert Scott (1867), has a glass mosaic of the Last Supper by Salviati and sculptured figures by Armstead. On the south of the Sanctuary are the early-14th-century oak Sedilia, with defaced paintings identified as Sebert, St Peter and King Ethelbert, and the tomb of Anne of Cleves (d. 1557), the fourth queen of Henry VIII, above which is hung a 16th-century Brussels tapestry.

Part of the SOUTH TRANSEPT and its aisle is known as the POETS' CORNER, to many the most interesting quarter of the abbey. On the east of the aisle are busts of John Dryden (d. 1700), by P. Scheemakers, and Henry Wadsworth Longfellow (d. 1882), by Brock, the latter placed here by English admirers of the American poet. Next comes the fine Purbeck marble altar-tomb, under a canopy, erected in 1556 for Geoffrey Chaucer (d. 1400), the father of English poetry. Beneath the pavement in front are the graves of Robert Browning (d. 1889) and Alfred, Lord Tennyson (d. 1892). On the east wall of the aisle outside, near the door admitting to the abbey, is a tablet (unveiled in 1954) to William Caxton (d. 1491), who in 1477 set up the first printing press in England on a site close by.

On the south wall of the aisle, above the door to the Crypt under the Chapter House (closed to visitors), is a medallion of Ben

Jonson (d. 1637), and to the right are a monument (restored in 1778) to Edmund Spenser (d. 1599), author of the *Faerie Queene*, buried near the Chaucer tomb, and a bust by Rysbrack of John Milton (d. 1674), with a monument below to Thomas Gray (d. 1771). On the pier is a bust of Adam Lindsay Gordon (d. 1870), the Australian poet, and a slab in the floor to the north of this marks the grave of Thomas Parr ('Old Parr'; d. 1635), who is said to have lived under ten sovereigns and attained the age of 152 years. On the west side of the screen between the transept and the aisle are monuments to many famous writers. The monument to William Shakespeare (d. 1616), by Peter Scheemakers, was erected in 1740 and is inscribed with lines from *The Tempest*. The carved heads at the corners of the pedestal represent Elizabeth I, Henry V, and Richard III. On the left are a bust of Dr Samuel Johnson (d. 1784), by Nollekens, and statues of William Wordsworth (d. 1850) and Thomas Campbell (d. 1844). Above these are busts of Samuel Taylor Coleridge (d. 1834), by Thornycroft, and Robert Southey (d. 1843), by Weekes, and above Shakespeare are plaques to John Keats (d. 1821) and Percy Bysshe Shelley (d. 1822). On the right are a bust of Robert Burns (d. 1796), by Steell, a statue of James Thomson (d. 1748), author of *The Seasons* and *Rule, Britannia*, and a tablet to the Brontë Sisters with a line from a poem by Emily, 'with courage to endure'.

In the floor in front of these monuments are the graves of Johnson, Garrick, Sir Henry Irving (d. 1905, the actor), R. B. Sheridan (d. 1816, the playwright), Charles Dickens (d. 1870), and Handel. Farther north are the graves of Thomas Hardy (d. 1928) and Rudyard Kipling (d. 1936). On the south wall of the transept are two 13th-century wall-paintings, uncovered in 1936. Here also is the entrance to the 13th-century CHAPEL OF ST FAITH (reserved for private prayer); formerly the revestry, it contains two 16th-century Brussels tapestries.

Over the door to the chapel is a monument to Oliver Goldsmith (d. 1774), with an epitaph by Dr Johnson and a bust by Nollekens, and to the right are a bronze medallion of John Ruskin (d. 1900) and a copy of the fine bust by Chantrey of Sir Walter Scott (d. 1832). On the west wall are a medallion of Jenny Lind (d. 1827), the 'Swedish nightingale', and a monument to the composer, George Frederick Handel (d. 1759), the last work of Roubiliac. By the first pier are busts of William Makepeace Thackeray (d. 1863), by

Marochetti, and Lord Macaulay (d. 1859), whose grave is near by, and farther on is a statue by Westmacott of Joseph Addison (d. 1719), and a monument to David Garrick (d. 1779), the actor. Near the innermost pier are memorials to William Camden (d. 1623), the antiquary, and to George Grote (d. 1871) and Bishop Thirlwall (d. 1875), the historians of Greece (who share a single grave); and on the pier east of this is a bronze bust of William Blake (d. 1827), by Epstein (1957).

A gate at the end of the SOUTH AMBULATORY gives access to the Choir Chapels (admission, see p. 440). On the left is an early-14th-century tomb said to contain the remains of Sebert (d. 616), the reputed founder of the church; on the back of the sedilia above it are defaced 14th-century paintings. On the right is the CHAPEL OF ST BENEDICT (closed), best seen from the transept. Near the railing is an alabaster tomb with the effigy of Simon Langham (d. 1376), abbot of Westminster and later archbishop of Canterbury and Lord Chancellor of Edward III. Between this chapel and the next is a small 13th-century altar-tomb containing the remains of children of Henry III and Edward I. Opposite are the backs of the tombs of Richard II and Edward III, with enamelled coats-of-arms and exquisite little brass statuettes on the latter.

The CHAPEL OF ST EDMUND, king and martyr, is separated from the ambulatory by a medieval oak screen. On the right, inside, is the remarkable tomb of William de Valence (d. 1296), Earl of Pembroke and half-brother of Henry III. It consists of a stone altar-tomb surmounted by an oak chest on which rests an effigy in oak covered with gilded copper plates and enriched with remains of Limoges enamel. On the left of this is the fine Jacobean monument of Edward Talbot (d. 1618), eighth Earl of Shrewsbury, and his wife, and on the north-east of the chapel is the seated figure in alabaster of Lady Elizabeth Russell (d. 1601), the oldest non-recumbent statue in the abbey. In the centre are the table-tombs of Robert Waldeby (d. 1397), archbishop of York, who accompanied the Black Prince to France, and of Eleanor de Bohun (d. 1399), Duchess of Gloucester, whose brass, showing her in the habit of a nun, is the largest and finest in the abbey. A slab near by marks the grave of Edward Bulwer Lytton (d. 1873), the novelist. On the east of the chapel are an alabaster tomb with the effigy of Frances,

Duchess of Suffolk (d. 1559), mother of Lady Jane Grey, and the small alabaster effigies, unfortunately mutilated, of two infant children of Edward III. Beside the screen is a fine alabaster tomb with the effigy in armour of John of Eltham (d. 1337), second son of Edward II.

The CHAPEL OF ST NICHOLAS, which follows, has a good 15th-century stone screen. On the right is the tomb of Philippa, Duchess of York (d. 1431), and next to this the monument of Elizabeth, Duchess of Northumberland (d. 1776), designed by Robert Adam and sculptured by Nicholas Read. The vault below the chapel is the burial-place of the Percys, Dukes of Northumberland, the only family with the right of interment in the abbey. In the centre of the chapel is the splendid marble tomb of Sir George Villiers (d. 1606) and his wife, parents of the Duke of Buckingham, with effigies by Nicholas Stone. On the east are the characteristic Elizabethan monuments of the wife and daughter of Lord Burghley, Elizabeth I's minister (1589), and of Anne, Duchess of Somerset (d. 1587), widow of the Protector. In the ambulatory opposite is an oak Retable or Altarpiece, French or English work of the late 13th century, richly decorated ('the most remarkable example of early medieval painting'), but sadly damaged by misuse.

The steps on the right lead up to the Henry VII Chapel (see below), those on the left to the CHANTRY OF HENRY V, built by John of Thirsk (1441). On the tomb of Henry V (d. 1422) rests his headless wooden effigy, robbed of its silver-gilt plates and its solid silver head in the reign of Henry VIII. The body of his queen, Catherine of Valois (d. 1437), Shakespeare's 'beautiful Kate', buried in the old Lady Chapel, was disinterred at its demolition, exposed to public view, and not buried here until 1776.

The chantry forms the entrance to the CHAPEL OF ST EDWARD THE CONFESSOR, the most sacred part of the abbey, built over the apse of the Saxon church and structurally the east end of the choir. In the centre is the large but mutilated Shrine of Edward the Confessor (d. 1066), long a goal of pilgrimage. The Purbeck marble tomb (one of the two in England still containing the body of its saint) was made in 1268 by Peter of Rome at the order of Henry III and still retains traces of its splendid mosaics. The recesses on each side enabled pilgrims to kneel in prayer or in hope of a cure from sickness. The golden feretory decorated with gold images of saints and precious stones, stolen at the Dissolution, was replaced by a wooden superstructure by John Feckenham (1556–60), the last abbot of Westminster, and is usually covered by a pall presented by Edward VII in 1902.

On the north side of the chapel are the magnificent tombs of Henry III (d. 1272), the builder of the abbey, and (right) his daughter-in-law, Eleanor of Castile (d. 1290), the first queen of Edward I. The king's tomb, of Purbeck marble decorated with glass mosaics, was designed by Peter of Rome, while Eleanor's tomb was made by Richard Crundale. Both tombs have splendid gilt-bronze effigies (the earliest in England) by William Torel, a London goldsmith, and both are covered by 15th-century testers or canopies. To the left is the plain altar-tomb of Edward I (d. 1307), with a now illegible 16th-century inscription, 'Scottorum malleus'. When the tomb was opened in 1774 his body (6 ft 2 in. long) was in good preservation, clothed in royal robes with a gilt crown. The 15th-century carved stone screen which forms the back of the high altar has scenes on the cornice from the life of the Confessor. Against it stands the CORONATION CHAIR, made of oak by Walter, the 'king's painter', for Edward I, and attached to this underneath is the famous STONE OF SCONE, a block of sandstone used as the coronation seat of the kings of Scotland at Scone Abbey from about 850 and carried off by Edward I in 1297 as a token of the subjugation of Scotland. In the chair, which was made to hold it, every English monarch since Edward II (except Edward V, who died young, and Edward VIII, who abdicated) has been crowned, but on these occasions the chair is covered with a cloth of gold and moved into the sanctuary before the high altar. Against the screen are the state sword (7 ft long) and wooden shield of Edward III.

On the south side of the chapel adjacent is the tomb of Richard II (d. 1400) and his first queen, Anne of Bohemia (d. 1394), with gilt-bronze figures and a painted tester. Next to this is the elaborate tomb of Edward III (d. 1377), with a gilt-bronze effigy, a finely carved oak tester above, and niches round the sides for statuettes of his twelve children of which only those on the outside survive.

Both these tombs are thought to be designed by Henry Yevele, who was master-mason to Edward III. At the end is the black marble tomb of Philippa of Hainault (d. 1369), queen of Edward III, with a white marble effigy by Henniquin of Liège.

The chapel is left by steps descending to the North Ambulatory, where visitors turn to the right for Henry VII's Chapel.

The Lady Chapel is invariably called the CHAPEL OF HENRY VII after its royal founder, for whom it was built in 1503–19. Attributed to Robert Vertue, the king's master-mason, it is the richest example in England of the late-Perpendicular Gothic style, the beauty of its decoration culminating in the exquisite tracery of the fan vaulting. 'On entering,' writes Washington Irving, 'the eye is astonished by the pomp of architecture and the elaborate beauty of sculptured detail. The very walls are wrought into universal ornament, incrusted with tracery, and scooped into niches crowded with statues of saints and martyrs. Stone seems, by the cunning labour of the chisel, to have been robbed of its weight and density, suspended aloft as if by magic, and the fretted roof achieved with the wonderful minuteness and airy security of a cobweb.' The chapel consists of a nave, with five smaller chapels radiating from the eastern apse, and north and south aisles entered from outside the 16th-century doors. These are of oak, plated with bronze, carved with heraldic devices referring to the ancestry of Henry VII and Elizabeth of York, whose marriage united the Houses of York and Lancaster and brought to an end the Wars of the Roses. On each side of the nave are the delicately carved stalls of the Knights of the Bath, an order founded by Henry IV in 1399 and reconstituted by George I in 1725, when the chapel was dedicated as the chapel of the order, with the Dean of Westminster as its dean. No installation of knights took place after 1812, however, until the ceremony was revived by George V in 1913, when the present banners were hung above the beautifully carved canopies of the stalls. Each stall bears copper plates with the arms of the present and former holders; the lower seats are for the esquires, three of whom attend each knight. The quaintly carved misericords beneath the seats are worth examination. A case at the west end of the chapel contains the sword used by

George VI at the service of installation of Knights of the Bath in 1951.

In a vault beneath the pavement between the door and the altar is the grave (without inscription) of George II (d. 1760), the last monarch buried in the abbey, and Queen Caroline of Anspach (d. 1737). The grave of Edward VI (d. 1553) is below the altar, which is a copy (1935) of the original by Torrigiani, destroyed by iconoclasts in 1641. Behind the altar is the splendid tomb of Henry VII (d. 1509) and Elizabeth of York (d. 1503), the masterpiece of Pietro Torrigiani of Florence, completed about 1522. It consists of a black marble sarcophagus with a carved frieze of white marble on which rest the fine gilt-bronze effigies of the king and queen. At the sides are gilt-bronze medallions with the figures of angels and saints, and the tomb is enclosed by a bronze grille of English workmanship. The royal remains actually rest in the vault below, and here also is buried James I (d. 1625).

The south chapel of the apse is almost filled by an over-elaborate monument to the Duke of Richmond and Lennox (d. 1624), cousin of James I. In the next chapel is the marble altar-tomb of Dean Stanley (d. 1881), with his effigy by Boehm. The east chapel, now the ROYAL AIR FORCE CHAPEL, was dedicated in 1947 to those of the flying forces who lost their lives in the Battle of Britain (1940). The excellent stained-glass window by Hugh Easton includes in its design the badges of the 63 fighter squadrons who took part in the battle and a line from Shakespeare, 'We few, we happy few, we band of brothers'. A hole in the stonework, caused by a bomb, remains. The ashes of Lord Trenchard (d. 1956), the 'father of the R.A.F.', are buried beneath the floor. In the next chapel is the Roll of Honour of the 1,497 airmen of Britain and her allies who fell in the Battle of Britain. The large monument is to John Sheffield, Duke of Buckingham (d. 1721), and a slab in front of it marks the grave of Anne of Denmark (d. 1619), queen of James I. The north chapel is filled with the over-ornate tomb of George Villiers, Duke of Buckingham (d. 1628), the favourite of James I and Charles I.

Oliver Cromwell, Henry Ireton (his lieutenant and son-in-law), Admiral Blake, and John Bradshaw, the regicide, were originally buried in the east chapel, but at the Restoration their bodies were exhumed and dishonoured.

Blake was reinterred in St Margaret's churchyard, but the heads of Cromwell, Ireton, and Bradshaw were struck off and exposed on the roof of Westminster Hall.

The SOUTH AISLE of the chapel (sometimes called the Lady Margaret Chapel) contains several fine tombs. The first is that of Margaret, Countess of Lennox (d. 1578), the mother of Henry Darnley (second husband of Mary, Queen of Scots), who is identified as the foremost figure on the south side. Next comes the splendid tomb of Mary, Queen of Scots (d. 1587), who was beheaded by Elizabeth I and buried first in Peterborough Cathedral, but was removed here by Mary's son, James I. This, the last royal tomb erected in the abbey, has an effigy in the attitude of prayer under the lofty canopy. The tomb on the east is that of Margaret Beaufort (d. 1509), Countess of Richmond and mother of Henry VII, a patron of learning and foundress of St John's and Christ's Colleges at Cambridge. A great benefactress also of the abbey, she died in the abbot's house (now the deanery). The tomb, another magnificent work by Torrigiani, supports a gilt-bronze effigy in which the exquisite modelling of the hands is particularly notable. The grille round the tomb was removed and sold in 1822, but rediscovered and brought back in 1914. At the east end is a large monument, by Kent and Scheemakers, to General Monck, Duke of Albemarle (d. 1670), who helped to restore the Stewarts, and a vault in front contains the graves of Charles II (d. 1685), Mary II (d. 1694) and her husband William III (d. 1702), and Queen Anne (d. 1714) and her consort Prince George of Denmark (d. 1708). The beautiful carving on the east wall is characteristic of the chapel. At the west end are a medallion by W. Goscombe John to Earl Cromer (d. 1916), the 'regenerator of Egypt', and tablets to the Marquess Curzon (d. 1925) and Cecil Rhodes (d. 1902).

The NORTH AISLE (or Elizabeth Chapel) is chiefly notable for the elaborate tomb (well restored in 1956) of Elizabeth I (d. 1603), the work of Maximilian Powtrain and John de Critz, with the effigy of the queen in white marble. Below the cornice of the canopy are the arms of monarchs of England beginning with Edward the Confessor and of others of Elizabeth's kin. In a recess is the ring traditionally given as a pledge of clemency by the queen to her favourite, the Earl of Essex, but intercepted by the Countess of Nottingham when he attempted to send it back on his condemnation. Mary I (d. 1558) is buried in the same tomb as her sister and successor. At the east end (the 'Innocents' Corner') are the tombs of two infant children of James I who died in 1606–7. The younger is represented in an alabaster cradle, an unusual but delicately carved monument by Maximilian Colt. A small 17th-century sarcophagus close by contains bones generally thought to be those of Edward V and his brother Richard, Duke of York, sons of Edward IV, the princes murdered in the Tower in 1483. In the vaults in front of the monument to Charles Montagu, Earl of Halifax (d. 1715), near the east end, are buried Joseph Addison (d. 1719), the essayist, and the Duke of Albemarle.

The easternmost of the chapels opening off the North Ambulatory is the CHAPEL OF ST PAUL. On the right are the tombs of Lord Bourchier (d. 1431), standard-bearer to Henry V; Francis, Lord Cottington, Chancellor of the Exchequer to Charles I (d. in exile in Spain, 1652); and the Countess of Sussex (d. 1589), founder of Sidney Sussex College at Cambridge. On the left, by the door, is a bust of Sir Rowland Hill (d. 1879), the originator of penny postage. The grille of Queen Eleanor's tomb, fine wrought-iron work of 1294 by Thomas of Leighton (Buzzard), can be seen on the other side of the ambulatory.

The CHAPEL OF ST JOHN THE BAPTIST is entered through the so-called Chapel of St Erasmus (originally of Our Lady of the Pew), in reality no more than a vestibule. It has 16th-century doors and remains of paintings, and over the entrance is a beautifully carved niche with a triple canopy, brought by Abbot Islip from the vanished Chapel of St Erasmus. The Chapel of St John contains tombs of 15th-century abbots and, in the centre, the large marble table-tomb of Thomas Cecil, Earl of Exeter (d. 1623), with effigies of himself and his first wife. His second wife declined the less honourable position on his left hand and is buried in Winchester Cathedral. The small tomb of 1305 to the north-east contains the remains of Humphrey and Mary de Bohun, grandchildren of Edward I.

The chantry CHAPEL OF ABBOT ISLIP is in two storeys, the lower (no admission), containing the grave of Abbot John Islip

(d. 1532), who completed the nave, separated from the ambulatory by a screen erected by the abbot himself and carved with his rebuses: an eye with a man grasping a slip of a tree, and a man slipping from a branch. The upper storey, fitted up as a memorial chapel to nurses, midwives, and ambulance workers who lost their lives in the Second World War, has a striking window by Hugh Easton (1950). In the ambulatory opposite, the backs of the tombs of Edmund Crouchback and Aymer de Valence are worth inspection.

The east aisle of the North Transept was formed by combining the CHAPELS OF SS. JOHN THE EVANGELIST, MICHAEL, AND ANDREW. At the entrance is the huge monument by Joseph Wilton to General James Wolfe (d. 1759), the hero of Quebec. On the left in the aisle is a memorial to Sir John Franklin (d. 1847), lost in the search for the North-West Passage, with an inscription by Tennyson. To the right is the unusual monument to Sir Francis Vere (d. 1609), a noted Elizabethan general, with his effigy below and four kneeling warriors supporting a slab with his accoutrements, and in the next chapel is an over-dramatic monument by Roubiliac to Lady Elizabeth Nightingale (d. 1734). In the north chapel is the large cenotaph of Lord Norris (d. 1601), and around the walls are memorials including statues by E. H. Baily of Thomas Telford (d. 1834), the engineer, by Flaxman of John Kemble (d. 1823), the actor, and by Chantrey of Mrs Siddons (d. 1831), the actress, inspired by Reynolds' 'Tragic Muse'; tablets to Sir Humphry Davy (d. 1829), inventor of the safety lamp, and Lord Rayleigh (d. 1919), the physicist; and a bust of Sir James Young Simpson (d. 1870), who introduced the use of chloroform.

The NORTH TRANSEPT contains the graves and monuments of many famous statesmen. On the east side are statues by John Gibson of Sir Robert Peel (d. 1850); by Brock of W. E. Gladstone (d. 1898; buried in front); by Boehm of Lord Beaconsfield (d. 1881); and by Chantrey of George Canning (d. 1827); and a monument to John Holles, Duke of Newcastle (d. 1711), by James Gibbs and Francis Bird. On the west are a large monument by the elder John Bacon to William Pitt, Earl of Chatham (d. 1778); and statues of Lord Palmerston (d. 1865) and Lord Castlereagh (d. 1822). Beneath the pavement are the graves of Henry Grattan (d. 1820), the Irish patriot, William Wilberforce, C. J. Fox, and the elder and younger Pitt.

In the centre of the West Aisle of the transept is the large monument by Flaxman to the Earl of Mansfield (d. 1793), Lord Chief Justice, and on the walls are busts of Warren Hastings (d. 1818), Governor-General of India, and Richard Cobden (d. 1865), the apostle of free trade. The north-west window (1911) illustrates Bunyan's *Pilgrim's Progress*. The NORTH CHOIR AISLE, by which the nave is regained, is often called the 'Musicians' Aisle'. Those commemorated here include (on the left) the composers Orlando Gibbons (d. 1625) and Henry Purcell (d. 1695), who was organist of the abbey (and is buried near by), and (on the right) John Blow (d. 1708), composer and likewise organist, and Dr Charles Burney (d. 1814), the historian of music. Also commemorated are William Wilberforce (d. 1833), chief opponent of the slave-trade (a good statue by Samuel Joseph), and several scientists, notably Sir Joseph Hooker (d. 1911), the botanist; Lord Lister (d. 1912), the founder of antiseptic surgery; and Alfred Russel Wallace (d. 1913) and Charles Darwin (d. 1882), the scientists who independently formulated the theory of evolution. The painted shields-of-arms date from the 13th century; the window in the third bay was given by J. W. Gerard, American ambassador in Berlin in 1914–17, in memory of British prisoners who died in Germany in the First World War. Against the screen at the east end of the Nave is a monument by Rysbrack to Sir Isaac Newton (d. 1727), discoverer of the law of gravity.

Newton is buried in the nave close by, and here also are the graves of the scientists, Lord Kelvin (d. 1907), Lord Rutherford (d. 1937), and Michael Faraday (d. 1867). Floor-slabs in the North Nave Aisle mark the graves of Charles Darwin and Sir John Herschel (d. 1871), the astronomer, while his father, Sir William Herschel (d. 1822), the discoverer of Uranus, and his son, also Sir William (d. 1917), the author of the fingerprint identity system, are also commemorated. The ashes of Ralph Vaughan Williams, the composer, were buried in the North Choir Aisle in 1958.

On the wall of the NORTH NAVE AISLE (third bay) is a monument to Spencer Perceval (d. 1812), assassinated in the House of Commons by a madman; the relief, by Westmacott, shows the incident. In the floor of the fifth bay a stone inscribed 'O Rare Ben Johnson' indicates the grave of the poet, Ben Jonson (d. 1637); the original stone is in the wall below the monument to Thomas Banks (d. 1805), the sculptor. In the west bay are floor-slabs to Ernest Bevin (d. 1951), the Labour statesman, and to Sidney and Beatrice Webb (d. 1947, 1943), the Fabian sociologists. At the west end is a large monument by Sir Richard Westmacott to Charles James Fox (d. 1806), the Whig politician.

Some of the windows in the aisle commemorate famous engineers, including Sir Charles Parsons (d. 1931) and Sir Henry Royce (d. 1933). The North-West or BELFRY TOWER, called by Dean Stanley the 'Whig Corner', contains monuments to the third Marquess of Salisbury (d. 1903), with a bronze effigy by W. Goscombe John, and to Viscount Howe (d. 1758), by Scheemakers, given by the province of Massachusetts, at that time still a British colony; and the busts of Lord John Russell (d. 1878), by Tweed of Joseph Chamberlain (d. 1914), and by Onslow Ford of General Gordon of Khartoum (d. 1885). Over the west door is a large monument to William Pitt the Younger (d. 1806), by Westmacott.

The CLOISTERS are reached by doors in the South Nave Aisle, that on the east showing rich but much-worn carving. The earliest and finest work, dating from the mid 13th century, is in the north-east corner; the remainder was recast in 1344–86. Opening off the east walk is the vestibule admitting to the CHAPTER HOUSE, a noble octagonal chamber, 60 ft in diameter, built in 1245–55, probably by Henry of Reims, the builder of the church. A slender central pier of clustered shafts supports the lofty vault, a supposed copy of the original and provided by Sir Gilbert Scott when he restored the chapter house in 1866. Visitors are provided with overshoes to avoid damage to the remarkably well-preserved 13th-century pavement, the finest of its kind in England. The motifs include the arms of Henry III, the legend of St Edward and the pilgrim, heraldic beasts, and a curious fish (the 'Westminster salmon'). The wall arcades were greatly restored by Scott, though in the original style; they were decorated with a series of 14th-century paintings of which little more than a fragment (the Revelation of St John) has survived (restored in 1920). The tracery of the six large windows, each 39 ft high, was restored by Scott, though again to the former design, and it is probably the earliest example of the 'Geometrical' or 'Early Decorated' style in England. In 1941 much of the glass was destroyed by bombing, but in 1951 the windows were reset including some of the old glass

(1882), illustrating scenes from the abbey's history (a memorial to Dean Stanley), and quarries of new glass (by Joan Howson and others) showing the arms of persons connected with the abbey. In the head of the noble doorway ('one of the most beautiful things in English art') is a circular tympanum with the figure of Christ in Majesty (introduced by Scott and not part of the original design), and on either side of this are pairs of censing angels and the beautiful figures of the Virgin and the angel of the Annunciation, 13th-century work of the highest order.

The Chapter House, built to the order of Henry III, has been called the 'cradle of all free parliaments', for here the Great Council met in 1257, and here Parliament assembled from 1352 until 1547, when St Stephen's Chapel in the Palace of Westminster became its regular meeting-place. From then until 1866 the chapter house was used as a repository for State papers. Above the steps on the south side of the Vestibule are tablets to James Russell Lowell (1819–91), the American author, minister in Britain in 1880–5, and to Walter Hines Page (1855–1918), American ambassador in 1913–18. On the north side is a Roman sarcophagus, probably of the 3rd century, with a Saxon lid, or possibly the original lid carved with a cross by the Saxons when they used it for a second burial. The coffin was found under the green on the north side of the abbey nave in 1869. The vestibule has a quadripartite vault supported by Purbeck marble columns and wall-shafts; in the tympanum over the entrance from the cloisters are remains of a carving of the Tree of Jesse. The flying buttresses of the chapter house were added in the 14th century, but the pyramidal roof is modern, replacing a flat roof destroyed about 1740.

On the south side of the vestibule is the entrance to the LIBRARY and Muniment Room (admission by special permission only), in part of the monks' dormitory, and beyond is the CHAMBER OF THE PYX, entered through a restored Norman doorway with two heavy doors secured by seven locks. Originally a sacristy, part of Edward the Confessor's church, it has a massive central pier and the oldest altar in the abbey. Later it became the royal treasury and the repository of the 'pyx' or chest containing the trial-plates of gold and silver used as standards of reference for the coins of the realm.

The East Walk of the cloisters is extended on the south by the 11th-century Dark Cloister which emerges in the yard of Westminster School (p. 111). On the left is the door into the NORMAN UNDERCROFT, the only other surviving part of the Confessor's church, consisting of five vaulted bays below the dormitory. It now contains the abbey Museum, which includes architectural fragments, old seals and charters, 14th–15th-century chests (one for copes), and the coronation chair made for Mary II. The wax effigies were carried at the funerals of persons buried in the abbey; the oldest is that of Charles II (d. 1685), the one of Elizabeth I being a copy made in 1760, and others are of Mary II (d. 1694), William III (d. 1702), the Duchess of Richmond ('La Belle Stuart'; d. 1702), Queen Anne, (d. 1714) and the Duchess of Buckingham (d. 1743) and her two sons. The figures of the Earl of Chatham and Lord Nelson are not funeral effigies, but were made to attract visitors to the abbey. Previously it had been the custom to show the embalmed bodies of royal persons at their funerals, though in some cases these were replaced by effigies of wood, several of which are preserved here. The oldest is of Edward III (d. 1377) and is perhaps the oldest wooden effigy in Europe; others represent Anne of Bohemia (queen of Richard II), Henry VII and his wife Elizabeth of York, Mary I, and Anne of Denmark (queen of James I).

A passage on the left farther on leads to the charming LITTLE CLOISTERS (restored after war damage), originally part of the monk's infirmary. The south walk of the main cloisters was the burial-place of the abbots from 1068 to 1214. Beside a former entrance to the Refectory (part of which survives) are 14th-century recesses which served as cupboards for towels. The large 18th-century recess in the west walk takes the place of the monks' lavatory or washing-place. On the wall near by are memorials by Gilbert Ledward to those of the submarine branch of the Royal Navy killed in the two World Wars and to Commandos and members of the Airborne Forces and Special Air Service who died in 1939–45. A passage extending the south walk leads out to Dean's Yard (p. 111). Another passage on the right opens to the picturesque ABBOT'S COURTYARD (no entry). On the east side of this is the DEANERY (once the abbot's lodging), rebuilt after its destruction by bombing, and on the west is COLLEGE HALL, the old dining room of the abbot, now used by Westminster School (see p. 111). The steps on the north side ascend to the JERICHO PARLOUR, built by Abbot Islip, a panelled ante-room to the JERUSALEM CHAMBER (admission only by permission of the Dean), formerly the abbot's retiring room and now the chapter-room. Built about 1370 by Abbot Litlington and restored in 1956, it has an unusual oak ceiling, an elaborate 17th-century overmantel of wood, and 16th–17th-century tapestries. Henry IV died in the chamber in 1413, thus fulfilling the prophecy that he would die in 'Jerusalem' (Shakespeare's *Henry IV*, Part 2, iv, 5).

WESTMINSTER CATHEDRAL Plan VIII, D 1

STATION: VICTORIA, ¼-m. W., on the Southern Region and the Circle and District lines. — MOTOR-BUSES in Victoria Street, see Route 4.

ADMISSION daily 6 a.m. to 9 p.m. (to 6 p.m. on Easter Monday, Whit Monday, Christmas Day, and Boxing Day). Services on Sundays every half-hour from 6 a.m. until 9, then at 10.10 (Prime and Terce) and 10.30 a.m. (Capitular High Mass), 12 noon, and 3.15 (Vespers, Compline, and Benediction) and 7 p.m.; on weekdays at 6 (first Friday in the month only) and every half-hour from 6.30 until 9, then at 10.10, 10.30 (High Mass), 3.30, 6, and 8. Tickets for Tower Lift, 1/-.

WESTMINSTER CATHEDRAL is the principal Roman Catholic church in England, the seat of the Archbishop of Westminster, who holds precedence over the other three provinces of England and Wales. It stands near the south-west end of Victoria Street, from which it is approached via Ashley Place. The vast and imposing church, designed by John Francis Bentley (d. 1902), is in an early-Christian Byzantine style, inspired to some extent by St Mark's at Venice, though the exterior strikes a highly original effect by its alternate bands of red brick and Portland stone. The foundation stone was laid in 1895, the fabric was completed and the church opened for service in 1903, and the consecration ceremony took place in 1910. The cathedral is 342 ft long inside, the nave (the widest in England) is 60 ft across, or 149 ft including the aisles and side chapels, and the height of the main arches is 90 ft, while the dome rises to 117 ft above the floor. The nave has room for a congregation of about 2,000 and the whole church covers an area of about 54,000 sq. ft. The singular square campanile (St Edward's Tower) is 284 ft high to the top of the cross.

The site for the cathedral was bought in 1884 by Cardinal Manning (1865–92), who succeeded Cardinal Wiseman, the first archbishop of Westminster (1850). The building was begun under Cardinal Vaughan (1892–1903) and completed under Cardinal Bourne (1903–35). The seventh archbishop, the Most Reverend William Cardinal Godfrey, was appointed in 1956 and died in 1963, and a new archbishop has yet to be appointed.

The cathedral is orientated from north-west to south-east, but, in the description below, the high altar will be regarded as on the east. Over the main entrance (used only on Sundays) is a tympanum with a mosaic by R. Anning Bell (1916) representing Christ in

Majesty with the Virgin and SS. Peter, Joseph, and Edward the Confessor. Above and behind this rises the narthex or vestibule, flanked by domed turrets, and higher still can be seen the west window of the nave. On each side of the great doorway are medallions with the figures of twelve archbishops of Canterbury.

The usual entrance is from Ambrosden Avenue by the north-west vestibule, on the left of which is the entrance to the tower-lift. From the narthex at the west end of the church a striking impression is obtained of its extent and harmonious proportions, though the brick walls and piers are for the most part still bare. When the scheme of decoration is complete the lower surfaces, to a height of about 30 ft, will be covered with variegated marbles, while the upper parts of the church, including the vaulting and domes, will be faced with mosaics illustrating the doctrines of the Church. Some idea of the intended effect may be obtained from the chapels that have been completed.

At the west end of the NAVE are two monolithic columns of deep red Norwegian granite, symbolic of the Precious Blood of Jesus to which the cathedral is dedicated. The nave itself is comprised of three large bays separated by massive piers rising to support great domes. The great rood, 30 ft in length, hanging from the arch at the east end, is by Christian Symons, and is painted with figures of Christ and the Mater Dolorosa. Over the aisles are galleries supported by great columns of dark green marble hewn from the quarry in Greece which supplied the marbles for the great basilica of Santa Sophia at Constantinople (A.D. 563). They have beautiful capitals of white Carrara marble, no two of which are carved alike. On the main piers are the fourteen Stations of the Cross, bas-reliefs in Hopton Wood stone from Derbyshire, beautifully carved by Eric Gill. The white marble pulpit was enlarged and redesigned as a memorial to Cardinal Bourne (d. 1935). The statue of St Peter at the north-west end of the nave is a copy of that in St Peter's at Rome.

In the south-west corner of the cathedral is the BAPTISTERY, with bronze gates and a large font of coloured marbles designed by J. F. Bentley. The altar here was erected in 1946 by the Royal Canadian Air Force to officers and men who fell in 1939–45. The statue of St John the Baptist is a copy in block tin of that by

Thorvaldsen on the cathedral at Copenhagen. An arcaded marble screen separates the Baptistery from the CHAPEL OF SS. GREGORY AND AUGUSTINE. On and above the altarpiece here (by Henry Holliday) are mosaics illustrating the conversion of England to Christianity. In the aisle east of this chapel is a mosaic by Boris Anrep to the Blessed Oliver Plunket, archbishop of Armagh, hanged at Tyburn in 1681. The CHAPEL OF ST PATRICK and the Saints of Ireland is decorated with Irish marbles. In niches round the chapel are the badges of Irish regiments who fought in the First World War, and a casket on the left of the altar holds the roll of honour. In the CHAPEL OF ST ANDREW and the Saints of Scotland, native granite and marble have been extensively used, while on each side of the altar are fine bas-reliefs by Stirling Lee of SS. Ninian, Margaret of Scotland, Bridget, and Columba. Beyond the CHAPEL OF ST PAUL THE APOSTLE (where the crib is set up at Christmas) is the SOUTH TRANSEPT, and from this opens the elaborately decorated LADY CHAPEL, the first part of the church to be completed. Behind the altar is a mosaic by Anning Bell of the Virgin and Child, and other mosaics by Gilbert Pownall include the heads of Isaiah, Ezekiel, Daniel, and Jeremiah.

The outer aisle of the chapel leads to the SACRISTY, from which a stair descends to the CRYPT (no admission), dedicated as the Chapel of St Peter and lined with Greek marble. In its south wall are four recesses in which are preserved some fragments of the True Cross, a mitre of St Thomas Becket, and other relics. On the west (immediately below the high altar) is the small Chapel of St Edmund, with an altar below which a relic of St Edmund Rich, archbishop of Canterbury (d. 1240), is preserved, and the tombs of Cardinal Wiseman (d. 1865) and Cardinal Manning (d. 1892), originally buried at Kensal Green. Cardinal Griffin (d. 1956) and Cardinal Godfrey (d. 1963) are also buried here.

The SANCTUARY is raised 4 ft 6 in. above the nave, so that it is easily visible from every part of the church. The altar table is a single block of Cornish granite, 12 ft long and 12 tons in weight, uncovered only on Maundy Thursday and Good Friday. Above the altar crucifix, which is 7 ft 3 in. high, rises a white marble canopy or baldacchino, supported by eight columns of yellow Verona marble on pedestals of verde antico. The choir stalls are of oak inlaid with ivory and ebony; the archbishop's throne, on the north, is a smaller copy of the papal chair in the basilica of St John Lateran in Rome. The arcaded galleries on either side are of marble. The cathedral ends on the east in a wide apse containing the RETRO-CHOIR, which is raised 13 ft above the floor of the nave. At the top of the steps leading to it is a bas-relief of Christ the King in Hopton Wood stone by Lindsay Clarke, while the mosaic of the great tympanum over the high altar, by Gilbert Pownall, represents Christ in Glory, with the twelve Apostles and the emblems of the Evangelists on either side.

From the NORTH TRANSEPT, on the wall of which is a mosaic of St Joan of Arc, opens the CHAPEL OF THE BLESSED SACRAMENT, reserved for private devotion. It is enclosed by a fine bronze-gilt grille surmounted by a 'pelican in her piety', while the altar-rails of similar metal are adorned with the Instruments of the Passion. The inner veil of the tabernacle is hung from gold wedding rings bequeathed by matrons for the purpose. The mosaics on the walls and ceiling, the work of Boris Anrep, were completed in 1962. On the north is the small CHAPEL OF THE SACRED HEART and St Michael, and opening off the North Transept is the CHAPEL OF ST THOMAS OF CANTERBURY, or Vaughan Chantry, with a cenotaph supporting the marble effigy of Cardinal Herbert Vaughan (d. 1903), the founder of the cathedral, who is buried at Mill Hill (Middlesex).

In the finely decorated CHAPEL OF ST JOSEPH, the easternmost opening off the north aisle, is the tomb of Cardinal Hinsley (d. 1943). The CHAPEL OF ST GEORGE and the English Martyrs has an altarpiece carved in low relief by Eric Gill (1946) and a figure of St George by Lindsay Clarke. The body of John Southworth, the 'parish priest of Westminster', hanged at Tyburn in 1654 and beatified in 1929, was brought here from Douai in France in 1930. The CHAPEL OF THE HOLY SOULS, the last on this side, has beautiful mosaics designed by Christian Symons.

The CAMPANILE is well worth ascending for the extensive prospect over west London. Among the places in view are Westminster Abbey and the Houses of Parliament to the north-east, with the County Hall and the new Shell Centre behind them and St Paul's Cathedral farther away; St James's Park and Palace and Buckingham Palace to the north, with the Green Park beyond; and Hyde Park and Kensington Gardens to the north-west, with the Albert Hall and Brompton Oratory to the left. Immediately west is

Victoria Station, which has Chelsea Hospital (just in view) to the left of it, while to the south-west can be seen Chelsea Bridge and south-eastward rises the new Vickers building. On the north horizon are the heights of Harrow, Hampstead, and Highgate; and to the south-east is the television mast at Crystal Palace, while in the distance to the south stretches a long length of the North Downs. The campanile, 273 ft high in itself, is 48 ft higher than the west towers of Westminster Abbey, but 63 ft lower than the Victoria Tower of the Houses of Parliament. The cross, 11 ft high, that surmounts it, contains a relic of the True Cross. The lift in the campanile is the third highest in the world, exceeded only by those in the Riverside Church, New York.

The ARCHBISHOP'S HOUSE is in Ambrosden Avenue, adjoining the cathedral, and the CLERGY HOUSE in Francis Street, on the south. The Great Corridor connecting the cathedral with the Clergy House was hung in 1956 with the Stations of the Cross painted by Roy de Maistre.

ZOOLOGICAL GARDENS Plan I, A 2

STATIONS: CAMDEN TOWN, over ½-m. NE., on the Northern line; REGENT'S PARK, over ⅔-m. S., on the Bakerloo line; GREAT PORTLAND STREET, over ¾-m. SE., on the Circle and Metropolitan lines; BAKER STREET, 1¼ m. SW., on the Bakerloo, Circle, and Metropolitan lines. — MOTOR-BUSES No. 74 from Camden Town Station and from Hyde Park Corner, Marble Arch, and Baker Street Station to the North Entrance; Nos. 3, 53, and 276 from Charing Cross, Oxford Circus, and Great Portland Street Station to Gloucester Gate, ¼-m. E. of the South Entrance. — WATER-BUSES, see p. 44.

ADMISSION to the gardens daily (except Christmas Day) 9 a.m. (10 in November–March) to 7 p.m. or sunset (gates closed ½-hour earlier); 5/- (in winter, and all Mondays, except Bank Holidays, 3/-; Sundays until 1 p.m., 7/-, winter 5/-); to the AQUARIUM, daily from 10 (1/-); to the CHILDREN'S ZOO, daily from 10.30 (1/-); children under 14, half-price. — INVALID CHAIRS, without attendant, are obtainable at any entrance (by previous arrangement) or from the Zoo Shop (5, on plan); Children's Push Chairs from the Zoo Shop and (in summer) the North Gate; 2/- all day (deposit 2/6). Dogs and other pets are not allowed in the gardens; smoking is not permitted in the houses.

FEEDING TIMES: *Pelicans* (12, on plan), 2.30; *Reptiles* (15), 2.30 (Fridays only); *Sea-Lions* (19), 12 and 3.30 in summer (in winter 2.30 only); *Seals* (23), 4.30 in summer (3 in winter); *Penguins* (24), 4 in summer (12.30 in winter); *Lions* and *Tigers* (27), 3 in summer (2 in winter), except Wednesdays; *Eagles* (34), 3.30 in summer (2.15 in winter), except Wednesdays. *Chimpanzees' Tea Party* (6), weekdays in summer at 4 (weather permitting); in winter in the Children's Zoo (26) at 3. — ANIMAL RIDES in the Broad Walk (2), weekday afternoons (weather permitting), April–October.

RESTAURANTS: REGENT RESTAURANT (42), with waitress service,

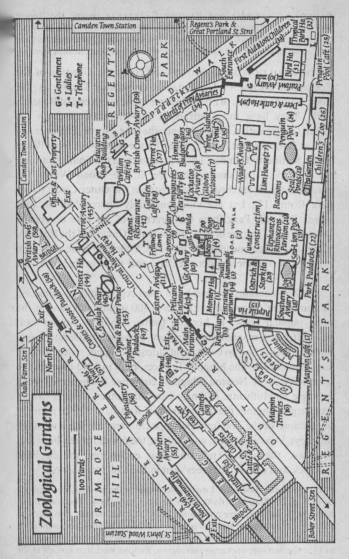

Zoological Gardens

100 Yards

G = Gentlemen
L = Ladies
T = Telephone

Camden Town Station

Regent's Park & Great Portland St Stns

REGENT'S PARK

PRIMROSE HILL

PRINCE ALBERT ROAD

REGENT'S PARK

Chalk Farm Stn
Camden Town Station
St John's Wood Station
Baker Street Stn

North Entrance
South Entrance
Main Entrance

First Aid & Lost Children (39)
Tropical Bird Ha (32)
Penguin Pool Café (25)
Bird Ha (31)
Peafowl Aviary (30)
Deer & Cattle Ha (29)
Children's Zoo (26)
Penguin Pool (24)
Seal Ponds (23)
Park Paddocks (22)
Lion House (27)
Raccoons
Sea-Lion Pool (19)
Elephant & Rhinoceros Pavilion (21)
Ostrich & Stork Ha (20)
Southern Aviary (18)
Reptile Ha (15)
Waders Aviary (28)
Homing Budgerigars (36)
Three Island Pond (35)
Deer (34)
Birds of Prey Aviaries
Owls' Aviary (33)
British Crows' Aviary (39)
Education Building
Offices & Lost Property
British Owls' Aviary (59)
Insect Ha (46)
Parrot Aviary (44)
Kodiak Bears
Cranes & Goose Paddocks (58)
Coypu & Beaver Ponds (45)
Elephant Paddock (47)
Pheasantry (56)
Northern Aviary (55)
North Mammal Ho (54)
Otter Pond (48)
Reptiliary (13)
Main Entrance
Eastern Aviary (11)
Monkey Ha
Small Mammals (14)
Entrance to Mammals
Gt Aviary (10)
Ravens' Aviary (9)
Fellows' Lawn
Giant Panda
Bean's Ho
Zoo Shop
Pelicans
Parrot Ha
Pavilion (40) Building
Pavilion Café (41)
Regent Restaurant
Garden Café (38)
Chimpanzees' Tea Party (6)
Cockatoo Aviary (8)
Gibbon Enclosure (7)
Camels (50)
Giraffes (51)
Antelopes (52)
Cattle & Zebra (53)
Deer (49)
Mappin Café (17)
Mappin Terraces (16)
Penguins
Bears
Goats
Broad Walk
(under construction) (2)

LG–30   465

PAVILION CAFÉ (41), and REGENT CAFETERIA (below the Regent Restaurant), all licensed, luncheons and teas; GARDEN CAFÉ (38), MAPPIN CAFÉ (17), and PENGUIN POOL CAFÉ (25), these three unlicensed, teas and light refreshments; REGENT BAR (42) and numerous refreshment kiosks.

The ZOOLOGICAL GARDENS, officially the Gardens of the Zoological Society of London, but universally known as 'the Zoo', occupy an area of about 36 acres at the north end of Regent's Park. They have three entrances: the Main Entrance in the Outer Circle, with a car park opposite; the North Entrance (p. 469) in Prince Albert Road, passed by the motor-bus from Baker Street Station to Camden Town Station; and the South Entrance (p. 468), near the south-east angle, in the Broad Walk. The gardens may be reached by motorists via the Outer Circle (compare Route 17), but are more enjoyably approached on foot across Regent's Park from the direction of the lake or via the Broad Walk. They are divided by the Outer Circle and the Regent's Canal into three unequal portions which communicate with each other by two tunnels under the drive and three bridges over the canal.

The Zoo contains the finest and most representative collection of animals in the world, with over 5,800 inhabitants, and is the most popular resort in London (some 2 million visitors each year). It has a magnificent aquarium, notable reptile and insect houses, many fine aviaries, and adequate open space for the larger mammals. The Mappin Terraces, built in 1913 through the generosity of J. Newton Mappin, comprise a huge reinforced concrete amphitheatre in which bears and other animals can be seen largely without the impediment of iron bars. Other interesting sections of the Zoo (especially for children) are the houses for monkeys, lions and tigers, and giraffes, the ponds for sea-lions and penguins, the giant panda and bear enclosures, the elephant paddock and the chimpanzees' den in the Children's Zoo.

The Zoological Society of London, the owner of the gardens, was founded in 1826 by Sir Stamford Raffles and Sir Humphry Davy. The collections, first opened in 1828, were augmented in 1831 by the animals previously in the Royal Menagerie at the Tower of London. Four giraffes were purchased in 1836 for £2,300, in 1835 the first chimpanzee seen in Britain arrived, and in 1850 the first hippopotamus was shown. Reptiles were first housed at the Zoo in 1849, and in 1853 the society built here the first aquarium in the world. The collections were further augmented in 1876, when the Prince of Wales (later Edward VII) presented the society with the animals acquired on his Indian tour. Uncommon animals raised in captivity in the Zoo include the takin, the first to reach Europe alive (1909), and the giant panda (1938). A few of the original buildings (by Decimus Burton) still survive, but new buildings, involving some rearrangement of the enclosures, are now being erected to the designs of Sir Hugh Casson and others.

The Zoo is most adequately explored by following the numbers given on the plan, an undertaking, however, requiring at least 2 hours for even a cursory survey. Visitors with less time at their disposal are advised to concentrate on the sections mentioned above. Opposite the MAIN ENTRANCE is the popular MONKEY HOUSE (1, on plan), containing chimpanzees, orang-utans, gibbons, mandrills, and gorillas. On the right of this is the BROAD WALK (2), where visitors may ride on elephants, camels, etc., and beyond are a house for SMALL MAMMALS (bush babies, etc.; 3) and enclosures for BEARS and the favourite GIANT PANDA (4). To the right of these is the Zoo Shop (5) and north of this is the lawn where the chimpanzees' tea party is held (6). Beyond the lawn are the GIBBON ENCLOSURE (7), with several examples of these acrobatic animals, and the interesting COCKATOO AVIARY (8).

From the lawn a return is made towards the entrance via the aviary for ravens (9); the GREAT AVIARY (10), with sacred ibises, etc.; the EASTERN AVIARY (11); and the PELICANS' ENCLOSURE (12). To the west of the entrance are a REPTILIARY (13), where smaller reptiles live in their natural state in summer, and the West Tunnel (leading to the northern parts of the gardens).

To the south-west of the main entrance is the AQUARIUM (14), perhaps the finest in the world, rebuilt in 1924, with fresh-water, marine, and tropical halls, containing some 3,000 fish and other amphibious creatures. Notable are the Giant Salamander from Japan, the largest amphibian, reaching over 5 ft in length (in the fresh-water hall), the sea-horses, turtles, dogfish, and dragon fish in the marine hall, and the lung fish in the tropical hall. To the east of the Aquarium is the REPTILE HOUSE (15), opened in 1927, where the animals live in natural conditions. Here can be seen alligators and crocodiles, chameleons, geckos, cobras and rattlesnakes, pythons, and boa constrictors (one nearly 25 ft long). Above the Aquarium rise the MAPPIN TERRACES (16), the lowest devoted to hogs, pigs, and peccaries, and those above to bears, including the favourite polar bears. On the highest terraces are Barbary wild sheep, mouflon and other mountain sheep, and wild goats. Near the foot is a penguin pool and the Mappin Café (17), and farther west is the Zoo Hospital, built in 1957 at a cost of over £60,000.

Beyond the Reptile House is the SOUTHERN AVIARY (18), with various sea-birds, etc., and farther on is the SEA-LION POOL (19), best visited at feeding-time. To the left is the OSTRICH AND STORK HOUSE (20), and beyond this is the site of the new ELEPHANT AND RHINOCEROS PAVILION (21). To the south are the PARK PADDOCKS (22), where llamas, alpacas, deer, etc., are kept in the open air, and farther on are the SEAL PONDS (23) and the PENGUIN POOL (24), always a centre of attraction. To the south-east of this, beyond the Penguin Pool Café (25), is the CHILDREN'S ZOO (26), where young visitors have the opportunity of handling tame animals. Here also are the Pony Stables and the Chimpanzees' Den.

The popular LION HOUSE (27), north of the Penguin Pool, contains also dens for tigers, leopards, jaguars, and pumas. To the north-east of it is the WADERS' AVIARY (28), and farther east is the old DEER AND CATTLE HOUSE (29), where the rhinoceroses are kept until their new home is ready. Beyond this is the PEA-FOWL AVIARY (30), with many fine specimens, and in the south-east angle of the gardens are the BIRD HOUSE (31), containing hornbills, toucans, talking mynahs, and birds of paradise, and the TROPICAL BIRD HOUSE (32), remarkable for its humming-birds, which fly about visitors' heads.

Near the SOUTH ENTRANCE is a post for first-aid and lost children (33). Beyond the entrance are the BIRDS OF PREY AVIARIES (34), with many eagles, vultures, and hawks, facing the THREE ISLAND POND (35), which has flamingoes and various waterfowl, and an aviary for Homing Budgerigars (36). Farther north is the PARROT HOUSE (37), with its fine array of cockatoos, macaws, and long-tailed parakeets. To the left is the Garden Café (38) and beyond are BRITISH CROWS' AVIARY (39) and the Education Centre (40). Some 30,000 schoolchildren visit the Zoo every year for lecture tours.

The East Tunnel, starting between the Pavilion Café (41) and the Regent Restaurant and Cafeteria (42), leads under the Outer Circle to the section bounded by the Regent's Canal. In this section, on the left, are the CENTRAL MAMMAL HOUSE (43), with many interesting species (mongooses, porcupines, tropical squirrels, etc.); the fine INSECT HOUSE (44), which should not be overlooked; ponds for COYPUS, large aquatic rodents, and BEAVERS (45); the popular house containing KODIAK BEARS (46); the ELEPHANT PADDOCKS (47; until 1964–5; see above); and the OTTER POND (48). On the right beyond this is a new bridge over the canal, and on the left is an entrance to the West Tunnel (which has notable copies of the Lascaux and Altamira cave-paintings). Farther on are houses built or reconstructed in 1962 for DEER (49) and CAMELS (50), of which there are several species, GIRAFFES (51), the tallest living mammals, ANTELOPES (52) and CATTLE AND ZEBRA (53). Deer and antelopes may also be seen on the slopes above the canal.

Another bridge over the Regent's Canal beyond these houses gives access to the northern section of the gardens. Here are the NORTH MAMMAL HOUSE (54), with many fine examples of the larger mammals (leopard, lynx, wolf, etc.), and the NORTHERN AVIARY (55), designed by Lord Snowdon and built in 1963, with many African and Indian birds. Beyond the new bridge are the PHEASANTRY (56), the OWLS' AVIARY (57), and the CRANES AND GOOSE PADDOCK (58), facing the NORTH ENTRANCE, and farther on is an aviary for BRITISH OWLS (59). From this a third bridge across the canal returns to the middle section of the gardens opposite the East Tunnel.

PLACES OF INTEREST IN OUTER LONDON

THE following short section on Outer London, including such pleasant suburbs as Hampstead, Highgate, Greenwich, and Dulwich, all with their points of interest, is arranged in districts, starting on the west from the Thames at Fulham, then working round north, east, and south to reach the Thames again at Battersea. The relative positions of the various districts is made clear on the road map on pages 28–9, and they are connected with Central London and with each other by numerous and frequent train and motor-bus services (compare pp. 33–42).

Fulham

STATION: PUTNEY BRIDGE, on the District Line. — RIVER LAUNCHES from Charing Cross or Westminster to Putney Pier, see p. 43.

FULHAM, approached from Chelsea (Route 8) by King's Road (Plan VI, F 2, 3) and from South Kensington (Route 10) by Fulham Road (VI, F 1, 2), stands on the north bank of the Thames, opposite Putney. It was once famous for its market gardens and later for its potteries, established about 1670. New King's Road ends at FULHAM HIGH STREET, on the left of which Ranelagh Gardens leads past Putney Bridge Station to the fashionable HURLINGHAM CLUB, in a house of about 1760 (best seen from the river). Part of the grounds was converted in 1954 into a public park, with an athletic stadium.

Near the north end of PUTNEY BRIDGE (built in 1886 by Sir Joseph Bazalgette and widened in 1933) is ALL SAINTS' CHURCH, the parish church of Fulham, retaining a 15th-century tower. The church itself, rebuilt in 1881 by Sir Arthur Blomfield, contains a 16th-century Flemish brass, a Gothic font of 1622, and many 17th-century monuments. In Fulham Palace Road, which leads to Hammersmith Broadway (see below), is the entrance to FULHAM PALACE, the residence of the bishops of London, who owned the manor of Fulham from about 691 until 1868. The most interesting part is the courtyard on the west, built by Bishop FitzJames in the early 16th century; the rest of the buildings belong to the 18th and 19th centuries. The site of the moat (reputedly dug by the Danes) is now a public garden, and between the palace grounds and the river is the BISHOP'S PARK, with an open-air theatre and a terrace that is a vantage point for watching the start of the Oxford and Cambridge Boat-Race (see p. 81).

Hammersmith

STATION: HAMMERSMITH, on the District, Metropolitan, and Piccadilly lines. — RIVER LAUNCHES from Charing Cross and Westminster to Hammersmith Pier, see p. 43.

HAMMERSMITH is reached from Kensington and the West End by way of Kensington High Street (Route 11; Plan VI, B 1) and its continuation, Hammersmith Road. This passes OLYMPIA, a huge exhibition building opened in 1886 and extended to the main road in 1930, and the brick Gothic building (by Alfred Waterhouse) of ST PAUL'S SCHOOL, a public school (650 boys) founded in 1509 by Dean Colet and moved here from St Paul's Churchyard in 1884. In the garden in front is a monument to the founder by Thornycroft (1900). Famous 'Old Paulines' include William Camden, the antiquary, John Milton, Samuel Pepys, the Duke of Marlborough, Judge Jeffreys, and Field-Marshal Lord Montgomery, whose headquarters were established here during the planning of the invasion of Normandy in 1944.

Hammersmith Road ends at HAMMERSMITH BROADWAY, a busy centre of traffic where several other roads converge (compare below). ST PAUL'S CHURCH, a large but uninteresting structure of 1882, a little to the south, contains a fine late-17th-century pulpit and a monument of about 1665 with a bronze bust of Charles I, probably by Le Sueur. To the south-west, beyond the Hammersmith Flyover (completed in 1961 as part of a new road out of London), is HAMMERSMITH BRIDGE, an unprepossessing suspension bridge of 1887, by Bazalgette, crossing the Thames to Barnes, in Surrey. LOWER MALL, skirting the river west of the bridge, retains several picturesque houses of the 18th century, while farther west is HAMMERSMITH TOWN HALL, built in 1939 to the designs of Berry Webber. Farther on, beyond Hammersmith Pier, is the UPPER MALL, with more picturesque old houses, including the charming Sussex House, of about 1726, and the DOVES INN, where James Thomson is said to have written part of *The Seasons*. KELMSCOTT HOUSE, built about 1780, was from 1878 until his death in 1896 the home of William Morris, who founded his tapestry works and printing press here. The first electric telegraph was constructed here, in 1816, by Sir Francis Ronalds. Northward from Hammersmith Terrace (about 1750) is ST PETER'S CHURCH, a Regency building by E. Lapidge (1829), and west of this is ST PETER'S SQUARE, an unusual but distinguished layout of the same period.

King Street, farther north, leads back from Chiswick High Road (in Middlesex) to Hammersmith Broadway, passing RAVENSCOURT PARK, on the west side of which is the fine ROYAL MASONIC HOSPITAL, built in 1931 by Sir John Burnet, Tait and Partners and extended in 1958 by the same architects. From the Broadway, Brook Green Road runs north towards SHEPHERD'S BUSH, with a large triangular green from which the broad Holland Park Avenue ascends eastward to Notting Hill Gate (Route 12). In Wood Lane, which goes on northward from Shepherd's Bush, are the vast new TELEVISION CENTRE of the BBC, to the designs of Graham Dawbarn (opened in 1960), and the WHITE CITY, a large open-air arena for sports and shows. In Ducane Road, on the left farther on, is the Hammersmith Hospital, incorporating the important POSTGRADUATE MEDICAL

SCHOOL of London University (founded in 1934), new buildings for which, by Lyons, Israel, and Ellis, were opened in 1962.

Paddington

STATIONS: PADDINGTON (Plan I, D 2) and EDGWARE ROAD (I, C 3) both on the Bakerloo, Circle, District, and Metropolitan lines; WARWICK AVENUE (I, C 2) and MAIDA VALE, on the Bakerloo line.

PADDINGTON (compare p. 19), is bounded on the south by Bayswater Road (Route 12) and on the east by EDGWARE ROAD (II, E 2–I, B 3), a long, straight and dismal thoroughfare following the course of the Roman Watling Street, which ran to St Albans and Chester. On the left, opposite Marylebone Road (Route 16), is the broad SUSSEX GARDENS (see p. 160), and Praed Street, farther on, leads to ST MARY'S HOSPITAL (1851), with a noted medical school (founded in 1854, and rebuilt in 1933), in the laboratories of which Sir Alexander Fleming discovered penicillin in 1943. Farther on in this street is PADDINGTON STATION (I, D 2, 3), the principal terminus of the Western Region, mostly designed by Isambard Kingdom Brunel, first opened in 1838 but reconstructed in 1850–4. The Great Western Royal Hotel, masking the south front, was built by Philip Hardwick in 1852.

On the left of Edgware Road a little beyond Praed Street begins the long winding Harrow Road (Plan I, C 1–3). This leads in a few minutes to PADDINGTON GREEN, the old village centre, with a statue of Mrs Sarah Siddons (d. 1831), inspired by Reynolds' 'Tragic Muse'. The actress is buried in the churchyard to the north-west (now a playing field). The first omnibus service in London started in 1829 from Paddington Green, running hence to the Bank. The adjacent ST MARY'S CHURCH (I, C 3), built in 1791 by John Plaw on the plan of a Greek cross, replaces that in which the painter Hogarth was married secretly in 1729. Harrow Road bears left farther on to cross a branch of the Grand Union Canal, but Warwick Avenue goes on past WARWICK GARDENS, a green retreat laid out in 1954 overlooking 'Little Venice' (compare p. 44). In Maida Avenue, which leads to the right from Warwick Avenue, skirting the Regent's Canal, is a CATHOLIC APOSTOLIC CHURCH in an early Gothic style, by J. L. Pearson (1894).

Maida Avenue ends at the junction of Edgware Road and MAIDA VALE, a broad thoroughfare deriving its name from the Battle of Maida (in Calabria), in which Sir John Stuart defeated the French in 1806. It still retains some of its mid-19th-century villas, but is now mainly lined by palatial blocks of flats in a variety of styles. In Kilburn Park Road, on the left near its north end, is the lofty and spacious ST AUGUSTINE'S CHURCH, a vaulted Gothic building, one of the finest designs of J. L. Pearson (1880). In the transepts are paintings by Marco Palmezzano, Filippino Lippi, Crivelli, and Titian, given by Lord Northcliffe, the newspaper owner.

Hampstead

STATIONS: BELSIZE PARK and HAMPSTEAD, on the Northern line; HAMPSTEAD HEATH, on the North London line (London Midland

Region; see p. 39); SWISS COTTAGE, on the Bakerloo line; and FINCHLEY ROAD, on the Bakerloo and Metropolitan lines.

ADMISSION to KEATS HOUSE, weekdays 10 to 6 (free; to library and museum, 9 to 7 or 8); to FENTON HOUSE, weekdays (except Tuesday) 10 to 1 and 2 to 5 or dusk, Sundays from 2 only (2/6; gardens only, 1/-); to KENWOOD HOUSE, weekdays 10 to 7 or dusk, Sundays from 2 (free; closed Good Friday and Christmas Eve and Day), to gardens daily 6 or 7.30 to 10 or dusk.

HAMPSTEAD, the most favoured residential suburb of London, is famous for its beautiful heath, its quaint streets and picturesque houses, and its wealth of literary and artistic associations. The newer part spreads over the south and west slopes of a considerable hill, the top of which is crowned by the delightful old village. This is approached from St John's Wood (Plan II, A 1) by way of Wellington Road and Finchley Road to SWISS COTTAGE, where a new civic centre (designed by Sir Basil Spence) is being built (1963), and thence by Fitzjohns Avenue, on the right of College Crescent; and from Camden Town (beyond I, A 3) by Chalk Farm Road and the broad HAVERSTOCK HILL.

Haverstock Hill, ascending past Belsize Park station and HAMPSTEAD TOWN HALL (1877), is extended by Rosslyn Hill. DOWNSHIRE HILL, on the right, with some good Regency houses, goes down past Keats Grove (formerly John Street), in which is the charming KEATS HOUSE, built in 1815 and known as Wentworth Place when John Keats lived there, from December 1818 to September 1820, his most creative period. The poet and his friend, Charles Armitage Brown, occupied the east half of the house, and the Brawne family the other half. The rooms in these, and the Chester Room, built on the east in 1838, contain interesting relics of Keats, his betrothed Fanny Brawne, and his friends; books owned and annotated by the poet; and letters written by him and his acquaintances. In the garden in front is the mulberry-tree under which the *Ode to a Nightingale* is conjectured to have been written. Adjacent is a public library containing a museum of portraits and early editions of Keats and his contemporaries, and works relating to the poet.

Keats Grove ends at South End Road, which passes Hampstead Heath Station in one direction, and in the other is extended by East Heath Road, skirting the lower part of the heath (see below). Paths on the right lead via the Hampstead Ponds, the source of the Fleet River, to PARLIAMENT HILL (319 ft), the southern extremity of the heath, affording a wide view over north London. Farther east are the Highgate Ponds, extending up towards the grounds of Kenwood.

WELL WALK, running left from East Heath Road farther up, passes the site of the wells that in the 18th century made Hampstead a fashionable spa. John Constable, the landscape-painter, lived at No. 40 (then No. 5) from 1826 until the year of his death, while Keats lodged after June 1817 at a house whose site adjoins the *Wells Hotel*. Flask Walk bears right from the end of Well Walk to gain (50 yds below the underground station) the HIGH

STREET, the extension of Rosslyn Hill (see above), retaining some of its original 18th-century houses (mostly disguised by modern shop fronts). Farther down is the ROYAL SOLDIERS' DAUGHTERS' SCHOOL, mostly built in 1855, but incorporating (on the north) part of the residence of Sir Harry Vane (1612–62), the Parliamentarian.

HEATH STREET, with many picturesque old houses, winds steeply up from Hampstead Station to the top of Hampstead Heath (see below). Hampstead Square, on the right, gives access to CHRIST CHURCH (1852), whose prominent spire is a landmark from many parts of London. In the other direction, Heath Street is prolonged by Fitzjohns Avenue towards Swiss Cottage. On the right before the junction opens CHURCH ROW, the finest street in Hampstead, with delectable terraces of 18th-century dwellings. At the end is ST JOHN'S CHURCH, the parish church of Hampstead, rebuilt in 1745–7, with a western extension of 1844, converted into a chancel in 1878. Other 19th-century work includes the ornate decoration of the Renaissance-style ceiling (by Alfred Bell; 1855) and the altarpiece by Sir Thomas Jackson (1878). In the north aisle is a bust of John Keats, sculptured by Anne Whitney of Boston and given in 1894 by American admirers of the poet. John Constable (d. 1837), who painted many of his landscapes in and around Hampstead, is buried in the south-east corner of the churchyard, the fine 18th-century wrought-iron gates of which were brought from the demolished seat of the Duke of Chandos at Canons, near Edgware. In the newer cemetery north of the road are the graves of George du Maurier (d. 1896), the author, Sir Herbert Beerbohm Tree (d. 1917), the actor-manager (both at the south end), and Sir Walter Besant (d. 1901), the historian of London, near the west side.

HOLLY WALK, ascending west of the cemetery, passes a Roman Catholic Chapel built for French refugees in 1816. ABERNETHY HOUSE, in which R. L. Stevenson and his future biographer, Sir Sidney Colvin, lodged in 1874, stands at the corner of Mount Vernon, which leads to HOLLY HILL, the northward extension of High Street from the underground station. On the left are the large MEDICAL COUNCIL RESEARCH LABORATORIES, built in 1880 as a hospital, and on the right, at the beginning of HOLLY BUSH HILL, is the picturesque house (restored in 1957) built in 1797 by George Romney, the painter, but occupied only until the following year, when he returned to Kendal, in Westmorland, broken in health. Hence THE GROVE goes on north to Hampstead Heath, passing FENTON HOUSE (N.T.), a delightful mansion of about 1693 with an attractive walled garden and beautiful furniture, porcelain, and early keyboard instruments, including a harpsichord of 1612 played on by Handel (lent by the Queen Mother). NEW GROVE HOUSE, farther on, was occupied in 1874–95 by George du Maurier, while ADMIRAL'S HOUSE (in Admiral's Walk, to the left) was the home in 1856–64 of Sir George Gilbert Scott, the architect, and John Galsworthy, the novelist, lived at GROVE LODGE, adjoining, from 1918 until his death in 1933. No. 3 LOWER TERRACE, opposite the west end of Admiral's Walk, was the first home in Hampstead of Constable (1821).

Lower Terrace ascends on the right to the Whitestone Pond (see below) and goes down in the other direction to Holly Hill, from which the long winding street of Frognal branches right, passing UNIVERSITY COLLEGE SCHOOL, a public day school (500 boys) founded in 1829 and moved here from University College, Gower Street, in 1907. Famous pupils include Lord Leighton, Joseph Chamberlain, Viscount Morley, and the Marquess of Reading. At its south end Frognal reaches FINCHLEY ROAD, traversing the west side of the hill on which Hampstead stands and connecting Swiss Cottage and Golders Green stations.

At the north end of Heath Street (compare above) is the WHITESTONE POND, commanding a varied and charming view said to extend into ten counties. The flagstaff just beyond marks the highest point (440 ft) of HAMPSTEAD HEATH, the finest 'lung' in the neighbourhood of London, a rugged sandy heathland (790 acres) spreading over the hills and valleys of a verdant range. Acquired by the L.C.C. between 1871 and 1927, it is still maintained largely in its natural state, partly grown with gorse and with a rich variety of trees. It is especially popular with Londoners on summer bank holidays, when a fair takes place near the Vale of Health. To the north of the flagstaff is JACK STRAW'S CASTLE, an old inn well known to Dickens and Thackeray, and commemorated by Washington Irving in *Tales of a Traveller* (badly damaged by bombing and to be rebuilt).

Beyond the inn the road divides, the right branch (Spaniards Road) leading towards Highgate. It runs along a ridge above the VALE OF HEALTH, where Leigh Hunt took a cottage after his release from prison (1816) and was visited by Keats, Shelley, Coleridge, and Lamb. The *Spaniards Inn*, farther on, is a picturesque 18th-century tavern, partly weather-boarded. Here the Gordon Rioters were overtaken while on their way to attack Lord Mansfield's house (1780). Beyond, on the right, is the entrance to KEN-WOOD HOUSE, a delightful mansion rebuilt in 1767–9 by Robert Adam for the first Earl of Mansfield, the famous Lord Chief Justice of George III. The wings on the north were added in 1793–6 by George Saunders, who also built the low service wing on the east, with the brewhouse and laundry (now a tea-room). Kenwood House was bequeathed to the nation by the first Earl of Iveagh (d. 1927), together with his magnificent collection of paintings, which include many fine English portraits of the 18th and early 19th century by Gainsborough, Reynolds, Romney, Raeburn, and Lawrence, and other notable pictures by Claude de Jongh (Old London Bridge, 1639), Van Dyck, Frans Hals, Rembrandt, Jan Vermeer, Pater, Boucher, Guardi, John Crome, and Turner. The portico is characteristic of Adam's work; the finest of the rooms is the Library (sometimes called the Adam Room) in the east wing, with delicate plaster-work by Joseph Rose and ceiling paintings by Zucchi. The lovely wooded grounds of Kenwood, laid out by Lord Mansfield and now the most beautiful part of Hampstead Heath, contain some splendid beeches and other fine trees.

North End Way descends from Jack Straw's Castle to Golders Green, in Middlesex, passing the *Old Bull and Bush Inn*, made famous by a music-hall song, and MANOR HOUSE HOSPITAL. Opposite is Ivy House, once the home of Anna Pavlova (d. 1931), the ballerina, and now a college of speech and drama of the Royal Academy of Music. Also on the left is an entrance to GOLDERS HILL PARK, the north-west extension of Hampstead Heath, with a secluded walled garden and deer enclosures. GOLDERS GREEN has a station on the Northern line, while a motor-bus (No. 210) runs back across the heath to Highgate and Finsbury Park Station.

Highgate

STATIONS: ARCHWAY and HIGHGATE, on the Northern line.

HIGHGATE, another favoured suburb on the north side of London, stands mostly on the top of the twin hill to Hampstead, and like its neighbour it preserves many attractive old houses. From Hampstead the best approach is by Hampstead Lane, passing Kenwood (see above), and from Central London it is most conveniently reached via the Archway underground station and Highgate Hill. ARCHWAY ROAD, which runs northward from the station, was constructed after 1812 to avoid the precipitous slope of Highgate Hill. On the right at the outset is WHITTINGTON COLLEGE, a group of Gothic almshouses built in 1882 under a bequest of Sir Richard Whittington (d. 1423). The lofty viaduct higher up was built over the road in 1897 in place of the former 'Highgate Archway'.

HIGHGATE HILL, ascending steeply from Archway Station, is the continuation of Holloway Road (compare p. 479). On the left, in about 250 yds, is the WHITTINGTON STONE, set here in 1821 on the site of that on which Dick Whittington is supposed to have sat when he heard Bow Bells chiming 'Turn again, Whittington, thrice Mayor of London'. Farther up is ST JOSEPH'S RETREAT, the chief house in England of the Passionist Fathers, with a Romanesque chapel of 1888 dominated by its dome. Close by is an entrance to Waterlow Park (see below) and higher up (just inside the park) is LAUDERDALE HOUSE, built in the early 17th century, but altered in the 18th century and restored in 1893, and now a refreshment house. After 1660 it was owned by the notorious minister of Charles II, the Duke of Lauderdale, who is said to have lent it to Nell Gwyn. The house stands on a terrace enclosed by an attractive garden. Nearly opposite is CROMWELL HOUSE, which has no associations with Oliver Cromwell, but was built about 1637 and has an elaborate oak staircase. This is the finest of the old houses in Highgate Hill and its extension, HIGH STREET, though many notable 18th-century houses have also survived.

Above the junction with High Street is another entrance to WATERLOW PARK, a beautiful retreat with several small lakes on the secluded slopes of the hill. Near the south-west gate in Swain's Lane are the entrances to the two parts of HIGHGATE CEMETERY, where many famous people are buried. The grave of Karl Marx (d. 1883), in the newer part to the left, is marked by an over-large bust of 1956. Swain's Lane climbs up to SOUTH GROVE, which leads right past Pond Square (with further old houses) to High Street, and left to the OLD HALL, built in 1691, perhaps on the site of Arundel House, where Sir Francis Bacon died in 1626, and to ST MICHAEL'S CHURCH, erected by Lewis Vulliamy in 1832, with a spire that is a well-known landmark. The east window contains glowing stained glass by Evie Hone (1955). The remains of Samuel Taylor Coleridge, poet and critic, were moved to the crypt from Highgate School in 1961. THE GROVE, which runs north from the church approach, is the most delightful street in Highgate, preserving many charming houses of the late 17th and early 18th centuries. In one of these (No. 3) Coleridge lived from 1823 until his death in 1834.

The Grove ends at HAMPSTEAD LANE, which leads west to Kenwood (see above) and east to the upper end of High Street at the *Old Gate House Tavern*, named from a former toll-house. Facing this is HIGHGATE SCHOOL (650 boys), a public school founded in 1565 by Sir Roger Cholmeley, Lord Chief Justice, but rebuilt in 1868 and added to subsequently. In NORTH ROAD, which starts beside the school, A. E. Housman wrote *A Shropshire Lad* at No. 17, one of a row of Georgian houses. Farther north, on the same side, are the distinctive HIGHPOINT FLATS, designed by Lubetkin and Tecton in 1936 and called by Le Corbusier a 'vertical garden city'. North Road, which retains other 18th-century houses, is prolonged by North Hill down to the outer end of Archway Road, while Southwood Lane, running parallel on the east at first, descends to Highgate Station near HIGHGATE WOOD, owned by the Corporation of London.

Islington

STATIONS: ANGEL (Plan IV, A 2), ESSEX ROAD, and HIGHBURY & ISLINGTON, on the Northern line; CANONBURY and HIGHBURY & ISLINGTON, on the North London line (L.M.R.; see p. 39).

ADMISSION to CANONBURY TOWER, usually on application to the Warden.

ISLINGTON HIGH STREET, running north from the Angel (p. 282), is prolonged by Upper Street to ISLINGTON GREEN, at the corner of which is a statue of Sir Hugh Myddelton, who brought the New River to London in 1613. Essex Road bears right from the green, but Upper Street goes on past ST MARY'S CHURCH, the parish church of Islington, built in 1754 and destroyed by bombing in 1940, except for its baroque steeple. Handsomely rebuilt in 1956 by Lord Mottistone and Paul Paget, it is embellished with fine woodwork and a large reredos with eight painted panels by Brian Thomas.

Canonbury Lane, on the right beyond ISLINGTON TOWN HALL (1925), leads to CANONBURY SQUARE, a characteristic layout of about 1800. To the north-east, in Canonbury Place, is CANONBURY TOWER, consisting chiefly of a lofty brick tower with a gabled wing on the west and a lower brick wing on the east. The chief survival of a country residence of the priors of St Bartholomew's (p. 267), it was mostly rebuilt about 1595 by Sir John Spencer, Lord Mayor of London. In 1616–25 it was leased by Sir Francis Bacon, and in 1763–4 Oliver Goldsmith lodged here. Two rooms in the west wing retain their rich Elizabethan oak panelling, and a gabled 16th–17th-century range survives (though much altered) east of the courtyard. The tower, together with a modern hall in the courtyard, is now the home of the Tavistock Repertory Company.

Canonbury Road runs south from Canonbury Square to Essex Road (compare above) and north to Highbury and Islington Station, from which Holloway Road goes on north-west through an uninteresting district to Highgate (see p. 477).

Stoke Newington

STATIONS: ESSEX ROAD, on the Northern line, DALSTON JUNCTION (E.R. and L.M.R.; see p. 39), and STOKE NEWINGTON (E.R.); and thence by bus.

STOKE NEWINGTON, one of the smallest London boroughs, is approached from Islington by Essex Road (see above), from which the winding Newington Green Road goes on to NEWINGTON GREEN. Hence the long Albion Road, retaining some villas and terraces of 1830, runs north to the old village centre. Here are the TOWN HALL (1937) and the OLD PARISH CHURCH of St Mary, rebuilt in 1563 and one of the few examples of an Elizabethan church, remarkable for its unusual brick south arcade. The north aisle, added in 1829 by Barry and destroyed in 1940, was restored in 1953 by C. M. Oldrid Scott, who also carried out other repairs. In the chancel is the tomb of John Dudley (d. 1580) and his wife Elizabeth, whose second husband was Thomas Sutton, the founder of the Charterhouse. The spacious NEW PARISH CHURCH, on the south side of the road, was built in 1858 in a florid early-Decorated style by Sir G. G. Scott, and supports a prominent spire 245 ft high, added in 1890 by J. Oldrid Scott. Restored in 1957 after war damage, the church has new stained-glass windows of the Life of Christ by Francis Skeat. CLISSOLD PARK, close by, containing a notable villa of about 1830, is skirted on the west by Green Lanes, which leads south to Newington Green and north past the New River Reservoirs to Finsbury Park, in Middlesex.

Church Street runs east from the Town Hall to the north end of STOKE NEWINGTON HIGH STREET, which follows the straight course of the Roman Ermine Street and preserves a fine group of Queen Anne houses at Nos. 189–91. It is extended south by Stoke Newington Road towards Kingsland Road (see p. 286).

Bethnal Green and Hackney

STATIONS: BETHNAL GREEN, on the Central line; HACKNEY DOWNS, on the Eastern Region.

ADMISSION to the BETHNAL GREEN MUSEUM, 10 to 6 (Sundays from 2.30; free; closed Good Friday and Christmas Day); to SUTTON HOUSE, on written application to the tenant (free).

BETHNAL GREEN, a populous borough long engaged in silk-weaving but now occupied to a large extent in the furniture trade, is reached from Shoreditch High Street (p. 285) by the drab Bethnal Green Road. Facing the east end of this is ST JOHN'S CHURCH, an original design by Sir John Soane (1828), and to the north, entered from Cambridge Heath Road, is the BETHNAL GREEN MUSEUM, a branch of the Victoria and Albert Museum, opened in 1872 in a building designed by Sir William Cubitt for the South Kensington Museum (p. 419). It houses a fine collection of costumes and Spitalfields silks; 19th-century British paintings; pottery and porcelain, glass, and silver; old furniture; and dolls and toys. Old Ford Road, starting north of the museum, leads in ½-mile to VICTORIA PARK, the largest open space in east London, with a boating lake, a swimming pool, and (on the north-east side) a pair of alcoves from old London Bridge.

Cambridge Heath Road is extended northward by Mare Street, the chief street of HACKNEY, a once squalid district where many blocks of flats have now sprung up. On the east of the street is ST JOHN'S CHURCH, the large parish church, built in 1797 on the plan of a Greek cross by James Spiller and handsomely restored in 1958 after a fire. It has 16th–17th-century monuments from the previous church, good 18th-century woodwork, and an unusual steeple added on the north in 1813. In the south-west corner of the churchyard rises the solitary tower, built in 1519, of the demolished old church. SUTTON PLACE, with a terrace of the early 19th century, leads east from the churchyard to Homerton High Street, in which Nos. 2–4 are SUTTON HOUSE (N.T.), a Tudor manor house of the early 16th century that later became the home of Thomas Sutton, the founder of the Charterhouse (p. 277). Though much restored, it contains good 16th-century panelling and stone fireplaces. To the north-east of the borough, on the Essex border, lie HACKNEY MARSHES, a large recreation ground watered by the river Lea.

Whitechapel and Bow

STATIONS: ALDGATE (Plan V, E 3), on the Circle and Metropolitan lines; ALDGATE EAST (V, E 3), WHITECHAPEL, STEPNEY GREEN, MILE END, BOW ROAD, and BROMLEY, all on the District and Metropolitan lines (Mile End is also on the Central line).

WHITECHAPEL, part of the borough of Stepney (see below), is largely inhabited by Jewish traders and craftsmen whose forerunners began to settle in this neighbourhood after the Russian persecution of 1881. Whitechapel High Street (p. 291) is prolonged by the broad WHITECHAPEL ROAD, the main thoroughfare, passing (on the right) THE LONDON HOSPITAL, the largest general hospital in the country, founded in 1740 but rebuilt here after 1748 and enlarged at various times. In Brady Street, on the left beyond Whitechapel Station, is a disused JEWS' CEMETERY (entrance at No. 37) containing the tomb of Nathan Meyer Rothschild (d. 1836), the English representative of the famous family of financiers.

From Cambridge Heath Road, which runs north to Bethnal Green (see above), Whitechapel Road is extended by the wide tree-lined boulevard of

MILE END ROAD, so called because it began one-mile from the old City wall at Aldgate. On the left at the outset is a bronze bust of William Booth (d. 1912), who began the work of the Salvation Army in the neighbourhood in 1865. Just beyond are the TRINITY ALMSHOUSES, established in 1695 for twenty-eight 'decay'd masters and commanders of ships or ye widows of such'. The attractive rows of dwellings, extended in the 19th century, were badly damaged by bombing, but have been taken over by the L.C.C., who thoroughly restored them in 1958. The chapel, on the north, was restored in 1960 as a welfare centre for handicapped people. Captain Cook, the explorer, lived after 1764 at No. 88, on the other side of the road. Farther on is STEPNEY GREEN, which leads south-east to St Dunstan's Church (see p. 482). ROLAND HOUSE (No. 29), purchased in 1914 for the Boy Scouts Association, is now a centre for scouting in the East End and an international hostel.

Mile End Road goes on past the SPANISH AND PORTUGUESE JEWS' HOSPITAL, established in 1665 and rebuilt in 1913. Behind is a small Jewish Cemetery (disused) opened in 1656, the first to be acquired by the Jews after their resettlement in England. Farther on is QUEEN MARY COLLEGE, since 1907 a branch of London University, but founded in 1887 and formerly called the East London College. The central buildings, of this period, were until 1953 the People's Palace, a cultural and recreational centre for east London suggested by the 'Palace of Delights' in Sir Walter Besant's novel *All Sorts and Conditions of Men*. A large extension to the west (1936) is decorated with reliefs by Eric Gill.

Crossing the Regent's Canal, Mile End Road, with early-19th-century terraces, continues to BOW, so called from an arched ('bow') bridge built over the river Lea in the 12th century, and famous for its porcelain in the 18th century; it is now the northern part of the borough of Poplar. In Bow Road are the POPLAR TOWN HALL, by E. C. Culpin (1937), with a civic theatre, and the long parish church of ST MARY STRATFORD BOW, on an island in the busy traffic. Rebuilt in the late 15th century, it has excessively narrow aisles, a good contemporary font, and a fine embossed ceiling in the chancel. The upper part of the tower, recast in 1829, has been reconstructed again after war damage. Bow Road descends eastward to cross the Lea to Stratford, in Essex.

Stepney and Poplar

STATIONS: TOWER HILL (Plan V, F 3), on the Circle and District lines; SHADWELL and WAPPING, on the Metropolitan line (New Cross branch); STEPNEY (EAST), on the Eastern Region line to Tilbury.

ADMISSION to the ST KATHARINE ROYAL FOUNDATION, usually on application to the Warden (free); to the DOCKS, by permission of the Port of London Authority only (see p. 298). — RIVER AND DOCK CRUISES, see p. 44.

STEPNEY, once notorious as a congested and poverty-stricken borough, includes the greater part of the 'East End' of London, with a population largely employed in the neighbouring docks or other seafaring activities.

Streets upon streets were completely devastated during the Second World War, and the slums have now been almost wholly replaced by large and airier blocks of flats designed by the L.C.C.

EAST SMITHFIELD, starting from the north end of Tower Bridge Approach (p. 300), is extended by THE HIGHWAY, previously Ratcliff Highway, a long street which formerly had an infamous reputation for its drinking dens for seamen. On the north rises ST GEORGE-IN-THE-EAST, one of the most imposing churches of Nicholas Hawksmoor (1715–23), gutted during the war but to be restored on an original plan by Arthur Bailey. Wapping Lane, on the right just beyond the church, leads between the two branches of LONDON DOCKS (first opened in 1805) to the eastward end of WAPPING HIGH STREET, running parallel to the Thames but mostly encompassed by huge warehouses. An alley beside the *Town of Ramsgate* inn, over ¼-mile west, admits to the Wapping Old Stairs made famous in a ballad. The notorious Judge Jeffreys was arrested near here in 1688, disguised as a sailor. The High Street is continued downstream by WAPPING WALL, passing a picturesque old inn, *The Prospect of Whitby*.

The Highway goes on past the church of ST PAUL'S, SHADWELL, rebuilt in 1820 by John Walters, and the KING EDWARD MEMORIAL PARK, overlooking a busy reach of the river, with a memorial slab (1922) to Willoughby, Frobisher, and other intrepid navigators who set sail in the 16th century from Ratcliff. In Butcher Row, which crosses the entrance to Rotherhithe Tunnel (see below) farther on to the left, are the buildings of the ST KATHARINE ROYAL FOUNDATION (compare p. 182), mainly dating from 1952. A cloister containing monuments from the Regent's Park church leads to the simple chapel, which has finely carved 14th-century stalls, with interesting misericords, and a Jacobean pulpit. The 18th-century Warden's House was previously the rectory of the demolished St James's church. The foundation now interests itself in social welfare work in the dock region.

Butcher Row ends on the north at CABLE STREET, which runs parallel to The Highway. In Stepney Causeway, to the left, are the head-offices of DR BARNARDO'S HOMES, established in 1866 and maintaining in various parts of the world more than 7,000 orphan children, purely by voluntary subscriptions and legacies. Over 160,000 boys and girls have been admitted by the institution, which never turns away a destitute child. Stepney Causeway and Cable Street (to the right) both lead to COMMERCIAL ROAD (p. 291), the main thoroughfare of Stepney. Belgrave Street, starting between the two streets, runs north again to ST DUNSTAN'S CHURCH, the interesting parish church of Stepney and the only medieval church in East London (apart from Bow), standing in a leafy churchyard until lately surrounded by a huge bombed area. Baptisms which take place at sea are frequently recorded in the church registers. Believed to have been founded in the 10th century, perhaps by St Dunstan himself, the structure is mainly of the 15th century. Notable in the chancel are the carved 13th-century sedilia and the canopied tomb of Sir Henry Colet (d. 1510), whose son, John Colet, afterwards dean of St Paul's, was vicar here in 1485–1505. Below the east window, which contains striking glass by Hugh Easton showing Stepney after the 'blitz', is set a remarkable late-Saxon stone rood-panel of the Crucifixion. In the south aisle can be seen the medieval rood-stairs and a curious stone brought from Carthage in 1663.

Commercial Road continues past Stepney (East) Station and Regent's Canal Dock. In Branch Road, between these, begins the approach to ROTHERHITHE TUNNEL, built in 1904–8 below the river to Rotherhithe. Close by in Commercial Road is the brick DANISH SEAMEN'S CHURCH, designed by Holger Jensen (1959) and containing wooden figures of St Peter and St Paul by C. G. Cibber, the Danish sculptor (1696). Farther east is the memorial hostel (1924) of the BRITISH SAILORS' SOCIETY, incorporated in 1818, and beyond this is ST ANNE'S, LIMEHOUSE, a characteristic church by Hawksmoor (consecrated in 1730), dominated by its steeple. From the end of Commercial Road, WEST INDIA DOCK ROAD bears to the right through Limehouse, a district which once had an unsavoury reputation. The narrow side streets, however, have lost their character since the bombing. On the left is Pennyfields, formerly the centre of the Chinese quarter, and on the right the *Railway Tavern*, better known as 'Charley Brown's', with an assembly of old curios. The road ends at the WEST INDIA DOCKS, opened in 1802 and extended south by Millwall Dock in 1868.

The line of Commercial Road is extended by EAST INDIA DOCK ROAD through the south part of the borough of POPLAR, which shares the marine interests of Stepney and also suffered disastrously during the war. On the north of the road is the new district of LANSBURY, named in honour of the Labour leader, George Lansbury (1859–1940), and the first part to be completed of a vast housing scheme planned by the L.C.C. over an area laid waste by bombing. It includes a modern market-place, the Trinity Congregational Church, in a contemporary style by C. C. Handisyde and D. R. Stark (1951), and a large new Roman Catholic Church by A. Gilbert Scott (1955), to an unusual design, with a massive brick tower raised over a central space. Farther east is ALL SAINTS CHURCH, the parish church of Poplar, built in 1823 by Charles Hollis, with an impressive Ionic portico and a successful steeple in the manner of Wren; the spacious and handsome interior has an unusual baldacchino over the altar. Near the gate of EAST INDIA DOCK, built in 1834–6, is the northern approach to BLACKWALL TUNNEL (1897), which passes beneath the Thames towards Greenwich, and within the dock (no admission) is the VIRGINIA SETTLERS' MEMORIAL, unveiled in 1951 to commemorate the 105 adventurers who sailed in 1606 from Blackwall to found the first permanent British colony at Jamestown, Virginia.

Rotherhithe and Deptford

STATIONS: ROTHERHITHE, SURREY DOCKS, and NEW CROSS, on the Metropolitan line from Whitechapel; DEPTFORD, on the Southern Region (compare p. 38).

ROTHERHITHE and its neighbour Deptford stand on the south bank of the Thames, opposite Stepney and Poplar, and are largely inhabited by dock-workers and others with seagoing connexions. From Tower Bridge Road (p. 299), Tooley Street and Jamaica Road run eastward towards Deptford, while Mill Street, on the left beyond St Saviour's Dock, leads to Bermondsey Wall, which winds through a forest of warehouses with occasional glimpses of the river. In Rotherhithe Street, the continuation, are the picturesque 18th-century *Angel Inn* and (1 mile from Dock Head) ST MARY'S CHURCH, the pleasant parish church of Rotherhithe, built in 1715 and containing good 18th-century woodwork. To the south of it is the 18th-century charity school, from which St Marychurch Street goes on to the east end of Jamaica Road. Opposite this, beside the NORWEGIAN CHURCH (1927), is the southern entrance to ROTHERHITHE TUNNEL (p. 483).

Lower Road runs south-east from Jamaica Road between the extensive SURREY COMMERCIAL DOCKS, the centre of the timber trade (first opened in 1807), and the mis-called SOUTHWARK PARK. It is extended by Evelyn Street to DEPTFORD (pronounced 'Det-ford'), long famous for its naval dockyard, founded by Henry VII in 1485 and closed in 1869. The Emperor Peter the Great worked as a shipwright here in 1698, and occupied the residence of John Evelyn, the diarist, at Sayes Court, the site of which is indicated by the small Sayes Park. The site of the dockyard is occupied by storehouses to the south-east of the former ROYAL NAVAL VICTUALLING YARD, opened in 1745 and closed in 1961.

To the north of Creek Street, beyond the end of the High Street, is ST NICHOLAS'S CHURCH, rebuilt in 1697 (except for the late-14th-century tower), but gutted by bombing and restored in 1957. The 17th-century woodwork, including a carving by Grinling Gibbons, has been returned, and a new tablet has been erected to Christopher Marlowe, who was slain in a brawl at Deptford in 1593 and is buried in the churchyard. To the south of the main road is ST PAUL'S CHURCH, a splendid building by Thomas Archer, consecrated in 1730, with a fine semicircular portico supporting a noble steeple, huge Corinthian columns inside, and rich plaster ceilings. Creek Street goes on east across the Deptford Creek, the mouth of the Ravensbourne, to Greenwich.

Greenwich

STATIONS: GREENWICH and MAZE HILL, on the Southern Region (see p. 38). — RIVER LAUNCHES from Westminster, Charing Cross, and Tower Pier, see p. 43.

ADMISSION to the CUTTY SARK, 11 to 5 or 6 (later in summer; Sunday from 2.30; 2/-, children 6*d*); to the ROYAL NAVAL COLLEGE (Chapel and Painted Hall), weekdays, except Thursday, 2.30 to 5 (free; also Sundays to the Painted Hall in May–September; to the Chapel for service on Sunday at 11); to the NATIONAL MARITIME MUSEUM, 10 to 6 (Sunday from 2.30; free; on closed Good Friday and Christmas Eve and Day: licensed restaurant in summer); to MORDEN COLLEGE, on written application to the Clerk to the Trustees (free).

GREENWICH (pronounced 'Gren-nidge'), one of the pleasantest suburbs of London, lies on the south bank of the Thames, nearly 5 miles below London Bridge by water. It has long been famous for its park, its hospital, and its observatory: the hospital now houses the Royal Naval College and the observatory has been moved to Sussex, but Greenwich has a maritime museum which should not be missed by any lover of the sea.

Greenwich High Road, the approach from the direction of London (A 206), passes the station and the TOWN HALL, a striking modern building by E. C. Culpin (1938), with a soaring clock-tower. At the end of the road is ST ALFEGE'S CHURCH, traditionally on the place where Alphege, archbishop of Canterbury, was martyred by the Danes in 1011. Henry VIII was baptized in the medieval building; the present church, designed in 1712 by Nicholas Hawksmoor and completed by John James, who also added the steeple (1730), was carefully restored in 1953, after severe war damage, by Sir Albert Richardson. The chiaroscuro decoration of the apse, by Thornhill (much damaged), has been repainted by Glyn Jones. In the church are the tomb of Thomas Tallis (d. 1585), the 'father of English church music', and a monument to General Wolfe (d. 1759), whose flag is also preserved.

Church Street runs north from St Alfege's to GREENWICH PIER, the terminal point of the river launches. Close by is the permanent berth of the CUTTY SARK, the last and most famous of the sailing clippers, launched at Dumbarton on the Clyde in 1869 and brought here in 1954, partly for use as an educational centre of the Mercantile Marine; after careful refitting, she was opened to visitors in 1957. Below decks is an interesting exhibition of old figureheads, prints and paintings, and maritime relics. A tunnel near the pier gives access under the river to the Isle of Dogs, in reality a large peninsula mainly occupied by docks, and a footwalk runs along the north front of the Royal Naval College to the *Trafalgar Tavern* (1837) at the north end of Park Row.

In King William Walk, which leads south from the pier to the National Maritime Museum, is the main entrance to the ROYAL NAVAL COLLEGE for the higher education of naval officers, moved from Portsmouth in 1873 and occupying the noble group of buildings erected mainly in 1696–9 by Sir Christopher Wren as GREENWICH HOSPITAL. This stands on the site of the royal palace of Placentia, begun in 1428 by Humphrey, Duke of Gloucester, and a favourite residence of the Tudor monarchs, Henry VIII and his daughters Mary I and Elizabeth I being born here, and Edward VI dying here in 1553. A new palace begun in 1664 for Charles II by John Webb was proceeded with after 1694 as a home for disabled seamen. The buildings, consisting of four separate blocks, were opened in 1705 (though not completed until 1750), but the hospital was abandoned in 1869 in favour of pensions. In the south-west block is the PAINTED HALL, completed in 1703 by Wren and so called from the effective wall and ceiling paintings by Sir James Thornhill, executed in 1708–27 (restored in 1957–60). The CHAPEL, in the south-east block, was designed by Wren, completed in 1752 by Ripley, and remodelled in 1789, after a fire, by 'Athenian' Stuart; it was redecorated in 1955. The fine pulpit, lectern, and font were made of wood from the old dockyard at Deptford; the altarpiece consists of a huge painting, 25 ft high, of St Paul shaking off the Viper, by Benjamin West. In the angle between King William Walk and Romney Road (south of the college) is the SEA-MEN'S HOSPITAL, built in 1763 as the Greenwich Hospital infirmary and altered in 1811 after a fire.

In Romney Road is one of the entrances to the NATIONAL MARITIME MUSEUM, a fascinating survey of naval history from Tudor times to the present day. There is another entrance on the east from Park Row, approached from Maze Hill Station via Park Vista. In the centre of the buildings is the QUEEN'S HOUSE, designed by Inigo Jones, a beautiful example of the Palladian style, begun in 1617 for Anne of Denmark, consort of James I, and completed in 1635 for Henrietta Maria, the queen of Charles I. It is connected by colonnades with wings on the east and west, added in 1805-16 to accommodate the Royal Hospital School for the sons of sailors and marines. The school moved to Suffolk in 1933 and the museum was opened here in 1937. The arrangement is mostly chronological, starting in the Queen's House with the Tudor and Stewart period (1485-1702), continuing in the Caird Galleries on the west with exhibits up to the close of the Napoleonic wars, and finishing in the East Wing, which brings the history up to the Second World War. Rooms IX and X in the West Wing contain a fine collection of portraits and personal relics of Lord Nelson, including the uniform worn by him at the Battle of Trafalgar. To the south is Neptune's Hall, with naval uniforms, ships' figureheads, etc., a model of Trafalgar, and a large assembly of ship models of the 18th–20th centuries. On the west of this opens the Barge House, containing the state barge of Mary II (1689), a barge built for Frederick, Prince of Wales (1732), and two 18th-century barges used by the Commissioners of the Navy. A wing extending on the west of the museum contains (on the ground floor) the interesting Navigation Room, comprising nautical instruments, globes, charts, etc. Above is the Print Room, which with the adjoining Students' Room (available for study on weekdays from 10 to 5) has many thousands of prints, drawings, and photographs. The main galleries contain ship models and mementoes of famous seamen, but are chiefly remarkable for the magnificent collection of naval scenes and seascapes by the Van de Veldes, Turner, and others, and the portraits by Kneller, Lely, Hogarth, Reynolds, Gainsborough, Romney, Copley, and many other famous artists.

Behind the museum rises GREENWICH PARK, a royal park laid out for Charles II by Le Nôtre, the landscape-gardener of Louis XIV, and notable for its sweet chestnuts, oaks, and hawthorns. The hill in the centre commands a wonderful view over Greenwich to east London and the Docks, with Tower Bridge and St Paul's to the left. The statue here of General Wolfe, by Tait Mackenzie (1930), was given by the Canadian nation. Near by is Flamsteed House, the former buildings of the ROYAL OBSERVATORY, established in 1675 primarily for the assistance of navigation. The zero meridian of longitude passes through the observatory and is marked on the path to the north. 'Greenwich time' remains the British Standard time, but owing to the growing pollution of the atmosphere the observatory was transferred in 1948–57 to Herstmonceux, in Sussex. The older part of the buildings, with the fine octagon room, is attributed to Wren, and the house, now an annexe of the National Maritime Museum (open during the same hours), contains instruments used by Flamsteed, Halley, and other early Astronomers Royal, and time-measuring instruments, including four chronometers made in 1736–64 by John Harrison. The mast on the turret above carries a time-ball that falls every day at precisely 1 p.m.

Near the west gate of the park is MACARTNEY HOUSE, where General Wolfe lived from the age of 11, and lower down, in CROOMS HILL, are several fine 17th–18th-century houses, including the Manor House of about 1700 and the charming Presbytery, built about 1630. In Chesterfield Walk, which runs south alongside the park, is the RANGER'S HOUSE, bought in 1753 by the Earl of Chesterfield and later occupied by Field-Marshal Viscount Wolseley.

To the south of the park stretches BLACKHEATH, an open breezy common, once the resort of highwaymen and the rallying-point of the Kentish rebels in 1381 (under Wat Tyler) and 1450 (under Jack Cade). THE PARAGON, at the south-east angle, designed by Michael Searles about 1790 and restored after war damage, is a noble crescent of seven villas connected by colonnades. Farther east is MORDEN COLLEGE, a home for City merchants founded in 1695 by Sir John Morden; the delightful building, confidently attributed to Wren, is well seen from the footpath passing north of the grounds.

Woolwich and Charlton

STATIONS: CHARLTON, WOOLWICH DOCKYARD, and WOOLWICH ARSENAL, on the North Kent line (S.R.) to Dartford; ELTHAM (WELL HALL), on an alternative line via Lewisham.

ADMISSION to the ROTUNDA, 10 to 12.45 and 2 to 4 or 5 (Sunday from 2; free); to CHARLTON HOUSE, on application to the Town Clerk, Town Hall, Greenwich, SE 10 (gardens open daily; free).

WOOLWICH (pronounced 'Wool-idge'), on the south side of the Thames some way below Greenwich, is a busy industrial and garrison town with the largest as well as the oldest military arsenal in Britain. BERESFORD SQUARE, the market centre of the town, lies between Woolwich Arsenal Station and the main entrance to the ROYAL ARSENAL, established in 1716 as the Brass Gun Foundry and now covering over 1,200 acres. Nearly 40,000 workers were employed here during the Second World War. Beresford Street, running north-west from the square, is extended by High Street past the approach to the WOOLWICH FREE FERRY (opened in 1889), with its quaint paddle-wheel steamers, to ST MARY MAGDALEN'S, the spacious parish church, built on a rise facing the river in 1729 and enlarged by a new chancel in 1894. Farther on is the former ROYAL DOCKYARD (closed in 1869), founded by Henry VIII, where the *Great Harry* was launched in 1515 and from which Sir John Franklin set out on his ill-fated expedition to the Arctic in 1845.

Woolwich New Road, starting south of Beresford Square, ascends near the huge ROYAL ARTILLERY BARRACKS, built in 1775–1802 facing the north side of Woolwich Common. Some distance south-west, reached from Repository Road, is the ROTUNDA, a prominent tent-like building designed by Nash and erected in St James's Park for the visit of the allied sovereigns in 1814. Moved here in 1819, it now houses an interesting artillery museum. The road skirting the east side of the common passes the former ROYAL MILITARY ACADEMY, familiarly known as 'The Shop', founded in 1741 and merged in 1946 with the Royal Military College, Sandhurst. The buildings were erected to the designs of Sir Jeffrey Wyatville in 1806, but have since been enlarged. For the continuation of the road over Shooters Hill to Well Hall and Eltham, see the *Penguin Guide to Kent*.

Green's End, ascending south-west from Beresford Square and passing the end of Powis Street, the chief shopping street of Woolwich, is extended past the TOWN HALL (1906) by Wellington Street, the beginning of the road to the older part of CHARLTON, now included in the borough of Greenwich. At the centre is ST LUKE'S CHURCH, a pleasing little brick building of 1630 with a gabled porch, enlarged by a north aisle (which has heraldic glass) in 1693 and by a new chancel in 1840. A little to the south stands CHARLTON HOUSE, an excellent Jacobean mansion with a three-storeyed porch, built in 1607 by Sir Adam Newton, tutor to Henry, Prince of Wales, and restored after bombing.

Camberwell and Herne Hill

STATIONS: ELEPHANT & CASTLE, on the Bakerloo and Northern lines and the Southern Region, and thence by bus; DENMARK HILL and HERNE HILL, on the Southern Region.

ADMISSION to SOUTH LONDON ART GALLERY, weekdays 10 to 6, Sundays 3 to 6 (free).

CAMBERWELL, an elongated borough that includes Dulwich and Crystal Palace, is reached from the Elephant and Castle by Walworth Road (see p. 304) and its long extension Camberwell Road, which leads to CAMBERWELL GREEN, shaded by a variety of trees. Thence Church Street runs east to ST GILES'S CHURCH, a lofty building in the early Decorated style by Sir Gilbert Scott (1844), with 14th-century sedilia and piscina, and grisailles of 13th-century glass in the west window. Farther on, in Peckham Road, is the SOUTH LONDON ART GALLERY, which has good loan exhibitions.

DENMARK HILL ascends to the south from Camberwell Green, passing KING'S COLLEGE HOSPITAL, founded in 1839 and moved to new buildings here in 1913. In Champion Park, the turning on the left beyond the railway, is the WILLIAM BOOTH MEMORIAL TRAINING COLLEGE of the Salvation Army, with statues of the founder and his wife (by G. E.

Wade) flanking the entrance to the large buildings, which were designed by Sir Giles G. Scott (1929). The main road continues past RUSKIN PARK (commemorating the residence in this locality from 1823 to 1871 of John Ruskin) and Red Post Hill (on the left), leading to North Dulwich Station (see below), to reach HERNE HILL. To the south-west of the station here is the pleasant BROCKWELL PARK, with the old hall of 1816 and a secluded old-world garden.

Dulwich and Crystal Palace

STATIONS: NORTH DULWICH, WEST DULWICH, SYDENHAM HILL, and CRYSTAL PALACE, all on the Southern Region (compare p. 38).

ADMISSION to DULWICH GALLERY, Tuesday–Saturday 10 to 4, 5, or 6; Sundays (April–September only) 2 to 5 or 6 (free); to the HORNIMAN MUSEUM, weekdays, except Tuesday, 10.30 to 6; Sundays from 2 (free).

DULWICH (pronounced 'Dul-lidge'), one of the quietest and most attractive suburbs of London, still retains to a large extent a rural atmosphere. This it owes in the first place to the benefactions of Edward Alleyn (1566–1626), the actor-manager and 'master of the royal beasts', who purchased the manor in 1605 and in 1619 founded the College of God's Gift, a trust which now maintains Dulwich College and several other schools, as well as the Dulwich Picture Gallery.

The road leading south from North Dulwich Station goes through DULWICH VILLAGE, which has many good Georgian houses. In the angle between Gallery Road (leading towards West Dulwich Station) and College Road are the OLD COLLEGE BUILDINGS, the 17th-century home of Alleyn's college, much altered in the 19th century and now comprising almshouses (part of the original foundation) and the offices of the trust. The chapel (entered from the cloister), recast in 1823, contains the grave of Edward Alleyn and a fine marble font of 1729 designed by Gibbs.

In College Road is the entrance to the DULWICH PICTURE GALLERY, the nucleus of which was a bequest of Edward Alleyn. This was greatly enhanced by paintings collected by Noël Desenfans, a French picture-dealer, for King Stanislaus of Poland (who abdicated before he could receive them) and bequeathed in 1807 to his friend Sir Peter Francis Bourgeois, the painter, who in 1811 left them to the college. The gallery, the first public art gallery opened in London (1814), was designed by Sir John Soane and has been well restored after its damage by bombing. The splendid collection is especially notable for its Dutch paintings (Rembrandt, Gerard Dou, J. van Ruisdael, Aelbert Cuyp, Hobbema, etc.) and its portraits by 17th–18th-century British artists (Lely, Kneller, Hogarth, Richard Wilson, Allan Ramsay, Gainsborough – especially of members of the Linley family – Reynolds, Romney, Hoppner, and Lawrence). The Italian School is represented by Raphael (two small panel paintings), Veronese, Domenichino, Guido Reni, Guercino, Carlo Dolci, Canaletto, and G. D. Tiepolo; the Flemish School by Rubens (including several fine sketches), Van Dyck, and the two Teniers; the Spanish School by Murillo (especially the lovely

Madonna with the Rosary); and the French School by Poussin (several characteristic works), Charles Le Brun, Watteau, and Lancret.

Opposite the old college is an entrance to DULWICH PARK, best seen when its azaleas are in flower. Lordship Lane, east of the park, ascends towards the HORNIMAN MUSEUM (by C. H. Townsend, 1902), at Forest Hill, worth a visit for its ethnographical collections and its musical instruments, and also possessing a fine library.

College Road goes on south from the gallery past DULWICH COLLEGE, a public school (1,500 boys) administered by the Alleyn Trust. The Italianate brick buildings, by the younger Charles Barry (1866–70), have been several times extended. Famous 'Old Alleynians' include Sir Ernest Shackleton, the Polar explorer, one of whose rescue boats is preserved in the grounds. The road ascends through the only surviving toll-gate in London to UPPER NORWOOD. An elevated plateau here is the site of the CRYSTAL PALACE, an immense structure of glass and iron, designed by Sir Joseph Paxton for the Great Exhibition of 1851 and transferred from Hyde Park in 1854. In 1936 it was completely destroyed by fire, except for the two lofty towers at each end, and these were pulled down in 1940. A soaring television transmitting mast, 708 ft high, was built here by the BBC in 1958. Part of the grounds has been converted into a public park, with a children's zoo, a boating-lake, and curious prehistoric animals in plaster, the only relic of the 1851 exhibition. On the rest a National Recreation Centre is being built, to designs of Hubert Bennett, with a large exhibition hall adjoining.

Kennington, Brixton, and Streatham

STATIONS: OVAL, on the Northern line; BRIXTON, STREATHAM HILL, and STREATHAM, on the Southern Region (compare p. 38).

KENNINGTON and its southern neighbour Brixton are working-class districts of little interest in the extensive borough of Lambeth. Newington Butts, running south-west from the Elephant and Castle (p. 303), is prolonged by Kennington Park Road, which ends at the junction of Harleyford Road, leading right past THE OVAL, the famous ground of the Surrey County Cricket Club, which was formed in 1844. In the angle between Camberwell New Road (on the left) and Clapham Road is ST MARK'S CHURCH, by D. R. Roper (1822); the interior, gutted by bombs in 1940, was partly restored in 1949. Viscount Montgomery's father was once vicar of the church, and the future field-marshal was born in 1887 in the vicarage near the Oval.

Brixton Road, starting east of the church, continues to BRIXTON, with the effective LAMBETH TOWN HALL (by Septimus Warwick, 1908). ST MATTHEW'S CHURCH, a little to the south, built in 1822, has its steeple at the east end and a 17th-century pulpit and lectern from the City. Hence the long Brixton Hill ascends to STREATHAM (pronounced 'Stret'm'), a favoured residential district mainly remarkable for its numerous huge blocks of flats. To the left near the beginning of Streatham Hill is the Italianate brick CHRIST CHURCH, by J. W. Wild (1842), 'perhaps the most original of Victorian churches', with a campanile, good mosaics in the apse, and stained glass by Walter Crane (1891). In Streatham High Road, some way farther down, is St Leonard's Church, the parish church, rebuilt in 1831 and altered at various times in the 19th century. The epitaph to Henry Thrale (d. 1781) is by Dr Johnson, who was a frequent visitor at Streatham Park, the home of the Thrales, which stood near the south side of Tooting Bec Common, ½-mile west of the church. In Aldrington Road, which runs south from the common, is the Romanesque brick St Alban's Church, by E. H. Martineau (1887). Gutted by fire in 1947, the upper parts were rebuilt (with an aluminium roof) by Sir Ninian Comper in 1954.

Clapham

STATIONS: Clapham Common, on the Northern line; Clapham and Clapham Junction, on the Southern Region.

Admission to the Museum of British Transport, weekdays 10 to 5.30 (1/-).

CLAPHAM, chiefly a middle-class residential district, is part of the extensive south-western borough of Wandsworth, the largest in London, including also Streatham, Balham, Tooting, Putney, and Roehampton. It is reached from Kennington (see above) by Clapham Road, which is joined at Stockwell by South Lambeth Road from Vauxhall (p. 308) and extended by Clapham High Street. Clapham Park Road, on the left of this, leads past Triangle Place, with the entrance to the Museum of British Transport, a growing collection of royal railway coaches, historic locomotives and road vehicles, and other exhibits illustrating every aspect of the history of rail, road, and canal transport in Britain. The large statue of James Watt (by Chantrey) was brought from Westminster Abbey.

The High Street ends at Clapham Common, on which a popular fair is held on summer bank holidays. In the north angle is Holy Trinity Church, built in 1775 by Kenton Couse, with a chancel added in 1902. A tablet on the south wall, outside, commemorates the 'Clapham Sect', an Anglican group that gathered in the houses round the common in the late 18th and early 19th centuries. Sir Charles Barry, the architect, died in 1860 at No. 29 North Side, a Georgian house on the site of that where Samuel Pepys died in 1703. Old Town, with a row of three charming Queen Anne houses (Nos. 39–43), north-east of Holy Trinity, leads towards St Paul's Church, built in 1815 on the site of a 12th-century structure. The chancel and transepts were added about 1890 in a Romanesque style by Blomfield; the north transept contains finely sculptured figures from the monument to Sir Richard Atkins (d. 1689) and his family. The church stands above the long uninteresting Wandsworth Road, which is extended by Lavender Hill to the busy cross-roads near Clapham Junction, claimed to be the busiest station in the world, with more than 2,500 trains passing every day. St John's Hill goes on towards Wandsworth, mainly given over to industry, and Putney, while Falcon Road leads north to the High Street of Battersea (p. 492).

Battersea

STATIONS: BATTERSEA PARK, and QUEEN'S ROAD, BATTERSEA (these two for Battersea Park), and CLAPHAM JUNCTION, all on the Southern Region. — RIVER LAUNCHES to Battersea Park, see p. 43.

ADMISSION to OLD BATTERSEA HOUSE, Saturday afternoons, October–April, on written application (enclosing a stamped addressed envelope; 2/-).

BATTERSEA, on the south bank of the Thames opposite Chelsea, is mainly concerned with industry, but retains some semblance of an old quarter round the church and the former village square. Albert Bridge Road, running south from the bridge (see p. 143), skirts the west side of the attractive BATTERSEA PARK, which stretches along the river to Chelsea Bridge and contains, besides the Festival Gardens (p. 75), a fine boating-lake and a sub-tropical garden. It was laid out in 1858 on the site of Battersea Fields, where the Duke of Wellington had fought a duel with the Earl of Winchilsea in 1829. Albert Bridge Road ends on the south at Battersea Park Road, which leads east towards Vauxhall, passing the BATTERSEA COLLEGE OF TECHNOLOGY, founded in 1891 (as the Battersea Polytechnic) and recognized by London University.

From Battersea Bridge Road, which runs parallel to Albert Bridge Road, Church Road leads west to ST MARY'S CHURCH, the parish church of Battersea (first mentioned in 1086), overlooking an industrialized reach of the river. Rebuilt in 1755 by Joseph Dixon, it retains from the previous church some 17th-century stained glass and several monuments, among them that of Henry St John, Viscount Bolingbroke (d. 1751) and his wife, with medallion portraits by Roubiliac. William Blake, the poet-visionary, was married here in 1782 to the 'heaven-provided' Catherine Boucher.

The *Raven Inn*, facing the old village square at the south end of Church Street, dates partly from the 17th century. Hence VICARAGE CRESCENT bears right past two fine 18th-century houses, in the second of which (the Vicarage) lived Edward A. Wilson (d. 1912), the Antarctic explorer Just beyond is OLD BATTERSEA HOUSE, built in 1699 and now containing fine collections of Pre-Raphaelite paintings and pottery by William de Morgan (d. 1917). From the end of Church Street, the narrow High Street goes on towards Clapham Junction (see above).

PUTNEY and ROEHAMPTON are described in the *Penguin Guide to Surrey*. Places of interest in the immediate neighbourhood of London include Chiswick (with Hogarth's House), Syon House, Osterley Park, Twickenham and Marble Hill House, Hampton Court and Bushy Park, Harrow-on-the-Hill, and Alexandra Park, all in Middlesex; the William Morris Gallery at Walthamstow, Epping Forest, and Waltham Cross and Abbey, in Essex; Dartford, Chiselhurst Caves, Bromley, etc., in Kent; and Wimbledon with its common, Kingston, Ham House and Petersham, Richmond and its park, and Kew with the Royal Botanical Gardens, in Surrey.

AISLE: wing or lateral division of a church, separated from the nave, chancel, or transept by a row of columns.

ALTARPIECE: structure of wood or stone above an altar, usually carved and/or painted.

AMBULATORY: aisle or corridor, especially one enclosing an apse.

APSE: semicircular or polygonal end of a chancel or chapel.

ARCADE: range of arches supported on piers or columns.

AUMBRY: recess or cupboard for sacred vessels used during Mass or Communion.

BALDACCHINO: canopy over an altar, generally supported on pillars.

BALUSTER: small shaft or column of varying diameter, often ornamented. *Balustrade:* series of balusters supporting a coping or rail.

BAPTISTERY: part of the church (containing the font) where baptism is administered.

BARBICAN: outer fortification, resembling a gatehouse, defending the entrance to a castle or town.

BAROQUE: style of architecture introduced from the Continent in the 17th century and characterized by a heavy extravagance in its ornamentation.

BARREL VAULT: *see* Vault.

BASILICA: rectangular building with colonnades on either side and a projecting apse.

BASTION: projecting work in the line or at the angle of a fortification.

BAYS: internal compartments of a building divided from each other only by piers or buttresses at the side.

BOSS: projection, usually ornamented, covering the intersection of the ribs of a vault.

BUTTRESS: structure of masonry or brickwork built against a wall to strengthen it. *Flying buttress:* one in the shape of part of an arch.

CANOPY: ornamental projection above a recess, altar, etc.

CAPITAL: head of a pier or column (*see* also Orders).

CHANCEL: eastern part of a church, formerly divided from the nave or crossing by a screen.

CHANCEL ARCH: enclosing arch at the west end of a chancel.

CHANTRY: endowment for a priest to say mass daily for a deceased person. *Chantry chapel:* one used for this purpose.

CHAPEL: place of worship inside or attached to a church, with an altar.

CHAPTER HOUSE: meeting place for the officiating clergy of a cathedral or of the members of a religious order.

CHARNEL HOUSE: building or chamber attached to or under a church for the reception of the bones of the dead.

CHOIR: part of the church where the service is sung.

CLASSICAL: in the style of the ancient Greeks and Romans (see also Orders).

CLERESTORY: upper part of the nave, chancel, or transept of a church, pierced with windows.

CLOISTER: series of covered passages, usually along the sides of a quadrangle, in a monastic or collegiate building.

COFFER: sunk rectangular or polygonal panel, usually in a ceiling.

COLLEGE: body of persons organized under one roof and devoted to common pursuits. Collegiate: containing a college or having one attached to it.

COLONNADE: range of columns, spaced at regular intervals.

COMPOSITE: see Orders.

CORBEL: bracket or projection from a wall, usually of stone, to support a roof vault or other weight.

CORINTHIAN: see Orders.

CORNICE: moulded horizontal projection at the top of a wall or other part of a building.

COVING: concave undersurface (like a large moulding) to a cornice, at the edge of a roof or ceiling, or under a rood-beam (hence also coved).

CROCKET: carved foliated ornament on a canopy, pinnacle, etc.

CROSSING: space at the intersection of the nave, transepts, and chancel.

CRYPT: underground room, especially one below the east end of a church.

DECORATED: the style of the middle period of English Gothic architecture, approximately 1280–1380 (see also Geometrical).

DEMI-FIGURE: the sculptured representation of the upper half only of a figure.

DETACHED SHAFT: see Shaft.

DORIC: see Orders.

EARLY ENGLISH: the style of the earliest period of English Gothic architecture, approximately 1190–1280.

EASTER SEPULCHRE: recess in a chancel or chapel to contain an effigy of Christ for Easter celebrations.

FAN VAULT: see Vault.

FERETORY: shrine or reliquary borne in a procession, or the place in a church where a shrine was kept.

FINIAL: ornamented top of a pinnacle, canopy, roof, etc.

FLYING BUTTRESS: see Buttress.

FOLIATED: carved or adorned with leaf shapes.

FONT: vessel to contain water for baptism.

FRESCO: wall painting done on the plaster while it is still wet.

GEOMETRICAL: the style of the earlier part of the Decorated period, so called from the window tracery, which was almost wholly in the form of circles or parts of circles.

GOTHIC: the style of architecture which followed the Romanesque and was characterized by the pointed arch. It is divided into Early English, Decorated, and Perpendicular.

GRISAILLE: painting or staining in grey monochrome to simulate shapes or ornament in relief.

GROINED: see Vault.

HAMMERBEAM: beam projecting at right angles from the top of a wall to support the roof members.

IONIC: *see* Orders.

KEEP: the main tower or stronghold of a medieval castle.

LANCET WINDOW: narrow window with a pointed arch.

LECTERN: reading-desk from which parts of the service are said.

LIERNE VAULT: *see* Vault.

LINENFOLD: stylized representation of linen in vertical folds, adopted as a pattern of decoration on panelling in the Tudor period.

MISERICORD: bracketed projection on the underside of a hinged stall seat, which, when turned up, afforded support to a person standing.

MOULDING: shaped edge of an arch, etc., with continuous grooves and projections, frequently ornamented with a regular pattern.

NARTHEX: enclosed vestibule or porch at the west end of a church.

NAVE: the main body of the church, separated by pillars from the aisles.

NORMAN: *see* Romanesque.

ORATORY: small private chapel in a house or castle.

ORDERS: system of parts and ornamentation distinguishing the styles of classical architecture, the Doric, Tuscan, Ionic, Corinthian, and Composite.

ORIEL WINDOW: bay window projecting usually from an upper storey.

PEDIMENT: triangular or segmental gable surmounting a portico, door, or window in classical buildings.

PERPENDICULAR: the style of the last period of English Gothic architecture, approximately 1380–1540.

PIER: solid pillar supporting an arch. *Clustered pier:* one made up of columns or shafts, generally banded together.

PILASTER: rectangular column built against a wall, forming a kind of flat buttress.

PISCINA: stone basin, usually set in the wall of a chancel or chapel, to contain water for purifying the vessels used in Mass or Communion (plural, *Piscinae*).

PORTCULLIS: gate made to slide in vertical grooves and close the entrance to a castle or ward.

PORTICO: porch whose roof is supported by columns.

POSTERN: small gateway at the back of a castle, forming a private entrance.

PREDELLA: platform or horizontal panel (or series of panels) below an altar on which persons or scenes subsidiary to those on the altarpiece are represented.

QUADRIPARTITE: divided regularly into four parts (as in the vaulting of a roof bay).

RAMPART: embankment or wall of earth or stone surrounding a fortified place.

RELIQUARY: casket or other repository for sacred relics.

RENAISSANCE: the style of architecture inspired by the classical revival in the 14th–16th centuries in Italy.

REREDOS: altarpiece.

RETRO-CHOIR: part of a cathedral or large church behind the high altar.

REVESTRY: vestry.

ROCOCO: style of architecture that followed the Baroque but was characterized by a lighter extravagance in its ornamentation.

ROMANESQUE: the style of architecture characterized by the round arch. It was current in England in the 11th–12th centuries, and is divided into Saxon and Norman. *See* also Transitional Norman.

ROOD: crucifix, usually placed above the entrance to the chancel in a medieval church. *Rood-beam:* beam supporting the rood. *Rood-loft:* gallery over the rood-screen. *Rood-screen:* screen across the west end of the chancel, under the rood-beam. *Rood-stairs:* stairs giving access to the rood-loft.

SACRISTY: room in a church for keeping vestments, books, and sacred vessels.

SANCTUARY: inner part of a chancel, where the altar is placed.

SAXON: *see* Romanesque.

SEDILIA (singular, *Sedile*): seats (usually three, of stone) for the officiating clergy, built on or into the chancel wall of the church.

SHAFT: column supporting a capital, often grouped together to form a pier or arranged singly for decorative effect. *Detached shaft:* one (possibly of a group) standing free of the main pier, etc.

SHRINE: chest or casket to contain sacred relics, or a tomb or sepulchre in which relics are deposited.

SPANDREL: flat surface between the shoulder of an arch and the moulding, etc., enclosing it, or between the shoulders of adjacent arches.

STALL: seat made of wood or stone and enclosed at the back and sides, usually one of a row for the choir and officiating clergy.

TESSELLATED: made up of small coloured cubes of stone.

TRACERY: ornamental ribwork, especially in a window (*see* also Geometrical).

TRANSEPT: transverse part of a cruciform church.

TRANSITIONAL NORMAN: style of the transitional period between the Romanesque and the Gothic, characterized by the change from the round to the pointed arch, which took place in about 1150–90.

TRIFORIUM: gallery or arcade in the wall above the arcade of the nave, chancel, or transepts, and below the clerestory.

TRIPTYCH: altarpiece consisting of a central carved or painted panel, with folding doors on either side the insides of which are also carved or painted. Similarly, *Polyptych*, with more than one central panel.

TUSCAN: *see* Orders.

TYMPANUM: space between the lintel of a doorway and the arch above it.

UNDERCROFT: vaulted space below a large room or building, especially a church or chapel.

VAULT: arched roof of stone or brick. *Barrel vault:* semicircular vault without ribs. *Fan vault:* vault whose ribs all spring from one point and spread out like a fan. *Groined vault:* roof having edges (groins) formed by the intersection of two or more vaults. *Lierne vault:* one having cross-ribs ('liernes') connecting the main ribs at or near the centres of their spans.

WARD: open space or court of a fortified castle.

INDEX

Place-names are printed in bold letters. Names beginning with Academy, College, Institute, Ministry, National, Royal, Society, and School will, as a general rule, be found under their specific heads: for instance, Institute of Actuaries, under Actuaries, Institute of; Royal Aeronautical Society, under Aeronautical Society, Royal. Abbreviations: Abp =Archbishop, Bp = Bishop.

INDEX

STREET PLANS OF CENTRAL LONDON

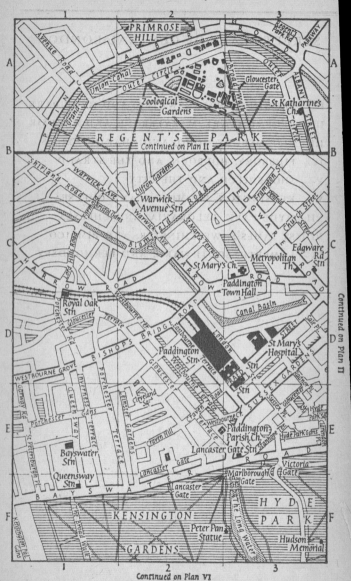

Continued on Plan II

Continued on Plan II

Continued on Plan II

Continued on Plan IV

Continued on Plan VIII

Continued on Plan III

Continued on Plan V

Continued on Plan IX

Continued on Plan IV

Continued on Plan I

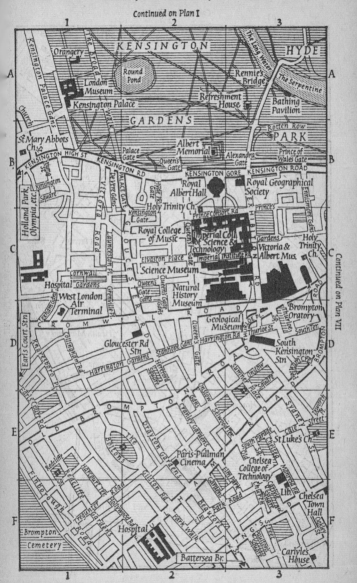

Continued on Plan II

Continued on Plan VI

Continued on Plan VIII

Continued on Plan III

Berkeley Hotel
London Library
Arts Council
Canada Ho.
Nelson Mon.
Charing Cross Stn.
Pier

Jermyn St.
New Zealand Ho.
CHARING CROSS
North'd Ave.
Hungerford Br.

PICCADILLY
Ritz Hotel
King St.
St James's St.
Royal Automobile Club
Admiralty Arch
Crown Estate Office
Whitehall Pl.

Green Park Stn.
Over-seas House
Travel Association
Queen's Chapel
Duke of York's Mon.
Admiralty
War Office
Royal Commonwealth Socy

GREEN
THE MALL
Marlborough House
Admiralty Horse Guards
Banqueting House
EMBANKMENT
VICTORIA

Lancaster House
St James's Palace
Scottish Office
Treasury
Foreign Office
Home Office
Cenotaph
New Scotland Yd
Westminster Pier

PARK
Queen Victoria Memorial
ST JAMES'S
Downing St.
K. Charles St.

Buckingham Palace
PARK
Government Offices
Middlesex Guildhall
Gt George St.
Stn.
Bridge St.
Westminster Br.
Parliament Sq.
Houses of Parliament

Wellington Barracks
Birdcage Walk
Q. Anne's Gate
St Margaret's Central Ch.

Queen's Gallery
Buckingham Gate
Petty France
St James's Pk Stn.
Westminster Abbey
Old Palace Yd
Jewel Tower

Westminster Theatre
Passport Office
Caxton St.
London Transport Offices
Dean's Yd
Westminster School

Blewcoat Sch.
VICTORIA STREET
Church House
Gt Smith St.
Great Peter Street
Westminster Tower Gdns.

Victoria Palace Th.
Howick Pl.
Greycoat Hosp.
Christian Science Ch.
Smith Sq.
St John's Ch.
Lambeth Br.

Victoria Station
Westminster R.C. Cathedral
Industrial Health & Safety Centre
HORSEFERRY ROAD
Westminster Hosp.

Royal Horticultural Society's Halls
VAUXHALL
VINCENT
Page Street
Thames House
London Fire Brigade

Warwick Way
BRIDGE ROAD
Vincent St.
Queen Alexandra's Military Hospital
ALBERT EMBANKMENT

Belgrave Road
REGENCY STREET
Tate Gallery
Royal Army Medical College

Bessborough St.
Vauxhall Br.
Vauxhall Walk

Churchill Gardens
Dolphin Square
GROSVENOR ROAD
Vauxhall Stn.
Harleyford Rd
Harleyford Rd

Nine Elms La.
Wandsworth Rd
Parry St.

Continued on Plan IX

IX · LAMBETH, SOUTHWARK, AND BERMONDSEY

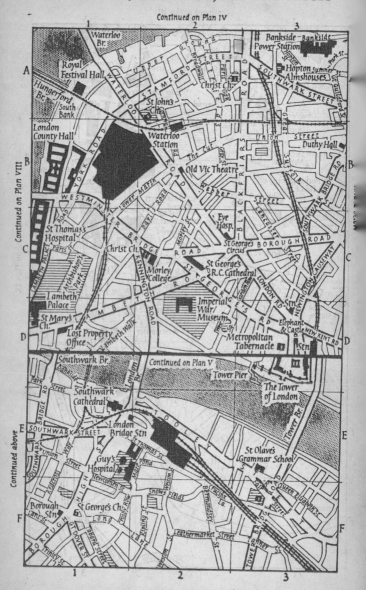

Continued on Plan IV

Continued on Plan VIII

Continued above

Continued on Plan V

Waterloo Br.

Royal
Festival Hall

Hungerford
Br.

South
Bank

London
County Hall

St John's
Ch.

Christ Ch.

Bankside Bankside
Power Station

Hopton sumner
Almshouses

SOUTHWARK STREET

Waterloo
Station

Old Vic Theatre

The Cut

Union   Street

Duthy Hall

St Thomas's
Hospital

Eye
Hosp.

BOROUGH   ROAD

Christ Ch.

St George's
Circus

Morley
College

St George's
R.C. Cathedral

Archbishop's
Park

Lambeth
Palace

St Mary's
Ch.

Lost Property
Office

Imperial
War
Museum

Elephant
& Castle

Metropolitan
Tabernacle

NEW KENT RD

Southwark Br.

Tower Pier

The Tower
of London

Southwark
Cathedral

SOUTHWARK STREET

London
Bridge Stn

Guy's
Hospital

St Olave's
Grammar School

Borough
Stn

St George's Ch.

Snows Fields

Leathermarket Street